TRANSFORMIN

ANNETTE IDLER &
JUAN CARLOS GARZÓN VERGARA

(eds)

Transforming the War on Drugs

Warriors, Victims, and
Vulnerable Regions

OXFORD
UNIVERSITY PRESS

OXFORD
UNIVERSITY PRESS

Oxford University Press is a department of the
University of Oxford. It furthers the University's objective
of excellence in research, scholarship, and education
by publishing worldwide.

Oxford New York

Auckland   Cape Town   Dar es Salaam   Hong Kong   Karachi
Kuala Lumpur   Madrid   Melbourne   Mexico City   Nairobi
New Delhi   Shanghai   Taipei   Toronto

With offices in

Argentina   Austria   Brazil   Chile   Czech Republic   France   Greece
Guatemala   Hungary   Italy   Japan   Poland   Portugal   Singapore
South Korea   Switzerland   Thailand   Turkey   Ukraine   Vietnam

Oxford is a registered trade mark of Oxford University Press
in the UK and certain other countries.

Published in the United States of America by
Oxford University Press
198 Madison Avenue, New York, NY 10016

Library of Congress Cataloging-in-Publication Data is available

ISBN: 9780197604359

Printed in Great Britain by Bell & Bain Ltd, Glasgow

Published in Collaboration with the Changing Character of War
Centre, University of Oxford

CONTENTS

CONTENTS

CONTENTS

CONCLUSION

LIST OF FIGURES AND TABLES

Figures

Tables

LIST OF CONTRIBUTORS

Editors

Annette Idler is the Director of Studies at the Changing Character of War Centre, Senior Research Fellow at Pembroke College, and Senior Research Fellow at the Department of Politics and International Relations, University of Oxford. She is also Visiting Scholar at Harvard University's Weatherhead Center for International Affairs. She holds a doctorate from the Department of International Development and St. Antony's College, University of Oxford. She is the author of *Borderland Battles: Violence, Crime, and Governance at the Edges of Colombia's War* (New York: Oxford University Press, 2019), which appeared in Spanish as Fronteras Rojas (Penguin Random House, 2021). She has published widely in journals including, e.g., *World Politics* and the *Journal of Global Security Studies* on the interface of armed conflict, organized crime, and security. She advises governments and international organizations on these matters and has served on the World Economic Forum's Global Future Council on International Security.

Juan Carlos Garzón Vergara is Global Fellow at the Wilson Center and a research associate at Fundación Ideas para la Paz (Colombia). He is a political scientist from the Universidad Javeriana (Colombia), and specialist in Theory and Armed Conflict Resolution at the University of Los Andes (Colombia). He received his master's degree in Latin American Studies at Georgetown University (USA). Garzón worked as an advisor of the Western Hemisphere Drug Policy Commission, a bipartisan, independent entity created by the US Congress. He was part of a team of analysts for the "Report on the Drug Problem in the Americas," produced by the Organization of American States, where he worked as a specialist in the Secretariat for Political Affairs (Washington DC) and as coordinator of the Mission to Support the Peace Process in Colombia. He has been an international consultant on security and development issues for the United Nations Development Programme (UNDP), the Inter-American Development Bank (IDB), the Norwegian Center for Conflict Resolution (NOREF) and Igarapé Institute (Brazil).

Chapter Contributors

Katherine Aguirre is research associate at the Instituto Igarapé and a Colombian economist with professional experience in the areas of violence and development. She has a master's in Development at the Graduate Institute in Geneva (Switzerland). Her research is focused on citizen security and peace, monitoring drug policy, and measurement of armed violence, including homicide, conflict and terrorism.

Kwesi Aning is the Director of the Faculty of Academic Affairs & Research, Kofi Annan International Peacekeeping Training Centre, Ghana and Clinical Professor of Peacekeeping Practice at Kennesaw State University, Atlanta. He holds a doctorate in Political Science from the University of Copenhagen, Denmark (1988) and a Bachelor of Arts (Hons) in History from the University of Ghana (1986).

David Bewley-Taylor is Professor of International Relations and Public Policy and founding Director of the Global Drug Policy Observatory (2013) at Swansea University, UK. In addition to numerous book chapters and journal articles, he has written two major research monographs, *The United States and International Drug Control, 1909–1997* (Continuum, 2001) and *International Drug Control: Consensus Fractured* (Cambridge University Press, 2012), and is co-editor of the *Research Handbook on International Drug Control Policy* (Edward Elgar, 2020). David was the founding Secretary of the International Society for the Study of Drug Policy (2006-07), has played an advisory role to governments and international organizations, and collaborated with and produced policy reports for a range of international non-governmental organizations.

LIST OF CONTRIBUTORS

Damon Barrett is a co-founder and Director of the International Centre on Human Rights and Drug Policy based at the Human Rights Centre, University of Essex. He is a lecturer at the School of Public Health and Community Medicine at the University of Gothenburg. He has spent the past decade working on the intersections between human rights and drug control. He holds a doctorate of law from Stockholm University, where he researched the child's right to protection from drugs in international law.

Pierre-Arnaud Chouvy, PhD, is a Geographer and Research Fellow at the French National Centre for Scientific Research. He specializes in the geopolitics of illicit drugs with a focus on Asia. He produces http://www.geopium.org.

Angélica Durán-Martínez is an Associate Professor in Political Science at the University of Massachusetts Lowell. She received a PhD in Political Science from Brown University, and an M.A. from New York University. Her bachelor's degree is from Universidad Nacional de Colombia. Her research focuses on violence, drug trafficking and drug policy, and their relations with democracy and the state. Her first book, *The Politics of Drug Violence: Criminals, Cops, and Politicians in Colombia and Mexico*, was published in 2018 by Oxford University Press.

Paul Gootenberg is SUNY Distinguished Professor of History and Sociology at Stony Brook University (New York) and Chair of History. He is a global commodity and drug historian who trained as a Latin Americanist at the University of Chicago and Oxford. His works include *Andean Cocaine: The Making of a Global Drug* (UNC, 2008), *Cocaine: Global Histories* (Routledge, 1999) and *The Origins of Cocaine: Peasant Colonization and Failed Development in the Amazon Andes* (with Liliana M. Dávalos; Routledge, 2018). From 2011-14 he chaired the Drugs, Security and Democracy fellowship (DSD) of the OSF and Social Science Research Council. Gootenberg is General Editor of the forthcoming *Oxford Handbook of Drug History* and President-elect of the Alcohol and Drugs History Society (ADHS).

Christopher Hallam is a research associate at the Global Drug Policy Observatory at the Swansea University. Christopher completed his PhD in 2016 at the London School of Hygiene & Tropical Medicine under the supervision of Professor Virginia Berridge. He is a historian of drugs and drug regulation, and has worked extensively for the International Drug Policy Consortium as a researcher and analyst of international drug policy.

Kasia Malinowska-Sempruch directs the Open Society Global Drug Policy Program, which provides grants to efforts advocating for an evidence-based approach to drug policy worldwide and encourages greater scrutiny of the international regime. She also teaches drug policy at the Department of International Relations of the New School in New York. Before joining OSF, she worked on issues related to the HIV epidemic at the United Nations Development Programme in New York and Warsaw. She holds a Master of Social Work from the University of Pennsylvania and a doctorate in Public Health from Columbia University.

Robert Muggah specializes in public security, migration, new technologies and smart cities. He is the co-founder of the Igarapé Institute and the SecDev Group. He is also a fellow at Princeton University and the Graduate Institute in Geneva. He is the author of eight books, including Terra Incognita (Penguin, 2020), and over 100 peer-review articles.

Clara Musto authored the book *Regulating Cannabis Markets: The Construction of an Innovative Drug Policy in Uruguay*. Her interest in this area comes from 2006, when she joined Proderechos, an NGO working on communication and politics for policy change. Clara then specialized in the regulation of illegal markets and drug policy evaluation and assisted the Uruguayan government on the regulation of cannabis.

Javier Sagredo is an expert consultant on drug policy of the EU International Technical Assistance in Bolivia. He has worked for more than 18 years on drug policy, citizen security and governance issues in Latin America and the Caribbean, both with the United Nations Development Programme and with the Organization of American States, where he has advocated for local sustainable and inclusive development-based solutions. He holds a law degree from the University of Salamanca (ESP) and University College Galway (IRL), a master's degree on European Integration from the Free University of Brussels (BEL) and a postgraduate diploma on Local Development and Decentralization from the University Alberto Hurtado of Santiago de Chile.

Carlos A. Pérez Ricart is Assistant Professor at the Center for Research and Teaching in Economics (CIDE), Mexico City. Prior to that, he was Postdoctoral Fellow in the Contemporary History and Public Policy of Mexico at the University of Oxford, where he was member of both the History Faculty and the Latin American Centre. He holds a PhD in Political Science and in Latin American Studies from a Comparative and Transregional Perspective at the Freie Universität Berlin, and has a degree in International Relations from El Colegio de México.

John M. Pokoo heads the Conflict Management Programme at the Kofi Annan International Peacekeeping Training Centre. He holds an M.A. in Contemporary War and Peace Studies, University of Sussex, Brighton. He is a PhD student at Rhodes University, Grahamstown, South Africa.

Philip Robins is an Emeritus Professor of the Politics of the Middle East at St. Antony's College, University of Oxford, where he has taught and researched since 1995. Before that he was the founding Head of the Middle East Programme at Chatham House, the Royal Institute of International Affairs in London. Robins has been researching drug policy in the Middle East since the early 1990s, and recently authored the ten-country study of Middle Eastern production, prevention and consumption of drugs entitled *Middle East Drugs Bazaar* (Oxford University Press, 2016). Robins has now retired from teaching but retains a keen research interest in both the Middle East and related drug policy.

Olga Sánchez de Ribera holds a master's and PhD in Criminology from the Institute of Criminology, University of Cambridge. She is a researcher associated at the Center of Society & Justice Studies, Pontifial Catholic University of Chile, and a consultant in evidence-based crime prevention at the Inter-American Development Bank. Her research interests include offenders' rehabilitation programs and evaluation, risk assessment, meta-analysis, and sex offending.

Mónica Serrano is a Research-Professor at El Colegio de Mexico, a Senior Fellow at the Ralph Bunche Institute and a Senior Research Associate at the Oxford Centre for International Studies. She was previously the coordinator of the North American Programme at El Colegio de Mexico and is a member of the International Advisory Board of the European FRAME Human Rights Project.

Ekaterina Stepanova heads the Peace and Conflict Studies Unit at the National Research Institute of the World Economy and International Relations (IMEMO), Moscow. From 2007 to 2009, she directed the Armed Conflicts and Conflict Management Program at the Stockholm International Peace Research Institute (SIPRI). Her research interests include the political economy of conflicts, with a focus on the illicit drug business. Her related publications include *The Role of Illicit Drug Business in the Political Economy of Conflicts and Terrorism* (Moscow, 2006) and 'Afghan Narcotrafficking: A Joint Threat Assessment' (New York: EastWest Institute, 2013).

Nicolas Trajtenberg is Lecturer in Criminology in the School of Social Sciences at Cardiff University and Associate Professor at the Department of Sociology in the School of Social Sciences at the Universidad de la República in Uruguay. He studied Sociology and Economics at the Universidad de la República and Criminology at the Universidad Autonoma de Barcelona, University of Oxford, and University of Cambridge.

ACKNOWLEDGEMENTS

This book is the result of a collaborative project sponsored by the One Earth Foundation and the Social Science Research Council, with inspiration from the academic journal *Global Governance*. Thanks to this project, we were able to convene a group of distinguished scholars and practitioners from across the globe to produce this edited volume with a view to stimulate debate across academia and the policy world. We would like to thank these organizations, as well as Pembroke College's Changing Character of War Centre and the Department of Politics and International Relations at the University of Oxford, the Research Council UK's Partnership for Conflict, Crime, and Security Research, and Harvard University's Weatherhead Center for International Affairs for their generous support.

There were many individuals without whom this volume would not be possible; here we would like to highlight the outstanding work by Mónica Serrano, Cleia Noia, and Roberta Spivak. We would like to thank Thomas G. Weiss, Director Emeritus of the Ralph Bunche Institute for International Studies at the City University of New York for hosting our seminar 'The International Drug Control Regime beyond UNGASS 2016: Perspectives from the Global South.' We enormously appreciate the time and energy that participants have dedicated to the seminar, in which the group of experts discussed the current and likely future developments in international drug control efforts with government and United Nations officials, as well as with members of civil society.

ACKNOWLEDGEMENTS

We are tremendously grateful to Michael Dwyer at Hurst Publishers for shepherding this book through to publication and also would like to express our gratitude to the anonymous reviewers of the manuscript for their excellent comments.

We also would like to thank Rupert York, Irene Arenas Almandós, María Alejandra Espinosa, Jerónimo Sudarsky, and Daniela Trujillo for their invaluable assistance in editing this volume.

Finally, we are deeply grateful to all contributors for their valuable efforts, their sharp chapters, and their commitment throughout this process.

Most importantly, we would like to acknowledge all those who fell victim to the multiple faces of the War on Drugs. This book shall help move beyond unnecessary suffering.

LIST OF ABBREVIATIONS

ACCORD	ASEAN and China Cooperative Operations in Response to Dangerous Drugs
AD	Alternative Development
AIDS	Acquired Immune Deficiency Syndrome
AQ	Al Qaeda
AQIM	Al Qaeda in the Islamic Maghreb
ARQ	Annual Report Questionnaire
ASEAN	Association of Southeast Asian Nations
ASOD	ASEAN Senior Officials on Drug Matters
ATS	Amphetamine-Type Stimulants
AU	African Union
BLN	Billion
BLO	Border Liaison Offices
BRICS	Brazil, Russia, India, China, and South Africa
BRQ	Biennial Reports Questionnaire
C3	The Crescent Three (Afghanistan, Pakistan, and Iran)
CARSI	Central America Regional Security Initiative
CCDAC	Central Committee for Drug Abuse Control (Myanmar)
CDDC	Compulsory Drug Detention Center

LIST OF ABBREVIATIONS

CELAC	Comunidad de Estados Latinoamericanos y Caribeños (Community of Latin American and Caribbean States)
CIA	Central Intelligence Agency
CICAD	Inter-American Drug Abuse Control Commission
CNB	Central Narcotics Bureau (Singapore)
CND	Commission on Narcotic Drugs
CNS	Central Nervous System
DEA	Drug Enforcement Administration, United States of America
DEVIDA	Comisión Nacional para el Desarrollo y Vida sin Drogas (National Commission for the Development and a Drug-free Lifestyle), Peru
DORA	Defence of the Realm Act
DSB	Drug Supervising Body
DTO	Drug Trafficking Organizations
ECDD	The Expert Committee on Drug Dependence of the World Health Organization
ECOSOC	United Nations Economic and Social Council
ECOWAS	The Economic Community of West African States
ECPCJS	ECOWAS Crime Prevention and Criminal Justice Centre
EMCDDA	European Monitoring Centre for Drugs and Drug Addiction
ELN	Ejército de Liberación Nacional (National Liberation Army), Colombia
EU	European Union
FAO	Food and Agriculture Organization
FARC	Fuerzas Armadas Revolucionarias de Colombia (Revolutionary Armed Forces of Colombia)

LIST OF ABBREVIATIONS

FATF	Financial Action Task Force
FBN	Federal Bureau of Narcotics (United States of America)
FBNDD	Federal Bureau of Narcotics and Dangerous Drugs (United States of America)
FSB	Federal Security Service of the Russian Federation
FSIN	Federal Penitentiary Service of the Russian Federation
FSKN	Federal Drug Control Service of the Russian Federation
GCC	Gulf Cooperation Council
GCDP	Global Commission on Drug Policy
GDP	Gross Domestic Product
GIABA	Inter-Governmental Action Group Against Money Laundering in West Africa
GIZ	Deutsche Gesellschaft für Internationale Zusammenarbeit (German Development Agency)
HIV	Human Immunodeficiency Virus
HLS	High-Level Segment
ICAD	International Conference on Alternative Development
IDCR	International Drug Control Regime
IFOR	Implementation Force
ILO	International Labor Organization
IMF	International Monetary Fund
INCB	International Narcotics Control Board
INL	Bureau of International Narcotics and Law Enforcement Affairs
INTERPOL	International Criminal Police Organization
IRD	Integrated Rural Development

LIST OF ABBREVIATIONS

IRI	International Republican Institute
ISAF	International Security Assistance Force
ISI	Inter-Services Intelligence of Pakistan
KMT	Kuomintang (Nationalist Party of China)
LACDD	Latin American Commission on Drugs and Democracy
LCDC	Lao National Commission for Drug Control and Supervision
LGBTI	Lesbian, Gay, Bisexual, Transgender/Transsexual and Intersex
LSD	Lysergic Acid Diethylamide
MAPS	Multidisciplinary Association for Psychedelic Studies
MAT	Medication-Assisted Treatment
MDMA	Methylenedioxymethamphetamine
MEM	Multilateral Evaluation Mechanism
MENA	Middle East and North Africa
MENAHRA	Middle East and North Africa Harm Reduction Association
MLN	Million
MT	Metric Tons
MVD	Ministry of Interior Affairs of Russia
NACD	Cambodian National Authority for Combating Drugs
NADA	Malaysian National Anti-Drugs Agency
NATO	North Atlantic Treaty Organization
NCF	Nederlandsche Cocaïnefabriek (Dutch Cocaine Factory)
NGO	Non-Governmental Organization
NPS	Novel Psychoactive Substances
NSDD	National Security Decision Directives, United States of America

LIST OF ABBREVIATIONS

NSP	Needle and Syringe Programmes
OAC	Opium Advisory Committee
OAS	Organization of American States
OECD	Organisation for Economic Co-Operation and Development
ONCB	Thai Office of the Narcotics Control Board
ONDCP	Office of National Drug Control Policy
OPGs	Organized Crime Groups (Russian abbreviation)
OST	Opioid Substitution Therapy
PAPS	Political Affairs, Peace and Security
PBC	Peacebuilding Commission
PCOB	Permanent Central Opium Board
PEN	Pre-Export Notification
PICS	Precursors Incident Communication System
PRC	People's Republic of China
PWIDs	People Who Inject Drugs
Rosfinmonitoring	The Federal Financial Monitoring Service of the Russian Federation
SALW	Small Arms and Light Weapons
SAP	Structural Adjustment Program
SDG	Sustainable Development Goal
SEA	Southeast Asia
SODC	Standing Office for Drug Control (Vietnam)
STD	Sexually Transmitted Disease
TB	Tuberculosis
UAE	United Arab Emirates
UK	United Kingdom
UN	United Nations
UNAIDS	Joint United Nations Programme on HIV/AIDS

UNASUR	Union of South American Nations
UNDCP	United Nations Drug Control Programme
UNDG	United Nations Development Group
UNDP	United Nations Development Programme
UNEP	United Nations Environment Programme
UNESCO	United Nations Educational, Scientific and Cultural Organization
UNFDAC	United Nations Fund for Drug Abuse Control
UNGASS	United Nations General Assembly Special Session
UNICRI	United Nations Interregional Crime and Justice Research Institute
UNHCR	United Nations High Commissioner for Refugees
UNODC	United Nations Office on Drugs and Crime
UNOWA	United Nations Office for West Africa
UNSC	United Nations Security Council
UPP	Unidade de Polícia Pacificadora (Police Pacification Units)
UPR	Universal Periodic Review
US	United States
US/NATO	United States Mission to the North Atlantic Treaty Organization
USAID	United States Agency for International Development
USSR	Union of Soviet Socialist Republics
VRAEM	Valle de los Ríos Apurímac, Ene y Mantaro (Valley of the Apurímac, Ene and Mantaro Rivers)
WCTU	Woman's Christian Temperance Union
WHO	World Health Organization

LIST OF TERMS

The following definitions and explanations are drawn from the United Nations Office on Drugs and Crime, *Terminology and Information on Drugs*, 3rd ed. (New York: United Nations, 2016), or, where identified as such, from World Health Organization (WHO), *Lexicon of Alcohol and Drug Terms* (Geneva: WHO, 1994), or United Nations Office on Drugs and Crime, *Early Warning Advisory on NPS* (Vienna: UNODC, 2015).

Term	Definition / Explanation
Abuse	Due to the ambiguity of the term 'abuse,' the WHO Lexicon has replaced this term with 'harmful use' and 'hazardous use,' which is defined as follows: Harmful use is a pattern of psychoactive substance use that is causing damage to health, physical (for example hepatitis following injection of drugs) or mental (for example depressive episodes secondary to heavy alcohol intake). Harmful use commonly, but not invariably, has adverse social consequences. The term was introduced in ICD-10 [International Classification of Diseases, Tenth Revision] and supplanted 'non-dependent use' as a diagnostic term. Hazardous use is a pattern of substance use that increases the risk of harmful consequences for the user. In contrast to harmful use, hazardous use refers to patterns of use that are of public health significance

Term	Definition / Explanation
	despite the absence of any current disorder in the individual user. In the context of international drug control, drug abuse constitutes the use of any substance under international control outside therapeutic indications, in excessive dose levels, or over an unjustified period of time.
Addiction	The terms 'addiction' and 'habituation' were abandoned by WHO in 1964 in favor of drug dependence. However, since those terms are still widely used, below is a definition of 'addiction.' 'Addiction' refers to the repeated use of a psychoactive substance or substances, to the extent that the user is periodically or chronically intoxicated, shows a compulsion to take the preferred substance (or substances), has great difficulty in voluntarily ceasing or modifying substance use, and exhibits determination to obtain psychoactive substances by almost any means.
Adulterants	A substance that is added to a drug to increase the quantity produced, enhance the pharmacological and psychoactive effect, or facilitate the administration of the drug. Adulterants may include sugars, caffeine, lidocaine or paracetamol. However, other adulterants may be more harmful, particularly when administered through injection.
Adverse Drug Reaction	In the general medical and pharmacological fields, 'adverse drug reaction' denotes a toxic physical or (less common) psychological reaction to a therapeutic agent. The reaction may be predictable, or allergic or idiosyncratic (unpredictable). In the context of drug abuse,

Term	Definition / Explanation
	the term includes unpleasant psychological and physical reactions to drug taking.
Agonist	A substance that acts at a neuronal receptor to produce effects similar to those of a reference drug. For example, methadone is a morphine-like agonist at the opioid receptors. Full agonist is a substance that produces a full response or the maximum effect at a given receptor. Partial agonist is a substance that produces a reduced response as it is unable to elicit the maximum effect or response.
Amphetamine (Amfetamine)	One of a class of sympathomimetic amines with powerful stimulant action on the central nervous system. The class includes amfetamine, dexamfetamine, and methamfetamine. Pharmacologically related drugs include methylphenidate, phenmetrazine, and amfepramone (diethylpropion). In street parlance, amfetamines are often referred to as 'speed.' See WHO, 1994, 15.
Analgesic	A substance that reduces pain and may or may not have psychoactive properties.
Antagonist	A substance that counteracts the effects of another agent. Pharmacologically, an antagonist interacts with a receptor to inhibit the action of agents (agonists) that produce specific physiological or behavioral effects mediated by that receptor.
Barbiturate	One of a group of central nervous system depressants that chemically are substituted derivatives of barbituric acid; examples are amobarbital, pento-barbital, phenobarbital, and secobarbital. They are used as antiepileptics, anesthetics, sedatives, hypnotics, and—less

Term	Definition / Explanation
	commonly—as anxiolytics or anti-anxiety drugs [...]. Acute and chronic use induces effects similar to those of alcohol. [...] See WHO, 1994, 18.
Decriminalization	The repeal of laws or regulations that define a behavior, product, or condition as criminal. [The term] is sometimes also applied to a reduction in the seriousness of a crime or of the penalties the crime attracts, as when possession of marijuana is downgraded from a crime that warrants arrest and a jail term to an infraction to be punished with a warning or fine. Thus, decriminalization is often distinguished from legalization, which involves the complete repeal of any definition as a crime, often coupled with a governmental effort to control or influence the market for the affected behavior or product. See WHO, 1994, 27.
Designer Drug	A novel chemical substance with psychoactive properties, synthesized specifically for sale on the illicit market and to circumvent regulations on controlled substances. In response, these regulations now commonly cover novel and possible analogues of existing psychoactive substances. The term was coined in the 1980s. See WHO, 1994, 29.
(Drug) Dependence	The term was introduced in 1964 by a WHO Expert Committee to replace addiction and habituation. 'Drug dependence' comprises a cluster of physiological, behavioral and cognitive phenomena of variable intensity, in which the use of a psychoactive drug (or drugs) takes on a high priority. It implies a need for repeated doses of the drug and

Term	Definition / Explanation
	indicates that a person has impaired control of substance use, as its use is continued despite adverse consequences. Psychological or psychic dependence refers to the experience of impaired control over drug use. Physiological or physical dependence involves the development of tolerance and withdrawal symptoms upon cessation of use of the drug, as a consequence of the body's adaptation to the continued presence of a drug.
Dose	A dose is the quantity of a substance which is required to elicit the desired response in the individual, both in medicine and for abuse purposes. This dose will vary depending on a number of factors, including the particular substance, its form, the route of administration, and the drug consumption history of the individual. Doses are therefore highly dependent on various effects, including past drug experiences, individual differences in weight and size and whether a drug is taken in combination with other substances (for example poly-drug use). Average doses are not generalizable or applicable to every person. Differences in the purity, potency and concentration of substances has implications on dosages and the amount that is consumed by an individual. For example, substances with high potency may require small doses, to produce similar pharmacological effects. While some substances are effective in milligrams or grams, others may exert their effect with as little as a few micrograms (1 microgram is equal to 0.000001 grams). Additional confounding

Term	Definition / Explanation
	factors exist that make accurate ranges of dosing information equivocal. There is a lack of information about social behavior and drug consumption patterns are highly variable, which in turn makes the level of use inexact. Data on average doses can therefore only provide certain estimates of use, which does not accurately reflect consumption patterns. In certain cases, the 'defined daily doses' used by the INCB for narcotic drugs and psychotropic substances, which is available in their technical reports, may provide further guidance. Drugs or substances that are used repeatedly over time can lead to the development of tolerance. During tolerance the body does not respond to the substance at the same dosage and therefore, higher amounts of the substance are required to achieve the desired effect.
Drug	In the context of international drug control, 'drug' means any of the substances in Schedule I and II of the 1961 Convention, whether natural or synthetic. A term of varied usage. In medicine, it refers to any substance with the potential to prevent or cure disease or enhance physical or mental welfare; in pharmacology it means any chemical agent that alters the biochemical or physiological processes of tissues or organisms.
Drug Testing	The identification and chemical analysis of drugs in seized material and biological specimens, that is, body fluids (urine, blood, saliva), hair, or other tissue, in order to assess the presence of one or more psychoactive substances.

Term	Definition / Explanation
Illicit Traffic	The manufacture, cultivation or trafficking in drugs or psychotropic substances contrary to the provisions of the conventions.
Injection	The administration of a drug [the way in which a substance is introduced into the body] through the skin using a syringe or any other injection tools. This route poses a serious public health risk as infectious diseases such as HIV or hepatitis can be passed from person to person through the sharing of injection equipment. Three methods of injection exist, namely intramuscular, intravenous (IV) or subcutaneous injections.
International Drug Conventions	The three main international drug conventions are: Single Convention on Narcotic Drugs of 1961 as amended by the 1972 Protocol establishes an international control system for narcotic drugs. Convention on Psychoactive Substances of 1971 establishes an international control system for psychotropic substances. United Nations Convention against Illicit Traffic in Narcotic Drugs and Psychotropic Substances of 1988, which provides comprehensive measures against drug trafficking, including provisions against money-laundering and the diversion of precursor chemicals.
Khat (Qat)	The leaves and buds of an East African plant, *Catha edulis*, which are chewed or brewed as beverage. Used also in parts of the Eastern Mediterranean and North Africa, khat is a stimulant with effects similar to those of amphetamine. Heavy use can result in dependence and physical and mental problems

Term	Definition / Explanation
	resembling those produced by other stimulants. See WHO, 1994, 44.
Legalization	Legal actions that make legal what was previously a criminalized behavior, product, or condition. See WHO, 1994, 44.
Licit Drug	A drug that is legally available by medical prescription in the jurisdiction in question, or, sometimes, a drug legally available without medical prescription.
Naloxone	An opioid receptor blocker that antagonizes the actions of opioid drugs. It reverses the features of opiate intoxication and is prescribed for the treatment of overdose with this group of drugs. See WHO, 1994, 47.
Narcotic Drug	In the context of international drug control, 'narcotic drug' means any of the substances, natural or synthetic, in Schedules I and II of the Single Convention on Narcotic Drugs, 1961, and that Convention as amended by the 1972 Protocol Amending the Single Convention on Narcotic Drugs, 1961. In medicine, a chemical agent that induces stupor, coma or insensibility to pain (also called narcotic analgesic). The term usually refers to opiates or opioids, which are also named narcotic analgesics. In common parlance and legal usage, it is often used imprecisely to mean illicit drugs, irrespective of their pharmacology.
New Psychoactive Substances	Term used by UNODC defined as 'substances of abuse, either in a pure form or a preparation, that are not controlled by the 1961 Single Convention on Narcotic Drugs or the 1971 Convention on Psychotropic Substances, but

Term	Definition / Explanation
	which may pose a public health threat.' See UNODC, 2015, 2.
Opiates and Opioids	Opiates are naturally occurring alkaloids of the opium poppy (Papaver somniferum L.), such as morphine, codeine, thebaine, etc. The term is often used interchangeably with opioids. However, opioids are synthetic compounds, which are derived from opiates but are not opiates themselves (see section 4). Opium, concentrate of poppy straw, morphine and heroin are under Schedule I of the Single Convention on Narcotic Drugs of 1961. See UNODC, 2016, 17.
Overdose	The use of any drug in such an amount that acute adverse physical or mental effects are produced. Overdose may produce transient or lasting effects, or death; the lethal dose of a particular drug varies with the individual and with circumstances.
Pharmaceutical Drugs	Drugs manufactured by the pharmaceutical industry or made up by a pharmacist. Industry terminology categorizes drugs as ethical drugs, available only on prescription, and over-the-counter or proprietary drugs, advertised to the consumer and sold without prescription. The list of drugs requiring prescription varies considerably from country to country; most psychoactive pharmaceuticals are only available by prescription in industrialized countries.
Psychedelic	The distinct feature of 'psychedelic' drugs is their capacity to induce states of altered perception, thought and feeling that are not experienced otherwise except in dreams or at times of religious exaltation; they can, but not necessarily, produce overt hallucinations.

Term	Definition / Explanation
Psychotropic or Psychoactive Substance	Any chemical agent affecting the mind or mental processes (that is, any psychoactive drug). In the context of international drug control, 'psychotropic substance' means any substance, natural or synthetic, or any natural material in Schedule I, II, III or IV of the 1971 Convention on Psychotropic Substances.
Scheduling of Substances	The schedules in the international drug control treaties were established to classify internationally applicable control measures that would ensure the availability of certain substances for medical and scientific purposes, while preventing their diversion into illicit channels. [...] In the Single Convention on Narcotic Drugs of 1961, as amended by the 1972 Protocol, narcotic drugs and their preparations are essentially listed in four schedules according to their dependence potential, abuse liability and therapeutic usefulness. [...] In the Convention on Psychotropic Substances of 1971, control measures are categorized in four schedules, depending on the relationship between the therapeutic usefulness and the public health risk of the substances. The four schedules use a sliding scale of those two variables: inclusion in Schedule I implies high public health risk and low therapeutic utility, and therefore the strictest control measures, whereas inclusion in Schedule IV implies the opposite: lower public health risk and higher therapeutic utility. See UNODC, 2016, vii–viii.

LIST OF TERMS

Term	Definition / Explanation
Sedative	Any of a group of central nervous system depressants with the capacity of relieving anxiety and inducing calmness. Major classes of sedatives/hypnotics include the benzodiazepines and barbiturates.
Stimulant	In reference to the central nervous system (CNS), any agent that activates, enhances or increases neural activity; also called psychostimulants or CNS stimulants. Included are amphetamine-type stimulants, cocaine, caffeine, nicotine, etc. Other drugs have stimulant actions which are not their primary effect, but which may be manifest in high doses or after chronic use.
Substances under International Control	Refers to substances listed in the schedules (for the 1961 and 1971 Conventions) and tables (for the 1988 Convention) which are annexed to these conventions.
Tranquillizer	A tranquillizer is a calming agent. The term can be used to differentiate between these drugs and the sedative/hypnotics: tranquillizers have a quieting or damping effect on psychomotor processes without—except at high doses—interference with consciousness or thinking.
Synthetic Drugs	The term 'synthetic drug' strictly refers to psychoactive substances that are manufactured through a chemical process in which the essential psychoactive constituents are not derived from naturally occurring substances. Synthetic drugs with long histories of illicit use include amphetamines and lysergic acid diethylamide (LSD). Amphetamines are synthetic drugs.

Term	Definition / Explanation
Withdrawal Syndrome	A group of symptoms of variable clustering and degree of severity which occur on cessation or reduction of use of a psychoactive substance that has been taken repeatedly, usually for a prolonged period and/or in high doses.

INTRODUCTION

FIFTY YEARS OF THE WAR ON DRUGS: A MOMENT OF UNCERTAINTY

Annette Idler and *Juan Carlos Garzón Vergara*

Five decades after President Nixon declared the War on Drugs on June 18, 1971, this war is back as a priority on the international community's agenda—or perhaps it has never left. Indeed, after Nixon's and Reagan's hardline approaches to the global drug problem,[1] practitioners, analysts, and diplomats alike feared the beginning of a 'War on Drugs 3.0.'[2] Far from the relaunch of a tested and proven strategy, however, the War on Drugs has become of great concern for both those who aim to reduce suffering through war around the globe and those who deplore the continued harm caused by narcotic drugs and psychoactive substances.

The War on Drugs came to mark how states responded to the drug challenge. It developed into the most prevalent embodiment of the international drug control regime (IDCR), a set of intergovernmental agreements on how drugs should be controlled between and within states, which saw its beginning with the signing of the first International Opium Convention in 1912.[3] Under the cover of the War on Drugs, governments blurred the distinction between crime fighting and war fighting,[4] and delegated much of drug policy implementation to institutions in charge of security rather than those dealing with public health, social policy, or development. The use of criminal law and punitive strategies became the cornerstone of drug policy in numerous countries, concentrating most of the budget and institutional capacities.[5]

In 2009, the international community agreed on the 'Political Declaration and Plan of Action on International Cooperation towards an Integrated and Balanced Strategy to Counter the World Drug Problem.' One of the proposed targets of this 10-year global strategy was to eliminate or reduce 'significantly and measurably' the illicit cultivation, production, manufacture, sale, demand, trafficking, distribution, and use of internationally controlled substances, the diversion of precursors, and money laundering. In 2014, a mid-term high-level review of the Plan resulted in the renewal of commitments, arguably without any serious evaluation of what had been achieved (or not).

In April 2016, the third United Nations General Assembly Special Session (UNGASS) on the world drug problem took place in New York. The meeting was intended as a response to the call from a group of Latin American countries—Colombia, Guatemala, and Mexico—to rethink and reorient drug policy by putting more emphasis on development and human rights-related issues, in addition to drug policy's coercive dimension. The mandate given by member states to the United Nations (UN) and agreed upon by the countries for this session was to assess 'the achievements and challenges in countering the world drug problem.' Rather than acknowledging the lack of progress in reducing the illicit production and consumption of drugs, the supporters of the current interpretation of the IDCR in the form of the War on Drugs tried to present the 'containment' of the problem as a success. Another opportunity to review the current approach was missed.

In August 2018, the administration of former US President Donald Trump sent out a 'Global Call to Action on the World Drug Problem,' encouraging other governments to sign up to it. According to the US State Department, 130 countries signed the document, which has a similarly prohibitionist and securitized tone to the 2009 UN Political Declaration. Trump's approach moved away from the agreement reached in the UNGASS 2016 Declaration that contains human rights considerations and a broader development agenda.

In March 2019, the international community met again, this time in Vienna in the context of a ministerial segment on drug policy organized by the Commission on Narcotic Drugs (CND), to review the progress made against the targets set in 2009 to reduce significantly the scale of the illegal drug market and decide on the strategy for the next years. The gathering of fifty-two member states and hundreds of civil society actors resulted in a ministerial declaration with reference to human rights obligations and the Sustainable Development Goals (SDGs). Reflecting the fact that some governments mainstreamed public health approaches and treatments of substance users at least to some degree over the past decade or so, this declaration suggests new targets focused on increasing the availability of controlled medicines, promoting alternatives to convicting and punishing drug dealers and users, and enhancing access to harm reduction services.

Despite these positive developments, a critical tone in the ministerial declaration is absent. It does not evaluate the progress—or lack thereof—made against the targets set a decade earlier to significantly reduce the scale of the illegal drug market. Notwithstanding the acknowledgement of the 'persistent and emerging challenges' identified in the document, the signatory countries held on to the objective of eliminating the market of narcotic drugs, reiterating the goal of 'actively promoting a society free of drug abuse.'

Still, decades of securitized drug policies have reinvigorated those voices who argue that policy change is imperative. Despite the progress made in some areas, the overall magnitude of drug demand has not substantially changed at the global level. The War on Drugs has failed to reduce the scale of illicit production or trafficking of drugs; indeed, it arguably has fueled the illicit drug trade. Illegal cultivation of opium poppy increased by 130 per cent between 2009 and 2018, and coca bush cultivation increased by 34 per cent in the same period. The estimated number of individuals who use drugs illicitly worldwide increased by 30 per cent (from 210 million to 271 million) between 2009 and 2017.[6] The Global Burden of Disease Study estimates that, globally, in 2017, there were 585,000 deaths and 42 million years of 'healthy' life lost as a result of the use of drugs.[7]

Securitized drug policies have also led to enormous economic costs, health impacts, and human rights violations. From heavily armed military forces fighting so-called narco-terrorists in Mexico and Colombia, and military coalitions chasing drug lords in Afghanistan, to merciless state forces imposing deadly punishment on consumers in Asia, the War on Drugs has produced thousands of deaths and contributed to substantial collateral damage. Meanwhile, trafficking organizations have developed increasingly sophisticated operations. Their destabilization capacity is now a serious concern for security strategists. Advances in communication technologies and the easy availability of information facilitate smuggling networks and trafficking rings that span across continents.

In light of this alarming situation, a rapidly growing number of civil society organizations and other stakeholders—including agencies of the UN system such as the UN Development Programme and the UN Human Rights Council, and coalitions like the Global Commission on Drug Policy formed by world leaders and intellectuals—have proposed alternative approaches. Some national governments have adopted less coercive measures that take into account their local and national interests and realities, including decriminalization, health-based interventions, the regulation of drug markets, and 'smart enforcement' approaches.[8] Novel policy approaches, such as the regulation of marijuana in Uruguay and an increased focus on 'flexibility' as exhibited by the legalization of cannabis for recreational use in several US states, have opened the door to experimentation. Canada has become the first G7 nation to legalize marijuana for recreational uses—this could be a breaking point in how this substance is regulated.

Overall, however, consensus on the way forward is missing in the global drug policy debate. Governments implemented reforms at the national level without revising the IDCR itself, thus the risk of falling back into the War on Drugs rhetoric—and practice—remains high. Indeed, as other scholars have argued,[9] escalating rather than terminating the War on Drugs—especially at the lower end of the supply chain—has become a 'new' possibility. At times, the international and national bureaucracies entrusted to implement and enforce prohibition norms for drug use even resisted these national reforms, reflecting the reluctance of important global players to move beyond the IDCR's interpretation as the War on Drugs. The European Union, for example, remains largely committed to the existing interpretation of the treaty framework; Russia and China strongly defend it on the basis of a 'prohibitionist equilibrium;' and the United States under President Joe Biden inherited the legacy of former President Trump's hardline approach, which is difficult to reverse swiftly.

Amid these diverging trends, the IDCR is at a crossroads. Will the international community move toward a modernized, yet traditionally coercive War on Drugs approach? Or will it transform the War on Drugs approach to redefine the meaning of 'putting people first' through a new paradigm based on a more comprehensive cost-benefit analysis than has been the case so far?[10]

Argument and Contributions

This book challenges simplistic and often biased accounts by asking how the War on Drugs has affected vulnerable regions across the world and what the ramifications have been for the IDCR. It constitutes the first comprehensive and systematic scholarly effort to theoretically, conceptually, and empirically investigate the impacts of the IDCR across issue areas and regions.[11] This volume uses the term War on Drugs (capitalized) to refer to a global phenomenon with multifaceted manifestations across different regions and issue areas. As Annette Idler points out in Chapter 1, these include the well-known US-led War on Drugs, but also the wars fought in other regions such as Myanmar, and the literal and symbolic wars against drug users across the globe.

This book's overarching argument is threefold, based on cutting-edge research and knowledge from experts on the ground. First, analyzing and mitigating the harmful impacts of the IDCR's interpretation in the form of the War on Drugs holistically requires people-centered rather than state-centric approaches. Second, the impacts of interpreting the IDCR in the form of the War on Drugs are 'glocal,' that is, they manifest themselves across the local and the global levels and thus cannot be addressed with state level forms of militarization alone.[12] Third, there are notable asymmetries among governments with regard to their vulnerabilities and capacities to respond to the challenge of the illicit production, trade, and use of drugs that do not necessarily coincide with the world's so-called North–South divide. The positions of governments of vulnerable regions both shape and have been shaped by the IDCR.

Through this threefold argument, the volume makes several novel contributions toward understanding, and ultimately tackling, the pressing challenges linked to the global War on Drugs.

First, this volume reveals the repercussions of securitizing global governance issues beyond drug policy. Critically evaluating the IDCR's securitization through the War on Drugs provides key insights into other global governance realms. Even though the United Nations Office on Drugs and Crime (UNODC) and the International Narcotics Control Board (INCB)—two pillars of the IDCR—made it explicit that the conventions do not require a War on Drugs and cannot be used to defend human rights violations, mandatory treatment, or the death penalty,[13] in practice many countries have interpreted and applied them from the perspective of intense criminalization. Hence the need to analyze the IDCR not only with a view to its intentions but also its results. The contributions in this volume challenge the binary framing of securitization versus desecuritization of drug policies that has shaped the debate so far by scrutinizing the War on Drugs from people-centered perspectives, for example by adopting a human security or a sustainable development lens. This conceptual move highlights how public policy labels such as the War on Drugs or the War on Terror create and perpetuate security issues based on biased threat perceptions. The labelling of the War on Drugs has turned it into a real war against multiple enemies. At the same time, it has shaped the international security agenda of the previous and current centuries by producing explosive, and rarely successful, mixes of counterinsurgency and counternarcotic strategies. This book challenges conventional thinking in defense and security sectors, whose military lenses create analytical blinders that neglect the diversity and complexity of the causes that these wars are intended to defend or defeat. The findings of this book thus also make rethinking securitized policy approaches such as the War on Terror or militarized responses to forced migration inevitable.

Second, the book offers a nuanced analysis of the multifaceted glocal impacts of the IDCR. It counters false dichotomies of global governance versus micro-level impacts by highlighting the glocal character of the IDCR and its local manifestations. Unlike existing works on drug control, this volume does not solely present research on either the institutional architecture (regime)[14] or on how illicit drug use and responses to it affect individual countries and regions,[15] but traces the links between the two. This book bridges the local and the global by tracing historical, current, and hypothetical future developments in international drug control efforts and the international interdependencies that arise from global illicit drug flows, assessing their impact on human rights, order, security, development, public health, and related socio-economic dimensions. The volume integrates analyses of criminal justice and human rights concerns with perspectives on health and human development, and considers metrics to measure advances in these dimensions. This approach allows us to contextualize drug use and its repercussions on public health within broader sociopolitical and economic trends as some countries become wealthier than others.

This volume also unpacks the dynamics behind illicit drug markets, the fluid motivations of the 'warriors,' and the multifaceted changing consequences for the 'victims' of this war, bearing in mind that the lines between warrior and victim are often blurred. Combining glocal and transnational perspectives, the book highlights the interconnectedness of the War on Drugs' cross-border impacts and evaluates how the IDCR may be revised with a view to reducing harm glocally. By doing so, it advances an important debate in the social sciences literature: on the local manifestations of global regimes.

Third, the book demonstrates common patterns of the impacts of the War on Drugs across vulnerable regions and elucidates why these regions have adopted certain positions. This becomes clear when historicizing and culturally contextualizing governments' perspectives in vulnerable regions across the globe. This volume departs from the conventional separation between developed and developing countries that prevails in the drug policy literature and that has perpetuated the global North–South divide. Instead, it adopts a 'vulnerabilities' approach: the chapters in Part II focus on those regions where international drug control initiatives severely undermine people's security and that lack the capacities to adequately cope with this situation. These regions include South America, Central America, West Africa, the Middle East and the Golden Crescent (Afghanistan, Iran, and Pakistan), the Golden Triangle (Laos, Myanmar, and Thailand), and Russia. To avoid portraying regions more homogenously than they are, the book discusses differences at local and national levels within each of the chapters, but it also derives conclusions that hold transnationally within each of the regions identified in this volume as vulnerable (see Chapter 1 by Annette Idler).[16] The local and national levels matter because drug policies and their ramifications differ within and across countries. Drug policies in South America, for example, cannot be understood without analyzing Uruguay, Bolivia, and Colombia separately: Uruguay as one of the first countries worldwide to legalize marijuana for recreational use; Bolivia, with its unique history of coca as a legal traditional product; and Colombia, with a counternarcotic policy that has been intertwined with counterinsurgency measures. Combining the examination of the local and national levels with a transnational approach, this volume analyzes entire regions by following the logic of production or transit sites to account for cross-border flows.

A Critical Moment in Global Affairs

The liminal state of the IDCR reflects the current critical moment in global affairs. At a time when global order is in flux, with the return of geopolitics to the center of the world stage on the one hand,[17] and rising rates of (low-intensity) violence on the other, rigorously scrutinizing how to move forward in the area of drug policies also sheds light on tackling other pressing challenges the world faces today. The War on Drugs constitutes an extreme case of the international security arena in a fractured world where traditional leadership from the United States and other Western powers can no longer be taken for granted. This extreme case highlights the need for a globally harmonized response to the drug problem, rather than the current model of clashing national policy approaches. It also elucidates the intractable links between local agendas and global geopolitics that shape the world's evolving security landscape. A more people-centered soft power approach, reflected in the SDGs, has partly sidelined conventional power politics. New emerging powers such as China, India, and Brazil have shaken up the old predictable power distribution, making a focus on vulnerable regions a *sine qua non* for understanding the world.

Geopolitical developments such as the end of the Cold War, 9/11, the rise of China on the world stage, and the Arab Spring have had dual effects on the regime. On the one hand, they have produced a shift of power among the regime's influential actors, including the five permanent members of the UN Security Council. On the other, they have triggered changes in the constellation of violent entrepreneurs involved in the illicit drug business and in how this business interrelates with other forms of transnational organized crime, armed conflict, and instability. Together, these developments suggest that grasping the world's interdependence and interconnectedness requires cutting across global, regional, and local phenomena rather than focusing on one of these levels in isolation.

Amid these shifts, a sustained and informed discussion on the multiple facets of transforming the War on Drugs is essential to overcoming the current moment of uncertainty surrounding the IDCR and paving the way to transforming other securitized policy areas such as counterterrorism and migration. This book intends to do just that by offering the necessary critical thinking, historical contextualization, and up-to-date evidence. The urgency of finding consensus on effective solutions to the world drug problem has triggered policy reports, briefings, and proposals, yet deeper and wider critical reflection on the IDCR is missing. Most contemporary drug policy studies serve advocacy purposes, for example to promote a public health approach or to defend human rights. They tend to focus on perspectives from specific stakeholders, particularly the United States or European governments. Against this backdrop, the goal of this book is to respond to the need for rigorous theoretical tools that guide evidence-based drug policies in a rapidly changing global context.

A Collaborative Effort

This book is the result of a collaborative project. The project's goals are to enhance understanding of the multifaceted impacts that the War on Drugs has had on vulnerable regions as well as of their respective positions in the regime, and to identify leverage points for change in international drug policy to strengthen people-centered approaches to the world drug problem.

The project brought together an international group of academic and policy experts who jointly adopt an approach conducive to these goals and a common language to analyze the various dimensions of the challenges of the IDCR's securitized interpretation. This approach has four distinctive features. First, it is multidisciplinary, to elucidate how the War on Drugs has affected various issue areas. It involves scrutinizing the IDCR from a variety of disciplinary angles, including international relations and political science, geography, history, sociology, criminology, and development studies. The experts with these disciplinary backgrounds include well-established scholars as well as early-career scholars, who bring to the subjects fresh new perspectives.

Second, the book's approach integrates various epistemologies. Historical and interpretivist approaches meet positivist perspectives, supported by a variety of different quantitative and qualitative methods, ranging from statistical analysis and systematic reviews of existing studies to ethnographic methods including interviews and observation. The book thus benefits from a dialogue between two groups of scholars: those whose work focuses on large-scale trends and shifts in drug policy, and those whose work builds on a bottom-up approach based on extensive fieldwork.

Third, leading experts from vulnerable regions, including countries such as Colombia, Ghana, Mexico, Russia, and Uruguay, contribute their expertise to this volume, in addition to renowned regional experts who have studied their respective regions for decades. Rather than perpetuating dominant Western perspectives, this book offers diverse expertise, facilitating rounded comparative insights that account for the particularities of each context.

Finally, this volume's approach is theoretically grounded in bodies of work on regimes, development, and security studies, and it also addresses the drug policy literature and practice. Comprising distinguished academics and experienced practitioners, the authors further theoretical debates, including on the securitization of other global governance realms, and bring in concrete country experiences and their direct work with multilateral organizations and governments.

The book's design can be loosely described as a structured, focused comparison. After outlining the evolution of the IDCR and its interpretation as the War on Drugs in the first part, the second part of the book presents various vulnerable regions across the globe. The third part focuses on the impacts of the interpretation of the IDCR as the War on Drugs across varying issue areas. A common set of questions informs each chapter (see the Annex for the guiding questions). This structure aims to elucidate the multifaceted impacts of the IDCR and the leverage points for transformation, while considering the realities of the respective regions. The questions evolve around the IDCR, its effectiveness, as well as stances of the various countries on it. This systematic approach facilitates dialogue and identifying connections between the various issue areas addressed in this volume. It culminates in concluding reflections on the War on Drugs thread that runs—sometimes explicitly, sometimes more implicitly—through the chapters.

In July 2015, the group of experts came together for a workshop in New York to critically discuss the state and the impact of the IDCR across regions and subject areas. They also engaged with policymakers, ambassadors, senior UN officials, and civil society representatives to explore how a scholarly rigorous book could inform long-term policymaking. After UNGASS 2016, the group further took stock of the advances and retrenchments in the international policy arena. This included analyzing the UN's review of the 10-year global strategy, which intended to significantly reduce the illicit drug market by 2019, as well as identifying opportunities for the post-2019 global drug strategy. The present book is the result of this in-depth engagement with the IDCR.

Outline of the Book

Chapter 1 develops the concepts and themes that theoretically underpin the book, which help move beyond the dichotomous understanding of drug policies as the securitized status quo of the War on Drugs on the one hand, and the desecuritization of drug policies on the other. These concepts include 'people-centered' security, the notion of the glocal in the context of the IDCR, and 'vulnerable regions'. The chapter demonstrates the analytical utility of a critical approach to drug policies, as it helps unpack the benefits of desecuritizing some drug policies without discarding the advantages of politicizing security in others.

Part I: The Changing Character of the War on Drugs

Equipped with the theoretical and conceptual tools from Chapter 1, Part I provides a historical background of the War on Drugs and the IDCR.

Chapter 2 asserts that, once the IDCR was established after the 1960s, drug consumption rates rose and drug supplies, trafficking routes, and trafficking organizations expanded and diversified. The chapter highlights three historical developments related to the current debate and crisis of the IDCR. First, it presents the major treaties and institutions that influenced the evolution of the IDCR; second, it analyzes the special role of the United States in the creation of norms and politics of the IDCR; and third, it surveys the long-term impacts of the IDCR on patterns of supply and use of two classes of global drugs, opiates and cocaine. The chapter finds that the global history of opiates since 1900 under the IDCR hardly represents a success story. Moreover, illicit cocaine expanded to unprecedented heights under the militarized IDCR.

Building on the historical background provided in Chapter 2, Chapter 3 presents more recent tensions around the policy direction that the so-called Vienna consensus entailed. The chapter explores the specific set of interwoven and interrelated themes that have challenged the IDCR. It explains the regulatory architecture of the IDCR, including the main stakeholders in the system and their interests, as well as the broader trends in the architecture. It argues that there are political differences among the various stakeholders that increasingly fracture the regime: while some states push for some type of reform, others resist change. The chapter concludes that there will be a turning point that is likely to either fragment or reconfigure the system.

Chapter 4 focuses on a particularly critical moment in the changing character of the War on Drugs: UNGASS 2016. It explains why

UNGASS 2016 produced high expectations for a breakthrough in the transformation of the War on Drugs, and why these expectations were subsequently not met. The lack of both a clear blueprint for reform and sound leadership among the countries that demanded adjustments to the IDCR were detrimental to advancing concrete changes. Overall, the chapter argues that UNGASS 2016 facilitated entry points for working toward more balanced and comprehensive drug policies, highlighting the importance of human rights, public health, and development. Nonetheless, it closed the door to substantial change in the interpretation of the IDCR and with it, to meaningful transformation of the War on Drugs.

Part II: Between Warriors and Victims: The War on Drugs across Vulnerable Regions

The second part of this volume zooms in on the regions identified as vulnerable to the world drug problem, the harmful impacts of the current interpretation of the IDCR, and the various faces of the War on Drugs. Just as drug flows have shifted across regions over time (as shown by Paul Gootenberg in Chapter 2), the book's regional rather than state-focused approach highlights the transnational logics of the illicit drug business. These transnational logics stand in stark contrast to national approaches to drug policy. The differing ways in which governments have adopted drug policies at the local and national levels reflect the diverging views that countries, UN agencies, and civil society organizations have of the IDCR (see Chapter 3 by Christopher Hallam and David Bewley-Taylor). Here surfaces another tension: the mismatch between what is labelled and measured as 'success' at the global level (see Chapter 14 by Robert Muggah and Katherine Aguirre), and the repercussions the IDCR has had in the form of the global War on Drugs. While Chapters 5 to 7 discuss mainly cocaine-related policies, Chapters 8 to 10 center on those related to opium.

Chapter 5 focuses on South America, the region where global cocaine flows originate, and where reform and debates about new domestic drug policies are likely to emerge. Despite the consensus on the need for change, this chapter argues there is little consensus on what this change entails, and that most governments still support the legal cornerstones of the IDCR. The chapter contends that three factors influence the region's endorsement for change: first, evolving US foreign policy; second, growing violence in the region; and third, changes in supply chain networks of cocaine. These have made intraregional and domestic markets more prominent, encouraging governments to recognize that drug policies have generated new problems. The chapter concludes by assessing the possibilities and obstacles for drug policy reform in the region.

Chapter 6 moves up the supply chain and north to Central America, the major transit zone between cocaine production in South America and the US market. Like Chapter 8, it highlights US influence and soaring violence as factors that determine the region's position in the international drug policy debate. The chapter argues that, instead of reducing harm in the region, the IDCR has triggered collateral damage in Central America that outweighs its success in deterring the illicit production, trafficking, and consumption of drugs. It shows that the negative effects of the IDCR are more visible in producer and transit countries because prohibitionist drug policies have transferred a large portion of social and financial costs onto them.

Chapter 7 moves from the South American production sites westward to the second-largest trafficking route toward Europe, with West Africa as a major transit zone. Revisiting the historical shifts in drug flows discussed in Chapter 2, this chapter traces West Africa's historical involvement in the illicit drug trade. It analyzes how poverty, corruption, fragility, and ineffective law enforcement and oversight of West African state institutions have contributed to the region's gradual transformation into a consumption zone, rather than a transit route for illicit drug flows. Calls for additional demand reduction interventions at the national level have therefore shaped drug policies in the region. The chapter concludes with a reflection on the usefulness of decriminalizing the illicit consumption of drugs.

While the previous three chapters focus on cocaine, the next three chapters center around opiates, the second major class of global drugs presented in Chapter 2. Chapter 8 discusses the IDCR in Pakistan, Afghanistan, and Iran where, toward the end of the twentieth century, the illicit use of drugs started to spread widely. The chapter argues that, despite the centrality of Afghanistan to the world's opiate market, it is only since 1979 and the Soviet invasion that it has had to confront multiple drug-related policy issues. Consequently, Afghanistan remains comparatively inexperienced in implementing drug policies. It shows that, as is the case with other countries coming to the IDCR challenge relatively late, the Crescent states rely much more on hard power than soft power solutions. The countries' assertions of national preoccupations in areas like judicial conduct reflect the region's highly distinct set of social mores and cultural values.

Chapter 9 explores the effectiveness (or lack thereof) of repressive policies in Southeast Asia, particularly Myanmar and Laos of the so-called Golden Triangle. It provides a detailed history as well as political and geographical discussion about the illicit drug trade, its decline, and resilience in the region. The chapter argues that opium production remains a significant challenge to sustainable development. Accordingly, forced eradication has proven to be ineffective. Furthermore, the chapter argues, the drug control community largely overlooks the fact that most drug control policies have been inadequate and counterproductive, leading to enormous human, societal, and economic costs in the region.

Moving on from opium production to transit and consumption sites, Chapter 10 assesses Russia's position in the IDCR. It explains that the country has undergone a shift in its dynamics and patterns of illicitly used drugs, and outlines Russia's unique circumstances as a major global illicit drug market and the single largest country market for Afghan heroin. The chapter also elaborates on Russia's composite stance on the liberalization of drug use and a reform or 'upgrade' of the IDCR. Building on Chapters 8 and 9, it argues that the shift to heroin dominance in 2000 was the result of two developments: first, the overproduction of opiates and unprecedented increase in Afghanistan's opiate output in the early twenty-first century; and second, the economic situation in Central Asia, including the growing dependence of the region's economies and populations on licit and illicit cross-border trade.

Part III: Between Securitization and People-Centered Policies: A Glocal Perspective on the War on Drugs

The third part of the volume demonstrates how a people-centered approach reveals the nuanced impacts that the IDCR in its predominant interpretation as the War on Drugs has had across policy domains. These include criminal justice, human rights, health, and development.

Chapter 11 addresses the prohibitionist argument that has historically dominated the IDCR discourse (see Chapter 2 by Paul Gootenberg), and falls under the broader 'securitization' agenda outlined in Chapter 1. Analyzing studies that deal with the link between narcotics and crime, the chapter evaluates whether existing empirical evidence backs up prohibitionist fears of rising crime through the illicit use of drugs. It shows that the association between the two does not necessarily imply causality, and that analysts disagree on how to interpret this connection. Furthermore, the chapter highlights a tendency to use non-representative samples of individuals within criminal justice populations with higher rates of drug prevalence in existing studies, thereby exaggerating the proportion of crime caused by the illicit use of drugs.

Adopting a human rights and health perspective, Chapter 12 further challenges the prohibitionist approach by calling into question the securitization/desecuritization dichotomy discussed earlier. It demonstrates the IDCR's impacts on people's security by highlighting systematic human rights abuses, most notably in drug control. Despite governments' efforts to contain human rights violations in several countries and regions, the ramifications for vulnerable groups continue to be a cause for concern. On the desecuritization side, the chapter discusses the need for accountability in the implementation of health measures, arguing that punitive approaches hamper harm reduction. It concludes that a treaty reform is necessary to undo historical injustices, amend undemocratic procedures, and reform the disproven theories underpinning contemporary international drug control.

Chapter 13 leaves the securitization debate behind and argues instead for a human development approach to drug policy. Taking the 2030 Agenda for Sustainable Development as a reference point, it reflects upon the basic premises that would be included in a development-based approach. Pinpointing the negative impacts that the War on Drugs has had on the most vulnerable people and on development more broadly, it contends that such an approach would improve the IDCR's effectiveness and reduce the harms associated with its implementation.

Chapter 14 integrates the critical views from across the domains of criminal justice, human rights, health, and development presented in Chapters 11 to 13 to suggest new drug policy metrics. It links back to the historical overview of the evolution of drug supply and use discussed in Chapter 2 by revealing how traditional drug policy indicators that reinforce the securitized War on Drugs discourse have justified and sustained the IDCR since the 1960s. Rather than proving the IDCR's success, such traditional indicators have exposed how severe the policy has been, for example by counting the number of people incarcerated for drug-related crimes, without showing its impact. The chapter thus proposes alternative goals, targets, and indicators to overcome the current limbo situation, better track the effects of a progressive drug policy, and shift to a more holistic drug policy paradigm.

The conclusion synthesizes the overall contribution of the book. It discusses how the War on Drugs has been a global phenomenon with nuanced manifestations at the local level across vulnerable regions, and how the character of the War on Drugs has changed over time. It points to the implications that the transformation of the War on Drugs paradigm can have for effectuating positive change in other areas of global affairs, such as the War on Terror.

1

WARRIORS, VICTIMS, AND VULNERABLE REGIONS
A CRITICAL PERSPECTIVE ON THE WAR ON DRUGS

Annette Idler

What started as a slogan in 1971—the War on Drugs—has triggered or perpetuated real wars not just on drugs, but also on drug users. These wars have inflicted large-scale human suffering across the various steps of illicit drug supply chains, from production to consumption, eroding licit livelihoods in production zones, increasing levels of violence along major trafficking routes, and undermining vulnerable people's health in market sites.[1] The mismatch between a predominantly coercive approach resulting from the War on Drugs paradigm, and the social, economic, and political manifestations of the illicit drug trade have also had 'hard' security ramifications beyond the illicit drug business. Given the networked character of multiple types of supply chains, it has contributed to the trafficking of arms, ammunition, and other goods that fuel conflict and spread violence across the globe (see Chapter 7 by John M. Pokoo and Kwesi Aning).[2] Together, these developments have reinforced global inequalities.

19

'The regulation of drugs should be pursued because they are risky, not because they are safe,' a 2014 report of the Global Commission on Drug Policy famously stated.[3] But the current interpretation of the international regime under which drugs are addressed is itself risky, as these illustrations show. Strategies to address the world drug problem have hardly changed:[4] numerous governments continue to destroy illicit crops and laboratories, detain or militarily target small-scale traffickers, and punish drug users. As discussed in the introductory chapter to this volume, not only do people continue to suffer under these measures, also the illicit drug trade continues to thrive. This questions both the means through which results are sought to be achieved and the results themselves.

This chapter argues that the world drug problem's primary framing as a national security issue by policymakers has greatly contributed to the international community's failure to curb the global illicit drug trade more effectively and to the human suffering that drug policies have caused. It holds that the drug problem only partly constitutes a threat to states; more substantively, it threatens the security of people. Often, it is not an issue of security at all, but one of public health, sustainable development, or other public policy realms. Accordingly, and borrowing from securitization theory and a critical approach to security, the chapter acknowledges that the world drug problem is indeed an urgent issue that requires extraordinary measures. However, it contends that such measures need to be adjusted to considerations of global security, rather than primarily of national security.

The chapter proposes a framework constructed around three main features, which allows to analytically unpack these distinct repercussions of the world drug problem at multiple levels. It discusses why these features are conducive to more effective drug policies and serve as entry points to transform the War on Drugs.

As a first feature, the framework embraces the concept of global security that includes people, in addition to political entities, as referent objects. This permits enhancing our understanding of the IDCR's impact on the security of individuals, (vulnerable) groups, and communities. Inspired by scholars who argue that security should be defined by actors other than the state,[5] a people-centered security lens serves 'to question how state elites use security and the merits of policies based on zero-sum, statist and militaristic understandings.'[6]

Second, the framework accounts for the drug problem's *glocality*. A 'glocal' analysis links a bottom-up approach with a macro-perspective on the illicit production, trade, and use of drugs in order to elucidate the manifoldness of challenges resulting from the drug problem as well as the impact of drug policies on a continuum ranging from the sub-state to the supra-state level. It sheds light on why governments need to adjust measures that are part of emergency action intended to respond to the drug problem to the most relevant level of analysis, rather than to prioritize state-level forms of militarization in a generalized manner. These levels of analysis include the global level via global governance measures in order to curtail, for example, global illicit supply chain networks that destabilize entire regions. They also concern the local level via targeted policies that address, for instance, the livelihood situations of farmers or traders.

Third, the framework focuses on *vulnerable regions* across the globe and their societies' perspectives on how to best tackle the world drug problem against the backdrop of their specific cultural, historical, and geographical context. Such a focus challenges the North–South divide that has been implicit in the discourse of the War on Drugs. It requires identifying the vulnerabilities of regions. These vulnerabilities arise from their geographic locations along illicit supply chains, their exposures to shocks and stresses, and shortcomings in their coping capacities.

Together, the framework integrates findings from various bodies of literature, including on: the IDCR and its associated policymaking processes that shape the War on Drugs discourse;[7] why and how the use of this discourse fuels wars across the globe;[8] and specific issue areas of the illicit drug trade, for example cultivation, drug violence, and addiction.[9]

Before developing the framework, a brief discussion of drug policies' framing as national security issue in the context of the War on Drugs is in order. Policymakers and analysts have been securitizing drug policies for decades, which is epitomized in the label that has been attached to drug policies—the War on Drugs. According to securitization theory, governments use the 'security' label through 'speech acts,' televisual images, and other nonverbal forms of communication to elevate issues above politics.[10] 'Security talk' (or visuals) prioritizes these issues on policymakers' agendas:[11] 'what makes a particular speech act [or other form of communication] a specifically "security" act—a "securitization"—is its casting of the issue as one of an "existential threat," which calls for extraordinary measures beyond the routines and norms of everyday politics.'[12] Through the speech acts or visuals, the 'securitizing actor' generates an audience's endorsement of 'emergency measures beyond rules that would otherwise bind.'[13] A successful securitization therefore 'has three components (or steps): existential threats [to a nation state], emergency action, and effects on interunit relations by breaking free of rules.'[14]

This securitization can be traced back to the key milestones of the current interpretations of the IDCR, such as political declarations and other policy documents: they portray the world drug problem as an existential threat to national security. Likewise, the preambles of the UN conventions present narcotic drugs as an existential threat.[15] The 1961 UN Single Convention on Narcotic Drugs states that 'addiction to narcotic drugs constitutes a serious evil for the individual and is fraught with social and economic danger to mankind.'[16] States should 'combat this evil.' This view was reinforced in 1971 when then US President Nixon declared 'drug abuse' to be the 'public enemy number one' and launched the War on Drugs.[17] Subsequent policy documents, notably the 1988 UN Convention against Illicit Traffic in Narcotic Drugs and Psychotropic Substances, which referred to the threat to the fabric of society, and to a 'danger of incalculable gravity' to youth, further contributed to the securitization of drugs. Since 1990, every political declaration on drugs has manifested similar language.

This continuous narrative of threat has perpetuated the IDCR's securitized character without reducing the social, economic, and human costs of the illicit production, trade, and use of drugs.[19] It served policymakers to justify extraordinary measures to address the problem. Examples include: eradicating illicit drug cultivation by toxic fumigating, which destroys both illicit and licit crops, and causes serious health problems in adults, children, and fetuses; enacting disproportionately severe forms of punishment for trafficking and consumption; and using the military rather than the police to tackle criminal violence.

The core components of securitization ('existential threats, emergency action, and effects on interunit relations by breaking free of rules'),[20] emblematic of the War on Drugs discourse, help explain three implicit assumptions of the prevailing interpretation of the IDCR. The first assumption is that the state lies at the center of drug policies because the *existential threat* concerns the state as the referent object of security. The second assumption is that, as a security challenge, the world drug problem requires governments to adopt a militarized response as a common approach to *emergency action*. The third assumption is that the ethnocentric perspective of the so-called Global North takes precedence over other perspectives, perpetuating an artificial North–South divide according to which the Western-biased perspective of the North is privileged in '*breaking free of rules*' when it suits them. But of course, especially in the realm of the War on Drugs, as Loader and Walker note:

> Security is ... destined to remain beyond our grasp. Not only does this mean that there can never ... be 'enough' security measures, which hold out a promise of protection while always also signifying the presence of threat and danger. It also warns us that responding to demands for order in the terms in which they present themselves (that is, ... 'wars' against drugs, or crime, or terror) can be little more than a bid to quench the unquenchable.[21]

Many scholars, including some representing the Copenhagen School who developed the securitization theory, thus call for desecuritizing drug policies. Accordingly, 'normal' political debates, including those around human rights, citizen security, sustainable development, and public health, would guide these policies, in addition to national security. Illicitly produced, traded, and used drugs would thus move back from 'securitized' to 'politicized,' effectively turning them into a part of broader public policy debates. Alternatively, they would become 'nonpoliticized,' in which case they would not even be a political issue.[22]

As the next section shows, the framework developed here moves beyond the dichotomous understanding of drug policies with the largely securitized status quo epitomized in the War on Drugs discourse on the one hand, and the call for desecuritizing drug policies on the other. It highlights that securitization can be helpful in some cases, but that, largely, the challenges that emanate from the world drug problem are more usefully treated in a different way.

The Case for Transformation: Changing the War Paradigm

Understanding the world drug problem through a framework that brings together the concepts of global, and hence people-centered, security, glocality, and vulnerable regions challenges the implicit assumptions (state-centrism, prioritizing militarization, ethnocentrism) of the IDCR's current interpretation as War on Drugs. Rather than falling into a binary of securitizing or desecuritizing drug policies, such a framework facilitates drawing on a portfolio of coercive (e.g., military, law enforcement) and transformative (e.g., development-focused, therapeutic) approaches that can be adopted in line with the particular issue that the illicit drug trade and the strategies to address it have generated.

Adequately balancing coercive and transformative approaches hinges on accounting for the experiences and perceptions of the people who are engaged in, and affected by, the illicit drugs business, hence the people-centered approach to security in this framework. This is consistent with a critical security studies approach that raises and addresses 'the concerns of referents other than the state/regime.'[23] It highlights that the security of individuals, groups, and communities—as well as their health, rights, and opportunities for development—are at risk along illicit supply chains, not only national security. Concepts that fall under the umbrella of such a people-centered approach include, for example, human security,[24] defined as freedom from fear, freedom from want, and dignity;[25] and citizen security, understood as the reduction of violence, threats, and fear through a mutually reinforcing state-society relationship.[26] Human development and the Sustainable Development Goals include citizen security as a major component of human well-being; they are intimately related concepts (see Chapter 13 by Javier Sagredo). Given that the drug problem's manifestations are multi-faceted and operate at the local and global level, the framework addresses this glocality. Any portfolio of approaches needs to be tailored to these different levels. Finally, the appropriateness, feasibility, and impact of distinct coercive and transformative approaches rest at least partly on the historical, cultural, and geographic context of a region and the societies living in it. This context, in turn, informs the region's vulnerability, the third conceptual underpinning included here.

The framework helps identify avenues for transforming the war paradigm in a way that makes drug policies more inclusive of 'the voiceless, the unrepresented, and the powerless.'[27] It expands what has mainly been a top-down approach focused on state elites by adding a bottom-up approach that embraces marginalized voices. By doing so, it serves as an entry point to promote emancipation, which is conducive to addressing the world drug problem because it frees people from constraints.[28] In the case of the illicit production, trade, and use of drugs, examples of these constraints include depriving coca or poppy farmers of alternative livelihoods in the absence of legal economic opportunities; committing violence against community members by drug cartels who consider them to be obstacles to their illicit businesses; disproportionately punishing small-scale traffickers; or engaging in human rights violations by government officials against drug consumers.

Alker (2005) claims that deciding whether securitizing a policy issue or politicizing security is more conducive to change 'must be answered empirically, historically, discursively.'[29] Transformation, then, is possible through two avenues. The first avenue takes seriously the experiences of those who feel threatened and considers these threats a security issue. The second avenue desecuritizes issues that are more effectively dealt with under a 'normal' political debate. Accordingly, addiction, for example, is dealt with under a debate on public health that involves weighing up options of therapeutic treatments rather than punishment. This requires balancing human rights, citizen security, sustainable development, and public health considerations, the themes that this book brings together as one holistic approach.

In what follows, the chapter demonstrates how the securitization of the world drug problem has imposed analytical blinders on those studying and shaping the IDCR. Removing these blinders suggests the need to shift the interpretation of the IDCR: from privileging state-centric to also accounting for people-centered security; from prioritizing militarization to embracing differentiated, glocal responses; and from perpetuating a Global North–South divide to adopting a vulnerable regions perspective.

i. From State-Centric to People-Centered Security

The first implicit assumption of the IDCR's interpretation in form of the War on Drugs is that the state represents the referent of security, hence the notion that drugs are a threat to national security. As Bailey sums up, national security 'is concerned with protection of the state, territorial integrity, and sovereignty, and essential state functions and agencies from threats by other states or trans-state actors, such as terrorism, organized crime, and the like.'[30] In the 1980s, in the context of the nuclear stalemate and increasing international interdependence through rising economic and environmental agendas, scholars and analysts increasingly criticized the militarily-focused concept of national security and studied security in a broader sense. With the end of the Cold War, the state's relevance also changed, as non-state actors and transnational actors such as non-governmental organizations and firms became increasingly influential in world politics. Accordingly, the global security agenda expanded to issues around identity and transnational organized crime. In this sense, the world drug problem is largely one that concerns global security; it lies outside the control of individual nation-states and affects people regardless of which state they belong to.[31]

Nonetheless, the IDCR is still anchored in the mostly state-centric UN conventions. They lend themselves to justifying a War on Drugs discourse that puts national security first. For example, the preamble of the 1988 UN Convention against Illicit Traffic in Narcotic Drugs and Psychotropic Substances states that 'illicit production of, demand for, and traffic in [drugs] adversely affect[s] the economic, cultural and political foundations of society … [and] links between illicit traffic and other related organized criminal activities … undermine the legitimate economies and threaten the stability, security and sovereignty of States.'[32]

Applying this logic in an undifferentiated manner means that those involved in the illicit drug trade are the state's enemies—warriors that need to be defeated to avoid that they victimize the state's own 'rank and file.' By alienating those involved in the illicit drug trade from the state, this logic impedes them from engaging in livelihoods that positively influence the security of the societies in which they are embedded. Given that the threat arising from the world drug problem is considered existential as well as external to the state and thus is presented as requiring radical measures rather than nuanced responses, the label 'enemy' is often applied in a generalized way to anyone involved, regardless of the severity or intentionality of their involvement.

Yet such generalizations are problematic. Even though states are responsible for designing drug policies and are the principal actors that form part of the IDCR as signatories of the conventions, the referent of security is not limited to the state. Certainly, links between various types of illicit flows including drugs and weapons for example do threaten the security of states in some cases; national security can be at risk. But this does not mean that all aspects of, and actors involved in, the illicit drug trade, are best understood through a state-centric lens. As the remainder of this section demonstrates, most of those involved in the illicit drug trade are not a threat to state security; their own security is at stake, and often due to the state's actions.

Blurring the Lines between Perpetrators and Victims

The War on Drugs paradigm has blurred the lines between perpetrators and victims. It portrays the world drug problem as 'enemy number one,' which has led numerous governments and analysts to categorize those involved in it as perpetrators. Using a people-centered viewpoint to unpack simplistic dichotomies such as 'perpetrators and victims' helps us understand why one person's perpetrator, or 'warrior,' is another person's victim. Consider for example poor poppy farmers in Afghanistan or Myanmar who face eradication of their illicit crops. These confrontations with heavily armed soldiers who take away their livelihoods alienate the farmers from the state. Poppy farmers have been stigmatized as being on the side of 'evil,' notwithstanding their poverty and lack of alternative livelihoods. In many conflict contexts, guerrillas and other armed groups draw on the illicit drug trade to sustain their fighting; they thus indeed jeopardize the state's security. If farmers cultivate crops illicitly in guerrilla-controlled territory, they are typically stigmatized as guerrilla collaborators. Universally adopted coercive drug policies turn these farmers into warriors 'by necessity,' involving them in the inescapable logics of war, even if they reject violence as a means to induce political change. For example, when the author of this chapter asked a coca farmer from the Andes about the expected arrival of the anti-narcotics officials on his land, he responded, 'What shall we do when they arrive, shall we fight?'

Accounting for the moral economy of these farmers questions punitive measures against illicit production,[33] including the opium ban in Afghanistan, manual illicit crop eradication in Myanmar and Thailand, or toxic sprayings in Colombia. These measures were motivated by lowering the threat of the influx of drugs into the United States and other Western states in order to protect their national security. However, at least since the 1970s, they have not only failed to substantially stall these flows but also endangered the security of the farmers cultivating the crops required for the illicit production of drugs (see Chapter 5 by Angélica Durán-Martínez, Chapter 8 by Philip Robins, and Chapter 9 by Pierre-Arnaud Chouvy).[34] Changing supply side dynamics by providing alternative livelihood opportunities for coca or poppy farmers puts people first in a holistic way. Chapter 9 highlights various models such as alternative development projects, integrated rural development, and sustainable livelihoods approaches that allow farmers to engage in alternative economic activities in regions where coca and poppy are cultivated and processed into cocaine or heroin. This includes regions such as the Andean region, the Golden Triangle (Laos, Myanmar, and Thailand), and the Golden Crescent (Afghanistan, Iran, and Pakistan). Another approach is to strengthen and regulate the markets for traditional products such as coca tea and medicine, or for new products such as energizing drinks, allowing farmers to continue cultivating coca or poppy in the absence of alternatives. Orienting coca or poppy production toward local, regional, and national markets rather than illicit international export can further create incentives for a more sustainable agriculture.[35]

In addition to people involved in production, those engaged in trafficking may be victims. Considering all traffickers equally as the enemy misses complex ethical considerations concerning the personal circumstances of these individuals. Powerful organized criminals often force small-scale smugglers to traffic drugs across borders in questionable conditions, especially in regions where legal economic opportunities are scarce. At border crossings between Colombia and Venezuela for instance, border guards found cocaine hidden in dead babies and people's stomachs. These have included cases of female traffickers who were single mothers living in poverty and forced to traffic drugs for these powerful criminal groups. The women may not report threats by the armed group to the police due to prior experience of abuse or of not being taken seriously because of their gender. If people traffic drugs voluntarily and independently, armed groups frequently charge them taxes.[36] Since these small-scale traffickers engage in illegal activities, they cannot seek protection from the state. As discussed below, sometimes state agents themselves take advantage of the vulnerable positions in which small-scale traffickers find themselves. As a result, the traffickers feel safer following the rules established by illegal actors who they depend on for protection rather than abiding by the rules of a state who does not provide protection.[37]

Further to material circumstances, the psychological motivations of those involved in, and affected by, the illicit drug trade need to be critically scrutinized. Perpetrators of violence (for example against law enforcement officials, rival drug gangs, or civilians encumbering their trafficking) can be vulnerable because they have been humiliated and shamed. Engaging in violence is often considered as conferring power to individuals,[38] who think they can use it to gain respect as well as dignity and to enhance their self-esteem.[39] In the absence of educational and economic opportunities, being a member of a violent drug gang can improve one's social status and provide a sense of belonging to a group. Purely coercive top-down drug policies fail to account for such motivations and are therefore unlikely to tackle the root causes of the illicit drug trade. Instead, they perpetuate the violent environment that has led these people to adopt such violent behavior in the first place.

The blurring of lines between perpetrators and victims is not limited to production and trafficking. It also characterizes the image of drug users. In Chapter 12, Damon Barrett and Kasia Malinowska-Sempruch find that stigmatizing *people* who use drugs rather than their *behavior* overlooks the reasons why people use drugs illicitly. Drug consumers, including addicts, are composed of a large and diverse group of people. However, the securitization of drug policies has led to treating them mostly as a homogenous mass, reinforcing stereotypes of the typical 'useless' drug user created through processes of marking and bounding.[40] Instead of identifying specific vulnerabilities and empowering vulnerable people with the skills to cope with and respond to difficult situations, individuals are considered 'amoral or immoral beings capable of the most heinous crimes imaginable.'[41] This leads to their 'discrediting and disempowerment relative to non-stigmatized individuals,'[42] and thus hinders their meaningful reintegration into society in the scope of rehabilitation.

Punitive measures that stigmatize vulnerable drug users also fuel another under-researched phenomenon: the nexus between stigma, radicalization, and violent extremism. Young, disenfranchised people who use drugs become even more marginalized through stigma, which can turn them into easy recruits for transnational terrorist networks. Such individuals may become radicalized and driven to join terrorist networks that stage attacks against those who they perceive as having rejected them.[43]

Viewing people as the referent of security thus has implications for how to think about illicit drug markets. If drugs are 'evil,' the logic that follows is that using them damages the social fabric of a society and threatens national security. If, however, citizens' physical and perceived security—in addition to national security—is considered important, responses to illicit drug markets are aimed at fostering inclusive societies instead of perpetuating a punitive system that jeopardizes the security of those in precarious situations. This reprioritization lies at the root of the harm reduction approach, a generalized ethic and related set of practices that sees the world drug problem through a public health lens (for a discussion of these practices see Chapter 12 by Damon Barrett and Kasia Malinowska-Sempruch). It facilitates 'maintaining the life and the health of people who use drugs rather than forcing or persuading them to achieve a drug-free lifestyle,' as the authors point out in Chapter 12. The benefits of such an approach for (suspected) drug users' security include reducing the psychological impact of stigma, of suffering abuse, and of human rights violations by other community members as well as by law enforcement officials.[44] It can help drug users integrate themselves into legal jobs and health services—from which they are excluded in many countries due to discrimination. As Nicolas Trajtenberg, Olga Sánchez de Ribera, and Clara Musto show in Chapter 11, it may also help them break through the vicious cycle of addiction that can lead drug users to commit crimes to have access to drugs or as an effect of being under the influence of drugs.

The Proportionality of Responses

Expanding the referents of security from the state to also include people suggests the need to establish proportional punishments for crimes committed by individuals involved in the illicit drugs business, instead of a generalized approach based on the perception of an existential threat. It acknowledges the complexities around disentangling the roles of victims and warriors many vulnerable people find themselves in. It also permits adopting stricter measures against those located in less vulnerable regions or belonging to less vulnerable groups who facilitate illicit trafficking in the background (see below). In many countries, punishment is disproportionately focused on minor drug offenders such as mules and small-scale traffickers. In Nigeria for example, the production, trafficking, and distribution of cocaine can result in life imprisonment, while possession or use carries sentences of up to 25 years of imprisonment.[45] In Ecuador under Law 108, until 2014 minor drug offenses could result in 25 years of imprisonment; the maximum sentence for homicide was 16 years.[46] Although it revised its drug laws, overall, Ecuador toughened rather than liberalized its drug laws.[47] In Peru, according to Article 2(24) (f) of the Peruvian Constitution, preventive police detention is normally twenty-four hours, but this can be extended to up to two weeks for illicit drug trafficking, terrorism, and espionage. Against this, only one out of every 3,000 imprisoned persons in Latin America serves sentences for money laundering—often among the 'high-end' form of transnational organized crime linked to the other steps of the illicit drug supply chain networks, including production and trafficking.[48] The disproportionately high rates of imprisonment of minor drug offenders has led to overcrowded prisons where small-scale traffickers face precarious security situations because of the lack of state control.[49] In countries such as Venezuela, so-called *pranes* manage the cocaine business from within prisons.[50] Indeed, prisons constitute major 'schools' for criminals, who become even more involved in the drug trade once they leave.[51] Scholars find that adjusting drug laws according to the principle of proportionality makes minor offenders less likely to become involved in violent crime. At the same time, doing so gives them the opportunity to receive treatment outside prison, which has been proven to be more effective than inside.[52] It could also reduce costs: Colombia spent US$1.184 billion on imprisonment for drug offenses between 2000 and 2015. Bolivia and Argentina spent US$6.5 million and US$1.3 million, respectively, in 2013 alone.[53]

Responding to Brokers

Analytically expanding the focus from national to also include people-centered security sheds light not only on the production and consumption 'ends' of the chain, but also on the role of the masterminds behind the illicit businesses who link the intermediate steps and nodes of illicit supply chain networks. The dichotomous lens of victims and perpetrators ignores these intermediaries, who are responsible for: buying the raw product that is processed into the drug; linking domestic producers to international traffickers; and arranging for dealers to distribute the product on the market. In some cases, these brokers are the kingpins that lead powerful criminal organizations and whose targeting has had mixed results.[54] Often, however, they are less 'public' figures who are well-connected with various different groups. Examples include the Russian arms dealer Victor Bout, the Venezuelan broker Walid Makled, and the Colombian broker alias 'Megateo.' Intermediaries stabilize illicit supply chains while fueling uncertainty among the people who interact with them as to whose rules of behavior to follow. Frequently, local community members do not know for whom the financiers and brokers (that is, intermediaries) work and whether complying with their rules provides protection or increases people's vulnerabilities.

Without fearing harsh punishment, small-scale offenders have more incentives to report to state agents on who forced them into trafficking or who charged them taxes. In the coca and cocaine producing countries of Bolivia, Colombia, and Peru, or in poppy growing regions of Myanmar, mistrust typically characterizes the relationship between rural communities and state authorities.[56] Fostering trust between communities and authorities, for example via community policing, generally increases people's willingness to cooperate with authorities. Such an approach, including implementing alternatives to imprisonment for drug offenses, can free up resources to improve intelligence on the intermediate stages of the supply chain to detect financiers or brokers who connect the various steps in the supply chain. This can lead to more successful operations to target powerful transnational criminal structures.

The heavy focus on the visible warriors who are often only small-scale traffickers means that powerful brokers have continued to benefit from the illegal business. According to the United Nations Office on Drugs and Crime (UNODC), the global illicit drug trade was worth US$320 billion annually as of 2007;[57] in 2017, other organizations estimated it to be between US$426 billion and US$652 billion.[58] Most of these funds go to violent non-state groups, not to poor farmers, small-scale traffickers, or dealers.[59] Those behind the business accumulate both financial and political power. By offering economic opportunities to communities that lack other feasible legal options, these violent non-state actors gain legitimacy while central governments lose support.[60] Especially in violent and fragile contexts, violent non-state groups typically control markets, territories, and/or populations, thereby challenging the state's legitimate monopoly on violence. In this sense, they are indeed the state's enemy, yet the state may not even be aware of them. Considering small-scale traffickers or farmers as enemies only helps powerful brokers catapult themselves into positions of illicit authority. Therefore, by providing legal livelihood opportunities and protection to local communities, states can ultimately ensure national security because such actions shrink the brokers' power base.

Some analysts argue that regulating drug markets reduces local people's vulnerability because licensed negotiators assume the function of intermediaries, with transparency regarding their identity and their employer. These negotiators could thus be made accountable for their actions, exposing farmers involved in the plant-based production of drugs to measures that are less arbitrary than the ones imposed by illicitly acting brokers and financiers.[61] As a result, armed groups would lose their ability to silence the farmers' voices and have less social control over these communities. This approach would enhance farmers' ability to speak out and design their own livelihood strategies. If only certain elements of the illicit drug market are regulated, investing more law enforcement resources toward detecting brokers rather than small-scale traffickers may also be effective. Removing brokers can interrupt the illicit supply chain of drugs.[62]

The long-term benefits of focusing on the mechanisms that connect the illicit supply chain steps for people's security arise from reducing the power of large-scale criminals, especially brokers. Yet the challenge of disrupting supply chains this way is the likely short-term downward security spiral. The detention of a broker does not go unnoticed by other illegal actors. Power struggles among potential successors contribute to violence and fear in such regions. People may be caught in the crossfire and mistrust increases, because power structures are no longer clear.

The State as Perpetrator

The 'all or nothing' thinking that applies to identifying 'perpetrators' and 'victims' in the illicit drug trade is also misplaced when it comes to defining who addresses or perpetuates the problem. Even if the national security discourse shifts to public security, it still focuses on the state. The concept of public security emphasizes the state's responsibility to protect people from threats by maintaining law and order. However, threats to citizens can emerge out of the governments' own activities.[63] Therefore, rather than perpetuating the belief that the 'good state' fights against 'bad drug lords,' one needs to acknowledge that actors involved in the illicit drug trade include corrupt government officials, regional elites, members of the police and the military, and community members.[64]

Decentering the state[65] through a people-centered approach challenges the Western top-down (elite-driven) thinking that has shaped the IDCR. In this account, the state is considered the principal actor that protects its citizens and decides what is good and bad for them. Such a perspective neglects states such as Guinea-Bissau, where state representatives are involved in drug trafficking and corrupt military officials deliberately turn a blind eye to traffickers to such an extent that some observers called it a 'narco-state.'[66] It also does not account for abuse of small-scale traffickers by prison officers and other officials in countries such as the United States or the United Kingdom.

What is more, state-centric IDCR interpretations ignore the lucrativeness of the drug interdiction business, where high investment in technological equipment and human capital may perpetuate the drug business itself. Powerful companies, particularly in the armaments industry, lobby state governments to keep on purchasing their equipment, often in return for political support. In brief, seeing the state as the 'cure' does not always reflect realities on the ground.

ii. From Prioritizing Militarization to Embracing Differentiated, Glocal Responses

The War on Drugs discourse portrays drugs as an existential threat to national security that needs to be addressed like other threats to the state, by urgent, military means. This discourse largely coincides with practices on the ground, as the chapters of this volume attest. At times, some dimensions of the illicit drug trade constitute a threat to national security and require targeted military means to mitigate them. Others, however, threaten the security of people rather than states.[67] In these cases, action is still urgent, and extraordinary measures may be required. Nonetheless, military force is hardly the most effective means, as is discussed below.[68] In fact, militarized governmental strategies have increased human suffering further: police and military forces in countries ranging from Mexico to Thailand and the Philippines have killed thousands of (in many cases innocent) people under the War on Drugs banner. For responses to the world drug problem to be effective and sustainable, they need to be adapted to the local, national, transnational, and global levels. A 'glocal' approach to drug policies moves away from a general militarized stance, and beyond the state level, toward a perspective that accounts for 'both local and global considerations' that span coercive *and* transformative approaches.[69]

To illustrate, consider a military approach employed to fight drug trafficking. The *modus operandi* of some Mexican or Colombian drug cartels have indeed resembled war tactics, as the bomb attacks and even shooting down of an airplane orchestrated by Colombian drug king pin Pablo Escobar infamously demonstrates.[70] In such cases, military means may be necessary. However, they are futile when addressing organized criminals who keep low profiles to avoid attracting attention from law enforcement officials. Likewise, the power of brokers as introduced above does not (solely) derive from military capabilities but from the capacity to corrupt, from strong networks across different sectors of society that provide protection, and from the ability to adapt and adjust to changing business environments in an agile manner. Drug policies that aim to interrupt illicit supply chains while also protecting people's security and respecting human rights require reforming the police and judicial systems rather than deploying military forces inconsiderately.[71] Another case in point is the urgent action of providing humanitarian relief to vulnerable refugees falling into the hands of drug cartels who control border crossings.[72] Here, as an extraordinary measure, rules related to long-winded bureaucratic procedures to provide humanitarian relief need to be transformed (rather than breached) to facilitate swift and effective protection to ensure these refugees' security.

People-centered approaches lack the resources that have been invested in militarization. Due to the deep-rooted and longstanding 'policy displacement' from a transformative toward a coercive approach (if there has been a displacement at all), budget allocations cannot be changed easily.[73] Policymakers have often justified militarization by citing the police's inability to tackle the drug problem and maintain public order, due to corruption endemic in the institution and citizens' disrespect toward the police. Even so, and regardless of whether corruption penetrates any institution initially set up to thwart lucrative illicit businesses, this does not change the fundamental dilemma. As

McDermott put it, 'soldiers are trained to eliminate an enemy, not arrest him, prepare a case against him and then bring him to trial.'[74] Investing resources in building the capacities of institutions who are set up to do the latter seems more effective.

Surely, there is movement in the system. To an increasing degree, states have been implementing responses on the transformative rather than the coercive end of the spectrum. Within the current IDCR framework, Uruguay regulates marijuana, and Canada and several US states legalized it for recreational use. As discussed in the introduction, such 'flexible' approaches have fueled tensions among proponents of the various IDCR interpretations and question universally securitized approaches with militarization as the extreme version.[75] They provide momentum for critically rethinking the War on Drugs across other substances, notably cocaine and heroin, under international control, and its repercussions on the 'glocal' level.

Local Level

A 'glocal' approach to analyzing the world drug problem and drug policies accounts for the distinct manifestations that both the 'problem' and the policies have at the local level (e.g., at specific production sites, trafficking routes, and markets) and the repercussions of drug policies on individuals and communities.

Concerning the production sites and trafficking routes, due to the tendencies of governments to adopt militarized responses to the drug problem, policies have focused on those areas affected by the illicit trade that attract most attention: so-called ungoverned spaces, where in fact non-state actors typically compete for governance functions. These regions feature brutal turf wars, violence against the population, or acts of retaliation against state actors, frequently interlinked with conflict dynamics, as in Afghanistan, Colombia, and Myanmar (see Chapter 8 by Philip Robins, Chapter 5 by Angélica Durán-Martínez, and Chapter 9 by Pierre-Arnaud Chouvy). Focusing military state action on seemingly ungoverned spaces does not diminish the illicit drug trade. Quite the contrary; most of the production is carried out in *illicitly governed* spaces where an illicit authority, for example organized criminals or insurgent groups, impose order and justice. Such spaces are critical for the illicit drug trade because, there, activities that sustain the drug economy go unnoticed. They are also safe havens for organized criminal structures and conflict actors, where they generate income that fuels violence and conflict in other regions.[76]

Caught in the War on Drugs paradigm, governments have largely ignored that the illicit drug trade has harmful impacts on local communities in these other regions that the state cannot see or categorizes as territory of the enemy rather than a region that features victims, as discussed above. In such illicitly governed (rather than ungoverned) regions, violence is virtually absent because the local population regards the violent non-state actor as a legitimate (illicit) authority and behaves according to its rules and norms. Still, the dominating violent non-state actor uses social control and psychological pressure to define the rules of behavior, and these rules are not rooted in a respect for human rights. Furthermore, people cannot turn to the state for support in cases of abuse; the local communities' voices are silenced. Benefiting from the shadow economy and an undemo-cratically imposed security and justice system, community members often support this illicit form of governance and indirectly nourish the drug trade through complicity.[77]

Analyzing the illicit drug trade's local manifestations demonstrates that state governments' lack of perceived legitimacy among communities facilitates the illicit drug production promoted by an illicit authority. Without empirical legitimacy, the state's presence is futile. Community members may only perceive the state as a valid alternative to an illicit authority if it demonstrates efficiency, efficacy, and credibility. Lund notes that, 'what is legitimate varies between and within cultures and over time, and is continuously (re-)established through conflict and negotiation.'[78] In historically neglected regions, governments can negotiate their legitimacy by demonstrating credible commitments to taking care of the coca or poppy farmers.

Structural shortcomings in marginalized rural coca or poppy growing regions thus cannot be rectified with military responses. To trump the illicit non-state authority, state-facilitated education, health, and employment opportunities as well as public goods such as roads and electricity are necessary. Such investments may even require a transnational approach because illicit authorities often span both sides of borders. By depriving violent entrepreneurs of their self-governed territories through providing governance functions, governments can dismantle non-state platforms for drug trafficking that otherwise persist even during intensified state military operations.

Finally, a nuanced glocal approach sheds light on the local political economy of a region, and its moral economy as mentioned above. This is relevant for international drug control frameworks to avoid unintended consequences because drug trafficking is interconnected with other illicit and licit economic cross-border activities. In Libya for example, arms and drugs were trafficked via routes that have historically been used to transport legal products.[79] Militarized measures to thwart illicit interlinked networks may undermine people's licit livelihood strategies: discouraging the trafficking of illicit goods via such routes needs to come along with protecting and promoting legal commerce in order not to jeopardize people's economic and food security. Gasoline smuggling across the Ecuador–Colombia border is another case in point. Although drug producers used it to process coca leaves into cocaine, many people were involved in this form of contraband because they used gasoline daily to operate their vehicles and boats. Even though it was illegal, they considered gasoline smuggling legitimate because alternative livelihood options were scarce. When the Ecuadorian authorities imposed stricter rules and limited the volume of gasoline that could be trafficked per day, many contrabandists ceased to earn enough income to cover their daily expenses. Furthermore, these stricter rules led local authorities to harass small-scale traffickers, while large-scale traffickers linked to the cocaine industry continued business as usual.[80]

Global Level

A glocal approach examines the world drug problem and the IDCR's impacts transnationally at the macro level. Such a perspective follows the logic of production, trafficking, and consumption dynamics regardless of state borders. Stephen Vertovec defines transnationalism as 'economic, social and political linkages between people, places and institutions crossing nation-state borders and spanning the world.'[81] The illicit drug trade epitomizes this concept in all dimensions.

Economically, the illicit drug business is based on the increase in value of drugs across borders. Socially, in transnational border areas, people on both sides suffer violence and abuse due to trafficking. Politically, drug cartels collude with state elites across borders to gain more profit. The transnational nature of the drug trade is historic, but globalization has reinforced this dimension and its repercussions. Through increasingly sophisticated and rapid means of communication and transportation, and the easy availability of instant information, 'globalization has brought benefits to many, it has also given rise to new concerns, manifest at times as local reactions to the spillover effects of events far away,'[82] as the UN Development Programme's 2014 Human Development Report summarizes it. This is true for events such as drug seizures, the discovery of new trafficking routes, or modes of drug production.

A methodological and theoretical transnationalism lens helps account for the dynamic cross-border nature of the illicit drug business, which cannot be tackled with militarized responses in defense of national security.[83] Drug routes have shifted across regions and continents throughout history due to changing political situations, as well as evolving market sizes and forms of transport and communication (see Chapter 2 by Paul Gootenberg). Likewise, variations in the impact of the predominantly coercively-oriented interpretation of the IDCR— for example, in advances in interdiction measures—across and within regions have produced a 'balloon effect' (shifts from one region to another) of cultivation, processing, transport, and consumption, as well as violence linked to the cross-border illicit drugs supply chain networks. For example, West Africa solidified as a major trafficking route in the mid-2000s, in response to heightened security searches and seizures by Dutch customs officials of flights arriving from the Netherlands Antilles. Similarly, while so-called drug violence has declined in Colombia over the last two decades, it has increased in Mexico.[84] And cocaine production declined in Peru and Bolivia in the late 1980s and 1990s, but only because it moved to Colombia before coca cultivation reemerged in Peru.

Regions are connected across continents through multiple overlapping supply chains of various types of drugs that interlink with other forms of transnational organized crime.[85] As mentioned above with regard to the relevance at the local level, drug trafficking routes are also used for other illicit cross-border activities including human trafficking, and arms and precursors smuggling, which often take the form of barter agreements in which drugs are exchanged for arms or other goods.

These illicit flows connect hubs of armed conflict and fragility across regions,[86] making a transnational, even global, perspective even more important to decouple the illicit production, sale, and use of drugs from conflict. In addition, terrorism is globally interlinked with drug trafficking. The most widely known link between the illicit drug trade and terrorism is the use of drug trafficking as an income source for terrorist activities, as is the case in Mali and the Sahel region where Al-Qaeda in the Islamic Maghreb (AQIM) is said to control parts of the drug trade.[87] In Somalia, the Islamist group Al-Shabaab derives income from trafficking heroin.[88] With organizational structures extending across the globe and multiple forms of trafficking being interconnected, militarily targeting individual groups who profit from the illicit drug trade may temporarily destabilize a single supply chain, but is unlikely to stop the illicit business rooted in resilient global illicit supply chain networks in the long term.[89]

Tracing these changes and connections across time and space allows us to identify patterns of vulnerability that hold across regions. They are linked to both the shifts in flows as well as policy responses to them, as will be discussed in the next section.

iii. From North–South Divide to Vulnerable Regions

The third element of the framework to analyze the drug problem considers the perspective of vulnerable regions in order to counter the ethnocentric North–South divide that has characterized the IDCR's interpretation in the form of the War on Drugs. The previous sections discuss why considering not only states but also people as referents of security alters the meaning of urgent action, and why prioritizing militarization as urgent extraordinary measure in response to the drug problem neglects the problem's root causes at the local level and its interdependence with other transnational challenges at the global level. This section builds on these points to clarify how to think differently about the voices and the audiences that propose and accept rule-breaking behaviors to thwart existential threats.[90]

Chapter 2 shows how the War on Drugs started as a US-led phenomenon, in which US politicians convinced a domestic audience of the need to counter the threat of drugs through extraordinary measures. This narrative of an external threat to a nation's future (young people who may become drug users) was also successful internationally, as the buy-in of governments across the globe demonstrates. These are not domestic audiences, though, but typically elites. Governments' rule-breaking behavior in the name of the War on Drugs has had predominantly negative effects on people across vulnerable regions affected by the illicit production, trafficking, and consumption of drugs, especially in the form of human rights violations, such as arbitrary detentions of ordinary citizens. If these audiences—that is, those directly affected by measures stemming from the War on Drugs—have a say in what kind of extraordinary measures are acceptable to counter the threat posed by the drug problem, the measures are likely to have less adverse effects on their lives. Additionally, current global asymmetries in the policymaking process and the impact of these policies may be reduced.

In order to account for the illicit drug business's global character, the securitizing actor (the actor who demands the measures) and the audience that agrees to them cannot be limited to the United States and the West, but need to include local constituencies across the world who are affected by securitized measures in response to the drug problem. To illustrate, consider the West's disdain for drug use, which is not necessarily shared by other cultures, and yet they are expected to follow its logic. Western countries often despise, or at best ignore, rather than respect traditional customs of drug use in non-Western cultures. Bolivia's difficulties in convincing other UN member states of the coca leaf's role in the country's historical traditions, which is similar to the tradition of consuming opium in countries like Iran, is a case in point.[91] The current War on Drugs paradigm largely ignores culturally conditioned perceptions of what is legitimate or illegitimate, of who is being victimized or supported, and of what people feel threatened by. Yet understanding these differences helps distinguish between those who choose to consume drugs, those who harm others by consuming drugs or who incentivize others to consume drugs, and those whose life circumstances make them more vulnerable to addiction to drugs.

An alternative to the Global North-South divide to think about which geographic spaces drug policies influence is to conceptualize them as vulnerable regions.[92] This conceptualization accounts for otherwise overlooked audiences. Borrowing from the literatures on human development, climate change, and natural hazards yields three main factors that shape a region's vulnerability in the context of the illicit drug trade: geographical location, exposure to shocks or stress, and a lack of coping capacities. Referring to climate change, O'Brien et al. argue that 'vulnerability is typically defined as a function of exposure to climate change, sensitivity, and the capacity to respond. [...] The most vulnerable are those who are highly exposed and sensitive to change and who have limited freedoms and capabilities to respond positively to change.'[93] Similarly, Nathan distinguishes between two features of vulnerability: exposure and insufficient capacities.[94] Dutta, Foster, and Mishra talk about exposure to 'shocks.'[95] Accordingly, vulnerability includes 'downside risks:' a country's proneness to shocks and its ability to recover from shocks. In the case of the illicit drug problem, vulnerable regions may be exposed to sudden events—shocks—or to long-term stress such as armed conflict or social unrest, absorbing resources and capacities. 'Insufficient capacities to prevent, prepare for, face and cope with hazards and disasters,'[96] as Cardona put it, reinforce their vulnerability.

Albeit to varying degrees, all regions included in this volume—located across the South and North—manifest these factors, (exposure through geographical location, shocks or stress, and a lack of coping capacities) that make them vulnerable to the undermining impact that the illicit drug trade and the IDCR's implementation in its interpretation as the War on Drugs has on order, security, health, and related socio-economic dimensions. Typically, their condition of vulnerability is further 'shaped by dynamic historical processes, differential entitlements, political economy, and power relations', as Wisner and Blaikie state.[97] Overall, there is a transnational thread of vulnerability: from farmers of illicitly cultivated crops and small-scale traffickers in Latin America or the Golden Triangle, to transit zone traffickers in West Africa or the Golden Crescent, to dealers and buyers in Russia and elsewhere. These three factors are briefly discussed in the next section.

Three Features of Vulnerability: Geography, Shocks and Stress, Lack of Coping Capacities

The first factor is geography. Regions facilitating illicit drug supply chains are vulnerable to the harmful impact of the illicit drug trade and policies to address them due to their locations. As Philip Robins puts it in Chapter 8, they are 'geo-narcotically' important. These include production sites, including areas where crops are cultivated illicitly (predominantly the Andean region, Afghanistan, and the Golden Triangle).[98] It also encompasses transit zones that host shifting trafficking routes. These are vulnerable for example due to porous borders, with corrupt state officials often reinforcing this porosity further. Such transit zones include, for instance, Mexico, West Africa, and Iran. They can also manifest 'strategic vulnerability,' as is the case in Pakistan due to its geostrategic location between fragile Afghanistan and hostile India. This location reinforces its vulnerability to harmful impacts of the illicit drug trade due to the difficulties it faces in coordinating drug policies with its neighbors.

Regions at the supply chain's end—that is, that comprise markets with a vast consumption population—can also be vulnerable, especially if they are located in certain 'neighborhoods' and the region's government(s) fail to address consumption in an adequate manner. As Ekaterina Stepanova discusses in Chapter 10, to some extent, Russia is a vulnerable consumption region because it is a close neighbor of the world's biggest opium producer, Afghanistan. In contrast to the strictly controlled US-Mexico border, Russia's borders with Central Asian transit states and their borders with Afghanistan are extremely porous. This porosity is partly what made it possible for Russia's opiate consumption to become comparable to that of the rest of Europe in the 2010s. Stepanova argues that transport infrastructure across these transit countries improved considerably over the last decade, but drug control capacities did not, which put additional stress on Russia.

In many cases, one region fulfils several functions in the supply chain, but this is not always reflected in policy responses. West Africa, for example, is a transit zone, but it is also becoming a market, as John Pokoo and Kwesi Aning note in Chapter 7. In Nigeria and Ghana, powerful local criminal structures increasingly control the lucrative illicit drug trade. Nonetheless, policies still treat the issue as a 'transit zone' problem in which foreign groups use their territories to conduct illicit business, rather than as a home-grown organized crime problem. Other examples include Thailand, a production site, a trafficking hub, and a consumer market, or Mexico, a production site for synthetic drugs and for poppy used to produce heroin, and a transit zone for Colombian cocaine. Even in the case of synthetic drugs, where the 'narco-geography' is less crucial because production does not depend on climatic and terrain conditions, geographic variables such as the proximity to large consumer markets still matter, as exemplified by Mexico's proximity to the United States.

The second factor that makes regions vulnerable to the harmful impacts of the illicit drug trade is exposure to additional shocks or stresses such as armed conflict. The illicit production and trade of drugs as well as other forms of organized crime typically thrive in armed conflict contexts because they are income sources that sustain fighting for a wide range of violent non-state groups.[99] At the same time, many armed actors shift their motivations for operating illegally and violently from ideological goals to profit once they get to benefit from the drugs business, thereby perpetuating the illicit economy. War economies are also convenient for others who have a stake in the illicit business: corrupt state officials, local elites, and even foreign troops. As the cases of Afghanistan, Colombia, and Myanmar—discussed elsewhere in this book—demonstrate, this 'conflict-crime nexus' applies to the Taliban in Afghanistan, the (now demobilized) Revolutionary Armed Forces of Colombia (FARC), the National Liberation Army (ELN), and right-wing groups in Colombia, and to various ethnic armed organizations such as the Shan State Army or the Ta'ang National Liberation Army (TNLA) in Myanmar.[100] In Afghanistan, analysts doubted the effectiveness of the US–Taliban peace deal struck in early 2020, given that the Taliban continued to make millions of dollars of profit from opium poppy cultivation—though this is not the only reason.[101] In Myanmar, opium production was part of political negotiations between state and non-state actors.[102]

And in Colombia, the drug problem was one of the six points of the peace deal between the FARC and the government, the continued involvement of other violent groups (and FARC dissidents) after the signing of this deal notwithstanding.[103]

The third factor that affects the vulnerability of regions is governments' limited capacities or political will to confront the drug problem in a way that reduces its negative impacts on order, security, health, and related socio-economic dimensions in a holistic way. These limitations frequently manifest themselves in high levels of corruption. They may be the result of state fragility or of a dysfunctional state–society relationship in which (some) citizens are deprived of their rights or lack protection. Even if regions are similarly exposed to risk, such as drug violence, harmful drug use, or addiction, their capacity to cope with these situations may differ. Evaluating the impact of the drug problem thus requires not only assessing a region's degree of exposure but also its capacities to deal with it. Iran, for example, is exposed to the influx of heroin from both Afghanistan and Pakistan, and the government has been unable to deal with it. The large drug supply means that heroin is cheap; a wrap of heroin is less expensive than a can of beer in some Tehran slums, as Philip Robins shows in Chapter 8. Limited coping capacities, or limited political will, also exist in the so-called Global North. In the United States, for example, the rural region of Appalachia is an epicenter of the nationwide opioids epidemic that has cost over 800,000 lives. Analysts cite the region's lack of economic opportunities, high unemployment rates, and underfunded social safety net as contributing factors to this situation.[104]

Within vulnerable regions, not all population groups are equally vulnerable.[105] John Friedman points to the lack of power as being a characteristic of vulnerability.[106] According to the Human Development Report 2014, 'human vulnerability is about the prospect of eroding human development achievements and their sustainability. A person (or community or country) is vulnerable when there is a high risk of future deterioration in circumstances and achievements.'[107] Robert Chambers,[108] discussing vulnerability in the context of poverty, considers vulnerability to be 'defenselessness, insecurity, and exposure to risk, shocks and stress.'[109] Societal groups such as the poor, the socially marginalized, or members of specific ethnic, racial, religious, or gender-oriented groups are particularly vulnerable. For example, certain racial groups are more likely to experience harsh punishment for drug trafficking than others. At the same time, the vulnerable regions discussed above comprise population groups that are considerably more exposed to the illicit drug trade's harmful effects and some of the policies established to address them.

Analytically starting from vulnerable regions, and vulnerable groups residing in these regions, rather than adopting a Western-biased approach to drug policies challenges the perpetuation of the status quo by questioning dominant power relations reinforced by the War on Drugs paradigm.[110] Considering people in vulnerable regions the audiences that take part in deciding whether, when, and how to operate outside the 'normal rules' in order to address the world drug problem ensures that responses are tailored to specific circumstances. Rather than preserving entrenched power relations, such a perspective reveals the agency of people who experience the IDCR's impacts particularly strongly. It opens avenues to enhance these regions' resilience by transforming the systems they are embedded in and building or strengthening institutions that are necessary to make such transformations sustainable.[111]

Conclusion

This chapter outlines the concepts and approaches that both inform and emerge from the in-depth studies of specific issue areas and regions in the following chapters. It presents a framework through which to analyze the world drug problem in a way that allows thinking outside the War on Drugs paradigm.

Changing a paradigm is a long-term process. In the case of the War on Drugs, this process resembles the shift from 'warfighting' to peacebuilding, with the latter being characterized by three features: first, it is a process that aims to address the root causes and the symptoms of armed conflict; second, it takes place at various levels of society—for example, at the grassroots—and in different spheres—for instance, in national governments and the international community; and third, neither the beginning nor the end of peacebuilding is clear-cut: it occurs before, during, and after conflict.[112]

Working toward sustainable peace does not preclude military action. In a similar vein, tackling the world drug problem from a critical perspective does not rule out military means in certain issue areas. Military pressure and punitive laws can be effective measures to address the drug problem—especially in contexts where the military capabilities of trafficking groups are indeed threatening a state's national security. However, the goal of such action is not to fight and defeat an enemy, but to achieve a situation that prioritizes human development, people-centered security, and respect for human rights in order to free people from constraints that do not let them enjoy these basic principles. Therefore, such measures need to be applied appropriately and balanced with other approaches.

Similarly, a people-centered approach is no panacea. Powerful business interests, lack of political will among governments, and problems in shifting resources are among the realpolitik that make it difficult to induce transformative change. Yet continuing to implement drug policies in the current 'business as usual' mode only fuels an ongoing spiral of violence.

Demonstrating how drug policies could possibly be changed is useful for examining how other policy realms, such as the War on Terror, could be transformed so that they address social inequalities, exclusion, and marginalization. Such paradigm shifts require buy-in from governments and local communities across the globe. They also require policy coherence among ministries of justice and interior, defense, and development agencies, and they must be coordinated on binational and international levels. The international community and, indeed, societies across the globe, will reap most of the benefits only after years, if not decades, of implementation. In the current political climate, driven by election cycles and other short-term considerations, such a delay makes it hard to advocate for change. Nonetheless, ultimately and paradoxically it is states that need to live up to the principle of shared responsibility if globally shared challenges such as the world drug problem are to be tackled.

Overall, while the IDCR has provided incentives for states to militarize responses to the world drug problem, this does not necessarily have to be the case. Employing 'security talk,' or 'war talk,'[113] governments have legitimized 'exceptional measures' such as a state of emergency, not least by pointing to the UN conventions that lend themselves to interpretations justifying 'more strict or severe measures.'[114] However, the conventions refer primarily to 'up-scheduling' drugs, as Paul Gootenberg in Chapter 2 and Christopher Hallam and David Bewley-Taylor in Chapter 3 discuss, while still calling for compliance with human rights, and stressing the availability of alternative options to coercive approaches. Hence, there is room for reinterpretation, perhaps a first step of a long-term transformation process.

There are also opportunities to tie the IDCR more closely to other priorities of the international community, such as the Sustainable Development Goals. As Javier Sagredo points out in Chapter 13, the consensus of all UN member states on the Sustainable Development Agenda can serve as an entry point to synchronize the IDCR with UN core objectives. For these policies to be truly transformative, they need to have the potential to 'amplify the voices of those who otherwise go unheard.'[115] These include the voices of marginalized people who tend to be excluded from high-level policy debates, such as coca or poppy farmers, small-scale traffickers, and drug consumers. Governments need to fight inequalities to overcome the artificial and often misplaced divide between warriors and victims. This can be the starting point of transforming the War on Drugs—which may have lost some strength in parts of the world but is still very much raging in others—into holistic people-centered drug policies within the context of an 'updated' IDCR.

PART ONE

THE CHANGING CHARACTER OF THE WAR ON DRUGS

2

BUILDING THE GLOBAL DRUG REGIME
ORIGINS AND IMPACT, 1909–1990s

Paul Gootenberg

The International Drug Control Regime (IDCR) is a modern
historical phenomenon, beginning in 1909 with the Shanghai
Opium Commission. It achieved its current status as a universal
comprehensive drug control regime after the 1964 entry into force of
the United Nations (UN) 1961 Single Convention on Narcotic Drugs,
and the major IDCR expansions of 1971 and 1988. In historical
terms, it was a milestone in international legal diplomacy, predating
conventions around human trafficking, chemical and nuclear
weapons, human rights and genocide, and global climate change. It
has had a lasting impact, unlike other conventions of the World War
I era.[1] By gradually defining and marking over time the boundaries
between legal regulated and medicinal drugs and those usages and
trades that became deemed illegal, the IDCR laid the ideological,
legal, and institutional framework for what is today often criticized as
a global drug 'prohibitionist' regime, as well as forming the basis for

the internationalized War on Drugs that accelerated after the 1960s. The UN drug regime has reflected, as detailed below, the expansion of American anti-drug ideals and influence on the twentieth century world stage. To a lesser extent, it has echoed the United States-led global War on Drugs which began after 1970. Several paradoxes mark the history of the IDCR. The first is that when the regime was in its 'weakest,' most plural form in the first half of the twentieth century, drug problems were receding, at least in Europe and the United States. However, once a uniform global control drug regime became firmly established after the 1960s, with US power behind it, the opposite occurred: the expansion and diversification of drug supplies, new illicit traffic routes and trafficking organizations, and rising rates of drug use. Drug-related violence, public health, and addiction worsened on a global scale (see Chapter 4 by Mónica Serrano for early interpretation of plural versus singular drug regimes).[2] Few model IDCR 'success stories' exist to speak of; in fact, no other global legal regime, after a century of concerted efforts, has led to such a perverse proliferation.

This chapter provides three areas of historical backdrop to the current debate and crisis of the IDCR. First, it periodizes the major treaties and institutions that marked its century-long evolution into its present form under the United Nations International Drug Control Programme (UNDCP). Second, it analyzes the special role of the United States in the creation, norms, and politics of the IDCR. And third, it surveys the IDCR's impact on two classes of global drugs: opiates and cocaine. In distinctive ways, the IDCR, global drug warfare and world geopolitical events ended up shifting the regions of illicit drug production, and often intensified illicit supplies and the conflicts surrounding controlled drugs.

Milestones in the Making of a Drug Regime, 1909–1990s

Behind today's embodiment of the IDCR lies more than a century of anti-drug politics, movements, meetings, legal conventions, treaties, and institutions. In a broad sweep, however, the IDCR can be divided into two long arcs of development: the birth of the international regime (1909–45) and the completion and consolidation of what most scholars consider a global prohibitionist regime (1945–91), albeit one with regulation of licit medical supplies and usage.[3]

The first era, 1909 to 1945, was the IDCR's formative stage. A small circle of 'big powers,' which were subsumed after 1920 into League of Nations agencies like the Opium Advisory Committee (OAC), worked to define and internationalize limitations on the supply of narcotic drugs, mainly opium and its derivatives morphine, codeine, and heroin. These campaigns advanced the idea of international drug restriction, and the methods of demarcating between legitimate— medicinal and scientific—use and illicit production. The League's central aim was to curtail the 'excess' supply of pharmaceutical trades. To achieve this, it began implementing systems of statistical reporting of medicinal drug needs, and spread models of national state regulation. However, these campaigns remained hobbled by political and personality conflicts, contending national drug interests and models of control, and weak information and enforcement mechanisms. They were mostly paralyzed along with the League of Nations at the start of World War II. Despite limited force, these debates and discourses around drugs helped legitimate distinctions between internationally sanctioned drug trades and those targeted for control. For the most part, these global drug flows and problems were declining in significance during the era in the United States and Europe where the movement originated, due to the effect of new national controls and cooperation by pharmaceutical firms.[4] Outcomes across Asia varied, both with regard to traditional opiates, and in stemming new flows of pharmaceutical drugs.

The second era, from 1946 to the early 1990s, centralized international drug control under the UN and its new institutions, for instance the 1946 Commission on Narcotic Drugs (CND), the 1961 Single Convention on Narcotic Drugs (1964), and today's UNDCP (1991). These agencies and treaties consolidated and expanded previously fragmented conventions into an integrated drug treaty system. Since the 1961 Convention, which combined eight previous treaties, the IDCR has been labelled a global 'prohibitions' regime, though it also regulates medicinal and residual commercial usage. It covers a comprehensive range of drugs, from opiates to cannabis, cocaine, and coca, and since the 1970s also synthetics, amphetamines, barbiturates, psychedelics, and designer drugs.[5] It mandates controls across the varied levels of illicit supply (drug growing and production, derivatives, precursor chemicals, trafficking, and financial flows), and entails obligations on most of the 193 member states of the UN. However, the drug control strategies instituted since World War II essentially projected the longer vision of US drug authorities: the criminalization of users of narcotic drugs and psychoactive substances, and particularly the interdiction of drugs at supply regions. They reflect public health, regulatory, or demand reduction strategies only to a very limited extent. Sanctioned by the UN, the regime is often described as 'promotional,' dependent on the will and legal cooperation of nations. In certain regions, such as the Americas, the IDCR depends on the overseas powers, enforcement programs, and intelligence of US anti-drug institutions, such as the Drug Enforcement Administration (DEA), the International Police Organization (INTERPOL), and other international policing agencies elsewhere.[6] Paradoxically, the realization of a modern prohibitions regime in the 1960s occurred alongside the unprecedented global expansion of illicit drug supplies and trafficking, drug cultures, and violence. Notable geographic shifts and changing mixes of global drug use occurred, but few cases of sustained drug eradication or long-term declines of consumption. Today, global use of cocaine, heroin, and cannabis, as will be shown later in this chapter, is far wider than in 1964. By the 2000s, this paradox of prohibition began to raise fundamental questions about the IDCR's effectiveness as a global regime.

Landmarks meetings, conventions, and treaties along the way to the IDCR system include:[7]

1909: SHANGHAI OPIUM COMMISSION. Organized by Bishop Charles H. Brent of the US Philippines, and progressive reformer Dr Hamilton Wright, the conference convened thirteen parties, including (but not limited to) European colonial powers in Asia (Britain, France, the Netherlands) and the Chinese and Siam dynasties. Disputes arose on the traditional medicinal use of opium. Specifics were tabled, unlike the prior 1907 '10 Year Agreement' between China and India to curtail opium trades.

1912–14 HAGUE OPIUM CONVENTIONS. Small conferences which pit US efforts, led by the State Department's Wright, to reduce world drug supplies against objections of colonial powers and European drug manufacturing interests. Licensing, record-keeping, and reporting of drug production was urged along with national regulatory laws. The principle of gradual restriction of opiates to 'medicinal and scientific' needs was introduced; thirty-four nations eventually agreed, with no set timetables.

1919–20s: PARIS, TREATY OF VERSAILLES. Signatories of the treaty ending World War I and member states of the League of Nations— excluding the United States—were required to adhere to the 1912 Hague Convention, including defeated drug manufacturers Germany and Hungary, committing them to the ideal of international control. Dozens of nations signed, including some Latin American states, without specified limitation commitments. The OAC (1921, or Special Advisory Committee on Opium and Other Dangerous Drugs) was formed to collect and study world drug data and laws.

1924–5: GENEVA INTERNATIONAL OPIUM CONVENTION. This was the first concerted attempt by the League of Nations, spearheaded by Britain, to institute drug limitations. The conference was undercut, among many problems, by the walkout of the US delegation led by Sen. Stephan Porter over the failure to set manufacturing limits and end colonial opium monopolies. The reporting of 'legitimate' drug imports-exports was established, and issues of coca and cannabis were raised. The League bodies expanded; the Permanent Central Opium Board (PCOB), a non-governmental expert committee, would persist until the 1960s.

1931: GENEVA, LEAGUE OF NATIONS DRUG LIMITATION CONVENTION (IMPLEMENTED 1933–4). Fifty-seven nations attended; the US returned, headed by State Department's Stuart Fuller. The core concepts of drug limitation were defined: systems of annual import needs were established, as on raw material stores, and an extension of control was implemented on 'derivative' drugs like codeine and ecgonine. National drug regulatory bodies would be required from here on. Rigorous statistical reporting and analysis would begin, to aid in the indirect shrinkage of global narcotic manufacturing, enforced by the DSB (Drug Supervising Body, 1933–67).

1936: LEAGUE OF NATIONS ILLICIT TRAFFIC CONFERENCE (1939: THE CONVENTION FOR THE SUPPRESSION OF ILLICIT DRUGS). Forty-two delegations attended. The convention recognized the displacement of narcotic trades to Asia, the non-compliance of producing states, and the need for international policing cooperation. A US proposal, led by the head of the Federal Bureau of Narcotics (FBN), failed to place limits on the growing of poppy and coca. The OAC *Illicit Traffic Subcommittee* was formed.

1939: PRODUCTION CONTROL TREATY TALKS TO COVER AGRICULTURAL INPUTS DERAILED BY WORLD WAR II. Until World War II, the IDCR existed on paper in a hodgepodge of compromise treaties based on statistical reporting mechanisms (export-import certificates, medicinal need estimates) and model national regulation. Many nations stayed outside the regime, including key opiate (Persia) and coca (Bolivia) producing sites. The focus on the trade of manufacturing powers made the system *de facto* one of shrinkage of 'excess manufacturing' supply. Broad limitation ideals and the concept of 'illegitimate' drugs took hold, despite few enforcement mechanisms. During World War II—an era of high production, scientific development, and hoarding of drugs—League institutions survived in the United States, managed by the US FBN.

1946: UN, CND. The CND was created in New York as an ongoing arm of the UN Economic and Social Council (ECOSOC). Designed by experienced 'inner circle' European refugee and British League drug controllers (Felkin, Renborg, Steinig) with US tutelage, it was later nicknamed 'The Gentleman's Club.' Originally, fifteen member states were involved, including coca and poppy growing states such as Peru and Turkey. League bodies persisted, but were enfolded under the policymaking CND, and moved to Vienna in the late 1950s. The Division of Narcotic Drugs remained to deal with opium issues. New source control initiatives began, such as the 1946 Indian opium reduction plan and the 1948–50 UN Andean Commission of Enquiry on the Coca Leaf. An ECOSOC resolution, prompted by the US, began the process of consolidating treaties and institutions into a 'Single Convention.'

1948: SYNTHETIC NARCOTICS PROTOCOL. This was an agreement to expand the 1930s reporting and limits to war-era synthetics such as Demerol, methadone, and poppy straw opium extracts.

1953: OPIUM PROTOCOL. A French diplomatic and US-sponsored treaty to specifically cut sources of raw opium to seven producing states, notably India, Iran, Afghanistan, Yugoslavia, and Turkey, under stringent quota controls of the DSB and PCOB. It was the first full supply-side treaty, but ratification failed due to complications, including the politics of Cold War alliances.

1961: UN SINGLE CONVENTION ON NARCOTIC DRUGS. This was the product of twelve years of negotiations and drafts, streamlining eight prior limitation treaties and conventions and supplanting even the failed 1953 Protocol. It was instituted in late 1964 with a US lag (1967), and remains the foundation of global drug control. A new central board was introduced, the INCB, consisting of eleven global experts, which eventually replaced former bodies, opium monopolies, pharmaceutical and other interest groups, with state input in the CND. Limitations were defined in four 'Schedules of Control,' including raw materials (poppy, coca) and governments were empowered to ban cannabis. All parties were required to criminalize scheduled drugs. Supply reduction 'at source' dominated conversations, and was also the focus of the US-sponsored 1972 Protocol. Illicit drug consumption was targeted in the US-funded 1971 UN Fund for Drug Abuse Control (UNFDAC).

1971: VIENNA PSYCHOTROPIC CONVENTION. Seventy-five governments negotiated—along with input from the World Health Organization (WHO), INTERPOL, and International Narcotics Control Board (INCB)—to expand the Single Convention to at least cover major classes of synthetic drugs such as amphetamines, barbiturates, and psychedelics, with provisions on drug treatment and manufacturing loopholes.

1988: ILLICIT TRAFFIC CONVENTION. Reflecting growing illicit international drug trafficking since the 1961 Convention, this US-instigated treaty criminalized precursor chemical trades, money laundering and related activities, and assets of the illegal drug industry. It enhanced cooperative law enforcement, multilateral legal assistance, extradition, and eradication programs of illicit crops.[8]

1991: UNDCP (NOW THE UNODC). This recentralized drug control functions and bodies in a supra-agency, following the United Nations General Assembly Special Session (UNGASS) special drugs meetings. Broader mandates, largely US-funded, were issued which integrated advancing drug intelligence and policing, alternative development, legal reform, and treatment. This generated the annual UN Global Drug Reports and anti-drug assistance missions. The original 1990s goals stressed the importance of a drug-free world against surging illicit drug use and traffic.

In summary, today's global prohibitionist regime came to fruition in the mid-1960s with the implementation of the 1961 Single Convention and with the institutions (CND, INCB, UNDCP), sometimes referred to as the Vienna Complex. The Single Convention consolidated, integrated and rationalized the statistical limitation tools which had been accumulating since the 1920s, and continued to define and limit legal pharmaceutical spheres. It specified the universality of drug limitation for all UN member states, with comparable criminalization regimes at all levels of drug trades. It instituted the first campaigns on source limitation across a growing spectrum of drugs, including poppy and coca growing and international trafficking. However, it still lacked usable enforcement powers, such as binding judicial sanctions or institutional policing forces.[9] Open wrangling among states receded with the Single Convention or post-war US regime dominance, but the IDCR has faced an even more serious set of challenges since the 1970s, including the rise of more professional illicit trafficking networks, powerful and violent transnational Drug Trafficking Organizations (DTOs), and new classes of drugs and drug use cultures.

The United States' Influence on the IDCR

Historians of drug diplomacy agree that the historical impetus behind the IDCR has largely come from the United States. This is not to say it is merely a US imposition, or that the dominance of US drug strategies was easily achieved. US diplomats acquired allies and opposition along the way; they suffered divisions themselves and endured compromises, retreat from drug institutions, and outright political and policy failures. However, it is true that the global prohibitions system in the 1961 Single Convention expanded longstanding US limitation ideals on a global scale, and that US power would expand yet further in the 1972 and 1988 accords. Some historians regard the US role in the twentieth century IDCR as analogous to the nineteenth century British crusade to abolish the African slave trade. The DEA and other drug 'Cops across Borders' agencies—global enforcement that only appeared after 1960—parallel the efforts of the Royal Navy in the slave trade, and early missionary discourse of individual 'enslaving' drug habits suggests a link.[10] However, whilst the British managed to eventually achieve their goal, at least in ending trans-Atlantic slave commerce, the US campaign to abolish enslaving drugs has had a different impact.

Historians and political scientists have a variety of explanations for the US role in global drug controls of the twentieth century, as well as for its particular biases.[11] Firstly, whereas nineteenth century attempts at international legal norms—for example, extradition laws and cooperative policing—bore a European legal imprint, its twentieth century equivalents, including the novel campaign of world drug control, have mostly reflected US judicial and policy norms. As the emerging power in modern global politics, the United States defined the international crimes it was attempting to contain.

Secondly, the absolutist moral vision of early US drug control, well-articulated by the late 1910s and early 1920s—a militant control strategy of extinction of 'excess supply' or 'limitation at its source'— has often been linked to 'American exceptionalism,' or what European diplomats referred to at the time as the 'American Plan.' Colonial powers (Britain, France, the Netherlands, and later Japan) were saddled with large Asian colonies which had sizeable drug-using populations, cultural traditions, and profitable colonial opium (or cannabis) revenue monopolies. In addition, many had 'farming' consignment systems, institutions paralleled in dynastic states such as Persia and Turkey. The United States had few such territorial ambitions. However, diplomats began to campaign around the 'opium problem' after the 1898 acquisition of the Philippines, which became—via Bishop Brent of the Philippines—the motive for the inaugural US international anti-narcotics campaigns in 1907–9, echoing earlier UK initiatives. The origins of US drug control in the Far East were thus in one sense a variant of US 'open door' policies towards Asia, redoubled in the 1930s by moral outrage against perceived Japanese drug imperialism in Manchukuo and Formosa. The United States would extend moral freedom to opium-oppressed Chinamen against rival colonial powers. Indeed, the US drug crusade abroad, though rooted in domestic, even local, anti-drug and racist attitudes, started before the United States formally achieved its own national drug control. In 1914, the pioneer US drug diplomat, Dr Hamilton Wright, persuaded Congress—generally wary of expanding federal power—to adopt the Harrison Narcotics Tax Act on the basis of Hague Convention treaty obligations.

Thirdly, US moral entrepreneurs saw industrial continental powers like Germany, Switzerland, and the Netherlands as captured or corrupted by massive global pharmaceutical interests in narcotics, opiate derivatives, and cocaine. Lucrative European drug export trades became regulated by the 1910s and 1920s in European quota cartels or trusts. In contrast, by 1920, the United States had fewer manufacturers of narcotics—for example, only two firms producing cocaine—and strictly banned their exports. Through corporate cooperation, US progressive reformers successfully regulated their output and distribution networks by the early 1920s.

Furthermore, the American stress on drug criminalization and limitation of drug sources likely reflected divergent twentieth century social policies. Most European states had substantive social hygiene or social medicine movements by the 1920s, in the form of social democratic or statist welfare policies spurred on by labor and in some cases fascist parties. These political movements legitimized the medicalized, national, and social approaches to problems of drug addiction. For example, in Britain the 1926 Rolleston Report paved the way to medical regulation, and later heroin maintenance; the pragmatic Dutch regulatory policy began even with its imperial East Indies drug industry in the 1920s. The origins of these social policies could differ (as in Britain versus France), but even the perception of a foreign threat in drugs—for example, the Defense of the Realm Act (DORA) used to ban recreational drugs in war-time Britain—did not lead to a punitive post-war national drug regime. In the United States, in contrast, punitive individual responsibility prevailed, sanctified by the Supreme Court's landmark 1919 interpretation of the Harrison Act towards criminalization. It grew harder over the decades, and its policies were only weakly and intermittently opposed by the conservative American Medical Association and some legal organizations.[12]

By 1930, American prohibitionist ideologies became institutionalized in the Federal Bureau of Narcotics (FBN), a small, anti-drug and medical supply regulatory bureaucracy with few overseas equivalents. The FBN was led for more than three decades (1930–62) by Harry J. Anslinger, a hardline former enforcement officer of alcohol Prohibition, who also served as the lead US drug negotiator abroad. Anslinger dominated US drug foreign policy for three formative decades after the death of Rep. Stephen Porter, a chair of the House Committee on Foreign Affairs and the force behind the US delegate walkout of the 1925 talks due to perceived surrender to European drug interests. The FBN was often outflanked by more compromising State Department foreign policy and narcotics officials, though Stuart Fuller (of the State Department) was also a pivotal early anti-drug official. Anslinger, however—in a story many times told—was not just a fanatical prohibitionist (and today the butt of many historical critiques and satire), but a deft politician of his time. For example, by the mid-1930s, he had quietly maneuvered the United States informally back into ongoing League drug proceedings, despite American public ambivalence about the League. Instead of alienating other drug diplomats, he forged lasting foreign alliances—for example, with Canada's Col. Sharman, a point-man into the British Commonwealth—and sheltered the exiled shell of the League PCOB regime on US soil during World War II. Behind the scenes, private foundations and publicists, mainly from the United

States, pressured the League for harder action. There were other active 'moral entrepreneurs' (or simply bureaucrats) in League drug control politics—Britons like Dame Rachael Crowdy, Sir Malcolm Delevingne (the dominant figure of the 1920s during US abstinence from League drug debates), Arthur Felkin, and Gilbert Yates. Other major figures included the Swede Bertil Renborg, Austrian Leon Steinig, Joseph Dittert from Switzerland, Charles Vaille from France, and Americans Helen Moorhead and Herbert May.[13] Yet none had the staying power or ideological influence of Anslinger.

As with later US drug politics, these energetic foreign initiatives often reflected bureaucratic interests: Anslinger justified the FBN budget and functions (against domestic critics who wished to reform the agency) with reference to overseas treaty obligations and successes. These were easier to claim than building a national consensus on drug policy. Anslinger went on to influence the structure, powers, and goals of the UN CND in 1946, though lost in its late 1950s transfer from New York to Vienna. He was the political author of the long post-1948 drive to hammer out the Single Convention on Narcotic Drugs, the core of the global IDCR, though he had championed first the stringent 1953 Opium Protocol. It ultimately included many long-coveted US concerns, such as the broad inclusion of cocaine and cannabis in global prohibitions, detailed raw material bans—including a 25-year period to the eradication of the Andean coca use—and concessions to US corporations such as the Coca Cola Company. He sat on the CND in its formative late 1940s years. It is an overstatement to say he dominated the body; Anslinger's political capital waned at home, as his prohibitionist principles were tarnished by poor politicking and corruption within the FBN. In an ironic career twist, Anslinger opposed the final version of the Single Convention, on the grounds that it undercut stronger opiate controls of the 1953 Opium Protocol—which would have permanently confined limited poppy sourcing to seven designated states.[14] Finally retired from the FBN by reformist Kennedy in 1962, Anslinger's objections delayed adherence to the new regime, ratified by the US Congress in 1967.

Nonetheless, US policies in the international arena likely drew from domestic opinion and were not simply the product of a few manipulative or powerful officials. For example, while all Western powers (and other states) associated orientalized drugs with race, the United States was a particularly conflictive multi-racial drug context. Strong American strains of racism animated anti-drug campaigns. They were anti-Chinese 'coolies' in the first opiate prohibitions, and anti-African American 'cocaine fiends' in Jim Crow era anti-cocaine fervor. Anti-Mexican propaganda ran through Anslinger's late 1930s 'reefer madness' cannabis campaign, whilst anti-Semitism and other 'mafia types' helped the construction of the international 'drug trafficker,' and fear of the passionately violent 'Latin' trafficker or urban 'crack-head' resonated throughout the 1980s US War on Drugs. Emotive prejudices were openly traded among the largely Protestant international entrepreneurs of the early twentieth century, much like Woman's Christian Temperance Union (WCTU) anti-alcohol campaigns. Hamilton Wright, for example, invoked race in his communications through the 1910s with his genteel European counterparts. Racism is also apparent in the cultural instincts of US and most other drug officials against varied indigenous 'drugs,' such as Andean coca leaf or regional drugs like East African Qat, or the South Asian popular pharmacopoeia of opiates and cannabis. Neo-colonial and colonial elites and medical authorities demanded action on their national drug problems, such as Egyptians in the 1920s who raised global concern with cannabis, used by Egyptian peasants. Similarly, Mexican authorities banned cannabis long before the issue heated up in the United States. On the other hand, potentially dangerous addictive drug production and cultures of the modern American and global pharmaceutical industries—synthetic psycho-actives like amphetamines (popularized by military use on all sides during World War II), and commercial 1950s–60s tranquilizers like Librium and Valium were slow to fall under international control, starting only in the 1970s. The same was true of 1960s drug culture psychedelics such as LSD (lysergic acid diethylamide) and later MDMA (Ecstasy). It was not just material US big pharma interests or bias for laboratory drugs. Rather, these were the consumer drugs of choice for the global white middle class.

The US nativist tradition of externalizing social tensions abroad— to the 'foreign' drug menace—has been a political and cultural element that reinforces the supply-side 'limitation at the source' philosophy of US, and with it UN, drug control. The iconography of drug threats was typically foreign in nature, an oriental snake squeezing the upright white citizen. The US War on Drugs has mainly played out in distant poorer 'third world' zones of Asia and Latin America, for instance Afghanistan and Colombia, populated in large numbers by poor people of color. A political and economic system that chronically fails to deal effectively with thorny social and political issues—such as racial discrimination and inequality—has fueled American demand proclivities and passions for drugs. In the modern world, the United States has become the core drug consuming nation, a condition dating to its foundational 'Alcohol Republic.' Popular fascination with drugged 'patent' medicines, which fell under regulation in 1906, later re-merged as consumption of modern pharmaceutical substitutes and the burgeoning illicit use of US recreational drug cultures in the 1960s.[15]

Drug historian David F. Musto labels this phenomenon 'The American Disease:' The United States, the world's most intensive drug consumer (including alcohol and medicinal manias), periodically swings between eras of permissiveness and repression. In reaction to intemperate desires, the United States plays the role of the world's leading puritanical prohibition nation. The US national temperance experiment (1919–33), inspired by religious fervor, was virtually unique among industrial nations, echoed only by intermittent Soviet, Finnish and Norwegian attempts to contain vodka. Few drug officials learned from the experience, with its explosion of bootleg markets, organized crime, and border smuggling, all for modest public health gains. Rather, ex-Prohibition officers such as Levi Nutt and Anslinger channeled failed moral fervor into the 'Export of Prohibitions'—Ethan Nadelmann's critical phrase—into the new crusade for globalized drug control.[16] Periodically, especially from Latin American elites, criticisms of hypocrisy are launched of lax US policies for curbing drug demand while demanding loyalty in a costly prohibition alliance.

The Cold War (1947–89) both reinforced and complicated the US focus on global drug prohibition. US influence on global drug policies soared in the post-war era when US drug laws and enforcement became increasingly punitive.[17] A fundamental political fact is that the US' communist antagonists in the post-1945 global system were tacit allies in global drug prohibitions, save for the principle of 'non-interference' by outside states or inspection. Post-war communist states, by their own authoritarian logics, were puritanical in the face of the challenge of alcohol, productivity, and social discipline in the Soviet Union and lingering nationalist and anti-subversion campaigns with opiates in China. The People's Republic of China (PRC) in the 1950s, for example, took draconian steps such as summary executions of dealers and addicts; its extensive secret police and informer networks, and closed borders made one of the rare 'success stories' in a century of drug suppression. Nonetheless, during the height of the Cold War, US officials turned a blind eye to drug trafficking by strategic anti-communist allies such as Chinese KMT [Kuomintang] exiles in the Golden Triangle in the 1950s, the 'French Connection' Corsican mafia in the 1960s, and the Contra militias of Central America in the 1980s. Other officials launched propaganda accusations of trafficking by communist states like China, North Korea, or Cuba. In the 1950s, Anslinger vocally joined these campaigns, in conflict with State Department priorities, to enhance the anti-communist credentials and indispensability of the FBN.

In some regions, especially Latin America, US power climaxed during the Cold War. By the 1960s, the United States had hitched its UN-sanctioned War on Drugs to the cause of anti-communism—broadly conceived as any threat to stability, law, or status quo. Latin American nations, informally within the US bloc, had been slow to adhere to League of Nations initiatives, largely viewing drug problems in terms of domestic social or racial hygiene. Diverse national policies, such as Mexico's experiment to medicalize addiction under Cárdenas in the late 1930s, Peru's tiny legal agro-industrial cocaine sector, or Uruguay's early (1970s) liberalization of drug possession, became buried in Cold War prerogatives. US-fostered anti-drug drives in post-war Mexico, Peru, Bolivia, and (by the 1980s) Colombia, became infused by strategic objectives, anti-subversion doctrines, and 'counterinsurgency' military training, equipment, and tactics that forged a long alliance between political elites, militaries, and expanding US drug agencies like the DEA.[18] Diplomatic sanctions, such as State Department 'decertification' of states that failed to fully cooperate on drug control, which was initiated in 1986, proved so politically biased as to lack credibility. The UN often provided a neutral fig leaf for such US interventions. As the Cold War wound down after 1989, some of these anti-drug conflicts took on a life of their own or merged into the rising US campaign in the 1990s of extirpating global terrorism, for instance in the case of Andean insurgencies which were quickly labelled as 'narco-terrorism.' This regional legacy of compliance is one reason that today's post-Cold War dissent from key Latin allies in the US drug war marks a historic shift.

Theoretically, the IDCR required a dominant power 'hegemon' to operate beyond the fractious drug politics of the interwar era. The unparalleled power and alliances of the United States after World War II provided that pillar. The war had devastated rival pharmaceutical industries in Germany and Japan—both under strict US narcotics control in 1945—and effectively ended (under explicit US political pressures) the lingering colonial opium monopolies of Asia. The post-war years saw Americans design, host, and underwrite the fundamental new UN institutions of drug control. At times, US drug diplomats set the agendas of these institutions, influenced appointments, and exercised a *de facto* veto or censorship powers. Opposing voices within the UN such as the WHO—which took a more epidemiological, medical, or social perspective on drugs—were largely shut out of CND policy, despite prescribed roles in drug scheduling. Even decades later, this was occurring—most infamously with a joint 1995 report by WHO–UNICRI (United Nations Interregional Crime and Justice Research Institute), which took issue with the monolithic Single Convention characterization of cocaine and coca use, and which was hurriedly suppressed by the UN under intense US pressure.[19] As indigenous rights became a UN prerogative, instituted by 1980s in the UN Working Group on Indigenous Peoples, the movement was insulated from drug issues—though questions soon began to emerge from Andean nations for a UN clarification on traditional coca leaf usage under the Convention. A similar walling off of drug policy occurred in response to the developmental and social concerns of the UNDP, United Nations Development Group (UNDG), and United Nations Educational, Scientific and Cultural Organization (UNESCO). In short, from the 1940s to 2000, US perspectives continued to inform UN thinking about global drugs, despite mounting evidence of the flaws of the Single Convention, and its incompatibilities with other core UN concerns. Even in 1998, during the last UNGASS on drugs, the UNDCP led by Pino Arlacchi, set official goals of a drug-free twenty-first century, which echoed the militarized wishful thinking of the Reagan and Bush administrations.

Critics have always existed of undue US influence in the early and modern IDCR. In the interwar era, staid European diplomats often took a jaundiced view of US initiatives as moralistic, one-sided, naïve, impractical, undiplomatic, and uncompromising. US officials accused Europeans and others of obstructionist protection of colonial and pharmaceutical interests. Generally, the United States regarded the League of Nations drug bodies as weak. Backed by growing informal power, US perspectives remained consistent over most of the century, and then dominant after 1945. This power likely stymied the expression and development of alternative global and local models of drug control to prohibition, criminalization of use, and source eradication control strategies. Alternatives included regulatory institutions (modifying state drug monopolies or supervised manufacturing quotas), demand reduction strategies (social epidemiology, public health, addiction treatment, and prevention), and the medicalization of harmful drug use (as in the former British drug maintenance system). US dominance lent biases in the types and classes of banned drugs, and was unrelenting with regard to the cultural preferences of ethnic or religious groups such as Bolivia's Aymara or Caribbean Rastafari.

Today, after a full century building the IDCR, and a half-century of history under global prohibition, such critiques are accumulating force. These issue from the global harm reduction movement, NGOs, the OAS, states, and citizen movements concerned with the collateral social violence, human rights abuses, political corruption, and regional destabilization generated by drug traffic, as in Latin America. These forces look a lot like the worldly reformers who began the regime a century ago and likely reflect the shifting basis of global power alliances. Within the United States, for a mix of reasons, public opinion has finally turned against the domestic War on Drugs, especially regarding cannabis. The term was officially retired during the medicalizing Obama era in Washington, though it was erratically revived by some Trump officials. Yet its punitive prohibitionist models still underlie the related IDCR.

Regime Impacts: Opiates and Cocaine, 1900–1990s

Historians focused on the complex institutional politics of the IDCR rarely identify the long-range impacts of the drug regime on patterns of drug supply and use. The question does attract speculation, accusation, or institutional denial, by both proponents and opponents of drug prohibition. Assessing outcomes requires a more systematic study of the long cost-benefits of the regime, isolating the causality of illicit drug flows, and comparing counterfactual policies.[20] Would today's drug challenges have occurred in any case, or have been worse or better without aspects of the regime? There are also many intervening contexts at the micro and macro levels: for example, changing drug technologies (new laboratory drugs and consuming techniques), intensified globalization and communications, and global political shifts and cultural changes that affect social tolerance of drugs.

This section begins with a panorama of modern opiates, which have changed forms and major zones of illicit supply throughout the century. These 'extensive' or geographic changes relate to geopolitical shocks as much as specific anti-opiate measures in the IDCR. The second case study, cocaine, demonstrates an 'intensive' IDCR impact, traced through the definitional process of becoming a criminal product with active trafficking and consumer networks. This occurred directly in the wake of the 1950s–60s finalization of the IDCR, which encompassed cocaine. Cocaine is also a proxy for US influence on the regime, given the long US impetus to place the drug on the international agenda and US anti-cocaine campaigns after 1980, acting as the regional power in its South American source regions. This drug war against Andean cocaine intensified source prohibition policy with paradoxical outcomes: enlarged and globalizing supplies of the drug, 'ballooning' of its commodity chains, and rising drug violence.

Opiates, smoking, and traditional medical usage of the drug in China and colonial Asia galvanized the international moral and legal campaigns for drug control at the start of the twentieth century. It took decades to bring cocaine, cannabis, and synthetic narcotic control mechanisms into an IDCR which had been conceived to end opiate use. Poppy (*papaver somniferum*) is the most universal of old-world preindustrial cures, with ancient prehistory across Eurasia and pre-existing commercial and political circuits which would be restructured by the IDCR and other events of the twentieth century. Opiate consumption also suffered use intensification, which was related to prohibition incentives to smuggling and pricing of concentrated drugs: the shifts from smoking of raw or mixed opium to modern refined injectable morphine and heroin by the 1930s, snorting of high-purity heroin, and recent waves of semi-synthetic opioid substitutes—that is, oxycodone, hydrocodone, fentanyl—drugs of comparable or greater harm or addiction potential.[21]

Gross numbers exist for global and regional opiates production, mainly raw opium harvests. At the start of the century, China (especially southern Yunnan and Sichuan) was the global epicenter of production in the aftermath of the contested nineteenth-century imperial trade from British India. China grew 35,000 metric tons of the crop, 85 per cent of world supply, comparable in terms of bulk to globally traded legal stimulants such as Brazilian coffee or Indian tea. Opiates also came from India (5,177 tons), Persia, Turkey, Afghanistan, the Crimea, the Balkans (Yugoslavia), today's Myanmar, and colonial Java and Indochina. Commerce for morphine-making European and Japanese pharmaceutical firms was largely a function of national colonies, which also had smoking opium monopolies for sales to Chinese labor in the diaspora and from Turkey and Bulgaria. In some states—for example, Persia and some East Asian colonies—monopoly revenues provided a vital quarter of state finances.

In the first wave of international drug control up to World War II, the emerging IDCR achieved significant reductions of opiates. Total harvests (metric tonnage) fell from 42,000 tons in 1906 to about 8,000 by 1934. The 1907 China–India limitation accord, the initial campaigns of Chinese nationalists, the early OAC and League statistical treaties, and voluntary colonial restriction (using state monopolies) were all working to reduce visible sales and traditional use. Moreover, Europeans successfully shrank the supply of manufactured drugs from pharmaceutical sectors—banned from export in the United States by 1920 and soon after Britain. The Geneva conventions notably shrank pharmaceutical trades: in the five years 1928–32 (admittedly during the Great Depression), morphine production fell from 6,840 to 1,516 kilos and heroin, of scant medicinal use, dramatically fell from 6,531 to 290 kilos.[22] These gains were offset, however, across the broader interwar era by a range of counter-effects. One aspect was diverted shadow sales from European firms, another were the new semi-illicit Japanese colonial drug enterprises from Formosa to the puppet state of Manchukuo in Manchuria. China's collapse into civil warlordism was a compounding factor, its armies financed in part by renewed opium sales. Pre-World War II stockpiling, partly of new semi-synthetics, and precursor diaspora or mafia long-distance morphine and heroin smuggling—the modern illicit trades—from illegal factories in Turkey and Shanghai to Europe and the United States both contributed to the rise.

Following World War II, two large pattern shifts registered in global opiates, as illicit heroin stabilized into an ongoing world trade.[23] These shifts corresponded to large-scale geopolitical divisions and shocks—the Cold War, decolonization, and their aftermaths—as much as to developments in the IDCR. The initial Cold War sparked the rise of the so-called 'Golden Triangle'—the hilly 'tribal' borderlands of Burma (now Myanmar), Thailand, and Laos—as the center of world poppy production and smuggling. The Golden Triangle accompanied the 1949 Chinese Revolution, which pushed opiate producing KMT (Kuomintang) exiles into ungoverned jungles and into alliances with independent Wa and Shan tribesmen. The PRC, meanwhile, launched a draconian cleansing of southern opiate provinces that cut crops to under 1,000 tons by the mid-1950s, pushing residual trades across its southern borders. Other post-war and Cold War events also worked to concentrate opium in the Golden Triangle: the phasing out (1946) of domestic legal opium sales in India and the end of the last colonial monopolies; Turkey's transformation into a strategically-placed US ally; the Persian opium ban (1955–8) with the overthrow of its nationalist monarchy and the new pro-US Shah of Iran; and the crackdown on the Levant 'French Connection' in the early 1970s. These events also sparked and intensified new Asian smuggling routes. For example, Pakistan stepped in as an opiate supplier to millions of Iranian smokers, with illicit output quadrupling to 800 tons by 1979, the year of the Iranian Revolution and its Islamic state drug crackdown. The cross-border politics of the long-running Indochinese wars (including US-sponsored secret armies, in addition to the war it was fighting in

Vietnam) also enhanced the Triangle. The Golden Triangle came to fill two-thirds of illicit world opiate supplies: from about 80 tons in 1945, to 700 by 1960, and 1,791 in Burma alone in 1993.[24] Its surplus increasingly flowed into globalizing heroin trades through such points as Hong Kong and Bangkok, organized by Asian, US, and European mafias. Apart from European cities, consumption by Vietnam vets and marginalized urban minorities led the way, partly reversed in the 1970s by methadone treatment programs. Secondary heroin-making zones also swung in and out of use, for example, Mexico's northern Sierra Madre region—another '*Triángulo Dorado*' [golden triangle]—close to clusters of US heroin demand.

A third opiates wave emerged, after 1980, in the shift to the now dominant 'Golden Crescent:' principally Pakistan and (by the 1990s) neighboring Afghanistan. Major world political events once again reshuffled opiate geographies. The Golden Crescent expanded as a substitute zone for the Golden Triangle in the post-Vietnam era, as UN, local governments, and DEA programs began to enter and tame the zone. In 1979, Pakistani opiates fell under a strict trade ban from the US-leaning Bhutto regime, creating a diversion into new kinds of heroin circuits, such as a growing population of domestic Pakistani addicts. Apart from Iran, the 1983 Soviet invasion of Afghanistan shook the opiate world in the late 1980s, giving it a new 'Islamic' cast. Resistance warlords and fragmentation of the country led to spreading dependence on poppy production until the 1989 Soviet withdrawal. By 1994, ungoverned and impoverished Afghanistan produced 3,416 tons of opiates, surpassing Burma as the global production pole. Afghanistan's meteoric rise as a 'narco-state' occurred under the Taliban regime (1994–2001), even with its late campaign to ban drugs. After 2002, as the battleground post 9-11 state in the US War on Terrorism, the North Atlantic Treaty Organization (NATO)-backed anti-Taliban regime has tolerated poppy due to the pragmatics of political survival. By 2007, the country produced 8,200 tons of illicit opium, mostly in Helmand province, some four times the known peak from the Golden Triangle, feeding burgeoning heroin networks into the ex-Soviet Union, China, and Europe. Mexico, on the other hand markets its 'black tar' heroin—now largely from Guerrero state—in the current US heroin epidemic. The drug vies with pharmaceutical opioids like Oxycontin (some smuggled from overseas mills) in rural and urban sites across the nation.[25] Since 2010, imported heroin has vied with potent full synthetics like fentanyl, mostly smuggled from Asia, which contribute to the current US 'opioid crisis'—responsible for some 30,000 deaths annually by 2018.

In short, the global history of opiates since 1900 and under the IDCR is hardly a success story. After the 1960s, a dramatic reversal occurred of the gains registered under initial regulatory efforts in the 1930s. Today's millions of heroin users worldwide are arguably as serious a challenge as the baseline China 'opium problem' of 1900. Heroin is now a grave cause for political concern in consuming frontiers like the Russian Federation, poised as many have noted to become the lead conservative force in global drug politics. The 'stimulus of prohibition,' Alfred McCoy's new term, manifests in hardening and hazardous forms of the drug, the transition from nineteenth century opium ingestion and smoking to twentieth century heroin shooting and snorting. Following the 1950s nadir of opiates, global heroin trades have approximately doubled decade by decade. At the start of the Single Convention era, world opiate supplies doubled from 1,200 tons in 1971 to 2,600 in 1987 to 4,285 tons in 1996, doubling again to about 10,000 tons in 2007.[26] The shift of supply basins and commodity chains, however, was not primarily an intensification impact of the US drug war, which was focused on the Western hemisphere. Nor was it fully attributable to Single Convention prohibition. Opiate shifts reflected the extensive political border shifts of the post-war world: decolonization, the Cold War and US proxy wars in Asia, Islamic revolutions, the fall of Communism and the Soviet Union, failing states, and today's War on Terror.

Cocaine, on the other hand, is easier to isolate and analyze in reaction to advancing restrictions and prohibition.[27] Cocaine is a modern drug, an alkaloid isolated in 1860 by German chemists from the benign traditional Andean coca leaf, *Erythroxylon coca*. European science aside—and a spectacularly brief era of diversion to Southeast Asia as a legal colonial crop—cocaine remained in the US global sphere across a series of Andean production hotspots. As an illegal drug after the 1960s, cocaine's history exemplifies the intensification of illicitness under the IDCR, which impacted the drug later than opiates (despite being noted in earlier accords). It began effectively with the 1960s and the start of the Single Convention, followed by the hemispheric US drug war, which was driven by cocaine between 1980 and 2005. This impact was perverse in terms of scale: illicit cocaine expanded to unprecedented heights under the militarized IDCR.

Cocaine enjoyed a three-decade legal expansion stage from 1885–1915 as a global medicinal commodity, after the revolutionary discovery of its use as a surgical anesthetic. By 1905, production was centered in eastern Peru, which produced 10 metric tons of 'crude cocaine,' a semi-processed paste like today's PBC *(Pasta Básica de Cocaína)* [Basic Cocaine Paste]. This was exported for refining and distribution by German pharmaceutical firms like Merck. US drug trades refined cocaine out of shipped coca leaf and produced a related boom in coca leaf goods, such as the extract used in Coca Cola (1887, decocainized after 1903), which was also briefly obtained from Bolivia. While legal cocaine had no ill effects on Andean producing areas, it did begin to stir opposition, particularly in the United States. Physicians quickly realized the drug's perilous side effects and potential as a drug of abuse, and so limited its usage.[28] However, by 1900 the drug's rapid price slide had led to its spread into patent medicines and into outcast cocaine recreational scenes, particularly—though not exclusively—in the United States. US states and localities banned sales and cocaine was covered, along with opiates, by the 1914 Harrison Act. The United States also worked to extend its anti-cocainism to the emerging global drug regime, with limited success until 1945; the other big powers were uninterested.

This interregnum, 1915–45, until the triumph of a cocaine prohibition regime, is noteworthy as a pluralistic era of cocaine history. Peru's legal cocaine fell into a steady decline as a global commodity as cocaine's circuits and politics diversified. In the United States, the drug was quickly brought under control by a tight regulatory pact among a small set of pharmaceutical firms and the ascendant FBN drug bureaucracy. Fears of unbridled consumption had vanished along with the drug by the 1930s. In Europe, declining profits and excess producers had by the 1920s led to its regulation by cartel and to isolated cocaine scenes. In Southeast Asia, on the other hand, two colonial powers—the Netherlands and Japan—forged entirely new circuits of the drug, hastening its decline in Peru. The Dutch seeded coca in Java as an intensive commercial colonial crop before the rise of anti-drug campaigns, and integrated this supply into Amsterdam's central state, the *Nederlandsche Cocaïnefabriek* (NCF) works. By the early 1920s, this dominated world medicinal markets, but as a core member of the anti-drug conventions (at The Hague), by the 1930s the Dutch were forced—under US pressure—to dismantle the industry. Japan, on the other hand, had by the 1930s fostered a colonial coca-cocaine industry—based on Formosa and modern pharmaceutical firms outside of League jurisdictions—with reputedly illicit outlets in India and China. There were, in short, a variety of world outlets and regimes of cocaine.

Cocaine was broached as a concern in League conventions, though no actual working restrictions ensued. Adverse scientific and League publicity lowered the prestige and commercial possibilities of the drug. Yet Peru, the drug's persistent producer, simply ignored League and US diplomats, though conducting its own lively debate on how to regulate cocaine as a national industry. Bolivia reacted by sending delegates to the 1925–6 Geneva conventions, who mounted a concerted defense of domestic coca leaf use, instigated by the SPY coca growers lobby. This proved enough to shelve League projects on raw material limits.[29] By the late 1930s, League officials had started to plan paper restrictions on coca, from a theoretical analogy to poppy-morphine controls, with scant cooperation from producer states. The remarkable fact is that in the absence of a prohibition regime, and despite a diversity of legal spaces for the drug—and for indigenous coca—cocaine fell into a steep decline. By the end of World War II, eastern Peru, the last primary producer, mustered less than 500 kilos of the marginal export. With the exception of some Asian reports, the drug was no longer a source of drug scares, social problems, or violence. A loose regime sparked no incentives for organized global illicit trades, beyond petty pharmacy thefts.

This stasis changed dramatically from 1945 to 1973, when the United States consolidated a prohibitions pact around cocaine, supported by the 1961 Single Convention, which brought both cocaine and coca leaf under UN control. American drug officials had never forgotten about cocaine, despite its disappearance in the United States and the scant concern or knowledge about the drug elsewhere in the world. The post-war era was an auspicious moment for action: the US had demolished and restructured the German and Japanese drug industries and forced an end to vestigial plantations in colonial Asia. US officials put coca and cocaine restrictions, with no opposition, near the top of the new UN CND agenda. The emerging Cold War gave US drug diplomats and even a few overseas drug agents more muscle in the Andes. In 1948, after a military coup in Peru, pro-US General Odría shut the last Peruvian cocaine workshops and criminalized the drug, which had been purposefully associated with the leftist opposition. By 1950, Peru had become a full-seated member of the CND.

Bolivia's story is more complex: undone by its 1952 Revolution, US anti-drug influence did not fully come into play until 1961, when—amidst scandals about its new illicit labs—Bolivia instituted its first national drug laws and the US assisted anti-cocaine campaigns. In 1948–50, the Andean states participated in a 'Commission of Enquiry on the Coca Leaf,' launched by the UN, which brought coca leaf prohibition projects to the Andes, though there was token opposition from local scientists. In short, the regime writ large expanded to include the cooperation of source states. Over the 1950s, these strictures took root and the long-negotiated 1961 Convention stipulated strict prohibitions on cocaine (save for residual medicinal, scientific, and commercial uses) and a 25-year plan to end coca use and associated cultivation in the Andes. Some analysts suggest that the 1961 and 1988 UN treaties have inadvertently left a legal grey area open for 'traditional use' of coca in countries like Bolivia and Peru. But the UN–US campaign went beyond paper. During the 1960s, for example, they sponsored—with the US Federal Bureau of Narcotics and Dangerous Drugs [FBNDD] and INTERPOL—a series of specific policing 'Study Missions' to South America, to intensify support and intelligence for wiping out cocaine and restricting coca leaf.

What officials hoped was that cocaine could be nipped in the bud as an illicit drug and opportunely eliminated from the world scene. A brief 1949 drug scare—the bust of the Balarezo cocaine smuggling ring from Peru to New York—gave the ban its impetus. However, the opposite occurred. From 1950 to 1973, criminalized cocaine makers in the Andes—first in Peru, then in Bolivia—began to form shadow circuits of the drug.[30] This was the first truly international commodity chain of illicit cocaine, linking coca leaf to PBC, to refining 'labs' to consuming and distribution scenes in Latin America, like Havana, and onto nascent cocaine scenes in cities like New York, Miami and Rio. The drug was routed through Chile, Cuba, and Mexico. Not just legal prohibition, but policing operations against the drug produced its opposite: the scattering of traffickers and price spikes incentivized a hemispheric network of cocaine. By the early 1970s, to the chagrin of UN drug officials, illicit cocaine involved hundreds of hardening smugglers and thousands of colonizing peasant growers in eastern lowland Bolivia and Peru. By 1973, illicit cocaine's turning point, these increasingly sophisticated carriers had managed to get more than a ton of the drug into the United States. No doubt local conditions drove peasants and smugglers to cocaine, but nascent global prohibition was failing—though, notably, it remained a relatively peaceful business.

The 1970s and 1980s ushered in the 'age of cocaine.' Events of 1973 proved crucial. The first was the Cold War US-inspired military coup in Chile, which quickly shifted smuggling routes and business centers of the illicit trade north to Colombia. This was the birth of the so-called Colombian 'cartels,' as in Medellín and Cali. Colombia had little prior exposure to cocaine, yet it had the perfect location and social conditions for smuggling and enlarging the trade. By 1977, 10 per cent of US youth had tried cocaine, a spectacular take-off for an essentially new and pricey drug. By 1980, centralizing Colombian rings processing Peruvian and Bolivian PBC had upped exports across the Caribbean to the United States to over 100 tons. This was ten times the 1905 peak of Peru's legal medicinal trade, and 200 times the total cocaine left on world markets before full prohibition in the late 1940s. By 1986, 22,000,000 Americans had tried the drug, and as the price plummeted at Florida entry points from $60,000 a kilo to $15,000 by 1990, it spread into novel low-cost markets like smokable 'crack' cocaine. Cocaine use also spread to Europe and parts of Latin America. In the mid-1990s, Americans alone—including 7,000,000 heavy users of the drug—spent about $38 billion on cocaine, half of all expenditures on illicit drugs. By the 1990s, the criminal capacity for making cocaine in the Andean ridge had swelled to well over 1,000 tons, peaking at about 1,400 tons, more than 2,000 times its pre-prohibition lows, with 14,000,000 heavy users worldwide.[31] Meanwhile coca, which had been slated by the Single Convention for full eradication by 1989, skyrocketed: Peru's Upper Huallaga Valley alone, which initially fueled the Colombian cartels, had 33,000 hectares in coca by 1979, peaking in the early 1990s at 120,000 hectares and 60,000 *cocalero* [coca leaf growers] families. Instead of vanishing, coca emerged as the key commodity of the eastern Andean ridge from Colombia to Bolivia. Meanwhile, with such high economic stakes, the trade was becoming dramatically more violent and destructive. Colombia collapsed into a protracted civil war in which the drug trade played an increasingly important role, making mid-1980s Medellin the world's most lethal city. Miami, US 'ghettos,' and remote peasant redoubts of the Huallaga all became hot danger zones along the cocaine trail. By the 1990s, US interdiction pressures on Colombia's cartels led to a rapid change in cocaine's commodity chain. Colombians began growing coca itself, turning it into a national business, and by 2000 Colombia led the world with 163,000 hectares. Caribbean routes changed, shifting to war-torn Central America to cross US borders via northern Mexico. By the 1990s, this lucrative shift in cocaine was the chief factor in the empowerment of the Mexican cartels, the Sinaloan, Juárez, and Gulf groups, a prelude to the explosive drug war violence and turmoil of Mexico after 2000. There have been other commodity chain shifts—cocaine has returned to Peru's VRAEM (*Valle de los ríos Apurímac, Ene y Mantaro*) region, and has spiraled again in the south of Colombia, with its globalizing consumption moving south to areas like Brazil. But it still largely remains a drug complex of the Western hemisphere. And more cocaine has been produced in 2020 (upwards of 2,000 tons) than at any time in the drug's licit or illicit history.

Some geopolitical events factored in cocaine's formation as an illicit drug, notably Cold War politics and the social miseries of Latin America's neoliberal 'lost decade' of the 1980s and 1990s. But its intensification was mainly produced by the drugs prohibition, institutionalized by the UN, which eliminated the drug's prior alternative spaces or institutions. By the 1960s, prohibition price incentives awakened both smuggler networks and poor peasant producers. However, the escalating US War on Drugs proved decisive, as formally declared by President Richard Nixon and instituted by the creation of a newly integrated drug war bureaucracy in the DEA, also in 1973. Without recounting in full the much studied and criticized US drug war, Nixon targeted marijuana, heroin, and amphetamines, thereby accidentally sparking the exponential 1970s rise in demand for and supplies of higher price cocaine. By the mid-1980s, interdiction, punitive domestic legislation, and militarized overseas drug operations were targeted against cocaine, with trafficking declared an official 'national security' threat by President Ronald Reagan (1986, National Security Decision Directive [NSDD]-221). During the 1980s, DEA and military budgets in this war soared from $100 million to over a billion dollars yearly. Fighting drugs cost the United States an estimated $10 billion in federal funds per annum during the 1990s.[32] Draconian laws against crack dealers and users, such as the 1986 Senate Anti-Drug Abuse Act, swelled federal prison populations from 300,000 to 2,000,000 by 2000. Ninety per cent of new inmates were Black or Latinos, reflecting 'racial disparity' in policing and sentencing practices. The United States became modern world history's most incarcerating nation. Integrated military operations like Operation Swordfish (against early Caribbean transit routes) were followed by US training, intelligence, and special forces on the ground in Peru, Bolivia, and Colombia, the 1989 Andean Initiative directed by US Army SouthCom and the CIA (Central Intelligence Agency). The United States became immersed in coca eradication drives, culminating in 1999's *Plan Colombia*, a comprehensive, decade-long drug war program that cost US taxpayers more than $8 billion, not to mention steep financial, human, and ecological costs to Colombia (see Chapter 5 by Angélica Durán-Martínez).

The impact of this drug war on overall cocaine availability proved negligible, with brief exceptions. Drug warring failed to stop cocaine and likely intensified it. The collateral damage of drug trafficking and interdiction has been enormous, notably its unprecedented waves of drug-related violence. After the prohibition price spikes of the 1950–60s, active intervention against cocaine—which the DEA intended to raise its price beyond the casual and hardcore user—likely worked to expand drug supplies, driving cocaine prices downward over a long three-decade stretch. The first recorded stable street price hikes of cocaine did not begin until after 2007.[33] This occurred inadvertently through two means. First, trafficking organizations simply offset the growing risks of interdiction (by 1990 this affected a significant share of Colombian cocaine) by seeding and spreading coca frontiers, thus raising above and ahead of demand stores of cocaine readied to smuggle. The well-known 'balloon' effect into new or safer cross-border territories was part of this process. Second, pressurized and fragmented trafficking organizations became more competitively efficient in intelligence, smuggling technologies, and the productivity of refining drugs and even coca varietals. In short, militarized supply interdiction badly backfired in the case of cocaine, creating a massive drug problem that would take decades to bring under control in the United States, and spreading its trade globally. By the 1990s, this war on cocaine was driven by the bureaucracies and budgets permanently invested in a failing strategy, and residual ideological fervor, including racism, rather than evidence of the policy's effectiveness and public health cost-benefits.

It is unclear how UN drug officials viewed the course of the US war against Andean cocaine, which became in effect the regional enforcement arm of the 1961 Convention. UN officials are less visible here than in Asian anti-opiate campaigns, which included substantive and negotiated programs of alternative development. The cocaine war occurred without UN objections, and the organization lent logistical and bureaucratic support in varied Office of National Drug Control Policy (ONDCP) Andean data and advising missions. As the threat of global trafficking spun out of control, US officials helped graft the 1988 Illicit Traffic Convention onto the 1961 Convention. The struggle against illicit drugs and DTOs, intensified by its earlier prohibitions, became folded into the UN mission. Meanwhile, the 1988 Convention along with the US drug war, widened the criminalization scope and powers of the IDCR regime. The target became international DTOs; after 2000, an umbrella anti-crime mission was explicitly renamed as 'Drugs and Crime' in the UNODC.[34] In the 1990s, as the UNDCP affirmed its commitment to a drug-free (including *coca*-free) world, other branches of the UN began to question the aims of the drug war. A jointly commissioned 1995 report by WHO–UNICRI took issue with the monolithic characterization of world cocaine and coca use, suggesting alternative public health approaches to the drug; this was hurriedly suppressed by the UN under US pressure. Only after 2000 did visible discrepancies begin to appear between US and UN roles in the Andean drug war, such as recent UN monitoring of Bolivia's heterodox coca policies.

Conclusion

At the close of the twentieth century, UN officials calculated that illicit drugs accounted for 8 per cent of global trade, phenomena inflated by prohibition and prohibition-based price estimates. About 4.2 per cent of the world's population were actively involved with illicit drugs, some 180,000,000 people, including the 14,000,000 regular users of cocaine, 13,500,000 opiate addicts, and 29,000,000 abusers of amphetamine. This historical policy outcome would surely have disturbed the signatories of the mid-century 1961 UN Single Convention, which instituted an IDCR based on a blueprint of global prohibition. Their goal was global abolition of both illicit drug supplies and use. The global scale of modern drug use would likely have also shocked the cosmopolitan turn-of-the-century idealists who gathered to debate drug limitation with a worrisome Chinese 'opium problem' in mind. The dramatic social violence and other social, health, and political hazards associated with the global drug war after 1970 would have been unthinkable to both sets of delegates: the 1990s drug-fueled civil war of Colombia, Mexico's drug-fired violent meltdown, and a snaking trail of late-century drug turmoil across the Middle East and South Asia, from Lebanon to Afghanistan. Confirmed drug warriors might argue—as some have—that these outcomes could have been worse had it not been for the 'containment' of international drug controls, but this remains a causality question for long-term social science analysis. The historical cases of cocaine and opiates sketched here—cocaine's dramatic birth and intensification as a hemispheric illicit drug after 1950, still uncontained, and heroin's extensive and still spiraling geopolitical shifts across Asia—largely belie that hypothesis. Yet UN officials during the formative years of the UNDCP in the 1990s remained committed to the American vision of a drug-free world of global prohibitions—a vision reaching heights of unreality.

3

THE INTERNATIONAL DRUG CONTROL REGIME
CRISIS AND FRAGMENTATION

Christopher Hallam and *David Bewley-Taylor*

Nearly two decades into the twenty-first century, the International Drug Control Regime (IDCR) faced significant—and arguably mounting—challenges. A general consensus has held together the regime since its foundation in its current form with the 1961 Single Convention on Narcotic Drugs; however, growing tensions around policy direction have resulted in the increasing fragmentation of this so-called Vienna consensus.[1] Specific issues such as the overweening focus on the law enforcement dimension of the treaties, the marginal role of human rights—and hence the difficult position of some aspects of the harm reduction approach within the IDCR—along with the problems surrounding access to essential medicines and the heterogeneity of the problem-landscape confronted by a monolithic colonial regime have all worked to generate tensions and systemic stress. Meanwhile, the longstanding dispute over the appropriate response to the recreational use of cannabis has escalated to a new pitch, with several jurisdictions initiating legally regulated markets for the drug's production, distribution, and consumption. While such actions at the subnational level within the United States as well as in Uruguay and Canada may well be justified on the grounds of pragmatism and public health, they are in direct violation of the treaties on which the IDCR is based. Those treaties entail a prohibition on the use of cannabis for anything other than medical and scientific purposes.

This chapter examines the state of play with respect to the tensions besetting the regime, and some of the options available to reform it and bring it into a more coherent and productive relationship with twenty-first century reality. Whether consensus-based reform will be possible is highly questionable, for alongside the fragmentation of the Vienna consensus is an enforced obligation amongst many of the countries and institutions involved to deny that such fragmentation is occurring at all. There remains a widespread, although increasingly strained, insistence that everything is 'business as usual,' with the international conventions maintaining their traditional role as the cornerstone of the global response to drugs and their associated vicissitudes.

The International Drug Control Regime and Pathways to Crisis

Consensus has held together the IDCR since the 1961 Single Convention on Narcotic Drugs, as amended by the 1972 protocol, which played a foundational role in ushering in what was then a realigned regime and shifting the priorities that had underpinned the old system, which had been based on the International Opium Convention of 1912. This consensus has been called by some scholars the Vienna consensus, as the United Nations (UN) bodies administering the regime have been based in that city since 1980. However, as we enter the third decade of the twenty-first century, this consensus is stricken by increasing levels of fracture and fragmentation, confronted by the complexities of a policy landscape that could not have been envisaged by those who constructed the regime in the aftermath of the Second World War.

A specific set of themes and issues have provided the focus for a growing challenge to the IDCR; these will be explored here, though it is important to bear in mind that they are an interwoven set of issues, each one impacting the others.

The new century has seen a rising, shared sense of the failure of attempts to control drugs by the tried and tested methods, a sense first registered in national contexts and expanding out through the traditional mass media and the new digital communication networks. This perception has arguably migrated from civil society into the institutions of the IDCR itself. It represents a perception of the futility of what has become known as the War on Drugs, and of the effectiveness of the IDCR: a multilateral system privileging a supply-side approach oriented around prohibition. Having penetrated the regime, this perception spread slowly at first, but has subsequently accelerated. At the 1998 United Nations General Assembly Special Session (UNGASS) on drugs, a renewed commitment was made by the international community of nations to a 'drug-free world,' with states pledging to eliminate or significantly reduce the illicit use and cultivation of the opium poppy, the coca bush, and the cannabis plant, supplemented by an equivalent objective regarding synthetic drugs and precursors. However, it was soon manifestly clear that this approach had already failed and would fail again. Indeed, for many observers there was a distinct sense of the absurd abroad when—at the mid-term review of progress in 2003—the Executive Director of the United Nations Office on Drugs and Crime (UNODC) issued a report entitled 'Encouraging progress toward still distant goals.'

By the time the next significant high-level meeting arrived in 2009, it was clearer still that little or no progress toward these objectives had been achieved, and that they remained 'still distant.' An influential report by Peter Reuter and Franz Trautmann, produced for the European Commission, concluded that: 'The global drug problem did not get better during the UNGASS period. For some countries (mostly rich ones) the problem declined but for others (mostly developing or transitional) it worsened, in some cases sharply and substantially.'[2]

Nonetheless, the institutions of the IDCR continued to hold their rhetorical ground. While it was becoming impossible to claim that drugs were being cleansed from the planet (there had been, briefly, a literal hope that the development of mycoherbicides that would kill poppy and coca plants, a biological scaling up of the War on Drugs),[3] the regime developed a new narrative of 'containment.' This narrative claimed that the illicit use of internationally controlled drugs had been successfully restricted to some 5 per cent of the adult population and that without drug control efforts there would be a veritable plague of consumers, bringing with it all of the associated health and social problems.[4]

In 2008, in the lead up to the high-level meeting, the Executive Director of UNODC Antonio Maria Costa produced the conference room paper that has come to be known as 'Fit for Purpose,' acknowledging what he described as 'unintended consequences' of the regime.[5] In this paper, he both elaborated on the containment narrative and described these unintended consequences: as 'a global black market' of illicit drugs, producers, and distributors; 'policy displacement,' in which funds that might have gone to public health go instead into security and law enforcement; 'geographical displacement' or the 'balloon effect,' as when supplies move between areas or jurisdictions in order to relieve the pressure of law enforcement; 'substance displacement,' where consumers move from one drug to another that is more potent or more available; and finally, 'the alienation of drug users,' their social stigmatization and exclusion from public health services. This paper by Costa and his close advisors represented a significant step in the progress of the regime's self-understanding, and reflected the inroads being made into the IDCR by the new discourses on drugs emanating from some regime members as well as from civil society and academia, even if its impact remained at first confined largely to the domain of rhetoric.

A second central factor in the fragmentation of the IDCR is represented by the issue of harm reduction, which is a generalized ethic and related set of practices focused on maintaining the life and the health of people who use drugs rather than forcing or persuading them to achieve a drug-free lifestyle. Emerging at the national, often local, level in the 1980s, this new and pragmatic approach to drug use emerged largely as a result of the advent of Human Immunodeficiency Virus (HIV) and Acquired Immune Deficiency Syndrome (AIDS), a deadly viral pathogen which could be transmitted through the sharing of needles and injection equipment. A public health orientation was therefore somewhat forced upon governments, and the response involved core harm reduction measures such as the greatly expanded provision of opioid substitution therapy (OST) and needle and syringe exchange. To those, including government officials, with an underlying ideological commitment to abstinence from all illicit drug use, these measures were viewed as highly controversial. They argued that such tactics encouraged drug consumption, were immoral, and among other things sent out the 'wrong message.' Others within government, particularly but not exclusively those in Europe, adopted a more pragmatic stance, and disputes between the two positions were soon enough heard in the forums of the IDCR.

Events at the High-Level Segment (HLS) of the 2009 Commission on Narcotic Drugs (CND), the UN's central policymaking body on the issue, provided a very visible demonstration of the break-up of the Vienna consensus, a process that was particularly evident in the conflicts surrounding harm reduction. Driven by the ideological and economic power of the United States, the UNODC and the International Narcotics Control Board (INCB or Board)—the watchdog of the UN drug control treaties—both spoke out against harm reduction, though many European states by then routinely included harm reduction measures in their national drug strategies. As a result of these divisions, there had been several heated debates at the CND in previous years. At the 2009 HLS, however, removal of all mention of harm reduction from the Political Declaration and Plan of Action resulted in the German ambassador Rudiger Ludeking leading a group of twenty-six mostly European countries in an 'interpretive statement.' In short, this statement meant that they would understand references to 'related support services' in the 2009 Political Declaration and Plan of Action to be referring to harm reduction.[6] He also requested that the statement be appended to the text, concluding a powerful item of support for harm reduction and demonstrating that the issue was of such importance that its absence would result in failure to sign. It was a clear indication that the old Vienna consensus was cracking.[7]

Further evidence was forthcoming at the same 2009 CND and crystallized around the classification of the coca bush. Bolivian President Evo Morales announced that he had come to Vienna to correct a historical error in the 1961 treaty, namely the prohibition of coca leaf chewing, an Andean cultural practice reaching back 3,000 years. Standing at the podium, President Morales held aloft a coca leaf and began to chew it ceremoniously, challenging Mr Costa to have him arrested. Having failed in its attempt to amend the Single Convention in order to comply with its recently re-written domestic constitution that permitted coca chewing, Bolivia was forced to withdraw from the Single Convention and rejoin with a reservation allowing coca chewing and the licit production of coca for that purpose.[8] They were eventually successful, but the struggle made clear the manifold difficulties involved in any attempt at reforming the drug control conventions via the mechanisms they contain for the purpose.

Another of the key contested domains is around cannabis, the drug with the world's highest number of illicit users and the object of widely differing policy proposals. Indeed, disagreements over the appropriate control of cannabis reach back to the early post-war period. A drug with an ancient medical profile, it was nonetheless decided at the CND in 1955 that cannabis had no therapeutic value, an essentially colonialist judgment that was also applied to its extensive cultural uses in South Asia, where eating cannabis and consuming cannabis drinks is embedded in numerous social functions such as wedding ceremonies and religious celebrations. Consequently, cannabis was included in Schedules I and IV of the Single Convention, a dual inclusion reserved for drugs that were considered extremely harmful and without any compensatory medicinal applications. Since cannabis policy has been the core issue that has moved states beyond 'soft defection' from the regime's punitive ethic[9] to an outright breach of the foundational treaty documents, it warrants discussion in a separate section below.

The diffuse sense of failure that marked the regime, the refusal to acknowledge the growing evidence base that underpinned those interventions characterized as harm reduction, the incoherence of the scheduling of drugs such as cannabis and coca as well as the widening divergence over policy prescriptions, sensitized observers to problems. These were articulated alongside further problems in both the design and application of the IDCR—all of these tied in with other UN issues. The result is a lack of systemic coherence, wherein the IDCR has failed to adequately articulate how it sits alongside other fundamental aspects of the UN project such as human rights and development, including in relation to the system-wide Sustainable

Development Agenda, and indeed the organization's objective of systemic coherence itself. Ironically, one of the primary goals of the first UNGASS on drugs—the 1990 UNGASS on Drug Abuse—had been to bring drug policies into harmony with the rest of the UN. The IDCR, however, continued to operate in ways that were at odds with the core UN objectives, in particular the imperatives of human rights, leading one UN official to describe human rights and drug control as existing in 'parallel universes.'[10]

The issue of human rights has continued to grow in its importance and visibility at the Vienna sessions of the IDCR, with organs such as the INCB increasingly vocal in their support of the inclusion of human rights in drug control. For example, Dr Viroj Sumyai, President of the Board, speaking at the fifth intersessional meeting of the sixty-second session of the CND in November 2018, stated that 'the fundamental goal of the UN drug control conventions is to safeguard the health and welfare of humankind by ensuring the availability of narcotic drugs and psychotropic substances for medical and scientific purposes while preventing their diversion and abuse.' This welcome formulation reverses the standard phrasing of the mission of the IDCR, which has generally begun with the prohibitive dimension, often mentioning medical access to controlled drugs as an afterthought.[11]

Nonetheless, the 2016 UNGASS on drugs demonstrated that the tensions and lack of agreement around the concept of human rights continue to be leading issues in the implementation of drug control, particularly around the use of the death penalty for drugs offenses, an issue that remained too controversial to include within the final text. While clearly representing some advances on previous soft law instruments, such as the 2009 Political Declaration, the outcome document of the 2016 UNGASS initially appeared to represent the weak product of what the Executive Director of the UNODC described as a 'very b-r-o-a-d consensus.'[12] As time has passed, however, energetic opposition to the document shown by the Russian Federation and its allies hints at the progress, within UN terms at least, that was made through the (albeit rhetorical) inclusion of health, human rights, and sustainable development.[13]

The Control Architecture

The fundamental objective of the IDCR is to restrict the production, distribution, and consumption of drugs to medical and scientific purposes. This is a dual imperative: it consists of an enabling dimension, which ensures access to drugs for those who need their therapeutic effects, and for research and development—and it consists of a restrictive dimension, which prevents by means of legislation the use of drugs for non-medical purposes, such as pleasure, relaxation, and philosophical exploration. Historically, the repressive function has been the dominant one: far more financial, human, and technical resources have been directed toward the suppression of non-medical drug use than have gone toward ensuring access to medicines and scientific research. In concrete terms, these polarities play into two principal methods of achieving drug control. These are 'commodity control' (the definition and regulation of the licit production, supply and possession of drugs) and 'penal control' (the suppression through criminal law of illicit production, supply and possession).[14] While the latter has come under increasing scrutiny, it is also important to note how indiscriminate prescribing and the resultant opioid crisis within North America since the 1990s also brings into question the regime's ability to effectively implement commodity control.

The present IDCR is administered by the UN. It is grounded in three international legal conventions: the aforementioned Single Convention on Narcotic Drugs of 1961, as amended by the 1972 Protocol; the Convention on Psychotropic Substances of 1971, and the UN Convention against Illicit Traffic in Narcotic Drugs and Psychotropic Substances of 1988 (see Chapter 2 by Paul Gootenberg). These conventions apply a range of 'schedules' or sets of control measures to the substances coming under their auspices. These range from very tight restrictions to loose and flexible controls, and are supposed to reflect levels of harm and addictiveness of substances on the one hand, and medical and therapeutic usefulness on the other. The CND makes the decision to schedule but is supposed to take into account the recommendations of the World Health Organization (WHO), which has the mandate to recommend on the levels of control, if any, that substances might require. This is one of the only important functions assigned to the health element of the regime.

There are several agencies and actors involved in the implementation and monitoring of the regime's operation: that is, the regime has some inbuilt self-monitoring capacities. Firstly, CND plays a pivotal role in its decisions. Its brief includes the conduct of an ongoing analysis of the global drug situation and the development of proposals—in the form of non-binding resolutions—designed to combat drug-related problems.

The International Narcotics Control Board (INCB) is the 'independent and quasi-judicial' control organ for the implementation of the drug control treaties.[15] The INCB was created under the Single Convention and established in 1968. It is, according to its mandate, technically independent of governments and of the UN, with its thirteen individual members serving in their personal capacities. The Board has the authority to assess worldwide scientific and medical requirements for controlled substances based on estimates from member states, and subsequently monitors allocations for imports and exports among parties to prevent leakage from licit sources into the illicit market. It fulfils a similar role in relation to precursor chemicals.[16] The Board also monitors compliance with the provisions of the drug control conventions.

The UNODC is the agency responsible for coordinating international drug control activities. It was established in 2002 and currently has around 500 staff members worldwide, though it employs numerous consultants and field workers. Its headquarters are in Vienna and it has twenty-one field offices, along with a liaison office in New York. The UNODC was established by the UN Secretary General in order to 'enable the Organization to focus and enhance its capacity to address the interrelated issues of drug control, crime prevention and international terrorism in all its forms.'[17]

The WHO is the UN specialized agency for health. It was established in 1948 and its objective, as set out in its constitution, is the attainment by all peoples of the highest possible level of health.[18] Health is defined as a state of complete physical, mental, and social well-being—not merely the absence of disease or infirmity. It is responsible for the medical and scientific assessment of all psychoactive substances and for advising the CND about the classification of drugs into one of the schedules of the 1961 and 1971 treaties. It is in this role of expert advisor to the policymaking and monitoring bodies that the WHO figures in the UN drug control system. The Expert Committee on Drug Dependence (ECDD) is the WHO body that conducts reviews of substances and makes recommendations to CND regarding the appropriate schedule of control within the conventions.[19]

The institutional bodies that form the framework of the IDCR are themselves inscribed in the drug control conventions and subsequent UN resolutions, which lay out their functions and composition. There is relatively little scope to change the tasks assigned to these drug control treaty bodies without first amending the conventions. However, there is little doubt that the INCB and its conservative supporters have at points devoted considerable attention to ensuring that the posts are occupied by those who share its views—a position that changed as the makeup of INCB shifted towards the inclusion of more open-minded elements. While the mandate of the Board and other bodies may be defined by the drug control conventions, the views of those in positions of significant power do count towards the tone and orientation with which such organizations operate.

The drug control conventions provide a certain amount of room for maneuver, and contain mechanisms for change for member states, though there is often an abyss between what is theoretically possible and what happens in practice. As touched on earlier, Bolivia sought to permit the use of coca, a practice its domestic constitution understood as a cultural patrimony. In this case, the 1961 Single Convention governing coca permitted Bolivia to propose an amendment to its provisions. In line with these provisions, the proposal was submitted to the UN Secretary General. Such proposals are circulated amongst the parties, and in the event that no state objects, after 19 months the treaty is amended in line with the proposal. Bolivia's proposal, as was expected, met with objections from a number of countries, particularly the US, leaving it with no realistic alternative but to leave the Single Convention and re-adhere with a reservation.

The difficulties experienced by Bolivia demonstrate the political differences that increasingly fracture the regime, and the impossibility of excluding the political domain from the legal. The interpretive frameworks imposed upon treaty law are themselves cultural and political. This was demonstrated by the appearance of a legal document in 2002, produced by the Legal Affairs Section of what was then the UN Drug Control Programme (now the UNODC) at the request of the INCB. The document was a response to INCB's query on the flexibility of the drug control treaties in relation to harm reduction and the legality of harm reduction measures. The resultant document was not made available to member states, presumably because the answers were not what the INCB wanted to hear—namely, that most of those health-related measures coming under the harm reduction umbrella were judged by the Section to be legal and permissible under the treaties. Furthermore, the Legal Affairs Section went so far as to make several statements that contradicted the INCB's unyielding commitment to the preservation of the regime in its current form— perhaps most importantly stating that:

> It is evident that new threats ... require that governments come up with new strategies to cope... It could even be argued that the drug control treaties, as they stand, have been rendered out of synch with reality since at the time they came into force they could not have possibly foreseen these new threats.[20]

The interpretive scope given to parties by the conventions does, then, allow for considerable domestic initiative and policy difference. There is space for countries to apply harm reduction measures, including those such as drug consumption rooms, which—while no longer regarding them as absolutely counter to the provisions of the conventions—the INCB often regards with ongoing hostility. This is a position maintained despite the advice it solicited from the Legal Affairs Section, which argued that the reliance on the concept of 'intent' in Article 3 paragraph 1 of the 1988 Convention precludes the possibility of legal breach by governments whose intent in providing such facilities is to reduce the harms associated with drug use and to bring users closer to medical and social support structures and personnel.[21]

It is not possible under the conventions to entirely remove drugs from criminal law. Moreover, states must treat trafficking or illicit production as 'serious' crimes. However, they are not required to criminalize personal use or possession, or to impose severe penalties in possession-related cases—a situation that leaves states legal space to pursue a range of decriminalization and depenalization approaches. In addition, there is no definition of 'medical and scientific' uses, an absence that provides the flexibility described above and applied by the Legal Affairs Section. Nonetheless, there are limits on what can reasonably be considered to constitute medical and scientific use. The thoroughgoing regulation of cannabis that was established in Uruguay, more recently in Canada and in some US states, for example, cannot according to careful legal scholarship be considered as scientific.[22] The increasing number of medical marijuana systems around the world and at different levels of governance, which involve a prescribing physician, can be considered legitimate, though even they have been subjected to repeated attacks by the INCB in its annual reports as failing the test of the genuinely medical. In some instances, this stance contains a degree of validity, as do charges relating to state responsibilities as laid out in the Single Convention. In others, however, the Board is arguably exceeding its mandate. In 2008, for example, the INCB noted its concern over 'medical cannabis' regimes, which it suggested may lead to expanded 'cannabis abuse,' affect adjacent states, and 'send the wrong message to the public.'[23]

Fragmentation and Complexity within the International Drug Control Regime

It has been customary practice amongst some, particularly international relations scholars, to refer to the IDCR, or the 'Global Drug Prohibition Regime,' as a normative mechanism determining the behavior of those countries who are signed up to its treaties and structures.[24] However, in the contemporary world the regime is increasingly complex and diverse, since regime members—that is to say, nation states—and the regime's bureaucracy and institutions contain both elements pushing for some type of reform and those seeking to resist any change in the regime's relationships with the exterior world. Taking a general overview, it is clear that over recent decades, the INCB—acting as an intervening variable within the regime—has positioned itself as the champion and defender of the regime in its current form. It has stood as a bulwark against change in rhetoric and practice, and against what it perceives to be a liberalization of the system.

The INCB has adopted a strong position against harm reduction, arguing that harm reduction is tantamount to legalization and an incitement to drug use, despite support for OST, needle and syringe programs (NSP) and other interventions in different UN bodies. It has criticized the practice of countries of which it disapproves, even though its mandate does not permit it to offer 'advice' to countries unless they specifically ask for it. The INCB's stance has been characterized as suffering from both 'mission creep' (exceeding its mandate) and 'selective reticence' (not speaking out when it should).[25] The Board, therefore, far from being a quasi-judicial and 'objective' body, is a political player within the system it is mandated to oversee.

The same is true of all of the UN agencies involved in drug control, though to varying degrees. The UNODC tends to operate as the public face of the IDCR, particularly with reference to the public utterances of its Executive Director, a post held between 2010 and 2020 by Mr Yury Fedotov, a career diplomat from the Russian Federation. Owing to Mr Fedotov's nationality, there were anxieties when he took up the post that he would use it to propagate the prohibitionist views of the Russian Government.[26] This did not prove to be the case, with Mr Fedotov taking up and developing the rhetorical line of his predecessor at the UNODC, Antonio Maria Costa, who—during the latter years of his tenure at least—defended the rebalancing of the regime toward health and human rights and away from the emphasis on punitive law enforcement. Nonetheless, the UNODC as represented by Mr Fedotov drew the line at any amendment of the conventions. Going further, he has reiterated the view that any suggestion of reform of the conventions threatens the stability of the regime.[27] Such exhortations appeared in his opening speech at the fiftieth CND in 2012, where he claimed that: 'Like any choir, we must sing in harmony. We cannot be out of tune. To ensure this, a commitment is required from all of us to acknowledge the importance of the Convention songbook.'[28] At this point in time, it was Bolivia and Uruguay who were admonished for singing out of tune, and consequently driving back the progress of the entire drug control project.

As we have seen already, the CND is a complex and heterogeneous assembly. Country delegations to CND meetings are made up of staff from diplomatic missions and from country capitals. Delegations are often weighted toward those with a law enforcement background rather than medical expertise, though this varies by country. As we illustrate in this chapter, countries maintain diverse positions on the most controversial elements of drug policy, such as harm reduction and cannabis control; nonetheless, a discourse of 'consensus' continues, on the surface at least, to hold sway in Vienna and New York on the occasion of high-level meetings. This consensus does not run very deep, and beneath it lies a field of tensions and conflicts; nonetheless, its hold on the drug control imagination is robust.

The WHO, which is—despite changes in the 2010s—a more marginal body within the IDCR than the Vienna-based drug control treaty bodies, has begun to engage the regime quite robustly over the problems of access to essential medicines. Approximately 80 per cent of the world population, or some 5.5 billion people, are estimated by the WHO to be without adequate access to medicines for the treatment of moderate to severe pain—that is, morphine and other opioids. Though it partnered with the INCB in administering the Access to Controlled Medications Programme, which was intended to address this huge problem, it is the WHO that has taken the lead in highlighting the clash between the restrictive and the enabling poles of the IDCR. The issue of ketamine has been in the foreground of this conflict (see Chapter 12 by Damon Barrett and Kasia Malinowska-Sempruch for a discussion of ketamine). The INCB has repeatedly used its annual reports and other public interventions to encourage member states to schedule ketamine under the provisions of the 1971 treaty. The WHO's Expert Committee on Drug Dependence (ECDD), which is mandated to review substances proposed for international control, recommended in three of its 'critical reviews' of the substance that there is no need to schedule ketamine, and that to do so would further restrict access to this vital anesthetic across rural areas and conflict zones in the developing world. The Expert Committee has stated that the restriction following on international scheduling could result in a 'public health disaster' accompanying the lack of ketamine for anesthesia. The WHO has at times been highly outspoken in regard to the attempt to internationally control ketamine and has worked hard to defend its health agenda within a regime that continues to be weighted toward law enforcement, though some adjustments have been made.

While the issue of ketamine has (probably temporarily) dipped off the radar, tramadol has emerged as a substance of similar concern.

The multiplicity of Novel Psychoactive Substances (NPS) represents a further set of new challenges to the IDCR. Although the regime has previously been confronted with new synthetic drugs to which it has adapted, the rapidity of the proliferation of NPS and the dynamism of their market penetration, particularly when combined with internet connectivity, represents a different scale of challenge. Some 803 substances were estimated to be in circulation by the 2018 World Drug Report,[29] representing unprecedented levels of stress on the system. In addition, although the domestic cultivation of cannabis has altered traditional producer-consumer distinctions, the relative ease with which NPS can be manufactured in 'kitchen sink laboratories' and the fact that producers can dispense with crop cultivation render the old geography of production, transit, and consumer zones obsolete. Similarly, research has come to light that indicates that heroin may be produced from engineered yeast, in effect making opioids available from sugar.[30]

The consequences of these developments are liable to be significant and profound, though it is too early to venture a clear idea of what they will mean for the IDCR. In one area, however, immediate effects have already begun to be registered, with previously unused clauses contained in the international drug control conventions now bringing about the provisional scheduling of the NPS mephedrone.[31] It is a matter of concern that such measures bypass the process of scientific review as it is normally carried out by the WHO—the drug is being scheduled prior to an ECDD critical review. Though the treaties do empower the CND to provisionally schedule prior to review when facing a significant threat, such actions represent a less than ideal state of affairs amidst the proliferation of NPS and the associated panic among some governments. In addition, although the WHO's Expert Committee does undertake a review on a provisionally controlled substance and may indeed recommend that the provisional controls should be removed, the CND is under no obligation to follow those recommendations. Historically, it has proved difficult to reverse the trend toward restrictive controls in the IDCR once the logic of the process is underway.[32] The effect is to further marginalize the role of the ECDD at a time when a scientific perspective is especially important in order to counter the panic that some governments have exhibited in the face of this new wave of psychoactive substances. The question of NPS featured prominently at the 2016 UNGASS.

In terms of countries that have played powerful roles as actors in the IDCR, historically the United States has been predominant, as explored in Chapter 2 of this volume. The twentieth century has rightly been called the 'American century.' As in many other issue areas, the US has used its financial, technological, and political power to influence the regime and to achieve its own objectives. Thus, the American War on Drugs has to a large extent directed and textured the international regime's more recent priorities and conduct, particularly after the 1988 Convention. The US played the leading role in setting the system up and has regularly used its diplomatic muscle to keep potentially dissident players in line. American support for a prohibitionist position has deep historical roots, and while it may have dovetailed with the country's geopolitical and military strategy, it was not purely cynical, but driven by an underlying morality that viewed drugs and addiction as incompatible with humanity and social life.[33]

Under the Obama administration, there was a sea-change in the direction of the overall American stance on drug control. Domestically, the administration reviewed its stance on drug consumers and began to view them as patients rather than moral or criminal miscreants. At the international level, this translated into a less obstructionist position at the UN in Vienna, including on the issue of harm reduction, albeit one that was not minded to considering reform of the conventions. To a varying extent, the US Federal Government also began to accept policy experimentation in other jurisdictions, for reasons which we will consider further below. These were linked to the decisions of several US states to establish legal, regulated cannabis markets. In short, the US is a shadow of the globalizing prohibitionist force it used to be, though this was to some extent rolled back under the auspices of the Trump administration. As in most issue areas, the policy positions on drugs—both domestic and international—under the Trump presidency were somewhat uncertain and fluid.

The country's erstwhile role as the cheerleader of a prohibitionist approach has lately been passed on to the Russian Federation, a country that has made methadone treatment illegal, which imprisons drug users in great numbers, and suppresses harm reduction practices despite its epidemic levels of HIV, HCV and TB (see Chapter 10 by Ekaterina Stepanova). At the CND, the Russian delegation rigorously adopts the hard line that the US abandoned. At the same time, it blames the United States and its allies—among other things—for their military failure in Afghanistan, which Russia views as the original cause of its explosion of domestic heroin use. Russia is supported in its hardline approach to drugs by a wide range of countries including Japan, Pakistan, and Egypt, as well as several other Asian and African states.

In terms of the trend toward change and reform in the IDCR, this has emanated most powerfully from Latin America (see Chapter 8 by Philip Robins, and Chapter 9 by Pierre-Arnaud Chouvy). The development became apparent with the Cartagena Summit in 2012, at which the Organization of American States (OAS) was mandated to examine alternative drug policies for the hemisphere. The region had been subjected to intense programs of securitization, often with US backing, with military interventions, armed proxies, defoliants, and crop eradication subjecting the populations, especially the poor, to extremes of hardship and ill-health. On the other side, the powerful drug trafficking organizations continued to scale up the violence of their response to the state and to defend their portion of the trade from rivals. Consequently, administrations and populations within Latin America had had enough of violence and corruption, and wanted to discuss different policy approaches. Within this context, it was a group of Latin American countries—Colombia, Guatemala and Mexico—that drove the rescheduling of the next planned UNGASS to 2016, the meeting having originally been scheduled for 2019. The latter remained the date of the UN high-level review of the targets contained within the 2009 Political Declaration and Plan of Action.

While the previous discussion represents some broad trends in the stakeholders in the IDCR and their interests, it is important to note that the regime is increasingly characterized by fragmentation, and fragmentation upon fragmentation. There is fragmentation between and within the regional groups, for example. Indeed, as could be seen at the 2016 UNGASS, although Latin America has expressed discontent with aspects of the present regime, there was and is no regional consensus on the direction of future travel: Uruguay argues that its regulated cannabis market does not constitute a breach of the conventions because under international law human rights treaties should take precedence over drug control treaties if there is a conflict between the two regimes. Bolivia supports the right of its indigenous population to grow coca but is opposed to the cultivation of cannabis. In Mexico, the primary concern is with the violence of the drug 'cartels,' while Colombia is preoccupied with the role of cocaine in the country's multi-sided civil conflict. Add to this scenario the changing balance in the IDCR, and the sustained patina of 'consensus' that denies that the regime is in a period of transition, and the situation becomes very complex indeed.

Cannabis in the IDCR: A New Level of Challenge to the System

In December 2013, Uruguay approved a law that would make the country's cannabis market legal, including not only consumption but cultivation and trade: the entire commodity chain from 'seed to sale' was to be legal and regulated by the state. Uruguay's President Mujica stated that 'the traditional approach hasn't worked. Someone has to be the first to try this.'[34] The country's government explained that it had taken this step because the methods inscribed in the IDCR had failed in their objectives, meanwhile filling prisons with small-scale users and enriching high-level criminals. The country's new, regulated system is intended to separate cannabis and its users from the market for more hazardous drugs such as *paco* (cocaine paste, widely used in Latin America), and to divert those funds that would otherwise go to criminal drug trafficking groups into education, public health, drug treatment, and prevention services. As already stated, Uruguay argued that the human rights justification of its new approach 'outranks' the 1961 Single Convention under which cannabis is classified, and with which it could be said to conflict.

Indeed, the INCB has insisted that Uruguay's regulated cannabis market *does* conflict with the Single Convention and puts the country in breach of it. It has repeatedly criticized Uruguay's move, calling cannabis 'an addictive substance with serious consequences for people's health.'[35] In a press interview, moreover, the then-president of the INCB, Raymond Yans, accused Uruguay of having a 'pirate attitude' toward the conventions, a judgment generating considerable anger in Uruguay and throughout Latin America, and which was way outside the Board's mandate. Other INCB members also expressed unease at Yans' intervention, stressing the lack of prior consultation and arguing that these statements did not represent the Board as a whole.[36] Perhaps not surprisingly, such a disrespectful attitude toward an elected government and its democratic decision was absent from Yans' conduct toward the United States, which was likewise in breach of the drug control treaties.

In 2012, the US states of Washington and Colorado moved through ballot initiatives to legalize and regulate the production, sale, and use of cannabis for recreational purposes. Although a shift in US policy—at least at a rhetorical level—was underway before 2012, it is possible to argue that the Obama administration's change in stance was influenced to some degree by this democratically-backed decision by two of its states, which have since been joined in the legalization of recreational use by other states and a federal district. As of mid-2020, eleven US states and Washington D.C.[37] permitted regulated cannabis markets, with several other ballots or legislative processes in the pipeline. Indeed, within the US it seems clear that the trend is toward reform of the domestic cannabis laws, at least at the state level. Despite some discussion, at the federal level the prohibition on non-medical use of the drug remains in place, and the US Government is fully supportive of the place of the international conventions and the regime they underpin.

As a way out of the conflicted position in which it finds itself in relation to the treaties, in 2014—and after considerable deliberation—the United States developed a 'new narrative' on the flexibility of the treaties. This position is often associated with its avowed originator, Ambassador William Brownfield, Assistant Secretary of State for International Narcotics and Law Enforcement Affairs (INL), and states that the US now proposes a more flexible approach to the interpretation of the treaties and a more tolerant approach to divergent national policies. The US refers to its kinder, gentler narrative as the 'four pillars' approach, in which the first pillar consists of defending the integrity of the treaties; the second pillar, that of 'flexible interpretation,' which understands the treaties as 'living documents' that adjust as the world changes around them; pillar three, 'tolerating different national policies,' which entails the acceptance of 'some degree' of differing national strategies for responding to drugs; and the fourth and final pillar, the shared belief, whatever the position of legalization and so on might be, that those transnational criminal groups that profit from production and trafficking should be energetically countered and, if possible, eliminated.[38] Despite such a stance, it was not to be long, however, before Washington demonstrated the limits of flexible interpretation when it was applied to other states.

The INCB, albeit with considerably more restraint and respect than it deployed when addressing Uruguay, disagreed with the Brownfield 'flexibility' narrative and held that the US was in breach of the Single Convention in allowing its citizens to partake in the non-medical use of cannabis. Some commentators welcomed the new US 'flexibility' stance, seeing it as a way forward from the impasse created around the drug control treaties, since it appears to permit changes to be made without the necessity of amending or redrafting the conventions—a remote political possibility in the present circumstances.[39] However, while it may be superficially appealing, the US State Department's 'flexibility' narrative has been subjected to powerful critiques from several academic and civil society commentators. Echoing earlier commentaries,[40] Martin Jelsma asks, 'Who gets to decide which flexible interpretation is acceptable under a more lenient regime and which one is not? Is the United States willing, for example, to apply the same principle to Bolivia's coca policy or to drug consumption rooms, or will it continue to condemn such practices?'[41]

The first sign of an answer to such questions was demonstrated in US public comment in 2015. In response to generalized discussions concerning decriminalization and the possible future creation of legal cannabis markets in Jamaica, US officials strongly opposed any moves on the grounds that it was a transit country.[42] Brownfield was critical, expressing his country's 'unease' and suggesting that Jamaica's proposals would add to the illicit traffic in the drug reaching the US. This raises the specter of the US as arbitrator of the applicability of the conventions, deciding whether a given policy measure should be assigned to the 'flexibility' pillar or to the 'integrity' pillar—neither of which have been signed up to or consulted upon by other countries. The legal grounding of the US position is extremely weak, while its political utility may be less than it appears at first sight.

The intensity of the challenge posed to the IDCR by changing attitudes to cannabis, however, increased considerably with the election of Justin Trudeau as prime minister of Canada in 2015. Influenced to a degree by events in Colorado and Washington state, Trudeau announced in April 2016 his government's aim of introducing legislation to create a regulated market for the recreational use of cannabis by early 2017. Following a somewhat extended legislative process, Bill C-45 came into law on 17 October 2018. However, rather than adopting the preferred approaches of the US Federal Government or officials in Montevideo and side-stepping the thorny issue, the Trudeau administration took the brave and honest decision to admit the resultant tensions that now existed in relation to Canada's international commitments. Indeed, in May 2018, Canadian Foreign Minister, Chrystia Freeland, acknowledged that C-45

> will result in Canada contravening certain obligations related to cannabis under the three UN drug conventions. I think we need to be open about that… [she continued, before going on to say that] the Canadian government is definitely open to working with treaty partners to identify solutions that accommodate different approaches to cannabis within the international framework.[43]

In an environment where amorphous 'untidy legal justifications' have been joined by the firm admissions of treaty breach by a G7 state, what courses of action are available to those governments seeking, for one reason or another, to reconcile domestic realities with international obligations?[44] A recent and welcome development is the reviewing of cannabis by the ECDD, a review which many argue is long overdue. Previously, cannabis had not been reviewed by the ECDD, and the only review ever carried out—allegedly by the Health Committee of the League of Nations in 1935—is of doubtful value and even disputed existence, as no records have survived the Second World War to substantiate its conclusions.

At its fortieth session in 2017, the Expert Committee began the process of reviewing cannabis, conducting a pre-review, which reported that the Expert Committee judged that a critical review was necessary. The critical review commenced in November 2018. Releasing the review's outcomes in January 2019, the ECDD recommended a series of changes in the scheduling of cannabis-related substances. Perhaps unsurprisingly, these did not include de-scheduling or downgrading the controls on cannabis for non-medical and non-scientific purposes.[45] Even so—and reflecting the strength of ongoing disagreement around medical cannabis within the CND—voting on the Committee's recommendations was postponed at both the 2019 and 2020 March sessions of the Commission.

With any substantive rescheduling regarding non-medical use unlikely in the foreseeable future, if ever, a second option would be to amend the 1961 Convention. Due to the nature of the mechanisms within the conventions for this purpose and divisions among regime members, this proposal is currently even more politically improbable. Although not without its drawbacks, a more realistic third option would be to utilize the tools used by Bolivia in relation to coca— denunciation and re-accession with a reservation permitting the use of cannabis within a given country.[46] Fourth would be the possibility of denunciation, based on the fact that the early acceptance of the treaties was driven by erroneous and outmoded data regarding cannabis. A final option is that of *inter se* modification. There are a range of jurists, scholars of international law, and drug control analysts considering pathways to reform, but we believe this is likely to be one of the most effective options currently available to reform-minded states, and as such will be discussed in the final section.

The IDCR: Which Way Next?

The powerful pressures exerted by the traditional reliance on consensus at CND, and the inertia and reluctance within the institutions of the regime to contemplate reform, mean that the overall political climate for treaty reform remains hostile. While tensions are increasing in relation to the (disputed) intersection between drug policy and the interconnected issues of human rights (see Chapter 5 by Angélica

Durán-Martínez), attainment of the Sustainable Development Goals (see Chapter 6 by Carlos A. Pérez Ricart), and UN system-wide coherence more broadly, it is cannabis that has generated compelling momentum for some type of regime reform and modernization. Those who continue to believe that the US flexibility narrative or other approaches based on scientific experimentation may offer a practical solution to the need for change are not unreasonably influenced by the regime's structural rigidity, and the hostility to change displayed by many of its members. However, they underestimate the dangers associated with such an argument not just within the realm of drug policy but also in international law more widely, of which these policies are just a small part.[47] However, the process of *inter se* modification may provide an alternative to either maintaining the status quo or accepting a dubious model that lacks a coherent legal basis, allowing the politically and economically powerful to decide what is and what is not an acceptable example of treaty flexibility. For Neil Boister and Martin Jelsma, amongst the options not requiring consensus, *inter se* modification provides a useful safety valve for collective action to adjust a treaty system which is arguably frozen in time.[48]

Although the mechanism is used relatively rarely, the option of *inter se* modification would enable a group of like-minded states to modify their relationship to the treaties to render them better adapted to the circumstances facing governments in the twenty-first century. The 1969 Vienna Convention on the Law of Treaties permits two or more parties to modify a treaty solely for themselves. As Article 41 states: 'Two or more parties to a multilateral treaty may conclude an agreement to modify the treaty as between themselves alone.'[49] There are limits to this process: parties can only conclude such an agreement so long as it 'does not affect the enjoyment by the other parties of their rights under the treaty or the performance of their obligations.'[50] The agreement must also be compatible with the 'effective execution of the object and purpose of the treaty as a whole.'

Legal experts have agreed that *inter se* modification is possible unless it is expressly prohibited under a given treaty; the international drug control conventions impose no such prohibition. However, it is early days for the exploration of the option as a potential legal foundation for a group of like-minded states to achieve a recalibration of their relations with the drug control treaties regarding cannabis. It remains to be seen how appropriate it might be as a strategy for regime modernization.[51] Those parties opposed to reform could, in theory, argue that, in view of an increasingly globalized and interconnected world, any such measure might impact upon countries that have not supported it.

Nonetheless, some areas of reform seem particularly amenable to these types of legal arrangements between like-minded states. Among a range of potential advantages over other options,[52] *inter se* modification could apply, for example, in the case of trade between national jurisdictions whose domestic laws permit licit markets in a substance, but which would be unable to trade under the conventions as they presently stand. Some believe that it would be suitable to allow supplies of cannabis from countries like Morocco to the coffee shop system in the Netherlands, or the Spanish cannabis clubs. Moreover, and perhaps more significantly, it can be argued that such a structure might help ensure that currently marginalized cannabis farmers are not excluded from any regulated markets that might emerge in traditional consumer states in the future. Similarly, the international conventions outlaw the export of coca leaf from Bolivia, where production is legal, to Argentina, where consumption is legal. As has been noted: 'An agreement among these, or other, sets of countries to modify the treaty, and thus permit trade between them, would seem to be a satisfactory arrangement difficult to challenge on the basis that it would affect the rights of other parties.'[53] Indeed, bringing the coca trade (which is currently carried out illegally as cross-border smuggling) under legal regulation would support the objectives of the IDCR by reducing the levels of illicit distribution and blocking the access of funds to transnational trafficking groups. Such arrangements between like-minded countries could also bring the parties into line with other international obligations lying outside the field of drug control. As Damon Barrett has demonstrated, despite Bolivia's dispute with the INCB and other parties that condemned it, its legalization of coca chewing and some production by indigenous people has strengthened the country's commitments to indigenous, human and cultural rights.[54]

The range of viability of *inter se* modification remains to be seen, and whatever progress is made towards the construction of a group of like-minded states, powerful players within the regime—countries such as the Russian Federation and its status quo allies—will be difficult to shift from their ingrained positions. Whatever strategy is adopted, it is crucial that the political will for change is present. That said, there may be a singular window of opportunity in that the US, amidst growing support for regulated cannabis markets within the country at the state level and some discussion of federal reform, may consider shifting its strategic focus on the drug. This observation must of course be tempered by the uncertainties which came from the Trump administration's mixed messages on the issue of drug policy generally. Nonetheless, the historical tactical choices it has made— stemming from the 'flexibility' narrative—are deeply problematic, for the reasons discussed above, and the US remains in partnership to an extent with the Russian Federation in that it refuses to openly contemplate any moves towards regime reform.

The Danish physicist Niels Bohr is credited with having remarked that 'prediction is very difficult, especially about the future.' With this in mind, there are several ways that the current fracturing of the regime may play out. For example, some countries may continue to make statements on the necessity of reviewing the treaty framework, such as the Czech Republic, Ecuador, Mexico, and others that have spoken out on the issue at recent CNDs. Such statements, of course, are not unimportant. They do not, however, equate to systemic moves to critically interrogate the effectiveness and current relevance of the existing legal architecture. It is possible that other broadly critical states will concern themselves with matters of health and human rights within the current boundaries of the treaties. This is not necessarily a bad thing, but it serves to sustain the larger structures of harm the IDCR in its present form presents through collateral damage.

The IDCR's improved performance depends largely on the frank recognition of the structural incoherence and conflicts that characterize it. Some reform-minded observers, having missed the opportunity at the 2016 UNGASS,[55] hoped that the 2019 Ministerial Segment of the CND would, if not trigger discussion of regime reform and modernization, then at least be a platform for the creation of some sort of advisory group or expert working group to deliberate the emerging and increasingly serious tensions between the treaties themselves and events on the ground. This idea has been around in various forms for some time, and is not uncommon in other regimes. It was particularly hoped this would arise in relation to cannabis, but also pertained to other issues including scheduling—where, as mentioned above, discord surrounds mandates and threatens the vital principle of relatively independent scientific review.[56] In addition, there are ongoing tensions between the IDCR and other UN projects and their founding treaties and themes, such as human rights, security (both narrowly and broadly defined) and development. It should be recalled how both human rights and the Sustainable Development Goals (SDGs) featured prominently in the outcome document from the 2016 UNGASS.

While the 2019 Ministerial Declaration failed to include reference to any such group, it is significant that the document did incorporate explicit commitments to 'strengthen international and interagency cooperation' and 'enhance coherence within the United Nations system at all levels with regard to the World Drug Problem.'[57] With the emergence of an increasingly sophisticated system-wide approach across the UN,[58] including notably in New York with engagement by the UN Secretary General's Chief Executives Board for Coordination, and the establishment of the UN System Coordination Task Team,[59] the omission of such a position would have been glaring. The Task Team has a mandate to look at data, and as such can consider examining the increasingly pressing issue of drug policy metrics and indicators. There is a growing awareness of not only a paucity of good-quality data on what has become known somewhat vaguely as the 'world drug problem,' but also that systems might, in fact, be measuring the wrong things and excluding important outcomes of a range of policy interventions.[60]

However, the stiffness of the opposition that these relatively mild measures to review the effectiveness of the drug control treaties may draw, in the absence of formal structures that exist in a range of other regimes,[61] should not be underestimated. It is likely that few parties to the treaties will want to rock the boat and will instead seek to negotiate their way through the current transitional period with as little conflict as possible. Moreover, while former President Mujica remarked that 'someone had to be first,' there is a reluctance among what might be seen as progressive states to lead the charge for reform and put their head even further above the parapet, for fear of reprimand from parts of the UN system and other member states. Unable to remain below the radar as had largely been the case with Uruguay, Canada experienced the full force of the Russian Federation's condemnation for its cannabis policy at the intersessional meeting of the CND in November 2018.[62] It seems likely that this was only the opening salvo in a protracted and determined campaign to defend the shape of the extant regime. Within such an environment, the formation of like-minded groups and a 'safety in numbers' approach certainly appears to be the most (geo)politically attractive way forward. In terms of other big beasts within the increasingly combative international drug policy arena, it appears—anecdotally at least—that off the record, the US State Department recognizes that its country is in breach of the conventions and seems relatively open (or resigned) to the inevitability of serious discussions of regime reform of one kind or another further down the line. The key question here is, how far down the line? It seems unlikely that despite the obvious—if studiously ignored—'Collapse of the Global Order on Drugs,'[63] the CND will be the venue for substantive collective discussion and associated moves toward systemic reform and structural modernization any time soon.

That said, from a more optimistic perspective regarding the concept of regime stasis, we should also note that consideration of 'reform' should not be confined simply to formal amendments of the legal texts of the conventions. Indeed, Bolivia's realignment of its relationship to the Single Convention regarding coca via withdrawal and recessions can be considered a modality of regime reform and change, as can possible future options including *inter se* modification. To be sure, agreement among a group or groups of like-minded states that does not involve consensus across the regime in its entirety links international drug policy reform to broader issues of change in the UN system, the shift away from universality and the inability to gain full accord in any issue area.[64]

These are some of the possible directions that processes of change may take, but what other levers might act upon the drug policy landscape and its implications for the IDCR? It is probable that much will hinge on the US state-level cannabis juggernaut and its increasing momentum.[65] It might be argued that the US Federal Government's initial reaction to Washington and Colorado was driven in part by a hope that the regulated markets would fail, that public opinion would shift back toward a repressive stance and policies would revert—that is, an optimistic holding strategy. This may yet play out, though it is becoming increasingly unlikely. Moreover, as further states move to establish legally regulated markets, they will learn from those that went before and, in theory, should be in a position to develop more optimized systems. It certainly seems that in 2012 Washington and Colorado learned from previous failed efforts in California.[66] We are now in a position where the US has more than a few 'rogue' states; by late 2018, one in five Americans lived in states that had opted to operate regulated cannabis markets, including the entire West Coast.

One of the biggest issues for cannabis policy within the US in 2016, and consequently the IDCR, was what would happen if California passed a law to legalize cannabis. Speaking in 2014, Alison Holcombe, former Director of the American Civil Liberties Union of Washington state, predicted that the move to a regulated market in California would represent a 'game changer, not only nationally but internationally.'[67]

In terms of transnational influence, this is particularly true south of the border. While recent moves in Mexico toward a regulated cannabis market should be seen as part of a complex and long-running process, at both a practical and political level it is difficult to see how Mexico will be able to sustain prohibitionist policies on cannabis, even with the support of the US Federal Government, when just across the border, California—the world's eighth largest economy—is operating a legally regulated market for cannabis. If President Andrés Manuel López Obrador follows through on legislation to legalize the possession, public use, growth, and sale of cannabis, other nation states within the region—including the Caribbean—or elsewhere may be encouraged, emboldened even, to follow. Moreover, if Mexico joins Canada as the second geopolitically noteworthy state in the hemisphere to shift to regulated markets, supporters of the regime in its current form will face mounting difficulties, including in labelling individual states as outlying miscreants that threaten the integrity of the regime.

When it comes to Europe, previously the continental locus for drug policy change,[68] it is obvious that the EU as a whole remains wedded to the current treaty framework. As a regional grouping, its stance may be understood as passive-active—supporting health and human rights within the existing boundaries and beyond—as opposed to the Association of South East Asian Nations, which is active in looking to create a drug-free region and world. Forecasting social, cultural, and political changes is always to some extent a throw of the dice. That said, Luxembourg's plan to establish a regulated recreational cannabis market (as announced in December 2018) has certainly forced analysts and politicians alike to start contemplating the repercussions of an EU member state embracing policy shifts that hitherto had been regarded as somewhat exotic, the product of events in the Western hemisphere. Indeed, before the release of the Coalition government's policy document outlining the proposal, shifts on cannabis policy in Europe were viewed as occurring through a gradual bottom-up process, for instance the launch of city-level experiments in the Netherlands and Switzerland.[69] New Zealand's decision to hold a referendum on a regulated cannabis market in late 2020 is a reminder that debates are also moving forward in other regions.

If, in light of the growing engagement with regulated cannabis markets in both national and subnational contexts, there is no substantial change in the IDCR, the strains upon it are likely to reach such proportions as to render the situation untenable in the not-too-distant future. This dynamic would pose threats to the stability of other elements of the regime, including perhaps its important functions relating to the provision of essential medicines. These are real risks associated with the US 'flexibility' model, which centers on an attempt to conceal the fissures and conflicts with which the regime is afflicted, keeping them out of sight and out of public discourse.

Overall, there is likely to be a tipping point at which the system will either have to be reconfigured, or fragment beyond the point of no return. Indeed, while not restricted solely to the issue of cannabis, observers of the 2020 session of the CND will have noted how at points the Vienna-based control system, long since straining, appeared on the verge of a meltdown. As one account of an earlier session put it, 'It has become increasingly evident that the sand of divergence has been getting into the gears of the CND's consensus functioning machinery, but never has it seemed so close to bringing it all to a grinding halt.'[70]

It is interesting to note, however, just how resilient the current regime is and ask what the timescale for substantive change might be. This resilience is no doubt the result of the massive effort invested in creating the IDCR in the first place, the inertia of the bureaucracy surrounding it, the functions it performs in terms of the licit trade, and the payoff for its current key supporters, especially Russia, China, and—in more complex ways—the US. The dispute over cannabis is at the heart of the regime's future direction, and resembles the way it absorbed and integrated many of the disagreements and changes that clustered around harm reduction interventions in previous years, particularly between 1998 and 2009. That said, the clear-cut treaty breaches surrounding cannabis are a new and significant variable. The core function of the regime is to restrict drugs to medical and scientific uses, and it is precisely this principle that is at stake in the current fractures. Paradoxically, what may ensure the continuing life of the regime over the long term is whether or not it possesses the ability to adapt to the modern world's relationship with drug consumption by allowing some currently scheduled substances to be consumed for non-medical and non-scientific purposes. Cannabis regulation may indeed reside at the beginning of that process, carrying the hopes of some and the fears of others.

4

A FORWARD MARCH HALTED
THE UNGASS PROCESS AND THE WAR ON DRUGS

Mónica Serrano

I believe that drugs have destroyed many lives, but wrong government policies have destroyed many more.

Kofi Annan

In September 2012, in three consecutive statements delivered at the United Nations General Assembly, the presidents of Colombia, Guatemala, and Mexico called on the United Nations (UN) to lead a far-reaching debate on the scope and limits of drug policy. In their statements, the three Latin American presidents alluded to the decisions reached at the southern Mexican city of Mérida in 2011, as well as during the 6th Summit of the Americas held in Cartagena, Colombia in April 2012. In addition to urging a significant reduction in drug demand, these countries had entrusted the Organization of American States (OAS) with the special task of assessing and preparing a 'frank' and 'thorough' report on the drug problem, as well as an honest assessment of the actions that had been taken to confront it.[1]

In his remarks to the UN in the autumn of 2012, and in the twilight of his presidential term, Felipe Calderón identified illicit drug trafficking, and the associated illicit markets in arms and human trafficking as major drivers of violence and violent deaths in Latin America. In his own country, Mexico, his government had confiscated over 150,000 weapons in the previous 6 years alone. This view was shared by the then-president of Guatemala, Otto Pérez Molina, who attributed no less than 40 per cent of homicides in his country to the violence associated with the illicit movement of drugs. The need to set off a long overdue international debate on the drug problem, which had caused so much havoc in the world and in Colombia, was in turn highlighted by former President Juan Manuel Santos. In line with this, and acknowledging the leading role played by the UN in discussions and efforts to tackle global problems from climate change to famines and pandemics, President Calderón demanded a global drug debate 'up to the challenges of the twentieth Century.'

Amidst the crises of security and violent trends affecting their countries, and with the certainty provided by half a century's track record on punitive drug control, the three Latin American heads of state called into question the rationale of policies of prohibition and supply control. In their view, not only had such efforts patently failed to halt drug consumption trends, they had also propelled the proliferation of thriving illicit drug markets and powerful criminal actors and organizations.

In the words of Felipe Calderón, 'the huge profits from buoyant black markets created by prohibition had incited criminal ambitions, increasing ever more the massive flow of resources towards criminal organizations.' Such resources had economically and politically empowered criminals, 'giving them a practically unlimited capacity to corrupt' and thus enabled them to 'buy whole governments and entire police corps, leaving societies in total helplessness.'[2] Concurring with this view, the then-presidents of Guatemala and Colombia underlined the need to openly acknowledge the flaws in dominant drug control policies and unending wars on drugs, and to consider alternatives routes, including regulatory options.[3] In their successive statements the three Latin American presidents conveyed the urgency of a much-needed change in drug policy.

Three months later, in early 2016, the General Assembly announced in its Resolution 67/193 its decision to convene a special session on the world drug problem with a view to assessing the progress that had been made in implementing the 2009 Political Declaration and Plan of Action. At that time, it seemed the desire to revisit the 'drug problem' had gathered momentum beyond the small group of countries calling for the drug debate.[4] Yet, once the process for the special session took off, the capacity of these countries to shape and influence the debate declined steadily. On the one hand, their failure to define a clear road map to UN General Assembly Special Session (UNGASS) beyond the vague notions of regulation and reform soon generated mistrust among those countries favoring prohibition and hardline drug control options. On the other, the efforts of Mexico, Colombia and Guatemala to gear the process towards New York, where all 193 UN member states were represented, and away from Vienna, soon met the bureaucratic resistance of the UN drug control system.

The end goal of the Latin American countries remained undefined, oscillating between regulation and marijuana legalization, and the re-opening of the drug control conventions. However, the logics and structures operating within the international drug control regime (IDCR) were pushed onto the defensive. It soon became evident that the ability of these countries to steer the debate towards a reform agenda depended not just on their vision, resources and diplomatic abilities, but on the broader international drug control context.

The way the process unfolded soon revealed three undeniable realities. The first concerned the lack of a clear blueprint for reform and sound leadership among the Latin American countries. Equally important were the wide differences in perceptions and positions on drug policy and drug control that cut across countries and continents around the world. Last but not least was the weight still carried by key actors and agencies, who were mostly responsible for the functioning and oversight of the regime and its three pillar conventions.[5]

The prospects for a dynamic Latin American leadership role vanished sooner than expected. Three major obstacles stood in the way. The first concerned Washington's decision to deploy a vigorous opposition campaign to any major revision of the IDCR. The Obama administration immediately made clear its concern over the moves taken by Colombia, Guatemala, and Mexico, and its determination to halt their impetus to revisit the IDCR regime. With different signals and gestures, the US Government demonstrated the limits to its tolerance on drug policy reform. Thus in the spring of 2012, days before the opening of a special meeting convened by President Otto Pérez Molina to discuss alternatives to drug trafficking in Central America, a high-level US delegation expressed Washington's opposition to any major change to prevailing regional drug control policies and strategies. In a first stop-over in Mexico City, the US delegation—headed by then Vice President Joe Biden, the Secretary for Homeland Security Janet Napolitano, and William Brownfield, the highest public official in charge of drug control policy in the State Department—bluntly expressed that the Obama administration was in no position to modify its stand against drug legalization.

In other words, while the Latin American heads of state were contemplating the feasibility of a new approach to illicit drug use that could both help turn off the tap to massive illicit flows and contain criminal violence, the US Government closed the door to regulation. In the view of Janet Napolitano, drug decriminalization was not a viable option to deal with the drug problem.[6] This message was immediately voiced in a meeting in Tegucigalpa, Honduras, where the US delegation met with the then-heads of state of Central America, presidents Porfirio Lobo Sosa from Honduras, Pérez Molina from Guatemala, Mauricio Funes from El Salvador, Daniel Ortega from Nicaragua, Ricardo Martinelli from Panamá, Laura Chinchilla from Costa Rica, and foreign minister Carlos Morales from the Dominican Republic. Not surprisingly, the pressure from Washington sufficed to ensure the failure of Guatemala's bid for regulation. Without further delay, the presidents of El Salvador, Honduras, and Nicaragua made clear their decision not to attend Pérez Molina's meeting, while Panama voiced its opposition to options for depenalization.[7]

When the Latin American presidents approached the international agencies and bodies responsible for the monitoring and implementation of the international drug conventions, they encountered their second major obstacle. While the pressures coming from Washington may have hampered the prospects for a viable Latin American leadership, the bureaucratic inertia of drug control agencies further disabled it. The first signs of resistance were manifest in the decision to postpone the special session from 2014 to 2016, and in the attempt to limit the debate to identifying and filling the lingering gaps in the 2009 Political Declaration and Plan of Action.[8] The Latin American countries succeeded in their efforts to convene a special session of the General Assembly on the world drug problem and, by enlisting the Third Committee, to broaden the scope of drug control measures to public health perspectives, human rights, and development. However, once the preparatory works for the special session gathered force, it became clear that the odds were stacked against them, and that their capacity to shape the debate would be significantly constrained by the gravitational force of the Vienna drug control bureaucracy.[9]

As soon as the Commission on Narcotic Drugs (CND), the regime's 'central policymaking body,' assumed a dominant role and started laying down the terms for the special session, the prospects for a conservative debate seemed ever more likely. On 15 March 2013, the Commission undertook to oversee the preparatory process for the special session with Resolution 56/12 and, by December of that year, General Assembly Resolution 68/197 had confirmed the Commission's role and formally requested this body to engage in the preparatory process. In March 2014, this was followed by a high-level review of the progress made in the implementation of the 2009 Political Declaration and Plan of Action and by the Commission's pledge, as stated in its Resolution 57/5, to conduct an 'adequate, inclusive and effective preparatory process of the special session.'[10] With the CND's tight control over the preparatory process established, the possibility of a critical and substantive debate significantly narrowed.[11]

But not all the obstacles standing in the way of a viable Latin American leadership were placed by actors and agencies favoring prohibition and punitive drug control. The third major obstacle to a credible Latin American leadership came from within the countries themselves, and was linked to domestic factors. Though the IDCR was clearly hostile to changes in drug policy, the domestic situation in Colombia, Guatemala, and Mexico was not particularly conducive to the consolidation of a strong regional leadership. While Colombia and Mexico faced heated presidential elections and the prospect of changes of government, Guatemala's President Otto Pérez Molina, a former general and a hugely controversial figure, had long confronted criminal accusations that would lead to his final arrest on corruption charges in early September 2015.[12]

The period between the General Assembly's 2012 decision to call a special session and the actual convening of UNGASS 2016 saw a prolonged tug-of-war between the Vienna drug control bureaucracy and those in the General Assembly in New York who favored an open and inclusive process with UN organs and agencies, as well as civil society, contributing 'fully to the preparations for the special session.' Not surprisingly, those committed to a substantial debate sought to mobilize and energize the General Assembly. More than anywhere else, it was in its reaffirmation of its commitment to address 'substantial issues, on the basis of the principle of common and shared responsibility,' and in full conformity with the purposes and principles of the UN Charter, 'international law and the Universal Declaration of Human Rights, and with respect for the sovereignty and territorial integrity of States' where the General Assembly's commitment to a truly meaningful special session became clear.[13] While these may have seemed minor differences of emphasis at the outset, they clearly reflected a significant divergence of perspectives between the CND's long-held control over drug control issues, and those seeking to energize the General Assembly. The final details for the special session were agreed toward the end of 2014 and were reflected in a number of organizational and substantive recommendations embodied in CND's Resolution 58/8.

In its Resolution 58/8, the Commission welcomed the General Assembly's decision to entrust the CND to lead the preparatory process, pledging to take all necessary measures to ensure 'an adequate, inclusive and effective preparatory process.' In a proposed General Assembly resolution, the CND sketched out the main details of the forthcoming special session. Both the secretary general and the president of the General Assembly (GA) would open the session, followed immediately by the heads of the main agencies of the UN drug control machinery—the CND, the Executive Director of the United Nations Office on Drugs and Crime (UNODC) and the International

Narcotics Control Board (INCB). A closing statement by the Director General of the World Health Organization (WHO) would then follow. A plenary or general debate would come next, in which representatives of regional and international organizations, member states, observer states and observers, as well as representatives of non-governmental organizations (NGOs)—to be selected by the GA president in consultation with the CND—would be given the floor to voice their views and perspectives. In addition, five parallel 'interactive and multi-stakeholder round tables' were announced, as well as a 'concise and action-oriented document' to be prepared by the Commission, which would include 'a set of operational recommendations' expected to be adopted at the plenary of the special session.[14]

By March 2015, when the special segment on the world drug problem took place in Vienna, the positions of Colombia, Guatemala, and Mexico had clearly shifted toward the center. While Guatemala maintained its critical stance towards punitive drug control policies, and suggested its commitment to continue exploring alternative strategies, the Central American country abandoned its pro-legalization stance on marijuana and pledged its commitment to observe the UN drug conventions.[15] In turn, Colombia highlighted the primacy of human rights and the urgent need to mainstream human rights in drug control strategies. Yet the prominence given by Yesid Reyes, Colombia's then minister of justice, to his country's contribution to the reduction of cocaine production and the dismantling of powerful drug cartels appeared to endorse orthodox drug control strategies.[16] Like his Guatemalan and Colombian counterparts, the Mexican Ambassador questioned the logic of punitive drug control and called for new solutions to the world drug problem while emphasizing that his country had spared no effort in the fight against the cartels, money laundering, and arms trafficking. Notably, the Mexican Ambassador opted not to take the special session as an opportunity to revisit drug control, but rather to underscore his country's commitment to the UN drug control conventions and the IDCR.[17] The moderation, not to say self-restraint showed by Colombia, Guatemala, and Mexico came as little surprise in the light of the US' statement, delivered by William Brownfield, which reiterated that the US would continue to promote international cooperation among judicial authorities, including through extradition, legal assistance and law enforcement, in accordance with the terms set by the international drug control conventions.[18]

Two months later, as part of the preparations for the special session, the General Assembly convened a significant high-level thematic debate. The event—which was intended to support the 'process towards the 2016 special session of the General Assembly on the world drug problem'—heralded some of the disagreements and divisions that would soon surface at UNGASS 2016.

The one-day event included a plenary session, in which eight prominent speakers participated, six of them from the Americas—including the three countries that had called for the UNGASS, together with the US, Jamaica, and the head of the OAS—plus the representatives from Afghanistan and Uganda. The session continued with two thematic sessions, one devoted to assessing the 'achievements and challenges of member states in countering the world drug problem,' co-chaired by Colombia and Portugal, and a second, co-chaired by Slovenia and Tunisia, on the 'importance for member states of implementing a multidimensional and multi-stakeholder approach in addressing the world drug problem.' The composition of the two sessions already suggested a rising division between an emerging group of countries that favored reform, and those who were ready to uphold the IDCR. While in the first session, the speakers represented two openly pro-reform countries—Uruguay and Ms Ruth Dreyfuss, former Swiss president and active member of the Global Commission on Drug Policy—in the second session, the views came from Thailand and Peru, two countries that at UNGASS would reaffirm their commitment to the three international drug conventions and to the viability of a world 'free of drug abuse.'

A year later, during the CND's 59th session, a draft outcome document (which the Commission had flagged since December 2014 among its substantive and organizational recommendations) was finally released. The draft document, entitled 'Our Joint Commitment to Effectively Addressing and Countering the World Drug Problem,' was circulated with a clear recommendation for its adoption the following month, at the plenary of the UNGASS on the world drug problem.[19]

As had been the case in May 2015, when the High-Level General Assembly Thematic Debate took place, the publication of the draft outcome document uncovered many of the fissures that would finally break out at UNGASS. While it is true that the outcome document was swiftly adopted by the General Assembly once UNGASS started on 19 April 2016, it is also the case that the chain of explanatory comments from several delegations left no doubt of the magnitude of the discord.[20]

Equally as important as the contrast between the hopes for reform and the wholehearted reaffirmation of the IDCR were the document's glaring omissions. The pressing arguments that had prompted Colombia, Guatemala, and Mexico to call for an urgent debate on the world drug problem were hardly registered. Instead, a number of paragraphs in the opening section, together with at least two 'operational sections' on supply reduction, and on 'cross-cutting issues in addressing and countering the world drug problem: evolving reality…emerging and persistent challenges and threats, including new psychotropic substances,' clearly heralded more of the same.[21]

Not only did a chain of paragraphs in the opening section reiterate the commitment of member states to 'effectively addressing and countering the world drug problem,' they also reaffirmed the validity of the IDCR's long-lasting goals, including the prevention and treatment of 'the abuse of narcotic drugs and psychotropic substances' and the prevention and countering of 'their illicit cultivation, manufacturing and trafficking.' The customary pledge to actively promote 'a society free of drug abuse' was followed by the explicit recognition of the three conventions—the Single Convention on Narcotic Drugs of 1961, as amended by the 1972 Protocol, the 1971 Convention on Psychotropic Substances, and the 1988 UN Convention against Illicit Traffic in Narcotic Drugs and Psychotropic Substances—as the 'cornerstone of the international drug control system.' Last but not least, the long-lasting role of the international drug control bureaucracy, and in particular the contribution of the CND and the UNODC, to 'addressing and countering the world drug problem' was praised highly, while the 'treaty mandated roles' of the INCB and the WHO were duly recognized.[22]

These paragraphs, together with the language used, especially in the 'operational recommendation' sections concerning supply reduction and persistent challenges and threats—including those coming from new psychotropic substances—provide evidence of the regime's powerful inertia. The elements of continuity become evident when reading through the paragraphs on supply reduction and persistent challenges and threats. This is nowhere clearer than in the measures considered to deal with supply reduction, to contain drug-related crime, and to countering 'emerging and persistent challenges, and threats.' Although many of the axioms included in these sections—from 'drug-related crime' to the 'links between drug trafficking, corruption and other forms of organized crime, including trafficking in persons, trafficking in firearms...and money-laundering'—are now widely seen as tangible consequences of the prohibition and drug control policies that the regime has long advocated, longstanding prescriptions prevailed.[23] Some of the specific pledges quoted in these sections are thus worth mentioning: 'intensifying our efforts to prevent and counter the illicit cultivation, production and manufacture of and trafficking in narcotic drugs and psychotropic substances' and to 'monitor current trends and drug trafficking routes and share experiences, best practices and lessons learned,' as well as 'strengthen the exchange of information and, as appropriate, drug-related criminal intelligence among law enforcement and border control agencies.'[24] These are the same tenets which have always formed the IDCR's direction; they are almost its *raison d'être*.

Of course, a set of arguments exists that would present the outcome document as a tribute to the efforts devoted to restructuring the IDCR. However, what the document said, what it ignored, and the debate it triggered laid bare the limits of the consensus around drug policy. First and most obviously, the document underscored the central position now given to demand reduction and prevention in drug control efforts. A second crucial point, highlighted both by the document and the ensuing debate, is the degree to which treatment of drug use disorders, rehabilitation, social reintegration, and the prevention and treatment of HIV/AIDS, hepatitis and other blood-borne diseases—including through medication-assisted programs and injecting equipment programs—have gained approval across regions.[25] Although the outcome document, significantly, omits to mention the term 'harm reduction,' the fact that these preventive measures have gained traction both among European nations and countries from other regions, ranging from Asia and Asia Pacific, to Africa and Latin America, is indicative of a forceful international reformist trend at play. However, the impulse towards reform also faced important checks. This was nowhere clearer than in how the sensitive issues of 'human rights, youth, children, women and communities' were presented as 'cross-cutting issues,' rather than as direct casualties of drug control policies, in particular those associated to a variety of wars on drugs. To the extent that human rights commitments were mentioned in the document, they were limited to imprecise pledges to carry out drug control efforts 'in full conformity with the principles of the Charter of the United Nations, international law and the Universal Declaration of Human Rights,' to help member states implement 'international drug control treaties in accordance with applicable human rights obligations' and to 'promote protection and respect for human rights and the dignity of all individuals in the context of drug programs, strategies and policies.'[26] Rather than calling attention to the negative human rights implications of prohibition's enforcement, these references chiefly signaled a modest effort towards humanizing drug control policies. The extent to which human rights are viewed as subsidiary by the IDCR can be seen in the difficulties that efforts to insert a reference to the death penalty in the outcome document encountered. The condemnation by Switzerland, Brazil, Costa Rica, Norway, and Uruguay of the use of the death penalty for drug offenses met a vocal resistance. Indonesia, on behalf of more than a dozen countries that still resort to the death penalty—China, Singapore, Yemen, Malaysia, Pakistan, Egypt, Saudi Arabia, Oman, UAE, Qatar, Kuwait, Bahrain, Brunei, Iran, and Sudan—vehemently defended the sovereign right to resort to the capital punishment for serious crimes, including drug production and drug trafficking.

Nonetheless, to get the debate going was in itself a significant achievement. However, as was to be expected, the broad range of statements delivered by more than 118 countries, ten or so regional and international organizations, and six representatives of civil society, reflected contrasting drug realities, political contexts, and institutional and human rights settings. The statements delivered by successive delegations revealed the many ways in which the problems of narcotic drugs and drug policy are being tackled by different countries around the world. They suggested diverse and sometimes patently diverging views about the world drug problem, and the topics and interpretations around which different countries and regions gravitated. The themes ran along a spectrum. At one end, China and Russia led the unconditional endorsement of the three international drug conventions and the validation of the IDCR. This contrasted to other approaches to drug control—including efforts to strike a balance between demand and consumption, and between law enforcement and public health approaches—in the middle, where the views of the US, some European states, and a few countries from other regions converged. As depicted by the US, the plan that best described this middle position is one 'that balances our approach between public health and law enforcement.'[27] At the other end of the band, there were countries from different regions that, calling attention to the human rights and public security implications of punitive enforcement, signaled their readiness to move toward public health approaches and decriminalization. The different ways in which participating countries approached these issues revealed conflicting understandings of the drug problem, and widely diverging views about how best to tackle it. Whether countries were represented at UNGASS by their health, interior, or foreign affairs ministers said much about their policy approaches. There were many significant signals—from the way countries chose to be represented at UNGASS, to the manner in which access to treatment and human rights were considered or thoroughly omitted—that allow us to identify the main controversies, to map reformist, conventional and obstructionist trends, and to locate the position of different countries in a drug policy constellation.

Fundamentally, the debate was a temperature-taking exercise that provided a sense of whether countries were willing to consider changes in drug policy, and to move toward reforming the IDCR. There had been hopes that the special session could produce some form of compromise in this direction, but drug policy showed yet again how deeply most countries were still divided.

If there was a region that expressed particular disquiet about the 'drug problem,' it was Latin America. The concerns expressed by the Dominican Republic on behalf of the thirty-three countries parties to the CELAC (Community of Latin American and Caribbean States) left no doubt of the regional perception of the drug problem as a significant threat. As was the case with other regions, however, there was a divide between countries like Uruguay, Colombia, Guatemala, Mexico, Saint Vincent and the Grenadines, and Trinidad and Tobago, which were critical of prohibition and wary of the pernicious effects of criminalization, and the ardent defenders of the IDCR represented in the region by Cuba, El Salvador, and Nicaragua.

Undoubtedly, the salience that the human rights dimension gained at UNGASS owes a great deal to European countries and the European Union (EU). As the Commissioner for International Cooperation and Development of the European Commission (speaking on behalf of the members of the EU and eight other European countries—Turkey, the former Yugoslav Republic of Macedonia, Serbia, Albania, Bosnia and Herzegovina, Ukraine, the Republic of Moldova, and Georgia) made clear, 'human rights are an integral part of any response to the drug problem.' True, references to human rights were a constant feature of European statements, but these basically revolved around calls for public health approaches, fair penalties and a condemnation of the death penalty for drug offenses. Despite this European convergence around human rights, like in Latin America, countries were divided. Denmark, Croatia, the Czech Republic, Cyprus, Greece, Iceland, Liechtenstein, Lithuania, Norway, and Switzerland all indicated their readiness to consider significant reforms; others, including France, Germany, Italy, Hungary, Spain, Georgia, Montenegro, and the former Yugoslav Republic of Macedonia validated in their statements repressive alternatives and the control of supply. Some of these countries also highlighted the potential links between drug trafficking, organized crime, and terrorism, a position that coincided with that held by Albania, Armenia, Belarus, Azerbaijan, and Kazakhstan.

China and Russia led the voices that vigorously opposed moves towards decriminalization and legalization. As China's State Counselor and Minister for Public Security, Mr. Guo Shengkun, expressed: 'Any form of legalization of narcotics should be resolutely opposed,' reaffirming his country's commitment to continuing 'the fight against narcotics.' In his turn, the Deputy Prime Minister of the Russian Federation, Mr. Alexander Khloponin—speaking on behalf of President Vladimir Putin—referred to the alleged nexus between drug trafficking, organized crime, and terrorism to celebrate the decision of the UN 'Security Council's qualification of illicit drug trafficking as a threat to international peace and stability.'[28]

With the notable exceptions of Australia and in particular New Zealand, the record of opinions reflected in the statements from countries in Asia and the Asia Pacific revealed by far the hardest positions on drug policy. The statement delivered by Mr. Nur Jazlan Mohamed, Deputy Minister of Home Affairs of Malaysia, on behalf of the Association of Southeast Asian Nations (ASEAN) countries— Brunei Darussalam, Cambodia, Indonesia, the Lao People's Democratic Republic, Malaysia, Myanmar, the Philippines, Singapore, Thailand and Vietnam—alluded to the two main points of an orthodox regional consensus: firstly, a 'commitment to a drug-free vision [and] a society free from drug abuse and its ill effects;' and secondly, a regional resolution 'against calls to legalize controlled drugs.'[29] Not surprisingly, in the chain of statements expressing unconditional support for the three conventions and highlighting the merits of prohibition, supply control and punitive enforcement, human rights considerations had little or no place. The impassioned statement of Mr. K. Shanmugam, Minister for Home Affairs and Minister for Law of the Republic of Singapore, dismissed right away what was perceived as a 'soaring rhetoric on the rights of people to access narcotics' and a false 'dichotomy— human rights and dignity... versus oppression.' The hardline regional approach to drug control was summarized by Mr. Shanmugam: 'it is possible to be tough on traffickers, to be tough in prevention, to be tough on drug abusers and, at the same time, to help abusers psychologically, medically and economically without having to feed them drugs.'[30]

Across Africa, an acute perception of vulnerability to booming and rapidly changing illicit drug markets and routes produced a regional sense of urgency. However, this sense—which in the statements of countries like Benin, Togo, and Cape Verde alluded to the risks to national stability and cohesion—did not translate into a regional consensus or a regional strategy. As was the case in Latin America and Europe, African countries remained polarized. At one end, West African countries, including Benin, Togo, Cape Verde, Ghana, Nigeria, Namibia, Zambia and Tanzania, readily endorsed prevention and public health approaches to the drug problem, and embraced the call to align drug control policies to human rights standards—with some of these countries also joining the transregional condemnation of the use of the death penalty for drug offenses. But at the other end, countries including Algeria, Burkina Faso, Cameroon, Kenya, Libya, Sudan, Tunisia, and the Sahel countries—Mauritania, Mali, Niger and Chad—swiftly framed the debate in security and law enforcement terms. Once these countries endorsed punitive enforcement and repressive supply control policies, human rights considerations were mostly sidelined or ignored.

One of the many surprising aspects of the debate is that when Latin American, European, or African countries—most notably Cameroon, Kenya, Tunisia, Sudan, Angola, and Morocco—alluded to the nexus of drug trafficking, organized crime, and terrorism, their representatives failed to address the role of prohibition in generating illicit drug markets, the transfer of vast illicit rents, and the ensuing drug-related corruption.

The analysis of regional trends across continents revealed the tensions and complexities underpinning the politics of drug control as these surfaced in UNGASS. Clearly, many forces operated simultaneously to complicate the realization of the goals that Guatemala, Colombia, and Mexico had originally envisioned. These countries also needed to take steps of their own to get their national strategies in order and offer a way forward. As UNGASS approached, the road to reform looked tough, but getting to that stage clearly depended on their ability to identify potential allies and opportunities. The different shades, tones, and signs that shaped the debate at UNGASS may not have offered a common or unified assembly, but provided Colombia, Guatemala, and Mexico with important analytical and policy insights to suggest a possible course of action.

An important principle of good leadership is to anticipate points of resistance and take steps in advance to navigate potential obstacles. UNGASS' notably complex alignments and permutations did not provide a propitious context or climate, but through the session, Colombia, Guatemala, and Mexico missed important opportunities.

Indeed, the inability of Latin American countries to provide credible leadership and a sense of direction to the discussion was an important factor in the way the debate proceeded, and in its final inconclusiveness. It is true that these countries were represented at the highest level, and that all three presidents called attention to the onerous human and institutional costs that prohibition policies and the War on Drugs had brought to their countries. A collective view appeared to be emerging among those for whom prohibition and the War on Drugs were major causes of the difficulties facing their countries. As former President Santos put it, not only had this war not been won, but it had left behind 'lives cut short, so much corruption and violence and so many young lives wasting away in prison.'[31] Mexico's former President, Enrique Peña Nieto in turn highlighted how 'the illegal trade in narcotics has led to death and violence, mainly in producer and transit countries.' Together, both presidents criticized the repressive, punitive approach that had clearly 'not succeeded in diminishing the worldwide production, trafficking or consumption of drugs.' Yet all that appears to have been agreed among these countries was that the special session would merely look 'beyond prohibition to effective prevention and regulation.'[32]

The three presidents shared the view that 'logic and common sense' dictated an 'in-depth and evidence-based review' and put forward a strong call in favor of a 'more humane drug policy.' However, in no way did their statements convey the sense of a common and clear stand on drug policy reform. Rather than anticipating how the debate might develop and taking steps to steer it, Colombia, Guatemala, and Mexico mostly reacted to the main themes and policy questions that had already been flagged in the outcome document. Their interventions did not add up to a plan. They conveyed a mixed bag of views and ideas without a sense of precision or clear direction. This is true whether we consider the views expressed in relation to the three conventions and the drug control system, their perspectives on human rights, or the contradictions underpinning their views on drug control policy, not to mention their heightened call to 'strengthen the common front against transnational organized crime.'

President Morales of Guatemala immediately embraced the final document's view about the three international drug control conventions as being 'sufficiently flexible to allow countries to implement drug policies according to their priorities and needs,' a view that was also fully endorsed by his Colombian counterpart, President Juan Manuel Santos. Likewise drawing on the final document, these statements referred to the need to address the 'global issue of drugs from the perspective of human rights,' in conformity with the Universal Declaration of Human Rights, avoiding relegating human rights and human rights conventions to 'second place with regard to drug conventions.' Undoubtedly, these human rights references, together with Santos's support for a moratorium on the death penalty for drug-related offenses were significant and reflected in the final document's broad shift of tack towards a human rights approach. Still, they were not clear enough to energize an urgent perspective about the incommensurate human and social costs attendant on drug control efforts and the fated human rights implications of prohibition and supply control policies. Indeed, there was little in these statements that alluded to the shattering human rights legacies of drug control, or to the urgent human rights concerns that had prompted these countries to call the special session in the first place. As was the case with the final document, the views expressed by Colombia, Guatemala, and Mexico failed to expose the many ways in which the aims of drug control and human rights may be inherently conflictual. They instead suggested that drug control efforts could be fine-tuned to conform to human rights standards.

The three former presidents were aware of the urgent need to 'redirect' global drug policy and international cooperation towards 'effective prevention and regulation,' and the views they expressed provided critical insights into the problematic world of prohibition and drug control. Peña Nieto, president of Mexico at the time, described drug trafficking as 'one of the most lucrative activities of organized crime and a decisive factor in its transnational growth,' which resonated with then President Santos's appeal 'to honestly recognize that just as our world is not free from alcohol, tobacco or violence, we will not have a drug-free world.' However, while sharing a common thread, these views were below the threshold of a common vision or agenda. Indeed, there was little to convey the message that, in the absence of much needed reform, the threats to democratic governability and human rights protection would only intensify.

Despite the spectacular failure of prohibition and punitive enforcement, each of these presidents went on to describe and extol the efforts that had been deployed by their countries as they struggled to contain the drug business. According to Santos, Colombia had crushed 'major cartels' which were once regarded as 'invincible in Medellín, Cali and the North Valley,' whereas Guatemala, tight resources notwithstanding, had 'complied with its international obligations, joining the struggle.' Mexico, in turn, reported how it had remained among the countries most committed to facing the drug problem.

At best, what the presidents' statements indicated was that the standard traditional approaches were very much still on the table. At worst, they seemed be heralding a new war on 'organized crime.' Those in any doubt might note how Peña Nieto described the efforts of his administration 'to reduce the supply of drugs' by 'facing up to organized crime' through better coordination, use of intelligence systems, the arrest of criminal leaders, and the dismantling of operational and financial structures. Similarly, Santos chose to highlight how Colombia would 'continue to combat organized crime, work to replace illegal crops with lawful alternatives and intercept boats and airplanes used to transport drugs, because for Colombia combating drugs is not only a moral imperative, but also a matter of national security.' If there was any expectation about the role that Colombia, Guatemala, and Mexico could play in providing leadership through the special session, their interventions revealed that this would not be the case. Any hopes from the drug reformist quarter faded once President Santos categorically affirmed that 'Colombia is not advocating the legalization of illicit drugs.'[33]

The analysis of the steps towards UNGASS 2016 and the chain of statements delivered over two consecutive days suggests that the three countries who requested the special session did just enough to make sure that UNGASS happened, but perhaps not enough to lay down the key arguments and coordinate delegations. The chance that without a proactive and committed leadership the debate could deliver an agenda for reform remained remote. If past General Assembly sessions teach us anything about the prospects for normative change, it is that where a significant group of countries are sympathetic to a given agenda, and have the capacity to coordinate and strategize, UN debates will most likely draw nearer the expected goal.

PART TWO

BETWEEN WARRIORS AND VICTIMS:
THE WAR ON DRUGS ACROSS
VULNERABLE REGIONS

5

SOUTH AMERICA

FROM ACQUIESCENCE TO REBELLION?

Angélica Durán-Martínez

South America sits at the center of the global drug production and trafficking chain. Due to its geographic proximity to the world's major drug consumer market, the United States, and its historical acquiescence to US agendas, South America has also been a faithful follower of the International Drug Control Regime (IDCR). Before 2009, it would have been difficult to predict that—as Hallam and Bewley-Taylor note in Chapter 3—the impulse for reforming drug policy and the IDCR would come from South America; very little defection from the IDCR had occurred there before. After 2009, however, South American leaders started to lead reform debates, and Uruguay became the first country in the world to legalize recreational marijuana in a radical challenge to the IDCR. This chapter explores the complex factors behind this transformation and future scenarios for drug policy. It argues that even though the region may continue leading reform debates and even pioneering new policies, key obstacles to reform remain. These obstacles include: a limited consensus across countries on what reforms entail; contradictions between a reformist discourse and traditional enforcement tools; weak political coalitions for reform; public opinion, which is changing, but is still skeptical; persistent problems with policing and justice systems; and a tendency to resort to traditional approaches in moments of crisis. Although it is unclear how much of the rhetoric will translate into change, or how far the change can go, a critical juncture opened debates unthinkable in the early 2000s.

A Changing Discourse

In 1993, Attorney General of Colombia Gustavo de Greiff participated in an international drug policy conference in Baltimore where he criticized drug prohibition and advocated for alternatives to deal with drug trafficking. In his words, 'We put Pablo Escobar [Colombia's most infamous drug kingpin] in jail. Nothing happened. Fighting drug trafficking is a lost cause.'[1] De Greiff had confronted one of Colombia's darkest periods in the fight against trafficking organizations during Pablo Escobar's narcoterrorist campaign. As attorney general, he implemented controversial policies such as offering reduced sentences to traffickers who surrendered themselves to authorities and confessed their crimes. De Greiff's comments did not go unheeded. Authorities in both the US and Colombia reacted harshly. Colombian President Cesar Gaviria—who eventually became a champion of drug policy reform—stated in a letter to de Greiff, 'Legalization is not the solution. If we had not fought with the firmness we showed, this country would easily be under the rule of criminals.'[2] The pinnacle of these criticisms was the cancellation of de Greiff's visa to the United States in 1995.

The reactions to de Greiff's unorthodox position on drug policy contrasted with the reactions to the declarations made by the Colombian Minister of Justice Yesid Reyes in 2015, as he toured the United States presenting a proposal for drug policy reform. Although recognizing achievements of the fight against drug trafficking, the minister advocated for a new approach that could grant 'greater autonomy for states to formulate policies that respond to their own local and national realities.'[3] This approach would include, among other measures, stopping the fumigation of coca crops, a policy sponsored and promoted by the United States government for decades. Although controversial, Reyes' declaration was supported by Juan Manuel Santos, the Colombian president at the time, and did not generate harsh criticism or cause the cancellation of his visa. The two episodes illustrate the change that the official debate on drug policy has undergone, as well as the changing environment in which to discuss drug policy,[4] not only in Latin America but around the world. They also illustrate the transformation of the interaction between the United States and South American governments in this policy realm, and the leadership of Latin American politicians on international drug reform debates.

This chapter argues that the opening of debates which would have been unthinkable even a few decades ago is the result of several factors: the accumulation of negative consequences of drug policies; increasing violence in the region, but particularly the impact of violence in Mexico (for a discussion of Mexico see Chapter 6 by Carlos A. Pérez Ricart); the realization that consumer markets had grown unattended for decades; changes in drug commodity chains (especially cocaine); and geopolitical changes in relations with the United States. The chapter also argues that gaps between discourse and practice, disagreements over what drug reform means, a changing but still skeptical public opinion, weak political coalitions for reform, and the need to reform other institutions like law enforcement and health systems, complicate drug policy reform in the short to medium term and create policy contradictions. Lastly, there is a clearer consensus about the need to change the status of marijuana, but more controversy regarding other drugs, and more clarity on alternatives to handle demand (use) than on those directed to reduce supply (production and distribution). These elements explain why, in moments of crisis, inertia creates the impulse to apply known policies that seem effective in the short run, even if their negative effects and lack of long-term sustainability are evident.

To advance these arguments, the chapter first summarizes the position of South America in the drug trade. Subsequent sections discuss how drug policy has evolved and its consequences; the discourse transformation and the reasons behind it; the obstacles to drug policy reform, and concludes briefly discussing future scenarios.

South America in the International Drug Trafficking Chain

South America is home to the world's three major cocaine producers, and this has been its major point of insertion into the global drug trafficking chain, where cocaine demand concentrates in the United States and Western Europe and supply in South America. Other elements also characterize the region's insertion in the chain: a growing, but not recent, consumption problem; an important role in heroin supply to the United States, and a diversification of trafficking routes since the early 2000s that has made more countries transit points for drugs. There are also increasingly notable south-south drug flows that reflect transformations in global drug commodity chains, especially of cocaine. By 2020, most drug flows in the region were still bound to major consumer markets in the United States and Europe, but cocaine flows have diversified due to declining and then stabilizing cocaine use in the United States between 2006 and 2014,[5] a high cocaine use prevalence in South America which has become one of the world's largest cocaine markets, and the multiplication of transit routes.

As Gootenberg argues in Chapter 2, coca and cocaine production have a long history in South America. Cocaine was not always criminalized; it constituted a small but legal industry in Peru up until the 1950s. Increasing worldwide criminalization radically transformed coca and cocaine production. The Cuban Revolution and Pinochet's 1973 coup in Chile led to the arrest of cocaine traffickers originally from those countries, thus relocating, empowering, and expanding the illegal networks that had started to emerge in the 1950s. These events shaped the geography of cocaine production that persists today, with Bolivia, Colombia, and Peru as the world's major coca and cocaine producers. The distribution of coca and cocaine production among these three countries has varied over time, partially in response to enforcement actions, in a dynamic that illustrates the balloon effects of drug policy described in the introduction to this volume. In the early 1990s, offensives against coca production in Peru and Bolivia prompted surges of production in Colombia. According to the United Nations Office on Drugs and Crime (UNODC), in 1990 Bolivia and Peru were responsible for 87 per cent of potential cocaine production worldwide; by 2000, Colombia represented 79 per cent of that potential. This dynamic was again reversed between 2000 and 2012, when the area of coca bush cultivation decreased by 52 per cent in Colombia while increasing by 37 per cent in Peru.[6] Since 2014, coca cultivation increased rapidly in Colombia reaching a historic high in 2017, while in Peru and Bolivia it declined partially as a result of new policies to handle coca crops, as discussed below.

Brazil's entry into the drug trade is also linked to cocaine, but differently than in Andean countries because the local market is more important. In the 1970s, cocaine entered illegal markets in Brazil and emerging criminal networks such as the *Comando Vermelho* increasingly engaged in managing imports and internal distribution of drugs.[7] Crack—a diluted, smokable form of cocaine—appeared in the 1990s and quickly spread among marginalized populations. By the late 2010s, the cocaine market in Brazil became the world's second-largest, representing 18 per cent of the global market in terms of users, mainly supplied by Bolivia. The country also serves as a transit point to markets in Europe and Asia.

Marijuana has also played a major role in South America's entry into global drug trafficking. In the 1960s, a boom in marijuana production made Colombia, along with other countries like Jamaica and Mexico, a central source of marijuana bound to the United States, and stimulated a highly profitable and often violent market.[8] In the 1970s, drug enforcement policies in Colombia—alongside increasing production of the seedless variety in Mexico—reduced the centrality of marijuana for the income of trafficking organizations and contributed to the rise of cocaine in Colombia's drug trade. Nowadays, marijuana is mostly produced within countries for their own domestic consumption or traded in intraregional drug flows. For instance, an estimated 80 per cent of marijuana produced in Paraguay (the largest producer in South America) is bound to Brazil and to a lesser extent Argentina, Chile, and Uruguay. Likewise, marijuana grown in Colombia reaches intraregional markets, Central America, and the Caribbean,[9] but it has also become more common in Colombia's own domestic market.

Opium and heroin have played an important, but more limited role in the region's drug trafficking chains. Colombia is a prominent opium producer in South America, and in 2013 it was still the main source of heroin in the US, but it reported decreases in opium and heroin production between 1997 and 2007, and again in 2011, though in 2014 poppy cultivation increased by 30 per cent.[10] By 2014, Mexico had surpassed Colombia as a source of heroin in the US, as indicated by the analysis of street samples. This trend was related to increases in the demand for heroin and synthetic opioids in the United States and in Mexico's poppy production (from 6,900 hectares in 2007 to 26,100 in 2014, and 30,600 in 2017, though figures are not directly comparable).[11] Since the 2010s, Mexican trafficking groups have increasingly engaged in the production and smuggling of synthetic opioids.

As a result of enforcement operations and changing market dynamics, in the 2010s more countries in South America appeared as transit points or even marginal drug producers. While in the 1970s and 1980s most cocaine produced in Colombia transited into the United States via maritime routes in the Caribbean, in the new millennium the routes are more complicated, including several inland points in Central America and Mexico. Countries in the Southern Cone became more important—although still comparatively minor—transit points for trafficking routes bound to Europe, with Venezuela and Brazil becoming significant transit points for cocaine routes through South and West Africa. Cocaine processing laboratories, and especially facilities for processing intermediate and low-quality forms of cocaine base aimed for intraregional markets, were reported in Argentina, Chile, Ecuador, and Venezuela. Methamphetamine facilities were detected in Argentina. The geography of drug flows in the 2010s was thus more diverse than in the previous two decades.

Another key characteristic of the region's drug markets since the 2000s has been growing local consumption. The Southern Cone used to concentrate consumption in the region, but since the early 2000s, countries that had previously been without large drug use problems reported growing marijuana and cocaine use, and also consumption of cheaper coca derivatives such as cocaine base—known as *paco* in Argentina or *basuco* in Colombia—or smokable forms of cocaine. In Uruguay for example, marijuana lifetime prevalence reportedly quadrupled between 2001, when it was first tracked, and 2014.[12] In the 2010s, local drug use became more widespread and noticeable for governments and citizens, yet the growing local use trend was not as recent as governments tended to present it, and often reflected prior inattention to complex long-term consumption trends. Available data from Rio de Janeiro, for instance, showed a decrease in cocaine use between 1989 and 2003 followed by an increase, thus underscoring the existence of older drug use problems.[13] In 2015, UNODC estimated an annual cocaine prevalence rate of 0.8 per cent for South America, higher than the 0.7 reported in 2004–5, but lower than the 1.3 per cent reported in 2013.[14] Similar ups and downs were reported for cannabis and opioids, showing either that trends are changing rapidly, or that the statistics are not reliable. Even though the growth of domestic drug markets has characterized drug commodity chains in South America in the twenty-first century, it is not just that such trends did not exist before. In some cases, drug use problems waned and reemerged, while in others, their growth may have gone unnoticed for some time.

Growing drug use rates since the late 2000s are associated with different factors. One prevailing explanation asserts that local drug markets increased as international trafficking organizations, under greater enforcement pressure, looked for easier markets to access. Another common explanation is that diversified trafficking routes allowed products to remain in transit countries. These factors played a role, and highlight some of the consequences of drug policies, but such prevailing explanations tend to ignore older drug use trends and the complex factors that explain drug use epidemics. Furthermore, many transit locations do not necessarily generate drug markets, international traffickers do not necessarily control local markets, and it takes time for a local market—especially open sale points, which have become a growing security concern in Latin America— to consolidate.[15] Although misconceptions abound in the assessment of drug use trends and their novelty, local markets are important, and a changing drug commodity chain has been a driving factor behind reformist discourses in the region. Paradoxically, responses to growing domestic trafficking also reflect the entrenchment of militarized drug policies and the contradictions between discourse and practice.

The War on Drugs in South America

The consequences of drug trafficking and the costs of drug enforcement have not been homogenous across countries and regions. However, it is safe to say that South America has borne a great burden of the violence and corruption derived from the operation of drug trafficking groups and of drug policy, especially in countries like Brazil and Colombia. The emphasis of the War on Drugs on the elimination of drug supply has transferred significant costs of enforcement to producer countries, often deepening the pernicious consequences of the drug trade.[16] Drug violence in South America has mostly been associated with disputes among drug traffickers, or between them and the state. This, however, does not mean that the victims of violence have been only criminals or state officials. For instance, in Rio de Janeiro disputes over control of growing cocaine markets led to a peak of 60 killings per 100,000 inhabitants in 1994,[17] and at the height of the narcoterrorist war in Medellin in 1991 the homicide rate was 381. Such death tolls cannot be simply reduced to criminals killing each other.

Drug violence can be attributed to the illegal status of drugs and the profits it generates, and to disputes between groups that cannot use legal means to enforce agreements. Prohibition is thus the backdrop that explains why criminal organizations are powerful in vast areas of these countries, given the huge profits that exist in illegal markets. Yet domestic political factors and power dynamics among different criminal groups account for variation in violence over time and space.[18] For example, in Bolivia and Peru, coca cultivation and trafficking organizations generate significantly less violence than in Colombia, where drug traffickers are more organized and confront the state, and where drug trafficking has fueled the internal armed conflict.[19]

By privileging militarized responses, drug policies have also fueled violence in several ways. Firstly, they increase human rights violations by law enforcers because policing frameworks tend to reward indiscriminate enforcement, are often guided by stereotypes, and advance get-tough-on-crime discourses.[20] Secondly, they can create leadership vacancies and fragment organizations, thus generating violent inter- or intraorganizational disputes. Thirdly, as drug laws become harsher they create greater opportunities for corruption and police abuse. In Brazil, for instance, militarized drug enforcement has fueled police corruption and violence as criminals bribe officials to prevent the enforcement of harsh laws, as police officers directly engage in criminality, or as enforcement actions stigmatize or target marginalized sectors of the population. It is estimated that police officers killed more than 11,000 civilians in Brazil between 2009 and 2013, while at the same time there was a reported increase in killings of off-duty police officers.[21] These numbers illustrate the lethality of police action as well as the potential vulnerability of police to corruption or violence if they refuse to cooperate with criminal actors. State responses to drug trafficking thus can deepen the problems they intend to address.

Civilian reactions to crime may further reproduce corruption and violence when paramilitary and vigilante groups emerge to combat drug traffickers. In Rio de Janeiro, militias emerged when groups of militarized police invaded *favelas* to prevent the entrance of drug lords and criminals, but then established protection rackets demanding payments from the population to maintain order and security. As militias grew more powerful, they engaged in illegal markets[22] and established close networks of collaboration with state authorities.

Drug trafficking also breeds instability when it is a funding source for rebel and other non-state armed actors, as occurred in Colombia and Peru. State responses may deepen the drug-conflict connection by minimizing the relationship between drugs and conflict to one of simple greed. This is illustrated in the 'narcoterrorist' discourse advanced by the US Government in the 1990s and reproduced by local governments. This discourse reduced rebel groups to the existence of illegal profits, ignoring that their formation preceded the escalation of drug trafficking, and that for groups like Sendero Luminoso or the FARC, drug trafficking not only represented economic resources but also social support. As a result, anti-narcotics policies aimed at weakening armed groups, such as crop fumigation, may have strengthened rebels by increasing their support among coca growers without any viable economic alternatives to coca cultivation.[23]

The corrupting power of organized criminals, along with the weakness or acquiescence of state institutions, has made corruption endemic in many law enforcement institutions, has affected electoral competition, and has reached high-level authorities. The goal of eliminating drug supply has sometimes led the US and local governments to turn a blind eye on corrupt military and police units, or on those engaged in human rights violations, if they are seen as 'effective' against traffickers—even though the protection of human rights became a key condition for disbursing military aid in the post-Cold War era through policies like the Leahy amendment.[24] An example is that of Vladimiro Montesinos, the chief of Peru's intelligence service under President Alberto Fujimori, who engaged in human rights violations and was directly connected to drug traffickers. Despite evidence about Montesinos's corruption, the United States did not question his actions because he was seen as successful in dismantling drug trafficking networks and prosecuting key traffickers.[25]

Drug trafficking organizations destabilize societies where social inequalities often make crime an attractive avenue of social advancement, even if the promise of social advancement is rarely fulfilled for most low-level criminals. The disproportionality of drug laws in terms of punishment, and the lack of differentiation between types of drug offenses, often reinforce such inequalities. Uprimny, Guzmán, and Parra[26] documented that in most South American countries, penalties for drug trafficking are larger than those for other serious crimes such as armed robbery, rape, and murder. In Bolivia, Colombia, and Peru, penalties for drug-related crimes are higher than those for murder. In Argentina, Brazil, Bolivia, Colombia, Ecuador, and Peru, maximum penalties for drug crimes equal, or exceed, those for rape. Penalties have grown over the years and most legislation treats different crimes, for instance street-level dealing, carrying drugs [often known as acting as a 'mule'], and trafficking large amounts of drugs, as essentially the same. In Peru, for instance, 'in less than sixty years the minimum penalty [for drug-related crimes] increased from two to twenty-five years and the maximum penalty to thirty-five years.'[27] As Madrazo argues, these trends reflect the constitutional costs of the War on Drugs: legal changes aimed at better enforcing prohibition often undermine constitutional protections by curtailing fundamental rights, undermining civilian controls over the military or accountability among branches of power, or undermining the legal security of citizens.[28]

Disproportional drug laws have augmented prison overcrowding and the violation of fundamental rights for those accused of drug crimes: in Bolivia, Brazil, Ecuador, and Peru, pretrial detention is mandatory for all drug offenses and can drag on for years. Throughout the region, many people are in prison for drug possession or participation at the lower end of the drug trafficking chain, while high-level traffickers make up a small percentage of the prison population. In Colombia, mid- and high-level traffickers constitute about 2 per cent of the total prison population for drug offenses.[29] This partially reflects that high- and mid-level traffickers are fewer in number in criminal organizations, but it also reflects the paradoxes of drug policies: those who have inflicted the most harm on society often bear relatively small penalties. Even though most prisoners are male, another trend associated with disproportional drug laws is the increasing number of women in prison: in Argentina, for example, an estimated 60 to 80 per cent of women are imprisoned for low-level drug offenses such as carrying or delivering drugs.[30] Imprisonment greatly affects marginalized populations, and perpetuates social exclusion, inequality, and poverty, without providing real alternatives for rehabilitation or reinsertion into legal activities (see Chapter 13 by Javier Sagredo for a discussion of these factors).

The disproportionality of drug laws also affects the treatment of drug users. Although less than in the United States or some Asian nations, the criminalization of consumers has been a problem in South America, even in countries where the personal use of drugs is legal. The focus on supply has led governments to ignore consumption problems that, though small compared to major consumer markets, have grown unattended. The governments' lack of attention to drug use as a public health issue generates problems such as inadequate treatment protocols and resources. Most treatment facilities in the region are privately owned, and many of them violate rights against patients or deploy treatment protocols not grounded in scientific evidence.[31]

Some enforcement operations and policies have been successful in dismantling criminal organizations or at disrupting drug trade flows. Indeed, the changing geography of the drug trade partially reflects those successes, but also their limitations. Operations that disrupt trade or organizations are often offset by the emergence of new organizations or by the displacement of trafficking dynamics to new locations. In the worst cases, they are offset by the high costs these operations entail and by their intended and unintended consequences. The most touted success is attributed to *Plan Colombia*, a large-scale program jointly funded by Colombia and the United States with the aim of drastically eliminating cocaine production and weakening the armed actors engaged in it. The plan, to which the US contributed about US $593 million on average each year between 2000 and 2008, illustrates the negative consequences of enforcement 'successes.' The governments of the United States and Colombia highlight how *Plan Colombia* reduced poppy and coca crops, decreased violence, and improved Colombia's security situation.[32] Measurements of coca and cocaine production are plagued with methodological difficulties, yet the UNODC calculates that the area of coca cultivated decreased from its peak of 161,700 hectares in 1999 to 86,000 in 2005–8,[33] and then to 48,000 in 2012; reductions of cocaine potential were smaller and more difficult to assess due to changing processing techniques and yields. Due to improvements in Colombia's security indicators, the US Government advocates for similar efforts in other countries.

Plan Colombia, however, entailed high costs and negative consequences. First, the direct cost associated with coca crop reductions was high considering the large number of hectares sprayed in the period. The most successful eradication policies were those that privileged less draconian measures like alternative development and interdiction instead of crop eradication and fumigation,[34] or which combined different approaches at the same time.[35] Overall, the cost-effectiveness of eradication efforts was low: Mejia and his collaborators estimate that each additional hectare of coca sprayed reduced coca acreage only by 0.10 to 0.15 hectares, while increasing environmental and health costs.[36] Second, state forces financially supported by *Plan Colombia* engaged in human rights violations as security was prioritized over human rights.[37] Third, despite improved security, military policies implemented through *Plan Colombia* targeted guerrillas more strongly than paramilitaries, even though the latter were also heavily engaged in drug trafficking. Dube and Naidu find, for example, that military aid was associated with increases in paramilitary presence and violence.[38] Fourth, there were high environmental and health costs associated with crop fumigation, and with the responses of coca growers who moved crops to natural reservations in response to eradication policies. Fifth, especially in the initial stages of the Plan, the counternarcotics component displaced communities affected both by fumigations and violence.[39]

Plan Colombia illustrates how policies that bring about the intended results of weakening criminal organizations or reducing crops are often offset by their costs or by the relocation of trafficking dynamics (balloon effects). Not all locations that could potentially be affected by changes in drug enforcement develop large-scale problems; local conditions matter.[40] However, reductions of coca cultivation in Colombia were offset by increases in Peru and Bolivia, and by the displacement of crops into areas previously marginal to the drug trade within the country, such as Nariño and the Pacific Coast. In consequence, despite changes in the geography of drug trade and the behavior of drug organizations, neither has been eliminated. Improved security has not stopped violence or localized criminal actors, who still constitute significant threats to citizen security in cities like Buenaventura and Tumaco, and in departments like Nariño and Choco.[41] As discussed below, an increase in coca cultivation between 2014 and 2017 led many observers to idealize the previous 'success' of *Plan Colombia* without considering the costs just described. Such type of reaction to crises exemplifies a common obstacle to reforming drug policy.

To summarize, the costs of drug enforcement in the region have been high. Even policies that reduce production or eliminate trafficking groups have entailed enormous costs, and have been offset by the displacement, not elimination, of drug trafficking and the violence associated with it. Increasing consciousness of these problems has been an important factor in the changing debate.

The Path to Changing Discourses: Geopolitics and New Policy Calculations

Until 2009, Latin America was a faithful follower of the IDCR, and this largely reflected the geopolitics of the Cold War within which international drug regulations emerged and which placed Latin America in a subordinate position to US power. With the US as a guardian of the IDCR, and with Latin America as a key stage where the United States waged the confrontation with the USSR (Soviet Union), the enforcement of drug policies in Latin America became inexorably linked to Cold War politics. Drug trafficking was attacked in those countries who were perceived as enemies, but a blind eye was turned on drug trafficking networks that involved potential allies. As the influence of the United States increased in South America, criticizing drug policy became taboo and little 'soft defection' in terms of alternative drug approaches existed. Acquiescence, however, was not only a top-down imposition; it was perpetuated by the ideological alignment of domestic sectors with the philosophy of drug criminalization and with using this philosophy to eliminate perceived social threats and political opponents. The vested interests of those who profit from militarized drug policies, such as security and bureaucratic agencies, also perpetuated acquiescence.

The acquiescence to the IDCR, however, has not been homogeneous, and at times it has been offset by the collusion between domestic elites and drug traffickers, or by the quiet resistance of governments. However, as the introduction to this chapter highlights, resistance often took place outside official government talk and did not materialize in major policy innovations. Prior to 2009, there were a few alternative drug policies, including Brazil's and Argentina's Needle Syringe Programs; the depenalization of drug consumption in Brazil (2006), Ecuador (1997), and Colombia (1994); and Bolivia's advocacy for de-scheduling coca leave and open resistance to US drug enforcement after Evo Morales was elected president. These policies were politically marginal and often limited in their implementation. For instance, most countries did not endorse Bolivia's advocacy for de-scheduling coca leaf, and measures like the depenalization of drug use remained in sharp contradiction with overall drug policy frameworks even in countries like Uruguay, where drug use was de-penalized in 1974. In Colombia, the constitutional provision allowing personal possession was legally challenged through reforms in 2009 and 2012, but most importantly, carrying small doses of drugs remained prosecuted; in practice, vulnerable populations bore the burden of such enforcement.[42] In Ecuador, the decriminalization of drug possession was not clearly regulated and, as a result, it remained at the judge's discretion to determine what amount of drugs constituted possession for personal use as opposed to trafficking intent.[43] Similarly, in Brazil regulations were unclear on how to distinguish possession for use from possession for trafficking and users remained subject to fines if they refused to provide community service or to enroll in treatment.[44]

In 2009 three former Latin American presidents created the Latin American Commission on Drugs and Democracy (LACDD), and issued a report calling for the need to rethink drug policy, making drugs a public health rather than a public security issue.[45] The report generated a cascade effect among world leaders, who shortly afterwards created the Global Commission on Drug Policy. The LACDD set a tipping point on drug policy discussions that many actors, especially non-governmental, had been championing for at least a decade. Former presidents Cesar Gaviria, Ernesto Zedillo, and Fernando Cardoso, who had been at the forefront of enforcing the IDCR, created the Commission and thus gave it a high profile. The reformist discourse further advanced when sitting presidents joined the call for reform. In 2012, Colombia's President Juan Manuel Santos advocated for an honest discussion on drug policy, followed by Guatemala's President Otto Pérez Molina. In the 2012 Summit of the Americas, the voices of sitting presidents calling for drug policy discussion multiplied, and as a result the Organization of American States (OAS) Secretariat agreed to prepare a report on alternative drug policy scenarios. Ever since, high-level discussions in intergovernmental organizations have proliferated, such as the 2014 Inter-American Drug Abuse Control Commission (CICAD), which met to debate drug policies in the region; the Community of Latin American and Caribbean States (CELAC)'s first meeting on the global drug problem in 2014; and the 2014 OAS special session on the world drug problem. Tellingly, Colombia was one of three countries (along with Guatemala and Mexico) which advocated for holding the 2019 United Nations General Assembly Special Session (UNGASS) on drugs three years earlier than scheduled. Indeed, the earlier occurrence of UNGASS in 2016 was a major achievement, even though the lack of radical changes during the session reflected the difficulties of moving the reformist discourse into practice.

This change in discourse was not unforeseeable, but the speed at which it evolved came as a surprise considering the high political cost of opposing drug policies prior to 2009. The political prominence of the actors endorsing the debate, including representatives of sitting governments, created a cascade effect that has lowered the cost of voicing opposition.

The reasons behind this transformation relate to the heavy cost that the enforcement of the IDCR has carried for Latin American countries. As already explored, a large proportion of the costs of law enforcement are passed from consumer to producer countries.[46] However, the costs of the War on Drugs and a greater consciousness of them cannot alone account for the timing of the change; if they did, the debate would have been endorsed by governmental sectors sooner, especially in countries like Colombia that had witnessed the worst consequences of drug trafficking and the War on Drugs in the 1990s. The reasons to endorse the debate vary across countries and were probably opportunistic for many presidents, but three factors are crucial. First, the role of the United States in the region has changed, opening the room for elites and policymakers to embrace ideas about reform with less concern about the consequences in terms of US support. Second, growing violence—and especially the explosion of violence in Mexico—may have acted as a catalyst for elite fears, making them more likely to consider alternative policy options. Third, a changing commodity chain of cocaine made intraregional and domestic markets more prominent and encouraged governments to recognize that drug policies have generated new problems. The next paragraphs explore each of these factors.

The waning US power in South America results from both political factors within the region and within the United States. Since the late 1990s—and to a great extent in response to citizens' discontent with the effects of neoliberal policies—several countries in the region elected leftist governments in a process colloquially known as the 'Pink Tide.'[47] While there are variations in the ideological preferences of these leftist presidents,[48] many of them shared either an opposition to US influence or at least a desire to increase government's self-determination. Drug policy, as a major arena of US influence, is naturally a place where these desires could materialize. Furthermore, changes in the global economic position of the United States deriving from China's economic influence in the region, and from Latin America's economic growth during the 2000s, reduced the US stronghold. At the same time, policy preferences changed within the United States. With the end of the Cold War, and especially after 9/11, the Middle East became the US main geopolitical concern, thus allowing greater policy independence in Latin America.[49]

Latin American governments thus became less willing to accept policies unilaterally imposed by the United States. The call for drug policy reform was at the same time the consequence and the prime example of US waning influence. The drug policy debate was even more significant considering that Colombia, perhaps the most reliable US ally in the region, led the debate under former President Juan Manuel Santos. Tellingly, until 2016 the US did not openly criticize calls for reform, a lack of reaction which was likely facilitated by the ideological position of Barack Obama's administration. This changed after Donald Trump was elected president. Trump appointed an attorney general that clearly opposed drug reform and marijuana legalization and put stronger pressure on Colombia's coca reduction policies. At any rate, the moral authority of the US Federal Government to condemn calls for reform in countries such as Uruguay has been undermined as radical challenges to the IDCR have occurred within the United States, with fifteen states having legalized recreational marijuana as of 2020.

The second factor explaining the shift in discourse is growing violence, and specifically the explosion of violence in Mexico (see Chapter 6 by Carlos A. Pérez Ricart), which may have galvanized elite support for reform and heightened the perception—and reality—both among governments and citizens, that the aforementioned costs of the IDCR have become unsustainable. Latin America's homicide rates surpass those of regions plagued by civil war: despite being home to only 9 per cent of the world's population, Latin America was the site of 30 per cent of the world's homicides as of 2017. Although this violence is driven by multiple factors,[50] drug trafficking is a major motor of it. The fact that Mexico's violence quickly exploded following the government's declaration of war against traffickers, and that it was partially connected to the enforcement 'successes' that disrupted Colombian trafficking, demonstrates that enforcement policies can fuel violence, thus legitimizing reformist voices.

Violence trends are not homogenous throughout South America, however. In the 2000s, Brazil and Colombia had the highest homicide rates in the region but saw a decline, while in Venezuela homicides sharply increased in the same period. This underscores how local conditions shape the consequences of drug trafficking and drug policy. Yet even for countries like Colombia where homicides declined in the 2000s, violence is still very high. Supporting the reformist discourse reflects the recognition of the costs imposed by drug trafficking and its enforcement, but may also allow governments unable to reduce violence to defer attention away from them.

The third condition facilitating change is the evolving drug commodity chain. Growing drug use in the region has compounded criticisms of the IDCR, while the declining cocaine markets in the United States (until 2014) may have reduced the US interest in concentrating efforts on eliminating cocaine supply. As noted above, while the causes of growing drug use are more complex than often recognized, the acknowledgement that balloon effects and more dispersed transit routes have contributed to regional drug use have elevated criticisms of the IDCR. In the words of an Advisory Commission on drug policy reform created in Colombia, 'The current drug use situation shows that drug problems in the country should be addressed with different and multidimensional lenses that facilitate the reduction of the adverse impacts of drugs on individuals and the society.'[51]

Potential for Transformation and Obstacles for Reform

The change in discourse in the scenarios where the drug policy debate takes place, and in reform advocates who increasingly include sitting high-level government officials and presidents, challenges traditional drug policy. The tipping point of South America's evolving position towards the IDCR was Uruguay's legalization of recreational marijuana in 2013, making it the first country to openly contest the prohibition of non-medical drug use. The International Narcotics Control Board challenged Uruguay's path-breaking decision[52] which was also praised in many other settings. Uruguay's legalization originated in an executive decision—not in a popular referendum, as occurred in US states like

Colorado—and this reflected that public support for reform was not the basis of the change.[53] In fact, while in the United States more than 50 per cent of the population supports marijuana legalization, in Uruguay support was not very high and the reform was possible, to a great extent, due to the popularity of then President José Mujica.[54] Since the late 2000s, other countries have initiated discussions regarding the need to create evidence-based policies, to advance autonomous drug policies, and to prioritize health outcomes.[55] However, the discourse is still far from a radical 'rebellion' against the IDCR—thus the question mark in the title of this chapter—due to a combination of domestic and international factors.

A common rhetoric runs through reformist discourse, which refers to the idea of advancing health, human rights, and development. Beyond this common rhetoric, however, there is no consensus on what these principles entail, and there is variation on how 'reformist' South American countries are. Nonetheless, the positions in each country change quickly, difficult reforms can rapidly become feasible, unlikely reform champions or opponents may emerge, and changes in political leadership affect the course of reform. The common rhetoric has spurred congressional and public debates on the need to reform drug regulations and increased support among political and opinion leaders for regulations legalizing or depenalizing medical cannabis, though there are stronger reform champions in some countries than others. As of 2020, Argentina, Chile, Colombia, Ecuador, Peru, Paraguay, and Uruguay have implemented medical cannabis regulations, although the paths to reform and actual content of the regulations vary widely, while Bolivia and Brazil have allowed limited medical uses. In Ecuador, a 2014 reform of the penal code differentiated types of trafficking based on quantities and established that drug couriers can be seen as victims of drug trafficking.[56] In Bolivia, President Evo Morales presented a reservation to the 1961 Convention in 2006, and advanced a 'coca yes, cocaine no' policy aimed at allowing coca production for legal and traditional uses while focusing eradication efforts on coca plots that exceed a legally allowed limit, and on cocaine interdiction. The policy, which privileges community self-regulation, appeared to contribute to an estimated reduction in coca acreage of 35 per cent between 2010 and 2015.[57] In 2012, Bolivia left the 1961 UN Single Convention on Narcotic Drugs to then rejoin with an exception that allows the chewing of coca leaves. Similarly, in 2013 Peru implemented an integral alternative development (AD) program credited with reducing coca cultivation, reversing the sustained increases of the previous 12 years.

In Colombia, changes in discourse and practice have appeared at the local and national level. Perhaps the most radical step was the suspension of the aerial fumigation of coca crops in 2015, in the context of the peace process with the FARC guerrillas. The final agreement signed between President Juan Manuel Santos' government and the FARC in 2016 included a chapter on drug issues. The chapter proposed to treat each aspect of the drug trafficking chain differently—for example, by depenalizing coca growers—to treat drug use as a public health issue, and to prioritize alternative development over forced eradication through the creation of a nationwide crop substitution program. As discussed below, some of these changes have not been fully implemented or were reversed after the election of a new president in 2018.

Throughout the 2010s, countries discussed enforcement alternatives to pure militarization, considering policies that address root causes of crime such as inequality, poverty, and weak state presence, and that treated drug use as a public health problem. One example is *De Bracos Abertos* [With Open Arms], a program designed 'to provide housing, food and work opportunities to crack users living on the streets' in one of the largest street crack markets in Sao Paulo.[58] Another example is the Police Pacification Units (UPP) program implemented in Rio de Janeiro since 2008, a military intervention designed at weakening criminal actors by targeting interventions at the most violent traffickers and announcing targeting in advance. A key component of the program was the attachment of military presence to the provision of social services in the intervention areas. The program reduced violence and other major crimes in some of Rio's *favelas* upon its implementation, though its results remain controversial, as discussed below.

Despite the emerging consensus on the need to change policies, and on some principles new regimes should include, there are obstacles to introducing or implementing policy changes. Opinions are diverse and there is little agreement on what particular policies, such as harm reduction, mean. While this does not necessarily represent an obstacle for individual countries to spearhead reform, it seems unlikely that in the short or medium term South America can advance a coherent position regarding reforms to international drug conventions. For example, although the region supported the call for the UNGASS 2016, there were diverse positions. Most South American countries recognized during UNGASS that the War on Drugs generated serious problems, and emphasized the need to respect human rights, to have balanced penalties at different levels of the drug trafficking chain, and to abolish the death penalty for drug crimes. At the same time, most countries reiterated the need to maintain the current drug conventions, and Colombia declared its opposition to legalizing non-medical uses of drugs. Only Ecuador mentioned the possibility of reevaluating a regime based on prohibition, and Uruguay—though critical of the existing drug policy model—expressed that the conventions were flexible enough to provide countries options to implement policies adapted to their own realities, in an effort to defend their own government's legalization of recreational marijuana. Bolivia remained relatively silent during the UNGASS discussions. UNGASS thus reflected, as Bewley-Taylor and Hallam discuss in Chapter 3, the fact that a major reform of the international conventions may not take place in the foreseeable future, and even a partial reform scenario between like-minded countries could be complicated by the varied opinions in South America. Besides a major reform in international instruments, reforms to domestic drug policy seem more plausible, but other hurdles exist in this area: contradictions between discourse and practice, and between different policies; a skeptical public opinion; the difficulty of creating political coalitions for reform; financial limitations and the need to reform other institutions; and the inertia that emerges during periods of crisis. Each one is explained in detail below.

Contradictions between Discourse and Practice

Alongside the renewed debate, many countries still implement 'iron fist' approaches to domestic and international trafficking. Policies aimed at dealing with local domestic drug markets exemplify these contradictions. In Colombia and Ecuador, governments supporting the drug reform debate also implemented 'wars' against micro-trafficking, emphasizing the destruction of drug use locations by military means, tougher penalties, and large-scale police/military deployments.[59] In Rosario, Argentina, large military operations to address growing and more violent trafficking organizations occurred in 2014.[60] In Ecuador, the reduction in penalties described above led to pardoning 4,000 inmates for minor drug crimes and entailed reforms in drug equivalency tables; however, this was revoked in 2015 with another reform that increased penalties, showing political inconsistency and pressures derived from growing drug problems. In 2012, the then President Rafael Correa announced the training of 4,000 army troops to combat crime and drug trafficking. At the same time,[61] he supported policies such as the decriminalization of drug possession for personal use, discussions about partial legalization of marijuana, and cracking down on unlicensed drug treatment facilities engaged in human rights abuses against patients.[62] In Uruguay, when Congress approved the new marijuana law, it also approved a law for compulsory reclusion of drug addicts. In Colombia, forced eradication operations and the renewed pressure to resume aerial fumigations in response to the extreme growth in coca cultivation since 2014—which reached an all-time high in 2017—complicated the implementation of the National Program for the Substitution of Illicit Crops created in the peace agreement with the FARC. Governments thus remain ambivalent about traditional militarized or iron fist approaches to combat crime, especially when facing a drug-related crisis.

Growing south-to-south cooperation also reflects the contradictions. South-to-south cooperation reflects the changing drug commodity chains and represents an opportunity to create new policy blueprints. Yet in practice, it is unclear whether this cooperation deviates from standard drug policies championed by the United States. For example, Brazil has had a growing influence on drug policy in Bolivia since the late 2000s, but the collaboration is focused on policing and militarized aspects. Likewise, Colombia's provision of police training for other countries has been guided by standard militarized frameworks. While it is clear that police and intelligence training are essential law enforcement tools, high-level cooperation on alternative drug policies is limited.

Skeptical Public Opinion

Significant sectors of the population remain opposed or skeptical to departures from existing drug legislation. In Uruguay, 54 per cent of the population still opposed legalization in 2017,[63] and while this number has declined over the years, it still may create hurdles for the successful implementation of the recreational regulatory regime. There is important variation across and within countries, which reflects changing ideas and norms about drug use, but also differing experiences with drug trade, drug use, and organized crime. Polls conducted in 2014–15[64] illustrated this variation: 43 per cent of the population supported legalizing or depenalizing drug production in Colombia, compared to 33 per cent in Uruguay, 23 per cent in Peru, 19 per cent in Argentina and 13 per cent in Bolivia. The support for depenalizing or legalizing drug use was similarly distributed, with 50 per cent in Uruguay, 43 per cent in Colombia, 40 per cent in Chile, 35 per cent in Argentina, 27 per cent in Peru, and 10 per cent in Bolivia. Another opinion trend working against drug policy reform is that significant sectors of the population support iron fist policies and the use of the military to combat crime and drug trafficking,[65] although this percentage also varies. According to *Asuntos del Sur*, while in Chile 49 per cent of the population believed that militarization was not an effective policy to reduce drug trafficking in 2015, the percentage fell to 15 in Peru and 16 in Bolivia.[66]

Public opinion can change rapidly, however, especially as the reform debate expands. There is growing support for reform among young people and in countries where governments advance a reformist discourse. There is also increasing—though still low—support for the medical and recreational uses of cannabis. In Colombia, support for depenalizing drug use among people under 35 years old increased from 30 per cent in 2013–14 to 43 per cent in 2014–15. When the medical marijuana bill was introduced in Congress, some polls found that 64 per cent of young people and men supported the proposal.[67] By contrast, in Argentina support decreased from 76 to 50 per cent in the same period,[68] coinciding with an electoral debate where candidates adopted a 'get tough on the drug trade' rhetoric.[69] This does not mean that public opinion simply follows the electoral-political debate, but rather underscores how the two influence each other, and their congruence is an important factor for reform.

Difficulty of Creating Political Coalitions

Another obstacle for domestic reform is the internal debate among political sectors. Pivotal political sectors oppose reforms, thus slowing down legal changes. In Colombia, the proposal for allowing medical cannabis introduced in 2014 moved slowly through Congress and generated stark opposition among prominent political figures such as former President Álvaro Uribe, leading the Santos government to implement a bounded version of the law through a decree that then became a law. The same occurred before and after the peace agreement with the FARC. The General Attorney, for example, opposed the depenalization of coca growers and favored the fumigation of crops. Some opposition is driven by ideological preferences, but it also reflects the incentives generated by the state-building process that standard militarized drug policies have entailed. Large bureaucracies and law enforcement in countries like Colombia have been inextricably linked to drug policy, and a shift of focus could potentially undermine the resources state bureaucracies and enforcement agencies receive. The biggest threat is that political swings can lead to radical changes in drug policy, as occurred in Colombia and Brazil after 2018, when presidents declaring positions of zero-tolerance to drugs were elected.

Financial Resources and the Need to Reform Other Institutions

Successful new policies depend on reforming other sectors and on having resources and infrastructure for implementation. In Uruguay, the implementation of legal marijuana sales in pharmacies took 4 years because the infrastructure did not exist, and significant resources were necessary to establish the state control system; as of 2020, only seventeen out of 1500 pharmacies had registered to sell marijuana. In Colombia, the resources needed to implement the National Program of Crop Substitution created in the peace agreement are enormous. As of 2020, 73,817 families have received subsidies but there is still little infrastructure and support to initiate sustainable substitution projects, which also require more effective and legitimate state presence, and broader development strategies.

Drug trafficking and its enforcement have generated and exacerbated corruption, impunity, and inequality, yet these problems will not simply disappear with changes in drug policy. For the positive changes mentioned at the beginning of this section to be successfully implemented, reforms will be required in the judiciary and police, alongside improvements in state presence and broad access to quality social services, among other things. For example, health-oriented drug policies require investment in treatment facilities, training specialists, and guaranteeing equitable access to health care. In Brazil, Dilma Rouseff's government's greater emphasis on drug treatment was coupled with opening treatment facilities, and was framed within a broader policy aimed at increasing coverage of community-based mental health care.[70] Similarly, new policing strategies require democratic and efficient police forces. Indeed, the successes of the UPP Program in Rio were undermined by corruption reports about UPP officers and by the limited implementation of the social component.[71] If the non-medical use of scheduled drugs was legalized, thus weakening the illegal organizations vying for its control, broader reforms to police institutions would be crucial to prevent illegal trafficking groups from moving into other illicit ventures where they can generate similar corrupt and violent dynamics, such as extortion or gambling.

Lack of Clarity in the Options, and Inertia in Times of Crisis

The last obstacle for drug policy reform is that, even though the debate is largely a product of a critical stance on militarized approaches to combat illicit drug supply, there is less clarity on how to tackle the supply side—and especially enforcement against criminal groups—than the demand side of drugs. Ideas about public health perspectives or depenalizing consumption and use seem clearer, even if contested. Proposals for the supply side are murkier. One idea that has gained prominence is that enforcement should not be indiscriminate, but should target organizations that generate the largest public security damage, and specifically those that generate more violence.[72] This approach has two important caveats. One is that focusing on violent organizations is to a large extent what enforcement actors have done historically, though not as part of a public and planned announcement but rather as an implicit prioritization of resources. A second caveat is that, because less openly violent actors may be more powerful or may have established strong social orders, focusing on the most violent may imply tolerating powerful criminals. The point is that finding enforcement alternatives to address organized crime is more challenging than finding alternatives to deal with low-level criminality. Similarly, while the consensus on the need to change marijuana regulations is more established, ideas on how to best deal with drugs like cocaine and heroin remain unclear and controversial. At any rate, as the reform debate grows and expands, new ideas on how to deal with these problems can emerge.

The ongoing debate on what the policy alternatives are, and the pressure of showing immediate results, may explain governments' inertia, always resorting to old and failed approaches when a crisis appears. For example, in Colombia the growth of coca crops by 257 per cent between 2013–17 led the government to insist on aerial fumigations—even though the evidence suggests that the increase, which slowed down in 2016–17, was due to multiple factors including expectations regarding the peace process and pressure from armed groups, and not just the suspension of fumigations, as many observers and government officials argued. Furthermore, insisting on fumigations ignored the fact that the municipalities which saw increases had been fumigated in the past, and thus that forced eradication and fumigations do not prevent replanting in the long-term and generate many negative side effects. Yet the possibility that alternative development brings small-scale—even if sustainable—results at a slow pace, made fumigation and forced eradication the most attractive and pernicious alternative. This kind of inertia is one of the biggest obstacles to reform.

Conclusion

In 2013, and in response to a mandate originating in the 2012 Summit of Heads of State of the Americas, the OAS presented potential scenarios for drug policy in the Americas. Broadly, the four scenarios considered were: the possibility of building a new consensus among countries in the Americas on policing strategies, focused on enhancing citizen security and institutional capacity; a scenario of policy divergence among countries, with some taking clearer steps towards depenalizing or legalizing non-medical uses of drugs; a scenario of advancing policies aimed at addressing the root causes of drug use and crime and strengthening communities without necessarily changing drug policies; and finally, a scenario of countries reneging on the obligations derived from international conventions. As this chapter has discussed, diverse positions and lack of clarity in terms of what reform means beyond a common rhetoric make the first and last scenarios unlikely. A consensus among countries appears difficult and the adoption of less draconian policing strategies can be hindered by a prevailing tendency to militarize responses to crime. A complete distancing from the UN conventions also seems unlikely, since all countries in South America—even those that have advanced strong reformist discourses—declare that they do not advocate for reforming the international conventions, and even if they do, they uphold the importance of respecting the conventions. In this sense, future drug policy in South America may look more like a combination of the other two scenarios. Each country may take a different route domestically, putting greater emphasis on implementing policies aimed at treating drug users and low-level criminals more humanely, and on shifting the focus from eliminating use and production to addressing the root causes of problems. One aspect that the OAS scenarios did not consider is that differences not only emerge among, but within countries, and due to domestic contradictions even the most reformist countries are likely to see gradual and often incoherent changes.

The future of drug policy change and thus of the transformation of the War on Drugs looks less radical than the reformist discourse may suggest, yet a word of optimism is necessary. A changing elite discourse is a necessary step for broad long-term changes. As many scholars of institutional change contend, policy and institutional reforms often result from cumulative changes and tipping points, rather than radical, one-time transformations. The diffusion of policy reforms often results from changes in how problems are framed, and this is where the changing debate is crucial. Thus, even if not radical or homogeneous, small changes may pile up, leading to perhaps more radical departures in the long-term. This can be facilitated if reformist sectors are able to strengthen their connections, and if reformist groups find a niche in key government posts. As Bewley-Taylor and Hallam discuss in Chapter 3 of this book, new policies and deviations create crucial legal conundrums in the functioning of conventions, and such contradictions can force countries to take clearer stances at the international level. Despite divergences among countries, and the persistence of conservative or contradictory policy preferences, South America is more prone to change than other regions of the world, as other chapters in this book explain.

6

MEXICO AND CENTRAL AMERICA
FLEXIBILITY AND FRAMEWORKS

Carlos A. Pérez Ricart

The International Drug Control Regime (IDCR) has received a hard blow from countries historically acquiescent to its policies. A strong expression of dissent and a sense of injustice have arisen among an important sector of civil society throughout Mexico and Central America. Moreover, the discontent is not only reflected in a vivid debate among non-governmental organizations (NGOs), but also shows in leaders and policymakers who share the perception that drug strategies should be reassessed urgently. In fact, the United Nations General Assembly Special Session (UNGASS) 2016 was the consequence of a call made by the governments of Mexico, Colombia and Guatemala in 2012 to discuss a novel approach to drug policy. However, despite the use of a new progressive discourse and some advances, legislative and judiciary reforms have been less promising. Legal practices and norms remain shaped by a repressive and prohibitionist approach.

161

More than other regions in the world, Mexican and Central American societies have paid a disproportionate price for following the current interpretation of the IDCR. Nowhere have these costs been more evident than in the human rights and human development dimension. This chapter argues that the IDCR has triggered a range of collateral damage and undesirable effects in the region, which far outweigh its relative success in detaining the illegal sowing, production, trafficking, and consumption of drugs. Instead of preventing harm, the current interpretation of drug control in the form of a War on Drugs in the region is causing it.[1]

This chapter has six sections. The first section aims to provide an overview of the current trends in the region's illicit drug chain. Despite the lack of reliable information (this remains a formidable obstacle), the section revisits the region's role in the illegal drug trade. The second section addresses the influence of the United States on drug policies in the region. The third section aims to analyze the so-called achievements of the IDCR. This part discusses the extent to which achievements have been real for the region. Section four is concerned with the negative effects of the IDCR. Section five addresses the region's position in the international drug policy debate. The chapter concludes with a discussion of the main challenges for the IDCR in decades to come. One question outlines the whole discussion: what are possible scenarios for drug policy in the region and what are the main obstacles and opportunities?

Mexico and Central America in the Context of the Global Drug Circuits

Countries in Central America are 'bridge countries,' that is, states that neither consume nor produce sizable amounts of drugs, 'but that lie on forward paths carved out between centers of production (Peru, Colombia, Bolivia) and key consumers markets.'[2] In contrast to Central American countries, marijuana and opium have been produced for decades in Mexico, and unlike its neighboring countries, it has a relatively large market of consumers—though unable to compete in size with the United States.

By the end of the 1970s, most cocaine from Colombia and Peru was shipped through the Caribbean, including transshipment via Jamaica,

Haiti, and the Bahamas. It was the shortest and easiest way to reach the United States. As the United States intensified its War on Drugs in the early 1980s (see Chapter 2 by Paul Gootenberg), trafficking routes were relocated. By transferring hundreds of agents to South Florida, US anti-drug enforcement hampered the coastal and air corridors of cocaine smuggling in the Caribbean which were used by Colombian drug trafficking organizations (DTOs). That move pushed trafficking overland through Mexico and Central America, drastically changing the region's role in the international drug market. The advantages of the Mexican–Central American corridor were thus discovered and exploited.

The increase of cocaine transiting through the region modified the complexity and the importance of DTOs in Mexico and Central America. By 1989, one-third of the cocaine imported to the United States came via Mexico with an upward trend, reaching more than 50 per cent in 1992.[3] The names and nationalities of the organizations have changed with time, but the percentage is nevertheless steadily rising: in 2015, the US Government estimated that approximately 83 per cent of the cocaine trafficked to the United States came through the Mexican–Central American corridor.[4] However, drug routes through the Caribbean have not been abandoned entirely; experts and the Drug Enforcement Administration (DEA) even predict a second heyday in the future.[5]

An important consequence of the money flowing toward Mexico from the late 1970s onwards was the recruitment of former soldiers and police officers into the ranks of DTOs. As early as 1977, a single and not particularly complex DTO in Mexico could move up to 2,000 kilograms of Peruvian cocaine base.[6] Traditionally family-based groups turned into small armies.[7] Blood ties were not a requirement for membership anymore. This shift in the constitution of trafficking organizations changed the history of Mexico. DTOs were able to professionalize their activities, establishing new distribution networks in the United States, and easily replacing prisoners and deceased members. However, the new model proved to have some deficiencies. As soon as a strong leader was eliminated, individual loyalties disintegrated, and 'outsiders' began to take control of the old family organizations. Violence among groups was a natural consequence of that shift.

Regarding Central America, the effects of the civil wars that affected many countries in the region in the 1980s laid the conditions for the establishment of criminal organizations.[8] As pointed out by two scholars, 'The peace process proved to be a fertile ground for a more extreme manifestation of fragility.'[9] The end of the civil wars in Guatemala and El Salvador reduced the size of their armed forces and intelligence services. Unemployed officers and government officials moved into illegal activities by offering their services and know-how to arms and drug traffickers.[10] Former rebel combatants who did not find a place in politics followed a similar path.[11] Moreover, in countries like Honduras, the military remained in charge of the security apparatus until 1998 and, even after that year, they maintained so much power that they were able to facilitate a *coup d'état* [putsch] in 2009.[12] Porous borders, illegal corridors, a surplus of weapons, and a general context of limited statehood, poor governance, and weak institutions only made things worse.

Another consequence of the civil wars that have affected the region in the last decade was the flow of thousands of refugees or economic migrants to the United States. Poor integration into society and financial inequality in the United States contributed to the creation of youth gangs whose activities degenerated into crime and distribution of drugs in big cities. The emergence of gangs also resulted in tougher laws in the United States, including the repatriation of convicted migrants to their countries of origin. As a result, nearly 46,000 convicts were deported to Central America between 1998 and 2005.[13] Partly due to lacking family links and limited Spanish-language skills, these people replicated gang structures in their home countries.[14] Once there, while maintaining transnational contacts with partners in the United States, they began to work closely with larger criminal networks in Guatemala, El Salvador, and Honduras.[15] This meant that even if some gang members could not control the chain of distribution of drugs, they played an important role in the protection of the shipments through 'their' territories.

i. Current Trends in the Region's Illicit Drug Sector

While cocaine trafficking is the most lucrative source of income for DTOs, there is an increasing trend regarding the trafficking of heroin, new psychoactive substances, and non-scheduled precursor chemicals to manufacture methamphetamine.[16] Meanwhile, marijuana trafficking has been reduced, most probably due to domestic cannabis production in the United States. Maritime transportation is an important method to smuggle drugs through Central America. Traffickers use speedboats, self-propelled semi-submersibles, and yachts to transport drugs along the coastline. Neither the US Coast Guard nor the local authorities can control the constant flow of vessels that depart from the Colombian, Ecuadorian, and Venezuelan ports on a daily basis. Ground transportation on its own is hindered due to geographical obstacles. The Darien Strip, a nearly impenetrable barrier of jungle between Panama and Colombia, makes the trafficking of drugs in large amounts impossible. A short sea voyage to Panama is inevitable. Once in northern Panama or Costa Rica, the narcotics are mainly transported over land through Mexico to the border between Mexico and the American southwest. Once there, the drugs are smuggled by passenger vehicles, subterranean tunnels, commercial cargo trains, or small boats departing from the West Coast or ultralight aircraft.[17]

Marijuana

Mexican marijuana has been a matter of concern for US narcotic policy for decades. However, in recent years, the share of US-consumed marijuana imported from Mexico has declined as some states in the US have regulated recreational cannabis.[18] It is probable that as legal production options continue to expand in the United States, less marijuana will be trafficked along the southwest border. Still, trafficking of marijuana makes up a significant share of the revenues of DTOs in Mexico and Central America.

The progressive development of a legal market of marijuana in the United States will have two probable effects. On the one hand, it might cut off a relatively small but still significant part of DTOs' funding.[19] However, it is unclear whether reductions in these revenues would lead to corresponding decreases in violence. On the other hand, as less marijuana will be exported, the amount of marijuana consumed in the region might increase, which is still low when compared to other parts of the world.[20] For the time being, tons of marijuana will continue to be cultivated every year in Mexico, Central America and the Caribbean.[21]

Opium and Heroin

Early in the twentieth century, Chinese migrants introduced opium poppies in Mexico. The plant grew with extraordinary results in the mountains of Mexico's northwest. By the early 1970s, Mexico had emerged as a major source for heroin in the United States when supplies from Southeast Asia were cut off. Nowadays, Mexico is the world's third-largest cultivator of opium poppy, following Afghanistan and Myanmar, and the biggest exporter to the United States.

Between 2010 and 2017, seizures of heroin and of illegal shipments of acetic anhydride increased along Mexican and Central American trafficking routes. This indicates a rise of opium production and a greater supply of heroin. However, the recent upsurge of fentanyl use in the United States has brought a new challenge to the opium industry in Mexico.[22] It is too soon to tell, but the fentanyl boom might reduce the demand for Mexican heroin in the long run.

Relatively successful eradication in Mexico has pushed some of the opium production to the south in recent years. The victim of this displacement has been Guatemala, where mountains in the northwest and the country's rich dark soil have been cultivated since the 90s by Mexican organizations and their allies in the country.[23] It is not a coincidence that the isolated provinces of San Marcos and Huehuetenango, where most of the opium poppy is harvested, were also areas disputed by the guerrillas.[24]

Cocaine

Cocaine remains the most important source of income for most DTOs. A great part of the cocaine that arrives in the United States is trafficked by Mexican organizations that purchase the narcotics from Colombian, Peruvian, or Bolivian producers and then smuggle them across the US border, where local and transnational distribution chains wait for the merchandise. In 2015, the DEA estimated that approximately 87 per cent of the cocaine trafficked to the United States passed through the Mexican–Central American corridor. The remaining 13 per cent flowed into the United States through the Caribbean corridor.[25]

The Central American share of the cocaine transshipments has grown in the last decade, elevating the stature of the sub-region in the international drug trade. By 2011, the volume of cocaine seizures in Central America was more than thirteen times the amount seized in Mexico, even though in the early 2000s more cocaine seizures were reported in Mexico than in Central America.[26]

By 2019, cocaine consumption and availability in the United States seemed to have gained a new momentum after some years of relative decline. This has generated a new increase in the trafficking of cocaine in Mexico and Central America. In 2018, the largest seizure of cocaine ever recorded in Central America took place in El Salvador (13,770 kg).[27] In the small state of Belize, where cocaine seizures were the exception, more than 1,300 kilograms of cocaine were seized during the first 9 months of 2019 alone.[28] In Guatemala, in the last 2 months of 2018 only, the government seized some 8,500 kg of cocaine. All these figures suggest that the trafficking of cocaine through the region will remain high for the foreseeable future.

New Psychoactive Substances and Non-scheduled Substances

Precursor chemicals used for the production of methamphetamine and other synthetic drugs, including fentanyl, are produced in China and then smuggled into the region. In a second stage, the methamphetamine produced in the region is smuggled across the southwest border between the United States and Mexico.[29] It is estimated that 70 per cent of the US supply of methamphetamine is trafficked through the port of San Diego.[30]

The increasing consumption of synthetic drugs in the United States and the greater availability of precursor chemicals has generated a boom in the illicit manufacture of amphetamine-type stimulants across the region. This may be the most important transformation of the drug market in recent years. The question of whether Central American republics will abandon their role as 'bridge countries' and enter the drug market as producers remains open. One thing is certain: the region has been transformed into a place of invention. New drugs are being produced without any of the standards a legal market would require. The use of basements and hidden locations is likely to have many negative outcomes, for instance ecological problems.

While China remains the source of most precursors, traffickers in the region have started using non-controlled pre-precursor chemicals such as alpha-phenylacetoacetonitrile (APAAN) and derivatives of phenylacetic acid in order to generate the precursor chemicals necessary for methamphetamine production.[31] Traffickers are also finding new ways of smuggling methamphetamine, from chocolate bars to liquids for conversion into crystal methamphetamine.[32]

Mexico may also become an important source of illicitly-produced fentanyl in the future. In November 2017, a Mexican Army patrol discovered a fentanyl production laboratory in the northwest.[33] Since then, new fentanyl production laboratories have been discovered almost on a monthly basis in different regions of Mexico. All of these suggest a growing presence of Mexican DTOs in the illegal fentanyl market.

On the Influence of the United States on Drug Policies in the Region

Efforts to reduce the supply of drugs through Central America to the United States can be traced back to the 1940s, long before the formal beginning of the War on Drugs in 1971. Since then, US drug policy in the region has been carried out through binational channels rather than through multilateral agreements or platforms. More than once, US policy has linked aid programs, loans and trade preferences to counternarcotics assistance. The US Congress has even required presidents to certify states that have cooperated in the United States' counternarcotics efforts, and to punish those that do not, in a policy which has often resulted in diplomatic tensions.

In the last two decades, United States drug policy has changed significantly. Firstly, compared to the amounts of money in counternarcotics assistance currently flowing from the United States to Central America and Mexico, previous numbers were insignificant. Secondly, current policy assistance for the region is less fragmented than it was in the last century when turf wars and other security priorities—i.e. the dynamics of the Cold War—came into conflict with counternarcotics politics.

Traditionally, Mexican, and Central American governments have been enthusiastic recipients of all kinds of security assistance, including equipment, specialized law enforcement training, and money. Questions about the metrics and indicators used to measure what is 'successful' have been left aside. Governments and economic elites in the region have had to accept the policies of the United States, partly because it was convenient for the objectives they pursued, partly because they were left with no alternative, and partly because it was convenient for the expansion of the drug control bureaucracy. In this sense, the War on Drugs has been an efficient way of regaining zones with little state presence, confronting state and non-state actors, and financing bureaucratic groups within the state. However, in some cases—and depending on the context—a radical discourse against drugs has brought political gains.

In the last decades, the United States has multiplied its efforts in Central America. A fundamental part of the relationship between the United States, Mexico and Central America runs along two frameworks: The Central America Regional Security Initiative (CARSI) and the Mérida Initiative.

CARSI was created in 2008 as part of a Mexico-focused counterdrug assistance package originally known as the Mérida Initiative. Mérida was split into a separate program (CARSI) in 2010 to involve more Central American countries and to become more responsive to their priorities. From 2008 to 2015, the US Congress appropriated an estimated $1.2 billion for Central America through Mérida/CARSI.[34] Through CARSI, the US Government provided equipment, training, and technical assistance to Central American law enforcement agencies, and aimed to strengthen the capacities of governmental institutions addressing security issues. However, a critical assessment of CARSI shows that the platform represented not a security strategy, but rather several programmatic initiatives operating independently from each other.[35] Thus, for example, US-supported law enforcement units failed to contribute to broader law enforcement reform. Equally, violence prevention programs have not been implemented. Drug seizures, arrests, and number of people trained continue to be used as metrics of success.[36]

The unexpected surge of unaccompanied minors and families from Central America to the United States in 2014 motivated the Obama administration to rethink their strategy towards the region. A new approach, the US Strategy for Engagement in Central America, was created. While it maintained the broader objectives of CARSI, the new strategy highlighted the relevance of transparency and governance in the region, and prioritized interagency coordination more than CARSI did. Regrettably, despite his pledge to maintain the strategy, former President Trump suspended much of the assigned budget in March 2019.[37] At the time of writing this chapter, the US narcotics policy towards the region is undergoing a transformation, the outcome of which is still unclear.

The United States has a separate cooperation framework with Mexico. Since 2008, as part of the Mérida Initiative, the United States has provided approximately $3.1 billion in training, equipment, and technical assistance 'to help strengthen Mexico's judicial and security institutions' (as of 2020).[38] The goals are broad, going far beyond law enforcement training: they include criminal justice reform and prevention efforts, drug demand reduction projects, and border security programs. Although $3.1 billion seems like a large sum of money, a part of this money has never left the United States—it goes towards the purchase of aircraft, software and other goods produced by US private contractors. Furthermore, it is a relatively small proportion of the total federal budget dedicated to security-related functions in Mexico, which totals approximately $7.7 billion per year (2018). Still, the Mérida Initiative represents a tenfold increase in US counternarcotics assistance to Mexico.[39] It was also symbolically relevant, representing a decisive break with diplomatic tradition which—with some exceptions—discarded the idea of a vigorous and decisive US anti-narcotics aid. For Mexico, Mérida was a break with a tradition of resistance toward US influence in that political space.

Besides the frameworks that the United States has with both Mexico and Central America, US agencies, the US Army, and the Department of State have found other ways to influence the region with drug-related frameworks. These include the North American Maritime

Security Initiative which Mexico, Canada, and the United States are part of; law enforcement cooperation agreements which include the participation of anti-drug agencies in detection and monitoring systems; agreements signed with the United States to allow access and use of facilities at airports in order to conduct aerial counternarcotics activities; a broad program of police training for Latin America; the sponsoring of conferences by law enforcement agencies; the formation of a transgovernmental network of mid-level officers by the DEA;[40] the funding through non-narcotic programs of organizational infrastructures; and judicial reforms.[41]

All these programs and efforts have been an important factor in perpetuating a specific approach within regional drug policies. The US counternarcotics program was accepted in exchange for the assistance. However, by focusing narrowly on counternarcotics, this kind of assistance has incentivized Central American countries and Mexico to stick to a 'traditional approach to drug law enforcement that prioritizes arrests over community-based approaches to reducing crime and violence.'[42]

The failure of the War on Drugs is most evident in the surge of unaccompanied minors trying to cross the Mexican border illegally to the US.[43] Throughout the summer of 2014, thousands of children from Central America's Northern Triangle arrived at the border with the hope of running away from countries immersed in violence. The millions of dollars invested by the United States in the development of criminal justice and law enforcement institutions have not stopped the migration flows.[44]

Any Achievements of the IDCR in the Region?

Neither Mexico nor its neighboring countries in the south feature large illegal consumer markets for drugs. Although the region is not an 'innocent bystander in the drug trade,'[45] compared to other regions, national surveys reveal low levels of consumption. Growing numbers of drug users in the region have historically been a strong argument for developing radical approaches. For example, based on the assumption that drug consumption had increased, former Mexican President Felipe Calderón (2006–12) justified the policies he implemented in order to combat trafficking in Mexico.[46] The strategy is not new; a similar argument was used by the Mexican government in the 70s as a way of justifying its eradication campaign.

Different surveys—although all with important shortcomings[47]— illustrate that the prevalence of narcotics has not increased significantly in the last decade. According to Mexico's National Survey on Drug, Alcohol and Tobacco Consumption 2017, marijuana had only been consumed by 2.1 per cent and cocaine by 0.8 per cent of respondents in the 12 months leading up to the survey.[48] However, evidence shows that stronger and less expensive drugs have been developed in Mexico and Central America, in order to reach a market with scarce economic resources.

It is possible to argue that although the IDCR has not solved 'the drug problem,' it has prevented higher levels of drug consumption in the region and an important number of deaths attributed to illicit substances. The argument has been highlighted by policymakers and has frequently been used to defend the IDCR. Nevertheless, low levels of consumption in the region can be explained due to the fact that the United States offers a more lucrative market for the DTOs.

In accordance with Article 12 of the 1988 Convention, which obliges exporting countries to inform importing countries of any planned export of precursors to their territory, all states in the region have been registered to the International Narcotics Control Board (INCB)'s Pre-Export Notification Online (PEN Online).[49] Similarly, national drug authorities use the International Import and Export Authorization System (12ES), which aims to administer the effective and efficient implementation of the import and export authorization regime for licit international trade in narcotic drugs and psychotropic substances.[50] Countries in the region are also involved in INCB Precursor Task Force of Project Prism and Project Cohesion, and many of the most important law enforcement agencies participate in the Precursors Incident Communication System (PICS), which enables 'worldwide and real-time communication and information sharing on precursors incidents (seizures, diversions and diversion attempts, shipments stopped in transit etc....) between national authorities.'[51]

Central American countries have established national coordination committees on drug control and crime prevention, and have also developed national strategies against drug and crime. Moreover, all countries have taken legislative and policy measures to meet their commitments under the above-mentioned conventions, including legislation to counter money laundering. Almost every Central American country has youth drug treatment centers. Similarly, national programs against addiction are run hand in hand with the UNODC and the Inter-American Drug Control Policy Commission of the OAS. Nevertheless, significant problems remain. Among others, ineffective drug interdiction programs on Nicaragua's Atlantic coast, shortage of opioid analgesics and palliative care programs in Panama and Costa Rica, and the lack of facilities for the treatment of drug use in El Salvador. A common concern was the absence of reliable data on the drug use situation for every country and the difficulty involved in acceding to psychoactive substances for medical purposes—one of the main goals of the IDCR. Finally, 'consumption of opioids for pain relief continues to be low, and some countries face a further decline in their already low levels of availability.'[52]

Mexico has been particularly obedient in placing precursor chemicals under national control.[53] As for the INCB, Mexico has played a leading role in Latin America in the area of precursor control and in the investigation of crimes involving the manufacture and sale of synthetic drugs, the confiscation and disposal of chemicals used in the manufacture of such drugs, and the dismantling of clandestine laboratories. During the 2010s, Mexico constructed an impressive regulatory framework, which involved the limitation of entry ports for precursor chemicals (only four from a total of forty-nine) and almost completely outlawed imports of pseudoephedrine and ephedrine.

However, paradoxically, the main achievements of the IDCR—for instance, the well-functioning control system aimed at preventing the diversion of chemicals—made places suffering from poor governance increasingly attractive for the clandestine manufacture of drugs. It is also debatable whether the policies successfully reduced the market size. Some research suggests that the alleged failures of prohibition in final markets may have been overstated in critical discourses.[54] However, the negative effects of the actual system are more visible in producer and transit countries since 'prohibitionist drug policies [...] have ended up transferring a large proportion of the costs' to them.[55] Even if supply reduction strategies may reduce and redirect drug trafficking,[56] the cost of negative outcomes and collateral damage far outweigh the few achievements of the IDCR in the region.

All in all, the analysis above indicates that the IDCR may have met its stated goal, stabilizing the consumption of narcotics and raising a 'well-functioning system to regulate the production, distribution and use of controlled drugs for medical and scientific purposes.'[57] However, the reduction is unmeasurable, and the system has proven to be more successful in some parts than in others. Moreover, neither UNODC nor other organizations offer sufficient evidence to show that, without the efforts of the IDCR, levels of consumption would be higher than the current ones. In contrast to the difficulty of showing the achievements of the IDCR, their harmful consequences are well documented for a region distinguished by its institutional fragility.

The Negative Consequences

i. Cycles of Violence, Corruption, and State (Il)legitimacy

The relation between crime and drugs is complex. However, there is little doubt that drug smuggling acts as a prime carrier and replicator of many criminal activities.[58] Besides lack of research and methodological shortcomings in a large number of studies, there is consensus that drug trafficking is both an important driver of homicide rates in the region, and one of the factors behind rising violence levels in the area. This is because actors in organized illegal enterprises lack legal devices to resolve disagreements. Thus, they rely on informal means of resolving conflicts and often resort to violence.[59] However, what proportion of crime is related to drug trafficking is still not clear. Since 2007, violence associated with drugs has grown in the region. Even if most of the media attention has focused on Mexico, the wave of violence has been particularly disturbing in the northern part of Central America. As in Mexico, most of the recent violence has been attributed to the role of the three countries in the drug chain. While this is part of the explanation, the involvement in the drug trade is only a 'symptom of underlying social-economic issues rather than a prime cause of violence and crime in itself.'[60] Proof of the complex relationship between crime and drugs is that some countries that score worse on poverty and development, such as Nicaragua, or play a similarly important role in the drugs chain, for instance Costa Rica, maintain low levels of violence and crime compared to others in the region.[61]

It has been said that 'hot spot' drug trafficking areas tend to experience higher rates of crime than 'non-hot spot' areas.[62] However, not every territory works that way. In the case of Guatemala, for example, the homicide rate decreased after 2006, despite the country's increasingly important role as part of the drug route to the United States.[63] In El Salvador, levels of violence dropped in 2012 and 2013 due to a truce among two of the more important gangs.[64] Even Honduras registered a 30 per cent drop in murder rates between 2011 and 2015.[65] The three examples suggest that violence among criminal groups is not necessarily linked to drug trafficking, or not always in the same way. The cases also exemplify the fact that declining violence sometimes has more to do with agreements between criminals than with government policies.

The variety of factors that explain the causes of the Northern Triangle's criminal violence notwithstanding,[66] production and trafficking of drugs undermines democratic stability and penetrates political institutions. As Mónica Serrano has observed, prohibition is the catalyst which enables a parasitic relationship between criminal groups and the state.[67] As political institutions fail to enforce the law, the feeling of mistrust towards justice institutions grows and legitimacy rates go down. Poor governance and institutional fragility worsen. The relationship becomes circular. A World Bank report from 2011 showed that, on average, crime victims in Central America 'have less trust in the criminal justice system, are more likely to approve of taking the law into their hands and believe less that the rule of law should be respected.' [68] It is not only an issue of public opinion, but of the state incapacity to enhance the rule of law needed to combat illicit activities in the long run.[69] The flow of money managed by drug traffickers makes it attractive for underpaid civil servants to work for DTOs—or better yet, to work for both.[70] In fact, one of the difficulties in analyzing drug trafficking in the region is that it is 'materially inseparable from the state's own administrative institutions.'[71]

Certainly, criminal networks can arise in regions with no or weak state presence. Nevertheless, they become much stronger when they emerge in contexts where some state institutions are co-opted or reconfigured by private interests.[72] In fact, research in Central America shows how drug organizations can effectively operate in countries with strong institutions as well as in countries with weaker ones. As stated by Fowler and Bunck, 'institutions are but one factor in determining the extent of bridge-state drug trafficking.'[73] That said, the impact of violence and corruption on the legitimacy of state institutions is especially relevant. That is particularly true in the Northern Triangle, where governance is already a concern and the licit economy is unable to meet the needs of populations. Even 'successful' examples of drug policy like eradication or punctual military interventions may cause a loss of confidence in state institutions.[74] This undermining of state legitimacy makes it more difficult for the system to provide public goods 'like justice or security, but rather generate a dynamic of crime, violence and corruption.'[75] Mexico and Central America have fallen into a so-called security trap.[76]

In Mexico, the surge of violence has been dramatic since the alliance between two DTOs—the Sinaloa Cartel and the Juárez Cartel—fractured in 2005. In response to an increasingly violent environment, former President Vicente Fox (2000–6) ordered an armed security operation against organized crime in the state of Tamaulipas. The government of Felipe Calderón carried out at least eleven similar operations between 2006 and 2012. This dramatic shift from previous administrations caused a cycle of violence never seen in Mexico before.[77]

The effects of the War on Drugs in Mexico have also been suffered beyond the border. The penetration of major Mexican syndicates into Central America, and particularly Guatemala, has triggered a long-term fight between a myriad of actors: cells of larger distant organizations, native *cartelitos,* and prominent families in the region.[78]

These cycles of violence do not affect populations equally. Vulnerable groups tend to suffer more than others. Thus, Central America and the Caribbean exhibit the highest rates of femicide in the world. Plausibly, these high rates—reaching 14.4 per 100,000 women in El Salvador— are connected with the drug war.[79] Furthermore, Central America and

Mexico constitute the only region where an increase in femicides has been registered in the last decade.[80] Women are victims of both zero-tolerance interventions that inadvertently increase insecurity among the civilian population, and drug traffickers who target women as 'drug mules' and execute them in order to send a public message to the authorities.[81]

Although women work mainly as growers, collectors, and low-level dealers, the increasing number of women imprisoned in Latin America is striking. From 2000 to 2015, the population of women prisoners in Latin America climbed 51.6 per cent, compared to 20 percent for men.[82] It is assumed that women represent, on average, around 5 per cent of the prison population in Central America; depending on the country, between 30 per cent and 90 per cent are accused of drug-related offenses.[83] The increase in the number of women imprisoned for drug offenses does not necessarily indicate an increase in the participation of women in drug-related crimes, but a rise in the prosecution in case of small-scale trafficking.[84]

Finally, another negative consequence associated with the emergence of a huge criminal black market is the rise of an internally displaced population. In El Salvador, for example, as many as 288,000 people fled their homes in reaction to criminal violence associated with drug trafficking. This accounts for 66 per cent of the 436,500 internally displaced people in Central America.[85] Even the most conservative surveys estimate the existence of around 280,000 internally displaced people in Mexico.[86] In contrast to Colombia—where the phenomenon has been recognized and quantified—policies in Mexico are non-existent, despite the creation of the Executive Commission of Assistance to Victims[87] in 2013, an underfunded institution without means to assist the problem of internal displacement of people.

These cycles of violence, promoted by prohibition, indicate that the focus of the IDCR needs to shift. Mechanisms guaranteeing access to justice and reconciliation for the communities that have been victims of drug violence, need to be implemented. What is more, these victims should be taken into account when discussing the future of the War on Drugs.

ii. Policy and Geographical Displacement

The IDCR's securitized interpretation in the form of the War on Drugs has promoted a system in which security and law enforcement concentrate almost all the attention, resources, and priorities. Meanwhile, human rights and public health concerns have been relegated and marginally acknowledged. In that sense, public policy has been *displaced*.

This policy displacement has triggered a logic of entrenchment and expansion within the drug control bureaucracy.[88] Based on wrong assumptions ('it's possible to eliminate the drug market') and big bureaucracies without civil control, a system of checks and balances has appeared in recent years.[89] In fact, the offensive against illicit drug use has proved transformative for regional counternarcotics and security policies: it has led to a major uptick in money allocated to federal agencies, resulting in large and unmanageable security institutions.[90] The Mexican case helps to explain the formation of a new 'narco-enforcement complex.' While the federal police tripled in size and saw their resources increased by a factor of four, the federal security budget almost doubled between 2006 and 2012.[91] Large-scale federal operations, the use of military personnel for law enforcement tasks, and an indirect militarized police approach have become the cornerstone of the Mexican security strategy.[92] In 2018, President López Obrador announced the creation of a National Guard, a hybrid institution composed mainly of military and former federal police. The force is scheduled to expand to an estimated 150,000 officers by 2023. There is little doubt that the institution will further militarize Mexican drug policy strategy.

The War on Drugs also includes costs at a constitutional level. Since 2006, Mexico has suffered the curtailment of fundamental rights, the curbing of federalism and state powers, and the undermining of legal security by conflating legal concepts and state functions.[93] Independent observers have detected a reduction in the fundamental principles of law, including the transformation of constitutional texts, interpretations, and practices in order to better face drug problems. The use of soldiers for counternarcotics functions and the excessive use of pretrial detention are just two examples of this. These 'constitutional costs'—which are justified by claims they are a way to better confront criminal organizations—are to be added to the list of costs of the War on Drugs. These changes have undermined longstanding commitments to specific constitutional principles, values, and rights.[94]

In a nutshell: a prohibitionist approach diverts resources from health, education, and other social needs. Moreover, drug enforcement has not been successful in terms of security. After years of steadily increasing budgets for security-related functions, levels of impunity remain high. By 2017, 93 per cent of estimated crimes went either unreported or uninvestigated.[95] The strategy has not been successful even by its own metrics. Militarization has contributed to the fragmentation and proliferation of DTOs which in turn has degenerated into a series of battles between trafficking cells. Second, decades of domestic drug enforcement, tighter interdiction, eradication programs, and repressive source control programs have not succeeded in substantially reducing levels of consumption or in raising the price of drugs. At best, drug law enforcement responses have led to a kind of fragmentation and displacement of criminal structures, and a geographical displacement of the global centers of drug production.

The drug industry displacement has been called the 'balloon effect' because 'squeezing (by tighter controls) one place produces a swelling (or an increase) in another place, though it may well [or not] be accompanied by an overall reduction'[96]—see Chapter 1 by Annette Idler. Different processes in Mexico, Central America, and the Andean region verify the hypothesis.[97] So, for example, as law enforcement efforts have been multiplied and cocaine seizures by the Mexican navy intensified, cocaine has increasingly been transported through Guatemala and Honduras.[98] The same process is taking place in relation to methamphetamines: due to increased law enforcement efforts in Mexico, Guatemala has been targeted as a new manufacturing base.[99]

The displacement of drug organizations is also part of the 'balloon effect.' The problem is not only in the geographical shift of the production of drugs, but also the fragmentation and dispersion of the organizations for survival.[100] In search of safer places, criminal groups move from one country to another. Although evidence remains unsystematic and anecdotal for the region, footprints of major Mexican and Colombian groups exist in the Central American Northern Triangle.[101]

Violence can also be displaced. Intervention in a given territory can have an impact in a distant one, efficient interdiction policies in one country increasing drug-related homicides in another. Even if the isolation of external variables from internal ones has been proved a difficult task,[102] some research suggests that the scarcity created by Colombian reduction of coca supply may have resulted in an estimated 21 per cent increase in homicides in Mexico for the period of 2006 to 2010.[103]

iii. Marginalization of Consumers and Over-Penalization

The IDCR's interpretation in the form of the War on Drugs promotes a system in which those who fall into the web of addiction find themselves penalized, marginalized, and excluded from the social mainstream.[104] With the exception of Costa Rica, drug possession is prohibited in all Central American countries 'to some extent or in certain circumstances.'[105] Despite the regional 'decriminalization' discourse, consumers continue to be detained, prosecuted, and even incarcerated in Mexico and Central America.[106]

Drug policy approaches dominated by strict law enforcement practices perpetuate the spread of hepatitis C, as well as HIV and other blood-borne diseases.[107] There are an estimated 16 million people who inject drugs in the world, 10 million of whom are affected by hepatitis C (see Chapter 12 by Damon Barrett and Kasia Malinowska-Sempruch). There is insufficient surveillance data for Mexico and Central America to estimate the size of their epidemics. However, it has likely been underestimated by public policy. It is estimated that 141,000 people have injected drugs in Mexico. The prevalence of hepatitis C antibodies among people who inject drugs (PWIDs) in Mexico is as high as 96 per cent.[108] In both Mexico and Central America, injecting opiates is also linked to HIV prevalence: 2.5 per cent of PWIDs are affected by HIV.[109] Honduras, Panama, and El Salvador also show relatively high numbers.[110] The illegality of injecting drugs has an adverse effect on the problem. Irrespective of the fact that harm reduction programs around the world have demonstrated the capacity to reduce the amount of disease, there are no examples of overdose programs or consumption rooms in any country in the region.[111] Only Mexico has operational needle exchange programs (NSP). Nevertheless, the coverage of the programs is very limited: NSP provisions remain under-resourced and the existence of the program depends on external funding.[112] In some areas, drug users have limited access to syringes through retail pharmacies.[113] Mexico is also the only country in the region that maintains OST programs. However, only a relatively small proportion of opiate users—18 per cent—have access to such programs in Mexico.[114] While some pilot programs have been developed at the local level in recent years, as of 2020 no needle and syringe exchange program was operative at a national level in the region's prisons.

An additional consequence of the punitive approach supported by the IDCR is the saturation of every prison system in the region. Prisoners have a higher risk of infecting themselves with HIV, tuberculosis, and hepatitis C due to needle and syringe sharing; in the Americas, the prevalence of HIV is around 3 per cent among people held in prison.[115] This can be attributed to the fact that drug users are vastly overrepresented in prison populations.[116] Thus, the problem becomes circular, since prisons in Mexico and Central America do not function as rehabilitation centers but rather as places of induction and recruitment for drug traffickers.

Like in other parts of the world, in Mexico and Central America health problems related to prohibition seem to outweigh the health benefits. Human rights obligations have been overlooked. There is what some have called 'a divorce between drug policies and human rights.'[117] The predominantly punitive interpretation of the conventions on which the IDCR is based has led to human rights abuses; however, these are given only a secondary role in UNODC reports and Commission on Narcotic Drugs (CND) discussions.

The Ongoing Debate

Unlike in other regions, a general agreement—at least a rhetorical one—exists in Mexico and Central America, namely that current strategies should be reassessed urgently. Leaders and policymakers share the perception that the region pays a disproportionate price for reducing drugs supply in violence, hijacked justice systems, and congested prisons.[118] Strong expressions of dissent with US policies came even from presidents in office. For example, former president of Guatemala Otto Pérez Molina (2012–15) proposed the depenalization of the transit of drugs by establishing a corridor through which cocaine could flow unhindered from South to North America. However, his imprisonment on charges of corruption in 2015 was a blow to the agenda promoted under his guidance. Much of the legitimacy his agenda had won was lost in an instant. Moreover, his successor Jimmy Morales did not show any intention to boost any of Molina's proposals. Another radical proposition came in 2011, when the President of Costa Rica Laura Chinchilla (2010–14) 'presented the outline of a funding mechanism based on a financial compensation scheme for drug seizures'[119] at an international donor conference in Guatemala. However, the interest the proposal initially gained quickly diminished.

Moderate criticism of the IDCR has been expressed within its framework. Mexico laid the way for a high-level General Assembly to discuss different aspects of global drug policy in 1993. That initiative culminated in the 1998 UNGASS. Mexico was also the promoter of the Multilateral Evaluation Mechanism (MEM) created in 1999, the objective of which was to counterbalance the certification process by the United States.[120] The experiment was flawed, but gave place to two platforms: the Latin American Commission on Drugs and Democracy, and subsequently the Global Commission on Drug Policy. Both panels have made calls for decriminalization, alternatives to incarnation, and greater emphasis on public health approaches.[121] While their recommendations and reports have only managed to enter academic literature and government reports as footnotes until now, their sole existence signals the emergence of a new public debate. More importantly, Mexico and Guatemala joined Colombia in requesting an international conference with the goal of taking necessary decisions. That joint declaration resulted in UNGASS 2016 and a new wave of discussions.

Despite this consensus to dissent, options for dealing with the tremendous flow of drugs through the region appear to be limited: no alternatives to prohibition have been discussed. There is little agreement among those actors that disagree with the actual regime on what an alternative policy should look like. This situation hinders the possibility to set a unified approach fitting all countries. Despite this inability to form a common block in UNGASS 2016, all leaders in the region recognized, on the one hand, the importance of pointing out the principle of shared responsibility and on the other, the urgency of distinguishing between policies for producers/transit countries and policies for consumer countries.

. The Mexican government claims to be open to a broad and global debate on the issue. As analyzed above, in practice the internal measures and strategies used are more law enforcement-oriented than before. As in other countries in the region, the law enforcement system still takes precedence over the health system as a tool of counterdrug policy. In fact, former President Peña Nieto called for the elimination of local police forces and for a strengthening of the War on Drug efforts.[122] Current President Andrés Manuel López Obrador retracted from his promise to pacify the country by taking troops off the street and sending them back to the barracks. Instead, he implemented the creation of the above-mentioned National Guard.

On the multilateral front, the Mexican government encourages the use of progressive language on the issue of shared responsibility between producer, transit, and consumer countries in UN resolutions.[123] In his address to the UN General Assembly during UNGASS 2016, former President Peña Nieto accepted that the solutions implemented by the international community 'have been frankly insufficient.'[124] Furthermore, he talked about moving 'beyond prohibition to effective prevention.' Despite the progressive language, UNGASS ended without significant changes to existing drug conventions,[125] and the new Mexican government does not seem willing to push for a meaningful change to the IDCR in the future.

Nevertheless, some advances have been made. The Mexican government approved the Law against Drug Dealing in 2009, which decriminalized consumption of small amounts of drugs for personal use (though threshold quantities were low), replaced criminal sanctions with treatment recommendations and established harm reduction as a state policy. Nonetheless, personal possession remains illegal and consumers are still criminalized.[126] The new law also (re)allows the use of traditional drugs by indigenous people.[127] More importantly, in an unexpected decision, the Mexican Supreme Court opened the door for people to grow their own marijuana in November 2015. The Court ruled that growing, possessing, and smoking marijuana for recreation is legal. The basis for the decision was that prohibition cut off the individual's free personal development, and that measures taken to prohibit this were disproportionate. Although the ruling did not approve the commercialization or sale of marijuana, this precedent will put some pressure on the Mexican Congress to create new rules for the production and sale of marijuana. Three years later, in October 2018, the Supreme Court deemed the country's marijuana prohibition law unconstitutional for the fifth time, a crucial threshold that allows the ruling to become jurisprudence.[128] This does not legalize recreational use of marijuana, but creates a precedent other Mexican courts must follow. Equally significant was the decision of Mexico's Interior Secretary, Olga Sánchez Cordero, to lead the fight in favor of the recreational use of marijuana and eventually opium poppies. She was one of the main driving forces of a section in the 2019–24 Mexican National Development Plan that includes a proposal to decriminalize prohibited drugs and shift priorities towards 'drug policy reform based on expanding treatment for drug addiction.'[129] The extent to which these promises will be translated into actual policy remains to be seen.

Will this lead to the creation of a regulated marijuana market, as exists in Uruguay and in some US states? It might be possible in the long run. Will this lead to a reconsideration of prohibition in relation to other drugs? Probably not. However, there is a lesson to be learned from the Mexican experience: it was a call from the judiciary, not from political actors, that drove the change. By arguing in terms of personal freedoms, the Mexican Court showed that even in a country where public opinion is opposed to marijuana decriminalization, change in drug policy is possible.[130]

Future Outlook—Moving beyond the War on Drugs?

Conditions for a significant change in drug policies are both constrained domestically and internationally. At the national level, many expect that there will be an increased budget for law enforcement tasks, a more persistent participation of armed forces in law enforcement activities, and a broader and stronger framework of cooperation with US agencies. Without any structural change, security budgets will continue to follow an upward trajectory. In addition to this, perverse incentives and indicators to measure 'success' (arrests and seizures, hectares eradicated, convictions, operations, and budget invested), and the tendency by law enforcement agencies to pump up results and goals will prevail over metrics oriented around public health, human rights, and safety objectives (see Chapter 14 by Robert Muggah and Katherine Aguirre for alternative indicators). As stated earlier, corrupt elites and political parties have benefited from the emergency status that prevails in Mexico and Central America; zero-tolerance politics and radical discourses continue—and will continue—to bring political gains, providing some kind of ceremonial presence for weak states still in the making. Despite a progressive discourse, one of the main obstacles to drug reforms is inside the political system of each country.

Understanding the long tradition of conservative policies in the region is important for analyzing the principal points of resistance to a change in drug policy. The punitive prohibitionist approach often associated with the IDCR has not been imposed from outside, either in Mexico or in Central America. Many punitive and prohibitionist policies were introduced in the early twentieth century, long before Shanghai, the League of Nations, and the CND were even designed. Indeed, US authorities 'first heard that marijuana turned ordinary people into ferocious maniacs' from Mexican sources.[131] Recreational marijuana was neither a casual nor a traditional part of Mexican life. Quite the opposite: negative representation of drug use as well as punitive practices were well established in the region. A study by Campos Costero has demonstrated that 'by the 1930s Mexico's drug-control options had already become severely limited.'[132] The IDCR reinforced a previous structure, but by no means established the foundations of the actual policies in the region. This fact, which is sometimes overlooked by proponents of a simple and linear process of policy diffusion, gives a different view of the relationship between domestic and international dynamics in the construction of the global regime.

Inside the formal structure of the IDCR, space for change also seems narrow. An eventual rescheduling of one of many illicit substances, marijuana, would not be sufficient to reduce drug-related violence, though it would represent an important step. However, as noted by Christopher Hallam and David Bewley-Taylor in Chapter 3 of this book, this is 'politically unlikely.' Other options such as the formation of a common block toward the amendment of the 1961 Convention seem equally improbable and insufficient. No government in the region seems prepared for 'engaging in a monumental diplomatic process that risked rupturing the global control system.'[133] Even a more radical alternative, such as the denunciation and 'recession' with a reservation permitting the use of cannabis would only put a patch over the fragmentation of the Vienna consensus. The option of 'modification inter se' seems improbable, as there are no like-minded states, and somewhat pointless in view of the region's needs (for the mechanisms of how this would work, see Chapter 3 by Christopher Hallam and David Bewley-Taylor).

Room for experimentation seems to be bigger outside the structures of the UN. A more likely journey will be the slow and tough construction of new frameworks through which countries can bypass the formal structure of the IDCR. The increasing importance of the OAS in the drug reform debate is a sign of independence. Unlike other efforts in the past, new interregional efforts may not succumb to 'regulatory capture' by the United States.[134] There are aspects of the current international scenario that could be helpful here: the United States is no longer the uncontested champion of a 'hardline punitive global counternarcotic regime,'[135] nor does it have the same influence over Mexico and Central America as in the last few decades. Thus, it is possible to envisage a shift toward decriminalization of drug consumption and the recognition of 'harm reduction' policy interventions as an important feature of drug policy. But how long will it take until governments in the region finally move away from incarcerating users and reduce penalties for low-level dealers? Probably a few years—with or without the conventions' authorization. Even if these eventual moves do not have any consequence in reducing the levels of violence, they will be remarkable developments in the debate from a human rights perspective.

A first step toward legislative reform would be to invest in frameworks which guarantee better and independent data collection, for instance price and purity series and epidemiological data. As has been previously noted, drug use surveys have important methodological and conceptual flaws.[136] Without credible data, it will be impossible to draw appropriate indicators and metrics for new policies. More importantly, an articulated agenda must be found within governments in the region. Until now, national anti-drug trafficking policies have had a competitive aspect more than a cooperative one. Under the circumstances, a successful interdiction or eradication policy in one country results in a threat to its neighbors as DTOs move their operations from one country to the next. Therefore, regional strategies based on a principle of shared responsibility are favorable to local anti-narcotics strategies.

Regarding the relationship with the United States, governments in the region will have to renegotiate resources for counternarcotics efforts. Support for civil society initiatives and free media should be prioritized—above all, in contexts where criminal funding plays a noteworthy role in shaping the operation of the justice and electoral systems. The United States can play a positive role in a shift toward reducing the effects of organized crime by supporting the fight against corruption and prevention of youth violence. The effects of organized crime may be reduced by funding more vigorous independent institutions like the International Commission against Impunity in Guatemala—whose mandate was unfortunately not renewed by the Guatemalan government in 2019—and similar efforts in Honduras through the Mission to Support the Fight against Corruption and Impunity. Violence prevention, community-oriented programs, and harm reduction projects should be prioritized. However, no program can single-handedly address the factors that drive crime and drug production. Future security strategies should be repackaged within a strategic framework that sets the reduction of poverty and inequality as a priority.

If the IDCR wants to preserve its most precious feature, the almost universal adherence it enjoys, it will have to show some flexibility regarding the possible developments that could take place in different regions and allow a larger interpretative room within the conventions.

A flexible IDCR means the construction of a framework in which different contexts and institutional arrangements should be considered. Mexico and Central America would be a good place to start.

7

WEST AFRICA
SECURITIZED DRUGS AS AN EXISTENTIAL THREAT?

John M. Pokoo and Kwesi Aning

In West Africa,[1] a region that features mixed functional capabilities of states and growing demand for the illicit use of drugs, applying strategies to comprehensively enforce the international drug control regime (IDCR) remains a challenge—with wide-ranging but differentiated repercussions on state and human security (for more on state and human security, see Chapter 1 by Annette Idler).[2] International methods deployed to control the non-medical use of trafficked drugs are often criticized[3] not because of their lack of thoroughness, but due to their skewed application in favor of supply reduction interventions and minimal focus on demand reduction. For example, one report described the over bearing supply reduction approach as 'securitization' in the form of the War on Drugs, and attributed the growth of the international drug trafficking sector to the excessive and securitized international counternarcotics approach which has inadvertently gifted an entire market to criminals.[4]

The Economic Community of West African States (ECOWAS) and the wider West Africa region is at the mercy of the international drug trade. It is a transit route due to its favored geographical, logistical, and governance conditions, which collectively provide an enabling environment;[5] increasingly, however, it is also a consumption zone. Some of the multiple impacts of international drug trafficking on West Africa include money laundering and state capture; transnational organized crime, including arms trafficking; and armed insurgencies, kidnappings, and terrorism.[6]

The above impacts of international drug trafficking on West Africa have attracted divergent analyses and policy recommendations.[7] For example, some of the analyses highlight the securitization of the illicit drug trade, and the associated measures implemented in countering this trade by governments, as a key contributory factor in anchoring both the expansion of the illicit drug economy and the 'global' dimensions of the trade (see Chapter 3 by Christopher Hallam and David Bewley-Taylor). Some focus on weak enforcement regimes, while others consider success stories from different geographical regions and make recommendations for the situation in West Africa.[8]

This chapter explores some of the options available to West African countries in addressing the drug problem, based on the institutional capabilities of governments in the sub-region. It argues that systemic governance and security deficits—including weak enforcement regimes, regional conflict complexes, corruption, and poor health infrastructure—create burdens for West African states to introduce a drug decriminalization regime. There is at present a strong ongoing campaign to decriminalize drugs.[9] A drug decriminalization regime in West Africa will require monitoring and enforcement measures. Failure in this regard could pose further human security risks to ordinary persons living farther away from the national capitals, where state institutions are often less functional. For example, investments meant to sustain a decriminalization regime could be diverted to nearer and more pressing challenges closer to the capitals, making monitoring in distant locations difficult, if not nearly impossible.[10] The proponents of decriminalization argue that a decriminalization regime helps to raise the health consciousness of states. Against this, this chapter argues that—given the poverty, corruption, fragility, and ineffective law enforcement and oversight potentials of West African states and their institutions—decriminalizing drugs will worsen the present situation. Decriminalization presupposes state ability to monitor, intervene, and provide support to users. Decriminalization also masks a strategic international effort to literally widen the market for drugs through legitimizing drugs across the world, leaving those jurisdictions that cannot cope with the health and other consequences to their fate. All available evidence suggests that the capacity of West African states to provide such support is at best weak or non-existent, as evidenced by consistent institutional failures to deal with malaria, tuberculosis (TB), human immunodeficiency virus infection and acquired immune deficiency syndrome (HIV/AIDS), and the Ebola virus. This chapter begins with a discussion of the historical involvement of West Africa in illicit drug trade and use.

Explaining the Problem of Drug Use in West Africa

In his 'West Africa's International Drug Trade,' Stephen Ellis[11] highlights the role of individual West Africans and the responses of particular political regimes in the sub-region in the global chain of drug trafficking, linking it to state formation in West Africa. Similarly, Kwesi Aning and Bah reveal the political and social dualism that exist in West African societies, a structural condition that allows drug traffickers to operate within informal networks that avoid detection by the formal state.[12] The drug problem in West Africa is not a recent phenomenon. Cannabis cultivation and use in the sub-region, for example, dates back to the 1950s, and links to the return of West African soldiers who had participated in World War II. Attention to the emergence of other drugs such as cocaine, heroin, and methamphetamine in the sub-region is of recent origin. Awareness has grown due to incidences of seizures at entry ports in West Africa, Europe, and North America from travelling West Africans and cargo shipments into the sub-region in the 1980s.[13] Since the 1990s, the intensity of drug trafficking and illicit use in the sub-region has worsened.

Understanding the deteriorating situation of drug trafficking in the sub-region requires analyzing the factors that motivate the involvement of West Africans in the international illicit drug trade. One of the above-mentioned historical perspectives focusing on Nigeria and other West African countries deploys political and economic processes in these countries to do so. It highlights the perceived alienation of particular identifiable groups—for example, Igbos in Nigeria—from official national political processes after the Biafra War in that country in the late 1960s, and identifies engagement in illicit activities as a response to political alienation.[14] This account becomes entangled with the economic down-turns of the 1980s following the implementation of the International Monetary Fund (IMF)-sponsored Structural Adjustment Programs (SAPs), which affected several other countries in the sub-region. It ushered in a period of sustained under-investment in key social and economic sectors, impoverishing individuals and communities in many parts of West Africa. The SAPs were considered Western-inspired economic interventions that contributed to the collapse of West African economies, triggering hardship and vulnerability for millions of West Africans. By this account, West Africans hold the West responsible for their economic plight and, therefore, they engage in illicit activities including drug trafficking as a wealth redistribution strategy. There is yet another historical account, which creates a triangular connection among ethnic groups in West Africa with their historical 'kinsmen' in Latin America from the period of the pre-colonial slave trade.[15] According to this account, the historical ties between social groups from West Africa and their counterparts in Latin America facilitated the socialization of West Africans involved in drug trafficking with markets and communities in Latin America. This re-establishment of historical socio-cultural affinities in turn promoted the movement of narcotic drugs from Latin America through West Africa to drug trafficking networks in other African Diaspora communities in Europe and North America from the 1980s onwards, when economic hardship and repressive political conditions in the sub-region generated an exodus of West Africans to Western countries.

In the Sahel parts of West Africa, there are accounts of some community leaders participating in the drug trade as a means of survival.[16] This account explores how the quest to control drug trafficking routes in northern Mali bring together rebel and terrorist groups, as well as government officials and tribal leaders, in intriguing alliances and forms of cooperation that sometimes lead to violent clashes. These clashes, however, are not necessarily over drugs per se, but more over the control of the trading routes which open up opportunities for other illicit activities. Control of such trading routes and the associated economic gains further strengthen clandestine operations even into territories that are deemed to be politically stable or secure. For example, three Malian trafficking suspects, Oumar Issa, Harouna Toure, and Idriss Abelrahman were arrested in December 2009 in Ghana, and were subsequently found to be members of the group Al Qaeda in the Islamic Maghreb (AQIM). They were negotiating cocaine shipments with the Revolutionary Armed Forces of Colombia (FARC), routing them from the west of Africa to the north and then on to Spain. They were eventually charged with plotting to transport cocaine across Africa with the intent to support Al Qaeda (AQ), its local affiliate AQIM, and FARC.[17]

By the 1990s, Guinea, Guinea-Bissau (a fragile state featuring a breakdown of rule of law and numerous archipelagoes with air-strips not linked to global aviation networks), Ghana (a functioning state with impressive aviation access, but also with strong informal networks co-existing with the official state) and Mali (which is located in northern West Africa and has fairly reliable aviation infrastructure) emerged as the major transit hubs in the eastern, western and northern parts of the sub-region. This emergence was spurred on by noted structural deficiencies across the sub-region, such as porous borders, weak institutions, corruption and political patronage, poverty, and ethnic or informal social networks.[18] However, these are not the only countries vulnerable to the international illicit drug transit trade in West Africa. Indeed, the structural challenges outlined above apply to all the countries in the sub-region. While there are documented cases of official political collusion in some countries,[19] the inherent historical trading ties and trading routes connect the land-locked countries in the sub-region to particular coastal states and facilitate the movement of narcotic drugs.

For example, in Guinea-Bissau—where there have been documented relationships between senior government and security officials and drugs cartels—competing local interests have led to the assassination of senior political and military figures.[20] In addition, there have been cases in Guinea where a cargo plane loaded with drugs was protected by presidential guards on arrival. Additionally, illicit drug deals were conducted inside the first lady's private residence and in the president's VIP salon, and cocaine was sent to Europe in the diplomatic pouch.[21] The son of the late former president of Guinea, Captain Ousmane Conté, admitted in 2008 (after the overthrow of his father's regime) that he was the godfather of the drug trade in that country.[22] Togo was also deemed a vital operational platform for drug trafficking activities, though the level of official collusion was shrouded in secrecy, enabling the concealment of the volume of these activities.[23] Until 2008, cocaine smuggling was not even banned in Sierra Leone.[24] This situation changed with the seizure of 703 kilos of cocaine—and the suspicion that the Minister of Transportation, Ibrahim Kemoh Sesay, and his brother Ahmed were involved in organizing the flight that delivered the cargo from Venezuela with fake Red Cross markings.[25] A 2014 report by the Global Initiative against Transnational Organized Crime indicated that illicit trafficking activities constitute one of the key factors underpinning the political crisis in Mali. The report notes that such activities have entrenched themselves into the Malian State structures. For example, there have been several examples of collusion within the Malian State apparatus and institutions, for instance political and military elites colluding both with traffickers and rebels in the northern parts of the country in an opportunistic relationship.[26] When it comes to consumption, accounts on Ghana[27] and to a larger extent, Nigeria,[28] exhibit strong class undertones in the profiles of those engaged in illicit drug use. Essentially, these studies associate drug use—mainly cannabis—with the underprivileged class.

Toward the Securitization of the Narcotics Threat

By the late 1990s, the prevalence of the illicit drug trade in terms of seizures and domestic consumption levels had resulted in West African states beginning to discuss the possible deleterious impacts of narcotics availability and consumption on states. ECOWAS member states started the process of securitization by recognizing the problem, discussing it amongst heads of state and at government summits. They adopted the appropriate protocols and conventions, and established specific units to highlight the dangers of drugs availability.[29] In the case of West Africa, a security community[30] was established by ECOWAS with its 1975 protocol, which can be characterized as 'a collective with a high level of transaction and communication in which non-violent dispute resolution is the norm.'[31] This particular usage of security communities as a lens is critical to understanding how the narratives about the possible threats posed by narcotics to state survival were eventually constructed. Buzan and Waever have argued that security communities provide a framework for understanding how such a community constructs 'securitizations' with its members.[32] The securitization framework was introduced into the international relations discipline by the Copenhagen School[33] in the 1990s as a new concept for security analysis (see Chapter 1 by Annette Idler), and was largely influenced by Buzan's work on broadening the concept of security beyond traditional military issues to include referent objects, such as environmental, economic, social, and political sectors.[34] Securitization was conceptualized as the act of casting an issue as one of 'existential threat'—here the issue of the availability, sale, trafficking and misuse of narcotic drugs—that requires extraordinary measures beyond the routine norms of everyday politics.[35] As Buzan et al. posited, 'in security discourse, an issue is dramatized and presented as an issue of supreme priority; thus by labelling it as security, an agent claims a need for and a right to treat it by extraordinary means.'[36] In other words, securitization theory argues that no issue is in itself a menace.[37] Security is thus viewed as a subjective condition, to be analyzed by examining the 'securitizing speech acts' through which threats become represented and recognized.[38] This model conceives security as a 'self-referential practice because it is in this practice that the issue becomes a security issue—not necessarily because a real existential threat exists, but because the issue is presented as such.'[39] The process of elevating an issue to an existential threat requires 'a securitizing actor' and a 'speech act.'[40] For this process to be successful, the actor has to be in a position of authority to make the securitization claim, the alleged threats facilitate securitization, and the securitizing speech act follows the grammar of security.[41] In other words, successful securitization has three components: [1] the presence of existential threats; [2] emergency action; and [3] effects on interunit relations by breaking free of rule.[42]

Alternative interpretations of securitization theory argue that 'if too much is securitized, security might become unexceptional and therefore securitization would not be politically effective.'[43] Other schools of thought express concern about the 'intellectual incoherence' of the subject as a result of excessive securitization.[44] Moreover, some show aversion to 'militarization and confrontation-orientation of traditional conception of security.'[45] Some have asserted that securitization is 'narrow in context, form and nature, with focus on the speech act of the dominant actors.'[46] However, this chapter adopts a more nuanced approach to the application of securitization, focusing on the opportunity to address certain issues without necessarily triggering a traditional military-type response, and the potential it represents for the idea of collective and communities of security.[47] Furthermore, this chapter argues that securitization can provide the necessary impetus for mobilizing the international community towards a desired action. Above all, as global understanding and conceptualization of security continue to evolve, so multilateral response mechanisms should continue to be recalibrated in tandem with recognized threats or securitized issues.

The three key conventions underpinning the IDCR seek to protect the health of people from the inappropriate use of narcotic drugs and psychotropic substances. The 1961 and the 1971 Conventions are based upon concern for the welfare of mankind, allowing the use of narcotic drugs and psychotropic substances exclusively for medical and scientific purposes. In addition, the 1988 Convention indicates—among many other things—that in cases involving individuals selling a small amount of drugs with the intent to obtain the money to maintain their habit as drug addicts, the legislation should identify and divert such minor matters away from the criminal justice system. Thus, Article 3, paragraph 4. (c) of the 1988 Convention states that 'in appropriate cases of a minor nature,' the parties may provide 'as alternatives to conviction or punishment' measures such as education, rehabilitation, or social reintegration, as well as treatment and aftercare. The above places enormous responsibility on states to guarantee adequate provision for such purposes.

In other words, while there are supply reduction measures within the framework of the IDCR, a lax response to related demand reduction measures could produce skewed and unintended outcomes. Thus, the emergence, transit, and usage of narcotics became an existential threat to human security in West Africa, as it constituted an 'extraordinary event and a matter of public health and security risk to other states.'[48]

Understanding the Drug Trafficking Environment in West Africa

Much of the conditions that create vulnerabilities to drug trafficking in West African countries are rooted in the nature of the states in the sub-region, as well as in the characteristics of the constituent sub-state actors (for the concept of vulnerable regions see Chapter 1 by Annette Idler). For example, relations between and among sovereigns are premised on notions of equality and interdependence.[49] However, the evolution of state sovereignty in sub-Saharan Africa was born of a mechanism to appropriate territories to extra-regional powers and dependence.[50] Consequently, African states continue to deal with a plethora of systemic challenges that are intrinsic to the very nature of their evolution. These challenges include denial of the monopoly over the use of force which has arisen from historical and persistent Cold War interventions that armed non-state actors on the continent;[51] denial of rights and social justice for particular social constituencies within jurisdictions;[52] and a directed development/modernization model not rooted in indigenous realities, but driven by extra-regional perceptions of development for Africa and maintained through engagements with the Bretton Woods Institution.[53] A combination of the above challenges together with corrupt practices in the African public spheres translates into persistent under-investment in critical social sectors and limits the expanse the state's presence in providing security and other social goods including health services, rehabilitation and psychosocial counseling services across most national sovereign territorial jurisdictions. These challenges reveal that issues such as narcotics drug use—assessed to be an existential threat—cannot be left to ordinary political and social procedures and processes, especially as such conditions could facilitate organized criminality and indiscriminate use of drugs. Furthermore, there is more danger in the association between methods of illicit drug use (for example, injection) with health hazards including the spread of HIV and other deadly diseases. Increasingly in West Africa, there is a clear association between drug usage and acquisitive crimes as well as behavioral challenges including aggression or violence (for the link between drug use and crime see Chapter 11 by Nicolas Trajtenberg, Olga Sánchez de Ribera and Clara Musto). Even with only poor statistical bases and data, analyzing police and correctional services' data shows that close to 80 per cent of Ghana's prison inmates have some association with drugs and crime.[54]

The West African sub-region is no longer just a transit route for drugs but also an increasing consumption zone. Traffickers pay some locals in kind instead of cash, fueling drug circulation on the local market. Since this occurs against the background of poor health infrastructure standards, regional voices such as Obot have called for more demand reduction interventions at the national level.[55] In some countries, human capital is being affected by increasing levels of consumption. For example, in Ghana, security officials have observed that many of the locations where drugs are used illicitly are either commercial or mining centers where there is easy access to money through legitimate work or robbery to sustain the addiction habit. The United Nations Office on Drugs and Crime (UNODC) estimates that some 35 to 40 tons of cocaine move through West Africa each year but consumption is perceived to have flattened or stabilized since 2009.[56] Indeed, the value of the cocaine trade in West Africa is more than the national budget for some of the economies in the sub-region.[57] Additionally, the former Executive Director of the UNODC, Yury Fedotov, expressed concern about drugs and crime in West Africa while briefing the United Nations Security Council (UNSC) in 2012. According to Fedotov, some 30 tons of cocaine and almost 400 kilos of heroin were trafficked through West Africa in 2011, and methamphetamine laboratories had been discovered in the sub-region.[58] For its part, ECOWAS acknowledged that drug trafficking is an enemy of the state and the rule of law, existing as a parallel power that rivals the legal system, making overcoming it imperative.[59] While the associated local drug consumption levels are worrying, the potential for corruption and state capture as well as other governance deficits including violence and money laundering could paralyze governments in the sub-region.

For example, the involvement of AQIM operatives in the Sahel, crossing the sub-region from its northern parts to the south to purchase drugs, heightens the security dilemmas of the region. In Mauritania, Niger, Mali, and Ghana, AQIM operatives have initially been arrested on drugs charges, with terrorism charges eventually added on. The nexus between narcotics dealers and terrorists is thus becoming clearer as criminal organizations in several West African states work with affiliates or sympathizers of AQIM to ship drugs to North Africa and onward to Europe.

On the consumption side, the World Drug Report published by the UNODC combines West and Central Africa in its desegregated analysis of global geopolitical drug demand and supply. According to the 2019 edition of the report, which captures data from 2013–17, the global death toll from drug use is on the rise, as 585,000 people died as a result of drug use in 2017. The report continues that 'prevention and treatment continue to fall far short of needs in many parts of the world. This is particularly true in prisons, where those incarcerated are especially vulnerable to drug use and face higher risks of HIV and hepatitis C transmission.' According to the report, between 25.7 million and 26.7 million people in West and Central Africa use cannabis annually, and between 1 million and 250 million people use cocaine. Furthermore, the report continues that between 300 million and 580 million people in the region inject drugs annually, while a further 16–50 million people who inject drugs suffer from HIV and hepatitis C.[60]

There is thus a very high rate of cannabis use in West Africa, and a rising usage rate for cocaine. Such sizable and surging consumption trends, in addition to the methods of use, have a wide range of adverse health consequences, including the transmission of HIV infection through injected drugs and the spread of AIDS.[61] The above notwithstanding, structures for dealing with addiction are insufficient,[62] prompting a 2013 African Union (AU) Conference of Ministers of Drug Control to stress that grouping drug users together with people with major psychiatric disorders runs the risk of turning people off from seeking treatment and obfuscates the specificity of care that drug addiction requires.[63]

The West African Response Framework

West African states have adopted a number of policy, legal, and institutional measures in response to drugs control in the sub-region. In December 2008, the ECOWAS summit adopted a political declaration on the prevention of drug abuse, drug trafficking, and organized crime in West Africa, pledging to accord drug control the priority it deserves at the highest level of government in member states as well as at the ECOWAS Commission. Several other narcotic drugs-related decisions of ECOWAS were:

- Resolution relating to Prevention and Control of Drug Abuse in West Africa (ECOWAS 1997).
- Recommendation C/98 on the establishment of a Regional Fund for Financing of Drug Control Activities in West Africa.
- Decision on the establishment of a Regional Fund for Financing Drug Control Activities (ECOWAS 1998).
- Decision on establishing the Inter-Governmental Action Group against Money Laundering in West Africa (GIABA) (ECOWAS 1999).

In 2007, following reports on rising drug seizures at ports in the sub-region, ECOWAS heads of state and government expressed serious concern about the expansion in drug trafficking.[64] As a result, the ECOWAS Commission was mandated to take urgent action. GIABA was authorized to determine the scale of the problem, using the recommendations arising from its activities to subsequently prepare for ECOWAS' strategy. As a result of this background preparatory work, two initiatives were undertaken. The first was a civil society organizations meeting on drugs in Abuja, Nigeria, on 16 October 2008. The second was the ECOWAS collaborative regional ministerial conference on drug trafficking and control in October 2008 at Praia, Cape Verde, with the assistance of UNOWA, UNODC, and the EU. It was titled 'Drug trafficking as a security threat in West Africa.' An outcome draft document later transformed into the Political Declaration cited above. In the operative sections of the Political Declaration, the ECOWAS Commission was directed to establish:

- A strong coordination mechanism to forge close links with member states government and civil institutions and organizations involved in drug control in order to achieve better coordination in the control of drug trafficking and abuse in the sub-region, and for that purpose.
- An ECOWAS Drug Control and Crime Prevention Division responsible for the overall coordination of regional initiatives undertaken in the area of drug abuse and crime prevention, treatment, and rehabilitation as well as the collection and analysis of data on crime and drug phenomenon in the sub-region.
- '[A]n appropriate structure under the direct supervision of the President of the ECOWAS Commission, responsible for overall coordination and monitoring of regional initiatives undertaken in the area of drug trafficking and drug abuse prevention.'
- The Crime Prevention and Criminal Justice Center (ECPCJS)[65] to serve as a focal point for mutual legal assistance both amongst ECOWAS members and non-members.
- The Department of Peace and Security under the Office of the Commissioner for Political Affairs, Peace, and Security (PAPS) was tasked with facilitating the formation of the Network of Drug Law Enforcement Agencies/Units within the framework of the West African Joint Operations for the coordination of efforts to combat drug trafficking and related transnational organized crime in the ECOWAS sub-region.

The most important aspect of the new ECOWAS approach is the responsibility by each individual state in addressing the issue. In other words, the regional solution will be the addition/result of the efforts made at national level.

The above measures have underlined the emergence of national technical focal agencies focusing on such targeted thematic issues as financial intelligence and economic and organized crime control. However, many of these national agencies display an inconsistent operational visibility—that is, they are under-resourced, unknown to the public and struggle to be accommodated within the national security agency set ups. There are a few exceptions—for example Nigeria, where the economic crime office successfully prosecuted high-profile cases and in doing so, asserted its relevance to Nigerian society.

The Situation in West Africa

In terms of the conditions that make the West African sub-region ideal for narco-trafficking, West Africa presents an ideal geographical choice for the narcotic drugs trade. As a result, it could become a space for unrestricted and indiscriminate illicit consumption of narcotic drugs were they to be decriminalized, as a result of the fragile capacities of the constituent states with weak public health infrastructure and porous land and sea borders. Furthermore, West Africa's numerous archipelagoes provide a safe haven for traffickers to elude detection. Again, West Africa already serves as a logistical hub and transit center for drug traffickers. Its geography, particularly Guinea-Bissau and Cape Verde, with their numerous uninhabited islands and archipelagos, alongside the sparsely populated but vast and unmanned territories of the Sahel, makes detection difficult and facilitates transit. The region boasts well-established networks of West African smugglers and crime syndicates,[66] and a vulnerable political environment that creates opportunities for such operations. In several West African countries, protracted civil wars, insurgency operations, and *coups d'état* have led to instability and diminishing human capital, social infrastructure, and productive national development assets. These phenomena have coincided with an increase in the number of armed groups operating in the region and an increase in flows of Small Arms and Light Weapons (SALW). Additionally, instability in North Africa and its subsequent impact on Mali has triggered flows of heavier weapons through the Sahel region and enhanced access to arms by violent groups, including terrorist groups.[67] In the case of Mali, drug traffickers have often exploited such instability to further their own interests. Armed groups, including terrorist groups, also pose significant transnational threats to both the traffickers and the states and peacekeepers in the sub-region. The Malian State, in particular, faces a challenge to its stability both from the influx of multiple trafficked goods and from the relationships among such groups as they intermingle with local communities, often providing safe passage and protection to traffickers in exchange for a percentage of the total face value of the trafficked goods, including narcotic drugs. Thus, there is an emerging intersection between drug trafficking and the expansion and variation in the activities of terrorist groups in West Africa. For example, the *modus operandi* of AQIM for funding its activities was once kidnappings—particularly of foreigners—and the protection of smuggling rackets in the Sahel. Since 2009, it has changed its operational tactics, extending its spheres of influence and activities to the more southerly states in West Africa. In the process, it has widened its range of commodities of value to include narcotics, petrol, migrants, and cigarettes as an economic resource mobilization strategy.[68]

The governance landscape in West Africa can be characterized as being under serious threat. The fragility of states in the region is deepening, especially in those states that are undergoing reconstruction from years of conflict and civil war. Most government institutions and agencies—for instance, the security services and judiciary—continue to be ineffective, inefficient, non-functional, corrupt, and subject to political manipulation and intimidation, making the state a threat to its own self.[69] In Guinea-Bissau, for example, endemic corruption in the military, judiciary, and civilian administration have made these institutions easy prey for outside criminal networks and drug traffickers.[70] Additionally, high-level elected officials and security personnel were found to be involved in a range of cocaine and heroin trafficking seizures in the late 2000s, indicating that both the formal and traditional governance and security systems of many West African countries are at risk from international drug trafficking cartels. Recent seizures and arrests in Guinea-Bissau and other West African countries have shed further light on how the work of trafficking networks are facilitated by a range of actors, including businessmen, politicians, members of the security forces and the judiciary, clergymen, traditional leaders, and youth.[71]

Apart from Nigeria, Sierra Leone, and Togo, none of the fifteen ECOWAS countries have dedicated areas of national budget to the treatment of drug-related illnesses.[72] These multifaceted challenges threaten the abilities and capabilities of the national drug-related technical agencies to function effectively on their own in the sub region.

What Opportunities Exist?

During the 2010s, the UNSC periodically discussed the growing threat posed by drug trafficking in West Africa and the Sahel region. The AU and ECOWAS expressed similar concerns. These concerns led to the adoption of several UN Security Council Presidential Statements in which the UN Secretary General was urged to consider mainstreaming the issue of drug trafficking into conflict prevention strategies, and integrated missions assessment and planning and peacebuilding support.

i. Narcotic Drug Control Regime in West Africa

The UNODC is the foremost UN technical agency assisting ECOWAS member states in the fight against drugs. Its medium-term strategy was adopted by the CND and the Commission on Crime Prevention and Criminal Justice, and is reflected in ECOSOC Resolution 2007/19. This resolution provided the overall results-based framework guiding the programmatic activities of the UNODC for the period 2008–11. It continues to operationalize its strategy through thematic and regional programs. While the thematic programs provide the framework for operationalizing the priorities laid down in UNODC's medium-term strategy, the regional programs operationalize the strategy geographically. Between 2008 and 2011, the thematic priorities of the Office related to organized crime, corruption, terrorism, criminal justice and reform, health and human development, anti-money laundering, and human trafficking. It pursued these priorities through advocacy, research, legislative and legal support, norm setting, and technical assistance.

In West Africa, the UNODC was instrumental in the processes leading to the adoption of the 'Political Declaration on the Prevention of Drug Abuse, Illicit Drug Trafficking and Organized Crimes in West Africa' in 2008. Among many other provisions, the Declaration calls upon 'Member States to develop and implement comprehensive and integrated National Drug Control Master Plans to tackle the drug problem in the short and long-term, with the support of local and international development partners and other relevant stakeholders' and to 'Take appropriate steps to make health care and social support available, affordable and accessible to those who abuse drugs and those dependent on drugs.'[73]

Subsequently, UNODC developed a plan of action jointly with the ECOWAS Commission for the period 2008–11. The Plan of Action was renewed indefinitely in 2012.[74] The Plan of Action has five thematic areas, focusing on: mobilization of national political and financial commitment; law enforcement and national/regional cooperation against drug trafficking and organized crime; effecting criminal justice; health and security problems associated with drug use; and reliable data gathering mechanisms for gauging the magnitude of drug abuse in West Africa. From the perspective of demand reduction, only one of the five objectives address health and security-related issues of drug users. In other words, the work of the UNODC relating to demand reduction is yet to manifest itself on the ground. Its impact in terms of empowering national actors to confront the international drug problem from the perspective of demand reduction remains a work in progress. Largely due to the nature and dynamics of the illicit drug environment in West Africa discussed above, demand reduction interventions in the sub-region remain low,[75] and there have been several seizures across the sub-region that point to complicity of individual national officials.[76]

This chapter has reviewed the context of West Africa in light of the ongoing debate as to whether or not to decriminalize narcotic drugs. Much ground has been covered in terms of the limited capacities of states in West Africa against the background of rising illicit drug use in combination with limited demand reduction measures to address issues of prevention and treatment. This chapter has also argued that, because of the limitations of the African state and the existential threats posed to West Africans by drugs, it is imperative to securitize the problem of narcotic drugs—though from a people-centered perspective. This would give the drug problem the remedial attention it needs, and thus, at least in the short term, seems more adequate than decriminalizing drug use without assuring the safety of drug users in the sub-region.

8

THE CRESCENT THREE STATES
WHICH WAY TO GO?

Philip Robins

It is welcome that a volume like this, dealing honestly with the past and debating the practicalities of the future, includes a chapter on the Middle East; so many comparable works do not.[1] Historically, countries like Iran and Turkey were major opiate producers, stretching back to an era well before the creation of the International Drug Control Regime (IDCR).[2] At the same time, the Middle East was also a significant focus for consumption. Who amongst those who have studied the phenomenon could forget the dual onslaught on Egyptian society in the 1920s and the 1930s from the 'white drug habit,'[3] combining opiates and coca?

Hashish, meanwhile, has become so ingrained in the social habits of certain parts of the Middle East—Egypt again—that it has become part of the national identity of many of its peoples, with even the urban poor saving up to purchase hashish for their wedding breakfasts. Only since the 1980s has the illicit drug spread deeply and widely across the region—notably among the Gulf Cooperation Council (GCC) states[4]—and become subject to the more punitive side of the IDCR response. In short, for these states drugs policy in the region has been both belatedly policy-ized,[5] and so transformed as to become effectively 'Americanized.'[6] Yet this has come at a time when the drugs response has been distinctly softened, at least in some non-Middle Eastern state contexts, notably South America.

Despite this auspicious point of departure, a focus on the region as a whole is required. The conception of the 'Middle East' briefly set out here has been confined to the countries of Afghanistan, Iran, and Pakistan, the 'C3.' Without being overly deterministic, as the field of 'critical geography' warns us against, one could argue that Afghanistan is generally regarded as a Central Asian nation, though it is without the rigid klepto-states that spring to mind regarding the sub-state system of Central Asia. Meanwhile, Pakistan belongs indubitably to South Asia.

Iran may be viewed—for example, because of the location of the Shia shrines in southern Iraq—as more clearly 'at home' in the Middle East. But in privileging geopolitics in this way, we would ignore the ethnic link between Iran and the fellow Shia, ethnic Hazara people of western Afghanistan.

This chapter argues we would do much better to conceive of Iran in more inclusive terms, as being a 'cusp state'[7] rather than belonging exclusively to the region of the Middle East—or indeed Southwest Asia, or any other restricted geographical expression that constrains our mental maps. Iran can plausibly claim to be part of multiple international sub-state systems, and that should be seen as a boon.[8] Moreover, as a cusp state Iran could be regarded as fitting into a range of different international regimes, unlike if it were merely a 'milieu state,'[9] strongly anchored in a single regional context.[10] If Iran had played its hand more deftly in terms of statecraft than it has often done, it might actually have found itself less frequently sanctioned by the international community than it has at various times since the 1990s.

This chapter will primarily focus on the C3, namely Afghanistan, Pakistan, and Iran. Afghanistan is clearly key, as the dominant hub relative both to neighboring countries and competitor producers in more 'faraway places' such as Myanmar. It will also include a consideration of Pakistan and Iran, the neighbors of Afghanistan most affected by its drug domination and lying adjacent to the Muslim Middle East (see Chapter 10 by Ekaterina Stepanova for how Russia is affected by Afghanistan's drug domination). The chapter will culminate by relocating Afghanistan and its woes in a mixed context of interregional competition and rivalry, then return to the Middle East, NGOs and states as a whole.

In the process, this chapter will make three broad arguments relating to the IDCR and the countries under review. First, it argues that in spite of the centrality of Afghanistan to the world opiate market today, it is only since 1979 and the Soviet invasion that it has had to confront such multiple, apparently intractable issues as persistent political violence or the fear of it.[11] Afghanistan therefore remains surprisingly inexperienced, especially at the state level, as far as drug-related issues are concerned.

Second, it contends that—as befits countries with a highly distinct set of social mores, cultural values, and circumstances such as tribalism, chronically endemic poverty, and the use of violence in seeking to realize a range of political goals—the societies concerned tend to reproduce themselves at moments of challenge and crisis, such as in the assertion of national preoccupations in areas like judicial conduct.

Third, it holds that countries coming to the challenge of the IDCR relatively late in the day have tended to rely much more on hard power solutions than their soft power equivalents, such as the adoption of the rule of law.

Output Increases

Since 2002, Afghanistan, Iran, and Pakistan have consistently accounted for more than 90 per cent of the global quantity of opium seized by law enforcement each year.[12] More than two-thirds of that amount comes from the deadliest of the Afghan provinces, Helmand. As for the Middle East overall, or even the Middle East and North Africa (MENA) countries generally, no dedicated country statistics are produced by the UN or any other agencies. The largest reduction in illicit morphine took place in Afghanistan, where it fell from 44 tons in 2012 to 24 tons in 2013.

It is not surprising that the countries that we refer to collectively as the 'developed world' still dominate the conduct of international affairs in its many practical dimensions. In the case of illicitly used drugs, this has been the case even more acutely. For example, the European powers played a prominent role during the life of the League of Nations during the interwar years. However, this reflected a rare institutional success for a multilateral organization, the reputation of which has tarnished since its demise in 1946.

The developing world has played a more dominant role since the end of the Second World War and the incorporation of all of the leading world states into a multilateral framework through the UN system and notably through the world's two superpowers, the United States and USSR. This power dynamic also applies to the less tangible sphere of world narratives, where the United States has been the dominant storyteller, whether of narratives based on events generated domestically, hemispherically, globally, or synthesized as a combination of these.

Nothing breeds success like success. The capacity and overall comparative effectiveness of the developed world makes it more likely to be able to accentuate that structural advantage. It has done so both coercively and diplomatically. The former has best been accomplished through the phenomenon that the US' Drug Enforcement Administration (DEA) has become. With regard to the leadership of the US in the elaboration of a set of diplomatic structures, and the norms and ideas that underpin them, neither the operationalization of diplomacy nor that of military power can be properly replicated by the underdeveloped world.

There have been marked changes in the production levels of opiates in Afghanistan. The pressure applied by China on neighboring producer countries in the Golden Triangle to desist from previous levels of production partly explains this.[13] This has taken place without there being any commensurate change in the opiate production levels in the Golden Crescent area, of which Afghanistan is the dominant player.[14] By 2007, Golden Crescent countries were producing some 92 per cent of the world's opium.[15]

The vast majority of these narcotics have been trafficked abroad, either via Iran through the Afghani province of Nimruz and then to

Europe, or by ships bound for further afield.[16] As with Pakistan and Iran, however, increasing volumes of drugs are staying on home turf, where they are consumed by younger men in particular. Opiate users are even to be found in the squalid residences of central Kabul. These young people have often turned to drugs because of some family catastrophe, such as an unscrupulous family member or parents who have died prematurely. Some drug users began consumption when they were as young as eight, sometimes prompted by family members determined that they be forced to work harder.[17]

Many drug-dependent Afghans have spent much of the last 30 years in Iran and Pakistan, where addiction rates have historically been high, in order to escape violence at home. Recently, such users have been returning home, bringing their addiction with them. There are now an estimated 1.3 million heroin users in Afghanistan, representing a roughly tenfold increase in consumption compared to the 130,000 people using the drug in 2005. As of 2016, 1 gram of heroin cost around US $6, and was available easily in the capital. Unemployment rates ran at an estimated 40 per cent of the population, which numbers 35 million people, in a symptom of the almost complete collapse of the Afghan economy.

The original US-led invasion of Afghanistan took place in 2001 in the aftermath of 9/11, as the Taliban drew opprobrium for its support for the forces of AQ.[18] The United States and the United Kingdom took heavy casualties while trying to pacify these areas in the early 2000s, having first been distracted by the US government's preoccupation with invading Iraq in March 2003. Subsequently, the US concentrated on the south of the country, where casualties were more manageable. The German and other ISAF (International Security Assistance Force) contingents—which were roughly 140,000 strong—concentrated on the north of the country and tended to avoid engagement.[19] The former President Obama oversaw a withdrawal of the ISAF forces, putting a debacle of some kind or other firmly on the cards. However, it was at least something short of that which took place.

The Taliban became divided as it sought a stable leadership successor to Mullah Omer. Mullah Mansour, who was reportedly close to Pakistan and the notorious Pakistani intelligence service (the IRI), took over initially, but was killed by a US drone on 22 May

2016 having apparently been under close surveillance for some time. Military confrontations resumed between the Taliban and state forces. Meanwhile, the US provided a fighting capacity comparable to that of the state.

Before the signing of the 'agreement for bringing peace' between the United States and the Taliban on 29 February 2020, attempts to generate peace talks on the ground were largely ineffectual. A mentality of trial by strength continued to dominate the landscape. An ad hoc body, named the Quadrilateral Coordination Group, was selected to explore ways of moving the peace process forward. It comprised officials from the US, Afghanistan, China, and Pakistan. Greater US flexibility on the presence of Iran, in particular, would have shown a lesson learned from the Syria peace talks, which saw hundreds of thousands of Syrian civilians perish before Iran and Syria were invited to attend in their own right.

The presence of China, together with the United States, as members of the formal Group was encouraging. Such a strong axis certainly has mediatory potential. However, despite the agreement reached in 2020, it is likely that much more suffering will be sustained in Afghanistan and Pakistan before the dispute can be labelled 'ripe' for resolution.

Afghanistan: The Focus of Opiate Destructiveness[20]

Unlike Iran and Turkey,[21] Afghanistan has 'little deep history'[22] of mass long-term cultivation of opium poppy. As such, Kabul's 'current hegemonic position' is 'only marginally rooted in history.'[23] It is only since the early 1970s that Afghanistan has emerged as a player of deep and enduring importance,[24] though in this case as a sub-state body, and not in itself as a 'narco-power.' This occurred because of the instability in the Golden Triangle countries located in Southeast Asia, exacerbated by opiate bans in Iran and Pakistan. It is therefore untenable to argue historicist inevitability when trying to explain the country's domination of the market.

It seems likely that Afghanistan will remain the most significant producer of poppy due to a complex interplay of elements. Afghanistan's emergence as an important center of poppy production is closely connected to a handful of national and sub-regional key factors. These include: state collapse (notably in 1996 at the hands of the *mujahidin* [mujahideen]); intermittent violence; desperate and entrenched levels of rural poverty; and invasion, notably at the hands of the Soviet Union in 1979 and the United States in 2001, when the firepower of the Afghans was massively dominated by those of the superpowers. The illegal drugs trade accounts for between 25 per cent and 33 per cent of the Afghan economy's total worth. As the vicious cycle has tightened, so illicit drug cultivation has become more difficult to shake. To quote the British drugs expert on Afghanistan David Mansfield 'poverty and poppy are intrinsically linked.'[25]

The expert community of those working on the vexed issue of crop spraying remains fundamentally divided. Allied to this debate is the issue of which chemicals could or should be considered for spraying purposes. Vying for policy supremacy is another, secondary clash, over the context in which such a policy should be played out. While some view spraying as best suited to policy elaboration, others argued for a security-focused framework.[26] When this argument surfaced around David Mansfield's work in 2010, it was never decisively put to bed. While Mansfield was clearly reluctant to flatly endorse eradication of poppy crops, a limited form of agreement was endorsed as long as the tactic was used 'strategically.' The international community seeks to re-establish the official state in Afghanistan, and thus hopes to once again break the power of the narco-state.

The nature of production has remained broadly constant over time. On pain of a punitive response, farmers are incentivized to sell their opium poppy at the 'farm gate.' They do so not necessarily out of any partisan moral stand or loyalty to their local political masters, but simply as a response to the shape of the prevailing rural political economy. It is a more mundane, though highly strategic calculation, concerning the notable shortage of credit available in the agrarian economy. This is used to create rural dependencies, which are necessary if farmers are to have access to the supply of seeds, fertilizer, and other primary inputs in time for the following year's harvest. The provision of essential inputs also helps to undermine other provisions, such as the alternative cropping method. It is generally agreed that wheat is the most viable of these alternatives. Other more recent examples, such as saffron, have been attempted, but apparently without success.

Taken together, the impact of the changes has been to establish what retired British spymaster Nigel Inkster has called 'a shadow state,' incorporating a 'widespread culture of impunity.' These dependencies are multiplied when one realizes that they are supplied by middlemen who know that most farmers do not have any sustainable methods for getting crops to markets. The prolonged period of civil conflict has resulted in the erosion of an already chronically poor security environment and infrastructure framework, from which the country has progressively suffered. This includes the quality of the rural road system, essential if crops are to be successfully transported to the market.

The middlemen pay a *de facto* 'tax' to whichever militia grouping has most reliably been able to deliver 'security' for the drugs consignments on the ground. Since 1996, that militia has been the Taliban. Increasingly since the early 2000s, Afghan groups have succumbed to the market-style logic of the treatment of opiates through a process of 'vertical integration' that facilitates the acquisition of a dominant position in the drugs production and supply process. Increasingly, the opium is refined into morphine base. Opium labs have increased in number in order to boost output, warehouse effectively and increase the speed and maneuverability of drugs distribution.[27]

The only time this model faltered was in 2000, when Mullah Mohamed Omar, the so-called moral head of the Afghan Taliban, issued an edict stating that opium was un-Islamic. This resulted in a moratorium on cultivation which saw output slide to 185 tons in 2000–1.[28] In a demonstration of how—under the right circumstances—it is possible to 'buck the market,'[29] the Taliban used their considerable monopoly on violence almost unilaterally to ensure that there would be no harvest comparable to previous years. As ever, it was a challenge to infer the reasoning behind such a move. The most plausible interpretation is that the organization were looking to curry political favor. Up to that point, the Taliban government had only been formally recognized by Pakistan, Saudi Arabia, and the UAE. Soon after, the 9/11 atrocity took place at the hands of AQ, with Kabul strongly implicated in the organization and funding of the attacks.

Impact from Outside

One might have expected that the quiet turbulence experienced around the future of the IDCR over the last few years would have provoked some considerable discussion about the future in the C3. However, there is little evidence to suggest this. The reason for such an omission has less to do with any ideological position in place, and more with practical issues of state capacity and what level of debate the C3 might be capable of generating.

For Afghanistan, which has been the most unpredictable of the C3 since the 1980s, issues to do with reform and change have had much to do with state size and fragility, and rather less to do with rational decision-making in the context of an engagement with public policy change. Whatever else might be taking place, if this is the nature of the research output, then it is a pity if it is resulting in an unwillingness or inability to contribute to the wider debate.

Such a contribution would otherwise be opportune. The future of the Afghan state is once again a source of debate. This is evident in the Obama administration's reluctance to ramp up US presence in the country, coming as it did against the sudden reinjection of insurgency that took place in Kunduz in September 2015. The US redeployment came against a backdrop of a serious and sustained program of training and investment, but one which failed to have a decisive impact on the robustness of the state against the challenges it faced. One of these has been the illicit drug trade, and the money laundering associated with it. Little was likely to come of the redeployment as a result. In 2020, then President Trump's decision to withdraw troops from Afghanistan changed the course once again, but will not necessarily bring any solution soon.

Toward Pakistan, the United States under Obama showed a comparable commitment to the installation of stability. However, Washington's impact was inevitably more circumspect than it was in Afghanistan. Hence the use of drone missiles for targeted attacks, as witnessed against Yemeni opposition and military leaders, rather than more mainstream political figures.

As far as drugs-related research driven by external parties regarding Iran is concerned, the promise is encouraging, though things are never quite as smooth as one might expect. Certainly, the presence of many multiple-tasked NGOs as a matter of routine is very welcome. Moreover, these bodies are to be active across society, regardless of whether one is focused on areas where there are more medical or sociological aspects to study. Owing to the scale of the problem of the illicit drug trade, it tends to be an area of societal activism that goes without interference from the hardline supporters of the regime.

Overall, the C3 states do not tend to concern themselves with drugs activism a long way from home. There is a deep and enduring preoccupation with the Muslim world and issues, such as Palestine, and their relationship with such matters. This is arguably less of a compulsion for the Iranian regime—as opposed to the populace— than either nationalist Pakistan or the totally distracted Afghanistan.

Likewise, there is little evidence that the C3 are seriously, profoundly, or continuingly engaged, especially in the major drugs-related issues of the day from a global or transregional perspective, such as cannabis consumption in Uruguay or study group meetings of former presidents. For both Afghans and Pakistanis there is no tradition of extended profile in Latin America. Iran on the other hand has such a broad profile, as suggested by the accusations of terror attacks in Argentina or attempts to muscle in on ad hoc partnerships like the BRICS countries, for instance over nuclearization during the first decade of the century. Nonetheless, though Iranians are genuinely preoccupied with the threatening nature of 'hard' drugs on their borders, this is not a pressing matter for the high politics of state, as nuclearization obviously would be.

Afghanistan is an incredibly important country geo-narcotically, especially as far as opiates—and more specifically heroin—are concerned. It is because Afghanistan is a weak and passive state that it is of interest to the states to be found all around it, and on the trafficking routes away from it. The Afghan state is mired in violent insurgency, chronic poverty, terrible uncertainty, and external intervention. With little capacity or opportunity to effect change, Kabul hardly has the luxury to be able to reflect on their drugs experience or policy.

The brief commentary above exposes the challenge facing the IDCR. On the one hand, Afghanistan has never been subject to as many or such intrusive interventions as with the IFOR involvement between

2001 and 2015—the policy was thrown somewhat into reverse by its partial return in 2015. However, the ability of the NATO-led forces to make an impact on the ground was negligible when compared to the resources committed and over such an extended period. If ever there was a demonstrable disequilibrium between the enormous costs, poor results, and disappointing outcomes of these interventions, it was Afghanistan.

Having established that there is great variation within the three states, and that despite being geographically proximate they lack 'shared stateness,' we may proceed to discuss whether or not the current IDCR is being implemented to the letter, or if its viability is already in doubt.

Pakistan: The Plunderer State

Mohammed Hanif has described Pakistan as a state made from plunder.[30] During the partition of India in the late 1940s, there was mass looting as those fleeing from indiscriminate violence risked losing their lives. Islamabad, the capital, was supposed to be land set aside for the benefit of working farmers. Those worthy aims have vanished. Most of the capital is now the preserve of the well-to-do. Corruption has fueled the transformation of agricultural land into upmarket dwelling places for the upper middle class. Politicians, generals, bureaucrats, and journalists were the main beneficiaries of the changing social class structure of the emerging state.

Meanwhile, the war in Pakistan has been raging since 9/11, the advent of the anti-terrorism age. During that time, American officialdom dubbed Pakistan 'a duplicitous partner.' The US subsidized the state in Pakistan to the tune of an estimated $33 billion, amidst repeated and fruitless attempts to start afresh. Pakistan's army and its intelligence have gone through the motions, though in reality they are said to seek to profit from contraband. Around one-third of all the drugs bound for Pakistan transit the coastal/interior area of Baluchistan. The big jump in the volume of drugs smuggling took place under the military dictatorship of the Pakistani president General Zia ul-Haq. Though Zia was killed in an air crash in August 1988, his political legacy has for the most part continued undisturbed.

Support for the insurgent Taliban came disproportionately from the madrassas in Baluchistan and Northwest Frontier Province, where the struggle for the future of Kashmir—the main leftover from the era of independence—is at its fiercest. The Pashtu ethnic and linguistic body deepened by common experience of a pared-back Islam and equally pared-back materialism were well placed to sweep across the border and join with their political allies the residue of their predecessors.

The Pakistani armed forces are organized, well equipped and well trained,[31] consisting of some 500,000 men. It has a track record of intervening in civilian national politics. India and Pakistan fought two wars during their early history. In 1971, there was a third, when India engineered the secession of East Pakistan (now Bangladesh), dangerously implying that Pakistan itself was not immune to division. Since then the India–Pakistan struggle has gone nuclear, increasing the potential strategic risk.

The Pakistani military enjoyed considerably more success in the resistance its intelligence wing, the Inter-Services Intelligence (ISI), mounted against the Soviet occupation of Afghanistan. This was partly because the ISI knew Afghanistan well. It would effectively dominate the resistance for the next two decades, while the political residue of its success is still discernible.[32] In the 1980s and 1990s, Pakistan's main politicians, Nawaz Sharif and Benazir Bhutto, complained that they had little control over the ISI. Money generated from drugs and criminal activities empowered the agency as a political force.[33]

In Pakistan, opium seizures increased in 2013 for the third consecutive year to reach 34 tons.[34] The previous year, the rate increased in Pakistan by 3.8 tons from 1.4 tons in 2012. Pakistan is part of the so-called 'southern route' which helps to facilitate the movements of opiates from Afghanistan either westward through Iran into Europe, or southward through the Gulf and into littoral states of the waterway (for the 'northern route' see Chapter 12 by Ekaterina Stepanova). The movement southward is facilitated by the large number of Pakistani expatriate workers who are employed in the Gulf states, despite the punitive risks of trafficking in these countries.

An estimated 600,000 Pakistani nationals become drug users every year. It is estimated that around 10 per cent of all college students are drug dependent.[35] Nearly half the country is illiterate. Around 20 per cent are generally malnourished. There is also a pronounced cross-over between opiate use and those who are HIV positive.[36]

To try to get to grips with the problem, the Pakistani government adopted what it labelled a Drug Control Master Plan in 2010. This represent attempts by the governments of Afghanistan, Iran, and Pakistan to identify ways of controlling drug trafficking, rehabilitating drug dependents, and creating public awareness about drug abuse. The aim of such cooperation has been to prevent drugs being smuggled from Afghanistan into its neighbors. Though valiant rhetorically, there are few signs that such aims can be successfully addressed. Afghanistan remains an intractable challenge for the C3 countries both at home and abroad.

Iran: The Idiosyncratic Actor

Third and most enigmatic of the C3, Iran remains nominally a revolutionary state and an Islamic state. The takeover took place in January 1979, following 2 years of turmoil. The revolution removed the serving monarch, Muhammed Reza Shah Pahlavi. The monarchy had existed in Iran for the best part of 2,000 years, though the Pahlavi dynasty itself had barely been in power for two generations. The Shah was eventually ousted by a rainbow coalition that included oil workers, politicized women, the left, and rural workers.

The Shah was weakened by a combination of factors. These included his close security association with the US, his terminal cancer diagnosis, and the fact that he had emasculated the military—his one ally—for fear that it might attempt to remove him. Chief among his adversaries were the Shia clergy and the 'bazaar,' whose trading interests had been threatened by the Shah's import substitution model of industrialization, which was a mainstay of his so-called secular, modernist 'White Revolution.'

'Hard' drugs had been available in Iran under the Shah for recreational purposes—principally in the form of opiates—particularly in the nineteenth century and around the time of the Second World War. It was even reported that the Shah himself liked to imbibe. A law was passed in 1955 to ban the cultivation of opiates. This was not by any means the first time an Iranian regime had attempted to assert its authority by

219

seeking to suppress the presence of drugs. The forces of conservatism and of radical change have vied to transform the country since the age of the pre-Pahlavi dynasty, the Qajars. This impulse is evident in the Shah's push for modernity in the early 1960s in opposition to the Shia clergy, in the clergy's own opposition to the 'Westoxification' evident just prior to the revolution, and in the zealotry of the 'Hanging Judge' Sadeq Khalkhali in the immediate aftermath of the revolution as he moved ostensibly to 'clean up' Pahlavi Tehran.

The definitive outcome of the revolution came in 1981 with the adoption of a restricted constitution, which held the values of Islam above all else. It was overseen by the dominant figure of the revolution, Ayatollah Ruhollah Khomeini, the revolution's leading clergyman. He would pioneer a new form of Shia Islamist government, *velayat-e-faqiq*. The leader of this Shia Islamist movement engineered a referendum outcome that would consolidate the political orientation of the revolution for two generations. However, this does not mean that the revolutionary outcome was popular, or had integrity. The Islamic Republic steadily became structurally unpopular due to a cluster of different factors, from regime corruption and the extensive use of capital punishment (for drug traffickers in name, but often with political activists in mind), through to the mass casualties sustained during the 1980–8 Iran–Iraq War. It is now estimated that the popularity split between pro and anti-revolution supporters is around 30 versus 70 per cent.

Meanwhile, the struggle for social power is as important as ever as far as the eventual fortunes of the revolution are concerned. This applies to the issue of drug policy at least as much as any other area. The Iranian regime believes it has a good story to tell, especially as far as improving its external relations are concerned. At least until the Trump administration began, both the United States and the United Kingdom broadly shared Iran's external policy. Throughout all the difficult days since the 2000s, and in contrast to disputes over human rights abuses, gay rights, and relations (or absence thereof) with Israel, not to mention nuclearization, the illicit drug trade was a rare and enduring example of a win-win benefit to both sides.

Take, for example, Iran's exemplary record on opiate interdiction. At 436 tons, Iran remained the country with the largest quantity of opium seized each year. In Iran, the volume of morphine seizures rose to 10.4 tons in 2016 from 7 tons in 2012. Most of these seizures were made without any substantial aid from those Western countries—or, for that matter, regional powers such as Saudi Arabia—all of which have much to gain from Iran's active cooperation.

It is doubtful, however, that the Iranian government will abandon its position any time soon. This is well illustrated by the nature of recent regime policy over the drugs issue, notably in the transition period between the liberal revolutionary Mohamed Khatami (in office, 1997–2005), and his successor, Mahmoud Ahmadinejad (2005–13), the hardline, regime anti-reformer. The former was long served by Mohammed Falah, the head of the Iranian Anti-Narcotics HQ. A progressive man who had, among other things, advocated and pursued a harm reduction strategy, he had been an effective advocate in discouraging Iranians from spreading drugs-related diseases.

When the Khatami presidency came to an end, it was widely supposed that a policy hardliner would replace Fallah, and indeed that was the initial outcome of the appointments procedure that took place. Speedily enough, a further round of hirings and firings took place. As the Ahmadinejad administration learned the range and depth of the problem at home, so the necessity of appointing a competent director who could implement a harm reduction program came to take priority. Heroin abusers who once faced capital punishment are now immune from arrest.[37]

Having said that, it would be misleading to suggest that Iranian anti-drugs policy is functioning in a joined-up manner, or that the situation on the ground is improving. Opiates have never been so prevalent in the country, especially heroin. The main concentrations of poor Iranians are resident in notorious areas, such as the slums of south Tehran. These areas are renowned for poverty and prostitution. Infamously in such areas, it is cheaper to pay for a wrap of heroin than to buy a beer.

Bringing the NGOs Back In

The chief, noteworthy exception to a growing hardline element in both state activism and policy engagement has been the emergence of NGO activism. The Middle East had no real tradition of independent

NGOs prior to the 1990s. Such bodies did exist, but they tended to be single-sector, corporatist organizations,[38] beholden to the dominant political regimes of the day. Pluralism or activism through competition was absent. It was only with the economic recession of the mid to late 1980s and the consequences of the First Gulf War in 1990–1 that the landscape began to seriously change.

As the broader prospects for change began to transform on the ground, so did the lot of the drugs-related NGOs. Initially, the change was represented by small, private technical organizations, often set up by those who had lost friends or relatives to drugs. An early leading light in the field was Um el-Nour, established in 1989. It was based on the Lebanese coast, gazing out onto the Mediterranean. By and large, these were low-profile organizations, mainly concerned with detoxification and rehabilitation rather than policy advocacy. And indeed, such bodies were often successful, though their modest size meant that there were unable to transform the situation. So, for the first two decades of its existence, Um el-Nour helped 3,305 people suffering from drugs-related afflictions, of whom 10 per cent were women.

The big breakthrough as far as advocacy was concerned also came from Lebanon, with the emergence of maverick anti-drugs campaigner, Elie Aaraj, who had been a small-scale medical activist in the 1970s. In 2007, he founded the Middle East and North Africa Harm Reduction Association (MENAHRA).[39] Immediately, the association's work gave it a regional platform. In turn, a more regional perspective on drugs helped to standardize the collection of comparable statistics. It also provided a forum for the regular exchange of response perspectives that could once again facilitate the work. Most importantly though, such activism helped the NGO communities to speak to the state both with authority and hard facts.

This is not to say that NGO activism has been straightforward during the 2000s and 2010s. As recently as the late 1990s, the small handful of Jordanian drugs charities would seek the permission of state figures before allowing interviews. Saudi Arabia's Wiqaya or the al-Anood Foundation are close today to where Jordanian organizations were then. The former exists to tap wealthy businessmen in order to fund mainly preventive work. The al-Anood, named after King Fahd's favorite wife, even had one of his sons, Prince Saud bin Fahd bin Abdul

Aziz, as its chief patron. However, this was not an automatic passage to funding and policy influence.

If any country has benefited from the expansion of the NGO sector in the region it is Iran, where the sector is both larger and more sophisticated than its counterparts to the west. There are many more dedicated drugs NGOs in Iran. They work at an outreach level in places like municipal parks, as well as providing palliative care. Interestingly, the use of Islam as an ideological support system is well established, and taken seriously. These techniques parallel other types of religiously motivated rehabilitation, such as the Christological programs in Beirut. Drug treatment services were developed in the early 2000s. Thousands of methadone clinics have been provided for, primarily in the private sector. There is also significant use of stimulants, notably crystal meth, in Iran. Concerns regarding the mental health of Iranians have arisen as a result.[40]

The Omitted Middle East: States and Societies Not Included

This chapter began by observing that studies of drugs in the Middle East are few and far between. They are hardly extensive wherever one looks. Iran arguably has the greatest, continuous coverage, reflecting its active status in the demand, supply, and trafficking domains. This is likely to continue. The Iranian authorities and the Iranian people have been striving to eliminate any or all of these stages for well over 100 years, hitherto to little profit.

Turkey is another country that receives research attention, though the focus is much less extensive than Iran's. It may be the case that as people trafficking from Turkey with the target destination of Western Europe has become something of a *cause célèbre*, the commodity trade will switch from people to narcotics. It is certainly the case that it is easier to smuggle heroin than humans, both because of physical scale and—dependent on other factors as well, like price—the margins that can be made on such criminality.

The fortunes of trafficking bring us back to the Middle East more generally. It has only been over a duration of perhaps three decades that opiates, and illicitly used drugs more generally, have become entrenched. Prior to the 1980s, drugs—mostly hemp-based—were modest in volume and smuggled from the Indian subcontinent for the specific use of Indian and other related migrant labor. As the numbers of laborers grew, and as the spending power of those in work also increased, so the supply and demand graph proved to be unstoppable.

The various states have broadly adopted two responses. The first was to ignore the phenomenon, based on the assumption that family cohesion and the prevalence of organized Islam would act as a warning to keep away from such socially undesirable activity. The state was lacking in its response, especially in the realm of health and law enforcement. There were few if any specialist medical personnel or detectives trained in investigative or laboratory activity. By default, those with drug problems had their condition problematized twice over. They were obliged to seek medical assistance in psychiatric hospitals, even though there were unlikely to be specialist medical facilities because addiction issues were so far from mainstream specialist medicine. Indeed, reports suggest that considerable stigma attaches itself in the region to the use of drugs when compared to alcoholism, the dominant specialism within the addiction branch of medicine, and one where there was no doubt about the Islamic invocation against the use of such substances.

Once states had transcended the non-engagement phase, so those like the Gulf states and others underwent a Jekyll & Hyde-style reaction within their individual jurisdictions. Their reactions largely took the form of a backlash, tending strongly towards the aggressive and the punitive. They increasingly came to resemble national security responses. Thresholds for punishment, notably incarceration and capital offenses, became hair-trigger decisions. Some of the responses were ludicrous. In Dubai, an automatic jail term of 4 years was triggered in the event of the discovery of cannabis residue on the exterior of some shoes.

Conclusion and Outlook

i. Afghanistan

Let us go back to the general fortunes of the C3, and the prospects for Afghanistan more specifically, in helping to concentrate our minds on the prospects for the future. Since the 2010s, it appears as if the council of despair has increasingly come to engulf the prognosis of illicitly used drugs. On the one hand, the growing intuition of former President Barack Obama was in favor of an early withdrawal of US forces, stating that American forces would be out by 2014. Meanwhile, the mood in the British foreign and security establishment was equally pessimistic. Obviously, the British could not go alone, like some nineteenth century colonial reprise. There was no third way.

There was, in any case, little appetite to continue on the part of the British following their extended and very bloody mauling at the hands of the Afghan Taliban in the southern province of Helmand.[41] When British views leaked out regarding prospects for the future they were usually clear, if not unequivocal. It has variously been referred to in apocalyptical terms as a 'War Without End?' or the 'unwinnable war on dangerous drugs.' A former British ambassador to Kabul, Sir William Patey, went even further and called to 'legalize the heroin trade.' This may not have been a particularly auspicious moment. But to paint Afghanistan as some sort of hopeless and never-ending conflict sounded like the box set of an Orientalist fantasy game, and hence was probably not particularly helpful.

If the Afghanistan conflict was unwinnable because of the nature of its physical geography, then unwinnability might well be part of the solution to the country's problem. If, on the other hand, part of Afghanistan's difficulties are the multiple problem areas that it faces—poverty, multiparty conflicts, and external interference—then concentrating on a single phenomenon such as war, conflict, or destruction may be the view of a struggle too narrowly cast.

Demonstrating that leadership and related issues are of central importance, sources on the ground—especially from among the Western law enforcement community in Afghanistan—hold differing views. They tend to differentiate the approaches of the two executive presidents over the issue of the illicit drug trade. Today's incumbent president, Ashraf Ghani, enjoys a reputation for being non-interventionist. This contrasts with his predecessor, President Hamad Karzai, a member of the Pashtun majority in the country. A third player on the domestic scene is the former foreign minister, Dr Abdullah Abdullah. Like Ghani, he is also a member of one of the minority constituent members of the Northern Alliance. He has not intervened to stymie any interventions.

The message most consistently emanating from among the foreign personnel based in Kabul and beyond is that corruption is the most endemic problem, interfering with benign attempts to improve the situation on the ground. Corruption is widely accepted as present in every transaction that takes place, whether in national government or in the negotiation of local contracts.

This situation is compounded by the fact that the associated problems of apparent sloth and incompetence help to crush attempts to move forward with virtuous initiatives such as the construction and creation of a stronger public sector ethos. Some Afghans, especially those working in the private sector, are viewed as inept and slow. This does not help the cause of those attempting to implement reform, especially if that involves the necessity for rapid reform.

Reform is moving at a slow pace. Such lack of speed causes immediate frustrations for the foreign donor community, because their time horizon is incredibly short. Ambassadors from the likes of the United States and the United Kingdom, and Western countries more generally, barely stay for a single year. Gone are the time horizons of the old colonial service, when an officer or official—think Thomas Russell in Egypt—might have dedicated most of their professional lives to the betterment of one country and one aspect of its affairs. As for Afghan officials, most honest educated officials have fled the country, either out of fear of attack, or because foreign jobs pay relatively well and are reasonably easy to secure, especially on the international quota system.

ii. Pakistan

Three crucial questions present themselves when seeking to evaluate the prospects for the relationship between drugs and society in Pakistan. First, can the strategic vulnerability of the Pakistani state and society—sandwiched as it is between a hostile India and a chronically weak Afghanistan—be ameliorated, especially in the areas beset by endemic levels of violence and the trafficking of opium poppy? (For a discussion of the concept of vulnerable regions see Chapter 1 by Annette Idler).

Second, in struggling to counteract this vulnerability, will the powerful ISI intelligence group permit itself to be dismantled or at very least brought under political control? The ISI enjoys a reputation for being unreformable. That reputation became more established and intractable through the 1970s into the 1980s, especially under the leadership of General Zia ul-Haq. That profile has grown over the course of the last three decades and will now be very difficult to throw into reverse.

Third, will the answers to the first two questions ensure that enough of a liberal democracy will emerge in the long run to secure the state from its enemies, whether they be tribal elements, Islamist militants, or simply greedy individuals and their institutions of rent-seeking support, like the military?

It remains the case that Pakistan's self-image is one of strategic vulnerability. That vulnerability originates from its adversarial relationship with India, and the wars that it has fought since independence. Their original relationship was a function of hostile relations which emerged in connection with the Kashmir question in the late 1940s following the partition of the Indian sub-continent.

Pakistan has been a democratic country, intermittently. One thinks of the two terms in office enjoyed by Nawaz Sharif's Muslim League, or the periods at the head of government led by the Pakistan People's Party. One thing that it has never enjoyed, however, is a liberal society. During the last government headed by Benazir Bhutto, for example, it became common knowledge shortly before her assassination that she had allowed her patrician husband of convenience, Asif Ali Zardari, to turn himself into a latter-day 'Mr. 10 per cent,' to his own eventual political and commercial benefit.

iii. Iran

The relationship between Iran and the US has been poor since 1979, ever since the Iranian people succeeded in ousting the last pro-US Pahlavi Shah. Coming at the height of the second Cold War, it was a strategic reversal of tremendous psychological impact, if not necessarily an entirely substantive one. Despite the absence of formal diplomatic relations, from the mid-1990s up until the Trump administration, the United States and Iran had been exploring ways in which the relationship might be stabilized and even improved. If truth be told, there were precious few ideas. In most realms, such as human rights and the Arab–Israeli peace process, the prospects for improvement seemed grim.

One area where potential exists has been in the realm of the trafficking and illicit use of drugs. Both Iran and the United States have serious drug problems. Both have massively expanded the law enforcement operations of the state to try to prevent 'hard' drugs flowing into the country. Interestingly, both states attempted to bring about reform in the operation of policy: for Iran, a persistence in the use of harm reduction; in the US, the medical use of marijuana.

A breakthrough came about in July 2015, when Iran and the United States concluded an accord to curtail Iran's alleged development of a nuclear capability.[42] It was widely assumed weaponization was set to follow. Subsequently, the preoccupation of both sides was speculation as to whether the other would allow them to implement the concessions permitted in the accord. For sure, neither side—the Supreme Leader's office or the US Senate—was uniformly euphoric about the plan. Both had suffered too much international embarrassment at the hands of the other side to expect a very warm reaction. For Iran, the negotiation was primarily about the removal of international economic sanctions. In the United States, the Obama presidency at the time was weak and could be exploited, as it was Obama's legacy that was of paramount importance. Even so, mutual convergence over the issue of illicit drugs as an important aspect of confidence-building measures was still very much in the fore. This changed again under former President Trump, with the United States withdrawing from the nuclear deal and re-imposing sanctions in 2018. From 2019 to 2020, tensions between Iran and the United States escalated further with the Persian Gulf crisis, when the United States built up its military presence in the region.

Can the two countries set aside 30 years of structural enmity? Can meagre levels of trust between the two sets of elites be enough to drive ahead with bilateral cooperation? If forced to choose between Iran and Saudi Arabia for cooperation, especially over the (Persian) Gulf, will Washington choose Tehran for preference?

9

THE GOLDEN TRIANGLE
REGRESSION THEN REFORM?

Pierre-Arnaud Chouvy

Mainland Southeast Asia is famous worldwide as the site of the so-called Golden Triangle, one of the two main areas of illegal opium production in Asia and one of the largest in the world, with Myanmar (also known as Burma) ranking second in the world after Afghanistan (670 tons of opium produced on 57,600 hectares in Myanmar in 2014 and 92 tons on 6,200 hectares in Laos).[1] While poppy cultivation and opium production had greatly abated in the Golden Triangle between the late 1990s and the mid-2000s, with a decline superior to 80 per cent, Burmese and Lao outputs respectively tripled and quadrupled between 2006 and 2014. This was in spite of multiple opium bans, numerous forced eradication campaigns and, to a lesser extent, various economic development efforts.[2] As Yury Fedotov, the former United Nations Office on Drugs and Crime (UNODC) Executive Director, emphasized, his agency's 2014 Southeast Asia Opium Survey 'shows that despite continued eradication efforts, opium production remains a significant challenge to sustainable development in the region;'[3] as if forced eradication had not been widely proven to be inefficient and even counterproductive, and as if economic development could only result from—rather than be a means to—drug supply reduction.

As Marina Mahathir stresses, 'More than thirty years ago when drug use and drug trafficking became an issue of great concern in Southeast Asia, governments responded by setting up the most punitive laws possible to control it.' Yet despite such laws, including the death penalty even for small-scale trafficking, 'the drug issue— production, trafficking, and consumption—in Southeast Asia has not gone away and indeed has only increased.'[4] If mainland Southeast Asia is infamous the world over for its large illegal opium and methamphetamine production, it is also known, despite few reliable estimates, for its very important consumption market of both opiates—especially in Malaysia, Burma, and Vietnam—and amphetamine-type stimulants, especially in Cambodia, Laos, and Thailand. The region and its constituent countries have implemented some of the world's most repressive and harmful policies and actions against not only illegal drug production and trafficking but also against illegal drug consumption.

The Association of Southeast Asian Nations (ASEAN) has long pushed for a zero-tolerance approach towards drugs in the region, something that has considerably affected the promotion of both alternative development (AD) programs and harm reduction and health-based addiction treatment services for drug users, especially opioid substitution therapies (OST) and needle and syringe exchange programs. As denounced by the International Drug Policy Consortium, 'the ASEAN drug-free target by 2015 has led to the intensification of ineffective law enforcement approaches with severe consequences on economic, health, and social issues, as well as jeopardizing the safeguarding of human rights.'[5] The failure of drug control in Southeast Asia is troublesome not only because illegal drug production and consumption have proven extremely resilient, but also because the inadequacy and the counterproductivity of most drug control policies and actions remains overlooked by large parts of the drug control community. In fact, the resilience—that is, the capacity to withstand perturbation and remain as or even more functional after disruptions of anti-drug policies and actions—of the illegal drug industry can be said to proceed from the vast array of unintended consequences of drug control policies and actions, and the ignorance of them.

The Golden Triangle: Nexus of Illegal Drug Production and Trade

The Golden Triangle, where most of the world's illegal opium originated from the early 1950s until 1990, before Afghanistan's opium production surpassed that of Myanmar in 1991, is located in the highlands of the fan-shaped relief of the Indochinese peninsula. The international borders of Myanmar, Laos, and Thailand run here; rugged hills and mountains, heavy monsoon rains, and lack of transport infrastructure have long protected rebel armies and illegal crop cultivation from the writ of central governments and anti-drug agencies. Yet after decades of the expansion of poppy cultivation in the three countries, opium production has progressively and momentarily receded, almost completely disappearing from Thailand in the 1990s, and seriously decreasing in Laos during the early 2000s. Regional poppy cultivation has abated, concentrating in northern and northeastern Myanmar, particularly in the Kachin and Shan states along the borders of China, Laos, and Thailand, where it had originated in the mid-nineteenth century after being imported from China.

Still, although Burmese opium production also decreased considerably between 1998 and 2006, it has—like that of Laos—proven to be geographically and historically resilient. Cultivation has reportedly almost tripled in Myanmar between 2006 and 2014 (from 21,600 hectares in 2006 to 57,600 hectares in 2014), even if it decreased again to 33,100 hectares in 2019. It quadrupled in Laos between 2007 and 2014 (1,500 hectares in 2007 to 6,200 hectares in 2014), then declined to 5,700 hectares in 2015 (latest available figures).[6]

Myanmar's turbulent political history since its independence in 1948 can be held responsible for Asia's longest illegal opium production: the opium economy and the war economy have clearly nurtured one another in a country that has suffered civil war for the past 60 years and where the world's longest armed insurgency is still taking place.[7] Indeed, as an extremely valuable economic resource, opium has often enabled warring factions to fund their respective war efforts. Opium production has also weighed upon strategic negotiations, offering both state and non-state actors opportunities to gain political leverage or create ad hoc strategic alliances.[8]

However, insofar as illegal activities are concerned, contemporary mainland Southeast Asia is known not only as a locus of illegal drug production but also as a drug trafficking hub and a significant drug consumer market; estimates report there are about 300,000 opiate users in Myanmar, a very high 0.80 per cent prevalence, surpassed only by Malaysia with 0.94 per cent.[9] Heroin and methamphetamine (*yaa baa*), an amphetamine-type stimulant, are produced mainly in Myanmar and trafficked heavily throughout the region. Heroin and methamphetamine are consumed regionally both in mainland and insular Southeast Asia, or exported to China via the province of Yunnan, to India via its northeastern states, or overseas, mostly to Japan, Australia, and North and South America.

Drug Supply Reduction in the Golden Triangle

The global regulation of opium production implies that opium poppy cultivation is forbidden, except for pharmaceutical purposes. However, opium control is not systematically or properly enforced everywhere: some countries lack the means—whether financial, material, or technical—to enforce anti-drug laws on their territory. Others suffer from having their writ challenged by anti-government forces and do not completely control their territory, and again others tolerate illegal crops in some sensitive areas of their territory, often out of (geo-) political realism—for instance, those states often and inaccurately called 'narco-states.'[10] Nonetheless, when these authorities that are confronted with illegal opium production become able and willing, for one reason or another, to enforce laws in all or part of their territory, they do it first and foremost by banning opium production.[11]

Opium bans differ from eradication, for they amount to interdiction of cultivation, not to forced destruction of standing crops. Successful interdiction results from the use of authority and power while forced eradication is achieved by force, although threat of force obviously makes bans more easily and widely respected. Therefore, a degree of political legitimacy is needed for opium bans to be issued, implemented, and respected.

Sixty years of Asian opium bans have demonstrated that drug supply reduction is very rarely effective—in fact, it is most often counterproductive. The Chinese 'success story' is unique because it took a full decade (the 1950s) to ban opium production, and because it was made possible by the very specific nationalistic and ideological context of the Chinese communist revolution. All other Asian opium bans were carried out hastily and with no or not enough economic alternatives. In Iran and in Turkey, the first opium bans failed, leading to renewed productions authorized by both governments (see Chapter 8 by Philip Robins). It took a theocracy to suppress opium production in Iran, at high human cost, and Turkey eventually opted for legal opium poppy cultivation; it is still a producer of concentrate of poppy straw for the pharmaceutical industry. In Afghanistan, the opium ban issued by the Taliban in 2000 basically failed out of success: the economic shock that it caused to the country and to the poorest of its farmers made the ban clearly counterproductive, as opium poppy cultivation expanded from 82,000 hectares in 2000 to 193,000 hectares in 2007, when the country's 8,200 tons of opium amounted to 93 per cent of global illegal opium production (see Chapter 8 by Philip Robins). Though Afghanistan's poppy areas fell by almost a fifth, from 224,000 hectares in 2013 to 183,000 hectares in 2014, 'the reasons for the dramatic reduction in cultivation do not lie with the actions of the Afghan government, or other external agencies, but with the repeated crop failure that has plagued the former desert areas of southern and southwestern Afghanistan.'[12]

According to the UNODC, in the late 2000s, Southeast Asia's Golden Triangle was near disappearing: Thailand had all but suppressed cultivation (and annual eradication campaigns are still conducted there), while Myanmar and Laos had significantly diminished their respective production. Yet many—including the UNODC—questioned the sustainability of these 'successful' opium bans, as AD was either absent or at least insufficient to make up for the loss of income of some the poorest of Asian farmers.

When opium bans are issued and implemented before alternative livelihoods have been promoted, developed, and made viable and sustainable, as it is too often the case, the very survival of most poor farming people is threatened: in the Wa region in Myanmar, for example, the UNODC explained that the opium reduction had resulted in a 'serious lack of cash, lack of food, and increased debt for many households' who ended being 'unable to purchase not only rice but also basic household necessities such as cooking oil, salt and clothing.'[13]

Most often, opium bans not only fail, prove counterproductive, and put countless lives at risk, they also go against the basic human rights and democratic values that the proponents of the global prohibitionist regime and the War on Drugs claim to be among their foremost objectives. Increasing poverty and threatening livelihoods is contrary to basic human rights. According to the Office of the United Nations High Commissioner for Human Rights, economic deprivation, understood as a lack of income, is a 'standard feature of poverty,' although 'poverty is not only deprivation of economic material resources but a violation of human dignity too.'[14] Most Asian opium bans have been and continue to be issued by authoritarian regimes in countries where human rights and democratic values are far from respected: this is the case in Myanmar, in Laos, in Thailand, and in Vietnam, to name only Southeast Asian countries. As opium bans are rarely efficient, even when imposed by authoritarian regimes, illegally cultivated crops are also often eradicated—that is, physically and forcefully destroyed before harvest.

Eradication is the forced destruction of a standing crop, whether manually (through the thrashing of poppy fields by hand), mechanically (through use of tractors, helicopters, planes), chemically (through use of herbicides such as glyphosate, paraquat, or Agent Orange), or even biologically (through use of fungi or mycoherbicides, also known as 'Agent Green,' such as *Pleospora papaveracea* against opium poppies or *Fusarium oxysporum* against coca bushes). Unlike opium bans, eradication relies on force and power, not on authority, and therefore easily leads to violence since—as has been the case in Thailand's Chiang Mai Province in 1967, in Pakistan's Swat Valley in the late 1980s, and in Afghanistan's Uruzgan Province in 2007—forceful destruction of standing crops is likely to be opposed by armed resistance.

Eradication also proves different from opium bans in that its consequences for opium farmers and their livelihoods are often worse.

234

Farmers who obey opium bans most often lose revenues, but not an entire crop; farmers who choose—out of conviction, fear, or relative economic ability—not to plant opium poppies in their fields can grow other crops; but farmers whose fields are eradicated lose an entire crop and often find themselves with no revenues at all. Worse, farmers whose fields are eradicated at a late stage, not long before harvest time, lose not only the various inputs—labor, seeds, water, fertilizers— invested in poppy cultivation, but cannot repay their debts when they have sold their crops in advance or have borrowed against takings, as is often the case for the poorest opium farmers in Afghanistan, Myanmar, and Laos. Eradication is therefore even more destructive than it first appears, as it basically targets the crops and the livelihoods of the most vulnerable segment of the drug industry: the farmers themselves and especially the resource-poor farmers among them (see Chapter 13 by Javier Sagredo).

Since opium production is a coping mechanism and a livelihood strategy that clearly proceeds from poverty and food insecurity, whether that poverty is war-related or not, eradication is likely to be counterproductive as it threatens highly precarious livelihoods, increases poverty, and raises opium prices. Yet, authorities often resort to and encourage eradication on the basis that opium farmers are breaking the law and expose themselves to legitimate repression. In this case, as with opium bans, a socioeconomic issue is addressed from a legal point of view: opium production is targeted as a cause of further problems (illegality, corruption, addiction, etc.) rather than as a consequence of other problems (poverty and low availability of physical, financial, and human assets). The causes of opium poppy cultivation are therefore ignored and even made more acute. Eradication is also promoted on the grounds that many opium farmers, whether in Afghanistan, Myanmar, or Laos, resort to opium production by choice (some say greed), and not by need. For example, in January 2007, the First Secretary for Counternarcotics at the British Embassy in Afghanistan stated in an interview about opium production in Helmand province:

> My feeling is that a lot of the poppy is grown here by people who are greedy, not needy, not by people who have to grow poppy. They're

growing it for a profit. They're not being forced to grow it, they choose to grow it, and they do it because they can get away with it.[15]

While some deny that opium production is linked to poverty, others contend that it is a cause rather than a consequence of poverty. There are those who argue that farmers, whether opium farmers or not, 'are rational economic actors with free choice over what crops they cultivate and who derive considerable riches from that choice.' According to such views, opium poppy is therefore 'a legitimate target for eradication—in fact, it is the only action that will deter farmers from the blind pursuit of profit.' To the proponents of eradication, 'the underlying assumption is that there are sufficient livelihoods available to farmers or that development agencies can "create" them quickly, providing "the carrot" to make "the stick" of eradication more politically acceptable.'[16]

Opium bans and forced eradication have long preceded economic development in drug control policies. In the early 1950s, China suppressed its massive opium production almost exclusively through an imposed ban that implied tens of thousands of arrests, thousands of capital executions, hundreds of thousands of propaganda and 'education' meetings, and a few eradication campaigns.[17] Yet, in the Yi areas of southwestern China, where opium poppies once covered up to 40 per cent of some counties' arable lands and where 50 to 80 per cent of local households (both Yi and Han) engaged in poppy cultivation, the authorities managed to reduce part of the cultivated areas by convincing Yi farmers to switch from opium to food crops.

Yet it was only years later, in 1972, that the world's first international crop substitution programs took place, in Turkey and, more significantly, in Thailand. Although the Single Convention on Narcotics Drugs was adopted in 1961 (ratified by Thailand in 1961 and by Turkey in 1967), the world's first development projects that aimed at reducing illegal drug crops were initiated in the early 1970s as a consequence of the strong anti-drug stance and focus of the Nixon administration. 1971 saw the official launch of the so-called War on Drugs by the Nixon administration and the coining of the 'Golden Triangle' expression by the US Assistant Secretary of State for East Asian and Pacific Affairs, Marshall Green (see Chapter 1 by Annette Idler).

The first international development project that was designed and implemented in order to reduce or suppress illegal agricultural production of drugs started in 1972 in Thailand (see Chapter 13 by Javier Sagredo). Until then, crop substitution had only been tried after opium bans were imposed, either in order to make forced eradication possible—as in the Yi and Tibetan areas of China—or as a way to make up for a brutal loss of income, as in Turkey. The fact that the first real crop substitution project took place in Thailand is easily understandable. Opium production had considerably increased in Southeast Asia following its suppression in China, spurring the emergence of the Golden Triangle. Production had hardly started in Pakistan, where prohibition was enforced only in 1980, or in Afghanistan, as Iran had just reversed its 1955 ban. Thailand, one of the very rare southern countries never to have been colonized, was a privileged partner in the US anti-Communist efforts.[18]

Thailand also experimented extensively with crop substitution and AD because of the very early personal involvement of its monarch, King Bhumibol Adulyadej (crowned in 1950), who initiated a crop replacement project as early as 1969 in an opium-producing village next to which he had recently built his new Phuping Palace. 'Among the most influential was his guideline that opium poppies not be destroyed until viable alternatives existed. The king realized that the radical removal of the hill people's source of income would imperil them.'[19] As a consequence, forced eradication would only be resorted to briefly in the early 1970s and would not resume before 1984, 12 years after the start of the first crop substitution project.

This was the first time that 'strategies were introduced to use development as an instrument of drug control.' Thailand would keep experimenting with development-based approaches to drug supply reduction for another 30 years and with resources never matched by any other country since. Crop substitution meant replacing opium poppies with crops that were legal, at least as lucrative as opium, not already overproduced in the lowlands, easily transportable to the lowlands, and easily marketable. Various crops were introduced in the highlands of Thailand in the 1970s, more or less successfully, and with unintended consequences—market gluts and decreasing prices, soil and stream pollution due to excess of chemical pesticides and fertilizers, etc.—including peaches, red kidney beans, cabbage, coffee, and cut flowers.[20]

Despite its initial promise, crop substitution quickly revealed its limits. Crop substitution indeed proved too simple—some would say simplistic—as development programs became focused less on the causes of poppy cultivation than on poppy cultivation itself: the main focus was on finding which legal crops could replace opium poppies, rather than addressing the causes of opium production in specific areas by specific communities. In Thailand and in the rest of the world— USAID started the first development project in South America's coca-growing areas in 1981, in Peru's Alto Huallaga Valley—the crop substitution approach was replaced in the 1980s by integrated rural development. From then on, 'the issue was less to find substitute crops than to introduce alternative sources of income and improve living conditions.'[21] Though it proved extremely useful, 'IRD (integrated rural development) as a development approach collapsed under its own weight.'[22] As a report on worldwide development practices stated: 'The projects were so complex that they were management nightmares, impossible to evaluate. Their long-term impacts were uneven, with some interventions being more effective than others in particular circumstances.'[23]

Therefore, the development approach to drug supply reduction was modified again in the 1990s and AD programs replaced 'integrated rural development' programs. AD programs differed from rural integrated development programs in their broader perspective, since 'the overall framework conditions for development' in a given country or area had to be taken into account and because AD had to be linked to 'other development issues and activities.'[24] At first altogether neglected in southern producing countries, then addressed as 'a medical problem in isolation from other development or community issues,' demand reduction was eventually added as a component of AD. In fact, both in Thailand and in Pakistan, the reduction of opium consumption had sparked an increase in heroin consumption and needed to be addressed in a socioeconomic way as well as medically.[25]

AD has been carried out in many unique ways, at different levels and times, through varying means in a range of countries and through an array of organizations and agencies. For example, the importance and timing of enforcement and repression (including forced eradication) has varied greatly from country to country.[26] Also, AD had come to 'mean different things to different people' in part because there was and still is 'no universally accepted definition of Alternative Development operating around the world across agencies and writers, despite the UNGASS definition of 1998.'[27] The Action Plan on International Cooperation on Eradication of Illicit Drug Crops and on Alternative Development, approved by UNGASS in 1998, defines AD as:

> a process to prevent and eliminate the illicit cultivation of plants containing narcotic drugs and psychotropic substances through specifically designed rural development measures in the context of sustained national economic growth and sustainable development efforts in countries taking action against drugs, recognizing the particular socio-cultural characteristics of the target communities and groups, within the framework of a comprehensive and permanent solution to the problem of illicit drugs.

The Action Plan further defines AD as 'a comprehensive approach of economic and social policy in view of generating and promoting lawful and sustainable socioeconomic options for these communities and population groups that have resorted to illicit cultivation as their only viable means of obtaining a livelihood, contributing in an integrated way to the eradication of poverty.' [28]

Yet in the early 2000s, 30 years after the UN and Thailand started the first international crop substitution project—and despite the lack of international consensus on what AD is—the surge of opium production in Afghanistan and the inefficiency of existing AD projects in Myanmar and Laos brought a new development concept to the fore.

After the crop substitution projects of the 1970s, the integrated rural development of the 1980s, and the AD of the 1990s, the record-high opium production in Afghanistan and the growing understanding that opium bans and forced eradication did not solve the causes of opium production—and often proved counterproductive—led to the emergence of the new 'alternative livelihoods' approach. Faced with renewed and unheeded opium bans, and with increasing but ineffective eradication campaigns, the 'emergence of an "alternative livelihoods" approach, which seeks to mainstream counternarcotics objectives into national development strategies and programs, is an attempt to respond to the causes of opium poppy cultivation and to create links with the wider state-building agenda.'[29]

This new approach is yet to be properly and successfully implemented in any country. It is true that the results of the economic approach to drug control have been rather disappointing, but AD cannot be dismissed altogether for having failed to address the illegal production of plant-based drugs. In fact, AD as a strategy has not failed because it was the wrong approach to drug supply reduction, but because it has barely been tried, and because drug supply reduction has constantly been considered distinctly from poverty reduction. While the links between poverty and agricultural drug production have been widely and convincingly demonstrated worldwide, drug supply reduction has mainly focused on interdiction and repressive measures such as crop bans and forced eradication. The vast majority of the funds, the material means, and human efforts that have been invested during almost 40 years of a global war on certain drugs have been used to design, implement, and reinforce repressive measures, which led to an increase in poverty—the main cause of illegal agricultural drug production—instead of alleviating it.[30]

Law Enforcement Against Drug Use

If drug supply reduction in Southeast Asia and elsewhere has suffered from its separation from poverty reduction, the same can be said of the difficulties faced by drug control policies and actions aimed at consumption. Indeed, drug consumption has long been and to some extent still is addressed not as a public health or a social issue, but as a matter of criminal justice: 'State responses to the phenomenon in the SEA region have been historically and still are largely dominated by penal considerations: arrest, fines, and varying periods of detention, criminal or administrative (whether in jail or under the guise of 'compulsory rehabilitation').'[31] Here, again, repressive measures can explain the failure and even the counterproductivity of drug control policies and actions.[32]

In Southeast Asia and China, the consumption of opiates particularly of amphetamine-type stimulants has always been addressed through the abstinence-based model, whether in jail or in compulsory detoxification centers. Repressive law enforcement measures and the large-scale incarceration of drug users have long been favored over harm reduction measures and other public health actions. In fact, drug users have been criminalized in the same way that opium farmers have been criminalized. Real drug wars have been waged at this level, such as when Thaksin Shinawatra, Thailand's prime minister (2001–6), launched the country's deadly War on Drugs in 2003. In a June 2004 report, Human Rights Watch explained that 'the government crackdown' in Thailand had resulted in the 'unexplained killing of more than 2,000 persons, the arbitrary arrest or blacklisting of several thousand more, and the endorsement of extreme violence by government officials at the highest levels.'[33] Yet most drug users interviewed by Human Rights Watch reported continuing to use heroin or methamphetamines during the drug war, 'albeit at a higher cost and less frequently.' The Thai War on Drugs largely failed, and as methamphetamine seizures kept increasing in Thailand, Thaksin had to call for a second War on Drugs in October 2004, this time with much less violence and publicity. Nevertheless, methamphetamine has still been widely produced in Myanmar and the rest of mainland Southeast Asia throughout the 2010s. Consumption and trafficking have risen so much that the *junta* [board] that seized power in Thailand in May 2014 perpetuated the previous harsh punitive measures aimed at drug peddlers, drug traffickers, and drug users—or at those even suspected of drug involvement. The *junta* declared a war on corruption and vice,[34] but not a new War on Drugs. Its anti-drug measures led to the arrest of close to 300,000 people (including about 140 officials) and sent over 200,000 suspected drug users in compulsory drug detention centers (CDDCs)—less than in 2013.[35] In the meantime, the *junta* seems to have acknowledged that waging Wars on Drugs was an ill-conceived, failed policy: in July 2015, Justice Minister General Paiboon Khumchaya declared at a public seminar that Thailand's long-lasting War on Drugs had failed, and that the suppression of certain drugs was a counterproductive policy goal that should be abandoned.[36]

In Thailand as in the rest of Southeast Asia, the War on Drugs is still largely a war on drug users and their criminalization has proved inefficient, if not counterproductive. As Fifa Rahman explains:

Criminal punishment of drug users has resulted in an undeniable social and public health cost. In recent times, however, there has been increased governmental and lawmaker understanding that a unilateral law and order approach to drug use simply does not make economic, social, and medical sense, and instead has resulted in increased crime, the spread of HIV, hepatitis C, and other blood-borne diseases, systemic human rights abuses, preventable overdose deaths, and numerous other social and economic costs to entire nations.[37]

Since the mid-1990s, ASEAN member states have increasingly relied on CDDCs—created in 1993 in Vietnam and as late as 2002 in Thailand—where confirmed (and even suspected) drug users are forcibly detained for rehabilitation.[38] Compulsory drug rehabilitation—or at least detention, since rehabilitation in such centers is very basic, if it exists at all—takes place in Cambodia, China, Laos, Malaysia, Thailand, and Vietnam,[39] where (according to the UNODC's latest data)[40] over 236,000 people were detained in over 1,000 CDDCs. Such detention is most often imposed 'without due process, legal safeguards, or judicial review.'[41] With very high relapse rates—70 per cent in Thailand and more than 95 per cent in Cambodia—due to treatments that are not evidence-based, and often administered by non-medical military or law enforcement personnel, CDDCs are known for being not only ineffective, but also hotbeds for violent treatment, human rights abuses, and high contamination rates of blood-borne diseases such as HIV and hepatitis C.[42]

Things are changing. A small decline in the number of CDDCs has been observed since 2011, and twelve UN agencies have issued a joint statement against such centers, calling on states to 'close compulsory drug detention and rehabilitation centers and implement voluntary, evidence-informed and rights-based health and social services in the community.'[43] Progress is clearly underway in the region; in Cambodia, the health ministry equipped approximately 100 health centers that implement 'community-based treatment' in 2017.[44] Vietnam wants to reduce its drug users held in CDDCs from 63 per cent in 2013 to 6 per cent by 2020, and Malaysia had converted eighteen of its twenty-eight CDDCs into Voluntary Cure and Care Centers by 2013.[45]

Yet progress is slow, and though most Southeast Asian countries have recently introduced and disseminated health care-based or medical approaches such as buprenorphine or methadone-based substitution therapies, most keep resorting to punitive drug control methods, notably in Vietnam where drug users remain subject to administrative detention for up to 2 years.[46] 'Because of important social, cultural, legal, or religious concerns, in all of these countries, the newly introduced health care or medical approaches did not replace but were allowed to coexist simultaneously with the traditional public security measures.'[47] This is in part because 'a significant barrier to progress is the difficulty in convincing policymakers of the need for the immediate closure of the CDDCs in the absence of adequate resources and facilities providing evidence-based treatment in the community,' and also because of the 'ongoing tensions' that exist between 'the public health imperative and public security concerns.'[48] In Thailand, progress is also on its way in the form of new legislation, which was being drafted in 2015 for submission to parliament. Thailand's law enforcement agencies now seem to agree that drug law reform is necessary and in his July 2015 speech, Justice Minister General Paiboon Khumchaya spoke of increasing voluntary rehabilitation services for drug users after acknowledging the failure of Thailand's compulsory rehabilitation system.[49] On 16 January 2017, the first amendments to Thailand's drug policy were adopted and implemented. The changes reduced penalties for possession, import and export, and production for sale.[50]

The situation in Southeast Asia is incredibly serious, whether on public health issues—most notably the propagation of the HIV and hepatitis epidemics among injecting drug users—or human rights violations, from compulsory detentions centers, to extrajudicial killings, to the death penalty. In October 2015, Jeremy Douglas, the UNODC Regional Representative for Southeast Asia and the Pacific, called for a shift from a 'sanction-oriented to a health-oriented approach to drug use and dependence' in an opening speech to the Regional Dialogue on Drug Policy and HIV in Southeast Asia. He stressed that

> it is clear that addressing the legal and policy barriers to accessing essential health services needed by people who use drugs is critical [because] these barriers result in people who use drugs facing stigma

and discrimination as well as criminalization and punitive policies being an entrenched part of the drug rehabilitation landscape in the region.[51]

The UNODC continues to call for a shift towards holistic and health-oriented approaches in national drug policies. In 2018, the Government of Myanmar and the UNODC collaborated on a new national drug policy that aims to contribute towards 'safe, secure and healthy communities.'[52]

Such calls for reform are all the more necessary when countries like Singapore, where 'the constitution does not contain any express prohibition against inhuman punishment' (torture is deemed inhuman but not the death penalty, even for drug offenses),[53] continues to praise ASEAN's zero-tolerance approach to drugs, stands firm against any legalization policies, and calls for the pursuit of the War on Drugs despite its obvious failure and likely counterproductivity.[54] This is what the second Minister for Home Affairs and Foreign Affairs of Singapore declared during the opening speech of the thirty-sixth ASEAN Senior Officials Meeting on Drug Matters (ASOD) in Singapore, when he renewed the vows for a drug-free ASEAN by 2015 despite the fact that the international and regional drug situation continued, in his own words, 'to be challenging, with higher production, higher trafficking, and higher consumption of heroin and methamphetamine.'[55] The Singaporean minister also stressed that the ASEAN is 'the only regional bloc that has maintained a drug-free focus' by strengthening its fight against the 'scourge of drugs.' He eventually warned other ASEAN member states against the reforms towards more liberal drug policies that are taking place in other regions of the world, and especially the 'de-criminalization of drug consumption.'[56] Such a statement shows how much drug control policies and actions still need to be reformed in Southeast Asia where most of the drug control bodies keep focusing on repression and criminalization of opium farmers and drug users.

The Build-up of Drug Control in Mainland Southeast Asia

In 1993, in an early step towards stricter drug control policies in mainland Southeast Asia, a number of countries, including China,

Myanmar, Laos, Thailand, and the United Nations International Drug Control Programme (precursor to the UNODC), signed a Memorandum of Understanding for Drug Control, to which Cambodia and Vietnam became parties in 1995. In December 1997, the ASEAN issued its Declaration on Transnational Crime and, in 1998, its foreign ministers signed a joint declaration committing association members to achieving a drug-free ASEAN by 2015. As a result, a regional framework called ASEAN and China Cooperative Operations in Response to Dangerous Drugs—or ACCORD—was launched. The commitment towards a drug-free ASEAN by 2015 gave the region a clear objective, while the ACCORD Plan of Action outlined a road map towards that objective, without specifying expected outcomes or providing an ad hoc menu of quantitative benchmarks.

This is in part because ACCORD has never been more than an attempt to create a framework of multilateral cooperation. It is merely a declaration of intent, aiming far beyond what is politically possible amongst member states that favor predominantly repressive drug control policies and actions. The operational arms of the ACCORD Plan of Action are four task forces, one for each pillar of action: the promotion of civic awareness ('advocating on the dangers of drugs'), the reduction of consumption ('by building consensus and sharing best practices in demand reduction'), the strengthening of the rule of law ('improved law enforcement cooperation'), and the elimination or significant reduction of production ('by boosting alternative development projects'). The ACCORD Task Forces meet annually to foster operational coordination through the creation of annual work plans involving the various national level drug control agencies: the Burmese Central Committee for Drug Abuse Control (CCDAC, established in 1975), the Cambodian National Authority for Combating Drugs (NACD, established in 1995), the Lao National Commission for Drug Control and Supervision (LCDC, established in 2001), the Malaysian National Anti-Drugs Agency (NADA, established in 1996), the Singaporean Central Narcotics Bureau (CNB, established in 1971), the Thai Office of the Narcotics Control Board (ONCB, established in 1976), the Vietnamese Standing Office for Drug Control (SODC, established in 2000), and their other regional counterparts.

The fact that the UN had failed to achieve a drug-free world by 2008 (as planned in 1998) did not deter the Southeast Asian nations from setting their own unrealistic goal of obtaining a drug-free region. In fact, as the 2008 mid-term progress report produced by the UNODC and the ASEAN made clear, the drug-free ASEAN goal was set without actually defining what drug-free meant and therefore making any progress toward such a goal impossible to identify.[57] While the same report acknowledged this, it also stated that 'the commitment of achieving a Drug-Free ASEAN by 2015' was 'still valid.'[58] The ASEAN was of course very far from being free of drugs at the end of 2015, but rather than acknowledging how unrealistic its goal was, the ASEAN chose to push back the deadline. On the other hand, the implementation date of the ASEAN Economic Community was brought forward from 2020 to December 31, 2015, which means that past and especially future advances in regional integration will further challenge the region's national law enforcement agencies. As a result, they will ease on trafficking and smuggling activities, making a drug-free ASEAN an even more distant goal.

To fight against transnational organized crime and especially against drug trafficking in an increasingly integrated regional economic market, the ASEAN created various communication and monitoring bodies, most notably the ASEAN Ministerial Meeting on Transnational Crime, the ASEAN Chiefs of National Police, the ASOD, and the ASEAN Airport Interdiction Task Force. In September 2015, these were joined by the ASEAN Narcotics Cooperation Center (ASEAN-NARCO) which is meant—oddly considering its late birth date and the fact that the 2015 deadline was pushed back to 2020 in 2013[59]— 'to further drive regional efforts in pursuing ASEAN Drug Free 2015.'[60] Such bodies were meant to make a drug-free ASEAN by 2015 an achievable goal, and also to monitor progress (or lack thereof). New bodies and projects keep being created to strengthen the drug control capacity and efficiency of ASEAN member states. Such initiatives include the Safe Mekong Project, which made cross-border cooperation a reality through joint operations from four participating states from January 2015 to March 2015 along the Mekong River. Myanmar, China, Laos, and Thailand, who have since launched the Safe Mekong Project Phase II, together arrested 3,398 people and seized

25,884,580 methamphetamine tablets, 52.54 kilograms of crystal methamphetamine, 1,556.9 kilograms of heroin, 48.9 kilograms of morphine, and 179.05 kilograms of opium in 2 months.[61] In 2019, the Safe Mekong Project was extended to 2023 for a third phase, which includes six countries, adding China and Vietnam to the original members.[62] More recent regional efforts include the ASEAN Work Plan on Securing Communities Against Illicit Drugs 2016–2025 and ASEAN Political-Security Community Blueprint 2025.[63] Such actions are obviously reminiscent of the failed War on Drugs which Thailand launched in 2003, and one wonders how disruptive and efficient such spectacular actions are expected to be when drug production, trafficking, and consumption have proven again and again to be extremely resilient.

The need for such ad hoc cooperative actions questions the efficiency and pertinence of the above-mentioned communication and monitoring bodies, as well as the effectiveness of the large-scale Border Liaison Offices (BLOs) mechanism that the UNODC has helped facilitate in the region. As explained in the 2008 ASEAN–UNODC mid-term report, 'BLOs bring together law enforcement units from both sides of a land or water border and put in place protocols for joint operations.'[64] At least seventy BLOs have been established along the borders of Myanmar (eight), Cambodia (eleven), Lao People's Democratic Republic (eighteen), Thailand (eighteen), Vietnam (eight), and China (seven).[65] One wonders why projects such as the Safe Mekong Project are needed when the BLO Program is officially presented as the premier method to enhance regional cooperation and integration, and achieve effective border management against drug trafficking and other trafficking and smuggling activities.

Conclusion

Neither the many and costly drug control efforts made by national governments, the ASEAN and the UNODC, nor the heavy costs paid by opium farmers, drug users and broader civil societies, have produced the expected results. The Golden Triangle is still a major area of illegal opium production, methamphetamines are still produced in bulk in various Southeast Asian countries, illegal drug use in the region has far from abated, and the ASEAN was no closer to being free of drugs in 2018 than it was in the late 1990s, when the utopian call for a drug-free region was first made. In fact in 2018, drug cases experienced an increase in the region, where over 90 per cent of drug offenses were conducted by ASEAN nationals despite measures taken by member states.[66] Neither the strengthening of repressive drug control policies nor the multiplication of drug control agencies, programs, and ad hoc projects have proven effective in reducing illegal drug production, trafficking, and consumption.

Despite the post-1971—that is, after the launch of the US-led global War on Drugs—surge in illegal production of opium, coca, and possibly cannabis,[67] some (the partisans of the containment theory) suggest that an 'increase in the size and scope of the illicit drug industry would have been far greater in the absence of law enforcement.'[68] Others adopt a more balanced approach:

> The consolidation and expansion of the control regime in the 1960s, 1970s, and 1980s, to include prohibition against consumption, did not prevent renewed expansion of opiate consumption or the tendency toward mass markets and widespread distribution networks—nor does the adoption of the more stringent policies appear to have caused them.[69]

Nonetheless, nobody can deny the many unintended consequences that drug control policies and interventions have generated, and the fact that most of these unintended consequences can be held responsible for the overall failure of the prohibitionist regime. The regime can also be blamed for generating seriously disruptive unintended consequences, evidenced by the resilience of the illegal drug industry, but also for uncountable collateral damage in the social, economic, political, environmental, and human rights areas. Allegedly unintended consequences of drug control policies and interventions that sustain the resilience of the illegal drug industry at various scales and levels—both over space and time—include crop displacement (one aspect of the so-called balloon effect), increased prices and production, worsened corruption, heightened armed violence (especially in the context of armed conflicts), and weakened counterinsurgency. In addition, social unrest, ethnic insurgency, environmental degradation, increased deforestation, destruction of legal crops, increased poverty and debt, school dropouts, prostitution, human smuggling and trafficking, needle sharing and spread of blood-borne diseases, health issues from poor quality of drugs, substance switch, increased street crime and violence, and deteriorations in human rights, all result from these approaches.[70]

Part of the difficulty in estimating and understanding the efficiency and the consequences, positive or negative, of drug control policies lies in their inadequate—or sometimes altogether non-existent—monitoring and evaluation. For example, while the UNODC rightly explains that its surveys are meant to 'assess the extent of opium poppy cultivation' and to gauge 'the effectiveness of opium bans and their implications,' it nevertheless fails to provide the information or, rather, the analysis, that is 'essential for developing effective strategies for sustaining the transition from an illicit economy to a licit economy.'[71] The UNODC never specifically explains why cultivation decreases or increases in a given country, state, province, or district. Worse, as stressed by David Mansfield in relation to Afghanistan, 'it is not unusual for the drug control community to attribute reductions in cultivation to its own actions even where there is insufficient evidence to support such a claim.'[72] As a result, the real drivers of rises and falls in cultivation are too often misunderstood and ignored, as is the inefficiency and sometimes the counterproductivity of some of the drug control actions designed and implemented by the drug control community.[73]

Apart from all the above-mentioned factors which help explain why the prohibition of certain drugs and the War on Drugs have failed both regionally and globally, corruption is a key issue that is too often ignored, including by the ASEAN and by the UNODC in their mid-term report on a drug-free ASEAN.[74] Myanmar ranks among the world's most corrupt countries, as Transparency International has found in its yearly reports over the last decade. In 2009, only Afghanistan and Somalia were found to be more corrupt than Myanmar, making it the 178th most corrupt country out of 180. Laos ranked 158th along with Cambodia, while Vietnam ranked 120th, and Thailand 84th (along with India). China fared a bit better as the world's 79th most corrupt country. On the other end, in 2019, Singapore was ranked the world's

4th least corrupt country, well ahead of the United Kingdom (12th), or France (23rd).[75] It is obvious that corruption hinders drug control efforts at various levels and especially at the trafficking stage.[76] The proceeds of the illegal drug economy feed corruption, as Willem van Schendel and Itty Abraham suggest when they describe how 'the act of enforcing a selected flow of people and objects across a border, from border patrols to customs, immediately allows for the possibility of rents to be charged for circumventing these rules and by the same token provides opportunities for smuggling of people and objects across these borders.'[77] The difficulty of coping with drug trafficking, therefore, results not only from poverty—which makes drug production and trafficking even more attractive economically—but also corruption. Indeed, a lack of resources and fragile domestic institutions also undermine the efforts against both drug production and drug trafficking.

Drug trafficking is only one aspect of the drug economy, and while the goals of a drug-free world or a drug-free ASEAN will never be reached, efforts can and should be made to minimize the harms caused by illegal drug production, trafficking, and consumption. Alongside demand reduction, harm reduction policies are of course a crucial tool against the spread of blood-borne diseases, notably along drug trafficking routes. On the other end, economic development is needed in order to provide alternative livelihoods for opium poppy cultivators: poverty, and more precisely food insecurity, is the main driver of opium production in mainland Southeast Asia. Nevertheless, economic development is not achievable without good governance; that is, without peace, political stability, the rule of law, and control of corruption.

The future of the international drug control regime (IDCR) in Southeast Asia, and more precisely in and around the Golden Triangle, depends first on the future of prohibitionist drug policies and actions. Whether the failure and the counterproductivity of the global prohibitionist drug policies and the accompanying War on Drugs will be acknowledged or not, internationally and officially, and whether it will be followed by reinforcing harm reduction policies both at the drug supply and drug consumption levels, or by more repressive strategies, will largely determine the anti-drug stance adopted by the ASEAN and its member states. Considering how repressive the anti-drug policies of the ASEAN and its member states have been for decades, regarding drug production and drug consumption, there is little hope that the regional or national policies will change drastically outside of global reforms; the upcoming reform of Thailand's drug legislation will most likely improve what are still very repressive drug laws, but is unlikely to grant the most progressive demands made by drug policy advocates.[78]

Despite the recurrent aggressive declaration of Southeast Asian officials, drug supply reduction policies and actions have been limited in scope, means, and efficiency during the past decades in Myanmar and Laos (Thailand being largely out of consideration due to its small historical importance as an opium producer and exporter). Forced eradication and AD projects are more costly and practically difficult to implement than actions aimed at drug trafficking groups and routes, as shown by the importance of counter-trafficking efforts versus the paucity of drug production control measures. The areal dimensions of illegal agricultural production often proves more difficult, both tactically and financially, to target than the reticulate dimensions of drug trafficking networks and routes. The old status quo—limited policies and actions unable to alleviate either drug production or drug consumption, and tacit acceptance of it by concerned authorities—is highly likely to endure as long as the same failed policies and actions remain the sole tools to address illegal drug production, trade and consumption, regardless of the ups and downs of illegal opium production in Myanmar and Laos, and despite a thriving regional drug consumption market for both opiates and ATS.

Therefore, there are two scenarios for the future of the IDCR in the region. The first scenario is that of a protracted status quo, according to which repressive drug control policies and actions will continue to be implemented, or even revamped and reinforced at various economic, human, and societal costs, despite their well-documented failure and counterproductivity, which will then only increase. This scenario is the most likely one in the short term, as global, regional, and national policies will take time to evolve toward more progressive and less counterproductive solutions. The second scenario, that of a revision and reform of repressive drug control policies and actions, is no less likely than the first one but can only occur in the longer term. Indeed, over time the existing status quo cannot prove viable, whether politically, economically, or socially. Innovative, efficient policies and actions will be necessary to address the various issues, both direct and indirect, inherent to the illegal drug industry. However, in order to see the second scenario take place in Southeast Asia, the IDCR will first have to evolve, something that has already started to happen with the reforms that have taken place in various South American countries or even in the United States. In the end, it is less the future scenario that is to be questioned than the timeline of its implementation.

10

RUSSIA
BEYOND THE GLOBAL SOUTH–NORTH FRAMEWORK

Ekaterina Stepanova

Russia's perspective on the International Drug Control Regime (IDCR) is to a large extent shaped by the scale, sources and specifics of its narcotics problem.[1] What is often overlooked in assessing Russia's position in contemporary debates over IDCR reform is how unique the Russian case is—not so much in terms of Russia's nominal role in the illicit drug trade, as in terms of the extremely radical and speedy shift in its narcotics situation in the post-Soviet period. Over a period of the two first post-Soviet decades, the narcotics situation in Russia shifted from being almost drug-free in Soviet times, to becoming one of the major global narcotics markets and the single largest country market for Afghan heroin. In the 2010s, Russia alone consumed a volume of opiates comparable to that consumed in the rest of Europe. By the end of the 2010s, the opiate curse was aggravated by the major rise in synthetic drugs in Russia's market.

The sheer scale and speed of this fundamental shift in Russia may have some analogues in other parts of the world—for example, in West Africa, which quickly turned into a major narcotics transit corridor from Latin America to Europe and a growing drug market. What is unparalleled, though, is the fact that the surge in drug use in post-Soviet Russia coincided with, and occurred largely because of, several other more fundamental shifts of the 1990s–early 2000s, including:

- The radical change of the economic order from a planned socialist economy to one of the wilder versions of the market capitalist economy.
- In social terms, a move away from an equitable and universal social welfare towards a very limited and uneven system heavily varying by social class and region, and from an egalitarian society to a highly unequal one.
- A shift from an authoritarian ideology-based state to, at first, a dysfunctional state on the verge of collapse, followed by a slow and difficult state-building process that led to the consolidation of a rigid, but functional and populist hybrid regime by the late 2000s.
- A sharp rise in general crime levels from the 1990s to the early 2000s, which only started to stabilize by the late 2000s.
- Colossal reduction in the area of territorial control. Russia had never existed as a separate state with its post-Soviet borders before, and it had new, porous, and unprotected state borders across Eurasia, including those with and through Central Asia.
- Internationally, Russia's role shifted from being one of the two global superpowers to being a regional power at first before becoming in the 2010s, a major macro-regional force. This was coupled with the long process of the search for a new national identity and identification of Russia's national interests, values, and place in the world.

All these processes developed 'at once' and helped shape the demand side of Russia's rapidly escalating narcotics problem. However, even these major shifts and social calamities, whose worst effects were felt back in the 1990s, had only created favorable demand conditions for Russia to emerge as a mid-size narcotics transit and consumer state. Primarily driven by a historically unprecedented surge in narcotics output from the world's largest center of opiate production—Afghanistan—the problem deteriorated later, in the early twenty-first century, escalating into a national catastrophe. Due to poor socioeconomic conditions in most of the Central Asian states that lie between Russia and Afghanistan, their limited state functionality, the reorientation of much of their economies to informal cross-border shuttle trade facilitated by a combination of open borders with both Afghanistan and richer northern neighbors (Kazakhstan and Russia), and the remnants of some relatively developed Soviet-built transport infrastructure, Central Asia naturally became a wide and major 'northern' transit corridor for Afghan opiates. As a result, Afghanistan quickly emerged as the single main source of the heroin which flooded and overwhelmed Russia's drug market, turning it from the mid-size consuming country of the 1990s to one of the largest end-markets in both Europe and Asia in the 2000s.

In the case of Russia, particularly in the critical stage of the 2000s–10s, the avalanche-like, practically unlimited narcotics supply from Afghanistan drove demand, rather than the other way around. In the later 2010s, Russia's hard drugs market became somewhat more diversified and demand-driven.[2] At that time, consumption of opiates, and especially heroin, remained high, while imported and domestically produced synthetic drugs also spread. However, this does not change the main pattern of Russia's narcotics challenge in the early twenty-first century, which reveals much about where Russia stands in terms of its drug control policy and in the debates on the IDCR reform, and why.

Russia's Role in the Illegal Drug Trade

While Russia's place in the illegal drug trade has changed significantly since the early 1990s, as of the late 2010s Russia's primary role in the illicit drug business has been that of a huge consumer market. Its hard drugs market has been mostly an end-market for imported drugs, dominated by heroin almost entirely originating from Afghanistan, and to a lesser extent, by synthetic drugs imported from China and

Eastern Europe. It is also a relatively minor transit state. In the early twenty-first century, manufacturing of narcotics—marijuana and, increasingly, synthetic drugs—remained relatively limited and mainly intended for domestic consumption.

i. Shift to Heroin Dominance in Russia's Hard Drugs Market in the 2000s

For Russia, the large-scale inflow of opiates, mainly heroin, of Afghan origin has become a particularly vital first-order human security challenge. The direct harm that the abuse of Afghan heroin caused to the life and health of the Russian population during the first two decades of the twenty-first century, and its dramatic impact on Russian society, outweighed cumulative harm from illicit use of all other types of controlled narcotics and psychotropic substances[3] in the Russian domestic market (and all other Afghanistan-related concerns that Russia has had).

The shift toward heroin dominance in the Russian hard drugs market had not occurred before the twenty-first century—even the socioeconomic hardships and traumatic transitions of the 1990s did not succeed in turning post-Soviet Russia into anything more than a mid-size consumer of drugs and a transit country for the illicit drug trade. A combination of three main factors is critical to explaining Russia's transformation into the single largest country end-market for the Afghan heroin in the 2000s.

Overproduction of Opiates in Afghanistan

The main factor has been the continuing overproduction of opiates, and the unprecedented increase in Afghanistan's opiate output in the early twenty-first century (especially since 2004), which far exceeds cultivation and production levels of the 1980s or 1990s. The last year of the Taliban's *de facto* rule (2001) saw the unprecedented decline, by Afghan and global standards alike, of the area of poppy cultivation to just 8,000 ha[4] (a reduction of 91 per cent) as a result of the effective Taliban poppy cultivation ban of 2000. In contrast, the deeply embedded Afghan opium economy significantly expanded in post-

Taliban Afghanistan during the US/NATO security presence. The first peak came in 2004–8; the second was from the mid-2010s through 2019. In 2017, poppy cultivation in Afghanistan reached its historical peak of 328,000 ha, according to data from the UN Office on Drugs and Crime (UNODC),[5] or 329,000 ha according to US Government data.[6] This represents an area that is forty-one times larger than the area of poppy cultivation in Afghanistan under *de facto* Taliban rule in 2001. The historical peaks for opium production in Afghanistan were reached, first, in 2007 (7400–8000 mt, depending on the data source) and then in 2017 (9000–9104 mt;[7] see Figure 10.1).

The rapid and major increase in poppy cultivation and opiate production in Afghanistan in the 2000s stimulated the expansion of Afghan opiate trafficking—and the sharpest increase during that decade was felt through the new, 'northern route' via Central Asia. This resulted in cheaper prices for the Afghan heroin on the Russian market in the 2000s, compared to the 1990s.

Figure 10.1: Poppy cultivation and opium production in Afghanistan, 1994–2019

1. Poppy cultivation in Afghanistan, 1994–2019, ha

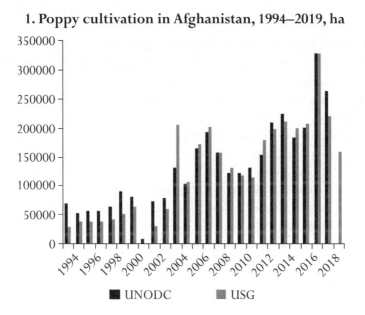

2. Opium production in Afghanistan, 1994–2019, mt

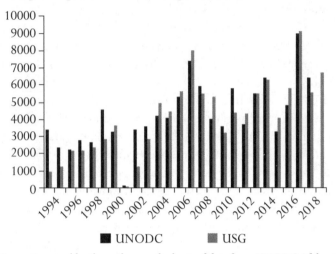

■ UNODC   ■ USG

Data Source: Prepared by the author on the basis of data from UNODC Afghanistan Opium Surveys (2002–2019) and US Department of State International Narcotics Control Strategy Reports (1994-2020).

Conditions Along the Transit Route

There are several explanations of why much of Afghanistan's surplus opiate (especially heroin) supply created by the overproduction in the 2000s, went northward via Central Asia to Russia. The economic situation in Central Asian states, especially Tajikistan and Kyrgyzstan, was worse than that of Afghanistan's western neighbors Iran or Turkey, as the second transit country along the more traditional 'Balkan' route to Europe. In contrast to the functional states of Iran and Turkey, most Central Asian states (especially Tajikistan and Kyrgyzstan) were marred by systemic dysfunctionality, instability, and the dominance of clan-based/patronage-clientele relations. Even in formally rigid autocracies, such as Uzbekistan, the central state control over distant peripheries was extremely limited. These conditions were compounded by a combination of:

- The growing dependence of the region's economies and populations on cross-border shuttle trade in both legal and illegal goods.

- Central Asia's porous borders with Afghanistan (in sharp contrast to, for instance, the more rigidly protected Afghan–Iranian border).
- Open border regimes between Central Asia (south of Kazakhstan) and the much more economically developed, resource-rich, and higher income northern states of Russia and Kazakhstan which have been united in a Customs Union since 2010 and in Eurasian Economic Union since 2015.[8]
- A visa-free regime with Russia and Kazakhstan and mass outflow of millions of legal and illegal labor migrants from Central Asia, especially from Tajikistan, Kyrgyzstan, and Uzbekistan, to Russia's lucrative and rapidly growing labor market of the 2000s. This made Russia the largest recipient of migrants in the Eastern Hemisphere.

In sum, this geographically huge, economically underdeveloped, and socially backward regional space directly to the north of the world's largest center of opiate production and trafficking (Afghanistan) was permeated by informal cross-border trade routes and the dynamic movement of people across poorly protected borders. At the same time, some key transport (rail, road) infrastructure had been maintained from the Soviet era, and was more developed than in parts of Pakistan bordering Afghanistan, for example. Furthermore, in relatively close regional proximity to the north, Central Asia borders a huge country at a qualitatively higher level of economic development and with much higher living standards (Russia), an almost limitless potential end-market for illicit goods.

While any cross-regional comparisons are extremely relative, in the early twenty-first century the gap in the level of socioeconomic development between Russia as the end-market and the main narcotics transit states of Central Asia—and the drug-producing Afghanistan—can be roughly compared to the gap between the USA as a narcotics consumer market and the drug-producing and transit states of South and Central America in the Western hemisphere. In other words, in terms of role and place in the illicit drug supply chain, Russia's function is similar to that of other states in the Global North. As of the 2000s, it emerged as a major end-market, with an incomparably higher level of socioeconomic development than the underdeveloped transit states of Central Asia, and the source country, Afghanistan. The principal difference was that, in contrast to the 'tough' and fenced US–Mexico border, the borders between Russia and Central Asia have featured a visa-free regime and are porous. Russia's border with Kazakhstan is the longest land border in the world, at twice the length of the US Mexican border. The borders between opiate producing Afghanistan and such transit Central Asian countries as Tajikistan and Turkmenistan have hardly been protected at all. Further risk factors across Central Asia that invite trafficking and which have remained relevant well through the 2010s include the widening gap between the region's growing trans and cross-regional trade connections and recently developing transport infrastructure on the one hand, and weak drug control and counternarcotics capacity, in addition to declining opiate interdiction levels in most Central Asian states (with the exception of Uzbekistan), on the other.

Demand Dynamics in Russia

The third factor explaining Russia's heroin curse is related to demand dynamics within Russia itself. While the traumatic transition, deep social crisis, and shock economic liberalization of the 1990s played their role in Russia's shift from drug-free to mid-size drug (ab)use/transit country, these factors were no longer the primary drivers of the 'heroin catastrophe' of the 2000s. When it comes to Russia, the rising—not declining—economic tide of the 2000s, in combination with relatively cheap prices due to major overproduction at the source, made heroin affordable to larger segments of the population, across regions and social groups. The fact that it is heroin rather than any other narcotic substance that became the hard drug of the first choice in Russia in the 2000s was primarily dictated and determined by the over-abundance of supply of this particular drug to the Russian market at the time (see points 1 and 2 above), in contrast to the limited supply of cocaine for example, which remained far more expensive and therefore an elite drug.

As a result of a combination of these three factors, by the 2010s, over 80 per cent of heroin that went out of Afghanistan via Central

Asia ended up in Russia (75–80 tons a year), even though trafficking via Central Asia accounted for just 25 per cent of Afghanistan's heroin exports (90 metric tons) and 15 per cent of opium exports (35–40 metric tons).[9] From 2011 to 2015, three-quarters of the total inflow of Afghan heroin along the northern route ended up in Russia.[10] Of importance here is not merely the volume, but the structure and ultimate destination of the 'northern' flow: while in the 1990s, Russia emerged as a transit state for and a modest consumer of Afghan opiates, in the 2000s, it started to absorb almost all incoming heroin, partly because it could now afford to, consuming almost as much as all of Europe did.[11]

The scale of the threat posed by the inflow of Afghan opiates has been different for Russia and Western/Central Europe, as the two large end-markets of comparable value. If by 2009 the size of the Western European opiate market (US$20 billion [bln]) still exceeded that of Russia and Kazakhstan (US$13 bln combined),[12] a later UNODC study for 2009–12 estimated combined annual gross profit from the Afghan opiates in Western and Central Europe at US$18.1 bln.[13] That equaled the highest available estimate of the value of the Russian opiate market (US$16–18 bln in 2014) made by the Organisation for Economic Co-operation and Development (OECD) financial watchdog, the Financial Action Task Force (FATF).[14] Structurally, while the Russian illicit drugs market was dominated by Afghan heroin for much of the early twenty-first century (at least until the late 2010s), the European markets were diversified. A long-term trend of stabilization and decline in opiate consumption in Western Europe has partially reversed only since the 2010s,[15] and for much of the 2000s and the 2010s it has been superseded by growing inflows of cocaine from South/Central America, including via West Africa, and the rise in illicit use of synthetic drugs, including new psychoactive substances. The United States has not been directly threatened by Afghan opiates, which account for between just 3 and 5–6 per cent of its heroin market.[16]

ii. Domestic Narcotics Market and Drug (Ab)use

The structure of Russia's domestic market and drug (ab)use displays some important differences compared to either major consumer states of the 'Global North,' or transit and drug-producing countries of the 'Global South.' These specifics make some of the stereotypes and conceptual frameworks developed on the basis of other regions' experience—such as the centrality of major 'drug cartels' to the trafficking process or the 'vulnerable populations' concept—not fully applicable, relevant or well-tailored to the Russian or the broader Eurasian context (for the concept of 'vulnerable regions' see Chapter 1 by Annette Idler).

The Role of Opiates in the Market Structure

By the 2010s, the Federal Drug Control Service (FSKN) estimated that Russia's heroin market was worth US$6 bln, followed by natural cannabinoid hashish (US$1.5 bln), also mostly of Afghan origin (see Figure 10.2).[17] According to Russia's FSKN, annual numbers of heroin users hovered at 1.5–1.7 million (out of 2.5 million active drug abusers, or 2 per cent of the total population),[18] which corresponds to the UNODC estimates putting the average annual number in 2011–15 at over 1.4 million.[19] These estimates referred to a period of growing heroin prices during and following an interim limited decline in opiate inflow to Russia recorded in 2008–12, as a direct result of a temporary decrease in Afghanistan's opiate output as a market reaction to previous overproduction and lower yields due to weather conditions.

Figure 10.2: Hard narcotics market value in Russia (bln USD), 2010

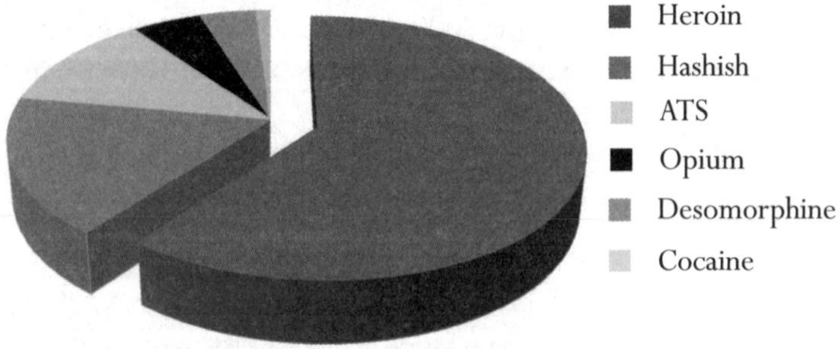

Data source: FSKN, 2011.
ATS refers to amphetamine-type stimulants, mainly amphetamine and methamphetamine.

For Russia's opiate market, the correlation of supply-demand drivers in favor of the growing and largely uncontrolled supply of the Afghan opiates along the northern route persisted into the 2010s, despite the rise in heroin prices coupled with worsening economic conditions in Russia, and growing use of and demand for other (mostly synthetic) drugs. This once again underscores the important but secondary role of demand factors inside Russia for its Afghan opiate market. The new major spike in Afghan opiate production in the mid to late 2010s led to the increase in opiate seizures and trafficking along the largest 'Balkan route' through Iran and Turkey to Europe, the development of the new 'southern route' to the Gulf, South Asia, and Africa, and a new resurgence in trafficking along the 'northern route' via Central Asia to Russia, following a limited temporary decline in 2008–12.[20]

Heroin supply to Russia continues to transit Central Asia (notably Tajikistan and Kazakhstan) and, to a lesser extent, the South Caucasus (as of the mid-2010s, mostly Azerbaijan). Russia serves as the end-market for these flows, with only small-scale heroin trafficking onwards to Belarus and the Baltic states.[21] Within Russia, Afghan heroin is mainly trafficked to three main hubs: the Moscow area, the area around Perm and Yekaterinburg, and the area around Novosibirsk and Irkutsk. From those hubs, heroin shipments are repackaged and distributed to large consumer markets across the country, including the European part, Western Siberia, and the Russian Far East.[22]

As shown by the publicly available set of the Ministry of Internal Affairs (MVD) and FSKN data on registered narcotics-related crimes for 2013–14, the main types of drug seized in those years (accounting for 80 per cent of all registered narcotics-related crimes in Russia) by overall value were cannabinoids, heroin, and amphetamines (see Figure 10.3). Natural cannabinoids, ranging from prevalent 'soft' marijuana to 'hard' hashish, were the most frequently seized drugs (33.8 per cent), with an average retail price of US$16.6/gram.[23] They were followed by more expensive heroin ((US$80/gram at that time), making up 24.9 per cent of all seizures.[24] All other drugs still lagged behind, with amphetamines accounting for 14.4 per cent and synthetic cannabinoids for 13.6 per cent. Cocaine—mostly trafficked via airports or Saint Petersburg and the Black Sea ports by drug couriers or concealed within maritime shipments originating in the Caribbean

Figure 10.3: Main narcotics seized in Russia in 2013-2014, by value, %

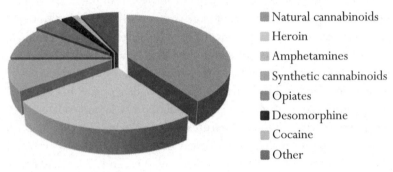

- Natural cannabinoids
- Heroin
- Amphetamines
- Synthetic cannabinoids
- Opiates
- Desomorphine
- Cocaine
- Other

Data source: MVD; FSKN

and South America—was one of the most rarely seized drugs (0.3 per cent) and the most expensive one (US\$178/gram).[25]

In contrast to the United States, the world's largest narcotics end-market—and, to an extent, to other main drug markets in the 'Global North'—drug trafficking into and within Russia has not been fully monopolized by a handful of large criminal cartels. The trafficking has been more fragmented and 'pluralistic,' with the spread of less structured and more flexible organizational models. Along with some larger cross-regional trafficking organizations, it has also involved (especially in interregional trade and retail distribution inside Russia) many smaller, more segmented, locally based groups, often ethnic, family or clan-based. While in the Western hemisphere, transnational drug cartels who traffic narcotics into the United States often also control distribution inside the United States, traffickers who bring in the Afghan heroin and hashish from Central Asia to Russia hardly control wholesale or retail distribution that may be carried out under the patronage of Russia's larger OPGs (Russian abbreviation for organized crime groups) which often originate from, are based in and dominate one of the country's regions.[26]

The Rise in Synthetic Drugs

Since the mid-2010s, Russia's drug market structure has started to change. While the inflow of opiates, especially heroin, remained high or even increased, the main change was in the rise in trade, production, and use of synthetic drugs.[27] As a result, synthetics have been gaining a larger share of the market and even surpassed opiates in narcotics seizures. Of the total of 21.8 mt of narcotics seized by all relevant Russian agencies in 2016, 1.4 mt were opiates (including 965–6 kilograms of heroin); 4 mt were synthetic drugs; 15 mt were cannabis products, and 1.4 mt were psychotropics (see Figure 10.4).[28] The new development was a shift to cathinone, cannabinoids, and synthetic opioids as the main synthetic drugs on the Russian market: in 2016, Russia became second only to the United States in the quantity of seized cannabinoids (0.7 mt) and reported the largest synthetic cathinone seizures (2 mt).[29]

Figure 10.4: Narcotics seizures in Russia, 2016, by type, mt

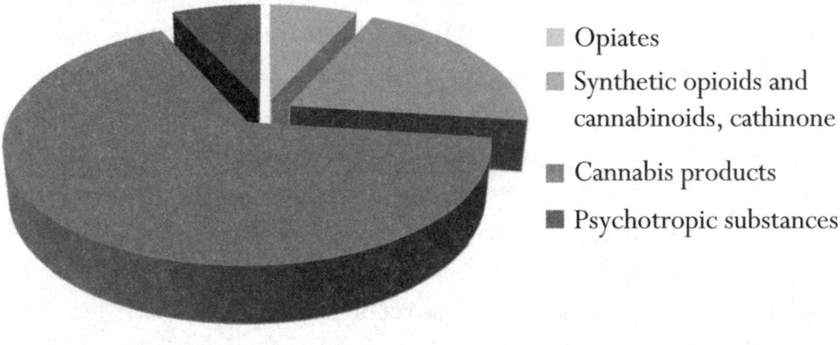

■ Opiates

■ Synthetic opioids and cannabinoids, cathinone

■ Cannabis products

■ Psychotropic substances

Data source: MVD; FSKN

At the end of 2018, the Russian Ministry of Interior Chief Directorate for Drug Control pointed at the growing role of synthetic drugs on the Russian market as the single largest trend, noting an increase of their share from 5.7 to 22.4 per cent over a period of 6 years since 2012. In market terms, growing demand and supply of synthetics, including synthetic opioids, was partly meant to make up for a temporary increase in heroin prices, due to a short-term relative decline in opiate production in Afghanistan between two major peaks in 2007 and in the mid-2010s. But, in contrast to the opiate/heroin inflows that come from abroad and are less dependent on fluctuations in demand at Russia's end-market, synthetics are only partly imported, increasingly produced at home, and more heavily demand-driven. In 2018 alone, the number of labs in Russia manufacturing synthetic drugs increased by 14 per cent.[30]

iii. Social Structure of Drug (Ab)use

Trends in overall drug use in Russia are not easy to discern, due to a lack of unified, consistent methodology, a breakdown in data collection efforts due to institutional transition on the drug enforcement side from a specialized drug control agency (the FSKN) to the MVD department since 2016, and disparities in data from different sources and estimates. According to sociological data provided in the draft 'Strategy of State Anti-Narcotics Policy of the Russian Federation through 2030,' as of 2020 the number of respondent who used drugs systematically or from time to time had reached 1.9 million, or 1.3 per cent of all respondents.[31] However, this only reflects a share of overall number of drug users, i.e., those respondents who were ready to admit drug use. The FSKN earlier estimated, relying on its own methodology, that as of 2015 the overall number of drug users in Russia could have reached 8–8.5 million people.[32] On the one hand, in 2013–18, a certain shift from opiate/opioid abuse to growing use of 'new' synthetic drugs and the 'recreational' and other 'controlled' use of psychoactive substances was recorded by sociologists.[33] On the other, the number of deaths from harmful drug use continued to grow for much of the 2010s, from 3750 deaths in 2011 to 4830 in 2017, and only somewhat declined in 2018 (4450).[34]

The available data on the social structure of drug (ab)use in Russia in terms of age, gender, regional/geographical distribution, social patterns, etc., points to a wide variety of patterns and allows for very broad generalizations only. First, as of the mid-2010s, the use of narcotics—accounting for 18.3 per cent of all (ab)use of psychoactive substances—lagged far behind the consumption of alcohol in Russia (80.7 per cent).[35] Second, harmful drug use is generally more prevalent in urban than in rural areas. Third, women use narcotics 4.7 times less frequently than men do (but are somewhat more likely to abuse hard substances).[36] Fourth, an integrated indicator of narcotics dependency and harm by age group shows the generally younger age—and greater exposure to related harm—among drug (ab)users, as compared to alcohol abusers. The critical 'switch' of the share of narcotics in total harmful use of psychoactive substances jumps from 7 per cent in those aged 15–17 years to 33 per cent in the 18–19-year age group, with the greatest harm and exposure in absolute terms (950 people out of 100,000) affecting those aged 20–39 years.[37]

The overall harm from illicit drug consumption to public health and human security in Russia is hard to overestimate: according to Russia's Security Council, the estimated damage to the national economy and society from the narcotics problem is equivalent to 3–5 per cent of Russia's Gross Domestic Product (GDP), comparable to the total size of Russia's public health budget.[38] Narcotics-linked mortality in Russia (mostly linked to the use of opioids) started to decline and fell from 9354 deaths in 2006 to 5249 cases in 2016, the lowest level in a decade.[39] However, it is hard to tell whether this decline came as a result of improvements in treatment, as it correlates with a parallel decline in first-time entrants into treatment for opioid (mostly heroin) use by three-quarters over the period 2006–17, and with a reduction in the proportion of drug treatments for opioids over time.[40] Russia remains one of the few countries where the number of new HIV/AIDS-infected people and related deaths continues to increase, with the intravenous use of non-sterile needles by a drug user (especially heroin/desomorphine addicts) remaining the main cause of infection (57.3 per cent of all infected).[41] In January 2016, the Federal Research and Methodological Center for Prophylactics and Countering HIV/AIDS registered the 1,000,000[th] HIV infection in Russia.[42] Over 40 per cent of Russians who get infected with HIV/AIDS are people who inject drugs (PWIDs).

Overall, the social structure of illicit drug consumption in Russia does not appear to conform to the 'vulnerable populations'-centered concept, developed primarily on the basis of cases and experiences of the Western hemisphere—with its overcrowded socially deprived *barrios* [neighborhoods] of the South and the inner-city 'grey' delinquency zones of the North—or Europe, with its fully shaped, disenfranchised and socially excluded migrant *banlieues* [suburban areas]. While more research has to be done in this field in Russia, beyond several broad trends (such as generally greater exposure of young males in urban settings), there is no evidence so far that illicit drug use has been primarily concentrated in, or most heavily affects, specific social groups, districts or segments in any systematic way, be it in terms of income levels, social role, or territorial distribution (for example, foreign labor migrant communities, or people living below poverty level, or populations of mid-sized corporate towns). So far, Russia displays neither isolated, consolidated migrant ghettos, as it is still at the first-generation labor migration stage, nor socially excluded inner-city districts, while areas in acute economic decay—ranging from small to mid-size former corporate towns across the country or rural areas—primarily suffer from alcohol consumption.

Instead, drug use tends to affect the entire cross-section of Russian society, including its mid and high-level income strata and its most economically advanced and developed cities. This is logical, given that most drugs are more expensive than alcohol, Russia's more widespread, first-choice psychoactive substance. Drug use is also spread across urban and rural, more and less industrialized, central and peripheral regions. If there are variations, it is more in terms of the dominant type(s) of drug; in more economically deprived regions, cheaper substitutes/surrogates for certain types of narcotics are more widespread, for example, desomorphine as a substitute of heroin and other synthetics. There are also variations which relate to the overall size of a region's population. The far more relevant category to the Russian case (than any specific 'most vulnerable' populations) is that of 'socially excluded' and 'socially deprived' groups—but that applies primarily to those who have already become drug users, and the way the society and the state still treats them (see section 3).

iv. Russia and Narcotics-Related Money Laundering

The UNODC estimated the value of the global trade in Afghan opiates at US$70 billion in the mid-2010s. According to the latest highest available estimate of the Russian opiate market, it could be worth US$16–18 bln, which would make up to 22.8–27.7 per cent of the global market.[43] While Russia shares some of both the vulnerabilities and the restraints to narcotics-related money laundering common for most large illicit drug end-markets, including Europe and the USA, it also displays some differences.

One of Russia's two key specifics in this regard is that, while narcotics-related money laundering may be relatively significant, not only is it outmatched by other sources of illicit revenues (for instance, other organized crime activities, tax evasion)—it also pales when compared to the two main sources of large-scale financial transactions which dominate Russia's illicit financial scene. These refer to (a) the misuse of a share of profits from trade in Russia's own vast natural resources and (b) more general syphoning of legal budget funds and flows. Both are conducted through misuse of domestic and foreign financial and legal entities, investments in real estate or security instruments, and luxury consumer goods.[44]

Russia's other feature, on which the previous one is conditional, is higher corruption at all levels of government compared to countries of an equivalent level of development: Russia stood at the 138th place out of 180 in the 2018 Transparency International Corruption Perception Index, at the same level as Iran, Lebanon, Mexico, and Papua New Guinea, with minimal fluctuations of annual score/place in 2012–18 indicating lack of progress.[45] This high level of corruption is coupled with well-developed modern banking/financial infrastructure and heavy involvement in international trade and trade regimes. Moscow and Saint Petersburg are evolving as macro-regional international trade and financial hubs—Russia's current isolation from Western financial markets due to sanctions adopted against the country since 2014 due to the crisis in Ukraine (and gradually tightened since then) notwithstanding. In addition, there are a considerable number of cross-border financial transfers, especially with the main transit region for narcotics to Russia (Central Asia), made through informal value transfer systems.

Given Russia's large illicit consumer market for drugs, all this constitutes a vulnerability and creates potential for drug-related money laundering—and has pushed the Russian government to improve the anti-money laundering legal and enforcement framework. Russia took efforts to get itself removed from the FATF blacklist in 2002, and built up its financial intelligence unit, Rosfinmonitoring. While in 2017, the US Government categorized Russia as a major money laundering country,[46] at the time of writing this chapter, the FATF did not identify Russia as a country having substantial money laundering and terrorist financing risks or strategic deficiencies in countering both.

Russia's Drug Control Policy and the IDCR

Historically, Russia had been at the outset of international drug control efforts. The Russian Empire took part both in the 1909 Shanghai Opium Commission, and in the work on the 1912 Hague International Opium Convention. In the 1990s, post-Soviet Russia suddenly faced a rapidly growing and deteriorating drug problem which it lacked technical expertise to deal with in all spheres: legal, medical/research, policing/law enforcement, customs and border control, and treatment/social rehabilitation. Consequently, Russia had to build its drug control system and policy almost from scratch. At that stage, the IDCR in general, and the UN Commission on Narcotics Drugs (CND) and UNODC support and experience in particular, proved timely and indispensable for Russia. In turn, Russia has become one of the strongest advocates of the UN-centered IDCR. The IDCR has been seen by Russia not only as a *sine qua non* hedge against global/transnational drug trafficking, but it has also played a pivotal role in helping Russia establish its own drug control system, despite all the difficulties of post-Soviet state- and economy-building. It helped Russia establish its basic drug control legal and technical framework. Russia became part of all IDCR conventions and sought to build and shape its own drug control system in line with these international obligations, although later than many other states. In 1998, the Russian Government signed an agreement with the UN Secretariat on urgent technical support in drugs and crime control and adopted its first-ever legal framework for drug control, the Federal Law 'On narcotics and psychotropic substances.'[47] Russia has taken an active part in all IDCR bodies, supported the growing role of the UNODC (headed, from 2010 to 2019, by former Russian diplomat Yuri Fedotov)[48] and has become one of the top ten 'Emerging and National' contributors to the UNODC budget.[49]

Following the 1990s, post-Soviet Russia became an active IDCR member and relied on it for support in shaping its own drug control system, which included all the mainstays of IDCR, including strict prohibitionism, reflecting the mainstream global approach supported by the majority of states. This approach was confirmed and reinforced by the launch of the 'Decade Against Drugs,' declared by the UN in 1998. In the following years, Russia's position on IDCR reform had been identical to the official UNODC line: the international community should follow the decisions of its official and universally recognized bodies, such as the Vienna-based CND.[50] In 2009, the CND unanimously reaffirmed the relevance of drug control conventions that form a comprehensive legal basis for international efforts in this area, and of lists of controlled substances that were all described as harmful to human health if not used for strictly medical purposes. According to this approach, calls for legalization essentially undermined international law.

With the failure of the UN 'Decade Against Drugs,' underscored by an increase rather than a decline in illicit global drug production, trade, and use by the end of the 2000s, voices in favor of more radical revision of the IDCR and of the mainstream methods of drug control—including prohibitionism—started to rise, mostly in the Western hemisphere. These voices reflected a diverse set of drivers and motivations. They ranged from pragmatic recognition of the ineffectiveness and high social costs of harsh anti-narcotics measures in supply countries (especially Latin American stakeholders) and of uneven supply-demand balance in global drug control reasons, to liberal ideological/value-based considerations and major commercial/business interests (including those of pharmaceutical companies) in the developed West. The debate was catalyzed by reports by the non-governmental Global Commission on Drug Policy (GCDP) that started to appear in 2011, and especially by its 2014 report 'Taking Control: Pathways to Drug Policies that Work.'[51] It was also fueled by its promoters' determination to bring it to discussion at the 2016 UN General Assembly Special Session (UNGASS), in an attempt to change the focus of global narcotics policies. Among other things, their hopes were partly stirred up by the Obama administration's softening approach to drug control, which left Russia as one of the main, or even the lead advocate of preserving the IDCR as it was—a role previously comfortably played by the United States—at the 2016 UNGASS meeting.

Notably, these discussions coincided with the period of sharp deterioration of overall relations between Russia and the West. While this new decline in Russia–West relations stemmed from geopolitical tensions, especially over the crisis in Ukraine in 2014, it spurred deep mistrust that affected all other spheres of mutual relations and cooperation, including IDCR discussions. Russia has become ever more suspicious of any 'liberalization' initiatives of Western origin, while on the other side it has started to be depicted by anti-prohibitionists, especially in the West, as almost the main obstacle on the way to what they see as 'progress,' i.e. the legalization of most or many types of narcotics, liberalization of global drug markets, and harm reduction.

While (at least on the harm/demand reduction side) this view has some merit, it is overly simplistic and Western-centric. It ignores the solid support of the core IDCR principles not just by Russia, but among most states of Asia, the Persian Gulf, and Africa. It only focuses on conservative elements in Russia's global approach, while ignoring (for example) progressive trends in Russia's take on supply reduction. These include Russia's new emphasis on socioeconomic development and on its search for negotiated peace solutions to armed conflicts in key drug-producing regions, notably Afghanistan, which are increasingly seen by Moscow as *sine qua non* strategies to create conditions for long-term reduction of deeply embedded drug economies in these regions (see section 4). It also poorly accounts for the way Russia's approach to the IDCR was shaped by, and reflected, the specifics of its own drug challenge.

At the global level, Russia's conservative, strictly prohibitionist position towards the IDCR did not only stem from its general 'protective' approach to the UN. Nor has it been just a natural progression from growing dominance of conservative, traditionalist values and preference for enforcement-style methods and solutions in Russia's domestic politics, projected into its foreign policy. To a large extent, Russia's conservatism in the sphere of international drug control was shaped by the fact that, in the early twenty-first century, Russia remained largely an end-market for major flows of drugs from abroad, dominated by opiates of Afghan origin, with this prevalence only somewhat challenged by the spread of synthetic drugs since the mid-2010s. This dictated a heavy emphasis on the need to impede the illicit drug trade and to support functional global systems of administrative control of narcotics circulation by all available means. It created a focus on the supply side of the problem, at the expense of its demand side. Nowhere has this approach been reflected more evidently than in Russia's insistence on the role of the IDCR as a global hedge against attempts at legalizing narcotic substances.

Prohibitionism and Opposition to Legalization

The debate at the 2016 UNGASS in New York provoked broad international discussions in which Russia reaffirmed and pushed forward its strict prohibitionist position.

While Russia formally acknowledged the 'growing disappointment with the results of countering the global narcotics threat' and 'the pressing need to restore trust in the states' efforts to fight drugs and to achieve real results in reducing this world peril,'[52] it also condemned any 'attempts to use the lack of breakthroughs in countering illicit drug circulation' as a 'pretext for calling for revision, or even deconstruction, of the IDCR.'[53] In particular, Russia dismissed the GCDP initiative as an attack on the international anti-narcotics system, in that it called for the legalization of certain types of narcotic substances, claimed that prohibitionism had exhausted itself, and that present methods—which the Commission considers overwhelmingly punitive—had proven ineffective and excessively costly. According to the head of Russia's FSKN at the time, 'the advocates of this approach try to manipulate the facts with an aim to show that it is the prohibitionist policy of the world community that leads to narcotics-related criminality.'[54] The GCDP reports were also seen in Moscow as an attack on the present UN-centered drug control system and, hence, on the UN. The most Moscow was ready to concede was a recognition that 'a new scale of narcotics challenge requires a new quality of response to it.' This led to a set of generalized and modest recommendations, such as 'strengthening of the three international anti-narcotics conventions, closing the gaps in their practical implementation and adapting them creatively to new realities.'[55]

Attempts at liberalizing the IDCR through legalization—at the time, the discussion mostly evolved around soft drugs—were seen by Russia as particularly harmful and worrying, even though it was recognized that it was 'gaining popularity.'[56] Russia's official arguments against legalization included a threat of 'creeping disintegration of the IDCR, depriving international anti-narcotics efforts of the common political and legal platform' and a potential 'to create a network of narcotics offshores around the world.'[57] Moscow questioned the use of legal trade in alcohol and tobacco as an argument to legalize drugs by stressing multiple negative effects of alcohol abuse 'as one of the main causes of death from heart attacks or accidents.' Russia also employed the standard 'entrance gate' argument, claiming that the use of soft drugs raises the probability of addiction and facilitates the switch to hard drugs, whilst soft drugs themselves may lead to psychological disorders from schizophrenia to deep depression.

With many allies in the non-Western world—especially in Asia, Eurasia, and Africa—on the same side of the argument as Russia, the 2016 UNGASS did not lead to major revisions of the IDCR. Its final document reaffirmed 'the world free of drugs' as the main goal, and did not mention any harm reduction programs. For Russia, rejecting harm reduction was less of an issue in itself—that is, a domestic social or medical issue of dealing with drug use through substitute therapy—as it was a secondary by-product of its strict prohibitionism according to which medication-assisted treatment (MAT) was seen as just another violation of the ban on the use of narcotic substances. It is worth noting that on this particular issue, Russia's position was shared by fewer non-Western states (about ninety out of 193) than its broader protection of the IDCR regime. Even states with harsh anti-narcotics policies, such as China and Iran, had introduced some forms of substitute therapy.

Since then, Russia's official stance on this issue and on broader IDCR reform has remained unchanged. On the eve of the presentation of the GCDP's seventh report in Mexico in September 2018, Russia's Deputy Foreign Minister Oleg Syromolotov described harm reduction programs, including methadone MAT, as an 'indirect way of legalization of narcotic substances through official medical system' and reminded listeners that Russia's 'Strategy for the state anti-narcotics policy through 2020' prohibited the use of substitute therapy for treatment of drug addicts.[58] Even Russia's rare MAT advocates acknowledged that the 2018 GCDP report 'is useful mostly for those countries that have already moved [from total prohibitionism] towards regulation of their drug markets,' but 'hardly applicable' to Russia.[59]

Domestically, the dissenting opinions of some medics and marginal, often *émigré* NGO activists notwithstanding,[60] legalization is simply not part of the national discourse or debate, and does not seem to be very relevant in the Russian context compared to the far more pressing and still insufficiently or poorly addressed concerns about prevention, decriminalization of use, treatment and rehabilitation (see below a special sub-section on these issues). As lead NGO activist Anna Sarang noted, 'for our country [Russia], decriminalization of the drug (ab)use is a more relevant issue—to ensure that drug users end up not in prisons, but in places where they can get real medical and social support.'[61]

The Russian government has stood united on these issues, from the federal level all the way down to the city and municipal authorities.[62] In the absence of any serious domestic national debate on the subject, the primary role in related discussions has shifted to the Ministry of Foreign Affairs and to the international debates around the IDCR. More remarkably, even the few dissenting views in Russia acknowledge that 'the Russian population shares the authorities' position in favor of repressive attitudes towards drug abusers.'[63] Furthermore, the society at large appears to be more conservative on many drug control issues than the government itself, whose position does not simply reflect broader social consensus on the general prohibitionist framework, but, in some ways—especially on part of the Ministry of Health policies—tries to moderate the prevailing public mood.

i. Drug Enforcement

Russia's drug control and enforcement policy has been generally restrictive and heavily securitized. Russia's drug enforcement system only took shape with the formation in 2003 of a 40,000-strong drug enforcement agency, on the basis of a former department within the MVD—first the State Committee on Drug Control, then the FSKN—as part of the national 'security sector.' It was meant to evolve as a specialized, independent investigative and policing capacity, separate from the large and corrupt MVD, to tackle narcotics-related organized crime, trafficking networks, and related money laundering. The MVD retained powers to carry out drug-related administrative and criminal detentions, sometimes also performed by Federal Security Service (FSB), and the cases are decided by courts.

The FSKN remained a separate leading drug enforcement agency (reporting directly to the Russian president) for 13 years through April 2016, when it was transferred back to the MVD again as a chief directorate headed by a deputy minister, absorbing many of the former FSKN employees. This move was primarily dictated by state budget constraints in the midst of economic and financial crisis in Russia, aggravated by the global collapse of energy prices in the mid-2010s. It was also part of the broader security sector reshuffling and optimization that involved, *inter alia*, concentration of all policing functions into a streamlined, leaner, more compact and focused MVD, while stripping it of its more militarized forces—transforming the former 'internal troops' and special forces into the newly established 'National Guard'—and partly making up for that institutional loss by bringing drug enforcement and migration control issues back under the MVD's control. The MVD and FSB are the main federal agencies conducting drug-related investigations.

Regardless of its institutional structure, Russia's drug enforcement system remained punitive/prosecution-oriented, though this is hardly unique to narcotics-related cases, and reflects the general state of criminal justice in Russia. Out of 100,000 narcotics-related court cases in 2010, in only 0.1 per cent of cases were defendants acquitted.[64] At the end of 2016, 26 per cent of the population of Russia's penal colonies (138,260 of the total of 519,491 people) were convicted on narcotics-related charges.[65] Among people convicted for narcotics-related crimes, drug users—convicted for illicitly buying and using drugs without the purpose of selling them—heavily outnumbered traders: in 2018, they comprised 79 per cent of all those convicted in drug-related cases.[66] In the late 2010s, approximately 200,000 drug-related crimes were registered annually, with no discernible change in the scale of illicit circulation of drugs.[67] Illicit drug manufacturing and trade are considered serious crimes, with a maximum sentence of 15–20 years. In December 2017, the Moscow Region (Oblast)

Court for the first time issued a life sentence for drug trading (which was the heaviest of several charges) in a case involving a Tajik gang leader engaged in trafficking of over 600 kilograms of heroin from Afghanistan via Tajikistan to Russia. The defendant had been previously released in Tajikistan following an extradition from Russia on similar charges in 2003.[68]

As FSKN increasingly took over drug control policy from 2003 to 2016, the drug enforcement system gradually became more securitized (for the securitization of drug policies more broadly, see Chapter 1 by Annette Idler). For example, FSKN took control from the Ministry of Health in deciding on the list of precursors to be banned and since 2014 even had the final say on the inclusion of new items on the list of controlled substances, under the pretext of the need to speed up the 'listing' process for dynamically emerging new narcotic and psychoactive substances. While following the FSKN downgrade to an MVD directorate, the Ministry of Health regained some of its functions, the lead role of '*siloviki*' (the security sector) in Russia's drug control was underscored in December 2016 by the presidential appointment of the minister of interior as chair of the State Anti-Drug Committee, which coordinates Russia's drug control policy.

The spread of synthetic drugs in Russia's domestic market required additional, and adjusted, enforcement and policing efforts. In 2017 alone, Russian law enforcement destroyed 150 labs producing synthetic drugs.[69] As synthetic drugs are sold online, including via the 'dark web,' more often than other drugs, the MVD and FSB had to intensify their efforts on this front—for instance, by shutting down the larger identified online marketplaces, in cooperation with Russia's internet and media watchdog agency Roskomnadzor.

Of the foreign influences on the Russian drug enforcement system, the US drug enforcement model appears to have exerted the strongest influence through leading by example, rather than from any conscious effort on the US side. The US experience in counternarcotics, a well-developed drug enforcement system, and strong specialized investigative and intelligence capacities in this field appealed to the Russians, and fitted the specifics of Russia's own law enforcement preferences. The US Drug Enforcement Administration (DEA) to an extent served as a model for FSKN. More broadly, in the early twenty-first century a degree of proximity could be observed between the two countries' drug enforcement policies at the federal level. Both have been heavily securitized, interdiction and supply-oriented—in contrast to prevailing European approaches, for instance, which emphasize demand reduction and treat the issue primarily as a health/law enforcement problem (see Chapter 12 by Damon Barret and Kasia Malinowska-Sempruch). This used to facilitate contacts and cooperation between the two services in drug enforcement—prior to the breakdown of US–Russia relations in 2014, which led to the placement of Viktor Ivanov (FSKN Director May 2008–April 2016) under the US sanctions regime, despite his non-involvement in Russia's policy on Ukraine, and to the discontinuation of the work of the Counternarcotic Working Group of the US–Russian Bilateral Presidential Commission. Nonetheless, a degree of proximity between the US and Russia's approaches to drug enforcement—as well as their positive assessment of the IDCR and the role of the UNODC—remained in place. The Obama administration, however, appeared to prefer that someone other than itself (for example, Russia) champion the prohibitionist, pro-IDCR and pro-UNODC discourse at the 2016 UNGASS. Still, as noted by Andrey Avetisyan, Russia's former ambassador to Afghanistan and the UNODC Regional Representative for Afghanistan, in October 2015: 'For us as the UNODC, the US–Russia format is the most comfortable, the most UNODC-friendly one.'[70]

Though restrictive, Russia's drug control and enforcement policy is hardly the strictest in the world. Since 1996, an open-ended national moratorium on capital punishment has been in place in Russia. Additionally, criminalization of drug use in Russia is not as strict as (for example) in Sweden: in Russia, minimal individual doses (6 or less grams of marijuana or 0.5 or less grams of heroin or cocaine) carry administrative, not criminal punishments. The intensification of bureaucratic infighting within the government due to a situation of declining funding and budget cuts even helped push FSKN, in its later years, towards rationalization and optimization of drug control policies, which at times had 'sideline' positive effects. For instance, in 2015 punishment for drug storage was differentiated into those (a) for personal use only, (b) retail distribution, (c) wholesale and (d) organized trade/trafficking, whereas previously these were all qualified as serious or particularly serious crimes. In the words of FSKN's director at the time, Viktor Ivanov, 'some heroin abuser Sidorov caught with 2.5 grams is treated by law in the same way as some Russian analogue of Pablo Escobar.'[71] With around 100,000 people convicted for narcotics-related offenses annually in the mid-2010s, and the government spending around 96 billion roubles a year on associated costs, FSKN proposed to allow courts at the stage of preliminary investigation to offer drug users medical treatment as an alternative to criminal prosecution.[72]

Overall, in the mid-late 2010s, there has been no appetite in several key sectors of the Russian government, including the presidential administration, for any major draconian drug policy restrictions or further restriction of the already harsh drug enforcement function. None of these, however, implied any liberalization of Russia's overall drug control and drug enforcement policy. In some aspects, it has or is expected to become more restrictive: for instance, following the autumn 2019 call from President Putin to criminalize 'online narcotics propaganda.' In July 2020, a new draft law in the Russian parliament called for the expansion of the crime of 'inducing to drug abuse' to include 'narcotics propaganda through the use of information-communication networks, including the internet,' to carry a sentence of up to 15 years in prison.[73]

ii. Demand Reduction, Treatment and Rehabilitation

Demand reduction remains the weakest spot in Russia's drug control policies, and is an area where both Russian state and society should intensify their efforts and focus. However, what is often overlooked, especially by Western observers in their critique of Russia's approach to demand, and especially harm, reduction, are the role of the IDCR in introducing and promoting demand reduction to Russia, and a series of steps undertaken in the late 2010s, notably by Russia's Ministry of Health, to humanize and improve the situation on the demand reduction and rehabilitation side. This is especially noticeable in the context of the dissolution of Russia's main drug enforcement agency (FSKN) as a separate entity in 2016 and the shift of its enforcement functions back to the MVD.

The IDCR and the UNODC, in particular, played a key role in familiarizing Russia—a country that in the first decades of dealing with the problem had been completely obsessed with addressing the supply side—with the idea, principles, and methods of demand reduction. As a result, in 2010 Russia's 'Strategy for the state anti-narcotics policy through 2020' for the first time proclaimed, alongside drug enforcement, the need for demand reduction, including through social rehabilitation of drug users. In the mid-2010s, the UNODC started to more actively support and promote demand reduction in Russia. Former UNODC Executive Director Fedotov was a strong advocate of demand reduction, very familiar with Russia's realities and specifics, and has been an authoritative voice influencing Russia's internal drug control policies, to the extent that it has been possible. While noting Russia's limited progress in this area, such as introducing prophylactic programs in schools, he repeatedly underscored the urgency of the problem. Among other things, he suggested the creation of a UNODC-based platform for the exchange of best practices and results of cutting-edge scientific research on drugs which Russia could benefit from. He encouraged greater reorientation of Russia's approach towards public health care of drug users at all stages from treatment to reintegration into a society, and insisted that methods of medical assistance to drug users should stem from scientific evidence, not ideology, superstitions, or personal convictions or preferences.[74]

The main treatment available to drug users in Russia is limited to detoxication, followed by rehabilitation: relief of withdrawal (abstinence) syndrome followed by psychological training, with the use of antipsychotic drugs, not agonist and antagonist agents. For Russia, harm reduction—and especially substitute therapy, including opioid treatment programs—remains the single most contentious aspect of demand reduction. In 1998, any substitute therapy was banned by the 'Law on narcotics and psychotropic substances.' Russia's January 2020 draft Strategy on State Antinarcotics Policy through 2030 stressed again 'the inadmissibility of substitute drug therapy methods with the use of narcotics, the legalization of "recreational" drug use, or unjustified expansion of the use of "narcotic analgesics."'[75]

Along with Turkmenistan and Uzbekistan, Russia remains one of just three post-Soviet states that have totally banned MAT. For over two decades, Russia's ban on MAT was still supported even by the Ministry of Health,[76] and remains the only aspect of drug policy that deviates from the official UNODC approach and from the World Health Organization's (WHO) recommendations. While the UNODC sees substitute therapy as having both positive and negative impacts, Russia denies it has any positive impact, viewing it as the worst manifestation of 'narcoliberalism' and little more than a justification for the legalization of certain types of drugs. Russia's drug control officials insisted that the emphasis should be placed not only on 'relieving the pain' of drug 'addicts,' but 'on the right of other people to live in a drug-free society and community.'[77] They believe that MAT 'is not therapy, as it does not cure, but freezes the problem and leads to lifetime narcotization.'[78]

That did not, however, stop a private citizen—long-time user Dmitri Poloushkin—in his attempt to contest the ban on MAT in Russia's Constitutional Court in March 2016, which he claimed violated his right to 'all available medical treatment' guaranteed by Article 41. Nor did it stop the first deputy head of the Federal Penitentiary Service of Russia (FSIN) Anatoly Rudyi, who unexpectedly spoke in favor of substitute therapy at the September 2018 meeting of the Presidential Council on Human Rights, explaining from his work experience that criminal justice methods cannot solve the problem of 'what is a market and can only be fought by market means.'[79]

The situation regarding the rehabilitation and social reintegration of former drug users also remains grim. There is no institutional coherence and coordination, or clarity about which agency or ministry will be responsible for demand reduction. Three different ministries (health, labor, and interior) divide responsibilities for drug user rehabilitation; for example, while medical rehabilitation centers are under the Ministry of Health, control over non-medical rehabilitation (outside the formal health system) is retained by the law enforcement (the MVD since 2016, and FSKN before that). A comprehensive national rehabilitation program is lacking, as is funding—like all other parts of the 'social sphere,' rehabilitation had been severely underfunded. By the mid-2010s, the Ministry of Health operated only eighteen medical rehabilitation centers and eighty-eight departments in clinics, in addition to four centers operated by regional authorities and a handful of specialized in-patient daycare stations, together making up just 3032 hospital beds for a population of 143.5 million, where the number of officially registered drug abusers alone exceeds 530,000.[80]

An earlier attempt to address the problem of underfunding and lack of attention to rehabilitation was through securitization of the sphere: in 2014, FSKN assumed the role of a chief curator and coordinator of the system of rehabilitation and resocialization of drug abusers, and direct control of non-medical rehabilitation centers—about 500 private and confessional structures which could serve up to 20,000 people annually. It was also empowered to provide financial, organizational, and technical support to NGOs that worked in this sphere.[81] This short-lived attempt to shift control over social rehabilitation to a drug enforcement agency (an analogue of the US DEA), had it been realized, would have had serious repercussions; most small and mid-size private rehabilitation centers and NGOs could not fulfil strict FSKN reporting and other requirements, while many patients would be deterred by privacy concerns.

On the one hand, the downgrade of FSKN through its transformation into a directorate under the MVD in 2016, mainly dictated by imperatives of financial optimization, implied overall decrease of funding for drug control policies in general; in reality, securitizing something is often the only way to ensure a proper level of funding and attention to the matter in Russia. On the other hand, there was also a silver lining for demand reduction and rehabilitation. While the end of FSKN as a separate agency was hardly driven by any conscious effort to soften the enforcement approach that continued to dominate Russia's drug control policy, sheer optimization stopped FSKN's 'grand plans' to practically monopolize the rehabilitation sphere, and led to the transfer of some social functions in drug control from the former FSKN to the health ministry. The ministry's traditionally 'softer' stance on drug control policy implied its certain humanization. So far, this has been reflected in its handling of the problems of rehabilitation centers, and of seriously ill patients' access to narcotic painkillers.

In 2014, the Ministry of Health was tasked by Premier Dmitri Medvedev with drafting a project on the interaction between the national health system and non-medical rehabilitation centers. In May 2018, it came up with its set of fourteen mandatory and ten optional recommendations for such centers to get a license, including not only basic sanitary and other standards, but also an obligation not to use inhumane treatment, violating human dignity.[82]

There has been growing flexibility on allowing the use of narcotic substances for medical treatment as pain-relievers and for research purposes—for example, Moscow State University got permission to use these substances for that end. In 2015, the federal antinarcotics legislation was amended to ensure access of medical patients in need of narcotic and psychotropic substances, which was spurred by a series of high-profile suicides among seriously ill patients. In 2016, the health ministry presented a road map for facilitating access to pain-relieving medical narcotics, mostly opioids, for about a million patients in need, especially oncological patients.[83] However, according to the International Narcotics Control Board (INCB), Russia remains thirty-eighth out of forty-two in Europe in terms of patients' access to narcotic painkillers; worldwide, it comes in at eighty-second.[84]

iii. The Effects of the IDCR and Other External Influences and Their Limits

How does this relate to any potential IDCR 'adjustment?' Could any potential IDCR adjustment—or, indeed, any external influence—affect or change Russia's drug control policies and practices?

While overall in the mid-late 2010s Russia did more to comply with the IDCR than before, and in a more well-rounded manner, it remains firmly opposed to any major IDCR reform. On the one hand, a combination of the scale of Russia's drug challenge, its law enforcement system, and the dominance of social conservatism in its national value system largely explains why the IDCR's effects for Russia itself are interpreted as positive and why, internationally, the IDCR has turned into one of Moscow's rare 'sacred cows.' On the other hand, while there are some serious problems in Russia's drug control policy, especially on the demand reduction, treatment, and rehabilitation side, they cannot be blamed on the IDCR. They primarily relate to Russia's own socioeconomic, sociopolitical and sociocultural contextual specifics, the preferences of its securitized regime and governance system, and dominant popular sentiments.

Could anyone—beyond some form of the 'adjusted' IDCR—deliberately influence Russia's domestic drug control policies from the outside, including in the area of demand reduction? If any direct political push for this comes from the West, it is a non-starter by default. That is not only due to Russia's principal disagreements with many Western countries on such aspects of drug policy as substitute therapy or legalization of soft drugs, nor even due to the worst deterioration of the Russia–West relations in the past 25 years, ongoing since 2014. Russia is unlikely to perceive any Western 'mentoring' in this area as sincere or benign—above all, because it partly blames the US/NATO 'security' involvement in Afghanistan in the 2000s–early 2010s for the state collapse/dysfunctionality, lack of security and comprehensive development, and the armed conflict in that country. All these are fundamental conditions for a major increase in opiate production in Afghanistan throughout the 2000s–10s which drove the avalanche-scale supply along the northern route to Russia. Against this background, attempts by anyone in or from the West to lecture Russia on any aspect of its drug control policy are likely to provoke (and have provoked), *inter alia*, a return call by Russia for the West to instead focus more on support for drug control and development assistance to Afghanistan.

If any specific external influences on Russia's drug control policies are conceivable, those are likely to come from countries with stricter prohibitionist policies, but far more advanced than Russia on the demand reduction side, for instance Sweden. This does not mean, however, that there are no valuable lessons to be learned by Russia from abroad, including from European drug control experience, despite significant differences in the overall approaches to drug policy. Russia and Europe are comparable, above all, as the two main end-markets for the Afghan opiates, each linked to Afghanistan by its own major trafficking route, the 'Balkan' or the 'northern.' As shown by the European experience, even within the IDCR framework, combining sustained demand reduction/treatment improvement, functional law enforcement capacity, and protected external borders—of the EU and some of the main transit states along the Balkan trafficking route, such as Iran—can help to reduce the volume of trafficking and the size of the domestic opiate market.

International/foreign drug control policies and best practices were not the only external influences on Russia's drug control policies. Also, the limited, but highly controversial Western sanctions imposed against Russia in the context of the Russia-West tensions, catalyzed by the crisis over Ukraine, had dual implications.

Broadly speaking, the dynamic interaction of Western sanctions and Russian countersanctions contributed to the spiral of further deterioration of Russia–West relations, and reinforced the Russian authorities' rejection of any form of 'liberalism' originating in and promoted by Western institutions, states and non-state actors alike, especially in civic, social, and political spheres—including drug control/regulation policies. More specifically, Russia tried to complicate the enforcement of sanctions by no longer updating much of the information and data that was previously available on its government websites in English. That move heavily affected Russia's financial intelligence body, Rosfinmonitoring, seriously limiting access to its information, including on narcotics-related and other money laundering matters.[85]

However, paradoxically, the sanctions/countersanction game helped Russia reactivate and liberalize a segment of its legal drug economy. Until recently, Russia has had to import almost 100 per cent of the legal narcotic substances required for medical purposes by its pharmaceutical industry. As of 2018, there were thirteen legal medical opioids registered in Russia, including nine considered vital, but none of them involved full-cycle production inside Russia, while nine out of ten main suppliers were based in countries who had imposed sanctions against Russia. To ensure Western import phase-out in the context of expanding sanctions, in December 2018 the government formally endorsed the resumption of cultivation of narcotic plants in Russia, for medical purposes and the pharmaceutical industry. This extended to opium poppy with high-level alkaloid content. To develop a full-cycle production of narcotic painkillers, Russia needed 100 hectares of cultivation area for required drug cultures.[86] While the MVD has been tasked with ensuring strict control over such cultivation, indirectly this move—dictated solely by pragmatic socioeconomic reasons—may contribute to slow, gradual liberalization of at least some segments of Russia's drug control policy.

The Evolution of Russia's Approach to Opiate Supply Reduction:
Development, Negotiated Peace, and Countering Money Laundering

International debates on drug control are not confined to the prohibitionism/legalization framework. They extend to the balance of supply–demand and respective drug control strategies, problems of alternative and general socioeconomic development, ways to integrate and balance various drug control methods, and strategies and countering narcotics-related money laundering. While often perceived and portrayed by advocates of the IDCR liberalization as one-sidedly conservative, it is in these areas that Russia's policies and approaches—which took time to evolve—are more forward-looking, and may even generate some progressive ideas.

Overall, Russia's approach to the world drug problem has two sides that should be analyzed together. On the conservative/ traditionalist side, Russia remains opposed to the rise of anti-prohibitionist and legalization tendencies, especially in the Western hemisphere, and their potential impact on the IDCR. However, on the progressive and reformist side, Russia increasingly emphasizes comprehensive socioeconomic development in major drug-producing and transit areas, which should extend beyond crop substitution and agricultural development, and the need for international support for such development. It has turned to backing—and even directly facilitating—a negotiated, peaceful solution to Afghanistan's armed conflict as a *sine qua non* condition for improving prospects for state functionality, development, and drug control in the country which is the largest supplier of opiates to the Russian drug market. Russia also increasingly focuses on targeting transnational narcotics-related money laundering, much of which takes place in the developed and economically advanced parts of the world. It is in these areas that the main prospects for Russia's international cooperation with states across the North–South and supply–demand divide lie.

From Insisting on Eradication to Emphasizing Comprehensive Development

Russia's approach to these issues took almost two decades to evolve. The main shift occurred from Russia's earlier, almost exclusive emphasis on strict enforcement strategies of supply reduction—eradication, interdiction, drug labs destruction—to a more balanced and comprehensive approach that not only implies integration of enforcement, development, and institution-building strategies, but also suggests a new concept of alternative development. This gradual evolution is best illustrated by Russia's approach to reducing the size of the Afghan opium economy.

For Russia, trafficking of narcotics from Afghanistan reached the scale of a 'heroin catastrophe' in the very period when the United States and NATO assumed control over the security of Afghanistan. In addressing this problem, Moscow faced marked indifference from Western players in Afghanistan. As a result, some segments of Russian security and expert elites developed a view according to which the rise in illicit drug production in Afghanistan during US/NATO presence in Afghanistan occurred primarily due to US/NATO presence.

The lack of direct threat from Afghan opiates to the United States, and the fact they were a lower threat for most NATO/EU members compared to Russia, in addition to a prioritization of security and counterinsurgency tasks for the United States and its NATO partners, explain why the West did not particularly emphasize counternarcotics in Afghanistan. To the extent that the United States started paying some attention to counternarcotics in the country in the late 2000s, it emphasized different aspects than Russia did. From the United States' viewpoint, backing massive eradication in Afghanistan was technically unfeasible and politically counterproductive, raising the risk of alienating peasants in drug-producing areas. An emphasis on large-scale interdiction could, in turn, alienate many friendly or neutral warlords, government-linked figures, and clans who profit from the illicit drug trade in Afghanistan no less—or even more—than insurgents do. Hence, in a radical departure from the US reliance on massive aerial eradication in Colombia, for example, in Afghanistan the Obama administration promoted a combination of alternative development (mostly crop substitution in select areas, such as the Helmand or Kandahar 'food zones') and limited interdiction efforts meant to target insurgency-linked actors only.[87]

In contrast, Russia had initially advocated for more radical counternarcotics measures in Afghanistan, calling for massive eradication, robust interdiction, and drug laboratory destruction by the Afghan government and its security backers (the US and NATO). Such calls were hardly realistic, and were primarily of a declaratory nature. It took time for the Russian government to realize the gravity and 'indivisibility' of the narcotics problem, and to officially upgrade it to a top national and human security concern. It also took time for Russia's counternarcotics sector to gradually familiarize itself with the specifics and sources of the Afghan opium economy. As a result, Moscow's policy started to evolve beyond its earlier 'eradication first' mantra.

Unlike its Western counterparts, Russia was not constrained by any direct security/counterinsurgency risks in Afghanistan, or consequently, by the need to ensure loyalty or neutrality of local strongmen, clans, and field commanders by closing its eyes to their active involvement in the drug trade. Along with UNODC, Russia was quicker than Western states to recognize the drug business' links to all types of Afghan political-military actors, including corrupt officials and warlords linked to the government, not just the Taliban insurgency. In 2011, Russia's top counternarcotics officials were the first foreign government representatives to point out the short-sightedness of attempts to fully conflate drugs and insurgency/terrorism in Afghanistan: at that time, the insurgents' annual revenues from taxing poppy crops and some of the opium trade in areas under their control was unlikely to exceed US$140–170 million,[88] which comprised no more than 6.5 per cent of the total US$2.6 bln-worth net value of the Afghan drug economy in 2011,[89] making the insurgency a relatively 'minority beneficiary' of the drug economy.[90]

Since the early 2010s, Russia has started to advocate a more comprehensive drug control and counternarcotics strategy in Afghanistan, promoting not only enforcement measures—policing, interdiction, drug laboratories destruction, and crop eradication—but also longer-term development strategies beyond crop substitution, with the goal of creating stable sources of income on a national scale as a socioeconomic alternative to the opium economy. Russia fully recognized that the Afghan opium economy had deep roots, and that its reduction required stable international support for the socioeconomic development of Afghanistan. As President Putin remarked in September 2012:

Nine percent of that country's GDP comes from drug trafficking. If you want to replace this 9 per cent, you have to pay—but no one wants to... Talk is not enough—what is needed is substantive economic policies and financial assistance. Nobody seems willing to provide that, to begin with.[91]

As noted by FSKN's head Ivanov at a BRICS Ministerial on the narcotics problem in April 2015, 'the task of effectively turning people away from growing poppy requires major infrastructure reforms and solutions in drug-producing states.'[92]

Ironically, it was Russia's drug enforcement agency that had been the most active lobbyist for Russia's comprehensive development strategy for Central Asia. FSKN's plan to set up the so-called corporation on cooperation with Central Asian states (a subsidiary of Russia's state foreign investment bank Vneshekonombank) to promote alternative development (AD) programs across the region was backed by President Putin, but was stalled by insufficient funding and interest on the part of the banking sector. On Afghanistan, FSKN commissioned Russia's most ambitious narcotics-related development initiative so far—a plan for comprehensive development, prepared for the 'G-8' 2014 Sochi summit that was cancelled due to sharp deterioration in Russia–West relations over the crisis in Ukraine. The plan was based on a key premise, which applies far beyond Afghanistan: alternative agricultural development alone does not provide a long-term economic solution to the problem of Afghan drugs; other sustainable, long-term alternative sources of cash-based income have to be created inside Afghanistan on a systemic basis at levels from micro to national, including industrial and infrastructure development and extraction of mineral resources. More specifically, since Afghanistan's industrial development—including existing resource extraction projects such as those funded by China and India—requires more water and energy than Afghanistan has, the first stage of the plan focused on solutions to the energy problem, and investment in hydro-electric power stations in the northern parts of that country.[93] Implementing such ideas depended on international investment and cooperation, including with the West. This level of international investment in Afghanistan's development has been and remains unlikely to materialize. Additionally, Russia's relationships with major donors are unfavorable for such plans. Nevertheless, Moscow's interest in and thinking on AD have been growing. Both at the 2016 UNGASS and beyond, Russia has become an active promoter of a comprehensive development agenda and support for drug-producing states, including (but extending beyond) crop substitution and agricultural development.

Support for the Peace Process in Afghanistan

Russia has gradually increased seizures of the Afghan opiates at its own borders, started to do more on demand reduction at home, and can certainly do more in pressuring its Central Asian partners to improve drug control. However, there is little that Russia can do about reducing the opium economy inside Afghanistan. Russia lacked any leverage on Afghanistan's internal developments and actors, especially on the insurgency that *de facto* controlled rural areas in the country's south, where up to half of the heroin destined for Russia originates. As Russia gradually lost hope that any force inside Afghanistan could exert pressure on the Taliban, it started to reach out to those actors who could—such as Pakistan. In the mid-2010s, as the Taliban emerged as a major local armed opponent of the Afghan branch of the Salafist-jihadist Islamic State (ISIS), Russia even started to establish limited contacts with the Taliban, albeit much later than most other regional and extra-regional stakeholders. In addition to anti-ISIS considerations, Moscow's interest has been to make sure that the Taliban's interests are confined to Afghanistan and do not extend to Central Asia, and to promote Russia's drug-control concerns in any negotiation process on Afghanistan.

Russia's foreign and security policymakers gradually came to realize that none of Russia's concerns about Afghanistan, including reducing the size of the Afghan opium economy, could be alleviated as long as the armed conflict there continues in full force. This has made Moscow genuinely interested in stabilization in Afghanistan—and the combination of the US/NATO-backed military pressure on the Taliban and Western support for the Afghan government has not achieved this, nor ever could. Considering that Russia itself cannot play any direct security role in Afghanistan, and has had very limited policy leverage there, the maximum it could do was to push for stabilization through a regionally inclusive peace process involving the main Afghan insurgent force (a task that required having contacts with all major parties in question, including the Taliban). This led Russia to establish the Moscow format of regional peace consultations on Afghanistan in 2017, and hosting and facilitating the Moscow inter-Afghan dialogue involving the Taliban in 2019. In addition, Russia engaged in bilateral discussions on the Afghan peace process with the United States since 2018, and extended them in 2019 to also involve China and Pakistan. It further supported both the US–Taliban talks since 2018,[94] and the US–Taliban agreement signed on 29 February 2019.[95]

Countering Money Laundering

Russia's growing emphasis on following the money trail can be seen as another way to improve the supply–demand imbalance in Russia's drug control policies, and those globally. Russia's international activities in this field include leading the FATF Eurasian Group on Combating Money Laundering and the Financing of Terrorism, which also involves all Central Asian states. At FATF, Russia initiated and chaired (on par with the UNODC Global Program against Money Laundering) a major 'strategic surveillance' and typological study on financial flows linked to the Afghan opiates, which was actively supported by Western, Asian and other countries, the IMF, and the World Bank. It revealed drug money laundering and accumulation networks extending as far as the UAE, China, Turkey, Hong Kong, Russia, Latvia, the Netherlands, and the British Virgin Islands.[96]

Conclusion

In the context of discussions around the 2016 UNGASS, a large part of the world—including Russia, most Asian and some other states—has firmly recommitted itself to the IDCR. This does not mean, however, that they are opposed to any adjustment, upgrade, and development of the present regime.

Russia's conservative approach to IDCR reform and broader international drug policy debates has been to a significant extent shaped by its position as one of the largest markets for illicit circulation and consumption of mostly imported drugs in the early twenty-first century, and as the largest end-market for Afghan heroin, as well as by the specifics of its own state/governance system and society, including dominant social values. Illicit circulation and consumption of drugs pose a major direct human security challenge to Russian society. In contrast to Europe, Russia's drug market remains less diversified. For two decades, Afghan heroin has dominated its hard drugs market. While foreign and domestically produced synthetic drugs have recently overtaken it, the new unprecedented highs in opiate production in Afghanistan in the late 2010s are likely to lead to new surplus heroin flows and a return to cheaper opiate prices at the main end-markets, including Russia. The situation is aggravated by five factors. First, slow socioeconomic development and often weak state functionality across the 'northern' route to Russia via Central Asian states; second, the role of cross-border informal trade, smuggling and informal migration flows for societies and economies of most Central Asian states; third, weak border and immigration control between Russia and Central Asia, and between Central Asia and Afghanistan; fourth, poor narcotics control in Central Asian transit states; and fifth, Russia's own underdeveloped demand reduction system.

For Russia, the main problems in drug control and the solutions to them go beyond the IDCR. On the supply side, they are more closely linked to the broader agenda of promoting long-term, comprehensive socioeconomic development at macro, meso, and micro-regional levels, and addressing problems with state functionality, bad governance, and corruption across the Central Asian/Eurasian region. In addition, supporting a negotiated solution for protracted armed conflict and upgrade of functionality and legitimacy of the Afghan state have been seen as *sine qua non* conditions for effective drug control and development which could help reduce the size of the Afghan opium economy. On the demand side, international prohibitionism versus legalization debates have minimal relevance in Russia's domestic context, where there is a broad societal consensus in favor of prohibitionism. In parallel, there also seems to be growing public support for introducing further restrictions on the use of such legal substances as tobacco and even alcohol. The main issue of the national debate on drug control in Russia has evolved around the need for a shift from the state-centered and enforcement-oriented system to the more human security-oriented paradigm that integrates enforcement and interdiction measures but emphasizes prevention, treatment and social rehabilitation. Health and social rehabilitation aspects, as well as prophylactic and preventive demand reduction strategies, remain the weakest segments of Russia's drug control system, even as in the second half of the 2010s there have been certain improvements in this sphere. These have been due mainly to the growing role of the Ministry of Health in Russia's drug policy—for example, in ensuring access of seriously ill patients to narcotic painkillers and in the rehabilitation of drug users. In this area, the relevant IDCR instruments and the broader international cooperation on drug control would be most useful for Russia. Some pragmatic 'liberalization' of Russia's drug regime also resulted, unexpectedly, from Western sanctions that stimulated import phase-out to lower Russia's dependence on Western products, including previously entirely imported narcotic substances for medical purposes. This led to the lift of the ban on limited domestic cultivation of narcotic cultures and manufacturing of narcotic drugs for medical purposes.

Internationally, Russia sees the world as divided over the issue of reforming the existing IDCR. It insists that efforts to reform the IDCR cannot be tailored to the interests of one group or type of state—for example, drug-supplier states—and that such efforts should be balanced and take into account interests, needs, and vulnerabilities of supplier states, significant transit (transit/consuming) countries, and main end-markets alike. Russia's prohibitionist and still mainly supply-centered position has been largely dictated by specifics of its own narcotics situation and domestic imperatives which for much of the early twenty-first century have been dominated by the need to counter the Afghan heroin challenge. Unless the size and output of the Afghan opium economy, related trafficking along the northern route, and heroin consumption in Russia drastically decline, and Russia's own drug market structure becomes more diversified and demand-driven, its position on the supply–demand equation, rejection of harm reduction, and its opposition to any more radical IDCR reform are unlikely to change fundamentally.

Overall, this also remains the prevailing approach across the broader macro-regions of Eurasia/East Asia. It is shared by most members of Shanghai Cooperation Organization, although even some of these states—including China and Iran—practice softer approaches to harm reduction, for example through substitute therapy. While much of Russia's international activity on drug policy is driven by its Afghanistan-centered 'Eurasian bias,' this bias also limits its global appeal. Throughout the 2010s, limited financial and institutional means for actively promoting Russia's drug control agenda constituted another constraint. Beyond Moscow's Eurasian partners, Russia's leverage over the broader international debate on the IDCR—while limited—has been and will be used wherever possible. Apart from having its voice heard at the UN tribune and in the IDCR bodies, Russia draws anti-narcotics concerns into the agenda of BRICS—the broadest transcontinental framework that it is part of.

Russia's drug control policy is not, however, one-sidedly conservative, nor confined to prohibitionism alone. Over the first two decades of the twenty-first century, this policy has undergone significant evolution from a tougher, almost entirely enforcement-oriented approach centered on supply reduction to a more balanced and comprehensive one. As a result, Russia has come to fully acknowledge the critical importance of a combination of enforcement and trafficking reduction with support for socioeconomic development in drug-producing and transit states, plus greater attention to demand reduction. Russia also takes a broad view of AD which goes beyond a primary focus on agriculture, and implies integration of infrastructure and industrial development at levels from local to national and regional. On this aspect—the need to fully integrate drug control and AD into broader socioeconomic development strategies—Russia closely shares views with many drug-producing states from Asia and Latin America. The imperative of comprehensive socioeconomic development as the primary long-term drug control strategy may form the main basis for Russia's cooperation and coordination with these states, including on the ways to reform and upgrade the IDCR—despite sharp differences on liberalization of prohibitionism as the mainstay of the IDCR.

PART THREE

BETWEEN SECURITIZATION AND PEOPLE-CENTERED POLICIES:
A GLOCAL PERSPECTIVE ON THE WAR ON DRUGS

11

DRUG USE AND CRIME IN THE CONTEXT OF THE WAR ON DRUGS

Nicolas Trajtenberg, Olga Sánchez de Ribera and *Clara Musto*

The IDCR and the Drug and Crime Link

The link between drugs and crime has been a core concern for both supporters and detractors of the International Drug Control Regime (IDCR).[1] Supporters of the IDCR prohibitionist status quo rely on the idea that the reduction of crime and violence are strongly dependent on being successful in the reduction of drug use.[2] From this perspective, efforts should be focused both on restraining drug supply and demand through investing resources in the criminal justice system, particularly in the enforcement of laws and sanctions aiming to control and deter producers, traffickers, and consumers. This should be complemented by prevention and treatment programs towards drug users or potential users.[3] Conversely, detractors of the IDCR have contended the causal contribution that policies by themselves can play in violence. More specifically, the prohibitionist emphasis on the criminal justice system, repression, and criminalization has proven to be not only largely ineffective in its goals of diminishing the demand and supply of drugs, but also enormously costly. According to estimations by the Alternative World Drug Report, the costs of drug law enforcement might be over $100 billion annually.[4] Furthermore, it is argued that the IDCR has counterproductive effects which aggravate violence through higher prices. Proponents of this argument say the IDCR increases violent competition among dealers, causes a rise in the corruption of criminal justice institutions, increases the problematic use of drugs and associated health problems, and provokes additional negative externalities through stigmatization and criminalization of drug users (see Chapter 6 by Carlos A. Pérez Ricart for an analysis of the collateral damages of prohibitionism in Central America and particularly Mexico).[5] As Paul Gootenberg claims in this volume, 'There are few model IDCR "success stories" to speak of.'

In this ongoing debate, much less attention has been paid to any systematic analysis of the empirical bases of the prohibitionist model in attempts to understand if drug use and crime are causally related and how. It is estimated that in 2017, 5.5 per cent of the world's population aged fifteen to sixty-four had used an illicit substance at least once in the previous year, and almost 13 per cent of people who illicitly use drugs are dependent. Cannabis is the most commonly used (188 million people), followed by opioids, amphetamine and prescription stimulants, ecstasy, and cocaine.[6] Empirical research shows there is a consistent association between the use of drugs and crime.[7] However, an association does not necessarily imply causality, and there is strong disagreement about how to interpret this connection and what type of policy consequences should be implemented.[8] Furthermore, a number of authors have identified a tendency in the existent researches to use uncritically non-representative samples of individuals within criminal justice populations with a higher rate of drug prevalence that exaggerates the proportion of crime caused by drugs.[9] Its problematic validity is due to the 'the collision of the dark figures, the unknown majorities of crime and drug use'[10] and to the associated fact that police discrimination plays a key role in the detention of offenders.[11] However, a methodic review of the available data specifically on the topic of drug use and crime for the Latin American case is still very much needed.

These doubts regarding the causal link between drugs and crime, in addition to the unfairness and inefficacy of 'tough and crime oriented' policies, have led some societies to explore more 'lenient and consumer oriented' alternative policies. These prioritize a public health approach and a focus on decriminalization and harm reduction; emphasize social costs associated with illegal drug use rather than illegal drug use in itself; and also in many cases, explicitly target the most problematic consumers rather than occasional harmless users.[12]

In this context, Latin America constitutes an interesting case. Prohibitionist policies following IDCR guidelines dominated the policy agenda on illicit production and use in this region for many decades. Here, the idea that drug users are fundamentally offenders has led to the consideration of the drug problem as mainly a criminal justice issue to be tackled through a War on Drugs,[13] despite the lack of compelling scientific evidence of its effectiveness.[14] Furthermore, Latin America is considered one of the most violent regions in the world in terms of the high incidence of crime, the variety of forms of violence and its persistence, partially due to problems regarding drug trafficking and organized crime.[15] As a result, some countries have started to shift their drug policies. For instance, Mexico, Brazil, Bolivia, Ecuador, and most notably Uruguay have started to review their policies in order to move towards more progressive drug reforms.[16] It is not yet clear why this radical change departing from IDCR guidelines took place in the Latin American region. According to Angélica Durán-Martínez in Chapter 5 of this volume, South America's new position towards drug policies was the result of past accumulation of failures and the enormous costs of enforcing drug prohibition; increasing levels of violence; a recognition of the previous lack of focus on consumer markets; and the change in the relationship between the United States and South American countries.[17]

These reform projects have faced strong social and political controversy both at the national and international level (see Chapter 3 by Christopher Hallam and David Bewley-Taylor).[18] One of the critical issues is the fear that these reforms will increase the levels of crime and violence in Latin American societies. However, one of the main problems in making or countering this argument is the lack of systematic information about the nature of the link between the use of drugs and crime on this continent.

Theoretically, drug use can be associated with crime in different ways. In 1985, Goldstein developed a cornerstone framework where drug use was connected with crime (i) through pharmacologic disinhibition; (ii) due to economic necessity and lack of means to finance drug consumption; or (iii) as a result of violence and crime inherent to illegal networks and markets where the drug is distributed.[19] However, some have argued for the inverse connection: it is involvement in crime that explains the use of drugs, either through criminal subculture or lifestyle or through obtaining extra economic resources.[20] A third position argues for an interactive link between both phenomena.[21] Some authors have shown that crime is initially more relevant in explaining the use of drugs, but later, drug use is key to understanding the continuity and persistence of criminal trajectories.[22] Finally, a fourth interpretation is that the empirical connection between drug and crime is spurious, and that both phenomena are produced by third causal mechanisms such as family structure, personality characteristics, criminal subcultures, and deviated peer groups or gangs.[23]

These different interpretations have implications for varying types of policy responses, including the possibility of generating a more rational, less punitive, and efficient drug control regime. There has been a general call demanding that governments provide better ways of constructing indicators and measuring the effectiveness of their drug policies (see Chapter 14 by Robert Muggah and Katherine Aguirre). In this context, it is important to evaluate the validity and reliability of the evidence supporting prohibitionist discourses that are trying to block the wave of more progressive drug policy reforms in Latin America. But in addition, it is also essential to analyze how evidence is interpreted and constructed to avoid a naïve perspective, under which policies are just the result of rational evaluation of objective empirical evidence. This study is an attempt to provide policymakers, researchers, and the general public with some empirical evidence of the baseline of this issue, and a critical view of how the problem has been researched. Therefore, the aim of this chapter is to inform potential changes in the IDCR by systematically reviewing published studies of illegal drugs use and crime in Latin American countries; analyzing disagreements and consensus regarding the topic; evaluating whether existing empirical evidence backs up prohibitionist fears; and discussing the main challenges for drug policy that the IDCR is likely to face in the near future. The objectives of this chapter more specifically are first, to review qualitatively Latin American studies. Secondly, it will conduct a meta-analysis using available studies to estimate the prevalence of illegal drugs use among adults and young offenders in Latin American countries; assess the extent of use of objective illegal screening tests (for example, urinalysis) to detect the illegal use of drugs; determine what drugs were most often used illegally by offenders. Third, the need for more research due to a scarcity of studies in this area is discussed, and tentative conclusions are accordingly drawn.

Methodological Approach

A systematic literature search on crime and drugs association was conducted using the following databases: Web of Sciences, Medline/PubMed and Scielo. A Google Scholar search was conducted to find any relevant papers which might have been missed. Studies published between 1990 and July 2015, with abstracts in Spanish, English and Portuguese were included.

The studies included between 1990 and 2015 had to meet some of the following criteria, discussing: (i) prevalence of illegal drug use and offense; (ii) information regarding type of offense committed immediately after consuming drugs; (iii) information regarding methods used to measure consumption of illegal drug; (iv) information regarding life consumption of any illegal drug; (v) gender; (vi) age range; (vii) the country where the studies were conducted in Latin America; (viii) and studies published in Spanish, Portuguese, and English. Both published and unpublished studies were considered.

These studies were the empirical base for a meta-analysis, a worldwide technique used by policymakers to guide policy decision-making. Its utility derives from the possibility of testing with more precision and power the significance, effect and size of the results of different independent studies by pooling all the data together through statistical analysis. In this way, it is possible to arrive at less biased conclusions and overcome well-known problems in narrative reviews, namely: reviewer bias; a lack of comprehensiveness; and a tendency to rarely examine and consider the quality of included studies.[24]

An in-depth narrative review of divergences found in the studies that have evaluated the use of illicit drugs and crime in Latin American countries follows. Those studies with enough quantitative data were included in our estimation of the prevalence of drug use among offenders. Studies were classified into three groups according to how the drugs–crime link was conceptualized and explored. We summarize key results of the twenty-three studies that presented available data to calculate the prevalence of committing an offense under the effects of illicit use of drugs, or immediately after. Furthermore, we examine if there are different prevalence rates between adults and young individuals, different types of drugs consumed by offenders, and different types of measurement of drugs.

Recent Studies and Developments in Drug Use and Crime Understanding in Latin America

The relationship between drugs and crime is under-researched in Latin America.[25] Although there is a large body of qualitative scientific research, when it comes to quantitative studies, the number is smaller. A total of forty-five studies were included in our qualitative systematic review. Out of these forty-five, only twenty-three were eligible for inclusion in our meta-analytical review since they provided enough data to allow the calculation of effect size.

The main reasons for exclusion from the meta-analysis were the following: studies that did not specify if the illegal drug was consumed close to committing the crime—for example, only reporting last year prevalence or life prevalence; attribution model studies that included only the fraction of crimes attributed to illicit use of drugs; studies that only reported licit use of drugs—for example, tobacco, alcohol, morphine, tranquillizers and sedatives such as the benzodiazepine family, diazepam, flunitrazepam or temazepam; methaqualone and barbiturates; and studies that did not discriminate between legal and illegal drug use.

Research studies were not equally distributed across the Latin American continent. More than one-third of the studies (seventeen) were carried out in Chile, followed by Argentina, Uruguay, and Colombia (five studies each), Costa Rica and Mexico (three studies each), Brazil (two), and only one study each in Venezuela, the Dominican Republic, Peru, Ecuador, Cuba, and Bolivia.

More than 80 per cent of the studies are based on biased samples from criminal justice populations; either prison samples (thirty studies) or arrested samples (six studies). Only seven studies included biological measures to detect illicit use of drugs, six out of seven of which were conducted in Chile. Forty-four per cent of the studies involved young individuals (under 20 years old), 27 per cent of the studies included adult subjects, and 27 per cent of the studies included a wide range of ages that included both young and adult individuals, or did not report the age of respondents. In terms of gender, approximately one-third of the studies did not report the gender distribution of the sample, 53 per cent of the studies included both genders, and five studies included only males.

The great majority of the studies (thirty-three) discriminated between the different types of illicit uses of drugs. Only eight studies included a generic measure of illicit use of drugs, and the two remaining studies included one specific measure of one type of drug (crack and marijuana, respectively). Regarding the type of offenses, almost 40 per cent of the studies did not distinguish among different types of deviant behaviors, including only a generic measure of crime or recidivism. The rest of the studies either included different types of crimes or antisocial behaviors, or included only a specific form of crime as a correlate of use of illicit drugs, such as homicide or violent behavior. Additionally, more than one-third of the studies (sixteen) included life or last 12 months prevalence, or were unclear about the measurement; five studies included last month prevalence; and the rest of the studies (twenty-two) included the most valid available measures such as consumption within the last 24 hours prior to the offense, reporting to have been under the effects of drugs while committing the offense, or urine tests. Almost half of the studies (twenty-one) did not have any control group. Less than one-third of the studies (thirteen) included a control group under a quasi-experimental design—for example antisocial youths versus non-antisocial youths, or recidivists versus non-recidivists. The remaining nine studies included normative data as a control group (for example general population or university students).

The studies included in this systematic review can be classified into three groups according to how the drugs–crime causal link is conceptualized and explored. First, studies that challenged a unidirectional causal role of drugs on crime and explored the opposite causal relationship. Only three papers were found in this category: a Colombian study by Nieto[26] which found that involvement in violent behavior was a significant predictor in a regression model of abuse of psychoactive substances in a sample of street individuals. A Chilean study[27] which showed that age of initiation in crime was on average antecedent to the age of initiation in the use of marijuana and cocaine, and additionally, recidivism was found to be a significant predictor of abuse and dependence of drugs.[28] Finally, Trajtenberg & Menese[29] reported that in Uruguay, the association between use of illicit use of drugs and crime involvement was partially explained away by personality traits (low self-control) and by having criminal peers for both conventional adolescents and for young offenders serving sentences in youth criminal justice institutions.

The second group of studies did not assume an explicit explanatory role of illicit use of drugs in crime. These studies were focused on exploring the association between both phenomena: five surveys of imprisoned offenders in Uruguay, Bolivia, Brazil, Costa Rica, and Ecuador;[30] a study of arrested adults in Uruguay that included self-report questionnaires, urine test and spirometry;[31] a survey of arrested individuals in Colombia;[32] a survey of adolescents at a youth center in Argentina;[33] and a Chilean study that compared youngsters from educational institutions and young offenders serving sentence in the youth criminal justice system.[34]

Finally, the large majority of the studies (73 per cent) explicitly assumed and/or attempted to evaluate empirically the antecedent causal role of illicit use of drugs in the explanation of crime, deviated behavior, recidivism, and problems with the criminal justice system.[35] Two studies failed to show that illicit use of drugs were playing a role in the explanation of crime. The study developed by Fundación Paz Ciudadania[36] used logistic regression to explain criminal recidivism among youth offenders in Chile; 'use of substances' was found to be not statistically significant as the independent variable. The second study was an analysis of temporal series between 1957 and 2002 in Venezuela, which showed that possession of illicit drugs was not significantly associated with the rates of homicide, injuries, robbery, robbery with violence, and drug crimes.[37] The empirical argument used by many of the remaining studies was that prison/arrested samples showed higher rates in different measures of illicit use of drugs—life prevalence, last year prevalence, last month prevalence, and 24 hours before crime prevalence[38]—when compared with similar age groups at a national level.[39] Some studies reinforced the causal interpretation in three ways: (i) showing that rates of arrests in the last year prior to imprisonment were greater for individuals with higher use of drugs prevalence rates;[40] (ii) including more refined and informative measures of drug use such as dependence/abuse—for example, how many days he/she used drugs in the last month or week previous to detention—and/or temperance (was the arrested individual visibly under the effects of drugs?);[41] and (iii) including alternative measures/tests of urine to complement the self-report questionnaires.[42]

Recent studies have employed a sophisticated argument for the causal interpretation of drugs, which is the Goldstein (1985)[43] tripartite framework with Pernanen, Cousineau, Brochu and Sun[44] specifications. This model involves estimating what proportion of crimes is committed to obtain resources to support drug consumption (economic compulsive),[45] is committed under the influence of a psychoactive substance (pharmacologic),[46] or is committed as a result of violence inherent to the workings of illicit drug markets. At present, studies included in this review have this type of estimation for the youth criminal justice system population of Chile,[47] Colombia, Uruguay and Peru,[48] as well as for the adult prison population of Argentina, Colombia and Chile.[49]

Only one Latin American study was found that was based on a sample of drug users: Eiranova and colleagues conducted a descriptive study of forty-six young male patients at an addiction clinic in Cuba, and found almost two-thirds of the patients exhibited violent conduct toward their family and other people, usually reproducing a learned behavior from childhood. Seven studies explored the causal link between drugs and crime, including samples not exclusively formed by offenders.[50] First, Brook and colleagues conducted a survey of 2837 adolescents between 1995 and 1996 in three cities in Colombia, which included several control, social, and psychosocial variables.[51] They found that the illicit use of drugs was one of the most significant risk factors for violent behavior. Second, Cordoba[52] compared 196 teenager offenders who had committed homicides with conventional teenagers from high schools in Colombia. He reported that the probability of committing homicide was associated with addiction to psychoactive substances, among other multiple risk factors. Third, a Chilean study on psychiatric disorders reported greater levels of abuse and dependence on marijuana and other psychoactive substances in youth offenders (n = 100) compared to high school students (n = 100).[53] A fourth study was a survey conducted by Brea and Cabral[54] in the Dominican Republic which compared fifty youth offenders and fifty conventional youths. The authors found statistically significant differences between the illicit use of drugs in youth offenders and conventional boys. In the regression model, the use of drugs was one of the three variables significantly associated with criminal behavior. Fifth, Alcalá et al. conducted an investigation of 581 teenagers in Chihuahua, México.[55] Although the use of drugs was not analyzed as an independent risk factor, it was included together with sexual activity as part of the component 'risk behaviors,' which was found to be a significant predictor in the regression model of antisocial and pre-criminal behavior. Sixth, Lüdke, da Cunha, Bizarro & Dell'Aglio[56] used the database of the National Survey on Risk and Protective Factors to analyze drug use and antisocial behavior in adolescents from low-income neighborhoods and public schools in five regions of Brazil. This study concluded that the frequency of arrest was significantly associated with last year's prevalence of cocaine, crack, and marijuana use. Similar results were obtained with involvement in drug trafficking and having problems with justice. Finally, Ruiz Martinez and colleagues compared a group of consumers of illicit drugs involved in crime with a group of consumers not involved in crime and a third group of non-consumers who were also not involved in crime (n = 150). This study found significant differences in the type of family bonds, family conflict, and intellectual and cultural activities between consumers and control groups of non-consumers.[57]

The meta-analysis conducted found an overall prevalence of consuming any illegal drug and committing a crime of 12 per cent. In other words, hardly more than one out of ten crimes committed could have its main motivation attributed to illegal drug use, a number considered low in statistical analysis literature. Given the high heterogeneity observed among the studies, we analyzed some variables that might be moderating the association between drugs and crime, such as the type of population, type of drug, and type of measure of the drug.

First, in population type, both adults and youth offenders showed similar prevalence (14 per cent and 11 per cent respectively). Secondly, regarding the type of drug, the most common types reported in the studies were cannabis, cocaine, and cocaine paste, with prevalence rates of 16 per cent, 7 per cent, and 10 per cent respectively. The prevalence of ecstasy, inhalants, and opium was very low (2 per cent, 4 per cent, and 1 per cent, respectively). However, the number of studies that did not specify the type of drug was high (40 per cent). Finally, with regard to the type of measurement to detect drugs, only six studies employed an objective method (urinalysis) to detect whether individuals had consumed immediately before committing the offense. The prevalence of these studies was higher (30 per cent) than those that employed a self-reported measure such as interviews or questionnaires (10 per cent).

Sensitivity analysis was carried out in order to illustrate the influence of specific studies, such as those published in Chile (n = 10). The overall results are not impacted by the inclusion of these studies—namely, the overall prevalence remains the same after excluding Chilean studies (11 per cent). Therefore, we can conclude that our results are robust.

Discussion of the Consensus and Disagreements on the Relationship between Drugs and Crime

This is the first study that has aimed to critically review and meta-analytically investigate the link between illicit use of drugs and crime in Latin America. Forty-five studies were identified as having enough data and using similar diagnostic criteria suitable for a critical review, with twenty-three studies having enough data to perform a meta-analysis. Below, we discuss the results from the systematic review and the meta-analysis, as well as the policy implications and limitations of this study.

Most of the studies included in our systematic review have relevant methodological limitations resulting in divergent results across the studies in different countries. First, the cross-sectional nature of all studies undermines the possibility of adequately evaluating the antecedent nature of illicit use of drugs in relation to crime.[58] Second, causal interpretation is also undermined by the type of sample used by most of these studies (arrested or imprisoned offenders). Criminal justice samples are not representative of offender populations. Not only do these samples overrepresent individuals with more serious, longer, and earlier criminal involvement,[59] but also offenders with higher drug use rates,[60] overestimating drug causal relevance on crime.[61] Additionally, these criminal justice samples might involve other unknown biases in potential key confounders, or third variables connected both with illicit use of drugs and crime. The critical issue is the lack of an adequate quasi-experimental research design which simulates a treatment and control condition and therefore allows a more reliable and precise evaluation of the specific explanatory role of drugs. The lack of adequate explanatory designs which include controls of key mediating and moderating causal factors runs the risk of seriously overestimating the causal incidence of illicit use of drugs.

Although the Goldstein–Pernanen models constitute a considerable improvement in the field, they do not overcome the aforementioned problems. Additionally, the validity of the counterfactual question involved in the estimation of the pharmacologic connection is problematic. Questions related to remembering what happened at the time of the offense, and what would have happened in an alternative scenario seems a cognitively challenging question for an average individual, especially for those offenders with problems of illiteracy, low cultural and human capital, and particularly substance abuse problems. Furthermore, there is a strong incentive for offenders to answer in a way that overstates the role of drugs as a neutralization or denial of responsibility technique.[62]

To summarize, although there are multiple possible causal connections between the illicit use of drugs and crime, quantitative studies in Latin America have mostly explored the role of illicit use of drugs as a causal antecedent of crime. Furthermore, methodological shortcomings regarding the type of population employed to examine this relation seriously limit the strength of this causal interpretation. Although there is some recent research with non-biased samples (that is, not formed exclusively by offenders), there has been little exploration of alternative causal links between both phenomena and third common causal mechanisms, with particularly little use of more theoretically oriented perspectives. The biased methodological nature of the research overestimates the relationship between illicit use of drugs and crime, favoring punitive and control-oriented drug policies embraced by the IDCR.

This meta-analytical review of studies reporting the prevalence of offenses committed under the effect of illicit drugs revealed important findings relating to population and drug types, as well as measurement issues. Overall, the prevalence of those committing an offense under the influence of an illegal drug in Latin America is low (12 per cent). However, this average offense prevalence under illicit drugs effects cannot be compared with any meta-analytical study from other continents, since there are no studies that account for this issue as far as the authors are aware.[63] Most epidemiological studies in Latin America have investigated the prevalence rates of illicit use of drugs in offenders, but very few have investigated the connections between illicit use of drugs and deviant behaviors in the general population. Therefore, there is a lack of research designs that include adequate control groups. Findings of the reviewed studies comparing the prevalence of illegal drug use in a general population with offender populations reported lower prevalence in the former group than the latter,[64] thus assuming strong support for a drug–crime connection. However, offenders are not a homogeneous group. They frequently show a range of problems or needs which are not shown in the general population. These include personality traits, criminal peers and subcultures, homelessness and mental health problems, unemployment and financial problems. Many of these factors are interlinked.[65] Therefore, before assuming a strong connection between drug use and crime, and implementing the resulting punitive laws and institutions, it is important to develop studies that include adequate control groups and valid measures of these different moderators to evaluate the full scope of the problem.

The reason that both youth and adult offenders showed very similar prevalence is unclear, since the studies do not report risk variables such as personality traits and criminal history. One possibility is that both adolescents and adults were life-course persistent offenders. The age-crime curve assumes that crimes are most prevalent during mid to late adolescence (16–20 years). The incidence of crime decreases with age in adulthood, but some continue to commit offenses afterwards.[66] Furthermore, variations across offenses have been reported. For instance, from the ages of 6 to 10 years of age, the prevalence of physical aggression tends to increase but tends to decrease at the age of 10 to 13 years of age. Among individuals who continue to exhibit deviant behaviors, these acts become most severe at around 15 to 16 years of age.[67] Since specific childhood and adolescent personality traits are related to drug use in young adulthood,[68] and conduct disorder is a predictor of drug-taking across adolescence,[69] one possibility is that adolescents and adults might show specific personality traits that mediate both drug consumption and criminal behavior. Another possibility is that the consumption of drugs is more associated with socioeconomic factors. The most common offenses reported by the studies were against property, which might be associated with drug acquisition. This hypothesis is also partially confirmed by those reviewed studies which showed through the counterfactual model that economic necessity plays a role in the explanation of crime. However, this association is unclear, since research has shown that those prone to emotional distress and antagonism are at greater risk for drug use, regardless of their economic situation.[70] Therefore, more longitudinal studies are needed to better understand the role of illicit use of drugs in the criminal trajectories of these offenders.

As expected, cannabis was the most prevalently used drug, followed by cocaine paste. Contrary to the global picture reported by the UN in Latin America, cocaine paste is nearly as prevalent as cannabis. Although correlations between stimulating drugs and violence-associated crime have not been found,[71] robust evidence suggests that the use of illicit drugs is associated with violent behavior and psychiatric symptoms and disorders in vulnerable persons.[72] It is clear that the relationship between illegal substance use and violence is complex, and that the interaction between substance abuse and pre-existing, concomitant, or resultant mental illness plays an important role[73] which has not been examined yet in Latin America studies. This might have important policy implications, as discussed below.

The lower prevalence of illegal drug use reported by studies that used self-report rather than urinalysis was expected. Therefore, the low average should be taken with caution since most of the studies relied on self-reports, thus representing a serious bias in the results.[74] However, because self-report measures are necessary to understand the complexity of causal and correlational attributes of drug use, studies have focused on determining what can be done to improve valid self-reporting.[75] Therefore, future studies should always include the percentage of agreement between biological and self-reported measures. This analysis would not only increase the validity of the results, but would also provide us with a better understanding of risk factors that might influence the association between illegal drug use and crime. A necessary next step in research is to explore the use of multilevel model studies in order to more adequately capture the ecological dimension of the relationship between drugs and crime. Latin American studies have argued about how the drug–crime link is dependent on the 'neighbor effect,' and the need to take into account its different nature in segregated and high-risk areas of the city.[76] However, at present—except for Brook and colleagues—the inclusion of contextual influences is generally included either as merely a variable in orthodox modelling[77] or in qualitative studies.[78] The correct identification of temporal antecedence is also a key component in the evaluation of causal relationships between phenomena. Therefore, the cross-sectional nature of most studies in Latin America is a serious limitation.[79] Only through longitudinal studies will it be possible to disentangle with more precision and reliability which specific connections between drugs and crime are more decisive, and what is the relevance of external social or individual factors. But more importantly, longitudinal studies will enable us to understand how all these components interact dynamically as individuals age in order to understand more clearly what the role of drug use in initiation, continuity, and desistance of crime is.

Published estimates of the prevalence of illicit use in the relation between drugs and violence vary greatly. After reviewing the pertinent publications, we attributed this variability to methodological differences between the studies, such as study design, study population selection, and settings. In addition, self-reports were used as the main source of information and, in most of the studies, there was a lack of information about the relevant moderating risk factors that would be necessary for understanding the associations in the study. Differences in study population selection and inclusion criteria of studies might explain the high variability between studies.

To summarize, this review has focused on the available research on illegal substance use and crime in Latin America from 1990 to 2015. The illicit use of drugs is consistently mentioned as occurring prior to or during the commission of many violent and criminal events, leading to a causal association between these two. As a result, there is a rejection of implementing non-punitive reforms that challenge the actual IDCR guidelines. However, this review shows that the prevalence of the relationship between illegal substance use and violence is low, and most of the times inadequately measured. This result should be interpreted with caution because most of the studies were based on questionnaires rather than a combination of subjective and objective measures. Specifically, this study showed that the prevalence was higher for objective measures (that is, urine sample). Furthermore, at present, studies cannot adequately capture the causal complexities of the drug–crime relationship, and particularly how it is moderated by a host of individual and environmental factors. More research is needed to examine the neurobiological, psychosocial, and ecological vulnerabilities of the subset of substance users and abusers who might be at risk for violent perpetration or victimization.

Main Challenges and Possible Scenarios for Drug Policy Development

Recent experiences in the regulation in the use of drugs, notably Uruguay, have awakened strong resistances among the more conservative sectors of societies who, assuming a 'jeopardy thesis,'[80] cannot but see a very dangerous institutional change due to the inherent criminogenic nature of use of drugs, among other negative consequences. One of the main reasons legislators support prohibitionist drug policies in Latin America (and in the rest of the world) is to reduce violence and state costs. However, available data contradicts these statements. Firstly, alcohol—which is the drug most consistently associated with both non-violent and violent behaviors[81]— is not only readily and legally available, but it is often sold by the state for profit.[82] Secondly, the existing scientific evidence strongly suggests that drug prohibition likely contributes to drug market violence and higher homicide rates (for the case of Latin America see Chapter 5 by Angélica Durán-Martínez and Chapter 6 by Carlos A. Pérez Ricart).[83] Thirdly, the cost of the drug control strategy is enormous. A total of $27.6 billion was requested to support the 2015 National Drug Control Strategy efforts to reduce drug use and its consequences in the United States.[84] Fourth, the limited nature of existent quantitative studies on the drug–crime link in Latin America constitutes a weak empirical base to support catastrophic forecasts about alternative policies that aim to regulate the illicit use of drugs.[85] Fortunately, the global drug policy debate is nowadays much more concerned with reliable scientific evidence that guides the development and evaluation of policies that work (see Chapter 14 by Robert Muggah and Katherine Aguirre).

However, despite empirical evidence, there is still strong resistance in the general public toward moving from prohibitionist drug policies to alternative policies, and to regimes focused on regulation and decriminalization that challenge the actual IDCR regime. Therefore, one of the main challenges for the future is not only to gather and evaluate empirical evidence that supports the need for alternative policies, but—equally importantly—how to build bridges with a still very distrustful and reluctant public opinion. In this sense, assuming a perspective that is too rationalist or cognitive might be an important strategic mistake. In order to overcome this key obstacle, a different perspective needs to be assumed. Some recent literature has shown that we judge first, and then look for reasons for that judgment. Haidt uses a metaphor to distinguish between two types of cognition: controlled processes (called 'the rider'), and automatic processes such as emotions and intuitions (called 'the elephant').[86] This metaphor is employed to argue that 'the rider acts as the spokesman for the elephant…it is skilled at fabricating post hoc explanations for whatever the elephant has just done.'[87] In other words, reasons are not used *ex ante* to inform judgment as the rationalist perspective has traditionally assumed, but *ex post* to convince others and ourselves that we are right. Therefore, if we want to change people's minds regarding the drug policies issue, focusing on empirical evidence and reasons (that is, the rider) will not be enough. We will have to focus on empathy and appeal to intuitions; we will have 'to talk to the elephants.'[88] Musto uses Haidt's framework to show the effectiveness of 'talking to the elephants' in Uruguay's campaign for cannabis regulation.[89] The way the moral and political debate was framed in the campaign, the type of arguments used, and particularly how it focused on people's intuitions and emotional reactions were decisive for achieving social change. Here, an important lesson might be learned and exported to other countries in the region that are discussing non-prohibitionist drug policy reforms in order to build more promising future scenarios.

Finally, this is not to say that legalization or regulation of drugs should be defended unconditionally. Instead, funding must be allocated for research and treatment to achieve a better understanding of which drugs make some individuals more aggressive, at what doses, and in what contexts. It seems that to move forward from prohibitionist regimes to policies based on the regulation of drugs, adequate ways to manage a particular subset of substance users with the risk of getting involved in violent behavior must be included. As a result, not only would practitioners be better able to treat problematic use and addiction, monitoring the withdrawal syndrome and associated symptoms, but governments would also be able to reduce costs. Cost-effective analyses reveal several issues. First, the savings in treatment programs are larger than the control costs. The costs of crime and lost productivity are reduced by $7.46 for every dollar spent on treatment.[90] Furthermore, drug treatment conducted within the community is extremely beneficial in terms of cost, especially compared to prison. Every dollar spent on drug treatment in the community is estimated to return $18.52 in benefits to society.[91] Second, not only would legalizing drugs save roughly $48.7 billion per year in government expenditure on enforcement of prohibition,[92] but also drug legalization would yield tax revenue of $46.7 billion annually, assuming legal drugs were taxed at rates comparable to those on alcohol and tobacco.[93]

However, this review has some limitations. First, the quality of the studies analyzed was low, mainly due to: biased samples; lack of adequate research design that includes control groups and controls for several confounders; the cross-sectional nature of studies; a lack of ethical procedures description; and potential conflicts of interests. Future studies that examine the present association should include a comparison of different levels of drug use and different levels of crime with adequate control groups.[94] Other confounder variables, such as personality traits, type of offense, criminal history, or socioeconomic status was often not reported, thus limiting the ability to assess their impact on illegal drug use and crime prevalence. The lack of longitudinal and multilevel studies has also limited our understanding of the nature and strength of the drug–crime link, its relationship with institutional and macro-level variables, and its potential policy implications. Additionally, most of the studies were reports, which might have a conflict of interest regarding drug policies. Recent literature in criminology has shown that different results in the evaluation of prevention policies might be due to systematic bias associated with conflict of interest.[95] Therefore, more peer review and unpublished studies with adequate measures of conflict of interest are needed in order to control this source of bias. Second, this review did not include alcohol. Studies that included both illegal drugs and alcohol reported that a high percentage of the offenses were committed under alcohol effects rather than illegal drugs effects. As a result, it is hypothesized that the alcohol–crime link might be stronger than illegal drug–crime link. Future systematic studies should examine this comparison and discuss the rationale behind a less prohibitionist framework towards alcohol than to other drugs. Third, although Chile was overrepresented among the selected studies, sensitivity analysis showed no differences when Chile was excluded from the analysis, demonstrating the robustness of results. More studies from other countries of Latin America are called for in order to understand what specific factors are influencing this relation in each country—for example historical, moral, cultural, political, and individual. Fourth, most of the studies used subjective measures (self-report). Future studies should combine subjective with objective measures (urinalysis), since this meta-analysis showed that the prevalence is higher in those studies that used the latter. Despite these limitations, the analysis and interpretation presented here further our understanding of this association, and suggest a direction for higher-quality additional studies to clarify risk factors and causal mechanisms, providing information to face the challenge of developing new drug policies.

12

HEALTH AND HUMAN RIGHTS CHALLENGES FOR THE INTERNATIONAL DRUG CONTROL REGIME

Damon Barrett and *Kasia Malinowska-Sempruch*

> *Everyone is entitled to a social and international order in which the rights and freedoms set forth in this Declaration can be fully realized.*
>
> Article 28, Universal Declaration of Human Rights

In recent decades, prison populations have steadily increased. There are 'likely well over eleven million' people in prison and pretrial detention worldwide.[1] Nobody knows how many are imprisoned for drug offenses, but it is in the millions, in some countries more than half of all prisoners. Approximately 1,320 people were executed for drug offenses between 2015 and 2017.[2] While the true figure is unclear, it is thought that as many as 20,000 people lost their lives to extrajudicial killings in the first 18 months of the Philippines' anti-drug campaign, which began in 2016.[3] In Mexico, drug-related violence increased dramatically following the 2006 decision of the Calderón administration to deploy the military to eliminate drug trafficking organizations. By 2018, over 20,000 people had been murdered every year.[4] Hundreds of thousands of people are in drug detention centers worldwide, arbitrarily detained and subject to serious abuses. United Nations (UN) agencies have called for their closure, including to help prevent the transmission of Covid-19.[5] In North America, the overdose crisis has seen year-on-year increases in mortality, with tens of thousands dying annually.[6] Global human immunodeficiency virus (HIV) targets are set to be missed by decades due to a lack of funding for harm reduction for people who inject drugs (PWIDs).[7] On the production side, millions have been displaced in Colombia, Afghanistan, Myanmar, and elsewhere due to crop eradication campaigns, which exacerbate existing insecurities. Yet record production of opium has been recorded in Afghanistan and of coca in Colombia. Mexico's production of opium has also grown significantly.[8]

The violence, corruption, abuse, and ill-health associated with drugs and the drug trade are well known. But today many consider the greatest harms to stem from the laws, policies and practices that have been put in place to tackle these phenomena. The International Drug Control Regime (IDCR) is regularly at the center of criticism, seen as being inflexible, failing to respond to contemporary challenges, historically unjust, and harmful in its implementation for security, development, and human rights. The longstanding global consensus that solidified through the twentieth century is now weakening, as starkly demonstrated by the legalization of the recreational cannabis market in Canada, Uruguay, and numerous US states. It has become common in recent years to call for a health and human rights-based approach to international drug control to be adopted.[9]

A full analysis of the health and human rights dimensions of drug control is beyond a single chapter. Many human rights and health issues will emerge in the regional and other thematic chapters in this volume. For our purposes, the wide variety of health and human rights issues is captured to the extent possible through discussions of (i) accountability for health failures and (ii) systemic human rights concerns within the IDCR. This is a somewhat artificial distinction, as they are connected, but it is helpful for a targeted analysis within a very wide subject area. In conclusion, this chapter offers some tentative suggestions for an agenda for systemic change at the international level.

Accountability for Health Failures

In the face of ongoing political commitments and massive effort in pursuit of the goals of the regime over many years, the UN drug control system has been beset by lack of agility and considerable problem-solving deficits. As discussed in the Introduction and Chapter 3 of this volume, the core aims of eliminating or significantly reducing demand and supply have not been met.[10] In contrast, the harms associated with drug use continue and in many ways have gotten worse, while the violence associated with the drug trade and drug enforcement has significantly escalated over the decades.

A review conducted in advance of the 2009 high-level UN meeting to agree a 10-year global drug strategy found 'no evidence that the global drug problem was reduced during the period from 1998 to 2007.'[11] In the United States, collated data on student drug use shows many fluctuations over the years but relatively steady overall prevalence of use.[12] In Europe, approximately 80 million people, a quarter of the population, have used illicit drugs at some point. A quarter of those age fifteen to sixteen have also done so.[13] According to the UN World Drug Report, 5.5 per cent of the world population uses illicit drugs—approximately a quarter of a billion people.[14]

The United Nations Office on Drugs and Crime (UNODC), however, argues that *prevalence* appears to be stable due to rising populations. But given that the 'elimination or significant reduction in demand' is a primary goal of the system, the total numbers are significant. Moreover, drug use is not the only health concern. The IDCR also regulates access to certain medicines. Yet about three-quarters of the world's population, mostly in the Global South, have no or insufficient access to opiates for pain.[15] Access to other controlled drugs for medical conditions is severely lacking. If these figures do not represent a failure to meet the regime's goals, what does?

i. Harm Reduction: Results, Yet Resistance

<u>Results</u>

It is estimated that 11.7 million people inject drugs around the world, documented in 158 countries and territories. Globally, it is estimated that 10 per cent of all new HIV infections occur through unsafe injecting practices. In many countries, incidence rates are far higher and in some, HIV prevalence rates among PWIDs are alarmingly high. The most affected regions are Eastern Europe, Southeast Asia, and the Middle East and North Africa. Worldwide, approximately 14 per cent of PWIDs are living with HIV, and over half with hepatitis C.[16]

Faced with the challenge of blood-borne viruses and other health harms such as wound infections and tuberculosis, as well as overdose deaths, many people who use drugs, social justice activists, and public health practitioners see the need for an alternative societal view on drug use. Harm reduction is the approach that emerged, one that aims to reduce social and health harms without 'necessarily' requiring people to stop using drugs.[17] This approach, more than almost all the other various drug policy strategies of recent decades, has been delivering results.

In those countries where HIV-related harm reduction has been brought to scale, HIV among PWIDs has been kept below 1 per cent. Countless HIV infections have been averted through such programs.[18] Overdose deaths among people who use opiates—which make up a significant proportion of overall fatalities—are preventable with an easily administered medicine called naloxone, and the establishment of safe injecting facilities allows for supervision of injections and immediate medical response, if needed. Thousands of lives have been saved with these methods. Opioid substitution therapy (OST) also significantly reduces overdose deaths, alongside reducing injecting; this remains the most effective form of opioid dependence treatment. Meanwhile, unnecessary injuries and hospitalizations are avoided daily through needle and syringe programs (NSP). Harm reduction is successful and cost effective.[19]

Today, ninety countries or territories across all regions implement NSP, though coverage and quality vary. Since 2012, according to the non-governmental organization (NGO) Harm Reduction International, NSP provision has increased in twenty-nine countries. Over eighty countries or territories, across all continents, implement OST.[20] There is now no credible argument that harm reduction is simply a European, Australian, or North American response, nor that it is hindered by cultural diversity, operating as it does across regions, cultures and religions.

Resistance

Despite the above successes, coverage of services remains poor overall.[21] Responses to HIV related to unsafe injecting practices have consistently fallen behind in funding and political attention, overshadowed by drug enforcement and colliding with drug-free visions for societies. Around half of all countries where injecting drug use has been identified have no NSP. Within countries, access to harm reduction is often a postcode lottery or an interminable pilot program reaching a handful of clients. In extreme cases, such services are illegal, as in the Russian Federation, which bans OST. Thailand continues to resist NSP, in contrast to its approaches to sexual transmission of HIV, and police are known to harass both people who use drugs and harm reduction workers. In response to overdose mortality, various US cities are poised to open safe consumption facilities but are held up by federal laws and face antagonism from the federal government.[22]

Just like the existence of harm reduction services, resistance to them is not confined to one region. However, that resistance shares a 'vision' of how to respond to drugs which is reflected in the IDCR, and against which harm reduction grates uncomfortably. Simply put, harm reduction is another way of looking at the problem, a critical drug policy, and one that does not support punitive approaches such as the criminalization of drug use or possession, and it works. It therefore generates heated debates at the UN Commission on Narcotic Drugs (CND), which has never recognized the harm reduction approach wholesale. However, CND has (at least in some cases) endorsed interventions that flow from harm reduction principles, such as the essential components of HIV prevention set out in technical guidance by the World Health Organization (WHO), UNODC and the Joint United Nations Program on HIV/AIDS (UNAIDS). It has also devoted resolutions to the specific challenge of overdose, including a recommendation to scale up naloxone access. The outcome Declaration of the 2016 UN General Assembly Special Session (UNGASS) on the world drug problem does not refer to harm reduction directly, but does endorse the provision of services to people who use drugs. The problem is that such interventions cannot work to scale if hampered by punitive approaches, which the CND also endorses. The proven effectiveness of harm reduction challenges the intended approach contained within the international system. This represents a system-wide confusion, reflected in the way countries implement public health interventions for people who use drugs, often on a scale that is too small to have an impact on infection rates,[23] at cross-purposes with criminal law enforcement and hindered by social stigma and human rights abuses.

The International Narcotics Control Board (INCB) used the platform created by the 2016 UNGASS as its first opportunity to speak more clearly in support of harm reduction. This came dramatically late, as for years it was at best grudgingly accepting of harm reduction following a long period of antagonism. The INCB has in the past gone so far as to call on governments to wean people off OST, equating the use of methadone or buprenorphine with 'drug abuse,' and has cautioned against HIV prevention measures that may 'facilitate drug abuse.'[24] This, alongside the CND's overall ambivalence, generates considerable system incoherence. Alongside HIV/AIDS and development agencies, human rights mechanisms within the UN have in the past decade increased their calls for a scaling up of harm reduction as a component of the right to the highest attainable standard of health and the right to benefit from scientific progress and its applications.[25]

ii. Controlled Medicines: Access, Governance, and the Right to Health

The Global Crisis in Access

The failure to ensure access to essential medicines controlled under the treaties is an especially stark and tragic example of the health failings of the drug control system, given the numbers of people touched by it, and how they are affected. It is estimated that 83 per cent of the world's population live in countries—overwhelmingly in the developing world—with low to non-existent access to controlled medicines, and inadequate access to treatment for moderate to severe pain.[26] This affects, for example, people with cancer, late-stage acquired immune deficiency syndrome (AIDS), those who have had accidents or undergone surgery, and women during childbirth. Medications for other conditions such as epilepsy are also affected, as are medicines such as methadone and buprenorphine used in the treatment of opioid dependence. It is a problem that is well known within the drug control system, by UN agencies and governments. Again, however, the extent to which the system itself plays a part in the structural causes of this crisis is not so readily accepted.

The Single Convention on Narcotic Drugs includes an estimates and statistical returns system, administered by the INCB and its secretariat, which is the primary international mechanism for attempting to reconcile the dual obligations of ensuring access while prohibiting uses outside of medical and scientific purposes. It is a model that emanates from the League of Nations, at a time when it was believed that if only the licit market could be controlled, the illicit market could be eliminated. In theory, the administrative system should ensure adequate stocks, but access on the ground is poor. There are many factors contributing to this situation, but among them are the overwhelming focus on enforcement and the fears of addiction generated by the longstanding drug control framework, which have contributed to a 'chilling effect' on access, including through overly restrictive drug laws and procurement and prescription processes.[27] A system designed to ensure access would not look like this.

A number of other substances with potentially important medical uses are listed in schedules under the 1961 and 1971 Conventions, which enshrine the determination that they should be subject to the most stringent controls in international law. This includes methadone, despite its daily prescription to hundreds of thousands of patients around the world and its role in the reduction of HIV transmission and overdose deaths. Cannabis, which is subject to the tightest of controls under the international system, is another important example, demonstrated by recent evidence on the use of cannabis tinctures in reducing epileptic seizures in children. Cannabis is also helpful in increasing appetite among cancer sufferers, and in various other ways. However, cannabis never went through the appropriate review procedure at the WHO to justify its control, and is only now being revisited through the appropriate review mechanism. It was written into the terms of the Single Convention on Narcotic Drugs and placed arbitrarily in the most stringent schedules of the regime. The evidence has long discredited this decision, even if political ideology still supports it.[28]

The use of lysergic acid diethylamide (LSD) and methylenedioxymethamphetamine (MDMA) in treating various mental health conditions is another controversy. MDMA, for example, has been shown to be highly effective as a component of therapy for post-traumatic stress disorder,[29] but research and especially any roll-out are hindered by national and international controls. There are signs of progress. In 2017, a multi-site study for research into MDMA-assisted psychotherapy was approved by the Food and Drug Administration in the US. The effort was entirely driven by the Multidisciplinary Association for Psychedelic Studies (MAPS), a civil society organization which took on board the fundraising for all of the research sites.

Health Governance and Scheduling

The above raises important questions about global health governance and the legitimacy of decision-making. Once substances enter onto the various schedules set out in the treaties, they carry binding legal obligations on all states parties, with knock-on effects even for those few states parties that have not yet agreed to be bound by the system. There are many problems with the scheduling system.[30] Some, however, are demonstrated by the controversy surrounding ketamine, widely used in human and veterinary medicine (see Chapter 3 by Christopher Hallam and David Bewley-Taylor for a discussion of ketamine). It is one of the few anesthetics available in rural parts of the developing world, and vital for surgeries. It is not currently under international control. But due to fears about recreational use in some states, there has been political pressure over many years from some governments and the INCB for ketamine to be scheduled under the 1971 Convention on Psychotropic Substances.[31] In 2015, China proposed that ketamine be brought under international control pursuant to the 1971 Convention, and it came to a vote of the

CND in March of that year. However, the WHO—which has a legal function under the Single and 1971 Conventions in this regard—has recommended three times against scheduling ketamine due to its low-risk profile as a public health concern, its high medical benefit and low-risk in its use as a medicine.[32]

Under the 1971 Convention, a two-thirds majority of CND members is required to bring a substance under international control. There are fifty-three members of the CND. Thirty-six states can, therefore, engage the obligations of all states parties to the 1971 Convention and the 1988 Convention against Illicit Traffic in Narcotic Drugs and Psychotropic Substances. As such, in the case of ketamine just two-thirds of CND members could have affected surgeries across the developing world, contrary to WHO advice. In the end, many states and civil society groups raised sufficient concerns that the vote was deferred. While this process was agreed to in drafting and accession to the treaties, it nonetheless raises democratic concerns. Simply put, many of the states that may have been affected would not have had a vote as they are not CND members. Others could have been outvoted and legally bound against their consent.

The ketamine question is also illustrative of the marginalization of the WHO in the drug control system. The WHO is the body mandated under the treaties to determine whether a substance meets the legal criteria for scheduling. In an opinion produced at the request of the chair of the CND, the UN Secretariat's Office of Legal Affairs found that the CND could legally overrule WHO and schedule ketamine against WHO advise.[33] This was based solely on the text of specific sub-paragraphs of the 1971 Convention. Not only was this an apparent misreading, but the undesirability of the outcome of this interpretation was also not discussed. A full legal analysis is beyond the scope of this contribution.[34] Simply put, however, the WHO review process sets the legal criteria for whether a substance can be before the CND for discussion in the first place. Unless those criteria are met, the CND is 'not authorized' to schedule, as noted in the commentary to the treaty.[35] It is an important check and balance against arbitrary decisions at the CND that must be protected if the health goals of the regime are to be taken seriously.

From Stocks to Access on the Ground: The Right to Health

While the drugs treaties include a system for ensuring adequate stocks, there is no explicit positive obligation to 'provide' medicines on the ground to those in need. Given the aim of the drugs treaties to ensure sufficient stocks, they could be interpreted as including an obligation to provide them on the ground to those in need. This reading is strengthened by the nature of the debates on this issue at the CND (indicating states parties' understanding of their obligations), but it is far from clear and would require fleshing out.

In this regard, the administrative aspect of the Single Convention is arguably underpinned—at least for states parties to both treaties— by Article 12 of the International Covenant on Economic, Social and Cultural Rights and Article 24 of the UN Convention on the Rights of the Child (to which all but the United States are parties). Access to essential medicines is considered a core minimum standard of this right, which is focused on meeting the needs of each individual.[36] Such medicines, as part of functioning health systems, must not only be available in the form of adequate stocks but geographically, financially and administratively accessible.

Recognizing the linkage to the right to health does not absolve the drug control system of its failings or shortcomings of implementation, but it does strengthen the normative basis for this crucial aspect, and potentially informs changes. For example, the right to health requires sufficient budgetary allocation, equity and non-discrimination in its implementation, and international cooperation for progressive realization.

Systemic Human Rights Concerns

i. Human Rights Abuses in Drug Control

Faced with an inability to eliminate or even significantly reduce demand, the UNODC has argued that the regime has been a success in helping 'contain' the problem, claiming that while overall use is up, overall prevalence is stable.[37] Whatever the merits of this claim, it has been achieved using certain methods. The costs of achieving any perceived 'containment' must, therefore, be factored into any determination of regime 'success.' In this regard, the human rights consequences of drug enforcement, which dominates the focus of policy, budgets, and efforts globally, must be taken into account. Consider the following brief snapshots:

The Death Penalty

While the true number is not known due to state secrets in China, Vietnam, and elsewhere, hundreds are executed for drug offenses every year.[38] While some would argue that this phenomenon has to do primarily with cultural contexts, this is demonstrably false. In fact, the adoption of capital drug laws increased following the adoption of the 1988 Drug Trafficking Convention.[39]

Over-Incarceration, Arrests, and Criminal Records

There are unknown millions in prisons around the world for drug offenses. There cannot be millions of major traffickers in the world, and the vast majority are in prison for minor, often non-violent, offenses. In some countries, penalties are excessively high for minor offenses. In Tanzania, for example, legislation intended to implement the drugs conventions allows for imprisonment of 10 years and/or a massive fine for drug use, possession of drugs or paraphernalia, or being on premises used for drug use without 'lawful and reasonable excuse.'[40]

Arrest and charge figures demonstrate clearly the targeting of low-level dealers and users by police. Even in countries where possession for personal use is not a crime, drugs present an easy opportunity for police to conduct searches and make arrests. In Brazil for example, after prison terms were removed for drug users but increased for traffickers, the total detainee population actually rose by 17 per cent from 2007 to 2010. There was a 62 per cent increase in those detained for trafficking. As a recent report noted, this 'indicates that some people who were detained for consumption ended up being accused of trafficking.'[41] Similarly in Mexico, despite 2009 reforms decriminalizing possession, 71 per cent of the activity of the office of the Attorney General had to do with possession.[42] Similar patterns are evident in Peru and Chile.[43] In this regard, aside from prison, we must consider criminal records, handed down so casually and regularly for possession. Many millions of families must face the future burdened by unnecessary criminal records, affecting life chances through employment, travel and in some cases social assistance.

Arbitrary Detention

There are hundreds of thousands of people who use drugs being arbitrarily detained in drug detention centers, primarily in Asian countries including China, Vietnam, Cambodia and India. Due to drug use or on suspicion of drug use—and sometimes merely by a recommendation of the police or a family member—people can be detained for months or even years. Aside from the initial violation of freedom from arbitrary detention, Human Rights Watch has documented severe abuses inside such centers, including denial of meals, beatings and forced labor, as well as high suicide rates.[44]

Police Violence

Central America has the highest regional homicide rate in the world, at 25.9 per 100,000 of the population.[45] This is a complex picture, but drugs are very much in the foreground, as Central America is an important trafficking route. In Mexico, violence has many root causes, but there is no question that the situation has deteriorated in scale and brutality since the militarization of the drug war in the country (see Chapter 9 by Pierre-Arnaud Chouvy). This speaks to the violence that follows both the drug trade and responses to it. Indeed, police and military violence additional to that inflicted upon communities by non-state actors is widespread. Killings and disappearances by Mexican police and military have been documented, while Thailand's 2003 War on Drugs is notorious for these kinds of abuses. Over just a few months, police gunned down over 2,000 people, many of whom had nothing to do with the drug trade.[46] Despite international condemnation, tens of thousands of extrajudicial killings by police have taken place in the Philippines.

Conflict

Drugs and conflict have long been intertwined. As the UN Development Programme (UNDP) remarked in relation to Colombia, the illicit drug trade is a 'center of gravity' in the conflict,[47] with guerrillas and paramilitaries alike profiting. In Afghanistan, meanwhile, 'the Taliban is profiting from the drug trade, as are various criminal gangs, which often are connected to the government, the Afghan police, tribal elites, and many ex-warlords-cum-government officials, at various levels.'[48] It is thought that between one and two-fifths of the Taliban's revenue is from drugs, while eradication has only increased political capital and undermined counterinsurgency through 'intense alienation of the affected population from the Afghan government and ISAF forces, and susceptibility to Taliban mobilization.'[49]

ii. Effects on Vulnerable Groups

While men make up the large majority of prison populations, women are disproportionately in prison for non-violent offenses, including drugs. Between 2006 and 2011, the female prison population in Latin America increased from 40,000 to more than 74,000, some facing sentences as high as 30 years, largely because of non-violent drug convictions.[50] In some countries, women are serving longer sentences for drugs than those imprisoned for rape or murder. Approximately 70 per cent of women in prison in the region are convicted or sentenced for drug offenses.[51] Globally, women are incarcerated for drug offenses more than for any other crime.[52] Many of these women are primary caregivers to small children, and were driven to such crimes through economic necessity. In some cases, children are born and spend their first years in prison; in others, they grow up knowing their mother from rare telephone conversations, given the wide distances between the prisons and their homes. Across the world, an unknown number of children are growing up with a parent unnecessarily incarcerated for non-violent drug offenses, and must face the associated stigma.

The above illustrates the impacts of drug enforcement on the children and young people in whose name such efforts are so often carried out. In Mexico, many tens of thousands have lost at least one

329

parent since 2006. Well over a thousand children have been killed.[53] In Colombia, Afghanistan, and elsewhere the impacts of crop eradication have been devastating for children, as families are driven into further debt and poverty. This is a vicious cycle. Faced with no other options, children must work and cannot go to school. In Afghanistan, faced with a family's starvation after eradication, girls are frequently bartered to pay opium debts to local drug lords.[54] As with other issues, rights abuses felt by adults are experienced also by children, both indirectly and directly. To grow up amid drug-related violence, for example, has the potential to generate long-term psychological harm.

It is by now well known that drug enforcement disproportionately targets racial and ethnic minorities. Studies in the US and UK have demonstrated clear institutional racism from surveillance to arrest to charges to imprisonment.[55] But we see similar dynamics elsewhere. In Brazil, for example, those facing the brunt of police abuses in the context of drug enforcement are young, and black or *pardo*—a term commonly used to refer to Brazilians of mixed ethnic ancestries.[56] While clearly an issue of race, this is also about the heavy policing of the urban poor, which over time erodes community cohesion and breeds further distrust towards the police.

The rural poor face similar targeting. Since the inception of the IDCR regime, the focus of control efforts has been on organic plant-based materials in the Global South. The vast weight of enforcement efforts were therefore concentrated in these areas, and it was not until the 1980s that the language of a 'balanced approach,' which is still unrealized, entered international diplomacy. The burden of global supply reduction remains focused on rural production, often by people struggling for month-to-month subsistence. Many live in areas without state presence, their only contact with the state being eradication teams or aerial fumigation planes. In Latin America, Afghanistan, Myanmar, and elsewhere, forced eradication has been shown to lead to violence, reduced family income, and food insecurity.[57] Caught between civil conflict and drug enforcement operations, indigenous peoples in Putumayo, Colombia, have been displaced, had food crops and livestock destroyed, and have been cut off from their lands and livelihoods. Similar situations are evident in Guaviare, representing a threat to these groups' 'material and cultural existence.'[58]

iii. Four Systemic Concerns

The above concerns have long been raised by UN agencies, researchers and human rights NGOs, as well as states, and reach across every facet of human rights protection. However, such abuses are too easily dismissed as the actions of wayward or over-zealous states or their agents. In recent years, it has been argued that abuses stemming from drug control are not just widespread but 'systemic,' with the international regime at the center of this critique.[59] This chapter offers four (non-exhaustive) concerns in this regard.

The Issue Is Negatively Framed upon a Narrative of Existential Threat

The threat posed by drugs and the drug trade has been a regular feature of political rhetoric for decades, and is enshrined in the preambles of the UN drugs conventions (for a more detailed discussion of the securitization of drug policies see Chapter 1 by Annette Idler). These refer, in the case of the Single Convention, to the 'evil' of addiction and the moral duty of states parties to 'combat this evil.' In the case of the 1988 Convention, they reference a threat to the fabric of society, and a 'danger of incalculable gravity' to children. The same or similar rhetoric has opened each political declaration on drugs since 1990. Drugs, then, are a threat to our civilized world, to democracy, and to a prosperous future. The drugs treaties are not themselves the source of this framing. The inclusion of such language represents government views, political strategies, media narratives, and—to an extent—public opinion.[60] Nonetheless, the effect on national policies of this global consensus on how to frame the problem should not be underestimated. This threat-based framing has many negative consequences. Here we focus on three.

The first is stigma, a rarely admitted yet intentional strategy behind the criminalization of certain behaviors. However, rather than stigma attaching to a behavior, it tends to attach to the people who engage in that behavior. In this way, while drug use may be stigmatized, it is people who use drugs who bear that stigma. Rural farming communities and poor people engaged in low-level drug offenses experience it too, tarred with the image of being part of the threat. This in turn has negative effects on health and social outcomes for those affected.

The second effect is resource imbalance. Simply, governments cannot politically sustain ramping up the level of rhetoric on such a threat without taking enforcement action. At the same time, securing resources to assist those who come to be seen as part of the threat is exceptionally difficult.[61] The UN has referred to this as the 'policy displacement' effect, with resources shifting from health to law enforcement as a negative outcome of the international regime.[62] State efforts and budgets are allocated overwhelmingly towards drug enforcement, which is also the arena in which the majority of rights abuses in drug control are felt.

The third effect is the fueling of intrusive and repressive measures, such as those outlined above. The threat narrative within the drug control regime legitimizes excesses in ways similar to those carried out in the War on Terror. In one of his final reports to the UN Human Rights Council, Professor Manfred Nowak, then UN Special Rapporteur on Torture, noted the various 'exceptional circumstances' or 'unique situations' used by government officials to explain acts amounting to torture and cruel, inhuman and degrading treatment. Among them was the threat posed by drugs.[63] Nowhere was this more clearly illustrated than in Indonesia's recent justification for its escalation of executions, referring to the drugs 'emergency' in the country, a claim contradicted by the evidence.[64]

What States Are Required to Do Under the UN Conventions Is Risky in Human Rights Terms

Consider, for a moment, the obligations undertaken by states parties to the UN drugs conventions. States agreed—among other things—to ban indigenous, traditional and religious practices; investigate, arrest and prosecute; extradite; eradicate crops; seize property; and even control speech due to the criminalization of incitement to use drugs. Some of this is not unique to drug control, but it is risky territory from a human rights perspective. That risk is then transposed into national systems around the world, sometimes in corrupt regimes where national human rights protections are poor. The approach adopted by the international community, in other words, provides the impetus and justification for a vast array of rights abuses, often committed by police and security forces.

The treaties cannot be absolved of this responsibility, being almost entirely absent of normative human rights content and safeguards. They operate as a floor, not a ceiling, explicitly encouraging states to go further. States parties are granted a permissive right to adopt 'more strict or severe measures.'[65] This permission must be restrained both by specific human rights protections, as well as by the general norm that the least restrictive means which achieve a given aim should be adopted.[66] The commentary to the 1961 Single Convention provides a clear example. In its discussion of 'more strict or severe measures' permitted under Article 39 of the Single Convention, the official commentary notes the death penalty for drug offenses as an example of one such measure;[67] the Indonesian Constitutional Court has in fact referred to this provision to uphold the death penalty for drug offenses.[68] While the commentary is careful not to 'condone' such a practice, international law on the death penalty has developed considerably. The commentary is out of date. Today it would surely have to conclude that capital punishment for drug offenses fails to meet the threshold of 'most serious crimes' for the purposes of Article 6(1) of the International Covenant on Civil and Political Rights.[69] In addition, it would have to recognize that state practice has clearly moved on, given the very small minority of states that continue to execute for drugs, and increasing votes in favor of successive General Assembly moratorium resolutions.[70]

The death penalty is an extreme example, so let us look at something more commonplace. Under the drugs conventions, the dominant approach to drug use and the drug trade is criminal law enforcement. It is a deterrence model. This is a significant driver of rights abuses, primarily because it does not work. Proper monitoring of this vast array of activities is impossible, so it becomes more intrusive in response— just in reference to schools, consider random drug testing, sniffer dogs, and searches of children's clothes and schoolbags. Moreover, as overall monitoring is impossible, enforcement becomes selective, focusing on more available and visible populations, be they street-based drug users or 'low-hanging fruit' in the supply chain. In this way, any intended deterrent effect gives way to discriminatory practices such as targeting of poorer areas, street-involved young people and ethnic minorities, exacerbated by arrest quotas and targets for police. Moreover, it is well known that certainty of punishment is far more effective than severity, yet in relation to drug laws, it is severity that tends to characterize responses. With no possibility of certainty of punishment for drug offenses, a more severe penalty is applied in the hope that it will act as a deterrent of itself and/or that when a person is caught, their punishment will act as an example to others.

In some cases, what the drugs treaties require is itself a direct violation of human rights. This is the case of the explicit ban on religious, traditional, cultural, or indigenous uses of certain plants. These were to be abolished by certain fixed times pursuant to Article 49 of the Single Convention. However, in various countries and regions such as the Andean region, India, Burma, and Afghanistan, this provision found itself up against centuries of cultural norms. Since 1961, international law has moved on, and the decision to ban traditional practices is one that now conflicts with a variety of international treaties and standards.[71] This includes 'free, prior and informed consent' of indigenous peoples on issues that affect them. Now considered to be a general principle in international law, such consent was never obtained in drafting the drugs conventions.

How Success is Measured Maps onto Human Rights Risk

Arrests, seizures of drugs, hectares of crops eradicated, and other aspects of state effort are considered indicators of success. These are also precisely those areas where human rights abuses are the most acute. In other words, states are commended for certain efforts, which may at the same time amount to or produce human rights violations. The death penalty again serves as an example. In Indonesia, for example, two Australians who had been captured with the assistance of the Australian Federal Police were later executed.[72] Thus, a major seizure and prosecution is seen as a success in drug control at the same time that the passing of such a sentence is a human rights failure.

Crop eradication is another case in point, whereby the hectares eradicated are regularly portrayed as success without evidence of actual overall reduction, and more importantly, without reference to the demonstrable effects on rural livelihoods, food security, internal displacement, and other areas of human rights concern. There is, in effect, no human rights scrutiny possible when state 'effort' and 'success' are seen to be the same thing.

There is no Effective Mechanism within the Drug Control Regime for Raising Human Rights Concerns

The only independent monitoring mechanism within the drug control system is the INCB, which unfortunately has a lamentable past record on human rights. With changes to its membership, however, it has become more vocal in its condemnation of rights abuses committed in the name of drug control, in particular the death penalty. However, these statements are often of a general nature, rather than singling out individual states. The board remains more likely to challenge specific states for adopting liberal drug laws, or certain harm reduction strategies such as drug consumption rooms. To take human rights seriously in monitoring the drugs conventions, the INCB will therefore have to become more forthright in its condemnation of specific actions by specific states, which will require more insight into the situation on the ground.

However, the INCB holds its meetings behind closed doors. Civil society may neither participate nor monitor deliberations. NGO submissions are not accepted for the INCB's flagship annual report, leading to bland restatements of government policy without crucial critical input. Importantly, apart from some narrow exceptions, this secrecy—which is anathema to the working methods that have developed within the UN[73]—is not required by the drugs conventions. Improved transparency and participation will also be needed.

At the CND, human rights debates are stunted and heated. States frequently suggest that while drug control is a matter of 'shared responsibility,' the measures undertaken that might violate human rights are an issue of domestic concern, protected by sovereignty. No state is ever directly criticized for its abusive actions. This flies in the face of the very purpose of human rights law. It was only in 2008, 42 years after its establishment, that the CND adopted a human rights resolution. It could be agreed on only after the death penalty, the indigenous peoples' declaration, and any mention of the Human Rights Council were stripped from the text. During the debates in Vienna, some delegations questioned the relevance of human rights and the relevance of the UN human rights system.[74] At the UNGASS in 2016, the death penalty was by far the most controversial topic, leading to deadlock in the negotiations running up to the event.

The net effect of this is that there is no official coordinated mechanism for holding states to account in an area that so evidently engages a vast array of human rights concerns. However, in the past decade, NGOs have begun using UN and regional human rights mechanisms to address these issues. This has resulted in a significant increase in focus on drug control from these mechanisms, including resolutions at the UN Human Rights Council and thematic reports from the secretariat.

Some Proposals for Systemic Chance

The above discussions have alluded to some areas where improvements to the international drug control system from a public health and human rights perspective could and should be made. Some of these are set out more clearly below. This is not to suggest that such international reforms will solve the many issues raised above; just that the international system is currently both a contributor to these problems, and a barrier to change. Many of these recommendations must be credited to civil society organizations working in drug policy and harm reduction advocacy, rather than the authors of this chapter.

i. Harm Reduction

The Declaration of Kuala Lumpur launched at the twenty-fourth International Harm Reduction Conference in October 2015 called for the initiation of a 'harm reduction decade,' following the UNGASS in 2016. It included a robust call for a radical redistribution of resources towards this effective and essential area of social, health and drug policy, and away from enforcement.[75] The proposal was not taken up at the UNGASS, but its challenge remains vital and invigorating.

During a harm reduction decade, the international community would be challenged to reassess its indicators of success and to measure itself on different criteria than those of the current system, based on time-bound and achievable targets. Even if not officially recognized, it is important for civil society and supportive governments to adopt an alternate vision and demonstrate, in comparison with the predictable failures of ten more years of the status quo, what harm reduction can achieve. Expanding service to the necessary scale and providing a comprehensive package, including safe consumption rooms and wide availability of naloxone, continues to be crucial, especially in light of the dramatic increase of overdose mortality.

ii. <u>Access to Controlled Medicines</u>

Access to essential controlled medicines should be extracted from the supply reduction and demand reduction pillars of the regime. A new pillar for the drug control system is required, one dedicated not to reducing supply and demand, but to 'ensuring supply and meeting demand.' Meaningful, time-bound targets for access to medicines on the ground should be set, with percentage increases by 2030 in line with the UN Sustainable Development Goals.

The WHO Expert Committee on Drug Dependence and the WHO Essential Controlled Medicines Department should receive greater funding. The WHO is in need of this funding to properly fulfil its role in the scheduling process and to assist states parties in their access to medicines targets.

iii. <u>Drug Policy Governance</u>

Decision-making around scheduling needs to be amended; it is fundamentally undemocratic. It should be reformed so that all decisions are made by a vote of all states parties. It is understood that this would require treaty amendment, which is unlikely in the short term, but perhaps a rule of procedure could be adopted whereby such decisions are, on good faith, adopted by a plenipotentiary meeting.

The ambiguity surrounding the legal functions of the WHO under the scheduling system should be addressed and ended. Member states should reaffirm, potentially via a resolution, that unless the legal criteria for scheduling are met via a WHO review, the CND is not authorized to place the substance under any schedule.

There should be a vote on contentious resolutions at the Commission on Narcotic Drugs. Except for scheduling decisions, the CND works solely on the basis of consensus. This tends to mask important disagreements, and to water down the potentially important language. While consensus is often important, it must not exclude voting where there is a legitimate need to understand where states stand on key issues.

INCB secrecy should be ended, and term limits introduced. There is no legal basis—apart from very specific circumstances—for the INCB's tradition of secrecy and exclusion of civil society. To improve its transparency and deliberations, as well as its understanding of situations on the ground, the INCB should learn from the working methods of similarly constituted UN human rights treaty bodies. These accept written shadow reports and oral interventions from NGOs, release summary records of meetings and webcast their sessions when government performance is reviewed.

Members of the INCB have also often served for terms in excess of 15 years. Such long-term membership can begin to erode impartiality. While members 'may' be re-elected under the Single Convention, states parties and WHO can—without the need for treaty amendment—decide not to put forward the same person for consecutive terms.

iv. Human Rights Accountability

For too long, the drugs question has been separated from other parts of the UN system. The Thirtieth Session of the UN Human Rights Council represented an important shift, where the human rights dimensions of 'the world drug problem' was discussed in a high-level human rights panel for the first time. This focus on drug control by the UN's existing human rights mechanisms is to be nurtured. Below are some specific ways to achieve this.

The international guidelines on human rights and drug policy should be implemented. The development of such guidelines, similar to those for HIV, business, or terrorism, is a recommendation that has been made for some time.[76] Since 2016, galvanized by the UNGASS, a global collaborative effort has been underway to produce these guidelines, coordinated by the International Centre on Human Rights and Drug Policy and the UNDP, and funded by GIZ, the German development agency.[77] The guidelines were completed in 2019 and presented at the CND. They bring decades of human rights jurisprudence to bear on key areas of drug policy, filling crucial normative gaps. The challenge moving forward, as usual, will be whether there is sufficient political will, even from a small number of states, to move from standard setting to implementation. The UN human rights system may use the guidelines as a normative benchmark for its future role in drug policy.

An annual thematic debate should take place at the Human Rights Council. The issues are far too broad and complicated to be addressed in occasional or ad hoc meetings. Human rights also remain a heated and difficult debate at the CND, where the expertise leans towards law enforcement, not human rights. An annual thematic day at the Human Rights Council such as is currently held on the rights of the child, indigenous peoples' rights, and other issues, should be initiated to develop international debate and agreement on standards over time. The above guidelines can inform such debates.

UN member states that are concerned about improving the human rights aspects of drug control should use the Universal Periodic Review (UPR) process at the Human Rights Council to question their counterparts about their drug control efforts. While the 'spirit of Vienna' does not allow for states to challenge each other on such issues at the CND, the UPR process is designed to do so within the framework of the Universal Declaration of Human Rights. NGOs have attempted this in the past, but without firm commitments from capitals that drug control is an important human rights theme, the questions do not get asked of countries under review.

Existing independent mechanisms should be more effectively harnessed. Special procedures of the Human Rights Council, which cover a wide range of areas from health to torture, should increase and strengthen their focus on drug policies during their thematic research and country missions. Treaty bodies overseeing implementation of the core UN human rights treaties should use their periodic reporting processes to press governments on the human rights effects of their drug policies.

However, a new mechanism should also be created. Drug control is well suited to a Special Rapporteur or Independent Expert that can unpack the human rights dimensions of the issue over time. This has been suggested before,[78] and was called for again by civil society representatives at the Thirtieth Session of the Human Rights Council. Some states were not supportive, reacting badly to any suggested new mechanism, but others saw the need, privately indicating support in principle to NGOs in attendance.

Since 1961, the world has transformed around the drug control system, which has remained like a rock in time-lapse footage, stagnant as everything else changes. The world population has tripled since the Single Convention was adopted, this increase taking place alongside massive migration to urban centers and widening health and income inequality in many places. These phenomena speak to the social determinants of health, within which the social determinants of drug-related harms must be considered. Globalization has transformed the drug trade and patterns of drug use, posing challenges which the current regime is ill-equipped to respond to. Technological advancements have accelerated in recent decades. The internet has changed the face of global communication and learning, affecting the way drugs are bought, sold, manufactured and moved. Novel psychoactive substances (NPS) and controlled drugs are frequently sold online, and methods to produce a wide range of plants and synthetics are available to anyone with an internet connection. Scientific understanding of the dynamics of drug use, drug-related harms, and the drugs trade have advanced significantly, as has our understanding of the nature and drivers of drug dependence and other drug-related harms. As we have seen, international law and the ways of working within the UN system have also moved on.

These factors and others speak to the need to innovate. Such innovation is hindered, however, by strategies for achieving health goals that have been legally embedded, perpetually, within the UN drug control conventions. In the early half of the twentieth century, government representatives could not have foreseen the world of today. The drugs conventions thus represent the legal formalization of hypotheses developed by those with literally no idea of the environment within which their laws would someday operate. Those hypotheses have long been disproven, while the negative consequences of pursuing them in health and human rights terms are all too apparent.

We, therefore, offer one final suggestion for systemic change: it must be ensured that treaty reform is on the table for debate. While treaty reform may not be sufficient to resolve the many problems we face, it seems increasingly necessary. To be sure, some issues can be resolved without treaty reform, including improving access to essential controlled medicines. Many human rights abuses carried out in the name of drug control can end immediately with sufficient political will. But many rights issues cannot be decoupled from the treaties, in particular the criminalization of the entire supply chain, and the security and development consequences of that choice, made internationally binding so long ago via the treaties. However unlikely treaty reform may be in the short or even medium term, to discount it would be to ignore those areas where treaty reform is necessary to undo historical injustices, to amend undemocratic procedures, and to reform the disproven theories underpinning international drug control.

13

THE 2030 SUSTAINABLE DEVELOPMENT AGENDA AND THE WAR ON DRUGS

Javier Sagredo

Introduction

> We are resolved to free the human race from the tyranny of poverty
> and want and to heal and secure our planet. We are determined to
> take the bold and transformative steps which are urgently needed to
> shift the world onto a sustainable and resilient path. As we embark
> on this collective journey, we pledge that no one will be left behind.[1]

The historical coincidence in timing of the approval of the 2030
Global Agenda for Sustainable Development with the discussions on
the effectiveness of the International Drug Control Regime (IDCR)
before and after the 2016 United Nations General Assembly Special
Session (UNGASS) allowed the international community to engage
in a more profound debate on the development dimensions of drug
control policies. This discussion has become crucial, considering the
increasing evidence of their negative impact on living conditions,

rights, liberties, and the welfare of specific groups, communities, territories, and countries.

An integrated and comprehensive political discussion on drug policy and its impact on development had never made it to the conference rooms of the UN Commission of Narcotic Drugs (CND) or been considered by its General Assembly in any of the past UNGASS. Previously, the debate had only been possible within the limited framework of the Alternative Development (AD) concept, one of the tools traditionally conceived and used to reduce the supply of plant-based drugs and a specific form of rural development frequently integrated within crop substitution and interdiction strategies.

The gradual appearance before and after UNGASS 2016 of new visions within this debate from national governments (mainly in Latin America), UN Agencies like the United Nations Development Programme (UNDP), development cooperation agencies, and civil society organizations working on drugs and development issues, has allowed for an increasing focus on the multiple connections and interactions between drugs, drug policy, and development. It has generated a growing surge of calls for the adoption of a development-based approach to drug policy, in order to improve its effectiveness and reduce the harms associated with its implementation.

There are many contradictions between the Sustainable Development Goals (SDGs) and their targets, and the objectives and impacts of drug control policies. These include considering how structural vulnerabilities and key capacities of countries, territories, populations, and individuals affect the possibilities to successfully deal with the enormous challenges that the drug phenomenon—and implementing drug policies under the present IDCR—pose.

In order to resolve these policy incoherencies, the 2030 Agenda— already signed and accepted by all UN member states—becomes a fundamental reference for developing and implementing a new breed of drug policy,[2] especially at a moment where there are profound divides over the need and scope for reform of the IDCR.

This chapter ponders the need to review the drug policy agenda in light of the 2030 Global Agenda for Sustainable Development, and to reflect upon some of the basic premises that a development-based approach would necessarily include. This need arises mainly from the disproportionately negative impact that drug control policies have on the most vulnerable, the group of people highlighted and prioritized by the 2030 Agenda. More generally, this chapter explores the wide and significant impact of policies emanating from the IDCR on development issues, something recently undertaken by important stakeholders like UNDP,[3] the Global Commission on Drug Policy (GCDP),[4] and other civil society organizations and networks.[5]

Drug Control and Development

The rapport between drugs, drug control policies, and development is complex and multidimensional. On the one hand, the elements that shape and influence human development in our communities determine how the drug phenomenon occurs in our societies. On the other, some aspects of the drug phenomenon—but mainly those policies traditionally developed to confront it—have an effect on sustainable development.

Yet drug control agencies and development institutions and communities have tended to operate in isolation from one other, under the 'shared irresponsibility' principle of ignoring each other. Nevertheless, there is a singular non-written common vision that has imprinted international and national responses by both communities of practice: treating the drug problem and its illicit markets as a malign tumor that needs to be isolated, combatted, and 'surgically removed from a healthy body.'[6]

The IDCR is anchored in international proposals initiated in the early twentieth century. Its legal framework, its interpretation and transposition in national policies—as well as its everyday implementation by drug control institutions—are based upon a framework of prohibition and abstinence, and founded more on ideological, moral, religious, political, and geostrategic interests (as well as intuition) than on evidence. These aspects also shape the underlying dominant social imaginary behind these measures. The matter is still purely conceived as a personal choice, and not as a problem rooted in profound social, economic and health-related disparities that need to be addressed from our common responsibility. As a result, these policies have been marked by fear of crime, violence, disease, exclusion and by rejection of those individuals linked in any way to drugs.

Therefore, most responses have traditionally based on the development of prophylactic measures like confinement (see Chapter 11 by Nicolas Trajtenberg, Olga Sánchez de Ribera and Clara Musto), exclusion and repression, both in regard to the communities and individuals involved in their production and trafficking as well as to those using them (see Chapter 2 by Paul Gootenberg). For example, at the global level, 18 per cent of the sentenced prison population are incarcerated for drug-related crimes (20 per cent in the Americas).[7] In the United States, according to 2020 data from the Federal Bureau of Prisons,[8] 45.7 per cent of the federal prison population is imprisoned for drug offenses. These responses have been applied without considering values and objectives that should have been given priority in guiding public action, such as the respect for human rights and fundamental freedoms or the well-being of all citizens.

Additionally, formal political support, even when openly expressed to confront drug-related problems, often dissolves in the reality of electoral and institutional dynamics. Few politicians are courageous enough to pose different options to address the problem, thereby taking the risk of being viewed by citizens and political rivals as facilitators of vice and corruptors of youth. Such political dynamics—added to social disengagement on the fate of the most excluded—have become a strong factor in preventing the development of alternative and innovative policy responses. They also are a key element in excluding important institutional sectors (education, health, social services, labor, local economic development), civil society, and community stakeholders from active involvement in constructing more complex and effective solutions.

Desperate voices for change from political actors in Latin American countries which have been strongly affected by and are vulnerable to drug-related problems (like the three governments—Colombia, Guatemala and Mexico—that asked for the revision of the international response to drugs in UNGASS 2016) are an exception in the midst of an international community which is not very enthusiastic about engaging in any modifications, or speaking out as strong defenders, of the actual regime.

Policies emanating from the IDCR mainly focus on a paradigm of drug control characterized by criminal law, enforcement, and abstinence approaches. They have rarely taken development issues into account. It has been circumscribed to the limited concept of AD programs, connected to eradication and interdiction efforts, and designed to provide legal economic opportunities to drug crop cultivators in rural areas where illicit crops are grown.[9] In fact, the word 'development' is absent from the texts of the 1961 and 1971 Conventions. It only appears once in the 1988 Convention, as 'rural development leading to economically viable alternatives to illicit cultivation,' under Article 14 dedicated to 'Measures to eradicate illicit cultivation of narcotic plants.'[10] These limited AD efforts have been neither effective nor sustainable, mainly because the root causes that sustain the cultivation of illicit crops and drug trafficking have not received the necessary attention, investment, or political will to solve them.

Nor have development programs and agencies usually recognized drug-related issues or the impact of drug policies (as well as other illicit economies) as elements to be accounted for. This is true even in territories or countries where they represent major factors affecting social, cultural, political, and economic dynamics, which still yield to law enforcement agencies in order to take care of the problem. The enormous scale of the illicit economy of drugs (estimated to be worth between \$426 billion and \$652 billion a year),[11] which represents more than four times the net global official development aid (\$144.2 billion),[12] leaves no aspect of development untouched. In many cases, the borders between licit and illicit are blurred; illicit economies generate job development and economic growth, food security, or access to land and markets, determine financial sector trends, and influence public goods and service delivery—including security—and political decision-making. Recent case studies in diverse regions (Tajikistan, Mali, Afghanistan and Colombia)[13] show a more complex picture of 'the role that illicit economies play in bolstering or undermining the state, in fueling or reducing violence and inequality, or in limiting or expanding wealth.'

Furthermore, some specific development policies (or their absence) can increase vulnerability to problems related to illicit

347

drug production, trafficking, and problem drug use. Illicit markets and economies become a survival option for many individuals and communities left aside by exclusive development policies and who lack many formal and legal options to obtain security and to be economically and socially included.

In these contexts, involvement in the drug trade cannot be simplified to a need/greed equation. Structural causes and consequences of the development and persistence of drug-related problems need to be fully understood and incorporated in sustainable development thinking, problem-solving, planning, and programming. The influence of drug economies and actors on development, livelihoods, and governance has to be fully understood in order to provide realistic responses to development problems. Maintaining these blind spots over the complexity of drug markets 'would be an act of gross negligence,'[14] because it could undermine development planning and investments, and possibly exacerbate drug-related problems.[15]

The 2030 Global Agenda for Sustainable Development, adopted by the UN General Assembly in September 2015, only makes a single reference to drugs in target 3.5, which aims to 'strengthen the prevention and treatment of substance abuse, including narcotic drug abuse and harmful use of alcohol.' Nevertheless, drug-related issues and policies affect nearly every aspect of development in many regions and countries, including poverty reduction, food security, human rights, health and well-being, education, social inclusion, gender equality, employment, environmental issues, human security, access to justice, inclusive political processes, governance, and the rule of law, among others. The negative impact of drug markets and drug control policies on the capacity of vulnerable communities, territories, and countries to attain good development results is something that needs to be contemplated by the development community within the 2030 Agenda for Sustainable Development and the SDG framework (see Chapter 1 by Annette Idler for the concept of vulnerable regions).

These harmful consequences of drug control policy on human development have been widely acknowledged. Still, key disagreements remain regarding approaches, with some countries still strongly focusing on abstinence, eradication, interdiction, and punishment, whilst others emphasize human rights, social inclusion, and development-based approaches. There are also growing concerns about tensions between the drug conventions and their implementation, and other international norms, mainly regarding human rights— for example with respect to health, criminal justice responses, or impact on women, youth, children, and other vulnerable populations (including minorities and indigenous groups, people with disabilities, and LGBTI populations).[16]

Alternative Development Policies: The Need for a Wider Perspective on Sustainable Development

International donors have promoted AD programs for decades to dissuade farmers from growing plants for illicit drug production, substituting them with legal crops, or other activities. The success of these programs has traditionally been measured against drug crop reduction locally or nationally, without accounting for other human development indicators or the displacement 'balloon effect' on other areas.[17] In most cases, AD policies have been directly aligned with drug control, public security, or trade priorities. Their strategies focus on repressive interventions in producing countries, rather than in the consumer markets, including forced eradication and fumigation, oppressive military enforcement, criminalization and stabilization, and consolidation strategies against insurgency. Additionally, poor design, fragmented implementation and poor funding have in many cases added to the failure to ensure local ownership or meaningful participation of farmers. All these elements have curtailed their effectiveness, augmented their negative impacts on development, and increased the vulnerability of poor target communities and neighbor or distant communities affected by the displacement of crops, production, violence from illicit actors and from institutional responses, all part of the War on Drugs' dynamics.[18]

Due to growing criticism of this limited vision of AD, in the 2010s, the international community tried to establish a set of guiding principles to 'serve as a reference point for future AD interventions and guide policy formulation in a way that improves the social, economic and political environment of small farmers and sustainably reduces illicit cultivation of crops used for the production of narcotic drugs.'[19] In 2011, a first draft was put together at a workshop in Thailand to prepare the International Conference on Alternative Development (ICAD).[20] This document built upon the practical experience of several decades of work promoting AD. It led to a new understanding of the importance of holistic policies,[21] in a move toward 'mainstreaming' AD into national, regional, and local development initiatives, as a necessary component of economic development targeting some of the world's poorest people. Nevertheless, when the international community met at ICAD the following year in Lima, in the final version of the document,[22] AD was once again placed as 'complementary' to 'law enforcement and illicit crop elimination' and 'in full conformity with the three drug conventions' (rather than with the UN SDGs), straying far from the original purpose of encouraging development ministries and agencies to invest their resources in improving livelihoods and reducing coca and poppy crops.

A second ICAD meeting took place in Thailand in December 2015, and the chair's summary[23] includes in its recommendations the fact that AD is 'intrinsically linked and complementary to the recently adopted 2030 Sustainable Development Agenda' and stresses the need 'to mainstream alternative development programs into national development plans, involving coordination between relevant governmental agencies in order to improve area-based, socioeconomic conditions of small farmer communities by providing necessary infrastructure and public services.' It also insists on the 'proper sequencing in the implementation of alternative development programs ... to allow smallholder farmers to have access to secured alternative livelihoods prior to the eradication of illicit crops.' It continues saying that 'the success of alternative development programs should not only be measured by illicit crop reduction estimates but also by using human development indicators' and calls for 'enhanced system-wide coherence and coordination on development and drug control policies amongst all relevant agencies.' Long-term investment, in addition to well-planned and sequenced experiences—like the one developed in the Doi Tung mountain area on the Thai side of the Opium Golden Triangle[24]—show the benefits of prioritizing human development objectives over criminalization and punishment, although they are not able to avoid negative externalities from the displacement of illicit crops to other areas.

Impact and Costs on Human Development of the Implementation of the IDCR

Fifty-five years of implementing policies emanating from the IDCR have left an indelible footprint on sustainable human development, imposing burdens on people and communities while deteriorating their social fabric.[25] UNODC[26] has partially recognized this since 2008 as a series of 'unintended' negative consequences of the current international drug control policies.

The creation of an enormous criminal black market through prohibition has fueled corruption, violence, and instability, threatening basic human rights, democratic governance, legal economies, citizen security, public health, and the environment.[27] Additionally, the implementation of drug policies has generated more harm than the issue they were expected to reduce, leaving a trail of human rights abuses (see Chapter 12 by Damon Barrett and Kasia Malinowska-Sempruch), including death, violence, discrimination, and marginalization of people linked to drug markets or use, mass imprisonment, restriction of basic liberties, exacerbation of poverty, negation of access to basic public goods and services. Furthermore, the militarization of public policy, deterioration of criminal justice and prison systems, unequal application of justice, punishment to users, and degradation of the environment have all followed in the wake of these policies.

The implementation of drug control policies has distracted key public institutional and budgetary resources from other development-oriented policies. As an example, drug control operations spending by governments globally exceeds US\$100 billion, almost the amount of net bilateral official development assistance (\$144 billion[28]) disbursed by OECD countries per year.[29] Many developing and middle-income countries with drug production and transit problems cannot afford considerable investments in drug control policies—which are mostly used to maintain enlarged anti-drug units and their expensive equipment, as well as to respond to the costs of mass criminalization and incarceration—and their subsequent negative productivity impact, considering the huge challenges for sustainable development that the new 2030 Agenda goals poses for their public sector, economy and society.

Some governments from Latin America and the Caribbean, as well as regional and sub-regional bodies (OAS, CELAC, UNASUR), have been active in denouncing the harmful consequences of present policies, mainly due to the negative effects the War on Drugs has had on their territories and populations. This also accounts for why three countries from this region asked to move forward to 2016 the UNGASS, initially scheduled for 2019 (see Chapter 5 by Angélica Durán-Martínez). Nevertheless, some differences then defined—and still define—a heterogeneous regional political scenario with countries like Ecuador initially asking for a complete revision of the conventions, and others like Peru, which—despite being a country with a significant presence of excess coca crops and a legal coca leaf market—defended the results of prohibition and the classical duet of forced eradication associated with AD.

An increasing body of evidence already synthesized by numerous actors, including civil society organizations and international health, human rights, development, and drug control agencies (such as the UNODC, UNDP, UNAIDS, WHO, UNHCR and UN Special Rapporteurs on Torture and the Right to Health),[30] has demonstrated additional harmful effects of drug control policies and related law enforcement practices on a number of development outcomes. Particularly, the reduction of poverty and promotion of sustainable livelihoods; human rights; economic development; health; governance and the rule of law; gender equality; the environment; and on indigenous peoples and traditional and religious practices.

A Disproportionate Impact on the Most Vulnerable

The negative impacts of drug policy have not been distributed evenly among or within countries, consolidating two major imbalances regarding who bears the costs of drug policies. One concerns the impact on the most vulnerable individuals, groups, and communities; the other on the most vulnerable territories and countries.

As Tokatlian notes:

> [...] vulnerable human groups who are severely harassed therefore end up dead, or in prison, or without access to health care or alternative opportunities for a decent life. In general, those who reap the greatest benefits from illegal trade enjoy wealth and investments that go untouched, despite the existing array of laws and restrictions of various kinds that are meant to deal with this issue; social standing among the well-to-do classes, who usually welcome the 'nouveau riche;' economic and political incorporation into the cracks between illegality and legitimacy and into a state (at the local, department and/or federal levels) that has been partially immobilized because of collusion between certain officials and criminal organizations.[31]

The first of these imbalances has to do with the uneven distribution of the IDCR's negative consequences within our societies, which has increased social divisions and economic inequities. Drug control laws have been 'tough on the weak and weak on the tough,'[32] impacting the poor and vulnerable disproportionately. Many of them are additionally victimized while living in spaces where criminal networks already impose their laws and interest, and where the drug war is being fought—that is, in poor urban communities and in isolated rural communities, where state presence as a whole is weak and mostly limited to the intervention of law enforcement and security agencies. It is not a coincidence that Latin America, one of the areas most affected by the War on Drugs, is also the most unequal and violent region in the world.

Most people linked to drugs as producers or sellers, the weakest links in the illicit traffic chain, do not profit significantly from their activities—for instance, poor farmers who depend on cultivating coca and opium to survive; poor small-scale couriers, sellers, and people who use drugs; or people who live in conflict zones. Furthermore, they become stigmatized and excluded from social, economic, and political formal participation, lacking the power and organizational capacity to express their views and make their voices heard to defend their interests. For poor people and communities—including those internally displaced, victims of land grabs, deportees, ex-prisoners, or for those whose livelihoods have been deteriorated by economic and development policies—participating in illegal activities is a form of social legitimation and offers an alternative survival economy.

Criminalization and Incarceration: Its Cost for Human Development

Special consideration has to be given to the recurrent use of penal measures (criminalization and incarceration) as a standard solution to confront all issues related to people's involvement with drugs all throughout the chain of production, distribution, and use. This exposure of a large number of people to the criminal justice system has generated enormous personal, family, social, and economic costs which have fallen mostly upon poor and marginalized groups, who comprise a huge percentage of those arrested, prosecuted, and incarcerated. For example, 68.6 per cent of incarcerated people never finished 9 years of school in El Salvador; the figure is 62.9 per cent in Peru, 60.6 per cent in Brazil, 60.4 per cent in Chile, and 51.1 per cent in Mexico.[33]

The international drug conventions (1961, 1971 and 1988) require the transposition of criminal sanctions for cultivation, production, sale, or purchase, but they do not oblige countries to impose any penalty (criminal or administrative) for drug use. The 1988 Convention does stipulate that states could consider possession for personal use a crime, but 'subject to its constitutional principles and the basic concepts of its legal system.'

The practical interpretation, transposition, and implementation of these conventions, with their focus on penal responses, have exacerbated the growth and the costs of the 'penal state,' generating substantial costs for development. Meanwhile, they have accentuated the poverty and marginalization of people who use drugs, and the poor and vulnerable people linked to production or trafficking. In many countries, it has also disproportionately affected women: most of the world's female prisoners are in prison for drug-related crimes (more than 60 per cent in Argentina, Brazil, and Costa Rica).[34]

This has caused greater social vulnerability, difficulties for their socioeconomic inclusion, and pushed these groups to almost direct dependence on illicit economies—and therefore to more exposure to criminal activities or associated violence. It has also increased the likelihood of criminal recidivism for those entering this cycle, many of whom are initially criminalized merely as consumers, without offering any pathways to solve their social, economic, or health problems.

Additionally, the space for abuse increases inversely to the capacity of law enforcement and justice institutions. In Latin America, one of the most dramatic stages for the War on Drugs, the malfunctioning of criminal justice institutions has generated a 'legitimacy crisis,' with most people perceiving the system as corrupt, inefficient, and favoring impunity. In 2018, the level of trust in the justice system was at its lowest (24 per cent) since 2003,[35] generating increasing support for harsher penal measures.

The rehabilitative function of prison systems has not been a priority. On the contrary, prisons have emerged as an overpopulated space that has fostered violence, human rights abuses, connection with criminal networks, and recidivism. According to the latest data,[36] eighty-six countries worldwide have critical overpopulation problems, with a prisoner occupancy rate higher than 120 per cent. Some, like the Republic of Congo, had a rate as high as 619.6 per cent in 2019. In regions like Latin America, prison overpopulation—fueled by disproportionate sentencing on drug-related crimes and excessive use of preventive population—is over the 120 per cent occupancy rate in most countries. The situation is worst in Guatemala and Bolivia, with occupancy rates of 372 per cent in October 2019 and 364 per cent in June 2018.[37]

Incarceration generates an enormous burden for prisoners and their families. On the one hand, it generates economic instability by saddling them with copious court fees, fines and debt, at the same time that their employment and economic opportunities are diminished. Many families lose income when a family member is removed from household wage earning, while those remaining must support their loved one financially, both in prison and afterwards. In many cases, women bear the brunt of the emotional and financial costs of incarceration, and its associated stigma, while trauma and isolation are relevant factors for the damaging of familial relationships, impeding families and communities from thriving. The existence of a previous criminal record affects later access to education, housing, voting, and other social services and civil rights.

Additionally, the inadequate conditions of prison settings, and the implementation of abstinence policies regarding drug use or sex among inmates—negating access to harm reduction tools like condoms or syringes—have also generated enormous associated health problems regarding infectious diseases, including STDs, HIV/AIDS, tuberculosis, and hepatitis, as well as overdoses. Families and their incarcerated loved ones frequently report post-traumatic stress disorder, nightmares, hopelessness, depression, and anxiety. Yet families have little institutional support for healing from this trauma, which would help them become emotionally and financially stable during and post-incarceration.

Criminalization has also exposed many consumers to repressive police practices, abusive situations, and the limitation of many of their basic civil, political, and social rights. It has pushed the most vulnerable's consumption into more hidden environments, hindering the implementation of articulated responses, the rapport of problem drug users with health and social services, and treatment or harm reduction programs. This facilitates the transmission of serious diseases such as AIDS, and puts many lives at risk.

The IDCR has given those in power an effective tool for social control to generate repression against vulnerable people linked—or suspected of being linked—to drug production, trafficking and use. At the same time, they are permissive—or not sufficiently efficient—with the few powerful illegal and legal actors participating in money laundering schemes.

It is not a surprise, then, that the communities and groups most affected by drug policies overlap with the same groups and communities mostly excluded from economic, social, and human development. Their problems associated with drugs and drug policy (from criminalization to lack of access to drug dependence treatments) become aggravated. These add up to the wide array of social and developmental difficulties connected to poverty and exclusion, which are concentrated in each individual, family, and community.

A Relevant Example: Impact on Children, Adolescents, and Youth[38]

While prohibitionist and repressive drug control policies have been justified by the real and potential harms associated with illicit drug use—public health problems, decreased productivity, unemployment, and poverty—the official drug control rhetoric emanating from the IDCR has always insisted with a special emphasis on the need for protection of the health, integrity, and rights of children, adolescents, and youth in order to avoid these harms. Because the initiation of drug use is more prevalent in these specific cycles of life, adolescents and young people have become the target of numerous prevention programs and campaigns against drug use—though many of these programs deliver ineffective, brief universal prevention, while not enough efforts are made on more effective selective or indicated prevention directed to young people initiating use or abuse. In some cases, youngsters are targeted and stigmatized up to a point where drug use is socially perceived as being almost exclusively performed by them.

Other impacts of drug policy on children, adolescents, and youth have not drawn similar attention. This includes the almost invisible imprisonment of youngsters—by the influence of their own families or by legal mandate—because of their suspected or real drug use, which is in many cases experimental and not problematic, in parallel with legal or semi-legal networks of detention centers where treatment is not evidence-based and many human rights are not respected. Criminalization policies and the profiling of poor youngsters have provoked additional negative consequences for many young individuals, directly connecting their lives with police repression, criminal justice and prison systems, as well as limiting quite early their options to continue studying or find a decent job. Adolescents and young people not working or going to school are more at risk of using substances (often of poor quality), becoming involved in drug dealing, or being victims of violence.

Negative impacts of the War on Drugs on poor rural and urban territories have also strongly affected children and adolescents. Many of them have joined the ranks of the victims or perpetrators of drug-related crimes and policies, and suffered the same negative impacts described above. The UN Special Rapporteur on the Right of Everyone to the Highest Attainable Standard of Mental and Physical Health has signaled that

> there has been insufficient attention to the many other ways in which children and their right to health are affected by drugs, the drug trade, and punitive state models... History and evidence have shown that the negative impact of repressive drug policies on children's health and their healthy development often outweighs the protective element behind such policies, and children who use drugs are criminalized, do not have access to harm reduction or adequate drug treatment, and are placed in compulsory drug rehabilitation centers.

Impact on the Most Vulnerable Countries

Costs have not been evenly distributed among different countries and regions. Some national or subnational realities present very different levels of vulnerability and/or resilience to different risks associated with the negatives consequences of drug policy, linked mainly to production and transit dynamics. In many of the territories linked to plant-based drug production and/or transit (like some regions in Afghanistan, Myanmar, Colombia, Peru, Honduras, Guatemala, and Mexico, among others), a mix of social, economic, political, governance factors and conflicts have contributed to the development and stagnation of drug-related problems, organized crime, violence, and social exclusion. They have also contributed to the multiplication of negative 'unintended' consequences of the implementation of drug policies that do not take into consideration all these elements.

On the one hand—and mostly relevant to developed countries whose drug problems are mainly associated with drug use—the IDCR legal framework and institutional architecture has allowed (not without some resistance, especially by an excessively militant INCB) the implementation of harm reduction, decriminalization, and social inclusion policies to tackle some of the most important 'unintended consequences' of the IDCR for their societies and citizens. This ability has also been reinforced by their greater resilience, which helps to solve these associated negative consequences.

On the other hand, the costs—economic, human, and social—on development have been disproportionally greater for those countries most vulnerable to the risks associated both with drug production and transit, and with the effects of the implementation of prohibitionist policies. As an example, in Mexico alone, the official number of confirmed homicides during the December 2006–November 2019 period (since former President Calderon's War on Drugs started) amounts to almost 275,000 people.[39] Just in 2019, 34,579 homicides were officially registered,[40] a number more than four times greater than the number of drug-related deaths in all twenty-eight countries of the EU (8,238 reported for 2017).[41] This is without even counting the disappeared (more than 61,000 people since 2006).[42] According to the UNODC, this sharp increase of homicides has been caused partly by what happened after the crackdown on the Mexican drug cartels that began in 2007. By 2011, the homicide rate had tripled—a rapid change that cannot be explained by long-term factors. The homicide rate then stabilized until 2015, when the cartels began to fragment and diversify, and the homicide rate started to rise again, resulting in an all-time high of more than 30,000 killings in 2017.[43]

Less developed and middle-income countries have to tackle these 'unintended consequences' within a straight-jacket of prohibitionist policies in the IDCR framework and those imposed by the logic of the War on Drugs, based on the strategy of attacking drug production at the source before it reaches the main markets. No room has been left to propose harm reduction recipes be applied for production or transit policies in order to mitigate the most extreme consequences of their 'international obligations' regarding the IDCR.

Often, weak local and national public structures have led these efforts. Overwhelmed by development-related obligations, they have lacked the capacity to significantly reduce drugs supply or demand. This is the case in rural communities or urban neighborhoods where organized criminals operate or traffic with open impunity. It is also reflected in the distress of people with addiction problems, who have limited or no access to effective and affordable treatment, and in the situation of prisons devoid of basic rehabilitation programs for those locked inside, including a significant number of drug users.

Public policy solutions have had to be implemented within local, national, and regional contexts tremendously vulnerable to the harms associated with illicit markets and to the effects of repressive policies: poverty, both rural and urban; inequality; lack of positive state presence; low accountability for the most powerful and limited access to justice for the rest; low access to basic public services or social protection; food insecurity and no access to natural resources or land tenure; lack of decent jobs and high informality within the economy; high levels of violence and insecurity; cultures that discriminate on the basis of class, race, ethnicity, religious, gender and sexual orientations; and limited fiscal space, among others.

The combination of a repressive approach and deficient state capacity has generated more harm than the drug phenomenon itself. It has further weakened public structures, mainly key political and security institutions[44] and criminal justice systems (see Chapter 5 by Angélica Durán-Martínez), because of their limited resilience to corruption or intimidation from criminals with enormous economic and armed power. In countries like Colombia, 'drug money has funded elections for at least three decades, and drug traffickers have gained influence in Congress and local governments.'[45] The use of extensive public resources to expand law enforcement efforts to fight organized crime—Mexico is spending US$9 billion a year, three times the GDP percentage that the US is allocating to fight drug trafficking, and Colombia increased public expenditure on security from 3.6 to 6 per cent of GDP in 2006[46]—has prevented many states from investing enough in other development areas. Similarly, the ubiquitous impunity in the laundering of assets derived from drug trafficking and other illegal businesses—even in countries with much greater institutional capacity[47]—demonstrates this weakening, and the collusion between organized crime and important sectors of financial and political institutions.

Agenda 2030 as the Main Reference for a Sustainable Human Development-Based Approach on Drug Policy

The concept of human development, developed in 1990 by the works of Amartya Sen and Mahbub Ul-Haq, represents a landmark in the way the international community understands development.[48] It recognizes that the true wealth of nations are their people, and that the main objective of development must point to the creation of conditions to allow people to experience long, healthy, and creative lives. Therefore, it is understood as a process that enlarges the choices, liberties, and capacities of people for their well-being and health, and which also enables their access to the necessary resources and knowledge to live decent lives.

This concept has profoundly inspired the new global 2030 Agenda for Sustainable Development, an ambitious blueprint for a better world, with broad, universal, and transformative goals. This Agenda rests upon five elements—people, planet, prosperity, peace, and partnerships—seventeen goals and 169 targets, which are 'integrated and indivisible and balance the three dimensions of sustainable development: the economic, social and environmental.'[49] During the September 2015 high-level meeting of the General Assembly, the 2030 Agenda received universal acceptance from all UN member states and a commitment to fully implement all its goals and targets.

The whole set of SDGs—which focus on ambitions such as ending poverty and inequality within and among countries, protecting human rights, promoting gender equality and empowerment of women, protecting the environment, generating prosperity and decent work for all—connect directly with the foundational ideas of human development in order to generate the conditions for people to thrive.

The changes that will be required to advance in this Agenda will only happen under certain policy coordination and coherence conditions, each government deciding 'how these aspirational and global targets should be incorporated in national planning processes, policies, and strategies,' while recognizing 'the link between sustainable development and other relevant ongoing processes in the economic, social and environmental fields.'[50] Therefore, each target and goal will need to be viewed in an interactive vision of impacts and synergies with other goals and targets, making analysis and action more complex and effective. One must understand the impact of one policy decision on other decisions, which is not always obvious or even considered.[51]

Public policies and interventions that exacerbate poverty and inequality, while negatively affecting the most vulnerable, increase stigma, exclusion and marginalization, limit women's empowerment, abuse basic human rights, erode democratic governance and transparency, fuel conflict or deteriorate health, have to be revised and reformed within a coherent policy framework that points to the SDGs as the main reference.

Specific sectoral objectives, like the ones traditionally pursued by drug policy—for instance, drug demand or supply reduction—have to be profoundly revised in order to contribute positively to this Agenda, transiting from a principle of 'do no harm' to a 'do the best reachable good.' Therefore, policies and specific interventions must be subject to an assessment of their impact, positive or negative, on development objectives and goals, in order for the international community to have a clearer picture of any present or predictable consequences on people, economies, or the environment. As a standard benchmark of decision making within the public sphere, the cost-effectiveness of policies and interventions must be continuously considered to avoid insisting on non-effective or expensive policies that make limited progress and impede effective or innovative interventions from being developed and financed.

The 2030 Agenda respects 'each country's policy space and leadership to establish and implement policies for poverty eradication and sustainable development' through 'nationally owned sustainable development strategies, supported by integrated national financing frameworks.'[52] This could be of special importance whenever national actors decide on specific challenges and trade-offs regarding inconsistencies between development objectives and other policies' impact on their population (including drug policy).

Contradictions between the 2030 Agenda and Drug Policy Implementation

There are many contradictions between the SDGs and their targets, and the objectives and effects of drug control policies. These policies negatively impact the capacity of countries and communities to reach those goals, especially those with greater vulnerabilities. Table 13.1 (see end of chapter) presents some examples of how negative effects of drug policies[53] correlate with thirteen out of seventeen specific SDGs.

In order to resolve these policy incoherencies, the 2030 Agenda needs to become a fundamental reference point for the development and implementation of a new breed of drug policy, especially in a moment where there are profound divides over the need and scope for IDCR reform.

Towards a Sustainable Human Development-Based Approach

A sustainable human development approach must be guided by the general principle that drug policy cannot become a factor that negatively affects communities or countries' sustainable development. On the contrary, drug policy should become an element to facilitate and promote sustainable and inclusive development for all, putting people first and leaving no one behind.

In this process, it will be crucial to build on a drug-control paradigm shift. We are advancing slowly from approaches that focus on antisocial behavior—based on the idea of the deviant or the criminal offender—to a medical-biological view, anchored in personal deficit and disease. But the international debate needs to progress on the recognition of people linked to drugs as citizens with all their rights, within a wider framework of sustainable human development.

This approach feeds on the main pillars of the UN (peace, security, development, and human rights) and the main objectives of the IDCR—improving the health and well-being of humankind—as well as on the basic principles of policy coherence, 'do no harm' and 'do the best reachable good.' It is based on the accumulated experience of those in the implementation of human development processes.

i. Breaking the Cycle of Standard and Ineffective Analysis and Responses: The Need for Complex, Innovative, Context-Specific and Human Development-Oriented Solutions

The consequences of adopting such an approach must change the way many drug control strategies are oriented and implemented. Governments, institutions, and societies must generate processes to overcome the traditional way in which public policy on drugs has been designed, implemented, monitored, and evaluated. This has often

363

been done on the basis of biased and fragmented analysis based on uninformed, incomplete, and incorrect cause-effect relationships. A new policy is needed in order to integrate drugs in a wider perspective, as part of a multidimensional human development strategy for specific territories or communities.

Local contexts present a different combination of risk factors associated with drug-related problems that make specific territories, populations, or groups more vulnerable to them. These problems and risk factors, as well as stakeholders involved, need to be identified and considered on their unique combination and specific interaction, in order to develop a set of articulated policies adapted to the situations they want to modify.

Therefore, holistic attention to social, economic, developmental, political, and cultural elements in intervention areas is needed to analyze the scope of the challenges ahead. Awareness of social and institutional perceptions, mapping of all stakeholders (legal and illegal) and power relations, is also key to understanding the complex interactions related to drugs in specific societies.

In correlation, responses will also require articulated action from the whole of the state, among different sectoral institutions—health, education, social, labor, justice, security—as well as coordination between different levels of administration (for instance, central and subnational governments) in order to generate solutions adapted to specific situations, challenges, and affected populations' life-cycle of needs.

ii. Assessment of the Impact of Drug Control Policies on Human Development and New Metrics of Success

It is also important to identify and estimate the factors which contribute to increasing the negative impacts and risks to human development, then to discuss and define the ways in which the elimination of those impacts could be strengthened, and resilience generated to a broad group of evolving risks.[54] The SDG framework could serve as a powerful reference to start evaluating not only the potential impact of planned policies on sustainable development, but also the past and present impact on developing policies.

So far, improvements in development results are not being considered by most governments over drug supply and demand reduction objectives. This prevents decision-makers, legislators, planners, or implementation actors from addressing them, generating blind spots and perverse incentives to increase, at any cost, the numbers of people arrested, prosecuted and jailed, as well as the number of illicit drugs seized (see Chapter 14 by Robert Muggah and Katherine Aguirre on the metrics of success for drug policy interventions). In 1999, the ECOSOC had already pointed out the importance of including human development metrics of success.[55] Therefore, both the capacity to produce positive development results—and the risks associated with generating interventions whose negative impact on sustainable development is significant—become crucial for drawing the lines that define and limit public policy intervention, and for debating and solving important policy dilemmas.

iii. Space for Development Agencies

Development practice needs to be considered by public policy-makers in order to define a new generation of effective development-based drug policy strategies and interventions based on innovative thinking that produces multidimensional solutions. This would allow an understanding of the drug problem not as a single reality, but as different problems related to drugs in different contexts.

At the UN, and in many countries, drug-related issues—even those directly linked to development processes, like AD—have traditionally been kept out of the scope and responsibilities of national development actors. They have mainly been coordinated by national drug commissions like DEVIDA in Peru or the Ministry of Counternarcotics in Afghanistan, and under drug control strategies—as was the case for the AD strategy under *Plan Colombia*. The limited results obtained by AD programs have demonstrated that agencies centered on fighting crime or dealing with criminal justice issues are not the best placed to coordinate, develop, and implement complex policies that have multiple interactions with development issues.

However, there are encouraging precedents in complex policy areas—such as conflict prevention and recovery, HIV/AIDS, or crime and violence prevention[56]—where involving development agencies that apply comprehensive and sustainable human development-based approaches has shown effective and sustainable results, away from one-sided securitization responses. The comprehensive focus of a sustainable human development-based approach would allow addressing both the causes and consequences of illicit drug markets, along with uncertainties, spillovers, trade-offs, and systemic risks in an effort to transform policies and challenging realities.

In this sense, a broader network of development organizations and actors engaged more seriously and systematically on drug issues should be generated. Enhanced linkages between development and drug entities will allow for a better understanding of the profound interrelationships between both fields[57] and for designing more effective and humane drug policies. Development work needs to become 'drugs-sensitive,' and the capacity of development agencies must be enhanced to engage with drug issues and to work in settings with large illicit economies. If affected countries or communities request the engagement of development agencies on drug-related issues, it could allow for a mitigation of the political risks associated with this paradigm change, as well as for overcoming institutional inertia and funding constraints. It is thus necessary to reorient resources away from law enforcement measures to strengthen development-based approaches.

The decision of UNDP and other development organizations to step into the pre and post-UNGASS debate is a promising move which hopefully will help others join in and promote this approach, but it needs to scale up from declaratory statements on best practices to actual experimentation and implementation.

iv. A Window of Opportunity for the UN to Advance in a System-Wide Sustainable Development-Based Approach to Drug Policy

The acknowledgement that illicitly produced drugs and sustainable development are inherently linked—as the 2016 UNGASS outcome document states—sets up the basis, both at national and at the UN level, to capitalize on the comparative advantage that other agencies have in implementing development programs.[58] A balanced IDCR redefinition of its institutional architecture, mandates, and responsibilities on drugs and development-related issues could allow programs like UNDP or other sectoral agencies like FAO, UNESCO, ILO, UNEP, UNWOMEN, UNICEF, UN-HABITAT, or UNHCR to actively participate with their knowledge and experience in the search for articulated solutions. This would also become an accelerator for redefining national institutional architectures on drug issues, allowing for more meaningful participation of diverse and necessary stakeholders under the basic principle of 'shared responsibility.'

This system-wide approach would eventually be reflected in the programmatic tools and policy frameworks defined by the different agencies in their cooperation with member states, like the UN Common Country Assessments, the UN Development Assistance Frameworks and the UN Country Programs, where 'Delivering as One UN' should materialize.

In order to establish a financial incentive, and as a counterweight to the dynamics of competition for donor funds among different agencies, the idea of a multi-donor and multi-agency fund for drug policy and sustainable development should be put forward. As previous experiences with other UN funds (like the Millennium Development Goals (MDG) Fund and the SDG Fund)[59] demonstrate, any project to be presented for funding would necessarily require the collaboration and interaction of a sufficient number of agencies or programs to assure the multidimensionality of the responses to the complex challenges on the drugs agenda and development. It would allow for additional innovation, new approaches and synergies among the different sectors involved.

Furthermore, civil society organizations have made growing calls for the 'creation of a special mechanism that would facilitate the integration of drug policy with the achievement of the 2030 Agenda' as 'critical to prevent drug policy from becoming siloed ... and to work effectively within the SDGs framework and the UN system as a whole.'[60]

Table 13

Examples of Drug and Drug Policy Related Issues that Negatively Affect the Capacity of Communities and Countries to Reach the SDGs

SDGs	Examples of drug and drug policy related issues that negatively affect the capacity of communities and countries to reach the SDGs
1. No poverty	• Greater exposure to risks in poverty environments due to a mix of social determinants such as higher availability of drugs and arms, lower urbanization levels, higher crime rates, earlier initiation ages, presence of dealing organizations, repressive police strategies, use of highly adulterated substances, higher number of relapse episodes, and presence of violence. • Long term incarceration caused by poor legal design, disproportionate long sentences and poor access to justice has become a big economic and social burden for most countries impacting, mainly, in the most disadvantaged individuals, families and communities, including youth, women and racial minorities. • People who suffer from addiction and their families are more at risk of losing their property, being unemployed, or having problems with the law, and they are more often victims of violence and discrimination.
2. Zero hunger	• Land grabs and displacement of rural inhabitants from non-state drug-related actors. • Implementation of repressive drug control policy causes loss of livelihoods, displacement, migration and criminalization of rural communities, fueling conflict.
3. Good health and wellbeing	Investments in security and supply reduction policies subtract enormous resources that could be used to invest in health and development policies.

SDGs	Examples of drug and drug policy related issues that negatively affect the capacity of communities and countries to reach the SDGs
	• Problem drug-use related deaths, infections, mental disorders, and disabilities due to lack of affordable treatment and rehabilitation services.
	• People with problem drug use denied or without access to basic services (housing, education, health, employment, social) and/or treatment because of lack of investment, criminalization of drug use and stigma and discrimination.
	• Lack of social (re)integration processes along with significant percentages of relapses and readmissions, limiting the chances of overcoming addiction problems and substantially reducing the efficiency of any investment in treatment and recovery systems.
	• Increase of prevalence HIV and other infectious diseases due to repressive measures and incarceration, and to the lack of effective prevention, treatment and harm-reduction policies directed to marginalized populations.
4. Good education	• Lack of response for the delivery of basic public goods and services, like education, due to improperly focused drug-policies.
	• Abstinence-based and prohibitionist policies, along with the lack of specialized services, result in the expelling of many adolescents and young people from the education system, hampering their progress and increasing the risks of being left behind or subject to violence and involvement in illicit economies.
5. Gender equality	• Female involvement in illicit drug trading due to economic and gender-inequality circumstances, such as single mothers needing a means by which to feed their family.

SDGs	Examples of drug and drug policy related issues that negatively affect the capacity of communities and countries to reach the SDGs
	• Disproportionate incarceration of women for their participation in the lowest levels of drug production or trafficking. Consequences of criminal punishment are felt differently by women, often with greater impact on their children and families. • Higher prevalence of gender-violence affecting female drug-users, with double vulnerability and stigma and the lack of specialized services. • Violence against women, macho culture, and obstacles to women's empowerment in areas controlled by drug-related organized crime. • Lack of gender-sensitive services do not allow access to treatment and recovery services for women. • Children, adolescents and women left behind may then engage in criminal activity or drug use as they struggle to cope with the lack of resources and support. • Deterioration of the insecurity perception change in routines and restriction of liberties, specially affecting women.
8. Decent Work and Economic Growth	• Loss of productivity and absenteeism because of harmful drug use. • Legal economic activities underperformance, increased costs of production of inputs (labor, land) and damage to productive dynamism because of increased unfair competition and market distortions by money laundering activities from drug money. • Inhibition of legitimate social and economic activity and lack of formal and legal economic alternatives for the poor, youth, women,

SDGs	Examples of drug and drug policy related issues that negatively affect the capacity of communities and countries to reach the SDGs
	indigenous populations and other excluded groups, because of illegal markets dynamics.
	• Subtraction of key human resources and innovation capabilities to the legal economy.
	• Long term incarceration caused by poor legal design and disproportionate long sentences has become a big economic burden for most countries impacting, mainly, in the most disadvantaged individuals, families and communities, including youth, women and racial minorities.
9. Industry Innovation and Infrastructure	• Investments in security and supply reduction policies subtract enormous resources that could be used to invest in development policies.
	• Entire regions, communities, and specific populations getting most of their income from drug-related illicit activities. Loss of fiscal space, affecting economic growth and employment generation due to lack of tax revenue generation.
	• Pre-eminence of illegal activities and perpetuation of a commodity and financial speculation mentality, hampering innovation.
	• Lack of response for the delivery of basic public goods and services due to improperly focused drug-policies. Investments in security and supply reduction policies subtract enormous resources that could be used to invest in industry, innovation, infrastructure and other development policies.
10. Reduced Inequalities	• Inhibition of legitimate social and economic activity and lack of formal and legal economic alternatives for the poor, youth, women, indigenous populations and other excluded groups, because of illegal markets dynamics.

SDGs	Examples of drug and drug policy related issues that negatively affect the capacity of communities and countries to reach the SDGs
	• Stigma associated with being a (former) problematic drug user and the increased likelihood of having a criminal record mean that obtaining and maintaining employment is more difficult.
	• Children, adolescents, and women left behind may then engage in criminal activity or drug use as they struggle to cope with the lack of resources and support.
	• People who suffer from an addiction and their families are more at risk of losing their property, being unemployed, or having problems with the law, and they are more often victims of violence and discrimination.
	• Pre-eminence of excluding and fear-based social representations that do not allow for changes in policies.
	• People with problem drug use denied or without access to basic services (housing, education, health, employment, social) and/or treatment because of lack of investment, criminalization of drug use and stigma and discrimination.
11. Sustainable Cities and Communities	• Violence, human rights abuses and major crimes committed by law enforcement agencies and justice system actors.
	• Violence, human rights abuses and major crimes against the population by non-state actors of the illicit drug market.
	• Deterioration of the insecurity perception change in everyday life routines and restriction of liberties.
	• Higher prevalence of gender-violence affecting female drug-users, with double vulnerability and stigma and the lack of specialized services.

SDGs	Examples of drug and drug policy related issues that negatively affect the capacity of communities and countries to reach the SDGs
	• Violence against women and macho culture in areas controlled by drug-related organized crime.
15. Life on Land	• Illegal cultivation of plant-based drugs is often pushed to remote areas of high ecological value. • Deforestation, land degradation, loss of endemic species and pollution of aquifer courses from chemicals used for the illegal production of drugs. • Deforestation and pollution from fumigation, eradication and destruction of illicit crop fields, drug-labs, drugs illicitly produced and chemical precursors. • Deforestation from narco-economies and extensive monoculture and cattle investments in protected or sensitive areas.
16. Peace Justice and Strong Institutions	• Violence, human rights abuses and major crimes committed by law enforcement agencies and justice system actors. • Weak state presence creates an environment conducive to illicit activity, and thereby allowing armed groups to use illicit drug economies to finance their activities. • Long term incarceration caused by poor legal design, disproportionate long sentences and poor access to justice has become a big economic and social burden for most countries impacting, mainly, in the most disadvantaged individuals, families and communities, including youth, women and racial minorities. • Violence, human rights abuses, and major crimes against the population by non-state actors of the illicit drug market.

SDGs	Examples of drug and drug policy related issues that negatively affect the capacity of communities and countries to reach the SDGs
	<ul><li>Deterioration of the insecurity perception change in routines and restriction of liberties.</li><li>Transgressions of basic human rights, as well as lack of civil and political rights enjoyment, because of disproportionate penal sentencing for drug related offenses (including death penalty) and mass incarceration of people linked to drugs.</li><li>Excessive use of criminal justice mechanisms, the disproportionality of penalties for drug offenses (including death penalty and long-term incarceration), abuse of pre-trial detention and the enforcement of mandatory sentencing laws have contributed to overload the judicial and prison systems, making them even more inefficient.</li><li>Impunity from human right abuses and major crimes due to corruption of and major threats to justice system officials and other public decision makers and administrative authorities.</li><li>Erosion of democratic governance, rule of law, and people's adherence to social norms and institutions by illegal actors by means of the 'normalization' of illegal activities, popular support, political and economic influence or protection from law enforcement and justice.</li><li>Use of key democratic institutions for illegal purposes.</li><li>Loss of income, unemployment, and food insecurity resulting from supply control programs often leads to frustration, antipathy to authorities, and social instability.</li></ul>

SDGs	Examples of drug and drug policy related issues that negatively affect the capacity of communities and countries to reach the SDGs
	• High sensitivity of drug issues along electoral processes, generating political problems for the promotion and approval of alternative policies and interventions. • Metrics and indicators for drug policy success are based in the specific and narrow traditional objectives of drugs demand and supply reduction without any other consideration of their impact on human rights, social inclusion or on any other elements of sustainable human development.
17. Partnerships for the goals	• Entire regions, communities and specific populations getting most of their income from drug-related illicit activities, without generating tax revenue. • Most vulnerable countries, mainly related to illicit production and transit of drugs, are most affected by the negative impacts and the costs of drug policy prohibitionist interventions. • Pre-eminence of prohibition and abstinence-based policies do not allow for the development alternative policies in developing countries.

14

RETHINKING DRUG POLICY METRICS TO MOVE BEYOND THE WAR ON DRUGS

Robert Muggah and *Katherine Aguirre*

After decades of politically charged debates over the War on Drugs, there is growing consensus that scientific evidence should be the basis for future policy and programming. Elected officials, drug tsars, public health specialists, and activists are virtually unanimous that data-driven scientifically informed responses are necessary to have any lasting impact on drug demand and supply.[1] This change in tone is a radical development. In the past, international and domestic drug policies were seldom forged or measured on the basis of reliable data and evidence. Rather, interventions to fight illicit drugs production, trafficking, and consumption tended to be guided by politically and ideologically informed metrics. Strategies that adopted forceful responses to drug control were premised more on a system of beliefs than scientific facts.[2] Predictably, the misalignment of data, metrics, and responses contributed in many cases to worsening the drug 'problem.'

There are encouraging signs that some of the persistent contradictions in contemporary drug policy are being recognized and reversed. Coalitions such as the Global Commission on Drug Policy (GCDP)[3] and a range of non-governmental and philanthropic organizations have helped bolster international commitment to evidence-based policy and practice.[4] In 2011, the Global Commission called for an alternative way of gauging the effectiveness and efficiency of drug policy. Specifically, it encouraged governments to 'establish better metrics, indicators and goals to measure progress' in achieving drug policy reform.[5] It acknowledged how the 'current system of measuring success in the drug policy field is flawed ... [and that] a new set of indicators is needed to truly show the outcomes of drug policies according to their harms or benefits for individuals and communities.'[6] It is, of course, one thing to call for better metrics and data collection, but quite another to set out a roadmap for how this might be done.

Divided into three sections, this chapter outlines a way to accelerate the shift away from the War on Drugs paradigm through the revision and reformulation of key metrics. It shows how traditional metrics have justified and sustained a repressive global drug control regime since the 1960s. It proposes alternative—albeit generic—goals, targets, and indicators to better track the effects of progressive drug policy.[7] This is not the first initiative to define parameters for monitoring the policy and practice of drug policy. Australia, Canada, and the United Kingdom have all developed mechanisms—influenced by existing international norms and standards—to measure the harms associated with illicit drug production and supply, and organized crime.[8] Nor will this chapter be the last attempt to rethink the underlying metrics of drug policy. The contribution is novel, however, in that it lays out an original framework based on evidence of what works rather than what is politically acceptable.

The first section revisits the conventional metrics applied by governments, international agencies, and non-governmental organizations (NGOs) around the world to monitor and enforce changes in drugs demand and supply. It also highlights the relevance and justification for new metrics to measure drug policy based on alternatives to punitive approaches. The authors find that traditional indicators tend to be narrowly focused on inputs and outputs designed to rein in production, interdiction, and consumption. There is less focus on the associated outcomes and impacts of drug policies, especially in relation to public security, population health, human rights, or development. Many existing indicators are not only outdated; they are counterproductive, a legacy of political and institutional interests that have prevailed since the mid-twentieth century.

The remainder of the chapter sets out the basic contours of updated goals, targets, and indicators to measure drug policy efficiency and effectiveness. The second section of the paper offers a historical perspective on the evolution of metrics. The authors consider how drug policy was evaluated before and after the consolidation of the International Drug Control Regime (IDCR). Conventional goals and targets emphasizing supply and demand reduction have justified and bolstered punitive legislation, policies, and programs. Section three proposes several general metrics to rethink drug policy, including two high-level impact objectives, six goals, sixteen targets, and eighty-six indicators. These were short-listed following extensive consultations with leading international experts in the fields of criminology, public health, human rights, and development. The final section includes recommendations to facilitate the process of the collection of new indicators, since the value of this framework will be in the ability of governments and others to implement it. The authors call for the strengthening of national drug observatories and a comprehensive review of available data.

From a Punitive to a Comprehensive Approach

The global debate and direction of drug policy for the past half-century has been largely informed by a crime control and criminal justice perspective. Put simply, this approach criminalized producers, retailers, and consumers of illegal narcotics. Traditional indicators mobilized to track domestic (and later global) implementation of drug control naturally mirrored this view, thereby perpetuating repressive policy and action. This narrow focus toward reducing the supply and demand for drugs not only failed to achieve its stated goals, but also generated adverse consequences for the safety and well-being of civilians. More recently, a change in perspective has emerged that puts security, rights, health, and development squarely at the center of drug policy. The GCDP and groups such as the Brookings Institution, the Drug Policy Alliance, International Drug Policy Consortium, Open Society Foundation, Transform Foundation, the Transnational Institute, and many others have been at the cutting-edge of these discussions. Indeed, an expert group convened by the International Peace Institute also proposed a framework of metrics aligned with the Sustainable Development Goals (SDGs).[9]

In the 1960s, several basic indicators were proposed to assess whether the goals of prohibition—with an emphasis on extinguishing drug production and supply—were being achieved. These included mapping the physical amount of land under cultivation (including coca, poppies, and cannabis), the extent of crops eradicated by different means (for example, slash and burn, fumigation, alternative products), the weight and volume of drugs being seized (for example, interdiction at borders, raids on sellers), the number of producers, traffickers, and users detained and imprisoned (for example, cartel leaders, low-level traffickers, addicts), and the extent of drug use in societies (for example, prevalence of consumption among teens, incidence of overdoses). International agencies such as the United Nations Office for Drugs and Crime (UNODC) were later enlisted by proponents of the global drug policy regime to track changes in these indicators over time.[10] In 2019, the World Drug Report was still reliant on these metrics, providing information on estimated trends in drug supply and use (cultivation, production and consumption). Its focus continues to be on plant-based drugs (cocaine, opiates and cannabis) together with synthetic and new psychoactive substances. While UNODC has reported on the risks and vulnerabilities associated with drug use, these issues occupy a lower order of concern relative to containing and disrupting supply and demand. The organization's analysis of drug policy developments is generally limited to the regulation of non-medical use of cannabis.

Notwithstanding the trillions of dollars invested in its maintenance, most of the desired outcomes of the IDCR over the past half-century have failed to materialize. What is more, unintended impacts have emerged, many of them undocumented by conventional monitoring systems. When the higher-order objectives of a policy demand results premised on enforcement, they can also create perverse incentives. In the case of drug policy, this has shifted the focus to expanding fumigation, maximizing drug seizures, and increasing arrests of producers, traffickers, and consumers. The law and order approach to drug policy did not, however, reduce drug production or demand, including addiction. Instead, it generated negative externalities such as sharp increases in violence and incarceration in precisely those settings where illicit drug production, trafficking, and consumption were occurring.[11] Among the many negative repercussions are, *inter alia*, an overall expansion of drug production, a decline in the cost of drugs, the spread of criminal markets, the corruption of political, law enforcement, and judicial systems in producer, transit, and consumer countries, and generally negative implications for human health, the environment, and long-term well-being.[12]

An unintended consequence of repressive approaches to drug policy has been their strong association with increases in organized and interpersonal violence.[13] According to one assessment, 'whilst drug market violence has traditionally been framed as resulting from the effects of drugs on individual users ... violence is increasingly being understood as a means used by individuals and groups to gain or maintain market share of the lucrative illicit drug trade.'[14] Narco-cartels, organized crime, and gangs are often involved in ruthlessly enforcing rules and defending territory from competitors. In the process, civilians—including those not entangled in the political economies of drug production, trafficking and retail—can become victims of informal justice or casualties of encounter violence.[15] Yet punitive drug policies—whether muscular military and police intervention or draconian penal laws targeting young people—aggravate the problem.[16] Paradoxically, it is often counternarcotics initiatives—efforts intended to curb illicit drug production, retail, and use—that are associated with the most egregious forms of violence, including tens of thousands of intentional homicides and disappearances a year.[17]

The debate on global drug policy over the past five decades has been influenced by very different aspirations than those proposed by the GCDP and like-minded organizations since 2011. Certain governments and intergovernmental bodies have endorsed approaches seeking to criminalize illicit production, supply and use of drugs. The expectation was that the threat of military action, more repressive policing, and tougher prison penalties would deter would-be drug manufacturers, traffickers, and users from availing themselves of narcotics. In addition to being inefficient, the War on Drugs is extremely costly: The Alternative World Drug Report estimates that global spending on counternarcotics exceeds $100 billion annually.[18] The effect is the fueling of a criminal black market with an estimated turnover of more than $330 billion annually.[19] The effectiveness of conventional approaches to addressing drug production, trafficking, and consumption are uneven. The UNODC reported in its 2019 *World Drug Report* that in spite of the tens of billions spent, 'prevention and treatment continue to fall short of needs in many parts of the world.'[20] The production of opium and manufacture of cocaine are still reaching record highs. For the UNODC, the status quo was tantamount to success: '... evidence shows that while the system may not have eliminated the drug problem, it continues to ensure that it does not escalate to unmanageable proportions.' Users of the most conventional drugs (heroin, cocaine, and cannabis) have increased: 'the number of people who use drugs is now 30 per cent higher than it was in 2009, when 210 million had used drugs in the previous year.'[21] Paradoxically, UNODC continues to praise 'increasingly effective law enforcement,' measured by the global interception rates of drugs.

Since the introduction of the IDCR, institutions responsible for compiling and disseminating data— including the Drug Supervisory Body (DSB) and the Permanent Central Opium Board (PCOB)—have also been responsible for overseeing the fulfilment of the provisions of drug control treaties. This, of course, generates a degree of moral hazard. The same can be said for UNODC, which is '... both the center for research and dissemination and a prime outlet for moral and political messages targeting drug.'[22] This is not limited to the drug policy arena. In the case of armed conflicts and heavy-handed policing, 'success' is often measured by the extent of casualties or desertions among insurgents, or the number of criminals killed or put behind bars. Such policies set up perverse incentives for armed forces and policing personnel to commit humanitarian and human rights violations, as the experience of Colombia's 'false positives' case so painfully reveals.[23]

There is a danger that policymakers focus on a discrete set of indicators that fulfil selective political and bureaucratic interests, rather than issues more relevant to the public interest. As is often the case in public policy, the focus of measurement tends to gravitate to measuring what is most visible, which in turn reflects the dominant power influences.[24] Current metrics of drug policy are 'valuable in terms of media management and providing the populace of countries with evidence that the authorities are achieving some success in their efforts to "solve" the drugs problem.'[25] This conceptual orientation has real-world implications. As noted above, the IDCR not only generated adverse consequences but also has subordinated equally—and potentially more—significant issues related to preserving and protecting the health, safety, and security of citizens.

Put succinctly, conventional drug policy metrics appear to be measuring the wrong variables. They explain 'how tough we are being, but do not tell us how successful we are' in achieving the overall goals of a progressive humane outcome.[26] Many of the traditionally applied indicators measure inputs and outputs but do not capture actual changes in the benefits or harms to individuals—including the unintended costs of repressive criminal justice measures. It appears that the bulk of policies and practices that are represented in global drug policy are not oriented toward improving human health, safety, and welfare. As stressed by the Global Commission, 'arresting and punishing drug users does little to reduce levels of drug use, taking out low-level dealers simply creates a market opportunity for others....'[27]

Most conventional indicators are process-oriented, in that they track the extent of drug crops sprayed, producers put out of business, and arrests and incarceration of traffickers and consumers. They do not, however, demonstrate whether drug supply or demand is increasing or declining. In most countries drug policy effectiveness is typically measured according to inputs—for example, dollars invested, police trained, and prisons built—and outputs (for example, number of interdictions of drug shipments, hectares of coca crops sprayed, and drug mules imprisoned) with less consideration of the outcomes and impacts of these interventions. Consider, for example, the longstanding goal of curbing drug trafficking. In fact, the variable 'drug trafficking' is frequently proxied by arrests and prosecutions of traffickers rather than the real impacts on the criminal organizations and their networks that manage trafficking and generate corresponding violence. Table 14.a (below) compares traditional indicators used in the context of the War on Drugs with newly proposed metrics to advance comprehensive drug policy.

Table 14.a

Comparing War on Drugs and Comprehensive Metrics for Drug Policy

War on Drugs Metrics	Comprehensive Metrics
Punitive enforcement-led approach emphasizing the criminalization of illicit production, supply and use of drugs.	A comprehensive approach designed to mitigate the harms generated by drugs with a focus on health, human rights, and security.
Focused on measuring the inputs and outputs associated with illicit drug production, interdiction, and consumption.	Focused on measuring the outcomes and impacts associated with drugs, and in particular ways of minimizing harms.
Narrowly-defined political and institutional interests and reflecting dominant international and domestic political influences.	Data-driven approach to tackling drugs with a focus on identifying solutions that minimize impacts on people and communities.
Process-oriented with an emphasis on repression: 'how tough we are.'	An emphasis on impact, outcome and output indicators: 'how successful we are.'
Failure to capture both higher-order and intended/ unintended consequences.	A recognition that a drug-free world is not feasible and a change in focus toward defining more practical, achievable, and relevant objectives consistent with existing drug treaties.

Source: Prepared by the authors.

Governments such as Bolivia, Canada, Colombia, Guatemala, Mexico, the Netherlands, New Zealand, Portugal, Spain, Uruguay, and a growing number of US states have started emphasizing the importance of new approaches, including a more balanced resort to criminal justice and the mitigation of harms generated by drugs.[28] As a result of the activism of transnational networks and domestic movements, the global discussion is re-orienting to include more engagement with themes related to safety and security, human rights, and public health as a means of reducing the negative effects of the production, distribution, and consumption of drugs.

In the process, many groups are calling for alternative metrics to prioritize, design, and monitor drug policy. These metrics should be organized in a comprehensive framework, even if national and subnational government authorities—in concert with citizen groups—ultimately decide the most appropriate approach suited to their local realities. The framework proposed here differs in many ways from the goals advanced by proponents of punitive approaches to drug policy. Indeed, the latter proposes few tangible measures for tracking changes in the health, safety, or welfare of people involved in or affected by drugs. Nor do they draw attention to ensuring value for money or a cost-benefit analysis of competing policy options. Yet these are precisely the kinds of priorities that all forward-thinking public policymakers urgently require.

There are ethical and efficiency-gains considerations when thinking about the higher order impacts of progressive drug policy. An ethical approach to drug policy should achieve improvements in safety, rights, health, and welfare while inflicting a minimal amount of harm on the least number of people. A key impact should be a reduction in scale of violence associated with drugs, including human rights violations, in addition to real and perceived safety and security. Meanwhile, an efficient approach should ensure that savings generated by a more targeted drug policy—returns from rehabilitated sellers and users being integrated into the labor market or the proportion of the budget once devoted to police and prisons being redirected to school and health expenditures—are channeled back into other productive social and economic sectors. The current approach to drug policy shaped by the War on Drugs paradigm with its emphasis on greater investment in military, law enforcement, and intelligence infrastructure coupled with incarceration, is what economists call 'unproductive' expenditure and garners few meaningful returns to society as a whole.

The overarching thrust of a comprehensive drug policy is thus intended to generate higher order impacts that improve well-being, and at a minimum do no intentional harm. Two basic expectations thus follow. First, comprehensive drug policy should improve health and welfare rather than diminish it. Second, such approaches should enhance the security and safety of drug users and the wider public alike. Moreover, selected indicators should allow for the measurement of both progress and results. This means monitoring drug policy differently. Rather than prioritizing the reduction of hectares under cultivation or numbers of traffickers arrested, the focus turns to enrollment of rural smallholder producers in vocational training and alternative livelihood projects, and exploring alternative sentencing possibilities for low-level non-violent offenders (see Chapter 9 by Pierre-Arnaud Chouvy on alternative livelihood approaches in the Golden Triangle).

While minimizing drug production, trafficking, and consumption are important considerations, they are means rather than ends of public policy. The real yardstick of successful drug reform should be whether it meaningfully improves the security and well-being of citizens. At a minimum, this means lowering mortality and morbidity associated with illegal drug use and reducing the stigmatization and criminalization of drug users. The goal is not to benefit drug producers, drug traffickers, and drug users, but rather society as a whole. A new framework with the proposed objectives and goals set out below could offer a roadmap. This is a significant methodological improvement on the current system of monitoring. The intention is not to be prescriptive, but rather to illustrate alternate pathways to drug policy that works.[29]

An Historical Perspective on Drug Policy Indicators

The history of the IDCR dates back to the beginning of the twentieth century (see Chapter 2 by Paul Gootenberg). Then—and to some extent even now—the focus was on limiting the production and consumption of opium. The 1909 International Opium Commission was the first example of international cooperation to control drugs. Information on production, trade, and consumption, and also revenue from opium accruing to governments was collected by the newly created International Opium Commission.[30] These early assessments were widely cited in the UNODC's 2008 report entitled 'A Century of International Drug Control' as a principal source of historical information on drugs (opium) during the emergence and development of an IDCR.

The International Opium Convention, signed in Geneva in 1925, required countries to collect data on illicit production, supply and use of drugs, and report findings to the Permanent Central Opium Board (PCOB). According to Article 24 of the Convention, one of the principle tasks of the Board was to oversee the statistical information sent by member states.[31] The focus then was on documenting drug stocks and consumption; the production of raw opium and coca; and the manufacture and distribution of heroin, morphine and cocaine. The original institutions responsible for generating statistics on drugs included the PCOB[32] and the Drug Supervisory Body (DSB), responsible for issuing a comprehensive assessment of global drug requirements.[33] The 1931 Geneva Narcotics Manufacturing and Distribution Limitation Convention Obligated parties to 'provide the PCOB with estimates of their national drug requirements—for domestic medical and scientific purposes.'[34] The PCOB was only mandated to track the trade, and any overage in production would be applied against a manufacturing country's estimates for the subsequent year. A supervisory body was created to administer and monitor the functioning of the system.

From 1948 onward, international drug control came under the auspices of the UN. The 1961 Single Convention on Narcotic Drugs resulted in a more rigid zero-tolerance and far-reaching system of control than earlier treaties. The Single Convention consolidated prior treaties and eliminated the onerous opium cultivation provisions from the 1953 treaty. The new treaty emphasized the risks drugs posed to the moral health of the humanity, highlighting the ways consumption contributed to the 'degeneration of the human race.' With virtually no recourse to scientific analysis, it regulated almost 100 substances, mostly plant-based products such as opium, cannabis, coca, and their derivatives. The Convention also created the International Narcotics

Control Board (INCB), combining the PCOB and the DSB into a single unified agency. This new organ was tasked with monitoring the application of the Convention and administering '... the system of estimates and statistical returns submitted annually by Parties.'[35] Synthetic products were also restricted, but with a less severe system of controls.[36]

The resulting classification of illicit drugs essentially defined the focus of metrics and data collection for the next 50 years.[37] The Single Convention consolidated previous treaties, calling for the tightening of controls on the production, distribution, and use of controlled substances—with an emphasis on supply side restrictions. Hence, prohibitionist approaches to drug control sanctioned crop eradication and the jailing of people associated with drugs without distinction, whether they were producers, petty traffickers, or non-violent and first-time consumers.

In the meantime, the rhetoric associated with the War on Drugs ratcheted up during the 1970s.[38] The fight against drugs assumed the character and dimensions of military action, and increasingly came to be framed in many countries as a question of national security. The broadening of the drug war opened space for the application of ever more stringent metrics to showcase state commitment to prohibition. These included the extent of military and law enforcement spending on drug interdiction, training of specialized units, assets committed to counternarcotics, and deployment of counternarcotics operations. Powerful states also increasingly pressured producer and transit countries into carrying out forced eradication of a specified number of hectares, to achieve arrests and seizure quotas, and demonstrate benchmarks for aggressive drug control. These measures were frequently made conditional on the receipt of official aid or more favorable terms of trade.

Today, the primary source of information on drug control is the UNODC's World Drug Report. The report provides periodic assessments of the global drug situation based on an Annual Report Questionnaire (ARQ) voluntarily submitted by member states. The UNODC acknowledges the existence of major data gaps and the uneven quality of information across countries.[39] It is worth recalling that the 1988 Convention against Illicit Traffic in Narcotic Drugs and Psychotropic Substances adopted by the UN General Assembly included a request for self-evaluations by member states (Biennial Reports Questionnaire; BRQ).[40] The BRQ is often introduced in the wake of United Nations General Assembly Special Sessions (UNGASS) and allows member states to report on the progress achieved in meeting declared objectives set by UNGASS. These reports are intended to monitor structures, methods of working, target populations, extent and coverage of programs, and difficulties encountered in the implementation of the Convention.[41]

Cracks in the IDCR first started to appear in the final years of the twentieth century. A growing uproar emerged over domestic social problems and public health crises associated with failures to contain drug supply and demand. Public authorities and activists alike expressed alarm at the expansion and spread of violent criminal markets across the Americas, Africa, and Asia, exploding prison populations in developed and developing countries alike, and the fact that the problem appeared to be getting worse, not better. At the same time, evidence began emerging of successful harm reduction options.[42] Some politicians, including Colombia's former President Santos, likened the situation to a 'stationary bicycle.'[43] In recent years a noticeable shift in the discourse of international organizations has also taken place, including the UNODC as well as the International Federation of the Red Cross, the Organization of American States (OAS), the World Health Organization (WHO) and others. Some of the institutions such as the WHO, the United Nations Program on HIV/AIDS (UNAIDS),[44] regional organizations such as the European Monitoring Centre for Drugs and Drug Addiction (EMCDDA)[45] and the OAS[46] have also started revisiting which drug metrics to monitor, together with investments in improving data coverage and quality.

Reframing Goals and Targets

The framework proposed below is not necessarily intended to be applied all at once, but rather to inspire new thinking and ideas on the locus of priorities. At its center are several goals that can, if pursued in an integrated manner, ensure a more effective and efficient approach to mitigating the harms generated by drugs. In total, two high-order impacts, six goals, sixteen targets, and eighty-six indicators were initially identified after reviewing hundreds of possible alternatives (see Table 14.b below). They include impact indicators,[47] outcome indicators (tracking the goals), and output indicators (tracking the targets).[48]

Table 14.b
A Framework for Comprehensive Drug Policy

High-Level Impacts	Impact Indicators
(1) Improve health and welfare of the population and	Lethal and non-lethal outcomes of drug-related violence.
(2) enhance security and safety of people involved with drugs and the wider public.	Migration and displacement of populations affected by drug violence. Opportunity costs of spending on responding to drug production, transit and use (on law enforcement versus other social sectors).

Goals and targets

Goal 1. End criminalization and stigmatization of drug users (outcome indicators)

Number of people detained/arrested/convicted for drug use in small quantities

Death penalty for any drug-related offenses

Employment rate of ex-drug users or ex-convicts (convicted for drug possession)

Educational enrollment/attainment of ex-drug users or ex-convicts (accused of drug possession)

Targets and output indicators	
1.1 Decriminalize drug use.	Existence of legislation that decriminalizes possession of drugs in small quantities for personal use
	Number of legislative proposals focused on drug decriminalization
	Number of civil society groups actively lobbying for drug decriminalization
	Number of individuals arrested/detained for offenses involving small quantities of drugs

1.2 Promote opportunities for former drug offenders.	Number of companies/firms that promote employment opportunities for former drug offenders/users
	Number of educational institutions (formal/vocational) promoting opportunities for former drug offenders/users
1.3 Reduction of bias in media reporting.	Number of media articles that attribute positions to credible scientific evidence
	Editorial positions on issues of decriminalization and harm reduction
	Reporting on regional and/or domestic press of strategies of drug policy

Goal 2. Curb drug use through public health measures

Number of drug overdose-related deaths

Number of deaths related to long-term health problems directly associated with drug use

Prevalence of drug-related infectious diseases (HIV, hepatitis B and C) among drug users

	Targets and output indicators
2.1 Create a national strategy for drug prevention.	Evidence of a national strategy focused on drug prevention
	National/state/municipal spending on drug prevention (as reported in budgets and as a proportion of total spending on drug policy)
	Number of persons entering prevention/harm reduction programs
2.2 Create a national strategy for harm reduction.	National/state/municipal spending on harm reduction (as reported in budgets and as a proportion of total spending on drug policy)
	Number of harm reduction interventions
	Number of accredited public hospitals/health institutions providing harm reduction programs

Goal 3. A more balanced approach toward incarcerating drug offenders – including decreasing offences for non-violent and first-time offenders

Persons referred to alternative sentencing for non-violent and small-scale drug-related offences

Proportion of prison population incarcerated for low-level drug offences

Overall level of overcrowding in prisons

Reported cases of torture and cruel, inhuman or degrading treatment of drug users (and indeed all prison populations)

	Targets and output indicators
3.1 Promote more proportionality of sentencing for drug users.	Proportion of non-criminal penalties for first-time and non-violent consumers
	Rehabilitation opportunities for repeat non-violent consumers
	Pre-trial detention for non-violent and first-time consumers
	Prison sentences (incidence and duration) for non-violent and first-time consumers
3.2 Promote more proportionality of sentencing for drug dealers.	Proportion of non-criminal penalties for first-/second-time and non-violent dealers
	Fines (as opposed to sentencing) for non-violent dealers
	Rehabilitation opportunities for repeat non-violent dealers
	Pre-trial detention for non-violent and first-time dealers
	Prison sentences (incidence and duration) for non-violent and first-time dealers

3.3 Promote more proportionality of sentencing for drug producers.	Proportion of non-criminal penalties for low-level/family-based producers
	Rehabilitation/alternative crop opportunities for non-violent producers
	Pre-trial detention for non-violent and first-time producers
	Prison sentences (incidence and duration) for non-violent producers
3.4 Increase support for alternative sentencing for drug-related crime.	Number of diversion mechanisms with a tested/demonstrated success rate
	National/state/municipal expenditures on diversion mechanisms
	Existence of legislation citing alternative sentencing options for first-time offenders

Goal 4. Target violent organized crime groups and drug traffickers

Number of arrests, convictions and incarcerations of people suspected of high-level trafficking, corruption and/or money laundering associated with drugs

Prison population of persons convicted for high-level organized crime involvement and/or affiliation

Prison population of those convicted of high-level illegal drug trade

Amount of confiscated assets from illicit drug markets, drug trafficking and money laundering

Prosecutions of cases of corruption associated with drug markets

Targets and output indicators	
4.1 Increase law enforcement efforts devoted to ending violent organized crime.	National expenditures on intelligence and anti-organized crime units
	Existence of legislation to tackle organized crime and large-scale drug trafficking (including assets apprehension)
	Existence of specialized law enforcement bodies focused on organized crime

4.2 Increase law enforcement efforts devoted to ending money laundering and corruption.	Existence of specialized law enforcement bodies focused on money laundering
	Creation of mechanisms to monitor, detect and confiscate drug-related laundered funds and assets
	Extent of confiscated assets from organized crime groups connected to drug trafficking and money laundering
4.3 Reduce corruption associated with drug markets.	Existence of legislation and explicit measures to punish corruption related to the drugs trade
	Creation of anti-corruption commissions or tasks forces within state institutions
	Existence of independent media entities monitoring corruption related to the drugs trade
	Existence of NGO(s) tracking corruption related to the drugs trade

Goal 5. Provide viable alternatives for illicit crop producers

Number of (former) illicit producers benefiting from alternative livelihood programs (by dollar value/by household)

Per capita income of former illicit producers before and after alternative livelihoods investment

Expenditures devoted to crop substitution and alternative livelihoods programs

5.1 Promote crop substitution.	Existence and publication of legislation setting out standards and procedures for crop substitution
	National expenditures on crop substitution and livelihood policies
	National programs planning and implementing crop substitution
	Extent of credits to smallholder farmers that implement crop substitution

5.2 Strengthen markets for alternative goods.	Existence of a national/subnational policy explicitly devoted to developing markets for alternative products
	Creation of institutions promoting transparency on prices of goods and services
	Safe credit and loan opportunities for small-holder farmers
	Subsidies for supporting trade associations
	Incentives to promote interaction between larger purchasers and smallholder farmers
5.3 Address structural factors contributing to the supply and demand for drugs.	Levels of social and economic development in communities producing drugs
	Underlying conditions of poverty
	Inequality
	Other indicators in the framework of SDGs

Goal 6. Experiment with different models of drug regulation

Profits of organized drug cartels and traffickers

Government tax revenue associated with controlled/regulated management of illegal drugs

Open illicit trafficking/selling of illegal drugs

Overdoses and associated morbidity with illicit use of poor quality/cut drugs

6.1 Standardize the scheduling of different drugs.	Existence of legislation that reflects re-classification of drugs
	Number of changes in regulations of reclassified drugs (from illicit to controlled)
	Existence of legislation in all countries that enables production and distribution of drugs for scientific research purposes
	Existence of legislation in all countries that permits cultivation, trade, and/or consumption of medical marijuana
	Existence of legislation that prescribes the regulation of drug availability (medical, retail, licensed sale)

6.2 Strengthen the regulatory system for managing production, selling and use of drugs.	Existence of systems for managing the production and transit of drugs
	Existence of oversight and management for dosage, preparation, pricing, packaging of drugs
	Existence of prescriptions for licensing, vetting, and training vendors
	Existence of rules for advertising, branding and promotion of drugs
	Existence of legislation for managing location of outlets, age controls and licensing arrangements for buyers for retail.

Implementing Comprehensive Drug Policy Metrics

The aforementioned framework could be implemented gradually, not all at once, with a prioritization of specific areas depending on the context. It can serve a heuristic function to help different layers of government better identify strengths and weaknesses in their existing legislation and practice. The framework is also aspirational, and its implementation will necessarily depend on a government's relative interests and actual capabilities. While there are invariably gaps between intention and practice, there are several ways that states might go about implementing the framework. A basic starting point is the strengthening of data collection, including via national drug observatories, and expanding internal reviews of what works (and what does not) in order to better identify priorities. Improved information on the scope of the challenges, but also the extent of domestic capacities, is fundamental. It may also be appropriate for governments to consider a simplified version of the framework, discussed at greater length below.

The collection and analysis of data associated with new indicators is comparatively straightforward. If the country in question has already established a national observatory for drugs, then it will be tasked with gathering relevant data in order to produce baselines. If there is no observatory, as is the case in several countries, the responsibility of harvesting information could be designated to a central national agency associated with the department of public health or safety. This entity would then be tasked with generating an inventory from a wide range of scientifically verified sources. The priority is that there is a single centralized repository for collecting, validating, organizing, and disseminating information to relevant ministries and departments. The institution could also be responsible for gathering data from departments and ministries responsible for police, defense, health, and home affairs, as well as statistical offices, attorney offices, penal agencies and other authoritative sources in civil society. The collection of more traditional metrics should continue, since they will offer a baseline for comparison.

Indicators for a progressive drug policy will not surface without strong leadership, careful investment and reflection. Many public entities are already overburdened and unable to take on new functions. Others may have an active interest in discouraging and subverting a more progressive approach to drug policy. Whatever the case, designated institutions will need to be incentivized to gather new data, including through the use of innovative methods. They may be required to make modifications to existing survey and census instruments. A review may be required to update and upgrade existing national data collection tools—including, for example, the Multilateral Evaluation Mechanism (MEM) of the Inter-American Drug Abuse Control Commission (CICAD).[49] These tools can be subtly amended to capture a wider range of information that could better assess the effects of drug policy on health, human rights, safety, and development. It may also be useful to develop public-facing tools, including interactive platforms, to expand public awareness and promote accountability.[50]

The design and development of a new drug policy framework will necessarily generate human resource, resource-related, and opportunity costs to institutions tasked with managing data and analysis. The prospect of collecting temporally, spatially, and demographically specific information on dozens of (new) metrics is daunting to even the most spirited civil servant. Importantly, though, few if any countries are starting from zero. Many governments and civil society groups are already collecting data on the indicators cited in the framework, though some may still require standardization, revision, and organization. Even so, it might be useful to consider a simplified and lightweight approach for those countries outside of North America and Western Europe that lack disaggregated data collection facilities. A more basic approach could, for example, reduce the number of indicators with just two per target. One of these might refer to a basic legislative framework or the application of a relevant policy intervention required to achieve the target, and the second could illustrate the implementation and safety or health impacts of such an intervention. The experimental application of a simplified framework could map out the extent of progress of a given country (see table 14.c below).

Table 14.c
A Simplified Approach to Monitoring Drug Policy Progress

Legislation / Programs (Yes / No)	*Implementation*
Goal 1. End criminalization and stigmatization of drug users.	
Is the possession of drugs in small quantities decriminalized?	Distinction of arrests by type and quantity of drugs
Alternatives for employment/ educational enrollment for ex-drug users or ex-convicts	People present in related education or employment programs
Goal 2. Curb drug use through public health measures.	
Is there a national strategy focused on drug prevention?	Spending on drug prevention / number of institutions / people in programs
Is there a national strategy for harm reduction?	Spending on drug prevention / number of institutions / people in programs
Goal 3. A more balanced approach toward incarcerating drug offenders—including decreasing offences for non-violent and first-time offenders.	
Existence of legislation that calls for more proportional sentences for drug users	Distinction of persons arrested by type and quantity of drugs

Legislation / Programs (Yes / No)	Implementation
Existence of alternative sentencing (rather than prison) for drug consumers	Number of people benefiting from alternative sentencing options
Existence of legislation implementing more proportional sentences for drug dealers	Distinction of persons arrested on drugs-related charges by type and quantity in their possession
Existence of alternative sentencing (rather than prison) for drug consumers	Number of people provided alternative sentencing options (dealers)
Existence of legislation implementing more proportional sentences for drug producers	Distinction of persons arrested by production of drugs by type and quantity
Existence of alternative sentencing (rather than prison) for drug producers	Number of people provided with alternative sentencing options

Goal 4. Target violent organized crime groups and drug traffickers.

Existence of legislation to tackle organized crime and large-scale drug trafficking	Number of agencies and spending on specific areas of organized crime investigation
Existence of legislation to tackle money laundering	Number of agencies and spending on specific areas of money laundering
Existence of legislation to tackle corruption associated with drug markets	Number of agencies and spending on specific areas of corruption associated with drug markets

Goal 5. Provide viable alternatives for illicit crop producers.

Existence of legislation setting out standards and procedures for crop substitution	Number of projects and general spending on crop substitution

Legislation / Programs (Yes / No)	Implementation
Existence of legislation setting out standards and procedures for the development of markets for alternative products	Number of projects and general spending on development of markets for alternative products

Goal 6. Experiment with different models of drug regulation.

Existence of legislation that reflects re-classification of drugs that enables production and distribution of drugs for scientific research and medical purposes	Number of producers and distributors of drugs for research and medical purposes; number of users per drug category
Creation of a regulatory system for managing production, selling and use of drugs	Existence of systems to manage the production and transit of drugs, mechanisms to oversee management of retail and / or controlled dosages for prescribed users; and rules for advertising and regulation of outlets

Data Source: Prepared by the authors

Conclusion

Taken together, new goals, targets, and indicators can help guide governments and civil societies in crafting and implementing a more comprehensive drug policy agenda. Such an agenda would fundamentally value the safety, health, and welfare of citizens. These are non-negotiable aspirations for any public policy. Moreover, the proposed framework is entirely consistent with the existing IDCR and its three conventions. The GCDP set out a practical roadmap for responsible drugs regulation and control. However, the framework elaborated here is intended to signpost, not prescribe, a pathway for positive change. It could be implemented in an incremental manner, allowing governments and societies to adapt and experiment on the basis of their needs and capacities. Some governments and societies have already made significant steps in revising their metrics in ways that suit their realities. Others have yet to start this journey. It may also be the case that public authorities and civic leaders want to test out specific goals or targets rather than pursuing them all at once.

Ultimately, each polity will need to critically reflect on what path is most appropriate and feasible. The establishment of metrics for drug policy should proceed cautiously, on the basis of a careful review of the evidence. While global solutions are needed in addressing illicit use of drugs,[51] there are no one-size-fits-all solutions, and governments should experiment with different approaches suited to regional and national realities. The design of metrics is, of course, political—not least since they set out explicit and implicit priorities, with the ability to shape the form and content of future investment. While there are many differences separating countries, most also share some basic priorities such as improving public health and reducing drug-related crime. At a minimum, the vast majority share the common objective of doing no intentional harm.

The adoption of a comprehensive drug policy agenda with associated metrics will not be simple or straightforward. There are many conceptual and methodological challenges related to data generation, standardization and sharing. The fact that current drug policy-related priorities are still premised on an outdated model means that new investments in information collection, interpretation, and dissemination will be required. This does not mean the status quo should prevail. On the contrary, new thinking is needed on how to mobilize political energy, public opinion, and scientific investments in the right direction. Policymakers and researchers alike must redouble their efforts to monitor and evaluate interventions to show what works and—just as importantly—what does not. There are simply too many risks associated with doing nothing, and the dividends of action now will be measured in safer, healthier, and more lawful societies tomorrow.

15

CONCLUSION

TRANSFORMING THE WAR ON DRUGS: A PATHWAY TO CHANGE THE CURRENT PARADIGM

Annette Idler and *Juan Carlos Garzón Vergara*

Since the United States' declaration of the so-called War on Drugs fifty years ago, this paradigm has gone global, with manifold faces across different regions, and it has changed its character over time.

This changing character is partly the result of changes in the world drug problem itself. Over the course of these five decades, new technologies have made illicit drug production more efficient. Globalization has allowed criminals to draw on more sophisticated communications and transport infrastructures to ship drugs along shifting trafficking routes and satisfy global demand. The internet has turned illicit drug markets into anonymous virtual spaces, accessible by consumers from practically any corner of the world. The proliferation of new synthetic drugs has added another, previously unthinkable dimension to the world drug problem, as their production and distribution is not tied to specific geographic spaces or harvesting cycles.

At the same time, governments have implemented the War on Drugs with gradually more sweeping measures, ranging from toxic aerial sprayings conducted by militaries in an attempt to eradicate the illicit cultivation of crops used for plant-based drugs, to artificial intelligence-based tools for tracing and interdicting drug shipments, to detecting and cracking down on cyberspace marketplaces that use platforms such as the Darknet. Responses to deal with new synthetic drugs have been militarized.

Justifications for a War on Drugs have changed over time as well. Depending on the *zeitgeist*, narratives have mutated from stressing the need to protect youth from illicit drug consumption and enhance social cohesion, to portraying trafficking groups from abroad as foreign substances that endanger the health of the body politic, to emphasizing the role of drug trafficking in financing terrorist groups, to name just a few.

Despite these changes, there has been a constant throughout the War on Drugs years: a large number of politicians, authorities, and local elites continue to consider the world drug problem a threat to national security, and to promise a drug-free society. Following a rhetoric that equates drugs with 'evil' and demands hard-and-fast solutions against the illegal drug market, citizen pressure has likewise contributed to the persistence of this paradigm, occasionally preventing the adoption of alternatives.

Still, the War on Drugs has not met its own objectives. Paul Gootenberg states in Chapter 2 that advocates of the War on Drugs argue that the negative outcomes might have been worse had it not been for the 'containment' achieved via international drug control measures. But whether or not this perspective is valid remains a causality question for long-term social science analysis and an unresolved public policy debate. Even if one accepts the statement that without adopting this paradigm the world would have a more serious problem, the cost-benefit balance continues to be unfavorable. As the former President of Colombia, Juan Manuel Santos, put it: 'Sometimes we all feel that we have been aimlessly pedaling a stationary bicycle. You look to your right, you look to your left, and yet you always see the same landscape—demand for drugs keeps rising and supply follows.'[1]

Indeed, implementing the International Drug Control Regime (IDCR) in the form of the War on Drugs has had tremendous costs and negative consequences. As several authors in this volume argue, this is because the largely unidimensional securitization of drug policies has led governments to justify extraordinary measures focused almost exclusively on the state's, rather than also on people's, security. What is more, governments' policy objective of demonstrating successful enforcement, rather than of mitigating the drug problem, has created perverse incentives. As Katherine Aguirre and Robert Muggah discuss in Chapter 14, governments and international agencies have measured 'success' as increases in crop eradication, drug seizures, and the arrests of producers, traffickers, as well as consumers, instead of assessing to what extent they have achieved to reduce harm caused by the world drug problem.

The contributors to this volume show that the War on Drugs has not only failed to reduce the size of the market, but generated new problems, such as the undermining health impact of toxic sprayings of coca cultivation in Colombia, or the lethal threat that fentanyl smuggled from China poses to US drug consumers while the government's focus has been on heroin and cocaine from South America. It has also produced 'collateral damage,' including people dying in extra-judicial killings in wars on drug users, as in the Philippines. And it has exacerbated the violence and insecurity that interventions were (supposedly) intended to remedy, as Mexico's soaring homicide rates demonstrate.

The War on Drugs' negative consequences are evident in vulnerable regions across the globe: they concern both the so-called Global South, where drug policies have been disconnected from development objectives, and the so-called Global North, where inequalities based for example on race have led to a disproportionately severe impact of drug policies on marginalized communities.

These consequences are particularly visible in producer and transit regions because prohibitionist drug policies have transferred a large portion of the economic and social costs to them. It is also in these regions that the nexus between illegal armed groups, terrorist organizations, and drug trafficking has perpetuated the securitization of drug policies particularly strongly.

Countries like Afghanistan, Mexico, and Colombia have seen real wars in the name of the fight against drugs, which have caused hundreds of thousands of victims. As Carlos A. Pérez Ricart states in Chapter 6, governments increased budgets for law enforcement tasks; armed forces participate persistently in what are supposed to be citizen security agendas and should be dealt with by the police. In West Africa, as John M. Pokoo and Kwesi Aning point out in Chapter 7, some observers criticize that methods to control the non-medical use of trafficked drugs prioritize interventions to reduce the supply, rather than the demand, of these drugs. However, the region has weak state governance capacities and a poor health infrastructure, especially in rural areas, making the implementation of demand-reducing programs and policies extremely difficult. Investing in reducing supply takes away resources required for a structural approach to building capacities across diverse governance areas and tackling the drug problem in a more holistic way.

In market regions, as in many parts of Southeast Asia, the War on Drugs has largely been a war on drug users. Disproportionately high criminal penalties have resulted in social and public health costs, including: increases in crime; the spread of HIV, hepatitis C, and other blood-borne diseases; and preventable overdose deaths. According to Pierre-Arnaud Chouvy in Chapter 9, in this region governments have invested heavily in drug control measures, and drug users and civil society more broadly have suffered considerably under these efforts. Yet the desired results never materialized. Also, in addition to persistent drug consumption, the Golden Triangle in particular continues to be a major area of illegal opium and methamphetamines production.

In Chapter 12, Damon Barrett and Kasia Malinowska-Sempruch highlight how experts criticize the law enforcement aspect of the IDCR under the influence of the War on Drugs for failing to respond to contemporary challenges. In its current interpretation, the IDCR is largely disconnected from governments' commitments to, first, upholding human rights and, second, enhancing human development.

First, regarding human rights, in many cases, drug policies under the banner of the War on Drugs have made constitutional protections void, contributed to the persistence of the death penalty, and led to over-incarceration, arbitrary detention, police violence, and extrajudicial killings with disproportionate effects on vulnerable groups. Women and young people have been especially burdened by this emphasis: one in four women imprisoned in Europe and Central Asia are inside for non-violent drug offenses, and, in Latin America, 70 per cent of women in prison are convicted or sentenced for drug-related crimes.

Second, the root causes, underlying conditions, and risk factors that contribute to the world drug problem also affect human development. Across production, transit, and consumer regions, the War on Drugs has largely been unresponsive to these causes. In many cases it has exacerbated them. They relate to structural inequalities and deep social vulnerabilities arising from unsatisfied basic needs, food insecurity, the lack of educational opportunities and employment, and deficient physical and financial infrastructures. This situation has created contradictions between the Sustainable Development Goals (SDGs) on the one hand, and drug policies implemented under the umbrella of the IDCR, on the other, as Javier Sagredo discusses in Chapter 13.

Christopher Hallam and David Bewley-Taylor show in Chapter 3 how this disconnect—and the heterogeneity of the problems it has caused—has created tensions and systemic stress. But substantial reforms will take time and face resistance, as evidenced in Chapter 4 by Mónica Serrano. To be sure, even if it is not a prominent theme in the UN conventions, the IDCR explicitly demands states to comply with human rights and suggests non-coercive responses to the world drug problem that are conducive to enhancing sustainable human development.[2] Nonetheless, as long as governments are able to draw on the War on Drugs narrative to justify erring on the side of (excessively) coercive and punitive measures while downplaying the need for more transformative approaches, this aspect of the IDCR will have little weight.

To begin moving forward on the path to change, this concluding chapter proposes to transform the current War on Drugs paradigm. One can assume that in a highly polarized context around the need— or lack thereof—to rethink the IDCR, policy and institutional reforms will not evolve from a radical, one-time transformation. Instead, they will be the result of cumulative changes and tipping points, as Angélica Durán-Martínez argues in Chapter 5.

In the short term, one can aspire to a more balanced interpretation of the IDCR, with a holistic, people-centered approach that champions human rights and sustainable development agendas. In the long term, most authors in this volume argue that the War on Drugs must end. Yet it will not end because one of the parties defeats its adversary, or the parties come to a negotiating table and reach an agreement. Instead, positive change requires a paradigm shift that is based on clear processes and open mindsets.

At the heart of this shift is the need to redefine the role of law enforcement and of the use of force by the state. As Annette Idler points out in Chapter 1, tackling the world drug problem from a critical perspective does not rule out securitizing, and indeed militarizing, certain issue areas. Accordingly, security institutions and the justice system have important contributions to make in order to tackle the world drug problem. However, these contributions need to center on prosecuting individuals and groups with the greatest capacities for violence and corruption because illegal drug markets provide an important source of power and revenue for such organized criminal groups. From this perspective, it seems nonsensical that—in the name of the War on Drugs—the limited coercive capacities of the state focus on persecuting small-scale growers, people who transport small amounts of substances, low-level offenders, or drug users.

Also, evidence shows that eliminating organized crime and illegal markets entirely is not viable.[3] In the best-case scenario, states can mitigate the negative consequences of illicit economies, transform the behavior of criminal groups to reduce harm, and lessen their social, economic, and institutional influences. Still, in many countries, drug laws have been conducive to heavy-handed enforcement, with low levels of oversight and high degrees of discretion and corruption. A primarily punitive approach has distorted the work of policing and criminal justice. It has prioritized goals that neglected the protection of people and respect for their rights.[4] Coercive actions should not aim to reach victory in a war-like fashion, but to work toward emancipation, according to which people are freed from the constraints that inhibit their abilities to enjoy basic principles such as human development, human security, and human rights.

The paradigm shift also needs to occur 'glocally.' Although the drug problem is global, many of its solutions are local. Cities and municipalities have greater flexibility to formulate interventions and apply novel policies. In fact, cities implemented many of the most sensitive and successful strategies, including providing drugs to prevent overdoses, syringe exchanges, and drug consumption rooms.[5] Instead of eradicating crops, some rural communities have moved coca and poppy crops to the legal economy in order to create alternative livelihoods.[6]

In order to transform the War on Drugs paradigm, it is important to recognize both its costs and consequences, and the capacities for identifying and developing alternatives. The contributors to this book offer concrete recommendations to advance this transformation:

1. Adopt a development-based approach to drug policy in order to improve its effectiveness and reduce the harms associated with its implementation. This approach must be guided by the general principle that drug policy should not negatively affect communities' or countries' sustainable development. The SDGs offer an opportunity to address the limitations of the current approach and to present new ideas that reduce harm, revitalize communities, and strengthen social safety nets.

2. Reduce harm caused by drug consumption via expanding social protection and health care services and providing comprehensive treatments such as safe consumption rooms and wide availability of naloxone, taking into consideration the local cultural contexts of the respective vulnerable regions.

3. Strengthen human rights accountability by adopting international guidelines on human rights and drug policies, and holding annual thematic debates on drugs and human rights at the Human Rights Council. An important step was the March 2019 launch of the 'International Guidelines on Human Rights and Drug Policy' by a coalition of UN member states, UN entities—including the United Nations Development Programme (UNDP), the United Nations Programme on HIV/AIDs (UNAIDS), and the World

Health Organization (WHO)—and leading drug policy and human rights experts.[7]

4. Emphasize policies to treat drug users and low-level criminals in a more humane way in countries where penalties for drug trafficking tend to be greater than those for other serious crimes like armed robbery, rape, and murder. Legislation must follow the principle of proportionality and thus assess penalties for different levels of trafficking and types of crimes (for example, street-level dealing versus trafficking large amounts of drugs). In line with such an emphasis, the UN System Chief Executives Board for Coordination made a collective commitment to 'call for changes in laws, policies and practices that threaten the health and human rights of people' and to 'promote alternatives to conviction and punishment in appropriate cases, including the decriminalization of drug possession for personal use.'[8]

5. Develop new goals, targets, and indicators to track the intended and unintended consequences of the IDCR and boost a more comprehensive and holistic drug policy agenda. Such an agenda would fundamentally value the safety, health, and welfare of citizens. Two key outcomes should be the reduction of violence and other human rights violations associated with drugs, and an increase in the experienced and perceived security by individuals, (vulnerable) groups, and communities. In December 2020, the Western Hemisphere Drug Policy Commission, an independent and bipartisan entity created by the US Congress, recognized the 'collective failure to control either drug abuse or drug trafficking,' and called for 'smarter international policies.'[9] This could be an opportunity for the administration of Joe Biden and Kamala Harris in the United States to both concentrate domestic efforts on addressing the nation's drug overdose crisis which has killed more than 500,000 people in the 2010s (including 71,000 in 2019 alone)[10] with a focus on harm reduction and promote a 'smart enforcement' approach internationally that embraces the use of innovative goals, targets, and indicators.

6. Consider the *inter se* modifications of the UN conventions, enabling a group of like-minded states to modify their relationships to the treaties. For example, modify UN

conventions to allow those states whose domestic laws permit licit markets for certain substances to trade with each other.

7. Advance domestic drug policy reforms. During the 2010s, several jurisdictions decriminalized and legalized recreational cannabis use. In what the International Narcotics Control Board considers a violation of the 1961 Single Convention on Narcotic Drugs, Uruguay was the first country to legalize the production, sale, possession, and recreational and/or medical use of cannabis; Canada was the first G7 nation that followed suit. Fifteen US states and the US capital, Washington D.C., did so too. In November 2020, Oregon became the first US state to decriminalize the possession of all drugs, including heroin, cocaine and methamphetamine, following in other countries' footsteps such as Portugal, the first country worldwide that decriminalized the consumption and personal possession of all drugs in 2001. The defection of other countries would continue to show a progressive weakening of the consensus in the IDCR, making evident the need for a change.

Together, these suggestions reinforce this book's urgent call for implementing holistic, people-centered drug policies.

As a final note, to conclude that the War on Drugs cannot be won and that it has yielded fewer positive results than was hoped for should ring alarm bells in other policy areas that have adopted similar approaches. For example, the 'War on Terror' in the post-9/11 world cannot be won through military victory alone. Tackling terrorism also requires establishing effective community policing, reducing social exclusion, and understanding that systems like *hawala* are embedded cultural practices, rather than mechanisms that fund terrorism per se.[11] Similarly, the 'War on Crime' in response to wildlife trafficking across Africa and Asia or to piracy off the shores of Somalia cannot be won militarily. Addressing these forms of crime requires capacity-building and investing in sustainable development to provide local communities with alternative livelihoods. Finally, even the 'war on coronavirus,'[12] declared by former US President Donald Trump in the context of the COVID-19 pandemic that hit the world in late 2019, cannot defeat the 'invisible enemy,' as UK Prime Minister Boris Johnson put it.[13] Instead, appeals to solidarity and empathy, for example to make people respect quarantine rules— as spearheaded by countries such as New Zealand or Germany—have proven to be more powerful. These are just some examples of when 'war talk' frames policy issues in a securitized, even militarized, fashion. Often, it would be more effective to address such policy issues with a holistic, people-centered approach that limits military responses to the areas where they are most needed.

Ultimately, it is hoped that this volume provides an impetus to debate other pressing issues of global affairs. Even if such challenges are unique to their respective times and places, the responses should be underpinned by the same overarching goals: to protect the most vulnerable groups, to revitalize the most affected communities, and to create the conditions that allow promoting sustainable and inclusive human development, and global security.

NOTES

INTRODUCTION: FIFTY YEARS OF THE WAR ON DRUGS: A MOMENT OF UNCERTAINTY

1. In 1971, then President Richard Nixon famously declared the War on Drugs, referring to drug abuse as the 'public enemy number one.' In the 1980s, then President Ronald Reagan reinforced the War on Drugs, expanding penalties and incarceration for drug offenses.
2. See for example Vann R. Newkirk II, 'The People Trump's War on Drugs Will Actually Punish,' *The Atlantic*, March 26, 2018, https://www.theatlantic.com/politics/archive/2018/03/killing-drug-dealers-opioid-epidemic/555782/.
3. Frank G. Madsen, 'International Narcotics Law Enforcement: A Study in Irrationality,' *Journal of International Affairs* 66, no. 1 (2012): 123–41.
4. Peter Andreas, *Killer High: A History of War in Six Drugs* (Oxford: Oxford University Press, 2020).
5. Jonathan P. Caulkins et al., *How Goes the 'War on Drugs?': An Assessment of U. S. Drug Programs and Policy* (Santa Monica, CA: Rand Corporation, 2005).
6. A 10 per cent increase in the global population in the same period accounts for some of this growth. UNODC, *World Drug Report 2019* (Vienna: United Nations, 2019).
7. Institute for Health Metrics and Evaluation (IHME), *Findings from the Global Burden of Disease Study 2017* (Seattle, WA: IHME, 2018).
8. According to Florentin Blanc and Michael Faure, 'smart enforcement' means that laws are not enforced via random routine controls, but that enforcement is grounded in assessing the risk beforehand, or that enforcement strategies are influenced by how the targeted community behaved. Florentin Blanc and Michael Faure, 'Smart enforcement in the EU,' *Journal of Risk Research* 23, no. 11 (2020): 1405-1423, https//doi.org/ 10.1080/13669877.2019.1673800.
9. See for example John Collins, 'Beyond UNGASS 2016: Drug Control Multilateralism and the End to the "War on Drugs,"' in *Militarised Responses to Transnational Organised Crime: The War on Crime*, ed. Tuesday Reitano, Sasha Jesperson, and Lucia Bird Ruiz-Benitez de Lugo, 1st ed. 2018 edition (New York: Palgrave Macmillan, 2017), 279–97.

10. Previous efforts were also intended to put people first. For example, in the Political Declaration of the General Assembly's Seventeenth Special Session in 1990, governments agreed on their determination 'to protect mankind from the scourge of drug abuse and illicit trafficking in narcotic drugs and psychotropic substances.' United Nations General Assembly, *Resolution S-17/2* on the *Political Declaration and Global Programme of Action adopted by the General Assembly at its 17th special session, devoted to the question of international co-operation against illicit production, supply, demand, trafficking and distribution of narcotic drugs and psychotropic substances* A/RES/S-17/2 (New York, February 23, 1990), https://undocs.org/en/A/RES/S-17/2.

11. For works that focus on some of these issues, see for example John Collins, ed., *Ending the Drug Wars: Report of the LSE Expert Group on the Economics of Drug Policy* (London: LSE, 2014); David T. Courtwright, *Forces of Habit: Drugs and the Making of the Modern World* (Cambridge, MA; London: Harvard University Press, 2001); Sir Richard Branson, *Ending the War on Drugs* (London: Virgin Books, 2016); Tom Kramer, Martin Jelsma, and Tom Blickman, *Withdrawal Symptoms in the Golden Triangle: A Drugs Market in Disarray* (Amsterdam: TNI, 2009); Emily Crick, 'Drugs as an Existential Threat: An Analysis of the International Securitization of Drugs,' *International Journal of Drug Policy* 23, no. 5 (Sep 2012): 407–14, https://doi.org/10.1016/j.drugpo.2012.03.004; David Bewley-Taylor, *International Drug Control: Consensus Fractured* (Cambridge: Cambridge University Press, 2012); David R. Bewley-Taylor, 'Towards Revision of the UN Drug Control Conventions: Harnessing Like-Mindedness,' *International Journal of Drug Policy* 24, no. 1 (1 Jan 2013): 60–8, https://doi.org/10.1016/j.drugpo.2012.09.001; Frank G. Madsen, 'International Narcotics Law Enforcement: A Study in Irrationality,' *Journal of International Affairs* 66, no. 1 (2012): 123–41; Paul Gootenberg, 'Talking Like a State: Drugs, Borders, and the Language of Control,' in *Illicit Flows and Criminal Things: States, Borders, and the Other Side of Globalization*, ed. Willem van Schendel and Itty Abraham (Bloomington: Indiana University Press, 2005), 101–27; Peter Andreas and Angélica Durán-Martínez, 'The Politics of Drugs and Illicit Trade in the Americas,' in *Routledge Handbook of Latin America in the World*, ed. Jorge Domínguez and Ana Covarrubias (New York: Routledge, 2014), 376–90; Henry H. Brownstein, ed., *The Handbook of Drugs and Society* (New Jersey: John Wiley & Sons, 2015).

12. Lexico Oxford Dictionary, 'Definition of Glocal in English,' 2020, https://www.lexico.com/definition/glocal

13. Juan Carlos Garzón Vergara, *Post-UNGASS 2016: Latin America and Drug Policy Perspectives* (Santiago de Chile: Consejo de Relaciones Internacionales de América Latina y El Caribe, 2017), https://consejorial.org/en/publicaciones/post-ungass-2016-latin-america-and-drug-policy-perspectives-2/

14. See, for example, Bewley-Taylor, *International Drug Control*; Madsen, 'International Narcotics Law Enforcement.'

15. See, for example, Pierre-Arnaud Chouvy, *Opium: Uncovering the Politics of the Poppy* (Cambridge, MA: Harvard University Press, 2010); Kramer, Jelsma, and Blickman, *Withdrawal Symptoms in the Golden Triangle*; Enrique Desmond Arias, *Drugs and*

Democracy in Rio de Janeiro: Trafficking, Social Networks, and Public Security (Chapel Hill: University of North Carolina Press, 2006); Dessa K. Bergen-Cico, *War and Drugs: The Role of Military Conflict in the Development of Substance Abuse* (Boulder: Paradigm Publishers, 2012).

16. Vulnerability may arise from geography (being a major production or transit region, or comprising a vast consumption population), exposure to external shocks and stress, and limited coping capacities (see Chapter 1 by Annette Idler).

17. Walter Russell Mead, 'The Return of Geopolitics,' *Foreign Affairs,* September 15, 2015, https://www.foreignaffairs.com/articles/china/2014-04-17/return-geopolitics; Stefano Guzzini, *The Return of Geopolitics in Europe?: Social Mechanisms and Foreign Policy Identity Crises* (Cambridge: Cambridge University Press, 2013); Abdel Monem Said Aly, 'The Return of Geopolitics,' *The Cairo Review of Global Affairs*, May 27, 2019, https://www.thecairoreview.com/essays/the-return-of-geopolitics/

1. WARRIORS, VICTIMS, AND VULNERABLE REGIONS

1. See, for example, Bruce Bagley, 'Globalisation and Latin American and Caribbean Organised Crime,' *Global Crime* 6, no. 1 (February 1, 2004): 32–53, https://doi.org/10.1080/1744057042000297963; Peter Andreas and Ethan Avram Nadelmann, *Policing the Globe: Criminalization and Crime Control in International Relations* (Oxford: Oxford University Press, 2006); Emily Crick, 'Drugs as an Existential Threat: An Analysis of the International Securitization of Drugs,' *International Journal of Drug Policy* 23, no. 5 (September 2012): 407–14, https://doi.org/10.1016/j.drugpo.2012.03.004. Jimmy Carter, '"El tiempo disponible para este trascendental esfuerzo es limitado": El Expresidente de EE. UU. y Nobel de Paz Jimmy Carter Escribe Sobre Proceso de Paz En Colombia,' *El Tiempo,* January 13, 2013, http://www.eltiempo.com/politica/jimmy-carter-escribe-sobre-proceso-de-paz-en-colombia_12512163-4; GCDP, *War on Drugs: Report of the Global Commission on Drug Policy* (Geneva: GCDP, 2011); El Tiempo, '"Perseguimos Cultivadores y Allá El Gringo Metiendo Varillo": Santos,' December 6, 2012, https://www.eltiempo.com/archivo/documento/CMS-12429983

2. Crick, 'Drugs as an Existential Threat,' 413.

3. Global Commission on Drug Policy (GCDP), *Taking Control: Pathways to Drug Policies That Work* (Geneva: GCDP, 2014).

4. By world drug problem I mean the undermining impacts on human rights, order, security, development, public health, and related socio-economic dimensions, or what MacCoun and Reuter refer to as 'addiction, crime, disorder, and disease' that stem from 'the illicit cultivation, production, manufacture, sale, demand, trafficking and distribution of narcotic drugs and psychotropic substances, including amphetamine-type stimulants, the diversion of precursors and related criminal activities.' Robert MacCoun and Peter Reuter, *Drug War Heresies: Learning from Other Vices, Times, and Places*, RAND Studies in Policy Analysis (Cambridge: Cambridge University Press, 2001); UNODC, 'Political Declaration and Plan of Action on International Cooperation towards an Integrated and Balanced Strategy

to Counter the World Drug Problem,' in High-Level Segment Commission on Narcotic Drugs (Vienna: United Nations, 2009), 7, https://www.unodc.org/documents/ungass2016/V0984963-English.pdf.

5. Cynthia Enloe, 'Margins, Silences and Bottom Rungs,' in *International Theory: Positivism and Beyond*, ed. Steve Smith, Ken Booth, and Marysia Zalewski (Cambridge: Cambridge University Press, 1996), 186–202; Edward W. Said, *Culture and Imperialism* (New York: Random House, 1994); Amitav Acharya, *Rethinking Power, Institutions and Ideas in World Politics: Whose IR?* (London: Routledge, 2014).

6. Pinar Bilgin, 'Critical Theory,' in *Security Studies: An Introduction*, ed. Paul D. Williams, 2nd ed. (London: Routledge, 2013), 103.

7. See, for example, David R. Bewley-Taylor, *International Drug Control: Consensus Fractured* (Cambridge: Cambridge University Press, 2012); David R. Bewley-Taylor, 'Towards Revision of the UN Drug Control Conventions: Harnessing Like-Mindedness,' *International Journal of Drug Policy* 24, no. 1 (2013): 60–68, https://doi.org/10.1016/j.drugpo.2012.09.001.

8. See for example, Winifred Tate, *Drugs, Thugs, and Diplomats: U.S. Policymaking in Colombia*, Anthropology of Policy (Stanford, CA: Stanford University Press, 2015); Paul Gootenberg, 'Talking Like a State: Drugs, Borders, and the Language of Control,' in *Illicit Flows and Criminal Things: States, Borders, and the Other Side of Globalization*, ed. Willem van Schendel and Itty Abraham (Bloomington: Indiana University Press, 2005), 101–27.

9. See, for example, Jonathan Goodhand, 'Corrupting or Consolidating the Peace? The Drugs Economy and Post-Conflict Peacebuilding in Afghanistan,' *International Peacekeeping* 15, no. 3 (June 1, 2008): 405–23, https://doi.org/10.1080/13533310802058984; Peter Andreas and Angélica Durán-Martínez, 'The International Politics of Drugs and Illicit Trade in the Americas,' in *Handbook of Latin America in the World*, ed. Jorge Dominguez and Ana Covarrubias (New York: Routledge, 2014), 376–90; Klaus von Lampe, 'Withdrawal Symptoms in the Golden Triangle: A Drugs Market in Disarray,' *Trends in Organized Crime* 13, no. 1 (March 2010): 87–108, https://doi.org/10.1007/s12117-009-9084-y.

10. Securitization theory was put forward by scholars belonging to the so-called Copenhagen School. See Barry Buzan, Ole Wæver and Jaap de Wilde, *Security: A New Framework for Analysis* (Boulder: Lynne Rienner Publishers, 1998), 5. Michael C. Williams, 'Words, Images, Enemies: Securitization and International Politics,' *International Studies Quarterly* 47, no. 4 (2003): 511–31.

11. Mark Shaw, 'Soldiers in a Storm: Why and How Do Responses to Illicit Economies Get Militarised,' in *Militarised Responses to Transnational Organised Crime: The War on Crime*, ed. Tuesday Reitano, Sasha Jesperson, and Lucia Bird Ruiz-Benitez de Lugo, 1st ed. 2018 edition (New York: Palgrave Macmillan, 2017), 11–21.

12. Buzan, Wæver, and Wilde, *Security*, 26.

13. Buzan, Wæver, and Wilde, *Security*, 5.

14. Buzan, Wæver, and Wilde, *Security*, 26.

15. Crick, 'Drugs as an Existential Threat.' For the emergence of the global prohibition regime even earlier see Chapter 1 by Paul Gootenberg, and Andreas and Nadelmann, *Policing the Globe*.

16. United Nations, *Single Convention on Narcotic Drugs* (New York: United Nations, 1961), preamble.

17. Richard Nixon, 'Remarks About an Intensified Program for Drug Abuse Prevention and Control,' Gerhard Peters and John T. Woolley, *The American Presidency Project* (Washington D.C., June 17, 1971), https://www.presidency.ucsb.edu/node/240238.

18. United Nations, *Convention against Illicit Traffic in Narcotic Drugs and Psychotropic Substances* (New York: United Nations, 1988), https://www.unodc.org/pdf/convention_1988_en.pdf.

19. Crick, 'Drugs as an Existential Threat.'

20. Buzan, Wæver, and Wilde, *Security*, 26.

21. Ian Loader and Neil Walker, *Civilizing Security* (Cambridge: Cambridge University Press, 2007), 11.

22. See, for example, Ole Wæver, 'Securitization and Desecuritization,' in *On Security*, ed. Ronnie D. Lipschutz (New York: Columbia University Press, 1995), 46–86; Columba Peoples and Nick Vaughan-Williams, *Critical Security Studies: An Introduction*, 2nd ed. (London: Routledge, 2015), 94.

23. Bilgin, 'Critical Theory,' 102.

24. For coupling a critical security approach with human security, see Edward Newman, 'Critical Human Security Studies,' *Review of International Studies* 36, no. 1 (2010): 77–94.

25. United Nations General Assembly, *Resolution 66/290. Follow-up to paragraph 143 on human security of the 2005 World Summit Outcome*, A/RES/66/290 (New York, October 25, 2012), https://undocs.org/A/RES/66/290.

26. Annette Idler, *Borderland Battles: Violence, Crime, and Governance at the Edges of Colombia's War* (New York: Oxford University Press, 2019).

27. See, for example, Ken Booth, *Theory of World Security* (Cambridge: Cambridge University Press, 2007) 105; Richard Wyn Jones, *Security, Strategy, and Critical Theory*. Critical Security Studies (Boulder: Lynne Rienner Publishers, 1999), 159.

28. Ken Booth, 'Security and Emancipation,' *Review of International Studies* 17, no. 4 (1991): 319; Booth, *Theory of World Security*.

29. Hayward Alker, 'Emancipation in the Critical Security Studies Project,' in *Critical Security Studies and World Politics*, ed. Ken Booth (Boulder: Lynne Rienner Publishers, 2005), 198.

30. John Bailey, 'Public and Citizen Security in South America: Trends, Controversies and Proposals,' in *Public Security in the Americas: New Challenges in the South-North Dialogue* (Washington D.C.: Georgetown University, 2003), 274.

31. John Baylis, 'International and global security,' in *The Globalization of World Politics: An Introduction to International Relations*, edited by John Baylis, Steve Smith and Patricia Owens, 8th ed. (Oxford: Oxford University Press, 2019), 240-255.

32. United Nations, *Convention against Illicit Traffic in Narcotic Drugs and Psychotropic Substances*. Although they do not overrule the conventions, more recent documents affirm the importance of a 'human-centred and rights-based approach firmly anchored by the 2030 Agenda.' United Nations System Chief Executives Board for

Coordination, *2nd regular session of 2018, New York, 7 and 8 November 2018: Summary of deliberations,* CEB/2018/2 (New York, January 2019), Article 19 c.

33. E. P. Thompson, 'The Moral Economy of the English Crowd in the Eighteenth Century,' *Past & Present* 50, no. 1 (February 1, 1971): 76–136, https://doi.org/10.1093/past/50.1.76; Annette Idler, 'Tracing Cocaine Supply Chains from Within: Illicit Flows, Armed Conflict, and the Moral Economy of Andean Borderlands,' in *Cocaine: A Moral Economy* ed. Enrique Desmond Arias and Thomas Grisaffi (Durham, NC: Duke University Press, forthcoming).

34. From the early 1930s to the later 1960s, some of these measures did forestall major flows into the United States and other Western states. David T. Courtwright, *Forces of Habit: Drugs and the Making of the Modern World* (Cambridge, MA: Harvard University Press, 2001).

35. Thomas Grisaffi, *Coca Yes, Cocaine No: How Bolivia's Coca Growers Reshaped Democracy* (Durham, NC: Duke University Press, 2019).

36. Idler, *Borderland Battles*, 206.

37. Idler, *Borderland Battles*.

38. See, for example, Hannah Arendt, *On Violence* (New York: Harcourt Brace, 1970), 13.

39. James Gilligan, 'Shame, Guilt, and Violence,' *Social Research: An International Quarterly* 70, no. 4 (2003): 1154.

40. Merrill Singer and J. Bryan Page, *The Social Value of Drug Addicts: Uses of the Useless* (Walnut Creek, CA: Left Coast Press, 2013), 16–17. Note that this does not include the cliché of cocaine-consuming investment bankers generally based in less vulnerable locations such as London or New York who are typically at the top end of the consumer hierarchy and categorized as non-threatening recreational drug users.

41. Singer and Bryan Page, *The Social Value of Drug Addicts*, 17.

42. Singer and Bryan Page, *The Social Value of Drug Addicts*; Erving Goffman, *Stigma: Notes on the Management of Spoiled Identity* (Englewood Cliffs: Prentice-Hall, 1963), 5.

43. Rajan Basra, and Peter R. Neumann, 'Criminal Pasts, Terrorist Futures: European Jihadists and the New Crime-Terror Nexus,' *Perspectives on Terrorism* 10, no. 6 (Dec 20, 2016), http://www.terrorismanalysts.com/pt/index.php/pot/article/view/554; Charlie Edwards and Luke Gribbon, 'Pathways to Violent Extremism in the Digital Era,' *The RUSI Journal* 158, no. 5 (October 1, 2013): 40–7, https://doi.org/10.1080/03071847.2013.847714; Rajan Basra, *Drugs and Terrorism: The Overlaps in Europe* (London: ICSR, King's College London, 2019), https://icsr.info/wp-content/uploads/2019/11/ICSR-Report-Drugs-and-Terrorism-The-Overlaps-in-Europe.pdf.

44. Count the Costs, *The War on Drugs: Promoting Stigma and Discrimination* (Bristol: Transform Drug Policy Foundation, 2015), http://www.countthecosts.org/sites/default/files/Stigma-briefing.pdf.

45. Jamie Bridge and Maria-Goretti Loglo, 'Drug Laws in West Africa: A Review and Summary,' *International Drug Policy Consortium and West Africa Commission on Drugs*, Briefing Paper, 2017, 3-4.

46. Sandra Edwards, 'A Short History of Ecuador's Drug Legislation and the Impact on its Prison Population,' in *Systems Overload: Drug Laws and Prisons in Latin America*, ed. Pien Metaal and Coletta Youngers (Amsterdam: TNI; Washington D.C.: WOLA, 2011), 52, http://www.druglawreform.info/images/stories/documents/Systems_Overload/TNI-Systems_Overload-ecuador-def.pdf; Transnational Institute, 'About Drug Law Reform in Ecuador,' *Drugs and Democracy*, June 2016, https://www.tni.org/es/node/22437#:~:text=The%20Law%20on%20Narcotic%20and,the%20process%20of%20being%20replaced.&text=This%20is%20the%20law%20that,of%20narcotic%20and%20psychotropic%20substances%E2%80%9D.

47. Arron Daugherty, 'Ecuador Toughens Drugs Laws, Muddles Policy,' *InSight Crime*, September 10, 2015, http://www.insightcrime.org/news-briefs/ecuador-president-proposes-tougher-punishment-for-microtraffickers.

48. Juan Carlos Garzón Vergara, *Tough on the Weak, Weak on the Tough. Drug Laws and Policing* (Washington D.C.: Woodrow Wilson Center, Latin American Program, 2015), 5, https://www.academia.edu/16414202/Tough_on_the_Weak_Weak_on_the_Tough_Drugs_Laws_and_Policing.

49. Annette Idler, 'Narco-Brokers and Financiers: The Key Elements in the Cocaine Business,' *Cocaine Route Programme: Combatting Transnational Organised Crime*, March 2015, http://www.cocaineroute.eu/flows/narco-brokers-financiers-key-elements-cocaine-business/.

50. Edward Fox, 'Prison Gang Leaders Order Hit on Police in Venezuela,' *InSight Crime*, November 20, 2012, http://www.insightcrime.org/news-briefs/prison-gang-leaders-order-hit-on-police-in-venezuelan-state.

51. Rodrigo Uprimny et al., *Curbing Addiction to Punishment: Alternatives to Incarceration for Drug Offenses*, trans. Hilary Burke, ed. Coletta Youngers (Mexico City: Colectivo de Estudios Drogas y Derecho, 2015).

52. Doug McVay, Vincent Schiraldi, and Jason Ziedenber, *Treatment or Incarceration? National and State Findings of the Efficacy and Cost Savings of Drug Treatment Versus Imprisonment* (Washington D.C.: Justice Policy Institute, 2004), http://www.justicepolicy.org/research/2023.

53. See Rodrigo Uprimny et al., *Curbing Addiction to Punishment*, 5.

54. See, for example, Carlos A. Pérez Ricart, 'La Kingpin Strategy: ¿Qué Es y Cómo Llegó a México?,' *Nexos. Prevención y Castigo. Blog Sobre La Política de Seguridad* (blog), October 21, 2019, https://seguridad.nexos.com.mx/?p=1646.

55. Annette Idler, 'The Logic of Illicit Flows in Armed Conflict: Explaining Variation in Violent Nonstate Group Interactions in Colombia,' *World Politics* 72, no. 3 (July 2020): 335–76, https://doi.org/10.1017/S0043887120000040. Financiers are little-known middlemen who buy the raw, or partly processed, material from farmers and ensure that it reaches the laboratories for further processing.

56. See, for example, María Clemencia Ramírez, *Between the Guerrillas and the State: The Cocalero Movement, Citizenship, and Identity in the Colombian Amazon* (Durham: Duke University Press, 2011); interviews by the author in coca growing regions in Colombia (2011-2018), and poppy growing regions in Myanmar (2020).

57. UNODC, *World Drug Report 2007* (Vienna: United Nations, 2007), 170.

58. Channing May, *Transnational Crime and the Developing World* (Washington D.C.: Global Financial Integrity, 2017), xi, https://secureservercdn. net/45.40.149.159/34n.8bd.myftpupload.com/wp-content/uploads/2017/03/ Transnational_Crime-final.pdf?time=1593529815.

59. Crick, 'Drugs as an Existential Threat,' 413.

60. Annette Idler and James J.F. Forest, 'Behavioral Patterns among (Violent) Non-State Actors: A Study of Complementary Governance,' *Stability: International Journal of Security and Development* 4, no. 1 (2015).

61. See, for example, Amanda Fielding and Nichola Singleton, *Roadmaps to Regulation: New Psychoactive Substances* (Oxford: Beckley Foundation, 2016), https://beckleyfoundation.org/wp-content/uploads/2016/05/Roadmaps-to-Regulation_NPS_20-06-2016.pdf.

62. Idler, 'The Logic of Illicit Flows in Armed Conflict.'

63. Charles Tilly, 'War Making and State Making as Organized Crime,' in *Bringing the State Back In*, ed. Peter B. Evans et al. (Cambridge: Cambridge University Press, 1985), 169–91.

64. Phil Williams, 'Transnational Organized Crime and the State,' in *The Emergence of Private Authority in Global Governance*, ed. Rodney Bruce Hall and Thomas J. Biersteker (West Nyack: Cambridge University Press, 2002), 161–82; Jonathan H. C. Kelman, 'States Can Play, Too: Constructing a Typology of State Participation in Illicit Flows,' *Crime, Law and Social Change* 64, no. 1 (August 1, 2015): 37–55, https://doi.org/10.1007/s10611-015-9568-4; Felia Allum and Stan Gilmour, eds., *Handbook of Organised Crime and Politics* (Cheltenham: Edward Elgar Publishing Limited, 2019), https://www.elgaronline.com/view/ edcoll/9781786434562/9781786434562.xml.

65. Krause and Williams, *Critical Security Studies*, ix–x.

66. Moisés Naím, 'The Drug Trade: The Politicization of Criminals and the Criminalization of Politicians' (working paper, prepared for the First Meeting of the Commission Geneva, 24–25 Jan 2011, Global Commission on Drug Policy, 2010).

67. See, for example, Keith Krause and Michael C. Williams, *Critical Security Studies: Concepts and Cases* (London: UCL Press, 1997).

68. See, for example, Paul D. Williams, *Security Studies: An Introduction*, 2nd ed. (London: Routledge, 2012), 136; Richard Falk, 'Toward a New Geopolitics?,' *Foreign Policy Journal*, August 17, 2012, https://www.foreignpolicyjournal.com/2012/08/17/ toward-a-new-geopolitics/.

69. For a conceptualization of these approaches on a continuum see Sasha Jesperson, 'Assessing Militarised Responses to Transnational Organised Crime,' in *Militarised Responses to Transnational Organised Crime: The War on Crime*, ed. Tuesday Reitano, Sasha Jesperson, and Lucia Bird Ruiz-Benitez de Lugo, 1st ed. 2018 edition (New York: Palgrave Macmillan, 2017), 1–10. Lexico Oxford Dictionary, 'Definition of Glocal in English,' 2020, https://www.lexico.com/definition/glocal.

70. Annette Idler, 'Colombia: Organised Crime, Politics, and Convenience,' in *Handbook of Organised Crime and Politics*, ed. Felia Allum and Stan Gilmour (Cheltenham: Edward Elgar Publishing Limited, 2019), 258–74.

71. Jeremy McDermott, 'Militarisation of the Drug War in Latin America: A Policy Cycle Set to Continue?,' in *Militarised Responses to Transnational Organised Crime: The War on Crime*, ed. Tuesday Reitano, Sasha Jesperson, and Lucia Bird Ruiz-Benitez de Lugo, 1st ed. (New York: Palgrave Macmillan, 2017), 271.

72. Julia Zulver and Annette Idler, 'Gendering the Border Effect: The Double Impact of Colombian Insecurity and the Venezuelan Refugee Crisis,' *Third World Quarterly* 41, no. 7 (2020): 1122–40; Annette Idler and Markus Hochmüller, 'Covid-19 in Colombia's Borderlands and the Western Hemisphere: Adding Instability to a Double Crisis,' *Journal of Latin American Geography* 19, no. 3 (2020): 280–88.

73. Commission on Narcotic Drugs, *Making Drug Control 'Fit for Purpose': Building on the UNGASS Decade. Report by the Executive Director of the United Nations Office on Drugs and Crime as a Contribution to the Review of the Twentieth Special Session of the General Assembly*, E/CN.7/2008/CRP.17* (Vienna: CND, 2008), https://www.unodc.org/documents/commissions/CND/CND_Sessions/CND_51/1_CRPs/E-CN7-2008-CRP17_E.pdf.

74. McDermott, 'Militarisation of the Drug War in Latin America,' 270.

75. John Collins, 'Beyond UNGASS 2016: Drug Control Multilateralism and the End to the "War on Drugs,"' in *Militarised Responses to Transnational Organised Crime: The War on Crime*, ed. Tuesday Reitano, Sasha Jesperson, and Lucia Bird Ruiz-Benitez de Lugo, 1st ed. 2018 edition (New York: Palgrave Macmillan, 2017), 283.

76. Idler, *Borderland Battles*; Idler and Forest, 'Behavioral Patterns among (Violent) Non-State Actors.'

77. Idler, *Borderland Battles*.

78. Christian Lund, 'Twilight Institutions: Public Authority and Local Politics in Africa,' *Development and Change* 37, no. 4 (2006): 693.

79. Tuesday Reitano and Mark Shaw, 'The Politics of Power, Protection, Identity and Illicit Trade,' Crime-Conflict Nexus Series (New York: United Nations University Centre for Policy Research, May 2017).

80. Interviews by the author with local community members along the Colombia-Ecuador border, 2011–2012.

81. Steven Vertovec, *Transnationalism*, *Key Ideas* (London; New York: Routledge, 2009), 1.

82. United Nations Development Programme (UNDP), *Human Development Report 2014: Sustaining Human Progress: Reducing Vulnerabilities and Building Resilience,* (New York: UNDP, 2014), http://hdr.undp.org/en/content/human-development-report-2014.

83. See, for example, Sanjeev Khagram and Peggy Levitt, *The Transnational Studies Reader: Intersections and Innovations* (New York: Routledge, 2008); Anna Amelina, Devrimsel D. Nergiz, Thomas Faist, Nina Glick Schiller, eds., *Beyond Methodological Nationalism: Research Methodologies for Cross-Border Studies*, Routledge Research in Transnationalism 24 (New York: Routledge, 2012).

84. See, for example, Deborah J. Yashar, *Homicidal Ecologies: Illicit Economies and Complicit States in Latin America* (Cambridge: Cambridge University Press, 2018).

85. Willem van Schendel and Itty Abraham, eds., *Illicit Flows and Criminal Things: States, Borders, and the Other Side of Globalization* (Bloomington: Indiana University Press, 2005).

86. See, for example, United Nations and World Bank, *Pathways for Peace: Inclusive Approaches to Preventing Violent Conflict* (Washington D.C.: World Bank, 2018), http://hdl.handle.net/10986/28337.

87. Lansana Gberie, *Crime, Violence, and Politics: Drug Trafficking and Counternarcotics Policies in Mali and Guinea* (Washington D.C.: Brookings Institution, 2015), 2.

88. Robert Rotberg, 'The Little-Understood Connection between Islamic Terror and Drug Profits,' *The Conversation*, February 16, 2016, http://theconversation.com/the-little-understood-connection-between-islamic-terror-and-drug-profits-53602.

89. The European Union's Cocaine Route Programme exemplifies how such an approach might take shape (see www.cocaineroute.eu).

90. For 'breaking free of rules,' see Buzan, Wæver, and Wilde, *Security*.

91. Grisaffi, *Coca Yes, Cocaine No*.

92. For a similar concept of vulnerable countries see United Nations General Assembly, *Resolution 70/1. Transforming Our World: The 2030 Agenda for Sustainable Development*, A/RES/70/1 (New York, October 21, 2015), Article 22, https://undocs.org/A/RES/70/1.

93. Karen O'Brien, Linda Sygna, and Jan Erik Haugen, 'Vulnerable or Resilient? A Multi-Scale Assessment of Climate Impacts and Vulnerability in Norway,' *Climatic Change* 64, no. 1 (May 1, 2004): 193–225, https://doi.org/10.1023/B:CLIM.0000024668.70143.80.

94. Fabien Nathan, 'Natural Disasters, Vulnerability and Human Security,' in *Facing Global Environmental Change: Environmental, Human, Energy, Food, Health and Water Security Concepts*, ed. Hans Günter Brauch et al. (Berlin; Heidelberg: Springer-Verlag Berlin Heidelberg, 2009), 1126, https://doi.org/10.1007/978-3-540-68488-6_87.

95. Indranil Dutta, James Foster, and Ajit Mishra, 'On Measuring Vulnerability to Poverty,' *Social Choice and Welfare* 37, no. 4 (2011): 743–61.

96. O. D. Cardona, 'The Need for Rethinking the Concepts of Vulnerability and Risk from a Holistic Perspective: A Necessary Review and Criticism for Effective Risk Management,' in *Mapping Vulnerability: Disasters, Development and People*, ed. Greg Bankoff (London: Earthscan, 2004), 37–51.

97. Ben Wisner and Piers M. Blaikie, *At Risk: Natural Hazards, People's Vulnerability and Disasters*, 2nd ed. (London: Routledge, 2004); Thomas E. Downing, et al. 'Integrating social vulnerability into water management,' NeWater Working Paper No. 5, 2006, Stockholm Environment Institute; Hallie Eakin and Amy Lynd Luers, 'Assessing the vulnerability of social-environmental systems,' *Annual Review of Environment and Resources* 31, no. 1 (2006): 365–94, https://doi.org/10.1146/annurev.energy.30.050504.144352.

98. The distinction between production, transit, and consumption sites becomes particularly blurred in the case of synthetic drugs.

99. See, for example, Phil Williams and Roy Godson, 'Anticipating Organized and Transnational Crime,' *Crime, Law and Social Change* 37 (June 2002): 318–20, https://doi.org/10.1023/A:1016095317864.

100. For the conflict-crime nexus see John De Boer and Louise Bosetti, 'The Crime-Conflict Nexus. Assessing the Threat and Developing Solutions,' Crime-Conflict Nexus Series (United Nations University Centre for Policy Research, May 2017).

101. Lindsay Maizland, 'U.S.-Taliban Peace Deal: What to Know,' Council on Foreign Relations, updated 2 March 2020, https://www.cfr.org/backgrounder/us-taliban-peace-deal-agreement-afghanistan-war.

102. Pierre-Arnaud Chouvy, Opium: Uncovering the Politics of the Poppy (Cambridge, MA: Harvard University Press, 2010).

103. See, for example, Williams and Godson, 'Anticipating Organized and Transnational Crime' for the role of peace agreements and illicit economies.

104. Beth Macy, 'America's Other Epidemic,' The Atlantic, May 2020, https://www.theatlantic.com/magazine/archive/2020/05/nikki-king-opioid-treatment-program/609085/.

105. United Nations General Assembly, Resolution 70/1, Article 23.

106. John Friedmann. Empowerment: The Politics of Alternative Development (Oxford: Blackwell, 1992).

107. UNDP, Human Development Report 2014, 15.

108. Robert Chambers, 'Vulnerability: How the Poor Cope,' IDS Bulletin 20, no. 2 (1989).

109. See also Amartya Sen, Poverty and Famines: An Essay on Entitlement and Deprivation (Oxford: Clarendon Press, 1981); Resources, Values and Development (Cambridge, MA: Harvard University Press, 1984) for the vulnerability, poverty, development nexus.

110. Securitization theory provides an analytical framework of the status quo but does not seek emancipation like other critical approaches that point to the problems of the status quo. Peoples and Vaughan-Williams, Critical Security Studies, 32.

111. For a discussion of the relationship between the concepts of vulnerability and resilience see Fiona Miller, H. Osbahr, E. Boyd, F. Thomalla, S. Bharwani, G. Ziervogel, B. Walker, J. Birkmann, S. Van der Leeuw, J. Rockström, J. Hinkel, T. Downing, C. Folke, and D. Nelson, 'Resilience and vulnerability: complementary or conflicting concepts?' Ecology and Society 15, no. 3 (2010):11; http://www.ecologyandsociety.org/vol15/iss3/art11/.

112. John Paul Lederach, Building Peace: Sustainable Reconciliation in Divided Societies (Washington D.C.: United States Institute of Peace Press, 1997).

113. Shaw, 'Soldiers in a Storm.'

114. United Nations, Single Convention on Narcotic Drugs, Article 39; United Nations, Convention on Psychotropic Substances (New York: United Nations, 1971), Article 23; and United Nations, United Nations Convention Against Illicit Traffic in Narcotic Drugs and Psychotropic Substances (New York: United Nations, 1988), Article 24.

115. Bilgin, 'Critical Theory.'

2. BUILDING THE GLOBAL DRUG REGIME

1. Peter Andreas and Ethan Avram Nadelmann, Policing the Globe: Criminalization and Crime Control in International Relations (Oxford: Oxford University Press, 2006), Chap. 1.

2. Paul Gootenberg, *Andean Cocaine: The Making of a Global Drug* (Chapel Hill: University of North Carolina Press, 2008).

3. See, for example, Ethan A. Nadelmann, 'Global prohibition regimes: The evolution of norms in international society,' *International Organization* 44, vol 4 (1990): 479–526, doi:10.1017/S0020818300035384.

4. On corporate controls, see Joseph Spillane, *Cocaine: From Medical Marvel to Modern Menace in the United States, 1885–1920* (Baltimore: Johns Hopkins University Press, 1999); for Germany, Richard Friman, *Narco-Diplomacy: Exporting the U.S. War on Drugs* (Ithaca: Cornell University Press, 1996), Chap. 2.

5. Please note that the control regime for these substances under the 1971 treaty is different (less stringent) than for substances regulated under the Single Convention.

6. Ethan A. Nadelmann, *Cops Across Borders: The Internationalization of U.S. Criminal Law Enforcement* (University Park: Penn State Press, 1993), Chaps. 3–5.

7. This following section relies on William B. McAllister, *Drug Diplomacy in the Twentieth Century* (London: Routledge, 2000), and David Bewley-Taylor, *The United States and International Drug Control, 1909–1997* (London: Continuum, 2001). There are many older accounts, for example, Peter D. Lowes, *The Genesis of International Narcotics Control* (Geneva: Lib. Droz, 1966).

8. The Convention also includes references to alternatives to incarceration as well as integrated rural development and asks states to consider traditional licit uses of crops.

9. For a specific discussion of UN enforcement powers, see Bewley-Taylor, *United States and International Drug Control,* 171–5: hardline critics label the IDCR a 'Promotional Regime,' 'Empty vessel,' 'Talking shop,' 'Figurehead,' 'Moral volunteerism,' though Bewley demonstrates the impact of the regime when combined with other forms of power.

10. Andreas and Nadelmann, *Policing the Globe,* Chap. 1.

11. The fullest account of US influence is Bewley-Taylor, *United States and International Drug Control* (also reflected in McAllister, *Drug Diplomacy in the Twentieth Century*); for early era, see especially Arnold H. Taylor, *American Diplomacy and the Narcotics Traffic, 1900–1939* (Durham: Duke University Press, 1969) and William O. Walker III, *Opium and Foreign Policy: The Anglo-American Search for Order, 1912–1954* (Chapel Hill: University of North Carolina Press, 1991) or his *Drug Control in the Americas* (Albuquerque: University of New Mexico Press, 1989). See also Kettil Braun, Lynn Pan, and Ingemar Rexed, *The Gentleman's Club: International Control of Drugs and Alcohol* (Chicago: Univ. of Chicago Press, 1975).

12. David F. Musto, *The American Disease: Origins of Drug Control* (New Haven: Yale University Press, 1973, and subsequent eds); a vast literature examines Anslinger's role, for example, John C. McWilliams, *The Protectors: Harry J. Anslinger and the Federal Bureau of Narcotics, 1930–1962* (Newark: University of Delaware Press, 1990); Jonathan Erien and Joseph Spillane, *Federal Drug Control: The Evolution of Policy and Practice* (Philadelphia: Pharmaceutical Products Press, 2004); William O. Walker III, ed., *Drug Control Policy: Essays in Historical and Comparative Perspective* (University Park: Penn State Press, 1992).

13. McAllister, *Drug Diplomacy in the Twentieth Century,* for biographies; many such actors left tracts and memoirs (Moorhead, LaMotte, Renborg), which became the basis of most pre-1970s literature on international drug control. See Matthew R. Pembleton, *Containing Addiction: The Federal Bureau of Narcotics and the Origins of America's Global Drug War* (Amherst: University of Massachusetts Press, 2017) for a new transnationalized view of Anslinger's and FBN politics.

14. Bewley-Taylor, *United States and International Drug Control*, Chaps. 3–4.

15. See Richard DeGrandpre, *The Cult of Pharmacology: How America Became the World's Most Troubled Drug Culture* (Durham: Duke University Press, 2006), Ch. 5, for innovative account.

16. Musto, *American Disease*; Ethan Nadelmann, 'U.S. Drug Policy: A Bad Export,' *Foreign Policy* 70 (Spring 1988): 97–108. The 'hegemon' analogy is from Robert Gilpin, *The Political Economy of International Relations* (Princeton: Princeton University Press, 1987).

17. Kathleen J. Frydl, *The Drug Wars in America, 1940–1973* (New York: Cambridge University Press, 2013); for view as straight U.S. (pharmaceutical) imperialism, see Suzanna Reiss, *We Sell Drugs: The Alchemy of U.S. Empire* (Berkeley: University of California Press, 2014).

18. David Weimer, *Seeing Drugs: Modernization, Counterinsurgency, and U.S. Narcotics Control in the Third World, 1969–1976* (Kent OH: Kent State University Press, 2011), Gootenberg, *Andean Cocaine*, Chap. 5; Friman, *Narco-Diplomacy*, Chaps. 4–5; William L. Marcy, *The Politics of Cocaine* (Chicago: Lawrence Hill Books, 2010).

19. Bewley-Taylor, *United States and International Drug Control, Ch.* 5, Epilogue; United Nations International Drug Control Programme, *World Drug Report* (Oxford: Oxford University Press, 1997), which begins to acknowledge the need for a wider view like public health. On indigenous issues, see Michael K. Steinberg, Joseph J. Hobbs and Kent Mathewson, eds., *Dangerous Harvest: Drug Plants and the Transformation of Indigenous Landscapes* (New York: Oxford University Press, 2004).

20. Robert McCoun and Peter Reuter, *Drug War Heresies: Learning from Other Vices, Times, and Places* (Cambridge: Cambridge University Press, 2001). There is also a big data problem, particularly around illicit trades, see Peter Andreas and Kelly M. Greenhill, eds., *Sex, Drugs, and Body Counts: The Politics of Numbers in Global Crime and Conflict* (Ithaca: Cornell University Press, 2011).

21. UNODC, *A Century of International Drug Control* (Vienna: UNODC, 2008) offers a distinctive picture, and explicitly analyzes drug trend outcomes (pages 81–91), positing that the IDCR has 'contained' illicit drugs to less than 5 per cent of global populations (less than allegedly used analogous drugs in 1907/08) and narrowed the range of production areas. While admitting IDCR 'unintended consequences,' it is still an official portrait, one rife with baseline and other conceptual problems. Sharply critical outcome perspectives include Alfred W. McCoy, 'The Stimulus of Prohibition: A Critical History of the Global Narcotics Trade,' in Steinberg, Hobbs, and Mathewson, eds., *Dangerous Harvest*, 24–111; Alfred W. McCoy, 'From Free Trade to Prohibition: A Critical History of the Modern Asian Opium Trade,' *Fordham Urban Law Journal* 28, no. 1 (2000): 304–49; or Bewley-Taylor, *United States and International Drug Control,* 175–206.

22. Kathryn Meyer and Terry Parssinen, *Webs of Smoke: Smugglers, Warlords, Spies, and the History of the International Drug Trade* (Latham, MD: Lowman & Littlefield Pubs, 1998), overall source for pre-1950 era (esp. Table 1, p. 21); McCoy, 'From Free Trade to Prohibition,' 320, consolidates quantitative data. See Frank Dikotter, Lars Laaman and Zhou Xun, *Narcotic Culture: A History of Drugs in China* (Chicago: University of Chicago Press, 2004), Chaps. 8–9, for reappraisal of Chinese results; John Jennings, *The Opium Empire: Japanese Imperialism and Drug Trafficking in Asia, 1895–1945* (Westport, CT: Praeger 1997).

23. Pierre-Arnaud Chouvy, *Opium: Uncovering the Politics of the Poppy* (Cambridge: Harvard University Press, 2010), broadly details these geographic-political-commodity shifts, superseding the (more conspiratorial) focus of Alfred McCoy's classic *The Politics of Heroin in Southeast Asia* (New York: Harper & Row, 1972; expanded versions, 1991, 2003, Lawrence Hill Books).

24. Chouvy, *Opium*, Chap. 3; McCoy, *Politics of Heroin*.

25. Sam Quinones, *Dreamland: The True Tale of America's Opiate Epidemic* (New York: Bloomsbury Books, 2015).

26. McCoy, 'From Free Trade to Prohibition,' 308, 315 (the 1990s heroin 'proliferation').

27. Much of the following section is based on my own research: Paul Gootenberg, ed., *Cocaine: Global Histories* (London: Routledge UK, 1999) and Gootenberg, *Andean Cocaine*.

28. Gootenberg, *Andean Cocaine,* Chaps. 1–3; Spillane, *Cocaine*. On Coca Cola, see Paul Gootenberg, 'Secret Ingredients: The Politics of Coca in US-Peruvian Relations, 1915–1965,' *Journal of Latin American Studies* 36, vol. 2 (2004): 233–66.

29. Gootenberg, *Andean Cocaine,* Chap. 5; Marcel de Kort, 'Doctors, diplomats, and businessmen: Conflicting interests in the Netherlands and the Dutch Indies, 1860–1950,' in Gootenberg, ed., *Cocaine: Global Histories*, Chap. 6.

30. Paul Gootenberg, 'The "Pre-Colombian" Era of Drug Trafficking in the Americas: Cocaine: 1945–1965,' *The Americas* 64, vol. 2 (2007): 133–76.

31. Gootenberg, *Andean Cocaine*, Chap. 7; Paul Gootenberg, 'Cocaine's Long March North, 1900–2010,' *Latin American Politics & Society* 54, vol. 1 (2012): 151–80.

32. Accessible account of the US drug war is Peter Andreas, *Smuggler Nation: How Illicit Trade Made America* (New York: Oxford University Press, 2013), Chap. 14; Peter H. Smith, ed., *Drug Policy in the Americas* (Boulder: Westview Press, 1992).

33. Gootenberg, 'Cocaine's Long March North.' For analysis, Michael Kenney, *From Pablo to Osama: Trafficking and Terrorist Networks, Government Bureaucracies, and Competitive Adaptation* (University Park: Penn State Press, 2007); U.S. Office of National Drug Control Policy, 'Coca in the Andes,' ONDCP, Policy & Research, April 2015; Daniel Mejía, *Plan Colombia: An Analysis of Effectiveness and Costs* (Washington D.C.: Brookings Institution, Latin America Initiative, 2014).

34. Bewley-Taylor, *United States and International Drug Control*, Chap. 5, epilogue; CF Antonio Maria Costa, preface to *A Century of International Drug Control* (Vienna: UNODC, 2008).

3. THE INTERNATIONAL DRUG CONTROL REGIME

1. Martin Jelsma and Pien Metaal, *Cracks in the Vienna Consensus: The UN Drug Control Debate* (Washington D.C.: WOLA, 2004), http://www.undrugcontrol.info/un-drug-control/cnd/item/2176-cracks-in-the-vienna-consensus.

2. Peter Reuter and Franz Trautmann, eds., *A Report on Global Illicit Drug Market 1998-2007* (Utrecht: European Commission, 2009), 16, https://www.tni.org/files/publication-downloads/global-illicit-markets-short.pdf.

3. Tom Blickman, 'Full Scope on the War on Drugs,' TNI, last modified July 18, 2005, https://www.tni.org/en/archives/act/2157.

4. UNODC, *World Drug Report 2006* (Vienna: United Nations, 2006), foreword.

5. Commission on Narcotic Drugs (CND), *Making Drug Control 'Fit for Purpose': Building on the UNGASS Decade. Report by the Executive Director of the United Nations Office on Drugs and Crime as a Contribution to the Review of the Twentieth Special Session of the General Assembly,* E/CN.7/2008/CRP.17 (Vienna: CND, 2008), https://www.unodc.org/documents/commissions/CND/CND_Sessions/CND_51/1_CRPs/E-CN7-2008-CRP17_E.pdf.

6. UNODC, 'Political Declaration and Plan of Action on International Cooperation towards an Integrated and Balanced Strategy to Counter the World Drug Problem,' in *High-Level Segment Commission on Narcotic Drugs* (Vienna: United Nations, 2009), https://www.unodc.org/documents/ungass2016/V0984963-English.pdf.

7. International Drug Policy Consortium (IDPC), *IDPC Proceedings Document on the 2009 CND and High Level Segment* (London: IDPC, 2009), https://papers.ssrn.com/sol3/papers.cfm?abstract_id=1425089. The countries were Australia, Bolivia, Bulgaria, Croatia, Cyprus, Estonia, Finland, Georgia, Greece, Hungary, Latvia, Liechtenstein, Lithuania, Luxembourg, Malta, the Netherlands, Norway, Poland, Portugal, Romania, St Lucia, Slovenia, Spain, Switzerland, the United Kingdom, and Germany.

8. IDPC, *IDPC Proceedings Document.*

9. David Bewley-Taylor, *International Drug Control: Consensus Fractured* (Cambridge: Cambridge University Press, 2012).

10. Paul Hunt, *Human Rights, Health and Harm Reduction: States' amnesia and parallel universes* (London: International Harm Reduction Association, 2008), http://www.ihra.net/files/2010/06/16/HumanRightsHealthAndHarmReduction.pdf.

11. IDPC 'President Sumyai Speaks on Drug Control and Human Rights at the CND,' IDPC, last modified November 27, 2018, https://idpc.net/incb-watch/updates/2018/11/president-sumyai-speaks-on-drug-control-and-human-rights-at-the-cnd.

12. David Bewley-Taylor and Martin Jelsma, *UNGASS 2016: A Broken or B-r-o-a-d Consensus? UN summit cannot hide a growing divergence in the global drug policy landscape* (Amsterdam: TNI, 2016), https://www.tni.org/files/publication-downloads/dpb_45_04072016_web.pdf.

13. United Nations Office on Drugs and Crime. 'Political Declaration and Plan of Action on International Cooperation Towards an Integrated and Balanced Strategy to Counter the World Drug Problem.' In *High-Level Segment Commission on Narcotic Drugs* (Vienna: United Nations, 2009), https://www.unodc.org/documents/ungass2016/V0984963-English.pdf.

14. Neil Boister, *Penal Aspects of the UN Drug Conventions* (The Hague: Kluwer Law International, 2001), 1–4.

15. 'INCB - International Narcotics Control Board,' INCB, 2020, http://www.incb.org/incb/index.html.

16. 'INCB,' INCB, http://www.incb.org/incb/mandate.html (site discontinued).

17. UNODC, *Operational priorities: guidelines for the medium term* (Vienna: UNODC, 2003), http://www.unodc.org/pdf/ed_guidelines_mediumterm.pdf.

18. 'World Health Organization,' WHO, http://www.who.int/governance/eb/constitution/en/index.html (site discontinued).

19. 'WHO Expert Committee on Drug Dependence,' Management of substance abuse, World Health Organization, 2020, http://www.who.int/substance_abuse/right_committee/en/.

20. United Nations Drug Control Programme (UNDCP) Legal Affairs Section, *Flexibility of treaty provisions as regards harm reduction approaches,* E/INCB/2002/W.13/SS.5 (Vienna: INCB, 2002), 6, http://fileserver.idpc.net/library/UN_HarmReduction_EN.pdf.

21. UNDCP Legal Affairs Section, *Flexibility of treaty provisions,* 5.

22. Rick Lines, and Damon Barrett, 'Cannabis Reform, 'Medical and Scientific Purposes' and the Vienna Convention on the Law of the Treaties,' *International Community Law Review* 20, no. 5 (2018): 436–55, https://doi.org/10.1163/18719732-12341384.

23. INCB, *Report of the International Narcotics Control Board for 2008*, E/INCB/2008/1 (Vienna: United Nations, 2009), 66, https://www.incb.org/incb/en/publications/annual-reports/annual-report-2008.html.

24. Ethan A. Nadelmann, 'Global Prohibition Regimes: The Evolution of Norms in International Society,' *International Organization* 44, no. 4 (1990): 479–526, http://www.jstor.org/stable/2706851?seq=1#page_scan_tab_contents.

25. IDPC, *The International Narcotics Control Board: Current Tension and Options for Reform* (London: IDPC, 2008), http://fileserver.idpc.net/library/IDPC_BP_07_INCB_TensionsAndOptions_EN.pdf.

26. IDPC, *IDPC Advocacy Note: Some Initial Priorities for Mr Fedotov, the new Executive Director of the United Nations Office on Drugs and Crime (UNODC)* (London: IDPC, 2010), http://fileserver.idpc.net/library/IDPC%20advocacy%20note%20-%20Appointment%20of%20UNODC%20ED%20FINAL%20VERSION.pdf.

27. This is a view implicitly echoed by Mr Fedotov's successor, Ms. Ghada Fathi Waly. Bewley-Taylor participant observation, CND March 2020.

28. IDPC, *IDPC Response to the UNODC World Drug Report 2012* (London: IDPC, 2012), 2, http://idpc.net/publications/2012/10/idpc-response-to-the-unodc-world-drug-report-2012.

29. UNODC, *World Drug Report 2018* (Vienna: United Nations, 2018), booklet 3, 9, https://www.unodc.org/wdr2018/en/drug-markets.html.

30. Rachel Ehrenberg, 'Engineered yeast paves way for home-brew heroin,' *Nature* 521, no. 7552 (2015): 267–8, http://www.nature.com/news/engineered-yeast-paves-way-for-home-brew-heroin-1.17566.

31. CND, *Background paper prepared by the United Kingdom of Great Britain and Northern Ireland related to its notification submitted on 23 January to the Secretary-General on*

the review of the scope of control of mephedrone, E/CN.7/2014/CRP.11 (Vienna: CND, 2014), https://www.unodc.org/documents/commissions/CND/CND_Sessions/CND_57/E-CN7-2014-CRP11_V1401524_E.pdf.

32.   A related problem arises from 'blanket bans' on substances with similar chemical properties. For a discussion of the recently established European approach, see Christopher Hallam, Dave Bewley-Taylor and Martin Jelsma, *Scheduling in the International Drug Control System* (Amsterdam: TNI; London: IDPC, 2014), 16–17, https://www.tni.org/en/briefing/scheduling-international-drug-control-system.

33.   James Q. Wilson, 'Against the Legalization of Drugs,' *Commentary*, February 1990, 21–8.

34.   Transnational Institute, 'Infographic: Why is Uruguay Regulating; Not Criminalising Cannabis?' last modified December 10, 2013, http://druglawreform.info/en/publications/item/5183-infographic-uruguays-pioneering-cannabis-regulation.

35.   United Nations Information Service, *Uruguay is breaking the International Conventions on Drug Control with the Cannabis Legislation approved by its Congress,* UNIS/NAR/1190 (Vienna: UNIS, 2013), https://www.incb.org/documents/Publications/PressRelease/PR2013/press_release_111213.pdf.

36.   'Posición del presidente de JIFE no representa opinión de ONU,' *Espectador. com*, December 13, 2013, http://historico.espectador.com/politica/280451/posicion-del-presidente-de-jife-no-representa-opinion-de-onu.

37.   Alaska, California, Colorado, Illinois, Maine, Massachusetts, Michigan, Nevada, Oregon, Vermont and Washington.

38.   'Foreign Press Centers,' U.S. Department of State, 2020, http://fpc.state.gov/232813.html.

39.   John Collins, 'The State Department's move to a more flexible diplomatic policy on drugs is a rational approach to a difficult question,' *The LSE US Centre's daily blog on American Politics and Policy*, December 1, 2014, http://bit.ly/1tuVypa. See also John Collins, 'Rethinking "flexibilities" in the international drug control system – Potential, precedents and models for reforms,' *International Journal of Drug Policy* 60 (2018): 107–14.

40.   Rick Lines, Damon Barrett and Patrick Gallahue, 'Guest Post: Has the US Just Called for Unilateral Interpretation of Multilateral Obligations?,' *Opinio Juris,* December 18, 2014, http://opiniojuris.org/2014/12/18/guest-post-us-just-called-unilateral-interpretation-multilateral-obligations/.

41.   Martin Jelsma, *UNGASS 2016: Prospects for Treaty Reform and UN System-Wide Coherence on Drug Policy* (Washington D.C.: Brookings Institution, 2015), 19, https://www.tni.org/files/download/treaty_reform_drug_policy_ungass2016.pdf.

42.   See David Bewley-Taylor and Malgosia Fitzmaurice, 'The Evolution and Modernization of Treaty Regimes: The Contrasting Cases of International Drug Control and Environmental Regulation,' *International Community Law Review* 20, no. 5 (2018): 421.

43.   Senate of Canada, 'The Standing Senate Committee on Foreign Affairs and International Trade Evidence' (declaration by Chrystia Freeland, Canadian Minister of Foreign Affairs, at the Standing Senate Committee on Foreign Affairs and

International Trade, Ottawa, May 1, 2018), https://sencanada.ca/en/Content/Sen/Committee/421/AEFA/54008-e.

44. For a more detailed discussion see David Bewley-Taylor, Martin Jelsma, Steve Rolles and John Walsh, *Cannabis Regulation and the UN Drug Treaties. Strategies for Reform* (Vancouver: The Canadian Drug Policy Coalition, 2016), http://fileserver.idpc.net/library/Cannabis_Regulation_UN_Drug_Treaties_April_2016.pdf; and Dave Bewley-Taylor, Tom Blickman and Martin Jelsma, *The Rise and Decline of Cannabis Prohibition. The History of Cannabis in the UN Drug Control System and Options for Reform* (Amsterdam: TNI; Swansea: Global Drug Policy Observatory, 2014), https://www.tni.org/files/download/rise_and_decline_ch4.pdf.

45. John Walsh, Martin Jelsma, Tom Blickman and Dave Bewley-Taylor, *The WHO's First-Ever Critical Review of Cannabis: A Mixture of Obvious Recommendations Deserving Support and Dubious Methods and Outcomes Requiring Scrutiny* (Washington D.C.: WOLA; Amsterdam: TNI; Swansea: Global Drug Policy Observatory, 2019), https://www.tni.org/en/publication/the-whos-first-ever-critical-review-of-cannabis.

46. David Bewley-Taylor, 'Towards a revision of the UN drug control conventions: Harnessing like-mindedness,' *International Journal of Drug Policy* 24, no.1 (2013): 60–8.

47. See Damon Barrett, Martin Jelsma and David Bewley-Taylor, 'Fatal Attraction: Brownfield's Flexibility Doctrine and Global Drug Policy Reform,' *Huffington Post*, November 18, 2014. See also: Lines, Barrett and Gallahue, 'Guest Post: Has the US Just Called for Unilateral Interpretation of Multilateral Obligations?' And see finally: Wells C. Bennett and John Walsh, *Marijuana Legalization is an Opportunity to Modernize International Drug Treaties* (Washington D.C.: Brookings Institution, 2014), http://www.brookings.edu/research/reports/2014/10/15-marijuana-legalization-modernize-drug-treaties-bennett-walsh.

48. Neil Boister and Martin Jelsma, 'Inter se Modification of the UN Drug Control Conventions. An Exploration of its Applicability to Legitimise the Legal Regulation of Cannabis Markets,' *International Community Law Review* 20, no. 5 (2018): 457–94.

49. Vienna Convention on the Law of Treaties, 18232 (1969), Article 41.

50. Ibid.

51. For detailed discussions on this option see Martin Jelsma et al., *Balancing Treaty Stability and Change: Inter se Modification of the UN Drug Control Conventions to Facilitate Cannabis Regulation* (Washington D.C.: WOLA, 2014), https://www.swansea.ac.uk/media/Balancing-Stability-and-Change.pdf; and Boister and Jelsma, 'Inter se Modification of the UN Drug Control Conventions.'

52. Boister and Jelsma, 'Inter se Modification of the UN Drug Control Conventions,' 492–3.

53. David Bewley-Taylor, Tom Blickman and Martin Jelsma, *The Rise and Decline of Cannabis Prohibition*, 65.

54. Damon Barrett, *Backgrounder: Bolivia's concurrent drug control and other legal commitments* (Colchester: International Centre on Human Rights and Drug Policy, 2011), https://www.tni.org/files/publication-downloads/international_legal_commitments.pdf.

55. Martin Jelsma, 'TNI calls for a wide-ranging and open debate that considers all options at UNGASS 2016,' TNI, last modified March 11, 2015, https://www.tni. org/en/un-drug-control/cnd/item/6148-tni-calls-for-a-wide-ranging-and-open-debate-that-considers-all-options-at-ungass-2016. See also https://www.tni.org/ en/publication/ungass-2016-background-memo-on-the-proposal-to-establish-an-expert-advisory-group.

56. David Bewley-Taylor, *International Drug Control*, 249.

57. CND, *Ministerial Declaration on Strengthening our Actions at the National, Regional and International Levels to Accelerate the Implementation of our Joint Commitments to Address and Counter the World Drug Problem* (Vienna: CND, 2019), https://www.unodc.org/ documents/commissions/CND/2019/Ministerial_Declaration.pdf.

58. Martin Jelsma, *UN Common Position on drug policy – Consolidating system-wide coherence* (London: International Drug Policy Consortium, 2019), https://www.tni.org/ en/publication/un-common-position-on-drug-policy-consolidating-system-wide-coherence.

59. See UN System Coordination Task Team on the Implementation of the UN System Common Position on drug-related matters, *What we have learned over the last ten years: A summary of knowledge acquired and produced by the UN system on drug-related matters* (New York: United Nations, 2019).

60. See for example, International Expert Group on Drug Policy Metrics, *Aligning Agendas: Drugs, Sustainable Development, and the Drive for Policy Coherence* (New York: IPI Publications, 2018); and David Bewley-Taylor and Marie Nougier, 'Measuring the "World Drug Problem": 2019 and Beyond' in *Collapse of the Global Order on Drugs: From the UNGASS 2016 to Review 2019,* ed. Axel Klein and Blaine Stothard (Bingley: Emerald Publishing, 2018), 49–65.

61. David Bewley-Taylor and Malgosia Fitzmaurice, 'The Evolution and Modernisation of Treaty Regimes. The Contrasting Cases of International Drug Control and Environmental Regulation,' *International Community Law Review* 20, no. 5 (2018): 403–35.

62. See 'Statement of the Permanent Representative of the Russian Federation to the International Organizations in Vienna Mr. Mikhail Ulyanov at the 5th intersessional meeting of the Commission on Narcotic Drugs' (statement, CND, Vienna, November 7, 2018).

63. Axel Klein and Blaine Stothard, eds., *Collapse of the Global Order on Drugs: From the UNGASS 2016 to Review 2019* (Bingley: Emerald Publishing, 2018).

64. See, for example, Kevin Rudd, 'Wresting Order from Chaos,' *The World Today,* June–July 2015, 14–15.

65. Tom Blickman, 'The Elephant in the Room: Cannabis in the International Drug Control Regime,' in *Collapse of the Global Order on Drugs: From the UNGASS 2016 to Review,* ed. Axel Klein and Blaine Stothard (Bingley: Emerald Publishing, 2018), 103.

66. Emily Crick, Heather J. Haase and David Bewley-Taylor, *Legally Regulated Cannabis Markets in the US: Implications and possibilities* (Swansea: Global Drug Policy Observatory, 2013), https://www.tni.org/files/gdpo1.pdf.

67. Emily Crick, Mark Cooke and David Bewley-Taylor, *Selling cannabis regulation: Learning from Ballot Initiatives in the United States in 2012* (Swansea: Global Drug

Policy Observatory, 2014), https://www.tni.org/files/publication-downloads/gdpo6.pdf.

68.   David Bewley-Taylor, *International Drug Control.*

69.   Blickman, 'The Elephant in the Room,' 103.

70.   IDPC, *The 2018 Commission on Narcotic Drugs. Report of Proceedings* (London: IDPC, 2018), 31, http://fileserver.idpc.net/library/CND-Proceedings-Report-2018_18.06.pdf.

4. A FORWARD MARCH HALTED

1.   Organization of American States (OAS), *The OAS Drug Report: 16 Months of Debates and Consensus*, OEA/Ser.D/XXV.4.1 (Washington D.C.: OAS, 2013), https://www.oas.org/docs/publications/LayoutPubgAGDrogas-ENG-29-9.pdf.

2.   Felipe Calderón, 'Speech at the 67th session of the United Nations General Assembly' (speech, UN headquarters, New York, September 26, 2012), http://webtv.un.org/meetings-events/general-assembly/general-debate/67th-session/watch/mexico-general-debate-67th-session/1862962046001.

3.   United Nations General Assembly, 'General Debate of the 67th Session 25 September 2012 to 1 October 2012,' last modified October 2012, https://gadebate.un.org/en/sessions-archive/67.

4.   The review was expected to include an assessment of the achievements and challenges in countering the world drug problem, within the framework of the three international drug control conventions and other relevant United Nations instruments. The notion of the 'drug problem' as defined by Peter Reuter and Robert MacCoun refers to the various dimensions that drugs and drug policy entail. Peter Reuter and Robert MacCoun, *Drug War Heresies*, Cambridge: Cambridge University Press, 2002. See also United Nations General Assembly, *Resolution 67/193. International Cooperation against the world drug problem*, A/RES/67/193 (New York, April 23, 2013), https://undocs.org/en/A/RES/67/193. See also *Political Declaration and Plan of Action on International Cooperation towards an Integrated and Balanced Strategy to Counter the World Drug Problem*, adopted by the General Assembly in its resolution 64/182 of December 18, 2009. See Official Records of the Economic and Social Council, 2009, Supplement No. 8 (E/2009/28), chap. I, sect. C.

5.   The IDCR rests on three main conventions—the 1961 Single Convention on Narcotic Drugs (as amended by the 1972 Protocol); the 1971 Convention on Psychotropic Substances and the 1988 Convention against Illicit Traffic in Narcotic Drugs and Psychotropic Substances—and has been managed by a number of bureaucratic structures, including the Commission on Narcotic Drugs (CND), the International Narcotics Control Board (INCB), and the United Nations Office on Drugs and Crime (UNODC). From at least the 1940s, the international drug control bureaucracy responsible for overseeing the implementation of the drug control regime has been heavily committed to the prohibition norm and to the US bias in favor of supply control. William B. McAllister, *Drug Diplomacy in the Twentieth Century* (London: Routledge, 2000), 100–39, 150; David Bewley-Taylor,

The US and International Drug Control 1909–1997 (London: Continuum, 2001), 43; David Bewley-Taylor, *International Drug Control. Consensus Fractured* (Cambridge: Cambridge University Press, 2012), 3–6.

6. Sara Miller Llana, 'Biden in Honduras: US Drug Policy Under Scrutiny,' *Christian Science Monitor*, March 6, 2012, http://www.csmonitor.com/World/Americas/2012/0306/Biden-in-Honduras-US-drug-policy-under-scrutiny; 'Biden ratifica postura de EU contra legalización de las drogas,' *El Universal*, March 4, 2012, http://archivo.eluniversal.com.mx/notas/834187.html; Luis Prados, 'El presidente de México pide a EE UU mayor control del tráfico de armas,' *El País*, March 5, 2012, http://internacional.elpais.com/internacional/2012/03/06/actualidad/1331000365_099669.html.

7. Amy Dudley, 'Vice President Biden Travels to Mexico and Honduras,' *The White House President Barak Obama*, March 7, 2012, https://obamawhitehouse.archives.gov/blog/2012/03/07/vice-president-biden-travels-mexico-and-honduras; 'Fracasa cumbre centroamericana para despenalizar la droga,' *Iberoamérica Central de Noticias*, March 26, 2012, http://www.icndiario.com/2012/03/26/fracasa-cumbre-centroamericana-para-despenalizar-la-droga/.

8. Interviews carried out in New York with Mexican diplomats and drug policy experts in the spring of 2014, spring 2016 and spring 2019.

9. In addition to securing the convening of UNGASS in 2016 in its paragraph 44, the 2012 annual omnibus resolution on drug policy, which was sponsored by Mexico and co-sponsored by 95 countries, included significant references to carry out drug control efforts in 'full conformity with the purposes and principles of the UN Charter, the Universal Declaration of Human Rights and human rights and fundamental freedoms' more generally. Although inserted in a mostly orthodox drug-control text, equally significant were the references to HIV prevention and treatment, including through 'care for injecting drug users' and the recognition of the important role played by civil society in addressing the world drug problem and the invitation to civil society to play a role in the design and implementation of drug demand and supply reduction programs. See United Nations General Assembly, *Resolution 67/193.*

10. United Nations General Assembly, *Resolution 68/197. International Cooperation against the world drug problem*, A/RES/68/197 (New York, February 18, 2014), https://undocs.org/en/A/RES/68/197. Resolution 57/5, in turn, reaffirmed the status of the CND as 'principal United Nations policymaking body on drug-related issues' and urged member states who had not done so, to consider ratifying or accessing the three conventions. See Commission on Narcotic Drugs, *Resolution 57/5: Special Session of the General Assembly on the world drug problem to be held in 2016* (Vienna: CND, 2014), https://www.unodc.org/documents/ungass2016/Background/CND_Res_57_5.pdf.

11. For a thorough analysis of the preparatory works leading to UNGASS 2016 and the control exerted by the drug control system see Mónica Serrano, *El Debate de la Sesión Especial de la Asamblea General de la Organización de las Naciones Unidas sobre el Problema Mundial de las Drogas de 2016* (Mexico City: Instituto Belisario Domínguez - Senado de la República, 2018).

12. Described by Guatemalan experts as 'a master of manipulation' Otto Pérez Molina had been elected president in 2011. Significantly, one of the trials involving Pérez Molina was shaped by prosecutors as a case of state capture. Then in 2016 the International Commission Against Impunity in Guatemala (CICIG) identified Pérez Molina's political party, Partido Patriota, as a criminal structure that had taken over state institutions. Francisco Goldman, 'From President to Prison: Otto Pérez Molina and a Day for Hope in Guatemala,' *The New Yorker*, September 4, 2015, https://www.newyorker.com/news/news-desk/from-president-to-prison-otto-perez-molina-and-a-day-for-hope-in-guatemala; Álvaro Murillo, 'Miguel Angel Gálvez. Juez a cargo del proceso de Otto Pérez Molina,' *El País*, November 13, 2015, http://internacional.elpais.com/internacional/2015/11/12/actualidad/1447364418_362897.html; José Elías, 'El expresidente de Guatemala, Otto Pérez, ligado a proceso por un nuevo caso de corrupción,' *El País*, July 27, 2016, http://internacional.elpais.com/internacional/2016/07/28/america/1469668078_832754.html; 'Corruption in Guatemala. Bad apples everywhere,' *The Economist*, June 11, 2016, http://www.economist.com/news/americas/21700418-ousted-president-accused-masterminding-kleptocracy-bad-apples-everywhere.

13. United Nations General Assembly, *Resolution 69/200. Special session of the General Assembly on the world drug problem to be held in 2016*, A/RES/69/200 (New York, January 26, 2015), https://undocs.org/en/A/RES/69/200; United Nations General Assembly, *Resolution 69/201. International cooperation against the world drug problem*, A/RES/69/201 (New York, February 12, 2015), https://undocs.org/A/RES/69/201.

14. The proposed five round tables would focus on: 1) Demand reduction and related measures, including prevention and treatment, health-related issues and availability of controlled substances for medical and scientific purposes; 2) Supply reduction and related measures, including responses to drug-related crime, countering money laundering and judicial cooperation promotion, as referred to in the CND resolution, 'drugs and crime;' 3) Cross-cutting issues: drugs and human rights, youth, women, children and communities; 4) Cross-cutting issues: new challenges, threats and realities in preventing and addressing the world drug problem in compliance with relevant international law, including the three drug control conventions, while strengthening the principle of common and shared responsibility and international cooperation and 5) Alternative development: regional, interregional and international cooperation on development-oriented balanced drug control policy and socioeconomic issues. See Commission on Narcotic Drugs, *Resolution 58/8: Special Session of the General Assembly on the World Drug Problem to be held in 2016* (Vienna: CND, 2014), https://www.unodc.org/documents/ungass2016/Background/CND_Resolution_58_8.pdf.

15. 'Declaración de Guatemala. CND, 9 de marzo 2014' (statement of the Guatemalan delegation at the Commission on Narcotic Drugs, March 9, 2014), https://www.unodc.org/documents/commissions/CND/CND_Sessions/CND_58/UNGASS_Statements/UNGASS_Statements_9March_Evening/58_Guatemala.pdf.

16. Yesid Reyes, 'Palabras del Doctor Yesid Reyes, Ministro de Justicia y del Derecho de Colombia, con ocasión del segmento especial del 58 periodo ordinario de sesiones de la comisión de estupefacientes' (speech delivered by Dr Yesid Reyes at the fifty-eighth session of the CND, Vienna, March 2015), https://www.unodc.org/documents/commissions/CND/CND_Sessions/CND_58/UNGASS_Statements/07_Colombia.pdf.

17. Juan Manuel Gómez Robledo, 'Statement on Behalf of the Government of Mexico by Amb. Juan Manuel Gómez Robledo, Undersecretary of Foreign Affairs for Multilateral Issues and Human Rights: Special Segment on preparations for UNGASS 2016' (statement delivered at the fifty-eighth session of the CND, Vienna, March 9, 2015), https://www.unodc.org/documents/commissions/CND/CND_Sessions/CND_58/UNGASS_Statements/UNGASS_Statements_9March_PM/16_Mexico_English.pdf.

18. William R. Brownfield, 'Assistant Secretary William R. Brownfield, Secretary's Special Remarks for the Opening of the Commission on Narcotic Drugs (CND) Special Segment on the Preparations for the UN General Assembly on the World Drug Problem, High-Level Segment' (speech delivered at the CND, Vienna, March 9, 2015), https://www.unodc.org/documents/commissions/CND/CND_Sessions/CND_58/UNGASS_Statements/13_USA.pdf.

19. United Nations Economic and Social Council, *Preparations for the special session of the General Assembly on the world drug problem: Revised draft resolution submitted by the Chair,* E/CN.7/2016/L.12/Rev.1* (Vienna: CND, 2016), https://undocs.org/E/CN.7/2016/L.12/Rev.1.

20. United Nations General Assembly, *Resolution S-30/1. Our Joint Commitment to Effectively Addressing and Countering the World Drug Problem*, A/RES/S-30/1 (New York, May 4, 2016), https://www.incb.org/documents/PRECURSORS/Resolutions-Precursors/GA-UNGASS-Res_S-30-1_2016.pdf.

21. The outcome document includes a 4-page opening section, and seven sections on operational recommendations on: 1) demand reduction and related measures, including prevention and treatment, as well as other health-related issues; 2) ensuring the availability of and access to controlled substances exclusively for medical and scientific purposes, while preventing their diversion; 3) supply reduction and related measures; effective law enforcement, responses to drug-related crime; and countering money laundering and promoting judicial cooperation; 4) on cross-cutting issues: drugs and human rights, youth, children, women and communities; 5) on cross-cutting issues in addressing and countering the world drug problem: evolving reality, trends and existing circumstances, emerging and persistent challenges and threats, including new psychotropic substances; 6) strengthening international cooperation based on the principle of common and shared responsibility and 7) alternative development; regional interregional and international cooperation on development-oriented balanced drug control policy, and socioeconomic-issues. United Nations General Assembly, *Resolution S-30/1.*

22. Ibid.

23. Ibid., paragraph k) and l), p. 10. f

24. Ibid., paragraph 3, p. 8 and paragraphs d) and f)., p. 9.

25. Ibid., 4–7.

26. Ibid., 2 and 4.

27. United Nations General Assembly, *Thirtieth special session: 4th plenary meeting*, A/S-30/PV.4 (New York, April 20, 2016), 14, https://undocs.org/en/A/S-30/PV.4.

28. United Nations General Assembly, *Thirtieth special session: 6th plenary meeting*, A/S-30/PV.6 (New York, April 21, 2016), 2, https://undocs.org/en/A/S-30/PV.6https://www.un.org/en/ga/search/view_doc.asp?symbol=A/S-30/PV.6.

29. United Nations General Assembly, *Thirtieth special session: 2nd plenary meeting*, A/S-30/PV.2 (New York, April 19, 2016), 12, https://undocs.org/en/A/S-30/PV.2.

30. United Nations General Assembly, *Thirtieth special session: 3rd plenary meeting*, A/S-30/PV.3 (New York, April 20, 2016), 28, https://undocs.org/en/A/S-30/PV.3.

31. Presidencia de la República de Colombia, 'Palabras del presidente de la República de Colombia, Juan Manuel Santos en la XXX Sesión Especial de la Asamblea General de la ONU sobre el problema mundial de las drogas' (intervention by President of the Republic of Colombia, Juan Manuel Santos at the thirtieth special session of the UN General Assembly on the world drug problem, April 21, 2016), http://es.presidencia.gov.co/discursos/160421-Palabras-del-Presidente-Juan-Manuel-Santos-en-la-XXX-Sesion-Especial-de-la-Asamblea-de-la-Organizacion-de-las-Naciones-Unidas-sobre-el-Problema-Mundial-de-las-Drogas;   United Nations General Assembly, *Thirtieth special session: 5th plenary meeting*, A/S-30/PV.5 (New York, April 21, 2016), https://undocs.org/en/A/S-30/PV.5.

32. Nieto addressed to Chief of States, UN Under-Secretary General, representatives of international and regional organizations, of UN agencies and representatives from civil society; United Nations General Assembly, *Thirtieth special session: 1st plenary meeting*, A/S-30/PV.1 (New York, April 19, 2016), 18, https://undocs.org/en/A/S-30/PV.1.

33. Presidencia de la República, 'Palabras del presidente de la República de Colombia.'

5. SOUTH AMERICA

1.   Richard O'Mara and Sandy Banisky, '80 People Try to Slay a Monster: Drug Conference Draws Participants from 18 Countries,' *Baltimore Sun,* November 17, 1993, http://articles.baltimoresun.com/1993-11-17/news/1993321086_1_legalization-of-drugs-colombia-national-drug.

2.   James Brooke, 'Colombians Press for the Legalization of Cocaine,' *The New York Times*, February 20, 1994, http://www.nytimes.com/1994/02/20/world/colombians-press-for-the-legalization-of-cocaine.html.

3.   El Tiempo, 'Colombia Pidió Autonomía en Política de Drogas,' *El Tiempo,* May 8, 2015, http://www.eltiempo.com/politica/justicia/colombia-pidio-autonomia-en-politica-de-drogas/15717615.

4.   Critical voices to the drug policy regime have abounded. Even at the time de Greiff appeared in Baltimore intellectuals and civil society actors made statements proposing radical changes in drug policy. Presidents like Virgilio Barco in Colombia (1986–90) at times raised concerns about the unevenness of drug policy pressure

on producer countries. The key difference, however, is that incumbent government authorities avoided positions like these publicly.

5. Available statistics in the United States suggest an increase in the monthly prevalence of cocaine use and of cocaine overdoses (excluding opioids) since 2014. See Beau Kilmer and Gregory Midgette, 'Mixed Messages: Is Cocaine Consumption in the U.S. Going Up or Down?' *The Rand Blog,* April 28, 2017, https://www.rand.org/blog/2017/04/mixed-messages-is-cocaine-consumption-in-the-us-going.html.

6. These calculations are based on data reported in UNODC's 2010 and 2014 World Drug Reports, yet the exact size of the changes remains controversial because the measurement of coca crops and cocaine production potential varies over time and between institutions. Statistics can be politicized as reflected in assessments of cocaine production potential in Bolivia. See Washington Office on Latin America, 'UN and US Cocaine Estimates Contradict Each Other,' July 31, 2012, http://www.wola.org/commentary/un_and_us_estimates_for_cocaine_production_contradict_each_other; Edward Fox, 'US Report on Colombia Cocaine Raises More Questions than Answers,' *Insight Crime,* August 1, 2012, http://www.insightcrime.org/news-analysis/us-report-on-colombia-cocaine-production-raises-more-questions-than-answers.

7. Michel Misse, 'Illegal Markets, Protection Rackets and Organized Crime in Rio de Janeiro,' *Estudos Avançados* 21, no. 61 (2007): 139–57.

8. Lina Britto, *Marijuana Boom: The Rise and Fall of Colombia's First Drug Paradise.* (Santa Barbara: University of California Press, 2020); Lina Britto, 'A Trafficker's Paradise: The "War on Drugs" and the New Cold War in Colombia,' *Contemporánea* 1, vol. 1 (2010): 159–77.

9. International Narcotics Control Board (INCB), *Report of the International Narcotics Control Board for 2014,* E/INCB/2014/1 (Vienna: United Nations, 2015), 63.

10. UNODC, *World Drug Report 2013* (Vienna: United Nations, 2014) 30. UNODC and Gobierno de Colombia, *Monitoreo de Cultivos de Coca 2014* (Bogotá: UNODC, 2015), 66.

11. UNODC, *México Monitoreo de Cultivos de Amapola 2015–2016 y 2016–2017* (Ciudad de Mexico: UNODC, 2018).

12. Maria Fernanda Boidi et al., 'Marijuana Legalization in Uruguay and Beyond,' (Miami: Florida International University, Latin America and Caribbean Center, 2015).

13. Michel Misse and Joana D. Vargas, 'Drug Use and Trafficking in Rio de Janeiro,' *Vibrant-Virtual Brazilian Anthropology* 7, no. 2 (2010): 88–108.

14. UNODC, *World Drug Report 2016* (Vienna: United Nations, 2016), 13.

15. Angélica Durán-Martínez, 'Drugs around the Corner: Domestic Drug Markets and Violence in Colombia and Mexico,' *Latin American Politics and Society* 57, no. 3 (2015): 122–46; Isaac De León Beltrán and Juan Carlos Garzón Vergara, *Urban Drug Markets and Zones of Impunity in Colombia* (Amsterdam: TNI, 2014).

16. John Collins, 'The Economics of a New Global Strategy,' in *Ending the Drug Wars: Report of the LSE Expert Group on the Economics of Drug Policy,* ed. John Collins (London: LSE, 2014), 9, https://www.lse.ac.uk/ideas/Assets/Documents/reports/LSE-IDEAS-Ending-the-Drug-Wars.pdf.

17. Mise, 'Illegal Markets.'

18. Angélica Durán-Martínez, *The Politics of Drug Violence: Criminals, Cops and Politicians in Colombia and Mexico* (New York: Oxford University Press, 2018).

19. Peter Andreas and Angélica Durán-Martínez, 'The International Politics of Illicit Trade in the Americas,' in *Routledge Handbook of Latin America in the World*, edited by Jorge Dominguez and Ana Covarrubias (New York: Routledge, 2014), 376–90.

20. Juan Carlos Garzón Vergara, *Tough on the Weak, Weak on the Tough: Drug Laws and Policing*, (Washington D.C.: Woodrow Wilson Center, Latin American Program, 2015).

21. David Gagne, 'Police Violence Continues to Plague Brazil: Report,' *Insight Crime*, November 11, 2014, http://www.insightcrime.org/news-analysis/police-violence-continues-to-plague-brazil-report.

22. Misse, 'Illegal Markets;' Misse and Vargas, 'Drug Use.'

23. Vanda Felbab-Brown, 'The Coca Connection: Conflict and Drugs in Colombia and Peru,' *Journal of Conflict Studies* 25, no. 2 (2005): 104–28.

24. Adam Isacson, 'The US Military in the War on Drugs,' in *Drugs and Democracy in Latin America: The Impact of US Policy*, ed. Coletta Youngers and Eileen Rosin (Boulder: Lynne Rienner Publishers, 2005), 27. The Leahy Amendment, named after his sponsor, is a law that prohibits the US Departments of State and Defense from providing military assistance to foreign military units engaged in human rights violations.

25. Isaias Rojas-Perez, 'Peru: Drug Control Policy, Human Rights and Democracy,' in *Drugs and Democracy in Latin America: The Impact of US Policy*, ed. Coletta Youngers and Eileen Rosin (Boulder: Lynne Rienner Publishers, 2005), 198.

26. Rodrigo Uprimny, Diana Guzmán and Jorge Parra, *Addicted to Punishment: The Disproportionality of Drug Laws in Latin America* (Bogotá: Dejusticia, 2012).

27. Ibid., 24.

28. Alejandro Madrazo Lajous, 'The Constitutional Costs of the War on Drugs,' in *Ending the Drug Wars: Report of the LSE Expert Group on the Economics of Drug Policy*, ed. John Collins (London: LSE, 2014), 56, https://www.lse.ac.uk/ideas/Assets/Documents/reports/LSE-IDEAS-Ending-the-Drug-Wars.pdf.

29. Pien Metaal and Coletta Youngers, eds., *Systems Overload: Drug Laws and Prisons in Latin America* (Amsterdam: TNI; Washington D.C.: WOLA, 2011).

30. Raúl Alejandro Corda, 'Imprisonment for Drug Related Offenses in Argentina,' in *Systems Overload: Drug Laws and Prisons in Latin America*, ed. Pien Metaal and Coletta Youngers (Amsterdam: TNI; Washington D.C.: WOLA, 2011).

31. Catalina Pérez Correa and Coletta Youngers, *En Busca de los Derechos: Usuarios de Drogas y Las Respuestas Estatales en América Latina* (Mexico City: Colectivo de Estudios de Droga y de Derecho, 2014).

32. Vanda Felbab-Brown et al., *Assessment of the Implementation of the United States Government's Support for Plan Colombia's Illicit Crop Reduction Components* (Washington D.C.: USAID Management Systems International, 2009).

33. Daniel Mejía and Pascual Restrepo, *The Economics of the War on Illegal Drug Production and Trafficking*, Documento CEDE no. 54 (Bogotá: Universidad de los Andes, 2013).

34. Ibid.

35. Felbab-Brown et al., *Assessment*.

36. Daniel Mejía, Pascual Restrepo and Sandra Rozo, 'On the Effectiveness of Supply Reduction Efforts in Drug Producing Countries: Evidence from Colombia' (unpublished manuscript, Universidad de los Andes, 2013).

37. Paola Fajardo-Heyward, 'Understanding the Effect of Security Assistance on Human Rights: The Case of Plan Colombia,' *The Latin Americanist* 59, no. 2 (2015): 3–27.

38. Oeindrila Dube and Suresh Naidu, 'Bases, Bullets and Ballots: The Effect of US Military Aid on Political Conflict in Colombia' (working paper No. w20213, National Bureau of Economic Research, Cambridge, MA, 2014).

39. Fredy Rivera Vélez, 'Ecuador: Untangling the Drug War,' in *Drugs and Democracy in Latin America: The Impact of US Policy*, ed. Coletta Youngers and Eileen Rosin (Boulder: Lynne Rienner Publishers, 2005), 231–61.

40. Ecuador, for example, shares social and geographic conditions for coca cultivation but it has not developed large-scale coca crops, even though it plays other roles in the drug trafficking chain (Rivera Vélez, 'Ecuador').

41. María Victoria Llorente and Rodolfo Escobedo, *Lo que Esconden las Cifras: En 2014 Bajaron los Homicidios, Pero Persisten las Dinámicas Criminales* (Bogotá: Fundación Ideas para la Paz, 2015), http://www.ideaspaz.org/publications/posts/1123.

42. Jorge Parra, '20 Años de la Despenalización de la Dosis Personal,' *La Silla Vacía,* May 12, 2014, http://lasillavacia.com/node/47362.

43. Rivera Vélez, 'Ecuador.'

44. Luciana Boiteaux, 'Drugs and Prisons: The Repression of Drugs and the Increase of the Brazilian Penitentiary Population,' in *Systems Overload: Drug Laws and Prisons in Latin America,* ed. Pien Metaal and Coletta Youngers (Amsterdam: TNI; Washington D.C.: WOLA, 2011), 30–9.

45. Latin American Commission on Drugs and Democracy, *Drugs and Democracy: Toward a Paradigm Shift* (Geneva: Latin American Commission on Drugs and Democracy, 2009).

46. Daniel Mejía and Pascual Restrepo, 'Why is Strict Prohibition Collapsing? A Perspective from Producer and Transit Countries,' in *Ending the Drug Wars: Report of the LSE Expert Group on the Economics of Drug Policy*, ed. John Collins (London: LSE, 2014), https://www.lse.ac.uk/ideas/Assets/Documents/reports/LSE-IDEAS-Ending-the-Drug-Wars.pdf.

47. Andy Baker and Kenneth F. Greene, 'The Latin American Left's Mandate: Free-Market Policies and Issue Voting in New Democracies,' *World Politics* 63, no. 1 (2011): 43–77.

48. Javier Corrales, 'The Many Lefts of Latin America,' *Foreign Policy,* November–December 2006.

49. Marc Eric Williams, 'The United States and Latin America,' in *Handbook of Latin America in the World*, ed. Ana Covarrubias and Jorge Dominguez (New York: Routledge, 2014) 199–211.

50. United Nations Development Programme (UNDP), *Human Development Report 2013-2014: Citizen Security with a Human Face: Evidence and proposals for Latin America* (New York: UNDP, 2013).

51. Comisión Asesora para la Política de Drogas en Colombia, *Lineamientos para un Nuevo Enfoque de la Política de Drogas en Colombia. Informe Final*, Bogotá, May 2015.

52. Martin Jelsma, 'INCB vs Uruguay: The Art of Diplomacy,' *TNI Weblog*, December 17, 2013, http://druglawreform.info/en/weblog/item/5214-incb-vs-uruguay-the-art-of-diplomacy#.UrDlNx-34hc.twitter; Boidi et al., 'Marijuana;' International Narcotics Control Board, *Report*.

53. Boidi et al., 'Marijuana.'

54. José Miguel Cruz, Rosario Queirolo, and María Fernanda Boidi, 'Determinants of Public Support for Marijuana Legalization in Uruguay, the United States, and El Salvador,' *Journal of Drug Issues* 46, no. 4 (2016): 308–25.

55. 'Latin America Rethinks Drug Policies,' *The New York Times*, May 26, 2015, http://www.nytimes.com/2015/05/26/opinion/latin-america-rethinks-drug-policies.html?_r=1.

56. Sara Ortiz, 'Las Mulas Podrán Ser Consideradas Víctimas,' *El Comercio*, April 24, 2014, http://www.elcomercio.com/actualidad/seguridad/mulas-podran-consideradas-victimas.html.

57. Coletta Youngers, 'Shifts in Cultivation, Usage Put Bolivia's Coca Policy at the Crossroads,' *World Politics Review*, December 5, 2013.

58. Geoffrey Ramsey, 'The Changing Face of Sao Paulo's "Crackland",' *InSight Crime*, April 29, 2014, http://www.insightcrime.org/news-analysis/the-changing-face-sao-paulos-crackland.

59. Fernando Medina, 'Más Policías para Intentar Frenar el Microtráfico,' *El Comercio*, September 22, 2015, http://www.elcomercio.com/actualidad/policias-microtrafico-droga-ecuador.html.

60. 'Golpeada por la Droga Argentina Observa la Experiencia Uruguaya,' *El Universal*, May 3, 2014, https://www.eluniversal.com.co/mundo/golpeada-por-la-droga-argentina-observa-la-experiencia-uruguaya-158627-HXEU251017.

61. The decision perhaps reflected his lack of trust in police forces that had been involved in an insurrection against him and were perceived as largely corrupt, see Geoffrey Ramsey, 'Ecuador to Expand Military Role in Fighting Crime,' *InSight Crime*, April 30, 2012, http://www.insightcrime.org/news-analysis/ecuador-to-expand-militarys-role-in-fighting-crime.

62. Geoffrey Ramsey, 'Ecuador Cracks Down on Inhumane Drug Treatment,' *The Pan-American Post*, November 13, 2013, http://www.thepanamericanpost.com/2013/11/ecuador-cracks-down-on-inhumane-drug.html.

63. José Miguel Cruz, María Fernanda Boidi, and Rosario Queirolo, 'The status of support for cannabis regulation in Uruguay 4 years after reform: Evidence from public opinion surveys,' *Drug and Alcohol Review* 37, no. 1 (2018): 429–34.

64. Asuntos del Sur - Observatorio Latinoamericano de Políticas de Drogas y Opinión Pública, *Estudio 2014–2015: Estudio Anual sobre Políticas de Drogas y Opinión Publica, América Latina* (Santiago de Chile: Asuntos del Sur, 2015). To my knowledge more recent cross-national surveys on drug issues are not available.

65. UNDP, *Human Development Report 2013–2014*.

66. Asuntos del Sur, *Estudio 2014–2015*.

67.   Fundación Ideas para la Paz, *Legalización de la marihuana medicinal: ¿Qué opinan los colombianos?* (Bogotá: FIP, 2014), http://cdn.ideaspaz.org/media/website/document/5487d40ca0e99.pdf.

68.   Asuntos del Sur, *Estudio 2014–2015*.

69.   Adam Dubove, 'Argentina's Presidential Hopefuls Aim to Further Militarize Drug War,' *The Pan-American Post*, September 25, 2015, http://panampost.com/adam-dubove/2015/09/25/argentinas-presidential-hopefuls-aim-to-further-militarize-drug-war/.

70.   INCB, *Report*.

71.   Geoffrey Ramsey, 'Making Rio's Pacification Work: The Limits of UPP Social,' *InSight Crime,* August 22, 2014, http://www.insightcrime.org/news-analysis/rio-pacification-limits-upp-social; Nicole Froio, 'Brazil's Favelas are in Big Trouble, Despite the World Cup Marketing Push,' *The Guardian*, May 18, 2014, http://www.theguardian.com/commentisfree/2014/may/18/brazil-favelas-big-trouble-world-cup-marketing-police-abuse-killings-security.

72.   Mark Kleiman, 'Surgical strikes in the drug wars: smarter policies for both sides of the border,' *Foreign Affairs* 90, vol. 5 (2011): 89–101; Benjamin Lessing, *Making Peace and Drug Wars: Crackdowns and Cartels in Latin America* (New York: Cambridge University Press, 2018).

6. MEXICO AND CENTRAL AMERICA

1.   The chapter deals exclusively with Mexico and Central America. The Caribbean has been examined superficially in the first part when the global drug circuits are analyzed.

2.   This chapter uses the definition as: Julie Marie Bunck and Michael Ross Fowler, *Bribes, Bullets and Intimidation: Drug Trafficking and the Law in Central America* (Pennsylvania: Pennsylvania State University Press, 2012), 1. Still, Guatemala and Belize produce some drugs. More on it in the next section.

3.   Bunck and Fowler, *Bribes,* 16.

4.   Bureau for International Narcotics and Law Enforcement Affairs, *2015 International Narcotics Control Strategy Report: Volume I: Drug and Chemical Control* (Washington D.C.: U.S. Department of State, 2015), 166.

5.   U.S. Department of Justice Drug Enforcement Administration, *2015 National Drug Threat Assessment* (Washington D.C.: DOJ, 2015), vi.

6.   Edward Allen Heath, 'Mexican Opium Eradication Campaign' (unpublished master's thesis, California State University, 1981), 36.

7.   Stephen S. Dudley, *Transnational Crime in Mexico and Central America: Its Evolution and Role in International Migration* (Washington D.C.: Migration Policy Institute, 2012).

8.   José Miguel Cruz, 'The Root Causes of the Central American Crisis,' *Current History* 114, no. 769 (2015): 43.

9.   Ivan Briscoe and Martín Rodríguez Pellecer, *A State under Siege: Elites, Criminal Networks and Institutional Reform in Guatemala* (The Hague: Netherlands Institute of International Relations, 2010), 3.

10. Julie López, 'Guatemala's Crossroads: The Democratization of Violence and Second Chances,' in *Organized Crime in Central America: The Northern Triangle*, ed. Eric E. Olson and Cynthia Arnson (Washington D.C.: Woodrow Wilson Center, 2011), 140–242.

11. Dudley, *Transnational Crime,* 7–8.

12. Cruz, 'The Root Causes.'

13. Dennis Rodgers, Robert Muggah, and Chris Stevenson, *Gangs of Central America: Causes, Costs, and Interventions* (Geneva: Small Arms Survey, 2009), 9.

14. Thomas W. Ward, *Gangsters without Borders: An Ethnography of a Salvadoran Street Gang* (Oxford: Oxford University Press, 2012).

15. Ana Arana, 'How the Street Gangs Took Central America,' *Foreign Affairs*, June 2005; Max Manwaring, *Street Gangs: The New Urban Insurgency* (Carlisle: Strategic Studies Institute, 2005); Tom Diaz, *No Boundaries: Transnational Latino Gangs and American Law Enforcement* (Ann Arbor: The University of Michigan Press, 2009).

16. International Narcotics Control Board (INCB), *Report of the International Narcotics Control Board for 2019*, E/INCB/2019/1 (Vienna: United Nations, 2020), 64.

17. U.S. Department of Justice Drug Enforcement Administration, *2015 National Drug Threat Assessment* (Washington D.C.: DOJ, 2015), 3.

18. U.S. Department of Justice Drug Enforcement Administration, *2018 National Drug Threat Assessment* (Washington D.C.: DOJ, 2018), 87.

19. Some scholars have suggested that around 15 per cent and 26 per cent of drug export revenues are attributable to cannabis. See: Beau Kilmer et al., *Reducing Drug Trafficking Revenues and Violence in Mexico: Would Legalizing Marijuana in California Help?* (Santa Monica: RAND, 2010), 3.

20. Organization of American States (OAS), 'Report on Drug use in the Americas 2019,' (OAS 2019).

21. INCB, *Report of the International Narcotics Control Board for 2019*, 70. Like in the past, Jamaica remains the largest producer and exporter of cannabis in Central America and the Caribbean.

22. Romain Le Cour Grandmaison, Nathaniel Morris and Benjamin Smith, 'The last harvest? From the US fentanyl boom to the Mexican Opium Crisis,' *Journal of Illicit Economies and Development* 1, no. 3 (2019): 312–29.

23. Bunck and Fowler, *Bribes*, 210–11.

24. Ibid., 211.

25. U.S. Department of Justice Drug Enforcement Administration, *2015 National Drug Threat Assessment*, 61.

26. UNODC, *Transnational Organized Crime in Central America and the Caribbean: A Threat Assessment* (Vienna: UNODC, 2012), 19.

27. INCB, *Report of the International Narcotics Control Board for 2019*, 71.

28. Bureau for International Narcotics and Law Enforcement Affairs, *2020 International Narcotics Control Strategy Report: Volume I: Drug and Chemical Control* (Washington D.C.: U.S. Department of State, 2020), 101.

29. U. S. Department of Justice Drug Enforcement Administration, *2015 National Drug Threat Assessment*, 45.

30. Kamala D. Harris, *Gangs Beyond Borders: California and the Fight Against Transnational Organized Crime* (Sacramento: California Attorney General, 2014).

31.   Bureau for International Narcotics and Law Enforcement Affairs, *2020 International Narcotics Control Strategy Report*, 83.

32.   U.S. Department of Justice Drug Enforcement Administration, *2014 National Drug Threat Assessment* (Washington D.C.: DOJ, 2014), 19.

33.   U.S. Department of Justice Drug Enforcement Administration, *2018 National Drug Threat Assessment*, 33.

34.   Peter Meyer, *U.S. Strategy for Engagement in Central America: Policy Issues for Congress* (Washington D.C.: Congressional Research Service, 2019), 4.

35.   Eric E. Olson, ed., *Crime and Violence in Central America's Northern Triangle: How U.S. Policy Responses Are Helping, Hurting, and Can Be Improved* (Washington D.C.: Woodrow Wilson Center, 2015), 6–7.

36.   Ibid., 4–5.

37.   Congressional Research Service, *U.S. Strategy for Engagement in Central America: Policy issues for Congress* (Washington D.C., updated November 12, 2019).

38.   Congressional Research Service, *Mexico: Evolution of the Mérida Initiative, 2007–2020* (Washington D.C., updated February 19, 2020).

39.   U.S. Agency for International Development, *U.S. Overseas Loans and Grants: Obligations and Loan Authorizations: July 1, 1945 – September 30, 2012* (Washington D.C.: USAID, 2012).

40.   Carlos A. Pérez Ricart, 'The Role of the DEA in the Emergence of the Field of Anti-narcotics Policing in Latin America,' *Global Governance* 24, no. 2 (2018): 171–93.

41.   Bureau for International Narcotics and Law Enforcement Affairs, *2020 International Narcotics Control Strategy Report*, 37.

42.   Eric E. Olson and Katheryn Moffat, 'Executive Summary,' in *Crime and Violence in Central America's Northern Triangle: How U.S. Policy Responses Are Helping, Hurting, and Can Be Improved*, ed. Eric E. Olson (Washington D.C.: Woodrow Wilson Center, 2015), 1–17.

43.   Haeyoun Park, 'Children at the Border,' *The New York Times*, October 24, 2014.

44.   José Miguel Cruz, 'The Real Failure in Central America,' *Miami Herald*, July 24, 2014.

45.   World Bank, *Crime and Violence in Central America: A Development Challenge*, (Washington D.C.: World Bank, 2011), 32.

46.   Beatriz Caiuby Labate and Pamela Ruiz Flores López, 'Critical Reflections on the National Addiction Surveys (ENAs) in Mexico,' *Drugs: Education, Prevention and Policy* 21, no. 6 (2014): 427–33.

47.   See Caiuby Labate and Ruiz Flores López, 'Critical Reflections.'

48.   Comisión Nacional contra las Adicciones, *Encuesta Nacional de Consumo de Drogas, Alcohol y Tabaco, ENCODAT 2016-2017* (Mexico City: Gobierno de México, 2017), 49.

49.   INCB, *Report of the International Narcotics Control Board for 2019*, 23.

50.   Ibid., 22.

51.   Ibid., 35.

52.   Ibid., 70.

53.   Including nitroethane, monomethylamine, phenylacetic acid, its salts and derivatives, and methylamine. Additionally, in 2014 the Federal Government

amended its Health Act and included midazolam, mephedrone, piperazine and synthetic cannabinoids as psychotropic substances subject to regulation.

54. See: Jonathan P. Caulkins, 'Effects of Prohibition, Enforcement and Interdiction on Drug Use,' in *Ending the Drug Wars: Report of the LSE Expert Group on the Economics of Drug Policy*, ed. John Collins (London: LSE, 2014), 16–24.

55. Daniel Mejía and Pascual Restrepo, 'Why Is Strict Prohibition Collapsing? A Perspective from Producer and Transit Countries,' in *Ending the Drug Wars: Report of the LSE Expert Group on the Economics of Drug Policy*, ed. John Collins (London: LSE, 2014), 26.

56. As suggested by: Juan Carlos Garzón and John Bailey, 'Displacement Effects of Supply Reduction Policies in Latin America,' in *The Handbook of Drugs and Society*, ed. Henry Brownstein (Oxford: John Wiley & Sons, 2016), 482–503.

57. Commission on Narcotic Drugs (CND), *Making Drug Control 'Fit for Purpose': Building on the UNGASS Decade. Report by the Executive Director of the United Nations Office on Drugs and Crime as a Contribution to the review of the Twentieth Special Session of the General Assembly*, E/CN.7/2008/CRP.17* (Vienna: CND, 2008), 12–13.

58. Mónica Serrano and María Celia Toro, 'From Drug Trafficking to Transnational Organized Crime in Latin America,' in *Transnational Organized Crime and International Security*, ed. Mónica Serrano and Mats Berdal (London: Lynne Rienner Publishers, 2002), 166.

59. For a review of the argument see: David A. Shirk and Joel Wallman, 'Understanding Mexico's Drug Violence,' *Journal of Conflict Resolution* 59, no. 8 (2015): 1348–76.

60. Liza Ten Velde, *The Northern Triangle's Drugs-Violence Nexus: The Role of the Drugs Trade in Criminal Violence and Policy Responses in Guatemala, El Salvador and Honduras* (Amsterdam: TNI, 2012), 2.

61. Garzón and Bailey, 'Displacement Effects,' 499.

62. Matthew C. Ingram and Karise M. Curtis, 'Violence in Central America: A Spatial View of Homicide in the Region, Northern Triangle, and El Salvador,' in *Crime and Violence in Central America's Northern Triangle: How U.S. Policy Responses Are Helping, Hurting, and Can Be Improved*, ed. Eric E. Olson (Washington D.C.: Woodrow Wilson Center, 2015), 266–7.

63. Igarapé Institute, 'The Homicide Monitor,' accessed February 2, 2016, https://igarape.org.br/en/homicide-monitor/.

64. The truce broke down after little more than a year.

65. Instituto Universitario en Democracia, Paz y Seguridad, *Observatorio de la Violencia*, Boletín Anual No. 40 (Tegucigalpa: Observatorio Nacional de la Violencia, 2016).

66. Ten Velde, *The Northern Triangle's*, 5.

67. Mónica Serrano and Mats Berdal, eds., *Transnational Organized Crime and International Security* (London: Lynne Rienner, 2002), 15.

68. World Bank, *Crime and Violence in Central America*, 9–10.

69. Paul Gootenberg, 'Talking Like a State: Drugs, Borders, and the Language of Control,' in *Illicit Flows and Criminal Things: States, Borders, and the Other Side of Globalization*, ed. Willem van Schendel and Itty Abraham (Bloomington: Indiana University Press, 2005), 114.

70. Ibid., 114.

71. Geoffrey A. Boyce, Jeffrey M. Banister, and Jeremy Slack, 'You and What Army? Violence, The State, and Mexico's War on Drugs,' *Territory, Politics, Governance* 3, no. 4 (2015): 463.

72. For the Mexican case, see: Carlos Antonio Flores Pérez, *Historias de Polvo y Sangre: Génesis y Evolución del Tráfico de Drogas en el Estado de Tamaulipas* (Mexico City: Publicaciones de la Casa Chata, 2013). For a discussion: Jorge Eduardo Garay-Salamanca and Eduardo Salcedo-Albarán, *Drug Trafficking, Corruption and States: How Illicit Networks Shaped Institutions in Colombia, Mexico and Guatemala* (Bloomington: iUniverse, 2015); Enrique Desmond Arias, 'The Dynamics of Criminal Governance: Networks and Social Order in Rio de Janeiro,' *Journal of Latin American Studies* 38, no. 2 (2006): 293–325.

73. Bunck and Fowler, *Bribes*, 13.

74. Miguel García Sánchez, 'Cultivos Ilícitos y Confianza Institucional en Colombia,' *Política y Gobierno* 21, no. 1 (2014): 95–126.

75. Juan Carlos Garzón Vergara, *Fixing a Broken System: Modernizing Drug Law Enforcement in Latin America* (Amsterdam: TNI, 2014), 12.

76. John Bailey, *The Politics of Crime in Mexico: Democratic Governance in a Security Trap* (London: Lynne Rienner, 2014).

77. Valeria Espinosa, and Donald B. Rubin, 'Did the Military Interventions in the Mexican Drug War Increase Violence?' *The American Statistician* 69, no. 1 (2015): 24. See also: Javier Osorio, 'The Contagion of Drug Violence: Spatiotemporal Dynamics of the Mexican War on Drugs,' *Journal of Conflict Resolution* 59, no. 8 (2015): 1403–32.

78. Briscoe and Rodríguez Pellecer, *A State under Siege*, 43.

79. Geneva Declaration Secretariat, *Global Burden of Armed Violence 2015: Every Body Counts* (Cambridge: Cambridge University Press, 2015), 92.

80. Ibid., 95.

81. Ibid., 96.

82. Working Group on Women, Drug Policies, and Incarceration, *Women, Drug Policies, and Incarceration: A Guide for Policy Reform in Latin America and the Caribbean* (Washington D.C.: WOLA, 2016), 8.

83. Corina Giacomello, *Women, Drug Offenses and Penitentiary Systems in Latin America* (London: International Drug Policy Consortium, 2013), 9.

84. Ibid., 1.

85. Internal Displacement Monitoring Centre, *Global Overview 2015: People Internally Displaced by Conflict and Violence* (Geneva: Internal Displacement Monitoring Centre, 2015), 9.

86. Ibid., 16.

87. Laura Atuesta, 'Addressing the Costs of Prohibition: Internally Displaced Populations in Colombia and Mexico,' in *Ending the Drug Wars: Report of the LSE Expert Group on the Economics of Drug Policy*, ed. John Collins (London: LSE, 2014), 49.

88. Eva Bertram et al., *Drug War Politics: The Price of Denial* (London: University of California Press, 1996), 132–3.

89. Sabina Morales Rosas and Carlos A. Pérez Ricart, 'Militarización, Obstáculo para la Gobernanza Democrática de la Seguridad en México,' *Revista Colombiana de Sociología* 38, no. 1 (2015): 83–103.

90. Alejandro Hope, *Plus Ça Change: Structural Continuities in Mexican Counternarcotics Policy* (Washington D.C.: Brookings Institution, Latin America Initiative, 2015), 6.

91. Ibid., 6.

92. Morales Rosas and Pérez Ricart, 'Militarización.'

93. Alejandro Madrazo Lajous, 'The Constitutional Costs of the "War on Drugs,"' in *Ending the Drug Wars: Report of the LSE Expert Group on the Economics of Drug Policy*, ed. John Collins (London: LSE, 2014), 55–60.

94. Ibid.

95. Instituto Nacional de Estadística y Geografía, *Encuesta Nacional de Victimización y Percepción sobre Inseguridad Pública (ENVIPE) 2018* (Mexico City: INEGI, 2018), 31.

96. CND, *Making Drug Control 'Fit For Purpose'*, 10.

97. Cornelius Friesendorf, *US Foreign Policy and the War on Drugs: Displacing the Cocaine and Heroin Industry* (New York: Routledge, 2007).

98. OAS, 'The Economics of Drug Trafficking,' in *The Drug Problem in the Americas* (Washington D.C.: Organization of American States, 2013), 13.

99. Bureau for International Narcotics and Law Enforcement Affairs, *2015 International Narcotics Control Strategy Report*, 62.

100. Bruce Bagley, *Drug Trafficking and Organized Crime in the Americas: Major Trends in the Twenty-First Century* (Washington D.C.: Woodrow Wilson Center, 2012), 7–8. See also: Juan Carlos Garzón Vergara et al., *The Criminal Diaspora: The Spread of Transnational Organized Crime and How to Contain Its Expansion* (Washington D.C.: Woodrow Wilson Center, 2013), 11.

101. Bunck and Fowler, *Bribes*, 378. For a brilliant analysis of the presence of Mexican and Colombian cartels in Guatemala, see López, 'Guatemala's Crossroads.'

102. Garzón and Bailey, 'Displacement Effects,' 484.

103. See: Juan Camilo Castillo, Pascual Restrepo, and Daniel Mejía, *Scarcity without Leviathan: The Violent Effects of Cocaine Supply Shortages in the Mexican Drug War* (Washington D.C.: Center for Global Development, 2014).

104. CND, *Making Drug Control 'Fit for Purpose,'* 11.

105. Catalina Pérez Correa, Rodrigo Uprimny, and Sergio Chaparro, 'Regulation of Possession and the Criminalisation of Drug Users in Latin America,' in *After the Drug Wars: Report of the LSE Expert Group on the Economics of Drug Policy*, ed. John Collins (London: LSE, 2016), 31.

106. Ibid., 36–7.

107. Global Commission on Drug Policy (GCDP), *The Negative Impact of the War on Drugs on Public Health: The Hidden Hepatitis C Epidemic* (Geneva: Global Commission on Drug Policy, 2013), 4.

108. Harm Reduction International (HRI), *The Global State of Harm Reduction 2014*, ed. Katie Stone (London: HRI, 2014), 78.

109. Ibid.

110. Anabela Garcia-Abreu, Isabel Noguer, and Karen Cowgill, *HIV/AIDS in Latin American Countries: The Challenges Ahead* (Washington D.C.: World Bank, 2003).

111. HRI, *The Global State of Harm Reduction 2014*.

112. Ibid., 80–1.

113. See: Robin A. Pollini et al., 'Not Sold Here: Limited Access to Legally Available Syringes at Pharmacies in Tijuana, Mexico,' *Harm Reduction Journal* 8, no. 1 (2011): 13.

114. HRI, *The Global State of Harm Reduction 2014*.

115. UNODC, *World Drug Report 2015* (Vienna: United Nations, 2015), 5.

116. Kate Dolan et al., 'People Who Inject Drugs in Prison: HIV Prevalence, Transmission and Prevention,' *International Journal of Drug Policy* 26, no. 1 (2015): 12–15.

117. Juan Carlos Garzón Vergara and Luciana Pol, 'The Elephant in the Room: Drugs and Human Rights in Latin America,' *SUR International Journal on Human Rights* 12, no. 21 (2015).

118. Amira Armenta, Pien Metaal, and Martin Jelsma, *A Breakthrough in the Making? Shifts in the Latin American Drug Policy Debate* (Amsterdam: TNI, 2012), 2.

119. Ibid., 5.

120. See: Camilo Granada, 'The OAS and Transnational Organized Crime in the Americas,' in *Transnational Organized Crime and International Security*, ed. Mónica Serrano and Mats Berdal (London: Lynne Rienner Publishers, 2002), 95–102.

121. GCDP, *Asumiendo El Control: Caminos Hacia Políticas de Drogas Eficaces* (Geneva: GCDP, 2014).

122. Enrique Peña Nieto, 'Por Un México En Paz Con Justicia, Unidad y Desarrollo' (Palacio Nacional, Ciudad de México, November 27, 2014).

123. See for example: Juan Manuel Gómez Robledo, 'Statement on Behalf of the Government of Mexico by Amb. Juan Manuel Gómez Robledo, Undersecretary of Foreign Affairs for Multilateral Issues and Human Rights: Special Segment on preparations for UNGASS 2016' (statement delivered at the fifty-eighth session of the CND, Vienna, March 9, 2015).

124. Presidencia de la República de México, 'In the world drug problem, let us shift from prohibition alone to effective prevention and regulation: Enrique Peña Nieto' (press release, April 19, 2016), https://www.gob.mx/epn/prensa/in-the-world-drug-problem-let-us-shift-from-prohibition-alone-to-effective-prevention-and-regulation-enrique-pena-nieto.

125. David Bewley-Taylor and Martin Jelsma, *UNGASS 2016: A Broken or B-r-o-a-d Consensus? UN summit cannot hide a growing divergence in the global drug policy landscape* (Amsterdam: TNI, 2016).

126. Pérez Correa, Uprimny, and Chaparro, 'Regulation of Possession.'

127. For an analysis on drug legislation and prison situation in Mexico prior 2009, see: Ana Paula Hernández, 'Drugs Legislation and Prison Situation in Mexico,' in *Systems Overload: Drugs Laws and Prisoners*, ed. Pien Metaal and Colleta Youngers (Amsterdam: TNI; Washington D.C.: WOLA, 2011), 60–70. For an analysis of the shortcomings of the law: Jorge Hernández Tinajero and Carlos Zamudio Angles, *The Law against Small-Scale Drug Dealing* (Amsterdam: TNI; Washington D.C.: WOLA, 2009).

128. Germán López, 'Mexico Just Took a Big Step toward Marijuana Legalization,' *Vox*, November 1, 2018, https://www.vox.com/world/2018/11/1/18051592/mexico-marijuana-legalization-supreme-court.

129. International Narcotics Control Board, *Report of the International Narcotics Control Board for 2019*, 74.

130. Parametría, 'La Legalización de la Mariguana, Apuntes para México (Encuesta Nacional en Vivienda),' February 12, 2014, http://www.parametria.com.mx/estudios/la-legalizacion-de-la-mariguana-apuntes-para-mexico/.

131. Isaac Campos, *Home Grown: Marijuana and the Origins of Mexico's War on Drugs* (Chapel Hill: The University of North Carolina Press, 2012). See also: Alexander E. Dawson, *The Peyote Effect: From the Inquisition to the War on Drugs* (Oakland: University of California Press, 2018).

132. Campos, *Home Grown*, 226.

133. John Collins, 'Development First: Multilateralism in the Post-"War on Drugs" Era,' in *After the Drug Wars: Report of the LSE Expert Group on the Economics of Drug Policy*, ed. John Collins (London: LSE, 2016), 13.

134. *Prima facie*, countries of the region have their own framework for interaction and collaboration: The Inter-American Drug Abuse Control Commission (CICAD) of the OAS. Nevertheless, CICAD has succumbed to 'regulatory capture' by the United States. The CICAD's structure has been traditionally dominated by U.S. funding and policy perspectives. See: Armenta, Metaal, and Jelsma, *A Breakthrough in the Making?*, 3.

135. Vanda Felbab-Brown and Harold Trinkunas, *UNGASS 2016 in Comparative Perspective: Improving the Prospects for Success* (Washington D.C.: Brookings Institution, 2015), 10.

136. Caiuby Labate and Ruiz Flores López, 'Critical Reflections.'

7. WEST AFRICA

1. The countries that constitute the Economic Community of West African States (ECOWAS) are Benin, Burkina Faso, Cape Verde, Cote d'Ivoire, The Gambia, Ghana, Guinea, Guinea-Bissau, Liberia, Mali, Niger, Nigeria, Senegal, Sierra-Leone and Togo.

2. UNODC, *World Drug Report 2014* (Vienna: United Nations, 2014); United Nations Security Council, *Special Research Report: Emerging Security Threats in West Africa* (New York: United Nations, 2011); Kwesi Aning, *Understanding the intersection of drugs, politics and crime in West Africa: an interpretive analysis*, Policy Brief Series No. 6 (Santiago de Chile: Global Consortium on Security Transformation, 2010).

3. Caroline Chatwin, *Towards More Effective Global Drug Policies* (London: Palgrave Macmillan, 2018).

4. Danny Kushlick, *International Security and the Global War on Drugs: The Tragic Irony of Drug Securitization* (Bristol: Transform Drug Policy Foundation, 2011).

5. Kwesi Aning, 'Transnational Security Threats and Challenges to Peacekeeping in Mali,' *Conflict Trends* 2 (2014): 11–17.

6. UNODC, *World Drug Report 2017* (Vienna: United Nations, 2017).

7. Isidore S. Obot, *Prevention and Treatment of Drug Dependence in West Africa*, WACD Background Paper No. 2 (Accra: WACD, 2013); Kwesi Aning and John M. Pokoo, *Drug Trafficking and Threats to National and Regional Security in West Africa*, WACD Background Paper No. 1 (Accra: West Africa Commission on Drugs, 2013); Stephen Ellis, 'West Africa's International Drug Trade,' *African Affairs* 108, no. 431 (2009): 171–96.

8. Lansana and Camino Kavanagh, *Not Just in Transit: Drugs, the State and Society in West Africa: An Independent Report of the West Africa Commission on Drugs* (Accra: WACD, 2014).

9. Sam Jones, 'West Africa needs to look at partially decriminalizing drugs, says think tank,' *The Guardian,* June 12, 2014, http://www.theguardian.com/global-development/2014/jun/12/west-africa-decriminalising-drugs-policy-report; Kelly Morris, 'Drug Crime and Criminalization Threaten Progress on MDGs,' *The Lancet* 376, no. 9747 (2010): 1131–23,.

10. See for example, David Bewley-Taylor. 'Why is West Africa Repeating the Failures of the Latin American Drug War,' Open Society Foundations, January 28, 2014, https://www.opensocietyfoundations.org/voices/why-west-Africa-repeating-failures-latin-american-drug-war.

11. Ellis, 'West Africa's International Drug Trade.'

12. Kwesi Aning and A. Sarjoh Bah, *ECOWAS and conflict prevention in West Africa: Confronting the triple threats* (New York: New York University, Center on International Cooperation, 2009).

13. Emmanuel Akyeampong, 'Diaspora and Drug Trafficking in West Africa: A Case Study of Ghana,' *African Affairs* 104, no. 416 (2005): 429–47.

14. Mark Shaw, 'West African Criminal Networks in South and Southern Africa,' *African Affairs* 101, no. 404 (2002): 291–316.

15. Akyeampong, 'Diaspora and Drug Trafficking in West Africa.'

16. Wolfram Lacher, *Organized Crime and Conflict in the Sahel-Sahara Region* (Washington D.C.: Carnegie Endowment for International Peace, 2012).

17. U. S. District Court, Southern District of New York, 'United States v. Oumar Issa, Harouna Touré, and Idriss Abdelrahman,' New York, 2009, http://www.justice.gov/archive/usao/nys/pressreleases/April12/issa/issatoureandabdelrahmanindictment.pdf.

18. Mark Shaw, *Illicit financial flows: Illicit narcotics transiting West Africa*, OECD Development Co-operation Working Papers 64 (Paris: OECD Publishing, 2019).

19. Kwesi Aning, 'West Africa's security dilemmas: state fragility, narco-terrorism and oil politics,' in *Africa South of the Sahara,* ed. Europa Publications (London: Routledge, 2012); See for example, Georgina Wood Committee, *The Georgina Wood Committee Report* (Accra, 2006), http://www.ghananewsagency.org/social/georgina-wood-committee-presents-it-report-to-government-854 (accessed on October 20, 2015. By September 2020, the reference to the report had been removed from the website.

20 Vanda Felbab-Brown, 'The West African Drug Trade in the Context of the Region's Illicit Economies and Poor Governance' (presentation to Conference on Drug Trafficking in West Africa, in Arlington, VA, October 14, 2010).

21. 'Guinea Narco-state revealed in TV confessions,' *Washington Times,* March 15, 2009, https://www.washingtontimes.com/news/2009/mar/15/guinea-narcostate-revealed-in-tv-confessions/.

22. Lasana Gberie, *Crime, violence, and politics: Drug trafficking and counternarcotic policies in Mali and Guinea* (Washington D.C.: Brookings Institution, 2015).

23. Godwin, E., 'Drug trafficking menace in Togo,' *Daily Graphic*, March 9, 2009, 3.

24. David Blair, 'Sierra Leone being targeted by Latin American drug cartels,' *The Telegraph*, February 27, 2009, https://www.telegraph.co.uk/news/worldnews/africaandindianocean/sierraleone/4863771/Sierra-Leone-targeted-by-Latin-American-drug-cartels.html.

25. Ibid.

26   Peter Tinti, *Illicit Trafficking and Instability in Mali: Past, Present and Future* (Geneva: Global Initiative against Transnational Organized Crime, 2014); Kwesi Aning and Lydia Amedzrator, 'The Economics of Militancy and Islamist Extremism in the Sahel,' in *Political stability and security in West and North Africa,* ed. The Canadian Security Intelligence Service (Toronto: Her Majesty the Queen in Right of Canada, 2014).

27   Henry Bernstein, 'Ghana's Drug Economy: Some Preliminary Data,' *Review of African Political Economy* 26, no. 79 (1999): 13–32. Akyeampong, 'Diaspora and Drug Trafficking in West Africa.'

28   Oluwole Famuyiwa, Olatunji F. Aina, and Olufunlayo M. Bankole-Oki, 'Epidemiology of Psychoactive Drug Use amongst Adolescents in Metropolitan Lagos, Nigeria,' *European Child & Adolescent Psychiatry* 20, no. 7 (2011): 351–9, https://doi.org/10.1007/s00787-011-0180-6.

29. 'ECOWAS Drug Unit Portal,' Economic Community of West African States (ECOWAS), https://edup.ecowas.int/. This portal has all the materials and processes towards highlighting the processes towards the acceptance of drugs as an existential threat.

30. See for example Emmanuel Adler and Michael Barnett, 'Security communities in theoretical perspective,' in *Security Communities* (Cambridge: Cambridge University Press, 1998), 3–24; also Benedikt Franke, 'Africa's evolving security architecture and the concept of multilayered security communities,' *Cooperation and Conflict* 43, no. 3 (2008).

31. Christian Bueger, 'Communities of security practice at work? The emerging African maritime security regime,' *African Security* 6, no. 3–4 (2013): 297–316.

32. See for example Ole Waever. 'Insecurity, security and asecurity in the West European non-war community,' in *Security Communities*, ed. Emanuel Adler and Michael Barnett (Cambridge: Cambridge University Press, 1998), 68–118.

33. Barry Buzan, Ole Wæver and Jaap De Wilde, *Security: a new framework for analysis* (Boulder: Lynne Rienner Publishers, 1998).

34. Barry Buzan, *People, States and Fear: National Security Problem in International Relations* (New Delhi: Transasia Publishers, 1987).

35. Buzan, Wæver and De Wilde, *Security*, 26.

36. Buzan, *People*.

37. Thierry Balzacq, *Securitisation Theory: How Security Problems Emerge and Dissolve* (London: Routledge. 2010), 1.

38. Ole Wæver, 'Securitization and Desecuritization,' in *On Security*, ed. Ronnie D. Lipschutz (New York: Columbia University Press, 1995), 55.

39. Buzan, Wæver and De Wilde, *Security*, 24.

40. Wæver, 'Securitization and Desecuritization.'

41. Ibid., 32.

42. Ibid., 26. For more on securitization process, see particularly Emmers, Ralf, 'Securitization,' in *Contemporary Security Studies,* ed. Allan Collins (Oxford: Oxford University Press, 2013), 131–43.

43. Michael J. Sheehan, *International Security: An Analytical Survey* (London: Lynne Rienner Publishers, 2005), 60.

44. Stephen Walt, 'The Renaissance of Security Studies,' *International Studies Quarterly* 35 (1991): 211–39.

45. Jef Huysmans, 'Migrants as a Security Problem: Dangers of "Securitising" Societal Issues,' in *Migration and European Integration: The Dynamics of Inclusion and Exclusion*, ed. Robert Miles and Dietrich Thränhardt (London: Pinter Publishers, 1995), 53–72.

46. Matt McDonald. 'Securitization and the Construction of Security,' *European Journal of International Relations* 14, no. 4 (2008): 564.

47. Richard Wyn Jones, 'Travel Without Maps: Thinking About Security After the Cold War,' in *Security Issues in the Post-Cold War*, ed. Jane M. Davis (Cheltenham: Edward Elgar Publishing, 1996), 198.

48. See for example, Obinna Franklin Ifediora and Kwesi Aning, 'West Africa's Ebola Pandemic: Towards Effective Multilateral Responses to Health Crises,' *Global Governance* 23, no. 2 (2017): 225–44.

49. Amy Niang, 'The imperative of *African* perspectives on International Relations (IR),' *Politics* 36, no. 4 (2016): 453–66.

50. Amy Niang, 'Rehistoricizing the Sovereignty Principle: Stature, Decline, and Anxieties About a Foundational Norm,' in *Recentering Africa in International Relations,* ed. Marta Iñiguez de Heredia and Zubairu Wai (London: Palgrave Macmillan, 2018), 121–44.

51. Mahmood Mamdani, 'Good Muslim, Bad Muslim: A political perspective on culture and terrorism,' *American Anthropologist* 104 no. 3 (2002): 766–75.

52. Paul Henri Bischoff, Kwesi Anig and Amitav Achaya, 'Africa in Global International Relations: Emerging approaches to theory and practice, an introduction,' in *Africa in Global International Relations: Emerging approaches to theory and practice*, ed. Paul Henri Bischoff, Kwesi Anig and Amitav Achaya (London: Routledge, 2016).

53. Branwen Gruffydd Jones, 'Africa and the Poverty of International Relations,' *Third World Quarterly* 26, no. 6 (2005): 987–1003; see also, Kwesi Aning and Kwaku Danso, 'Ghana: Identity Formation and the Foreign and Defence Policies of a Small State,' in *African Foreign Policies: Selecting Signifiers to Explain Agency*, ed. Paul-Henri Bischoff (Abingdon: Routledge, 2020).

54. Aning and Pokoo, *Drug Trafficking*. See also Kwesi Aning and Samuel Aning. *National drug laws, related legislation and prison population in Ghana*, Background Paper for the WACD (Accra: West Africa Commission on Drugs, 2015), especially pp. 24–40. See also Etannibi Alemika et al., *Harmonizing Drug Legislation in West Africa - A Call for Minimum Standards*, WACD Background Paper No. 9 (Accra: WACD, 2014).

55. Obot, *Prevention and Treatment*.

56. For the narcotics drugs market in West Africa, see: UNODC, *Transnational Organized Crime in West Africa: A Threat Assessment* (Vienna: UNODC, 2013). See also Shaw, *Illicit financial flows* and 'The global drugs trade shifts to west Africa,' *The Economist*,

451

November 21, 2019, https://www.economist.com/international/2019/11/21/the-global-drugs-trade-shifts-to-west-africa.

57. Gberie, *Crime, violence, and politics.*

58. United Nations Security Council, *Statement by the President of the Security Council,* S/PRST/2012/2 (NewYork, February 21, 2012).

59. Aning and Pokoo, *Drug Trafficking.*

60. UNODC, *World Drug Report 2019* (Vienna: United Nations, 2019), booklet 2, https://wdr.unodc.org/wdr2019/prelaunch/WDR19_Booklet_2_DRUG_DEMAND.pdf.

61. United Nations General Assembly, *Resolution S-17/2 on the Political Declaration and Global Programme of Action adopted by the General Assembly at its 17th special session, devoted to the question of international co-operation against illicit production, supply, demand, trafficking and distribution of narcotic drugs and psychotropic substances,* A/RES/S-17/2 (NewYork, February 23, 1990), https://undocs.org/en/A/RES/S-17/2.

62. Obot, *Prevention and Treatment.*

63. Aning and Pokoo, *Drug Trafficking.*

64. See ECOWAS, 'The Thirty-First session of the Authority of Heads of State and Government: Final Communiqué' (Ouagadougou, Burkina Faso, January 19, 2007).

65. This Center's establishment was recognized as far back as 1999. In Article 46 of the 1999 Protocol relating to the Mechanism for Conflict Prevention, Management, Resolution, Peacekeeping and Security, the threat of drugs, to the sub-region was recognized; however, characteristic of ECOWAS and its leaders, nothing was done.

66. Ellis, 'West Africa's International Drug Trade.' See also: Fiona Mangan and Matthias Nowak, *The West Africa–Sahel Connection* (Geneva: Small Arms Survey, 2019).

67. Afua A. Lamptey, *Tackling the Aftermath of Libya's 'Arab Spring': Addressing the Small Arms Issue* (Accra: Kofi Annan International Peacekeeping Training Centre, 2013), https://media.africaportal.org/documents/Aftermath-of-Libya-1.pdf.

68 Aning, *Understanding the intersection*; Aning, 'Transnational Security Threats.'

69. Kwesi Aning and Festus Aubyn. 'The security situation in West Africa,' in *Africa South of the Sahara*, ed. Europa Publications (London: Routledge, 2012), 25–30.

70. Ibid.

71. Kwesi Aning and Lydia Amedzrator, 'Security in the Sahel: Linking the Atlantic to the Mediterranean,' in *Transatlantic security from the Sahel to the Horn of Africa,* ed. Riccardo Alcaro and Nicoletta Pirozzi (Rome: Edizion Nuova Cultura, 2013), 59–70; 'Sahara desert gun battle yields drugs haul, says France,' *BBC News*, May 19, 2015, http://www.bbc.com/news/world-africa-32796372; see also: *The Economist*, 'The global drugs trade.'

72. Obot, *Prevention and Treatment,* 8–9.

73. ECOWAS, 'Political declaration on the prevention of drug abuse, illicit drug trafficking and organized crimes in West Africa,' (Abuja, UNODC, December 2008), https://www.unodc.org/westandcentralafrica/en/ecowaspoliticaldeclaration.html.

74. The Plan of Action was renewed indefinitely under clause 42 of a communique issued at the end of the Forty-First Ordinary Session of the ECOWAS Authority

of Heads of State and Government at Yamoussoukro, Cote d'Ivoire, June 28–29, 2012, https://www.ecowas.int/wp-content/uploads/2015/02/41st-ECOWAS-Summit-Yamoussoukro-28-29-June-20121.pdf.

75. Obot., *Prevention and Treatment.*

76. Gberie, *Crime, violence, and politics*; Aning, 'Transnational Security Threats.'

8. THE CRESCENT THREE STATES

1. It is because of the tendency to ignore the experiences of the illicit drug trade in the Middle East that the author of this chapter was encouraged to write the most recent book on the subject, Philip Robins, *Middle East Drugs Bazaar: Production, Prevention and Consumption* (New York: Oxford University Press, 2016).

2. For the best, recent piece of work, specifically on heroin in a global perspective, see Letizia Paoli, Victoria A. Greenfield and Peter Reuter, *The World Heroin Market: Can Supply Be Cut?* (Oxford: Oxford University Press, 2009).

3. Sir Thomas Russell Pasha, *Egyptian Service, 1902-1946* (London: John Murray, 1949).

4. That is to say Saudi Arabia, Kuwait, the UAE, Bahrain, Qatar, and Oman.

5. By which is meant establishing an apparently coherent and consistent approach, even if such a systematic approach turns out to be largely spurious. For example, it was only in the 1970s–80s that the US placed concerted pressure on senior Egyptian officials to remove the public sale of illicit narcotics.

6. In the sense of following a chiefly American agenda, meaning a conservative approach to the big decision-making issues.

7. Marc Herzog and Philip Robins, eds., *The Role, Position and Agency of Cusp States in International Relations* (Abingdon: Routledge, 2014).

8. For these purposes, a cusp state is defined as being 'a state that lies uneasily on the political and/or normative edge of what is widely believed to be an established region [aka multi-milieu solidarity group].' Ibid., 1.

9. Milieu states may be understood as 'states that have decisively more in common with what subjectively is claimed to be the core values of an aspirant or established region than with the ambivalences epitomized by the existence of cusp states.' Ibid., 1.

10. Herzog and Robins, *The Role, Position and Agency.*

11. Afghanistan has seen a 30-fold increase in its potential opium production, from an estimated 200 tons in 1980 to 4,500 tons in 1999 and 6,100 tons in 2006. See Paoli, Greenfield and Reuter, *The World Heroin Market,* 118.

12. The sort of bold, decisive statement about the supply of heroin so beloved by writers and commentators in the 1990s and 2000s. For a recent, random and rather effective demonstration of such a phenomenon in practice see Julien Mercille, *Cruel Harvest. US Intervention in the Afghan Drug Trade* (London: Pluto Press, 2013), 1.

13. Howard W. French, 'Heroin grips poor town in rural China,' *International Herald Tribune,* December 24–26, 2004.

14. Thomas Fuller, 'Notorious Golden Triangle loses sway in the opium trade,' *The New York Times,* September 11, 2007, https://www.nytimes.com/2007/09/11/world/asia/11iht-golden.1.7461246.html.

15. Such figures should be taken with a pinch of salt. For a long time, especially in the 1990s, UK law enforcement officers routinely briefed that 90 per cent of all the heroin in Western Europe passed through Turkey, a statistic that was roughly accurate, but used instrumentally in order to elicit a political response.

16. Mujib Mashal, 'Afghanistan's river of solace,' *International New York Times*, March 10, 2016, 2.

17. Tahir Qadiry, 'Afghanistan, the drug addiction capital,' *BBC Magazine*, April 11, 2013, https://www.bbc.com/news/magazine-22091005.

18. For a good introductory book on the Taliban see Ahmed Rashid, *Taliban* (London: Tauris, 2010).

19. Mujib Mashal and Andrew E. Kramer, 'Russia Pulls Back from Cooperating with U.S. on Afghanistan,' *The New York Times,* February 20, 2016, https://www. nytimes.com/2016/02/21/world/asia/russia-pulls-back-from-cooperating-with-us-on-afghanistan.html.

20. Opiates are not the only drugs illegally on sale in Afghanistan. For instance, the so-called 'Afghan black' was a prominent hemp drug produced in the mid-1970s.

21. During most of the nineteenth century, most of the European demand for opium was supplied by the Ottoman Empire, the predecessor state of Turkey.

22. William B. McAllister, *Drug Diplomacy in the Twentieth Century* (London: Routledge, 2000).

23. Paoli, Greenfield and Reuter, *The World Heroin Market,* 112.

24. Nigel Inkster, 'Drugs: a war lost in Afghanistan,' *Foreign Policy*, May 29, 2012, https://foreignpolicy.com/2012/05/29/drugs-a-war-lost-in-afghanistan/.

25. David Mansfield and Adam Pain, 'Evidence from the field: Understanding changing levels of opium poppy cultivation in Afghanistan,' in *The Politics of Narcotic Drugs: A Survey,* ed. Julia Buxton (London: Routledge, 2011), 21.

26. 'Afghanistan: Narcotics battle,' *Oxford Analytica*, October 5, 2010.

27. UN confirmed that chemists are being imported into Afghanistan in order to step up the production of heroin in labs set to operate in the country. See 'Afghan Drugs Crisis,' *Financial Times*, July 30, 2008.

28. Cyrus Hodes and Mark Sedra, *The Search for Security in Post-Taliban Afghanistan* (London: Routledge, 2007).

29. Declan Walsh, 'Flower Plower,' *The Guardian*, August 16, 2008. The article argues that the Taliban have taken to the reinstitution of the poppy crop since the end of the 2000 ban.

30. Mohammed Hanif, 'Pakistan doesn't owe you a free mansion,' *International New York Times,* May 13, 2016.

31. But one which Owen Bennett Jones warns us 'enjoys a better reputation than it deserves.' See Owen Bennett Jones, *Pakistan: Eye of the Storm* (New Haven: Yale University Press, 2003), 278.

32. Hilary Synnott has written that 'Like so many troubling aspects of Pakistan's life, the transformation of the ISI intensified following the Soviet invasion of Afghanistan.' See Hilary Synnott, *Transforming Pakistan: Ways Out of Instability* (London: Routledge and IISS, 2009), 58.

33. 'Pakistan: Intelligence Services,' *Oxford Analytica,* November 7, 2006.

34.   UNODC, *World Drug Report 2015* (Vienna: United Nations, 2015), 44.

35.   Huma Yusuf, 'The Drugs of War,' *The New York Times*, November 9, 2012, https://latitude.blogs.nytimes.com/2012/11/09/the-war-in-afghanistan-brings-drugs-to-pakistan/.

36.   Azam Ahmed, 'That Other Big Afghan Crisis: The Growing Army of Addicts,' *The New York Times*, November 2, 2013, https://www.nytimes.com/2013/11/03/world/asia/that-other-big-afghan-crisis-the-growing-army-of-addicts.html.

37.   Donald G. McNeil Jr, 'Issue of drug enforcement vs. treatment splits the U.N.,' *International New York Times*, October 28, 2015, 11.

38.   For instance, the Libyan National Society for Anti-Drugs and Mental Stimulants. The charity was established in 1994.

39.   Afari Rahimi-Movaghar, Masoumeh Amin-Esmaeili and Behrang Shadloo, *Assessment of Situation and Response of Drug Use and its Harms in the Middle East and North Africa* (Beirut: MENAHRA, 2012).

40.   Rahimi-Movaghar, Amin-Esmaeili and Shadloo, *Assessment of Situation*, 29.

41.   Helmand is the deadliest province in Afghanistan. See Rod Nordland, 'Afghan Graft Hobbles Fight against Drugs,' *International New York Times*, April 7, 2016, 4.

42.   The negotiation took place between Iran, the recalcitrant state, and the US, arguably the only state capable of standing up to Iran. In practice, the rest of the UN's P-5 was also represented, thereby making the negotiation *de facto* fully multilateral.

9. THE GOLDEN TRIANGLE

1.   UNODC, *Southeast Asia Opium Survey 2014* (Bangkok: UNODC, 2014), 11.

2.   Ibid.

3.   Ibid., foreword.

4.   Marina Mahathir, 'Drug Law Reform in Southeast Asia,' in *Drug law reform in East and Southeast Asia*, ed. Fifa Rahman and Nick Crofts (Lanham: Lexington Books, 2013), vii.

5.   International Drug Policy Consortium (IDPC), 'Regional Advocacy, East and Southeast Asia,' accessed November 17, 2015. http://idpc.net/policy-advocacy/regional-work/east-and-south-east-asia

6.   UNODC, *Southeast Asia Opium Survey 2014,* 13; UNODC, *Transnational Organized Crime in Southeast Asia: Evolution, Growth and Impact 2019* (Bangkok: United Nations, 2019), 7.

7.   The Karen National Union (KNU) has fought Burma's central government since the country's independence in 1948.

8.   Pierre-Arnaud Chouvy, *Opium: Uncovering the Politics of the Poppy* (Cambridge, MA: Harvard University Press, 2010).

9.   UNODC, *Southeast Asia Opium Survey 2014*, 5.

10. Pierre-Arnaud Chouvy, 'The Myth of the Narco-State,' *Space and Polity* 20, no. 1 (2015): 26–38, https://doi.org/10.1080/13562576.2015.1052348.

11. Chouvy, *Opium: Uncovering the Politics of the Poppy*; James Windle, *Drugs and Drug Policy in Thailand* (Washington D.C.: Brookings Institution, Latin America Initiative, 2015); Vanda Felbab-Brown, *Enabling War and Peace: Drugs, Logs, Gems, and Wildlife in Thailand and Burma* (Washington D.C.: Brookings Institution, 2015).

12. David Mansfield, '"Economical with the truth": The limits of price and profitability in both explaining opium poppy cultivation in Afghanistan and in designing effective responses,' in *Reconstructing Agriculture in Afghanistan*, ed. Adam Pain and Jacky Sutton (Colchester: Practical Action Publishing, draft version, 2007).

13. UNODC. *Opium Poppy Cultivation in the Golden Triangle. Lao PDR, Myanmar, Thailand* (Bangkok: UNODC, 2006), 25.

14. United Nations Human Rights Office of the High Commissioner, 'Human rights dimension of poverty,' accessed September 19, 2007, https://www.ohchr.org/EN/Issues/Poverty/DimensionOfPoverty/Pages/Index.aspx.

15. Ahto Lobjakas, 'Afghanistan: Multipronged Drug Eradication Effort Set for Helmand,' *RFERL*, January 30, 2007, https://www.rferl.org/a/1074381.html.

16. Mansfield, '"Economical with the truth,"' 15.

17. Zhou Yongming, *Anti-Drug Crusades in Twentieth-Century China: Nationalism, History, and State Building* (Lanham: Rowman & Littlefield, 1999), 95–108.

18. Chouvy, *Opium: Uncovering the Politics of the Poppy*; Windle, 'Drugs and Drug Policy in Thailand.'

19. UNODC, *Opium Poppy Cultivation in the Golden Triangle,* 123; Ronald D. Renard, *Opium Reduction in Thailand 1970–2000: A Thirty-Year Journey* (Bangkok: UNDCP, 2001), 76.

20. Renard, *Opium Reduction in Thailand 1970–2000,* 57–68.

21. Christoph Berg and Alexander Seger, *Drugs and Development in Asia: A Background and Discussion Paper* (Eschborn: Deutsche Gesellschaft für Technische Zusammenarbeit, 1998), 10.

22. UNODC, *Thematic Evaluation of UNODC Alternative Development Initiatives* (Vienna: UNODC, 2005).

23. Ibid., 23.

24. Chouvy, *Opium: Uncovering the Politics of the Poppy*; Berg and Seger, *Drugs and Development in Asia,* 10.

25. Berg and Seger, *Drugs and Development in Asia,* 10; Chouvy, *Opium: Uncovering the Politics of the Poppy.*

26. Berg and Seger, *Drugs and Development in Asia,* 40.

27. David Mansfield and Adam Pain, 'Alternative Livelihoods: Substance or Slogan?' *Issues Papers 14650, Afghanistan Research and Evaluation Unit* (2005), https://doi.org/10.22004/ag.econ.14650; UNODC, *Thematic Evaluation,* ix.

28. Commission on Narcotic Drugs, *Draft Action Plan on International Cooperation on Eradication of Illicit Drug Crops and Promotion of Alternative Development Programmes and Projects* E/CN.7/1998/PC/7 (Vienna: ECOSOC, 1998), 3, 6.

29. Mansfield and Pain, 'Alternative Livelihoods,' 1–2.

30. Chouvy, *Opium: Uncovering the Politics of the Poppy.*

31. Nick Crofts et al., 'Law Enforcement and Drug Policy in Southeast Asia,' in *Drug law reform in East and Southeast Asia*, ed. Fifa Rahman and Nick Crofts (Lanham: Lexington Books, 2013), 59.

32. Chouvy, *Opium: Uncovering the Politics of the Poppy*; Pierre-Arnaud Chouvy, 'A Typology of the Unintended Consequences of Drug Crop Reduction,' *Journal of*

Drug Issues 43, no. 2 (2013): 216–30; Windle, *Drugs and Drug Policy in Thailand*; Felbab-Brown, *Enabling War and Peace.*

33. Human Rights Watch, *Not Enough Graves, the War on Drugs, HIV/AIDS and Human Rights Violations* (New York: Human Rights Watch, 2004), 1.

34. Prashanth Parameswaran, 'Thailand's Junta to Declare War on Corruption,' *The Diplomat*, May 29, 2015.

35. King-Oua Laohong, 'Drug-Free Communities an Elusive Goal, ONCB Chief Admits,' *Bangkok Post*, November 16, 2015. In 2013, drug-related arrests and compulsory drug treatment detentions respectively amounted to 431,000 and 485,000: Irin News, 'Rethinking Thailand's war on methamphetamines,' *The New Humanitarian,* January 13, 2014, http://www.irinnews.org/report/99449/rethinking-thailand-s-war-on-methamphetamines.

36. Patrick Tibke, 'Drug law reform coming to Thailand, but how far will it go?' IDPC, July 16, 2015, http://idpc.net/blog/2015/07/drug-law-reform-coming-to-thailand-but-how-far-will-it-go.

37. Fifa Rahman, 'Alternatives to Criminal Justice: Drug Courts, Drug Diversion, and Decriminalization,' in *Drug law reform in East and Southeast Asia*, ed. Fifa Rahman and Nick Crofts (Lanham: Lexington Books, 2013), 245.

38. Adeeba Kamarulzaman and John L. McBrayer, 'Compulsory drug detention centers in East and Southeast Asia,' *International Journal of Drug Policy* 26, no. 1 (2015): S33–S37.

39. Simon Baldwin and Nicolas Thomson, 'Compulsory "Rehabilitation" in Asia: Problems and Possible Solutions,' in *Drug law reform in East and Southeast Asia*, ed. Fifa Rahman and Nick Crofts (Lanham: Lexington Books, 2013), 140.

40. Anne Bergenstrom and Sonia Bezziccheri, 'Phasing out Drug Detention Centres in East and South East Asia' (UNODC poster, second Regional Consultation on Compulsory Centres for Drug Users in Asia and the Pacific, Kuala Lumpur, Malaysia, October 2012, https://www.unodc.org/documents/southeastasiaandpacific//poster/CCDU_Poster_08_3_Jun_2013.pdf.

41. Nick Watts, 'Compulsory Drug Treatment in Southeast Asia – Neither Ethical Nor Effective,' *Global Politics*, May 2, 2015, http://global-politics.co.uk/wp/2015/05/02/compulsory-drug-treatment-in-southeast-asia-neither-ethical-nor-effective/.

42. Ibid.

43. United Nations Joint Programme on HIV/AIDS, International Labour Organization, Office of the High Commissioner for Human Rights, United Nations Development Programme, United Nations Educational, Scientific and Cultural Organization, United Nations Population Fund, United Nations High Commissioner for Refugees, United Nations Children's Fund, United Nations Office on Drugs and Crime, United Nations Entity for Gender Equality and the Empowerment of Women, World Food Programme, and World Health Organization, *Joint Statement: Compulsory Drug Detention and Rehabilitation Centres* (New York: UN, 2012), http://www.unaids.org/en/media/unaids/contentassets/documents/document/2012/JC2310_Joint%20Statement6March12FINAL_en.pdf.

44. Alessandro Marazzi Sassoon, 'Study Calls for Closure of Compulsory Drug Centres,' *The Phnom Penh Post,* January 19, 2017, https://www.phnompenhpost.com/national/study-calls-closure-compulsory-drug-centres.

45. Kamarulzaman and McBrayer, 'Compulsory drug detention centers,' S35; Malaysia's Ministry of Home Affairs, *Country Progress Report of Drug Control – Malaysia* (Putraya: Malaysia's Ministry of Home Affairs, 2014), http://www.na.gov.la/files/aifocom11/Doc_for_AIFOCOM/COUNTRY%20REPORT/(11)%20Annex%20M-%20Country%20Report%20of%20Malaysia.pdf.

46. Kamarulzaman and McBrayer, 'Compulsory drug detention centers,' S34.

47. Marek Chawarski, Richard Schottenfel and B. Vicknasingam. 'Law Enforcement and Drug Policy in Southeast Asia,' in *Drug law reform in East and Southeast Asia*, ed. Fifa Rahman and Nick Crofts (Lanham: Lexington Books, 2013), 271–90.

48. Kamarulzaman and McBrayer, 'Compulsory drug detention centers,' S35-S36.

49. Tibke, 'Drug law reform coming to Thailand.'

50. Gloria Lai and Patcharavalan Akbar, 'Thailand amends drug law to reduce penalties and ensure more proportionate sentencing,' IDPC, February 15, 2017, https://idpc.net/blog/2017/02/thailand-amends-drug-law-to-reduce-penalties-and-ensure-more-proportionate-sentencing.

51. Transform Drug Policy Foundation, 'The Truth Behind the UNODC's Leaked Decriminalisation Paper,' October 20, 2015, https://transformdrugs.org/the-truth-behind-the-unodcs-leaked-decriminalisation-paper/.

52. UNODC, 'New national drug policy announced for Myanmar,' February 20, 2018, https://www.unodc.org/southeastasiaandpacific/en/myanmar/2018/02/new-national-drug-control-policy/story.html.

53. Patrick Gallahue et al., *The Death Penalty for Drug Offences: Global Overview 2012. Tipping the Scales for Abolition* (London: International Harm Reduction Association, 2012), 14.

54. Association of the Southeast Asian Nations, 'Statement by the Association of Southeast Asian Nations at the 5th Intersessional CND Meeting of the 61st Commission on Narcotic Drugs' (statement, UNODC, Vienna, November 7, 2018), https://www.unodc.org/documents/commissions/CND/2019/Contributions/November/MS_Statements/7_November/ASEAN_Statement_for_7_Nov.pdf.

55. Masagos Zulkifli, 'The 36th ASEAN Senior Officials Meeting on Drugs' (opening speech, Association of the Southeast Asian Nations, Singapore, August 24, 2015).

56. Ibid.

57. UNODC Regional Centre for East Asia and the Pacific, *Drug-Free ASEAN 2015: Status and Recommendations* (Bangkok: UNODC, 2008), 5–6.

58. Ibid., 85.

59. Association of Southeast Asian Nations, 'Joint Declaration for a Drug-Free ASEAN' (ASEAN declaration, October 12, 2012), https://asean.org/?static_post=joint-declaration-for-a-drug-free-asean.

60. Association of Southeast Asian Nations, 'ASEAN Launches Narcotics Cooperation Centre in Bangkok,' September 19, 2014.

61. Life Chiang Mai, 'Four nations meet in Chiang Mai for Safe Mekong Project,' April 29, 2015.

62. ASEAN Narcotics Cooperation Center, 'Workshop on Formulation of the 5-Year Master Plan (2019-2023) under the Safe Mekong Operation Project among 6 Countries,' April 16, 2018, https://aseannarco.oncb.go.th/ewt_news.php?nid=387&filename=index___EN.

63. Claudia Stoicescu and Gideon Lasco, *10 Years of Drug Policy in Asia: How Far Have We Come?* (London: IDPC, 2019), https://www.aidsdatahub.org/resource/10-years-drug-policy-asia-how-far-have-we-come.

64. UNODC Regional Centre for East Asia and the Pacific, *Drug-Free ASEAN 2015*, 77.

65. UNODC Regional Centre for East Asia and the Pacific, *Border Liaison Offices in Southeast Asia 1999–2009* (Bangkok: UNODC, 2010). Detailed BLO numbers date from 2009: more recent data was not made available.

66. Jonathan Evert Rayon, 'Creating a Drug-Free ASEAN: How Far Have we Come?' *ASEAN Studies Center*, May 21, 2019, https://asc.fisipol.ugm.ac.id/2019/05/21/creating-a-drug-free-asean-how-far-have-we-come/.

67. Chouvy, *Opium: Uncovering the Politics of the Poppy*.

68. James Windle and Graham Farrell, 'Popping the Balloon Effect: Assessing Drug Law Enforcement in Terms of Displacement, Diffusion, and the Containment Hypothesis,' *Substance Use and Misuse* 47, no. 8–9 (2012): 868–76.

69. Letizia Paoli, Victoria A. Greenfield, and Peter Reuter, 'Change is Possible: The History of the International Drug Control Regime and Implications for Future Policymaking,' *Substance Use and Misuse* 47, no. 8–9 (2012): 923–35.

70. Pierre-Arnaud Chouvy, ed., *An Atlas of Trafficking in Southeast Asia. The Illegal Trade in Arms, Drugs, People, Counterfeit Goods and Natural Resources in Mainland Southeast Asia* (London: I.B. Tauris; Bangkok: IRASEC, 2013), 214; Chouvy, 'A Typology of the Unintended Consequences;' Felbab-Brown, 'Enabling War and Peace.'

71. UNODC, *Southeast Asia Opium Survey 2014*, 49.

72. David Mansfield, 'Where have all the flowers gone? The real reasons for the drop in the poppy crop in Afghanistan in 2015,' *Alcis*, October 20, 2015, https://stories.alcis.org/where-have-all-the-flowers-gone-7de7b34e8478#.enfwvwq2e.

73. Chouvy, *Opium: Uncovering the Politics of the Poppy*.

74. UNODC Regional Centre for East Asia and the Pacific, *Drug-Free ASEAN 2015*.

75. Transparency International, 'Corruption Perceptions Index 2019,' 2020, https://www.transparency.org/en/cpi/2019/results.

76. Chouvy, 'The Myth of the Narco-State.'

77. Willem van Schendel and Itty Abraham, eds., *Illicit Flows and Criminal Things: States, Borders, and the Other Side of Globalization* (Bloomington: Indiana University Press, 2005).

78. Tibke, 'Drug law reform coming to Thailand.'

10. RUSSIA

1. The use of terminology in this chapter reflects the dominant usage patterns in Russia, shaped by its prohibitionist approach to IDCR. The term 'narcotics' is used in this chapter as it is defined in the draft 'Strategy of State Anti-Narcotics Policy of the Russian Federation through 2030,' Ministry of Internal Affairs of

the Russian Federation, January 16, 2020, p. 4, https://regulation.gov.ru/Files/ GetFile?fileid=4b8e646e-9121-4dd0-b0f1-71e5fe668cb8. The draft strategy defines 'narcotics' as 'narcotic substances, psychotropic substances and their precursors included in the List of Narcotic and Psychotropic Substances and Precursors, Subject to Control in the Russian Federation, analogues of narcotic and psychotropic substances; new potentially dangerous psychoactive substances, and plants, containing narcotic or psychotropic substances or their precursors, as listed in List of plants, containing narcotic or psychotropic substances or their precursors, Subject to Control in the Russian Federation'. See also: 'List of Narcotic and Psychotropic Substances and Precursors, Subject to Control in the Russian Federation,' enacted by Government decree no. 681 of June 20, 1998 (last updated on March 13, 2020), in Russian, http://base.garant.ru/12112176/#ixzz6SFc8JlXu; 'List of Plants, Containing Narcotic or Psychotropic Substances or their Precursors, Subject to Control in the Russian Federation,' enacted by Government decree no 934 of November 27, 2010 (last updated on August 9, 2019), http://pravo.gov.ru/ipsdata/?docbody=&prevDoc=102135282&backlink=1&&nd=102143353.

2. In line with Russia's rigid prohibitionist approach, the official drug control and enforcement agency—Federal Drug Control Service (FSKN) in 2003–16, succeeded after 2016 by a branch of the Ministry of Internal Affairs—has not differentiated between 'soft' and 'hard' drugs and even rejects such differentiation as a form of propaganda for, and a path to, 'drug abuse.' Russian health authorities sometimes make this distinction but often stress its 'relative' nature. The basic distinction that also makes it into the Russian public and media discourse is made between opiates and cocaine as the main 'hard drugs,' and drugs produced from cannabis as 'soft drugs,' but it gets more blurred when it comes to synthetic drugs. As used in this chapter, the term 'hard drugs' applies to drugs displayed in Figure 10.2 (heroin, opium, hashish, and cocaine). Of synthetic drugs, it includes amphetamines, methamphetamine, desomorphine and several other ones, but not MDMA/ecstasy, LSD, 'spices' (synthetic cannabinoids), and 'salts' (synthetic cathinones).

3. See List of Narcotic and Psychotropic Substances and Precursors, Subject to Control in the Russian Federation.

4. UNODC and Islamic Republic of Afghanistan Ministry for Counternarcotics, *Afghanistan Opium Survey 2018: Cultivation and Production* (Kabul: UNODC, 2018), 6.

5. Ibid.

6. Table 'Worldwide Illicit Drug Crop Cultivation 2011–2019,' in Bureau for International Narcotics and Law Enforcement Affairs, *2020 International Narcotics Control Strategy Report: Volume I: Drug and Chemical Control* (Washington D.C.: U.S. Department of State, 2020), 22.

7. UNODC and Islamic Republic of Afghanistan Ministry for Counternarcotics, *Afghanistan Opium Survey 2018*, 6–7; see Table 'Worldwide Potential Illicit Drug Production 2009–2017,' in Bureau for International Narcotics and Law Enforcement Affairs, *2019 International Narcotics Control Strategy Report: Volume I: Drug and Chemical Control* (Washington D.C.: U.S. Department of State, 2019), 23.

8. Customs Union became an integral part of the Eurasian Economic Union formed in 2015. Of other Central Asian states, Kyrgyzstan joined the EEU and Customs Union in 2015.

9. UNODC, *World Drug Report 2011* (Vienna: United Nations, 2011), 71; UNODC, *The Global Afghan Opiate Trade: A Threat Assessment* (Vienna: UNODC, 2011), 44; Bureau for International Narcotics and Law Enforcement Affairs, *2013 International Narcotics Control Strategy Report Volume I: Drug and Chemical Control* (Washington D.C.: U.S. Department of State, 2013), 277.

10. UNODC, *Afghan Opiate Trafficking Along the Northern Route* (Vienna: UNODC, 2018), 66.

11. UNODC, *World Drug Report 2011,* 72–3.

12. UNODC, *World Drug Report 2010* (Vienna: United Nations, 2010), 48.

13. UNODC, *Drug Money: The Illicit Proceeds of Opiates Trafficked on the Balkan Route* (Vienna: UNODC, 2015), 7, 9.

14. Financial Action Task Force (FATF), *Financial Flows Linked to the Production and Trafficking of Afghan Opiates* (Paris: FATF/OECD, 2014), 5.

15. As shown by an increase in heroin-related deaths in the UK in 2012–14 and in estimates of problem opiate users in France, and by growing heroin prevalence rates in Italy in 2008–14. United Nations Office on Drugs and Crime, *World Drug Report 2016* (Vienna: United Nations, 2016), 27–8; European Monitoring Centre for Drugs and Drug Addiction, *France: Country Drug Report 2017* (Luxembourg: European Union, 2017).

16. International Narcotics Control Board, *Report of the International Narcotics Control Board for 2011,* E/INCB/2011/1 (Vienna: United Nations, 2012), interview with DEA experts, November 2012; Ekaterina Stepanova, *Afghan Narcotrafficking: A Joint Threat Assessment*, report by Joint U.S.-Russia Working Group on the Afghan Narcotrafficking (New York: EastWest Institute, 2013), 13.

17. Viktor Ivanov, Director of the FSKN, quoted by: Interfax, March 23, 2012.

18. FSKN, 'On the narcotics situation in the Russian Federation and the result of countering illicit circulation of narcotics (January–March 2012),' 2012, http://www.fskn.gov.ru/pages/main/prevent/3939/4052/index.shtml.

19. UNODC, *Afghan Opiate Trafficking*, 66.

20. UNODC, *World Drug Report 2016*, xiii, 29–30.

21. UNODC, *World Drug Report 2018* (Vienna: United Nations, 2018), booklet 3, p. 17, http://www.unodc.org/wdr2018/prelaunch/WDR18_Booklet_3_DRUG_MARKETS.pdf.

22. UNODC, *Afghan Opiate Trafficking*, 71.

23. Alexei Knorre and Dmitry Skugarevsky, *How MVD and FSKN Fight Drugs: Comparative Analysis of the Two Agencies Effectiveness*, Analytical Notes on Law Implementation (Saint Petersburg: Institute of Law Implementation Problems, European University in Saint Petersburg, 2015), 11, 14.

24. Ibid. Heroin was the most frequently seized narcotic in seventeen, and opium in one out of Russia's eighty-three subjects/regions at the time, but those eighteen regions were all the most densely populated ones and included the central part of European Russia (Moscow and all regions around it), as well as several Volga

regions, a couple of large Siberian regions and Kaliningrad. The number of heroin seizure cases roughly equaled all (natural and synthetic) cannabinoid-related cases (in 2013, 3360 vs. 4153 cases, and in 2014, 4013 vs 2618 cases, respectively). See a clickable map of drug seizures by MVD and FSKN in 2013-2014, by region, produced by EUSP Institute of Law Implementation Problems: http://atlasjustice. com/drugmap/region.html.

25. Ibid.

26. Stepanova, *Afghan Narcotrafficking*, 31; UNODC, *Afghan Opiate Trafficking*, 122.

27. UNODC, *World Drug Report 2018,* booklet 3, p. 20.

28. Ibid., 15; Bureau for International Narcotics and Law Enforcement Affairs, *2018 International Narcotics Control Strategy Report: Volume I: Drug and Chemical Control* (Washington D.C.: U.S. Department of State, 2018), 157.

29. UNODC, *World Drug Report 2018,* booklet 3, p. 62.

30. First Deputy Head of MVD main directorate for drug control Kirill Smurov, Ministry of Internal Affairs of the Russian Federation (MVD) press release, December 6, 2018, https://xn--b1aew.xn--p1ai/mvd/structure1/glavnie_upravlenija/gunk/ novosti/item/15179154/.

31. Ministry of Internal Affairs of the Russian Federation, 'On the Strategy of State Anti-Narcotics Policy of the Russian Federation through 2030,' January 16, 2020, https://regulation.gov.ru/projects#npa=98716. For the draft text of the Strategy in Russian, see: https://regulation.gov.ru/Files/GetFile?fileid=4b8e646e-9121-4dd0-b0f1-71e5fe668cb8.

32. 'FSKN has reported on the Russian drug addicts' preferences,' *Interfax*, April 23, 2015.

33. See results of a set of surveys conducted from 2013 to 2018 by experts of the Institute of Sociology, Russian Academy of Sciences. Margarita Posdnyakova, 'New narco-situation in Russia,' *Review of Russian Foundation for Fundamental Sciences: Humanities and Social Sciences* 2, no. 95 (2019): 77–89, https://www.isras.ru/publ. html?id=7168.

34. Ministry of Internal Affairs of the Russian Federation, 'Draft Strategy of State Anti-Narcotics Policy of the Russian Federation through 2030,' 9, https://regulation. gov.ru/Files/GetFile?fileid=4b8e646e-9121-4dd0-b0f1-71e5fe668cb8.

35. All data in this passage are from a study by a group of Russian medical researchers: Ju.V. Mikhaylova et al., 'Increased drug addiction among children, adolescents and the young in Russia,' *Social Aspects of Public Health*, no. 3 (2014), http://vestnik. mednet.ru/content/view/572/30/lang,ru.

36. Ibid.

37. Ibid.

38. 'Patrushev: harm from narcotics in Russia equals health budget,' *Novosti Mail.ru*, February 25, 2013.

39. 'Basic Functioning Indicators of the Narcological Service of the Russian Federation.' Set of statistical handbooks for 2008–2017, released by NRC on Addictions – branch of V.Serbsky NMRCPN. Quoted in: UNODC, *World Drug Report 2018*, 20.

40. Ibid.

41. Prof. Vadim Pokrovski, head of Federal Research and Methodological Center for Prophylactics and Countering HIV/AIDS, quoted in: I. Tyazhlov, 'Russia is one of the few countries where cases of HIV-infection and deaths from HIV-AIDS are on the rise,' *Kommersant*, May 4, 2015.

42. V. Pokrovsky, quoted by Interfax.ru, January 20, 2016.

43. FATF, *Financial Flows*, 5.

44. FATF, *Second Mutual Evaluation Report of the Russian Federation: Anti-Money Laundering and Combating the Financing of Terrorism* (Paris: FATF/OECD, 2008), 7.

45. Transparency International, 'Corruption Perceptions Index 2018,' 2019, https://www.transparency.org/cpi201.

46. Bureau for International Narcotics and Law Enforcement Affairs, *2018 International Narcotics Control Strategy Report: Volume II: Money Laundering and Financial Crimes* (Washington D.C.: U.S. Department of State, 2018), 14.

47. Federal Law 'On Narcotic and Psychotropic Substances,' January 8, 1998, in *Russian Law Collection*, 1998. V. 2. Art. 219.

48. While the UN Secretary General made that choice in light of multiple considerations, it also reflected the recognition of the gravity of narcotics challenge faced by Russia.

49. These are governments that have either started contributing to the UNODC budget recently and/or provide funding to UNODC activities in their own countries: http://www.unodc.org/unodc/en/donors/emerging-and-national-donors.html.

50. Yuri Fedotov, 'Yuri Fedotov: "I am surprised that the Global Commission calls for legalization of ecstasy and cannabis",' *Security Index* 17, no. 4 (2011): 25–6, http://www.pircenter.org/media/content/files/0/13406273380.pdf.

51. GCDP, *Taking Control: Pathways to Drug Policies that Work* (Geneva: GCDP, 2014), https://www.globalcommissionondrugs.org/reports/taking-control-pathways-to-drug-policies-that-work.

52. Permanent Mission of the Russian Federation to the International Organizations in Vienna, 'Statement by the Russian President's Special Representative on international cooperation in the fight against terrorism and transnational organized crime, Anatoly Zmeyevsky, at the High-Level Segment of the 57th session of the UN Commission on Narcotic Drugs, Vienna, March 13, 2014,' 2014.

53. Ibid.

54. Government of Russia, 'Statement by Viktor Ivanov, head of State Anti-Narcotics Committee, Director of FSKN' (statement delivered at the BRICS Ministerial meeting, Moscow, April 22, 2015).

55. Ibid.

56. 'FSKN head spoke against legalization of soft drugs,' *Interfax*, April 21, 2015.

57. Permanent Mission of the Russian Federation to the International Organizations in Vienna, 'Statement by the Russian President's Special Representative.'

58. Ministry of Foreign Affairs of the Russian Federation, 'Deputy Foreign Minister Oleg Syromolotov's answer to a journalist's question on drug harm reduction programs, Moscow,' press release, August 6, 2018.

59. Anna Sarang, head of Andrei Rylkov Foundation (declared a 'foreign agent' NGO in Russia), quoted in: Valeria Mishina, 'The War on Drugs is lost: Global Commission

on Drug Policy invites states to legally regulate the drug market,' *Kommersant*, September 24, 2018, 4, https://www.kommersant.ru/doc/3750948.

60.   See, for example, a debate between Lev Levinson (representing the dissenting view) and Yuri Kroupnov (one of the strongest advocates of the mainstream harsh, conservative approach): Yu. Kroupnov, and L. Levinson, 'Is the War on Drugs Lost?' *Security Index* 17, no. 3 (2011): 85–98.

61.   Quoted in Mishina, 'The War on Drugs is lost.'

62.   As noted by Head of Moscow City Parliament Health Committee, 'any legalization of drugs paves the way for the full narcotization of the society.' Quoted in: V. Nekhezin, 'Legalization of drugs: Russia is still against,' *BBC Russian Service*, September 10, 2014.

63.   Narcologist Vladimir Mendelevich of the Kazan State Medical University, quoted in: Mishina, 'The War on Drugs is lost.'

64.   Kroupnov and Levinson, 'Is the War on Drugs Lost?' 96.

65.   Alexei Knorre, *Narcotics Crimes in Russia: Analysis of Court and Criminal Statistics*, Analytical Note (Saint Petersburg: Institute of Law Implementation Problems, European University in Saint Petersburg, 2017), https://www.openpolice.ru/docs/analiticheskaya-zapiska-narkoprestupleniya-v-rossii-analiz-sudebnoj-i-kriminalnoj-statistiki.

66.   '228th in grams and terms,' *Kommersant*, June 18, 2019, https://www.kommersant.ru/doc/3999368?from=doc_vrez.

67.   Ministry of Internal Affairs of the Russian Federation, 'Draft Strategy of State Anti-Narcotics Policy,' 7–8.

68.   'Russian Court has Sentenced a Drug Trader for Life for the First Time,' *Rosbusinessconsulting*, December 21, 2017.

69.   'FSB impeded the work of two large producers of synthetic drugs,' *Rosbusinessconsulting*, July 24, 2018.

70.   Andrey Avetisyan, 'Presentation at the 6th meeting of the Joint US-Russia Working Group on the Afghan Narcotrafficking,' Moscow, October 6, 2015.

71.   Quoted in: 'FSKN proposed to differentiate punishment for illicit drug storage depending on the degree of public danger,' *Interfax*, March 30, 2015.

72.   'FSKN head proposed to allow courts to stop criminal prosecution of drug abusers who go through treatment,' *Interfax*, March 30, 2015.

73.   'A draft law to criminalize narcotics propaganda online has been submitted to State Duma,' *Rosbusinessconsulting*, July 9, 2020, https://www.rbc.ru/rbcfreenews/5f0707079a79470540e6ef03.

74.   Fedetov, 'Yuri Fedotov: "I am surprised that the Global Commission calls for legalization of ecstasy and cannabis".'

75.   Ministry of Internal Affairs of the Russian Federation, 'Draft Strategy of State Anti-Narcotics Policy,' 16.

76.   Ministry of Health of the Russian Federation, 'Position of Ministry of Health of Russia Regarding the Opioid Substitute Therapy,' March 11, 2016.

77.   Government of Russia, 'Statement by Viktor Ivanov.'

78.   Mikhail Gabrilyants, adviser to the head of FSKN, remarks at the 6th meeting of the Joint US-Russia Working Group on the Afghan Narcotrafficking, Moscow, October 5, 2015. He also referred to methadone and buprenorphine as 'chemical handcuffs.'

79. Quoted in: 'I may be saying scary things for a man in uniform,' *Kommersant*, September 19, 2018.

80. V. Kozlov, 'FSKN is given the capacity to rehabilitate,' *Kommersant*, August 4, 2014.

81. The Russian Government, 'Decree of the President of the Russian Federation no. 507, July 10, 2014;' Kozlov, 'FSKN is given the capacity.'

82. 'Rehabilitation of drug users in Russia will meet new standards,' *Vesti.Medicina*, May 10, 2018, https://med.vesti.ru/novosti/obshhestvo-i-zakonodatelstvo/reabilitatsiya-narkomanov-v-rossii-budet-prohodit-po-novym-standartam.

83. 'Medicines should be available to those suffering from pain,' *Kommersant*, April 4, 2016.

84. Quoted in: 'Foundation call for the Ministry of Health to decriminalize pain reliever,' *Rosbusinessconsulting*, August 24, 2018.

85. Bureau for International Narcotics and Law Enforcement Affairs, *2018 International Narcotics Control Strategy Report: Volume II,* 170.

86. See 'Cabinet of Ministries has approved cultivation of narcotic plants for medicines,' *Rosbusinessconsulting*, December 26, 2018.

87. Thom Shanker and Elisabeth Bumiller, 'U.S. shifts Afghan narcotics strategy,' *The New York Times*, July 23, 2009.

88. UNODC, *The Global Afghan Opiate Trade*, 22, 30; Ekaterina Stepanova, 'Illicit drugs and insurgency in Afghanistan,' *Perspectives on Terrorism* 6, no. 2 (2012): 4–18.

89. UNODC and Islamic Republic of Afghanistan Ministry for Counternarcotics, *Afghanistan Opium Survey 2011* (Kabul: UNODC, 2011), 77.

90. V. Ivanov, quoted in 'White death across Russia,' *Voice of Russia*, November 22, 2011.

91. Vladimir Putin's interview to *Russia Today*, September 6, 2012, http://rt.com/news/vladimir-putin-exclusive-interview-481.

92. Statement by V. Ivanov at the BRICS Ministerial meeting.

93. Institute for Demography, Migration and Regional Development, *A New Generation of Alternative Development Programs for Elimination of Drug Production in Afghanistan* (Moscow: Institute for Demography, Migration and Regional Development [Russia]; Belarus: Center for Strategic and Foreign Policy Studies, 2014).

94. For more detail, see Ekaterina Stepanova, *Russia and the Afghan Peace Process*, Program on New Approaches to Research and Security in Eurasia (PONARS Eurasia) Policy Memo no. 618 (Washington D.C.: Elliott School of International Affairs, George Washington University, 2019), https://www.ponarseurasia.org/wp-content/uploads/attachments/Pepm618_Stepanova_Oct2019.pdf; Ekaterina Stepanova, 'Russia and the search for negotiated solution in Afghanistan,' *Europe-Asia Studies*, October 26, 2020, https://www.tandfonline.com/doi/abs/10.1080/09668136.2020.1826908?journalCode=ceas20.

95. On U.S.–Russia Joint declaration welcoming the signing of the U.S.–Taliban deal, see: Office of the Spokesman, U.S. Department of State, 'Joint Statement on the Signing of the U.S.–Taliban Agreement,' Media Note, March 6, 2020, https://www.state.gov/joint-statement-on-the-signing-of-the-u-s-taliban-agreement/.

96. FATF, *Financial Flows*, 35.

11. DRUG USE AND CRIME IN THE CONTEXT OF THE WAR ON DRUGS

1. In the last half of the century, drug policies have been guided by the International Drug Control Regime (IDCR) based on three main pillars: the 1961 Single Convention on Narcotic Drugs, the 1971 Convention on Psychotropic Substances, and the 1988 Convention Against the Illicit Traffic in Narcotic Drugs and Psychotropic Substances. For a historical overview of the evolution of the main laws, norms, and institutions of the IDCR see Chapter 2 by Paul Gootenberg.

2. Andrew J. Resignato, 'Violent Crime: A Function of Drug Use or Drug Enforcement?' *Applied Economics* 32, no. 6 (2010): 681–88, https://doi.org/10.1080/000368400322291.

3. Trevor Bennett and Katy Holloway, *Understanding Drugs, Alcohol and Crime* (Berkshire: Open University Press, 2005).

4. Steve Rolles et al., *The Alternative World Drug Report*, 2nd ed. (Bristol: Transform Drug Policy Foundation, 2016).

5. David Boyum and Peter Reuter, 'Reflections on Drug Policy and Social Policy,' in *Drug Addiction and Drug Policy. The Struggle to Control Dependence*, ed. Phillip B. Heyman and William N. Brownsberger (Cambridge: Harvard University Press, 2001); Robert MacCoun, Beau Kilmer, and Peter Reuter, 'Research on Drugs-Crime Linkages: The Next Generation,' in *Toward a Drugs and Crime Research Agenda for The 21st Century: Special Report* (Washington D.C.: National Institute of Justice, 2003), 65–95; Juan Carlos Garzón Vergara, *Consertando Um Sistema Falido: Modernizando a Aplicação Das Leis de Drogas Na América Latina*, Série sobre Reforma Legislativa de Políticas sobre Drogas No. 29 (Amsterdam: TNI; London: IDPC, 2014).

6. UNODC, *World Drug Report 2019* (Vienna: United Nations, 2019).

7. Trevor Bennett, Katy Holloway, and David Farrington, 'The Statistical Association between Drug Misuse and Crime: A Meta-Analysis,' *Aggression and Violent Behavior* 13, no. 2 (2008), 107–18, https://doi.org/10.1016/j.avb.2008.02.001; Richard Hammersley, 'Pathways through Drugs and Crime: Desistance, Trauma and Resilience,' *Journal of Criminal Justice* 39, no. 3 (2011): 268–72, https://doi.org/10.1016/j.jcrimjus.2011.02.006; Josine Junger-Tas, Incke Marshall and Denis Ribeaud, *Delinquency in International Perspective: The International Self-Reported Delinquency Study (ISRD)* (Amsterdam: Kugler Publications, 2003).

8. Toby Seddon, 'Explaining the Drug–Crime Link: Theoretical, Policy and Research Issues,' *Journal of Social Policy* 29, no. 1 (2000): 95–107, https://doi.org/10.1017/S0047279400005833.

9. Jan M. Chaiken, and Maria R. Chaiken, 'Drugs and Predatory Crime,' *Crime and Justice* 13 (1990): 203–39; Jan Keene, 'A Case-Linkage Study of the Relationship between Drug Misuse, Crime, and Psychosocial Problems in a Total Criminal Justice Population,' *Addiction Research and Theory* 13, no 5 (2009): 489–502; Alex Stevens, 'Weighing up Crime: The Overestimation of Drug-Related Crime,' *Contemporary Drug Problems* 35, no. 2–3 (2008): 265–290, https://doi:10.1177/009145090803500205.

10. Alex Stevens, 'When Two Dark Figures Collide: Evidence and Discourse on Drug-Related Crime,' *Critical Social Policy* 27, no. 1 (2007): 82

11.   Stevens, 'Weighing up Crime.'

12.   Bennett and Holloway, *Understanding Drugs, Alcohol and Crime*; Robert MacCoun and Peter Reuter, 'Evaluating Alternative Cannabis Regimes,' *British Journal of Psychiatry* 178, no. 2 (2001): 123–8, https://doi.org/10.1192/bjp.178.2.123.

13.   Jane A. Buxton, Mark Haden, and Richard G. Mathias, 'The Control and Regulation of Currently Illegal Drugs,' *International Encyclopedia of Public Health* 2 (2008): 7–16, https://doi.org/10.1016/B978-012373960-5.00356-7.

14.   Alex Stevens, Mike Trace, and Dave Bewley-Taylor, *Reducing Drug-Related Crime: An Overview of the Global Evidence* (London: Beckley Foundation, 2005); Peter Reuter and Alex Stevens, *An Analysis of UK Drug Policy: Executive Summary* (London: United Kingdom Drug Policy Commission, 2007).

15.   Peter Imbusch, Michel Misse, and Fernando Carrión, 'Violence Research in Latin America and the Caribbean: A Literature Review,' *International Journal of Conflict and Violence* 5, no. 1 (2011): 88–154; UNODC, *World Drug Report 2011* (Vienna: United Nations, 2011); UNODC, *World Drug Report 2014* (Vienna: United Nations, 2014).

16.   David Bewley-Taylor, Tom Blickman, and Martin Jelsma, *The Rise and Decline of Cannabis Prohibition. The History of Cannabis in the UN Drug Control System and Options for Reform* (Amsterdam: TNI; Swansea: Global Drug Policy Observatory, 2014); Garzón Vergara, 'Consertando Um Sistema Falido.'

17.   Another factor that might have played a role is the increasing numbers of use and misuse of drugs in the region. UNODC, *World Drug Report 2011*.

18.   An illustrative example was when Raymond Yans, president of UN's International Narcotics Control Board (INCB), directly accused the government of Uruguay of having a 'pirate attitude' for going against the UN's conventions on drugs. Martin Jelsma, 'The INCB vs Uruguay: The Art of Diplomacy,' *Transnational Institute*, December 17, 2013, http://druglawreform.info/en/weblog/item/5214-incb-vs-uruguay-the-art-of-diplomacy#.UrDlNx-34hc.twitter.

19.   Paul J. Goldstein, 'The Drugs/Violence Nexus: A Tripartite Conceptual Framework,' *Journal of Drug Issues* 39 (1985): 143–74.

20.   Richard Wright, Fiona Brookman, and Trevor Bennett, 'The Foreground Dynamics of Street Robbery in Britain,' *British Journal of Criminology* 46, no. 1 (2006): 1–15, https://doi.org/10.1093/bjc/azi055.

21.   Mark Simpson, 'The Relationship between Drug Use and Crime: A Puzzle inside an Enigma,' *International Journal of Drug Policy* 14, no. 4 (2003): 307–19, https://doi.org/10.1016/S0955-3959(03)00081-1.

22.   Chaiken and Chaiken, 'Drugs and Predatory Crime.'

23.   Ronald Akers, *Social Learning and Social Structure: A General Theory of Crime and Deviance* (New York: Routledge, 2009); Travis Hirschi and Michael R. Gottfredson, 'Self-control theory,' in *Explaining Criminals and Crime: Essays in Contemporary Criminological Theory,* ed. Raymond Paternoster and Ronet Bachman (Los Angeles: Roxbury, 2001), 81–96; Stephen Pudney, 'The Road to Ruin? Sequences of Initiation to Drugs and Crime,' *Economic Journal* 113, no. 486 (2003): 182–98.

24.   Paul D. Ellis, *The essential guide to effect sizes: Statistical power, meta-analysis, and the interpretation of research results* (Cambridge: Cambridge University Press, 2010).

25. Lucía Dammert, 'Drogas e Inseguridad en América Latina: Una Relación Compleja,' *Nueva Sociedad*, no. 222 (2009): 112–31.

26. Carlos José Nieto Silva, 'Consumo de Drogas en Tres Etapas de la Vida de Habitantes de Calle de Bogotá: Predictores de Consumo y Comparación con una Muestra de Población Infantil y Adolescente de Brasil' (master's diss., Universidad Federal de Rio Grande do Sul, 2011).

27. Instituto de Sociología, *Estudio de prevalencia y factores asociados al consumo de drogas en adolescentes infractores de ley* (Santiago de Chile: Pontifica Universidad Católica de Chile, 2007).

28. However, this study also explores the causal role of drugs on crime using the Goldstein – Pernanen et al. counterfactual model of imputation.

29. Nicolas Trajtenberg and Pablo Menese, 'Self-control, differential association and the drug–crime link in Uruguay in the context of the legalization of Marijuana,' *Aggression & Violent Behavior* 46 (2020): 180–9.

30. Mario Alberto Saens Roja et al., 'Privados de Libertad y Drogas: Experiencias en un Régimen de Confianza,' *Medicina Legal* 15, no. 12 (1998); Celina Manitas, 'Das Descobertas Privadas Aos Crimes Públicos: Evolução Dos Significados Em Trajectórias de Droga-Crime,' *Revista Toxicodependencias* 63 (2003): 674–706; UNODC, *Consumo de Drogas en Población Privada de Libertad y la Relación entre Delito y Droga,* Cuarto Informe Conjunto (New York: UNODC, 2010); UNODC, *La relación delito y droga en adolescentes infractores de la ley*, Quinto Informe Conjunto (New York: UNODC, 2010).

31. UNODC, *Consumo de Drogas en Población Privada de Libertad y la Relación entre Delito y Droga.*

32. Joanne Klevens, Ofelia Restrepo, Juanita Roca, and Adriana Martínez, 'Los Escenarios del Delito en Cinco Ciudades,' *Revista de Salud Pública* 1, no. 3 (1999): 245–54.

33. Edith Serfaty et al., 'Violencia y riesgos asociados en adolescentes,' *Revista Argentina de Clinica Neuropsiquiatrica* 10, no. 3 (2001).

34. Paula Alarcón Bañares et al., 'Validación del Cuestionario de Auto-Reporte de Comportamiento Antisocial en Adolescentes: CACSA,' *Paidéia (Ribeirão Preto)* 20, no. 47 (2010), https://doi.org/10.1590/S0103-863X2010000300002.

35. Boundaries between explanatory and descriptive goals are blurry. Although in some cases it is clear that a particular study has explanatory goals (for example, using more sophisticated statistical analysis such as regression, or applying the Pernanen counterfactual model) in other cases it is less clear. In this last case we also considered as explanatory those studies that despite using less sophisticated statistical analysis (for example bivariate statistics) nevertheless explicitly argued that their results had explanatory implications.

36. Fundación Paz Ciudadana, *Construcción de indicadores de reinserción social de adolescentes infractores de la ley penal* (Santiago de Chile: Fundación Paz Ciudadana, 2010).

37. However, Freddy A. Crespo, and Mireya Bolaños G., 'Delitos Violentos: Entre los Vapores de la Drogadicción,' *Capítulo Criminológico* 36, no. 3 (2008): 101–41, also analyzed a sample of imprisoned offenders in the Region Los Andes Penitentiary Center where they found a statistically significant relationship between involvement in violent crimes and use of drugs before arrest.

38. Another indicator usually used is age of initiation since studies show that imprisoned and arrested individuals start using drugs at an earlier age than the general population (see for example Paula Hurtado, *Consumo de Drogas en Detenidos: Aplicación de la Metodología I-ADAM en Chile* (Santiago de Chile: Fundación Paz Ciudadana, 2005); Instituto de Sociología, *Estudio de prevalencia*).

39. Fundación Paz Ciudadana, *Consumo de Alcohol y Delincuencia en Chile* (Santiago de Chile: Fundación Paz Ciudadana, 2003); UNODC, *Consumo de Drogas*; UNODC, *La Relación Delito y Droga.*

40. Hurtado, *Consumo de Drogas en Detenidos*; Fundación Paz Ciudadana, *Consumo de Alcohol y Delincuencia.*

41. UNODC, *Consumo de Drogas en Población Privada de Libertad y la Relación entre Delito y Droga.*

42. Javiera Carcamo, *Consumo de Drogas en Detenidos: Estudio I-ADAM 2010* (Santiago de Chile: Fundación Paz Ciudadana, 2011); Constanza Hurtado and Pilar Larroulet, 'Consumo de Drogas y Validación de Auto Reporte en Cárceles Chilenas,' in *VII Congreso de Investigación Sobre Violencia y Delincuencia* (Santiago de Chile: Fundación Paz Ciudadana, 2012), 135–47.

43. Goldstein, 'The Drugs/Violence Nexus.'

44. Kai Pernanen et al., *Proportions of Crimes Associated with Alcohol and Other Drugs in Canada* (Ottawa: Canadian Center on Substance Abuse, 2002).

45. The economic compulsive connection involves not only showing that individual commits crime to obtain resources to use drugs but also that he/she has dependence/abuse to drugs.

46. The pharmacologic attribution requires two conditions. Not only the individual has to commit the crime under the effects of drug use, but also the counterfactual condition must be met: the individual should not have done the crime if he/she had not been under the effects of drugs.

47. Eduardo Valenzuela and Pilar Larroulet, 'La Relación Droga – Delito: Una Estimación de la Fracción Atribuible,' *Estudios Públicos* 119 (2010): 33–66.

48. UNODC, *La Relación Delito y Droga.*

49. UNODC, *Consumo de Drogas*; Hurtado and Larroulet, 'Consumo de Drogas.'

50. Irina Eiranova González-Elías, Ariane Hernández Trujillo, and Ángela Otero Mustelier, 'El ciclo de la violencia en consumidores de sustancias tóxicas,' *MEDISAN* 17, no. 12 (2013): 9081–8. Although the following also include samples of non-offenders, they all explicitly lack explanatory ambitions or goals: Karla Selene López García, and Moacyr Lobo da Costa Junior, 'Conduta anti-social e consumo de álcool em adolescentes escolares,' *Revista Latino-Americana de Enfermagem* 16, no. 2 (2008): 299–305; Isabel C. Salazar-Torres, María Teresa Varela-Arévalo, Luisa F. Lema-Soto, Julián A. Tamayo-Cardona, and Carolina Duarte-Alarcón, 'Evaluación de las conductas de salud en jóvenes universitarios,' *Revista de Salud Pública* 12 (2010): 599–611; María Elena Villarreal-González, Juan Carlos Sánchez-Sosa, Gonzalo Musitu, and Rosa Varela, 'El consumo de alcohol en adolescentes escolarizados: propuesta de un modelo sociocomunitario,' *Psychosocial Intervention* 19, no. 3 (2010): 253–64.

51. David W. Brook et al., 'Early Risk Factors for Violence in Colombian Adolescents,' *American Journal of Psychiatry* 160, no. 8 (2003): 1470–8.

52. Franklin Escobar Córdoba, 'Riesgo Para Cometer Homicidio en Jóvenes Bogotanos: Un Estudio Multimétodo' (PhD diss., Universidad Nacional de La Plata, 2006).

53. Pedro Rioseco et al., 'Prevalencia de trastornos psiquiátricos en adolescentes infractores de ley. Estudio caso-control,' *Rev Chil Neuro-Psiquiatr.* 47, no. 3 (2009): 190–200.

54. Mayra Brea and Edylberto Cabral, 'Factores de Riesgo y Violencia Juvenil en República Dominicana,' *Revista PsicologiaCientifica.com* 12, no. 15 (2010).

55. Imelda Alcalá-Sanchez et al., *Prevención del Delito en Jóvenes, Mediante Colectivos Juveniles de Arte Libre* (Chihuahua: Dirección de Seguridad Pública Municipal, 2012).

56. Fernanda Lüdke et al., 'Uso de drogas e comportamento antissocial entre adolescentes de escolas públicas no Brasil,' *Trends Psychiatry Psychotherapy* 34, no. 2 (2012): 80–6.

57. Ana Olivia Ruíz Martínez et al., *Family Functioning of Consumers of Addictive Sustances with and without Criminal Behavior* (Mexico City: Universidad Autónoma del Estado de México, Universidad del Valle de México, 2013).

58. William R. Shadish, Thomas D. Cook, and Donald Thomas Campbell, *Experimental and Quasi-Experimental Designs for Generalized Causal Inference* (Boston: Houghton Mifflin, 2002), 171–206.

59. Bennett and Holloway, *Understanding Drugs, Alcohol and Crime.*

60. Chaiken and Chaiken, 'Drugs and Predatory Crime.'

61. Stevens, 'Weighing up Crime.'

62. Manitas, 'Das Descobertas Privadas;' Gabriel Kessler, *Sociología del Delito Amateur* (Buenos Aires: Editorial Paidos, 2004), 296.

63. Bennett, Holloway, and Farrington, 'The Statistical Association,' conducted a meta-analysis using data from US, Europe, and Australia but they did not compare prevalence rates but rather the odds of offending of drug users and non-drug users.

64. Carcamo, *Consumo de Drogas*; Fundación Paz Ciudadana, *Consumo de Alcohol y Delincuencia*; UNODC, *La Relación Delito y Droga.*

65. Ministry of Justice (of the UK), *Transforming Rehabilitation: A Summary of Evidence on Reducing Reoffending* (London: Ministry of Justice, 2013).

66. Terrie E. Moffitt, 'Adolescence-Limited and Life-Course-Persistent Antisocial Behavior: A Developmental Taxonomy,' *Psychological Review* 100, no. 4 (1993): 674–701, https://doi.org/10.1037/0033-295X.100.4.674.

67. Rolf Loeber et al., 'Findings from the Pittsburgh Youth Study: Cognitive Impulsivity and Intelligence as Predictors of the Age-Crime Curve,' *Journal of the American Academy of Child and Adolescent Psychiatry* 51, no. 11 (2012): 1136–49, https://doi.org/doi:10.1016/j.jaac.2012.08.019.

68. Judith S. Brook et al., 'Longitudinally Predicting Late Adolescent and Young Adult Drug Use: Childhood and Adolescent Precursors,' *Journal of the American Academy of Child and Adolescent Psychiatry* 34, no. 9 (1995): 1230–38, https://doi.org/10.1097/00004583-199509000-00022.

69. James G. Barber, Floyd Bolitho, and Lorne D. Bertrand, 'Intrapersonal versus Peer Group Predictors of Adolescent Drug Use,' *Children and Youth Services Review* 21, no. 7 (1999): 565–79, https://doi.org/10.1016/S0190-7409(99)00039-0.

70. Angelina R. Sutin, Michele K. Evans, and Alan B. Zonderman, 'Personality Traits and Illicit Substances: The Moderating Role of Poverty,' *Drug and Alcohol Dependence* 131, no. 3 (2013): 247–51, https://doi.org/10.1016/j.drugalcdep.2012.10.020.

71. Katrin M. Kirschbaum et al., 'Illegal Drugs and Delinquency,' *Forensic Science International* 226, no. 1–3 (2013): 230–34, https://doi.org/10.1016/j.forsciint.2013.01.031.

72. Joseph B. Kuhns and Tammatha A. Clodfelter, 'Illicit Drug-Related Psychopharmacological Violence: The Current Understanding within a Causal Context,' *Aggression and Violent Behavior* 14, no. 1 (2009): 69–78, https://doi.org/10.1016/j.avb.2008.11.001; W. Alexander Morton, 'Cocaine and Psychiatric Symptoms,' *Primary Care Companion to the Journal of Clinical Psychiatry* 1, no. 4 (1999): 109–13, https://doi.org/10.4088/PCC.v01n0403; Thor Norström and Ingeborg Rossow, 'Cannabis Use and Violence: Is There a Link?' *Scandinavian Journal of Public Health* 42, no. 4 (2014): 358–63, https://doi.org/10.1177/1403494814525003.

73. Mark S. Gold, Steven T. Gold, and Michael Herkov, 'Drugs and Violence in The USA,' in *Encyclopedia of Violence, Peace, and Conflict,* ed. Lester R. Kurtz, 2nd ed. (Amsterdam: Academic Press, 2008), 590–606.

74. Stephen Magura and Sung-Yeon Kang. 'Validity of Self-Reported Drug Use in High Risk Populations: A Meta-Analytical Review,' *Substance Use & Misuse* 31, no. 9 (1996): 1131–53.

75. Lana Harrison, 'The Validity of Self-Reported Drug Use in Survey Research: An Overview and Critique of Research Methods,' *NIDA Research Monograph* 167 (1997): 17–36.

76. Brea and Cabral, 'Factores de Riesgo;' Brook et al. 'Longitudinally Predicting;' UNODC, *Consumo de Drogas.*

77. Instituto de Sociología, *Estudio de prevalencia.*

78. Kessler, *Sociologia del Delito.*

79. Lüdke et al., 'Uso de Drogas;' Nieto, 'Consumo de Drogas en Tres Etapas.'

80. According to Albert Hirschman, *The Rhetoric of Reaction: Perversity, Futility, Jeopardy* (Cambridge: The Belknap Press, 1999), the jeopardy thesis argues that a change or reform is unacceptable because its costs and negative consequences are so high that it endangers previous basic accomplishments.

81. For an example of Uruguay, Nicolas Trajtenberg and Manuel Eisner, *Hacia una Política de Prevención de la Violencia en Uruguay* (Cambridge: University of Cambridge, 2014).

82. Peter N. S. Hoaken and Sherry H. Stewart, 'Drugs of Abuse and the Elicitation of Human Aggressive Behavior,' *Addictive Behaviors* 28, no. 9 (2003): 1533–54, https://doi.org/10.1016/j.addbeh.2003.08.033.

83. Dan Werb et al., 'Effect of Drug Law Enforcement on Drug Market Violence: A Systematic Review,' *International Journal of Drug Policy* 22, no. 2 (2011): 87–94, https://doi.org/10.1016/j.drugpo.2011.02.002.

84. The White House, *National Drug Control Budget: FY 2016 Funding Highlights* (Washington D.C.: The White House, 2016).

85. Of course, many of the reviewed studies caution about assuming that correlation analysis necessarily leads to causal analysis and explicitly warn about the lack of

consensus about the causal role of drugs, the limited nature of their samples, and type of analysis done (Crespo and Bolaños, 'Delitos Violentos;' Fundación Paz Ciudadana, *Consumo de Alcohol y Delincuencia*; Nieto, 'Consumo de Drogas en Tres Etapas'). What is more, in many cases it is argued for the need to consider unobserved common latent factors or more broadly include the social context of both phenomena. However, there is more speculation about third common factors hypothesis than actual empirical evaluation. Despite all these problems, these studies still help to reinforce the self-evident direct causal link between drugs and crime in politicians, policy-makers, and more generally in the public debate.

86.   Jonathan Haidt, *The Righteous Mind: Why Good People Are Divided by Politics and Religion* (New York: Pantheon Books, 2012).

87.   Haidt, *The Righteous Mind*, 54.

88.   Ibid., 57.

89.   Clara Musto-Dutra, 'Talking with Elephants. Issue's Framing and Public Opinion Dynamics on the Regulation of Cannabis in Uruguay' (presentation, 'Crimes against Reality' event, University of Hamburg, Hamburg, 2015).

90.   C. Peter Rydell and Susan S. Everingham, *Controlling Cocaine - Supply Versus Demand Programs* (Santa Monica: RAND Corporation, 1994).

91.   The Justice Policy Institute, *Substance Abuse Treatment and Public Safety* (Washington D.C.: The Justice Policy Institute, 2008).

92.   Jeffrey A. Miron, *The Budgetary Implications of Drug Prohibition* (Cambridge, MA: Department of Economics, Harvard University, 2010), 1–39.

93.   Jeffrey A. Miron and Katherine Waldock, *The Budgetary Impact of Ending Drug Prohibition* (Washington D.C.: Cato Institute, 2010), http://www.cato.org/pubs/wtpapers/DrugProhibitionWP.pdf.

94.   For example, Bennett et al., 'The Statistical Association.'

95.   Manuel Eisner, 'No Effects in Independent Prevention Trials: Can We Reject the Cynical View?' *Journal of Experimental Criminology* 5, no. 2 (2009): 163–83, https://doi.org/10.1007/s11292-009-9071-y; Manuel Eisner and David Humphreys, 'Measuring Conflict of Interest in Prevention and Intervention Research: A Feasibility Study,' in *Antisocial Behavior and Crime Contributions of Developmental and Evaluation Research to Prevention and Intervention*, ed. Thomas Bliesener, Andreas Beelmann and Mark Stemmler (Gottingen: Hogrefe Publishing, 2012), 165–80; Anthony Petrosino and Haluk Soydan, 'The Impact of Program Developers as Evaluators on Criminal Recidivism: Results from Meta-Analyses of Experimental and Quasi-Experimental Research,' *Journal of Experimental Criminology* 1, no. 4 (2005): 435–50, https://doi.org/10.1007/s11292-005-3540-8.

12. HEALTH AND HUMAN RIGHTS CHALLENGES FOR THE INTERNATIONAL DRUG CONTROL REGIME

1.   Roy Walmsley, *World Prison Population List*, 12th ed. (London: Institute for Criminal Policy Research and Birkbeck University, 2016), 2.

2.   Gen Sander, *The Death Penalty for Drug Offences: Global Overview 2017* (London: Harm Reduction International, 2018).

3. 'Philippines: Duterte's "Drug War" Claims 12,000+ Lives,' Human Rights Watch, January 18, 2018; Ted Regencia, 'Senator: Rodrigo Duterte's Drug War has Killed 20,000,' *Al Jazeera*, February 21, 2018.

4. Laura Calderón, Octavio Rodríguez Ferreira and David A. Shirk, *Drug Violence in Mexico: Data and Analysis Through 2017* (San Diego: Justice in Mexico, Department of Political Science & International Relations, University of San Diego, 2018), https://justiceinmexico.org/wp-content/uploads/2018/04/180411_DrugViolenceinMexico-12mb.pdf.

5. UNAIDS, ILO, OHCHR, UNDP, UNESCO, UNFPA, UNHCR, UNICEF, UNODC, UN Women, WFP and WHO, *Joint Statement: Compulsory Drug Detention and Rehabilitation Centres* (New York: United Nations, 2012); UNAIDS, ILO, OHCHR, UNDP, UNESCO, UNFPA, UNHCR, UNICEF, UNODC, UN Women, WFP and WHO, *Joint Statement: Compulsory Drug Detention and Rehabilitation Centres in the Context of Covid-19* (New York: United Nations, 2020).

6. F. B. Ahmad, L. M. Rosen and P. Sutton, 'Provisional Drug Overdose Death Counts,' National Center for Health Statistics, last reviewed Sep 16, 2018, https://www.cdc.gov/nchs/nvss/vsrr/drug-overdose-data.html.

7. Catherine Cook et al., *The Case for a Harm Reduction Decade: Progress, Potential and Paradigm Shifts* (London: Harm Reduction International, 2016), 6.

8. UNODC and Islamic Republic of Afghanistan Ministry for Counternarcotics, *Afghanistan Opium Survey 2017: Cultivation and Production* (Kabul: UNODC, 2017); UNODC and Gobierno de Colombia, *Colombia: Monitoreo de Territorios Afectados por Cultivos Ilícitos 2016* (Bogotá: UNODC, 2017).

9. See, for example, Global Commission on Drug Policy, *War on Drugs: Report of the Global Commission on Drug Policy* (Geneva: GCDP, 2011). Steve Rolles et al., *The Alternative World Drug Report: Counting the Costs of the War on Drugs* (Bristol: Count the Costs, 2012); United Nations General Assembly, *Right of Everyone to the Enjoyment of the Highest Attainable Standard of Physical and Mental Health*, A/65/255 (New York, August 6, 2010); Damon Barrett, 'Reflections on Human Rights and International Drug Control,' in *Governing the Global Drug Wars*, ed. John Collins (London: LSE, 2012), 56–62.

10. UNODC, 'Political Declaration and Plan of Action on International Cooperation Towards an Integrated and Balanced Strategy to Counter the World Drug Problem,' in *High-Level Segment Commission on Narcotic Drugs* (Vienna: United Nations, 2009), 1–6.

11. Peter Reuter and Franz Trautmann, eds., *A Report on Global Illicit Drug Markets 1998–2007* (Utrecht: European Commission, 2009).

12. Lloyd D. Johnston et al., *Monitoring the Future National Survey Results on Drug Use, 1975–2012: Volume I: Secondary School Students* (Ann Arbor: Institute for Social Research, University of Michigan, 2013). For a snapshot see pp. 48–52 for rates of lifetime use of any illicit drug among 10th to 12th graders and young adults aged 19–28 years, from 1991–2012.

13. European Monitoring Centre on Drugs and Drug Addiction, *European Drug Report 2014: Trends and Developments* (Lisbon: EMCDDA, 2014).

14. UNODC, *World Drug Report 2019* (Vienna: United Nations, 2019), 7.

15. Marie-Josephine Seya et al., 'A First Comparison Between the Consumption of and the Need for Opioid Analgesics at Country, Regional and Global Level,' *Journal of Pain and Palliative Care Pharmacotherapy* 25, no. 1 (2011): 6–18.

16. Harm Reduction International (HRI), *The Global State of Harm Reduction 2016*, ed. Katie Stone (London: HRI, 2016), 9.

17. 'What is Harm Reduction?' HRI, 2010, http://www.ihra.net/what-is-harm-reduction.

18. Chris Beyrer et al., 'Time to Act: A Call for Comprehensive Responses to HIV in People Who Use Drugs,' *The Lancet* 376, no. 9740 (2010): 551–63.

19. Cook et al., *The Case for a Harm Reduction Decade*, 11.

20. HRI, *Global State of Harm Reduction 2016*.

21. HRI, *Global State of Harm Reduction 2016*.

22. 'Special Response: Over 100 Researchers and Practitioners Respond to Rod Rosenstein on Safe Injection Sites,' *Points: The Blog of the Alcohol and Drugs History Society*, September 20, 2018, https://pointsadhsblog.wordpress.com/2018/09/20/special-response-over-100-researchers-and-practitioners-respond-to-rod-rosenstein-on-safe-injection-sites/.

23. Louisa Degenhardt et al., 'What Has Been Achieved in HIV Prevention, Treatment and Care for People who Inject Drugs, 2010–2012? A Review of Highest Burden Countries,' *International Journal of Drug Policy* 25, no. 1 (2014): 53–60.

24. International Narcotics Control Board, *Report of the International Narcotics Control Board for 2008*, E/INCB/2008/1 (Vienna: United Nations, 2009), para. 343; INCB, *Report of the International Narcotics Control Board for 2011*, E/INCB/2011/1 (Vienna: UN, 2012), para. 106.

25. Damon Barrett and Peter Gallahue, 'Harm Reduction and Human Rights,' *Interights Bulletin* 16, no. 4 (Winter 2011): 188.

26. Marie-Josephine Seya et al., 'A First Comparison.'

27. See for example, Juliane Kippenberg and Laura Thomas, *Needless Pain: Government Failure to Provide Palliative Care for Children in Kenya* (New York: Human Rights Watch, 2010), 47–9. See also Joan Marston, 'Why Should Children Suffer? Children's Palliative Care and Pain Management,' in *Children of the Drug War: Perspectives on the Impact of Drug Policies on Children and Young People,* ed. Damon Barrett (New York: IDebate Press, 2011), 219–36.

28. David Bewley-Taylor, Tom Blickman and Martin Jelsma, *The Rise and Decline of Cannabis Prohibition: The History of Cannabis in the UN Drug Control System and Options for Reform* (Amsterdam: TNI; Swansea: Global Drug Policy Observatory, 2014).

29. Michael C. Mithoefer et al., 'The Safety and Efficacy of ±3,4-Methylenedioxymethamphetamine-Assisted Psychotherapy in Subjects with Chronic, Treatment-Resistant Post-Traumatic Stress Disorder: The First Randomized Controlled Pilot Study,' *Journal of Psychopharmacology* 25, no. 4 (2011): 429–52.

30. Christopher Hallam, David Bewley-Taylor and Martin Jelsma, *Scheduling in the International Drug Control System* (Amsterdam: TNI; London: IDPC, 2014).

31. For an overview see Commission on Narcotic Drugs, *Updated Information Provided by the International Narcotics Control Board on the Implementation of Commission on*

Narcotic Drugs resolutions 49/6 'Listing of Ketamine as a Controlled Substance' and 50/3 'Responding to the Threat Posed by the Abuse and Diversion of Ketamine,' E/CN.7/2014/CRP.2 (Vienna: CND, 2014).

32. World Health Organization, 'Ketamine: Expert Peer Review on Critical Review Report,' presented at the 35th Expert Committee on Drug Dependence, Mammamet, Tunisia, June 4–8, 2012.

33. CND, *Legal Opinion from the Office of Legal Affairs of the Secretariat*, E/CN.7/2015/14 (Vienna: CND, 2015).

34. See, however, Transnational Institute, *International Control of Ketamine: Legal and Procedural Considerations About the Mandate of the Commission on Narcotic Drugs with Regard to Scheduling Decisions under the 1971 UN Convention on Psychotropic Substances* (Amsterdam: TNI, 2015).

35. United Nations, *Commentary on the Convention on Psychotropic Substances Done at Vienna on 21 February 1971,* E/CN.7/589 (Vienna: United Nations, 1976), para. 2.22, p. 71.

36. Committee on the Rights of the Child, *General Comment No. 15 (2013) on the Right of the Child to the Enjoyment of the Highest Attainable Standard of Health (art. 24)*, CRC/C/GC/15 (New York: United Nations Convention on the Rights of the Child, 2013); Committee on Economic, Social and Cultural Rights, *General Comment No. 14 (2000): The Right to the Highest Attainable Standard of Health (article 12 of the International Covenant on Economic, Social and Cultural Rights)*, E/C.12/2000/4 (Geneva: United Nations Economic and Social Council, 2000).

37. UNODC, *World Drug Report 2008* (Vienna: United Nations, 2008), 25–35, 212–18.

38. Patrick Gallahue and Rick Lines, *The Death Penalty for Drug Offences: Global Overview 2015: The Extreme Fringe of Global Drug Policy* (London: HRI, 2015).

39. Rick Lines, Damon Barrett and Patrick Gallahue, 'The Death Penalty for Drug Offences: "Asian Values" or Drug Treaty Influence?' *Opinio Juris*, May 21, 2015.

40. United Republic of Tanzania, *Drugs and Prevention of Illicit Traffic in Drugs Act, Section 16(2)* (Dodoma: United Republic of Tanzania, 1996).

41. Center for Legal and Social Studies (CELS), *The Impact of Drug Policy on Human Rights: The Experience in the Americas* (Buenos Aires: CELS, 2015), 18.

42. Ibid.

43. Ibid.

44. See, inter alia, Human Rights Watch (HRW), *'Skin on the cable': The Illegal Arrest, Arbitrary Detention and Torture of People Who Use Drugs in Cambodia* (New York: HRW, 2010); HRW, *Somsanga's Secrets: Arbitrary Detention, Physical Abuse, and Suicide Inside a Lao Drug Detention Center* (New York: HRW, 2011).

45. UNODC, *Global Study on Homicide 2019* (Vienna: UNODC, 2019), booklet 2, p. 16.

46. HRW, *Not Enough Graves: The War on Drugs, HIV/AIDS, and Violations of Human Rights* (New York: HRW, 2004).

47. UNDP, *El conflicto, callejón con salida: Informe Nacional de Desarrollo Humano para Colombia 2003* (Bogotá: UNDP, 2003), 305.

48. Vanda Felbab-Brown, *No Easy Exit: Drugs and Counternarcotics Policies in Afghanistan* (Washington D.C.: Brookings Institution, 2015), 3.

49. Ibid., 3, 9.

50. Coletta Youngers, 'Behind the Staggering Rise in Women's Imprisonment in Latin America,' *Open Society Foundations Voices*, January 6, 2014, http://www.opensocietyfoundations.org/voices/behind-staggering-rise-womens-imprisonment-latin-america.

51. Pien Metaal and Coletta Youngers, eds. *Sistemas sobrecargados: Leyes de drogas y cárceles en América Latina*, trans. Amira Armenta, Beatriz Martínez and Luis Enrique Bossio (Amsterdam: TNI; Washington D.C.: WOLA, 2010), http://www.dejusticia.org/files/r2_actividades_recursos/fi_name_recurso.192.pdf.

52. Laura Turquet, *Report on the Progress of the World's Women 2011-2012: In Pursuit of Justice* (New York: UN Women, 2011).

53. Aram Barra and Daniel Joloy, 'Children: Forgotten Victims of Mexico's Drug War,' in *Children of the Drug War: Perspectives on the Impact of Drug Policies on Young People,* ed. Damon Barrett (New York: IDebate Press, 2011), 29–42.

54. Atal Ahmadzai and Christopher Kuonqui, 'In the Shadows of the Insurgency in Afghanistan: Child Bartering, Opium Debt, and the War on Drugs,' in *Children of the Drug War: Perspectives on the Impact of Drug Policies on Young People,* ed. Damon Barrett (New York: IDebate Press, 2011), 43–59.

55. See for example Niamh Eastwood, Michael Shiner and Daniel Bear, *The Numbers in Black and White: Ethnic Disparities in the Policing and Prosecution of Drug Offences in England and Wales* (London: Release, 2014).

56. Jailson de Souza e Silva and André Urani, *Brazil: Children in Drug Trafficking: A Rapid Assessment,* Investigating the Worst Forms of Child Labour No. 20 (Geneva: International Labour Organization, 2002).

57. For examples see Damon Barrett et al., *Recalibrating the Regime: The Need for a Human Rights Based Approach to International Drug Policy* (Oxford: Beckley Foundation, 2008).

58. CELS, *The Impact of Drug Policy on Human Rights*, 45.

59. For example, see Damon Barrett, 'Reflections on Human Rights and International Drug Control,' in *Governing the Global Drug Wars*, ed. John Collins (London: LSE, 2012).

60. Fernanda Mena and Dick Hobbs, 'Narcophobia: Drugs Prohibition and the Generation of Human Rights Abuses,' *Trends in Organized Crime* 13, no. 1 (2010): 60–74.

61. On HIV/harm reduction funding see Catherine Cook et al., *The Funding Crisis in Harm Reduction: Donor Retreat, Government Neglect and the Way Forward* (London: International Harm Reduction Association, 2014).

62. CND, *Making Drug Control 'Fit for Purpose': Building on the UNGASS Decade. Report by the Executive Director of the United Nations Office on Drugs and Crime as a Contribution to the Review of the Twentieth Special Session of the General Assembly*, E/CN.7/2008/CRP.17* (Vienna: CND, 2008).

63. Human Rights Council, *Report of the Special Rapporteur on Torture and Other Cruel, Inhuman or Degrading Treatment or Punishment, Manfred Nowak: Addendum: Study on the Phenomena of Torture, Cruel, Inhuman or Degrading Treatment or Punishment in the World, Including an Assessment of Conditions of Detention*, A/HRC/13/39/Add.5 (New York: United Nations General Assembly, 2010), para. 44.

64. Claudia Stoicescu, 'Indonesia Uses Faulty Stats on "Drug Crisis" to Justify Death Penalty,' *The Conversation*, February 5, 2015.

65. United Nations, *Single Convention on Narcotic Drugs* (New York: United Nations, 1961), Article 39; United Nations, *Convention on Psychotropic Substances* (New York: United Nations, 1971), Article 23; United Nations, *Convention Against Illicit Traffic in Narcotic Drugs and Psychotropic Substances* (New York: United Nations, 1988), Article 24.

66. For an overview of the jurisprudence of the European Court of Human Rights see Eva Brems and Laurens Lavrysen, '"Don't Use a Sledgehammer to Crack a Nut": Less Restrictive Means in the Case Law of the European Court of Human Rights,' *Human Rights Law Review* 15, no. 1 (2015): 1–30.

67. United Nations, *Commentary on the Single Convention on Narcotic Drugs, 1961. Prepared by the Secretary-General in accordance with paragraph 1 of Economic and Social Council Resolution 914D (XXXIV) of August 3, 1962* (New York: United Nations, 1973), 449–50, para. 2.

68. *Edith Yunita Sianturi, Rani Andriani (Melisa Aprilia), Myuran Sukumaran, Andrew Chan, Scott Anthony Rush, 2-3/PUU-V/2007 IDCC 16* (October 30, 2007), https://www.hr-dp.org/contents/173.

69. For an overview of jurisprudence on 'most serious crimes' see Rick Lines, 'A "Most Serious" Crime? The Death Penalty for Drug Offences in International Human Rights Law,' *Amicus Journal* no. 21 (2010): 21–8.

70. United Nations General Assembly, *Resolution 69/186. Moratorium on the Use of the Death Penalty*, A/RES/69/186 (New York, February 4, 2015).

71. These include: the Convention on the Elimination of Racial Discrimination (1965); the Covenant on Economic, Social and Cultural Rights (1966); the Covenant on Civil and Political Rights (1966); the UNESCO Convention for the Safeguarding of Intangible Cultural Heritage (2003); the UNESCO Convention on the Protection and Promotion of the Diversity of Cultural Expressions (2005); the Convention on Biological Diversity (1992) and the Nagoya Protocol to the Convention on Biological Diversity (2011); and the UN Declaration on the Rights of Indigenous People (2007).

72. 'Bali Nine: Andrew Chan and Myuran Sukumaran Executed by Firing Squad,' *ABC News*, April 29, 2015. Note that Sukamaran and Chan were claimants in the above-mentioned Constitutional Court case that upheld the death penalty for drug offenses.

73. Damon Barrett, *Unique in International Relations? A Comparison of the International Narcotics Control Board and the UN Human Rights Treaty Bodies* (London: International Harm Reduction Association, 2008).

74. The debates were not recorded, but Damon Barrett was a civil society representative on the UK delegation at the time, participating in the debates.

75. HRI, *Declaration of Kuala Lumpur: Official Declaration of the 2015 International Harm Reduction conference* (London: HRI, 2015).

76. Damon Barrett et al., *Recalibrating the Regime*; United Nations General Assembly, *Right of Everyone to the Enjoyment of the Highest Attainable Standard of Physical and Mental Health*, A/65/255 (New York, August 6, 2010).

477

77. International Centre on Human Rights and Drug Policy, UNAIDS, WHO and UNDP, *International Guidelines on Human Rights and Drug Policy* (Essex: International Centre on Human Rights and Drug Policy, 2019), https://www.humanrights-drugpolicy.org/site/assets/files/1/hrdp_guidelines_2019_v19.pdf.

78. Tom Obokata, 'The Illicit Cycle of Narcotics from a Human Rights Perspective,' *Netherlands Quarterly of Human Rights* 25, no. 2 (2007): 159–87.

13. THE 2030 SUSTAINABLE DEVELOPMENT AGENDA AND THE WAR ON DRUGS

1. United Nations General Assembly, *Resolution 70/1. Transforming Our World: The 2030 Agenda for Sustainable Development,* A/RES/70/1 (New York, October 21, 2015).

2. The outcome document of the 2016 United Nations General Assembly special session on the world drug problem notes that 'efforts to achieve the Sustainable Development Goals and to effectively address the world drug problem are complementary and mutually reinforcing,' UNODC, 'Outcome Document of the 2016 United Nations General Assembly Special Session on the World Drug Problem: Our Joint Commitment to Effectively Addressing and Countering the World Drug Problem,' in *Thirtieth Special Session General Assembly* (New York: United Nations, 2016).

3. UNDP, *Addressing the Development Dimensions of Drug Policy* (New York: UNDP, 2015).

4. Global Commission on Drug Policy, *Drug Policy and the Sustainable Development Agenda* (Geneva: GCDP, 2018), http://www.globalcommissionondrugs.org/wp-content/uploads/2018/09/ENG-2018_SDGPaper_WEB.pdf.

5. See Steve Rolles et al., *The Alternative World Drug Report*, 2nd ed. (Bristol: Transform Drug Policy Foundation, 2016); International Drug Policy Consortium (IDPC), *Taking Stock: A Decade of Drug Policy: A Civil Society Shadow Report* (London: IDPC, 2018), http://fileserver.idpc.net/library/Shadow_Report_FINAL_ENGLISH.pdf.

6. Eric Gutierrez, *Drugs and Illicit Practices: Assessing their Impact on Development and Governance* (London: Christian Aid, 2015).

7. Commission on Crime Prevention and Criminal Justice, *World Crime Trends and Emerging Issues and Responses in the Field of Crime Prevention and Criminal Justice: Note by the Secretariat*, E/CN.15/2016/10 (Vienna: United Nations Economic and Social Council, 2016), https://undocs.org/E/CN.15/2016/10.

8. Data from September 29, 2018, see: Federal Bureau of Prisons, 'Statistics: Offenses,' https://www.bop.gov/about/statistics/statistics_inmate_offenses.jsp.

9. UNDP, *Addressing the Development Dimensions*.

10. United Nations, *Convention Against Illicit Traffic in Narcotic Drugs and Psychotropic Substances* (New York: United Nations, 1988), https://www.unodc.org/pdf/convention_1988_en.pdf.

11. Channing May, *Transnational Crime and the Developing World* (Washington D.C.: Global Financial Integrity, 2017), https://www.gfintegrity.org/wp-content/uploads/2017/03/Transnational_Crime-final.pdf.

12. OECD ODA Data, 2017, https://data.oecd.org/oda/net-oda.htm.

13. Gutierrez, *Drugs and Illicit Practices*.

14. Ibid.

15. William A. Byrd and David Mansfield, *Afghanistan's Opium Economy: An Agricultural, Livelihoods and Governance Perspective* (Washington D.C.: World Bank, 2014).

16. Human Rights Council, *Implementation of the Joint Commitment to Effectively Addressing and Countering the World Drug Problem with Regard to Human Rights: Report of the Office of the United Nations High Commissioner for Human Rights*, A/HRC/39/39 (New York: United Nations General Assembly, 2018), https://undocs.org/en/A/HRC/39/39.

17. UNDP, *Addressing the Development Dimensions*.

18. From Julia Buxton, *Drugs and Development: The Great Disconnect*, Policy Report 2 (Swansea: Global Drug Policy Observatory, Swansea University, 2015), https://www.hr-dp.org/files/2015/07/19/The_Great_Disconnect.pdf.

19. Commission on Narcotic Drugs, *International Workshop and Conference on Alternative Development in Chiang Rai and Chiang Mai, Thailand, 6–11 November 2011*, E/CN.7/2012/CRP.3 (Vienna: CND, 2012), https://www.unodc.org/documents/commissions/CND/CND_Sessions/CND_55/E-CN7-2012-CRP3_V1251320_E.pdf.

20. CND, *Report of the Workshop portion of the International Workshop and Conference on Alternative Development ICAD, Chiang Rai and Chiang Mai, Thailand, 6–11 November 2011* (Vienna: CND, 2012).

21. Coletta Youngers, 'UN Guiding Principles on Alternative Development: Opportunity Lost,' *Open Society Foundations Voices*, November 22, 2013, https://www.opensocietyfoundations.org/voices/un-guiding-principles-alternative-development-opportunity-lost.

22. United Nations General Assembly, *Resolution 68/196. United Nations Guiding Principles on Alternative Development,* A/RES/68/196 (New York, February 11, 2014).

23. International Conference on Alternative Development 2 (ICAD2), *International Seminar workshop on the implementation of the United Nations Guiding Principles on Alternative Development: Chair's Summary* (Bangkok, 2015), https://www.unodc.org/documents/ungass2016/Contributions/IGO/ICAD2/Chairs_Summary.pdf.

24. Javier Sagredo Fernández, *Nurturing Sustainable Change: The Doi Tung Case 1988-2017* (Bangkok: Mae Fah Luang Foundation, 2017).

25. Understood as 'the sense of belonging to a community and the existence of spaces for collaboration.' UNDP, *Human Development Report 2013-2014: Citizen Security with a Human Face: Evidence and Proposals for Latin America* (New York: UNDP, 2013), 8, https://www.undp.org/content/dam/rblac/img/IDH/IDH-AL%20Informe%20completo.pdf.

26. UNODC, *World Drug Report 2008* (Vienna: United Nations, 2008), 21, 212, http://www.unodc.org/documents/wdr/WDR_2008/WDR_2008_eng_web.pdf.

27. UNDP, *Addressing the Development Dimensions*.

28. OECD ODA Data, 2017, https://data.oecd.org/oda/net-oda.htm.

29. UNDP, *Addressing the Development Dimensions*.

30. See contributions for UNGASS from different UN Entities, intergovernmental organizations and other stakeholders at the UNGASS 2016 official website: https://www.unodc.org/ungass2016/en/contributions.html.

31. Juan Gabriel Tokatlian, *Drugs and the Peace Process in Colombia: A Moderate Radical Step* (Oslo: Norwegian Peacebuilding Resource Centre, 2014), https://noref.no/Publications/Regions/Colombia/Drugs-and-the-peace-process-in-Colombia-a-moderate-radical-step.

32. Juan Carlos Garzón Vergara, *Tough on the Weak, Weak on the Tough: Drug Laws and Policing* (Washington D.C.: Woodrow Wilson Center, Latin American Program, 2015), https://www.wilsoncenter.org/publication/tough-the-weak.

33. UNDP/CAF 2013 Prison Surveys, developed for the UNDP, *Human Development Report 2013–2014: Citizen Security with a Human Face*, see: http://hdr.undp.org/en/content/citizen-security-human-face for its executive summary and https://www.undp.org/content/dam/rblac/img/IDH/IDH-AL%20Informe%20completo.pdf for the complete report.

34. Grupo de Trabajo sobre Mujeres, Políticas de Drogas y Encarcelamiento, *Mujeres, Políticas de Drogas y Encarcelamiento: Una Guía para la Reforma de las Políticas en América Latina y el Caribe* (Washington D.C.: WOLA, 2016), https://www.oas.org/es/cim/docs/WomenDrugsIncarceration-ES.pdf.

35. Latinobarómetro survey 2018, see: Corporación Latinobarómetro, *Informe 2018* (Santiago de Chile: Corporación Latinobarómetro, 2018), 47, http://www.latinobarometro.org/lat.jsp.

36. Institute for Criminal Policy Research at Birkbeck University of London, 'World Prison Brief,' https://www.prisonstudies.org/.

37. Ibid.

38. The World Health Organization (WHO) defines 'Adolescents' as individuals in the 10–19 years age group and 'Youth' as the 15–24 years age group, while 'Young People' covers the age range 10–24 years. See: 'Adolescent health in the South-East Asia Region,' WHO, Adolescent Health.

39. Data from the Executive Secretariat of the National Public Security System of Mexico, 'Víctimas y Unidades Robadas,' 2020, https://www.gob.mx/sesnsp/acciones-y-programas/victimas-nueva-metodologia?state=published.

40. Ibid.

41. European Monitoring Centre on Drugs and Drug Addiction, *European Drug Report 2019* (Lisbon: EMCDDA, 2019), https://www.emcdda.europa.eu/edr2019_en.

42. As recognized by President López Obrador in January 2020. See: Denisse López, 'El resultado de la guerra contra el narcotráfico: más de 61.000 desaparecidos y miles de fosas clandestinas,' *infobae,* January 7, 2020, https://www.infobae.com/america/mexico/2020/01/07/el-resultado-de-la-guerra-contra-el-narcotrafico-mas-de-61000-desaparecidos-y-miles-de-fosas-clandestinas/.

43. UNODC, *Global Study on Homicide 2013* (Vienna: UNODC, 2014).

44. Francisco E. Thoumi, 'Competitive Advantages in the Production and Trafficking of Coca-Cocaine and Opium-Heroin in Afghanistan and the Andean Countries,' in *Innocent Bystanders: Developing countries and the War on Drugs*, ed. Philip Keefer and Norman Loayza (New York: Palgrave Macmillan and The World Bank, 2010), 215.

45. United Nations General Assembly, *Background Note of the Thematic Debate of the 66th Session of the United Nations General Assembly on Drugs and Crime as a Threat to Development* (New York: United Nations, 2012).

46. Philip Keefer and Norman Loayza, eds., *Innocent Bystanders: Developing Countries and the War on Drugs* (New York: Palgrave Macmillan and The World Bank, 2010).

47. Christopher M. Matthews, 'Justice Department Overruled Recommendation to Pursue Charges Against HSBC, Report Says,' *The Wall Street Journal,* July 11, 2016, http://www.wsj.com/articles/justice-department-overruled-recommendation-to-pursue-charges-against-hsbc-report-says-1468229401, based on U.S. House of Representatives, Republican Staff of the Committee on Financial Services, *Too Big to Jail: Inside the Obama Justice Department's Decision Not to Hold Wall Street Accountable* (Washington D.C., July 2016), http://financialservices.house.gov/uploadedfiles/07072016_oi_tbtj_sr.pdf.

48. UNDP, *Human Development Report 1990* (New York: Oxford University Press, 1990).

49. United Nations General Assembly, *Resolution 70/1. Transforming our World.*

50. Ibid.

51. Douglas Frantz, 'The Romeo and Juliet of Economic Transformation,' *OECD Insights Blog*, January 16, 2016, http://oecdinsights.org/2016/01/16/the-romeo-and-juliet-of-economic-transformation/.

52. United Nations General Assembly, *Resolution 70/1. Transforming our World.*

53. Based on table from UNDP, *Addressing the Development Dimensions*, 30–2.

54. UNDP, *Human Development Report 2014: Sustaining Human Progress: Reducing Vulnerabilities and Building Resilience* (New York: UNDP, 2014).

55. In resolution 1999/30 the ECOSOC called for 'a significant increase in cooperation between the United Nations International Drug Control Programme and the United Nations Development Programme, in view of the special role of the latter body as a coordinator for development activities within the United Nations system, and to that effect recommends that: (a) Drug-related indicators be jointly developed by the United Nations International Drug Control Programme and the United Nations Development Programme for inclusion in the human development report of the United Nations Development Programme.' ECOSOC, *Resolution 1999/30. Review of the United Nations International Drug Control Programme,* E/RES/1999/30 (New York: United Nations, 1999).

56. UNDP, *Human Development Report 2013-2014: Citizen Security with a Human Face.*

57. Nossal Institute for Global Health, *Dependent on Development: The Interrelationship between Illicit Drugs and Socioeconomic Development* (Melbourne: Nossal Institute for Global Health, 2010).

58. Ibid.

59. 'History,' Sustainable Development Goals Fund, http://www.sdgfund.org/history.

60. IDPC, *Advocacy Note: On the Road Towards the 2019 Ministerial Segment (Version 2)* (London: IDPC, 2018).

14. RETHINKING DRUG POLICY METRICS TO MOVE BEYOND THE WAR
     ON DRUGS

1.   David Bewley-Taylor, *Towards Metrics that Measure Outcomes that Matter* (Swansea:
      Global Drug Policy Observatory, Swansea University, 2016), https://www.
      swansea.ac.uk/media/Towards-Metrics-that-Measure-Outcomes-that-Matter-1.
      pdf; Susan MacGregor, Nicola Singleton, and Franz Trautmann, 'Towards Good
      Governance in Drug Policy: Evidence, Stakeholders and Politics,' *International
      Journal of Drug Policy* 25, no. 5 (2014): 931–4.
2.   Francisco E. Thoumi, *Debates y Paradigmas de las Políticas de Drogas en el Mundo y
      los Desafíos para Colombia* (Bogotá: Academia Colombiana de Ciencias Económicas,
      2015).
3.   The Global Commission on Drug Policy at http://www.globalcommissionondrugs.
      org/, last accessed May 29, 2020.
4.   Brookings Institution, 'Improving Global Drug Policy: Comparative Perspectives
      and UNGASS 2016,' *Brookings Institution*, April 29, 2015, https://www.brookings.
      edu/research/improving-global-drug-policy-comparative-perspectives-and-
      ungass-2016/.
5.   Global Commission on Drug Policy, *Taking Control: Pathways to Drug Policies that Work*
      (Geneva: GCDP, 2014), https://www.globalcommissionondrugs.org/reports/
      taking-control-pathways-to-drug-policies-that-work.
6.   GCDP, *War on Drugs: Report of the Global Commission on Drug Policy* (Geneva: GCDP,
      2011), 13, http://www.globalcommissionondrugs.org/wp-content/themes/
      gcdp_v1/pdf/Global_Commission_Report_English.pdf.
7.   These goals and targets are distilled from expert opinion gathered from leading
      drug policy specialists, together with the Global Commission on Drug Policy
      (GCDP). The proposed goals, targets, and indicators are designed to provide
      strategic direction to policy-makers and practitioners intent on changing course
      and getting control over narcotic drugs and psychoactive substances. They can and
      should be adapted and contextualized to meet specific country needs. They may
      require expansion or contraction depending on the needs on the ground. Either
      way, they are intended to provoke a critical reflection on the direction of drug
      policy, and the possible alternatives that can lead to a more holistic outcome. A
      detailed description of the framework is available at Robert Muggah, Katherine
      Aguirre and Ilona Szabo de Carvalho, *Measurement Matters: Designing New Metrics for
      a Drug Policy that Works*, Strategic Paper 12 (Rio de Janeiro: Igarapé Institute, 2015),
      http://igarape.org.br/wp-content/uploads/2015/01/AE-12-Measurement-
      mattes-07h-jan_.pdf.
8.   Andrew Goodwin, *Measuring the Harm from Illegal Drugs: The Drug Harm Index
      2005,* Online Report 22/07 (London: Home Office, 2007), http://webarchive.
      nationalarchives.gov.uk/20110220105210/rds.homeoffice.gov.uk/rds/pdfs07/
      rdsolr2207.pdf; Ziggy MacDonald et al., *Measuring the Harm from Illegal Drugs Using
      the Drug Harm Index*, Online Report 24/05 (London: Home Office, 2005), https://
      webarchive.nationalarchives.gov.uk/20110218140608/http://rds.homeoffice.
      gov.uk/rds/pdfs05/rdsolr2405.pdf; Peter Johnston et al., *Developing and Applying*

an *Organized Crime Harm Index: A Scoping and Feasibility Study*, Report No. 011 (Ottawa: Public Safety Canada, 2010), http://publications.gc.ca/collections/collection_2012/sp-ps/PS4-99-2010-eng.pdf; Alison Ritter, 'Methods for Comparing Drug Policies - The utility of Composite Drug Harm Indexes,' *International Journal of Drug Policy* 20, no. 6 (2009): 475–9.

9. International Expert Group on Drug Policy Metrics, *Aligning Agendas: Drugs, Sustainable Development, and the Drive for Policy Coherence* (New York: IPI Publications, 2018), https://www.ipinst.org/wp-content/uploads/2018/02/1802_Aligning-Agendas.pdf.

10. See, for example, the work of the UNODC in producing its World Drug Report. UNODC, *World Drug Report 2019* (Vienna: United Nations, 2019), https://wdr.unodc.org/wdr2019/.

11. There are many settings in which punitive drug policies generated extensive negative outcomes such as the case of Colombia. Other cases are Brazil, China, Guinea, Mali, Myanmar, Thailand, the USA, Vietnam and other countries in a review led by Brookings Institution. Daniel Mejia, *Plan Colombia: An Analysis of Effectiveness and Costs* (Washington D.C.: Brookings Institution, Latin America Initiative, 2014), https://www.brookings.edu/wp-content/uploads/2016/07/Mejia-Colombia-final-2.pdf.

12. The Alternative World Drug Report identified seven ways in which the War on Drugs generates negative effects including: the undermining of international development and security; fueling of conflict; threats to public health; spreading of disease and associated mortality; undermining of human rights; promoting of stigma and discrimination; creation of organized crime and enriching of criminals, impacts on deforestation and pollution; and wastage of billions on ineffective law enforcement. Steve Rolles et al., *The Alternative World Drug Report: Counting the Costs of the War on Drugs* (Bristol: Count the Costs, 2012), http://www.countthecosts.org/sites/default/files/AWDR.pdf.

13. Bruce D. Johnson, Andrew Golub and Eloise Dunlap, 'The Rise and Decline of Hard Drugs, Drug Markets and Violence in Inner-City New York,' in *The Crime Drop in America,* ed. Alfred Blumstein and Joel Wallman (Cambridge: Cambridge University Press, 2000), 164–206; Ian Martin et al., 'Violence Among Street-Involved Youth: The Role of Methamphetamine,' *European Addiction Research* 15, no. 1 (2009): 32–8, https://doi.org/10.1159/000173007; Alfred Blumstein, 'Youth Violence, Guns, and the Illicit-Drug Industry,' *Journal of Criminal Law & Criminology* 86, no. 1 (1995): 10–36; Robert Burrus, 'Do Efforts to Reduce the Supply of Illicit Drugs Increase Turf War Violence? A Theoretical Analysis,' *Journal of Economics and Finance* 23, no. 3 (1999): 226; Malcolm W. Klein, Cheryl L. Maxson, and Leah C. Cunningham, 'Crack, Street Gangs, and Violence,' *Criminology* 29, no. 4 (1991): 623–50.

14. Dan Werb et al., 'Effect of Drug Law Enforcement on Drug Market Violence: A Systematic Review,' *International Journal of Drug Policy* 22, no. 2 (2011): 87, https://doi.org/10.1016/j.drugpo.2011.02.002.

15. Robert Muggah and John P. Sullivan, 'The Coming Crime Wars,' *Foreign Policy*, September 21, 2018, https://foreignpolicy.com/2018/09/21/the-coming-crime-wars/.

16. Michael Tonry and Matthew Melewski, 'The Malign Effects of Drug and Crime Control Policies on Black Americans,' *Crime and Justice* 37 no. 1, (2008): 1–44.

17. Mesoamerican Working Group, *Rethinking the Drug War in Central America and Mexico* (Mexico City: Mesoamerican Working Group, 2013), https://www.ghrc-usa.org/wp-content/uploads/2013/12/Mesoamerica-Working-Group_Rethinking-Drug-War-Web-Version.pdf.

18. Steve Rolles et al., *The Alternative World Drug Report.*

19. The IDPC has stated that the drug strategy has failed, as the effects in the reduction of global supply are scant, and the negative effects on health, human rights, security, and development are huge. International Drug Policy Consortium (IDPC), *IDPC Drug Policy Guide: 3rd Edition* (London: IDPC, 2016).

20. UNODC, *World Drug Report 2019.*

21. Ibid.

22. Christopher Hallam and David Bewley-Taylor, 'Mapping the World Drug Problem: Science and Politics in the United Nations Drug Control System,' *International Journal of Drug Policy* 21, no. 1 (2010): 1–3.

23. Katherine Aguirre, 'Política de drogas: midiendo el fracaso y redefiniendo el éxito,' *La Silla Vacía,* February 10, 2015, http://lasillavacia.com/elblogueo/blog/politica-de-drogas-midiendo-el-fracaso-y-redefiniendo-el-exito-49552.

24. Consider, for example, the primary goals set by the 1998 United Nations General Assembly Special Session (UNGASS) on Drugs in New York: 'these objectives comprised "eradicating or significantly reducing" the illicit production of plant-based drugs, limiting the illicit manufacture and trafficking of synthetic drugs and the "significant and measurable" reduction of the demand for illicit drugs.' UN General Assembly, 'Assembly Special Session on Countering World Drug Problem Together Concludes at Headquarters, 8–10 June' (press release GA/9423, New York, June 10, 1998), https://www.un.org/press/en/1998/19980610.ga9423.html.

25. David Bewley-Taylor, *Towards Metrics.*

26. GCDP, *War on Drugs.*

27. Ibid.

28. U.S. Government Accountability Office. *Lack of Progress on Achieving Strategy National Goals* (Washington D.C.: GAO, 2015), http://www.gao.gov/assets/680/673929.pdf.

29. At the outset, the indicators would track and monitor the evolution of the targets and goals. The structure of indicators is intended to allow scientific evaluations of the effectiveness of the progressive drug policy. As noted by the Global Commission: 'a new set of indicators is needed to truly show the outcomes of drug policies according to their harms or benefits for individuals and communities,' GCDP, *War on Drugs,* 13.

30. See the *Report of the International Opium Commission, Shanghai, China, February 1 to February 26, 1909* (Shanghai: North-China Daily News and Herald, 1909), https://archive.org/details/cu31924032583225. In this report the number of opiates available for consumption were set as 'domestic opium production plus imports less exports.' The reliability of the information generated by the IOC report is

widely contested. In fact, the British delegation stated 'the figures dealing with the growth of the poppy and the consumption of opium are, as a rule, nothing more than rough estimates or mere expressions of opinion,' Timothy Brook and Bob Tadashi Wakabayashi, eds. *Opium Regimes: China, Britain, and Japan 1839–1952* (Berkeley: University of California Press, 2000), 215.

31. The PCOB did not have the right to question the statistics submitted by governments and could only request an explanation if it 'received sufficient evidence that a country acted as a center of illicit traffic of drugs.' UNODC, *A Century of International Drug Control* (Vienna: UNODC, 2008), https://www.unodc.org/documents/data-and-analysis/Studies/100_Years_of_Drug_Control.pdf.

32. The PCOB did not have the right to question the statistics submitted by governments and could only request an explanation if it 'received sufficient evidence that a country acted as a center of illicit traffic of drugs.' UNODC, *A Century of International Drug Control.*

33. 'The OAC requested information related to imports, exports, re-exports, consumption, reserve stocks, etc. Conservative estimates suggest that the world production of opium and coca exceeded medical and scientific needs by a factor of ten.' UNODC, *A Century of International Drug Control.*

34. Jay Sinha, *The History and Development of the Leading International Drug Control Conventions: Prepared for the Senate Special Committee on Illegal Drugs* (Ottawa: The Parliament of Canada, Library of Congress, 2001), http://www.parl.gc.ca/content/sen/committee/371/ille/library/history-e.htm.

35. Sinha, *The History and Development of the Leading International Drug Control Conventions.*

36. The influence and pressure of the multinational pharmaceutical industry had an effect on weakening controls for synthetics substances (such as amphetamines, barbiturates, benzodiazepines and psychedelics).

37. The Single Convention established four schedules to categorize various types of substances. Each schedule reflected a different level of control: 'among the most controversial classifications on the list, the coca leaf appears in List I and cannabis appears in both Lists I and IV, the latter reserved for the most dangerous substances.' Owing to the lack of information on psychotropic substances, they suffered fewer restrictions than plant-based products. Martin Jelsma, 'The Development of International Drug Control: Lessons Learned and Strategic Challenges for the Future' (working paper prepared for the First Meeting of the Global Commission on Drug Policy, Geneva, January 24–5, 2011), 4.

38. The term was first introduced by President Richard Nixon in 1971 when he identified drug abuse as 'public enemy No. 1.' Jelsma, 'The Development of International Drug Control,' 6.

39. For example, 'one major problem is the irregularity and incompleteness in ARQ reporting by Member States. Irregular reporting may result in absence of data for some years and may influence the reported trend in a given year. Secondly, submitted questionnaires are not always complete or comprehensive, and thirdly, much of the data collected are subject to limitations and biases. These issues affect the reliability, quality and comparability of the information received.' UNODC,

World Drug Report 2013 – Methodology (Vienna: United Nations, 2013), 1, https://www.unodc.org/unodc/secured/wdr/wdr2013/Methodology_2013.pdf.

40. The INCB did not impose international sanctions against non-complying countries. There are no formal sanction mechanisms in the Political Declaration or Action Plans. Information was received from less than 60 per cent of member states. UNODC, *A Century of International Drug Control*. The Board is empowered to 'recommend' embargoes to states party when they find a government in violation. Concerning governments that do not submit statistics, the Board can create estimates.

41. Stefano Berterame and Riku Lehtovuori, 'Treatment Data Indicators in the UNODC Data Collection System' (PowerPoint presentation, Vienna, UNODC, 2003), https://slideplayer.com/slide/740114/.

42. Sinha, *The History and Development of the Leading International Drug Control Conventions.*

43. Mille Bojer and Adam Kahane, 'Project: Scenarios for the Drug Problem in the Americas,' Reos Partners, accessed May 20, 2020.

44. The public health system has extensive experience with tracking and evaluating interventions. The work of the WHO is especially important, principally in relation to drug use and HIV. Also, the WHO has developed specific guidelines for setting targets, implementing, and monitoring public health approaches to harm reduction.

45. The EMCDDA provides information on drugs and drug addiction in the EU, including data related to treatment and prevalence, drug-related infectious diseases, high-risk drug use estimate, levels of drug-related deaths, drug-related crime in the form of drug seizures, types of offense, price, purity and use in prison, and country responses. European Monitoring Centre for Drugs and Drug Addiction, 'Data and Statistics,' accessed May 29, 2020, http://www.emcdda.europa.eu/data/stats2015.

46. The OAS has the Multilateral Evaluation Mechanism (MEM) which is an instrument designed to measure the progress of actions taken by the thirty-four member states of the Inter-American Drug Abuse Control Commission (CICAD). 'CICAD: Multilateral Evaluation Mechanism (MEM),' OAS, What is the MEM?, accessed May 20, 2020.

47. The collection of impact indicators is the first step to developing scientific evaluations of drug policy interventions.

48. Outputs consist of indicators of different activities generated by the specific intervention. Outcomes measure the results of concrete activities and imply the effects or impacts of interventions. A description of these categories can be found at http://www.enterprise-architecture.info/Images/Documents/mfo-outcomes.pdf and https://openknowledge.worldbank.org/bitstream/handle/10986/2699/526780PUB0Road101Official0Use0Only1.pdf?sequence=1.

49. This survey requests information on institutional strengthening, demand reduction, supply reduction, control measures, and international cooperation. Indicators that can be useful to track a change in drug policy include the indicators on alternatives to incarceration for drug-dependent criminal offenders (recommendation 8, question 50), sustainable alternative development and law enforcement initiatives

(recommendation 14), national organizations for the control of drug trafficking and related crimes (recommendation 20), and money laundering (recommendation 25), OAS - CICAD, *Hemispheric Report: Evaluation Report on Drug Control: Sixth Evaluation Round* (Washington D.C.: OAS, 2015). By 2019, the Inter-Governmental Group (IWG) of the MEM is in the Seventh-Round evaluation.

50. See, for example, https://igarape.org.br/en/issues/drug-policy/drug-policy-monitor/ as an example of such a platform focused on regional innovations in drug policy in the Americas.

51. 'The global nature of the problem requires a response based on international cooperation and universal coverage.' Moreover, as with all multilateral agreements, the drug conventions need to be subject to constant review and modernization in light of changing and variable circumstances. UNODC, *World Drug Report 2013 - Methodology*.

15. CONCLUSION

1. Juan Manuel Santos, 'Answers to War,' *New Statesman*, June 13, 2013, https://www.newstatesman.com/politics/politics/2013/06/answers-war.

2. Article 14.2 of the UN Convention against Illicit Traffic in Narcotic Drugs and Psychotropic Substances asks states to 'respect fundamental human rights'; see United Nations, *Convention Against Illicit Traffic in Narcotic Drugs and Psychotropic Substances* (New York: United Nations, 1988), https://www.unodc.org/pdf/convention_1988_en.pdf. Article 20 of the UN Convention on Psychotropic Substances of 1971 encourages 'early identification, treatment, education, after-care, rehabilitation and social reintegration' of drug users; Article 22 includes provisions for alternatives; see United Nations, *Convention on Psychotropic Substances* (New York: United Nations, 1971). Also, the International Narcotics Control Board (INCB), an independent, quasi-judicial expert body established by the Single Convention on Narcotic Drugs of 1961, stated in its Annual Report for 2015 that the international drug control treaties do not mandate a 'war on drugs.' INCB, *Report of the International Narcotics Control Board for 2015* (Vienna: United Nations, 2016).

3. Vanda Felbab-Brown, *Focused Deterrence, Selective Targeting, Drug Trafficking and Organized Crime: Concepts and Practicalities*, Modernizing Drug Law Enforcement Report 2 (London: IDPC, 2013).

4. Juan Carlos Garzón Vergara, *Tough on the Weak, Weak on the Tough: Drug Laws and Policing* (Washington D.C.: Woodrow Wilson Center, Latin American Program, 2015).

5. Juan Carlos Garzón Vergara, 'Worried about Illegal Drugs? Change the Policy and Think Long-Term,' *Georgetown Journal of International Affairs,* June 26, 2018, https://gjia.georgetown.edu/2018/06/26/illegal-drug-policy/.

6. Vanda Felbab-Brown, 'What Colombia Can Learn from Thailand on Drug Policy,' *Brookings*, May 4, 2017, https://www.brookings.edu/blog/order-from-chaos/2017/05/04/what-colombia-can-learn-from-thailand-on-drug-policy/. Andrés Bermúdez Liévano and Juan Carlos Garzón Vergara, *El Catálogo de las*

Pequeñas Soluciones: Alternativas para Sustituir los Cultivos Ilícitos en Colombia (Bogotá: Friedrich Ebert Stiftung and Fundación Ideas para la Paz, 2020).

7.   International Centre on Human Rights and Drug Policy, UNAIDS, WHO and UNDP, *International Guidelines on Human Rights and Drug Policy* (Essex: International Centre on Human Rights and Drug Policy, 2019), https://www.humanrights-drugpolicy.org/site/assets/files/1/hrdp_guidelines_2019_v19.pdf.

8.   United Nations System Chief Executives Board for Coordination, *2nd Regular Session of 2018, New York, 7 and 8 November 2018: Summary of Deliberations*, CEB/2018/2 (New York, January 2019).

9.   Western Hemisphere Drug Policy Commission, *Report of the Western Hemisphere Drug Policy Commission* (Washington D.C., December 2020), https://foreignaffairs. house.gov/_cache/files/a/5/a51ee680-e339-4a1b-933f-b15e535fa103/AA2A 3440265DDE42367A79D4BCBC9AA1.whdpc-final-report-2020-11.30.pdf.

10.   Western Hemisphere Drug Policy Commission, *Report of the Western Hemisphere Drug Policy Commission*.

11.   See, for example, Maryam Razavy, 'Hawala: An Underground Haven for Terrorists or Social Phenomenon?' *Crime, Law and Social Change* 44, no. 3 (2005): 277–99, https://doi.org/10.1007/s10611-006-9019-3; Rajan Basra and Peter R. Neumann, 'Criminal Pasts, Terrorist Futures: European Jihadists and the New Crime-Terror Nexus,' *Perspectives on Terrorism* 10, no. 6 (2016), http://www.terrorismanalysts.com/pt/index.php/pot/article/view/554. Countering violent extremism work is an example of the intent to shift the War on Terror paradigm into a more holistic approach.

12.   Demetri Sevastopulo and Katrina Manson, 'Donald Trump Urges Americans to Support "War" on Coronavirus,' *Financial Times*, March 17, 2020, https://www. ft.com/content/f4c7dce8-6883-11ea-800d-da70cff6e4d3.

13.   Boris Johnson, 'We Are Fighting an Invisible Enemy,' Instagram Post, June 3, 2020, https://www.instagram.com/p/CA_CS8GgI38/.

BIBLIOGRAPHY

ABC News. 'Bali Nine: Andrew Chan and Myuran Sukumaran Executed by Firing Squad.' April 29, 2015.

Acharya, Amitav, *Rethinking Power, Institutions and Ideas in World Politics: Whose IR?* London: Routledge, 2014.

Adler, Emanuel, and Michael Barnett. 'Security Communities in Theoretical Perspective.' In *Security Communities*, edited by Emanuel Adler and Michael Barnett, 3–24. Cambridge: Cambridge University Press, 1998.

Aguirre, Katherine. 'Política de drogas: midiendo el fracaso y redefiniendo el éxito.' *La Silla Vacía*, February 19, 2015, http://lasillavacia.com/elblogueo/blog/politica-de-drogas-midiendo-el-fracaso-y-redefiniendo-el-exito-49552.

Ahmad, F. B., L. M. Rosen, and P. Sutton. 'Provisional Drug Overdose Death Counts.' National Center for Health Statistics. Last reviewed September 16, 2018. https://www.cdc.gov/nchs/nvss/vsrr/drug-overdose-data.html.

Ahmadzai, Atal, and Christopher Kuonqui. 'In the Shadows of the Insurgency in Afghanistan: Child Bartering, Opium Debt, and the War on Drugs.' In *Children of the Drug War: Perspectives on the Impact of Drug Policies*, edited by Damon Barrett, 43–59. New York: IDebate Press, 2011.

Ahmed, Azam. 'That Other Big Afghan Crisis: The Growing Army of Addicts.' *The New York Times*, November 2, 2013. https://www.nytimes.com/2013/11/03/world/asia/that-other-big-afghan-crisis-the-growing-army-of-addicts.html.

Akers, Ronald. *Social Learning and Social Structure: A General Theory of Crime and Deviance*. New York: Routledge, 2009.

Akyeampong, Emmanuel. 'Diaspora and Drug Trafficking in West Africa: A Case Study of Ghana.' *African Affairs* 104, no. 416 (2005): 429–47.

BIBLIOGRAPHY

Alarcón Bañares, Paula, Ricardo Pérez-Luco, Sonia Salvo, Gloria Roa, Katherine Jaramillo, and Carla Sanhueza. 'Validación del Cuestionario de Auto-Reporte de Comportamiento Antisocial en Adolescentes: CACSA.' *Paidéia (Ribeirão Preto)* 20, no. 47 (2010): 291–302.

Alcalá-Sanchez, Imelda G., Claudia Arlett Espino, Carlos Gonzalo Ibáñez-Alcalá, and Rafael Humberto Delgado Limas. *Prevención del Delito en Jóvenes, Mediante Colectivos Juveniles de Arte Libre.* Chihuahua: Dirección de Seguridad Pública Municipal, 2012.

Alemika, Etannibi, Kwesi Aning, Frederic Loua, and Augustin Cisse. *Harmonizing Drug Legislation in West Africa - A Call for Minimum Standards.* WACD Background Paper No. 9. Accra: West Africa Commission on Drugs, 2014.

Alker, Hayward. 'Emancipation in the Critical Security Studies Project.' In *Critical Security Studies and World Politics*, edited by Ken Booth, 189–213. Boulder: Lynne Rienner Publishers, 2005.

Allum, Felia, and Stan Gilmour, eds. *Handbook of Organised Crime and Politics.* Cheltenham: Edward Elgar Publishing Limited, 2019. https://www.elgaronline.com/view/edcoll/9781786434562/9781786434562.xml.

Andreas, Peter. *Smuggler Nation: How Illicit Trade Made America.* New York: Oxford University Press, 2013.

Andreas, Peter. *Killer High: A History of War in Six Drugs.* New York: Oxford University Press, 2020.

Andreas, Peter, and Angélica Durán-Martínez. 'The International Politics of Illicit Trade in the Americas.' In *Routledge Handbook of Latin America in the World*, edited by Jorge Dominguez and Ana Covarrubias, 376-90. New York: Routledge, 2014.

Andreas, Peter, and Kelly M. Greenhill, eds. *Sex, Drugs, and Body Counts: The Politics of Numbers in Global Crime and Conflict.* Ithaca: Cornell University Press, 2011.

Andreas, Peter, and Ethan Avram Nadelmann. *Policing the Globe: Criminalization and Crime Control in International Relations.* Oxford: Oxford University Press, 2006.

Aning, Kwesi. 'Comprehending West Africa's Security Dilemmas: State fragility, narco-terrorism and oil politics.' In *Africa South of the Sahara*, edited by Europa Publications, 49–53. London: Routledge, 2012.

Aning, Kwesi. 'Transnational Security Threats and Challenges to Peacekeeping in Mali.' *Conflict Trends* 2 (2014):11–17.

Aning, Kwesi. *Understanding the Intersection of Drugs, Politics and Crime in West Africa: An Interpretive Analysis.* Policy Brief Series No. 6. Santiago de Chile: Global Consortium on Security Transformation, 2010.

490

Aning, Kwesi, and Lydia Amedzrator. 'The Economics of Militancy and Islamist Extremism in the Sahel.' In *Political Stability and Security in West and North Africa,* edited by The Canadian Security Intelligence Service. Toronto: Her Majesty the Queen in Right of Canada, 2014. https://www.canada.ca/content/dam/csis-scrs/documents/publications/NorthWestAfrica_POST_CONFERENCE_E_SOURCE.pdf.

Aning, Kwesi, and Lydia Amedzrator. 'Security in the Sahel: Linking the Atlantic to the Mediterranean.' In *Transatlantic Security from the Sahel to the Horn of Africa*, edited by Riccardo Alcaro and Nicoletta Pirozzi, 59–70. Rome: Edizion Nuova Cultura, 2013.

Aning, Kwesi and Samuel Aning. *National Drug Laws, Related Legislation and Prison Population in Ghana*. Background Paper for the WACD. Accra: West Africa Commission on Drugs, 2015.

Aning, Kwesi and Festus Aubyn. 'The Security Situation in West Africa.' In *Africa South of the Sahara*, edited by Europa Publications, 25–30. London: Routledge, 2012.

Aning, Kwesi, and A. Sarjoh Bah. *ECOWAS and Conflict Prevention in West Africa: Confronting the Triple Threats*. New York: New York University, Center on International Cooperation, 2009.

Aning, Kwesi, and Kwaku Danso. 'Ghana: Identity Formation and the Foreign and Defence Policies of a Small State.' In *African Foreign Policies: Selecting Signifiers to Explain Agency*, edited by Paul-Henri Bischoff. Abingdon: Routledge, 2020.

Aning, Kwesi and John M. Pokoo. *Drug Trafficking and Threats to National and Regional Security in West Africa*. WACD Background Paper No. 1. Accra: West Africa Commission on Drugs, 2013. https://www.globalcommissionondrugs.org/wp-content/uploads/2017/02/Drug-Trafficking-and-Threats-to-National-and-Regional-Security-in-West-Africa-2013-04-03.pdf.

Arana, Ana. 'How the Street Gangs Took Central America.' *Foreign Affairs*, June 2005. https://www.foreignaffairs.com/articles/central-america-caribbean/2005-05-01/how-street-gangs-took-central-america.

Arendt, Hannah. *On Violence*. New York: Harcourt Brace, 1970.

Arias, Desmond Enrique. *Drugs and Democracy in Rio de Janeiro: Trafficking, Social Networks, and Public Security*. Chapel Hill: University of North Carolina Press, 2006.

Arias, Desmond Enrique. 'The Dynamics of Criminal Governance: Networks and Social Order in Rio de Janeiro.' *Journal of Latin American Studies* 38, no. 2 (2006): 293–325.

Armenta, Amira, Pien Metaal, and Martin Jelsma. *A Breakthrough in the Making? Shifts in the Latin American Drug Policy Debate*. Amsterdam:

Transnational Institute, 2012. https://www.tni.org/files/download/dlr21.pdf.

ASEAN Narcotics Cooperation Center. 'Workshop on Formulation of the 5-Year Master Plan (2019-2023) under the Safe Mekong Operation Project among 6 Countries.' April 16, 2018. https://aseannarco.oncb.go.th/ewt_news.php?nid=387&filename=index___EN.

Association of Southeast Asian Nations. 'ASEAN Launches Narcotics Cooperation Centre in Bangkok.' September 19, 2014.

Association of Southeast Asian Nations. 'Joint Declaration for a Drug-Free ASEAN.' ASEAN declaration, October 12, 2012. https://asean.org/?static_post=joint-declaration-for-a-drug-free-asean.

Association of Southeast Asian Nations. 'Statement by the Association of Southeast Asian Nations at the 5th Intersessional CND Meeting of the 61st Commission on Narcotic Drugs.' Statement by the ASEAN, UNODC, Vienna, November 7, 2018. https://www.unodc.org/documents/commissions/CND/2019/Contributions/November/MS_Statements/7_November/ASEAN_Statement_for_7_Nov.pdf.

Asuntos del Sur - Observatorio Latinoamericano de Políticas de Drogas y Opinión Pública. *Estudio 2014–2015: Estudio Anual sobre Políticas de Drogas y Opinión Publica, América Latina.* Santiago de Chile: Asuntos del Sur, 2015.

Atuesta, Laura. 'Addressing the Costs of Prohibition: Internally Displaced Populations in Colombia and Mexico.' In *Ending the Drug Wars: Report of the LSE Expert Group on the Economics of Drug Policy*, edited by John Collins, 49–55. London: LSE, 2014.

Avetisyan, Andrey. 'Presentation at the 6th meeting of the Joint US-Russia Working Group on the Afghan Narcotrafficking.' Moscow, October 6, 2015.

Bagley, Bruce. *Drug Trafficking and Organized Crime in the Americas: Major Trends in the Twenty-First Century.* Washington D.C.: Woodrow Wilson Center, 2012.

Bagley, Bruce. 'Globalization and Latin American and Caribbean Organized Crime.' *Global Crime* 6, no. 1 (Feb 2004): 32–53. https://doi.org/10.1080/1744057042000297963.

Bailey, John. *The Politics of Crime in Mexico: Democratic Governance in a Security Trap.* London: Lynne Rienner Publishers, 2014.

Bailey, John, ed. 'Public and Citizen Security in South America: Trends, Controversies and Proposals.' In *Public Security in the Americas: New Challenges in the South-North Dialogue.* Washington D.C.: Georgetown University, 2003.

Baker, Andy and Kenneth F. Greene. 'The Latin American Left's Mandate: Free-Market Policies and Issue Voting in New Democracies.' *World Politics* 63, no. 1 (2011): 43–77.

BIBLIOGRAPHY

Baldwin, Simon, and Nicolas Thomson. 'Compulsory "Rehabilitation" in Asia: Problems and Possible Solutions.' In *Drug law reform in East and Southeast Asia*, edited by Fifa Rahman and Nick Crofts, 139–50. Lanham: Lexington Books, 2013.

Balzacq, Thierry. *Securitization Theory: How Security Problems Emerge and Dissolve.* London: Routledge, 2010.

Barber, James G., Floyd Bolitho, and Lorne D. Bertrand. 'Intrapersonal versus Peer Group Predictors of Adolescent Drug Use.' *Children and Youth Services Review* 21, no. 7 (1999): 565–79.

Barra, Aram, and Daniel Joloy. 'Children: Forgotten victims of Mexico's Drug War.' In *Children of the Drug War: Perspectives on the Impact of Drug Policies on Young People,* edited by Damon Barrett, 29–42. New York: IDebate Press, 2011.

Barrett, Damon. *Backgrounder: Bolivia's concurrent drug control and other legal commitments.* Colchester: International Centre on Human Rights and Drug Policy, 2011. https://www.tni.org/files/publication-downloads/international_legal_commitments.pdf.

Barrett, Damon. *Children of the Drug War: Perspectives on the impact of Drug Policy on Young People.* New York: IDebate Press, 2011.

Barrett, Damon. 'Reflections on Human Rights and International Drug Control.' In *Governing the Global Drug Wars*, edited by John Collins, 56–62. London: LSE, 2012.

Barrett, Damon. *Unique in International Relations? A Comparison of the International Narcotics Control Board and the UN Human Rights Treaty Bodies.* London: International Harm Reduction Association, 2008.

Barrett, Damon, and Patrick Gallahue. 'Harm Reduction and Human Rights.' *Interights Bulletin* 16, no. 4 (Winter 2011): 188–94.

Barrett, Damon, Martin Jelsma, and David Bewley-Taylor. 'Fatal Attraction: Brownfield's Flexibility Doctrine and Global Drug Policy Reform.' *Huffington Post*, November 18, 2014. http://www.huffingtonpost.co.uk/damon-barett/drug-policy-reform_b_6158144.html.

Barrett, Damon, Rick Lines, Rebecca Schleifer, Richard Elliott, and David Bewley-Taylor. *Recalibrating the Regime: The Need for a Human Rights Based Approach to International Drug Policy.* Oxford: Beckley Foundation, 2008.

Basra, Rajan. *Drugs and Terrorism: The Overlaps in Europe.* London: ICSR, King's College London, 2019. https://icsr.info/wp-content/uploads/2019/11/ICSR-Report-Drugs-and-Terrorism-The-Overlaps-in-Europe.pdf.

Basra, Rajan, and Peter R. Neumann. 'Criminal Pasts, Terrorist Futures: European Jihadists and the New Crime-Terror Nexus.' *Perspectives on Terrorism* 10, no. 6 (2016). http://www.terrorismanalysts.com/pt/index.php/pot/article/view/554.

Baylis, John. 'International and global security,' in *The Globalization of World Politics: An Introduction to International Relations*, edited by John Baylis, Steve Smith and Patricia Owens (8th ed). Oxford: Oxford University Press, 2019.

BBC News. 'Sahara Desert Gun Battle Yields Drugs Haul, says France.' May 19, 2015. http://www.bbc.com/news/world-africa-32796372.

Bennett Jones, Owen. *Pakistan: Eye of the Storm.* New Haven: Yale University Press, 2003.

Bennett, Trevor, and Katy Holloway. *Understanding Drugs, Alcohol and Crime.* Berkshire: Open University Press, 2005.

Bennett, Trevor, Katy Holloway, and David Farrington. 'The Statistical Association between Drug Misuse and Crime: A Meta-Analysis.' *Aggression and Violent Behavior* 13, no. 2 (2008), 107–18. https://doi.org/10.1016/j.avb.2008.02.001.

Bennett, Wells C., and John Walsh. *Marijuana Legalization is an Opportunity to Modernize International Drug Treaties.* Washington D.C.: Brookings Institution, 2014. http://www.brookings.edu/research/reports/2014/10/15-marijuana-legalization-modernize-drug-treaties-bennett-walsh.

Berg, Christoph, and Alexander Seger. *Drugs and Development in Asia: A Background and Discussion Paper.* Eschborn: Deutsche Gesellschaft für Technische Zusammenarbeit, 1998.

Bergen-Cico, Dessa K. *War and Drugs: The Role of Military Conflict in the Development of Substance Abuse.* Boulder: Paradigm Publishers, 2012.

Bergenstrom, Anne, and Sonia Bezziccheri. 'Phasing out Drug Detention Centres in East and South East Asia.' UNODC poster presented at the second Regional Consultation on Compulsory Centres for Drug Users in Asia and the Pacific, Kuala Lumpur, Malaysia, October 2012. https://www.unodc.org/documents/southeastasiaandpacific//poster/CCDU_Poster_08_3_Jun_2013.pdf.

Bermúdez Liévano, Andrés, and Juan Carlos Garzón Vergara. *El Catálogo de las Pequeñas Soluciones: Alternativas para Sustituir los Cultivos Ilícitos en Colombia.* Bogotá: Friedrich Ebert Stiftung and Fundación Ideas para la Paz, 2020.

Bernstein, Henry. 'Ghana's Drug Economy: Some Preliminary Data.' *Review of African Political Economy* 26, no. 79 (1999): 13–32.

Berterame, Stefano, and Riku Lehtovuori. 'Treatment Data Indicators in the UNODC Data Collection System.' PowerPoint presentation, Vienna, UNODC, 2003. https://slideplayer.com/slide/740114/.

Bertram Eva, Morris Blachman, Kenneth Sharpe, and Peter Andreas. *Drug War Politics: The Price of Denial.* London: University of California Press, 1996.

BIBLIOGRAPHY

Bewley-Taylor, David. *The United States and International Drug Control, 1909–1997*. London: Continuum, 2001.

Bewley-Taylor, David. *International Drug Control: Consensus Fractured*. Cambridge: Cambridge University Press, 2012.

Bewley-Taylor, David. 'Towards a Revision of the UN Drug Control Conventions: Harnessing Like-Mindedness.' *International Journal of Drug Policy* 24, no.1 (2013): 60–8.

Bewley-Taylor, David. 'Why is West Africa repeating the failures of the Latin American drug war.' Open Society Foundations, January 28, 2014. https://www.opensocietyfoundations.org/voices/why-west-Africa-repeating-failures-latin-american-drug-war.

Bewley-Taylor, David. *Towards Metrics that Measure Outcomes that Matter*. Swansea: Global Drug Policy Observatory, Swansea University, 2016. https://www.swansea.ac.uk/media/Towards-Metrics-that-Measure-Outcomes-that-Matter-1.pdf.

Bewley-Taylor, David, Tom Blickman, and Martin Jelsma. *The Rise and Decline of Cannabis Prohibition: The History of Cannabis in the UN Drug Control System and Options for Reform*. Amsterdam: Transnational Institute; Swansea: Global Drug Policy Observatory, 2014. https://www.tni.org/files/download/rise_and_decline_ch4.pdf.

Bewley-Taylor, David, and Malgosia Fitzmaurice. 'The Evolution and Modernization of Treaty Regimes: The Contrasting Cases of International Drug Control and Environmental Regulation.' *International Community Law Review* 20, no. 5 (2018): 403–35.

Bewley-Taylor, David, and Martin Jelsma. *UNGASS 2016: A Broken or B-r-o-a-d Consensus? UN summit cannot hide a growing divergence in the global drug policy landscape*. Amsterdam: Transnational Institute, 2016. https://www.tni.org/files/publication-downloads/dpb_45_04072016_web.pdf.

Bewley-Taylor, David, Martin Jelsma, Steve Rolles, and John Walsh. *Cannabis Regulation and the UN Drug Treaties. Strategies for Reform*. Vancouver: The Canadian Drug Policy Coalition, 2016. http://fileserver.idpc.net/library/Cannabis_Regulation_UN_Drug_Treaties_April_2016.pdf.

Bewley-Taylor, David, and Marie Nougier. 'Measuring the "World Drug Problem": 2019 and Beyond.' In *Collapse of the Global Order on Drugs: From the UNGASS 2016 to Review 2019*, eds. Axel Klein and Blaine Stothard, 49–65. Bingley: Emerald Publishing, 2018.

Beyrer, Chris, Kasia Malinowska-Sempruch, Adeeba Kamarulzaman, Michel Kazatchkine, Michel Sidibe, and Steffanie A. Strathdee. 'Time to Act: A Call for Comprehensive Responses to HIV in People Who Use Drugs.' *The Lancet* 376, no. 9740 (2010): 551–63.

Bilgin, Pinar. 'Critical Theory.' In *Security Studies: An Introduction*, edited by Paul D. Williams, 93–106. London: Routledge, 2013.

Bischoff, Paul Henri, Kwesi Aning, and Amitav Achaya. 'Africa in Global International Relations: Emerging approaches to theory and practice, an introduction.' In *Africa in Global International Relations: Emerging approaches to theory and practice*, edited by Paul Henri Bischoff, Kwesi Aning, and Amitav Achaya. London: Routledge, 2016.

Blair, David. 'Sierra Leone Being Targeted by Latin American Drug Cartels.' *The Telegraph*, February 27, 2009. https://www.telegraph.co.uk/news/worldnews/africaandindianocean/sierraleone/4863771/Sierra-Leone-targeted-by-Latin-American-drug-cartels.html.

Blanc, Florentin, and Michael Faure. 'Smart enforcement in the EU.' *Journal of Risk Research* 23, no. 11 (2020): 1405–23. https//doi.org/10.1080/13669877.2019.1673800.

Blickman, Tom. 'The Elephant in the Room: Cannabis in the International Drug Control Regime.' In *Collapse of the Global Order on Drugs: From the UNGASS 2016 to Review,* edited by Axel Klein and Blaine Stothard, 103. Bingley: Emerald Publishing, 2018.

Blickman, Tom. 'Full Scope on the War on Drugs.' The Transnational Institute. Last modified July 18, 2005. https://www.tni.org/en/archives/act/2157.

Blumstein, Alfred. 'Youth Violence, Guns, and the Illicit-Drug Industry.' *Journal of Criminal Law & Criminology* 86, no. 1 (1995): 10–36.

Boidi, María Fernanda, José Miguel Cruz, Rosario Queirolo, and Emily Bello Pardo. 'Marijuana Legalization in Uruguay and Beyond.' Miami: Florida International University, Latin America and Caribbean Center, 2015.

Boister, Neil. *Penal Aspects of the UN Drug Conventions.* The Hague: Kluwer Law International, 2001.

Boister, Neil, and Martin Jelsma. 'Inter se Modification of the UN Drug Control Conventions. An Exploration of its Applicability to Legitimise the Legal Regulation of Cannabis Markets.' *International Community Law Review* 20, no. 5 (2018): 456–92.

Boiteaux, Luciana. 'Drugs and Prisons: The Repression of Drugs and the Increase of the Brazilian Penitentiary Population.' In *Systems Overload: Drug Laws and Prisons in Latin America,* edited by Pien Metaal and Coletta Youngers, 30–39. Amsterdam: Transnational Institute; Washington D.C.: Washington Office on Latin America, 2011.

Bojer, Mille, and Adam Kahane. 'Project: Scenarios for the Drug Problem in the Americas.' Reos Partners. Accessed May 20, 2020. https://reospartners.com/projects/scenarios-drug-problem-americas/.

Booth, Ken. 'Security and Emancipation.' *Review of International Studies* 17, no. 4 (1991): 313–26.

Booth, Ken. *Theory of World Security*. Cambridge: Cambridge University Press, 2007.

Boyce, Geoffrey A., Jeffrey M. Banister, and Jeremy Slack. 'You and What Army? Violence, The State, and Mexico's War on Drugs.' *Territory, Politics, Governance* 3, no. 4 (2015): 446–68.

Boyum, David, and Peter Reuter. 'Reflections on Drug Policy and Social Policy.' In *Drug Addiction and Drug Policy: The Struggle to Control Dependence*, edited by Philip B. Heyman and William N. Brownsberger, 239–64. Cambridge: Harvard University Press, 2001.

Branson, Richard Sir. *Ending the War on Drugs*. London: Virgin Books, 2016.

Braun, Kettil, Lynn Pan, and Ingemar Rexed. *The Gentleman's Club: International Control of Drugs and Alcohol*. Chicago: University of Chicago Press, 1975.

Brea, Mayra, and Edylberto Cabral. 'Factores de Riesgo y Violencia Juvenil en República Dominicana.' *Revista PsicologiaCientifica.com* 12, no. 15 (2010).

Brems, Eva, and Laurens Lavrysen. '"Don't Use a Sledgehammer to Crack a Nut": Less Restrictive Means in the Case Law of the European Court of Human Rights.' *Human Rights Law Review* 15, no. 1 (2015): 1–30.

Bridge, Jamie and Maria-Goretti Loglo, 'Drug Laws in West Africa: A Review and Summary,' *International Drug Policy Consortium and West Africa Commission on Drugs*, Briefing Paper, 2017.

Briscoe, Ivan, and Martín Rodríguez Pellecer. *State under Siege: Elites, Criminal Networks and Institutional Reform in Guatemala*. The Hague: Netherlands Institute of International Relations, 2010. https://www.clingendael.org/sites/default/files/pdfs/20100913_cru_publication_ibriscoe.pdf.

Britto, Lina. 'A Trafficker's Paradise: The "War on Drugs" and the New Cold War in Colombia.' *Contemporánea* 1, vol. 1 (2010): 159–77.

Britto, Lina. *Marijuana Boom: The Rise and Fall of Colombia's First Drug Paradise*. Santa Barbara: University of California Press, 2020.

Brook, David W., Judith S. Brook, Zohn Rosen, Mario De la Rosa, Ivan D. Montoya, and Martin Whiteman. 'Early Risk Factors for Violence in Colombian Adolescents.' *American Journal of Psychiatry* 160, no. 8 (2003): 1470–8. https://doi.org/10.1176/appi.ajp.160.8.1470.

Brook, Judith S., Martin Whiteman, Patricia Cohen, Joseph Shapiro, and Elinor Balka. 'Longitudinally Predicting Late Adolescent and Young Adult Drug Use: Childhood and Adolescent Precursors.' *Journal of the*

American Academy of Child and Adolescent Psychiatry 34, no. 9 (1995): 1230–8. https://doi.org/10.1097/00004583-199509000-00022.

Brook, Timothy, and Bob Tadashi Wakabayashi, eds. *Opium Regimes: China, Britain, and Japan 1839–1952*. Berkeley: University of California Press, 2000.

Brooke, James. 'Colombians Press for the Legalization of Cocaine.' *The New York Times*, February 20, 1994. http://www.nytimes.com/1994/02/20/world/colombians-press-for-the-legalization-of-cocaine.html.

Brookings Institution. 'Improving Global Drug Policy: Comparative Perspectives and UNGASS 2016.' *Brookings Institution*, April 29, 2015. https://www.brookings.edu/research/improving-global-drug-policy-comparative-perspectives-and-ungass-2016/.

Brownfield, William R. 'Assistant Secretary William R. Brownfield, Secretary's Special Remarks for the Opening of the Commission on Narcotic Drugs (CND) Special Segment on the Preparations for the UN General Assembly on the World Drug Problem, High-Level Segment.' Speech delivered at the CND, Vienna, March 9, 2015. https://www.unodc.org/documents/commissions/CND/CND_Sessions/CND_58/UNGASS_Statements/13_USA.pdf.

Brownstein, Henry H., ed. *The Handbook of Drugs and Society*. New Jersey: John Wiley & Sons, 2015.

Bueger, Christian. 'Communities of security practice at work? The emerging African maritime security regime.' *African Security* 6, no. 3-4 (2013): 297–316.

Bunck, Julie Marie, and Michael Ross Fowler. *Bribes, Bullets and Intimidation: Drug Trafficking and the Law in Central America*. Pennsylvania: Pennsylvania State University Press, 2012.

Bureau for International Narcotics and Law Enforcement Affairs. *2013 International Narcotics Control Strategy Report: Volume I: Drug and Chemical Control*. Washington D.C.: US Department of State, 2013.

Bureau for International Narcotics and Law Enforcement Affairs. *2015 International Narcotics Control Strategy Report: Volume I: Drug and Chemical Control*. Washington D.C.: US Department of State, 2015. https://2009-2017.state.gov/documents/organization/239560.pdf.

Bureau for International Narcotics and Law Enforcement Affairs. *2018 International Narcotics Control Strategy Report: Volume I: Drug and Chemical Control*. Washington D.C.: US Department of State, 2018.

Bureau for International Narcotics and Law Enforcement Affairs. *2018 International Narcotics Control Strategy Report: Volume II: Money Laundering and Financial Crimes*. Washington D.C.: US Department of State, 2018.

Bureau for International Narcotics and Law Enforcement Affairs. *2019 International Narcotics Control Strategy Report: Volume I: Drug and Chemical Control*. Washington D.C.: US Department of State, 2019.

Bureau for International Narcotics and Law Enforcement Affairs. *2020 International Narcotics Control Strategy Report: Volume I: Drug and Chemical Control*. Washington D.C.: US Department of State, 2020.

Burrus, Robert. 'Do Efforts to Reduce the Supply of Illicit Drugs Increase Turf War Violence? A Theoretical Analysis.' *Journal of Economics and Finance* 23, no.3 (1999): 226–34.

Buxton, Jane A., Mark Haden, and Richard G. Mathias. 'The Control and Regulation of Currently Illegal Drugs.' *International Encyclopedia of Public Health* 2 (2008): 7–16. doi:10.1016/B978-012373960-5.00356-7.

Buxton, Julia. *Drugs and Development: The Great Disconnect*. Swansea: Global Drug Policy Observatory, Swansea University, 2015. https://www.hr-dp.org/files/2015/07/19/The_Great_Disconnect.pdf.

Buzan, Barry. *People, States and Fear: National Security Problem in International Relations*. New Delhi: Transasia Publishers, 1987.

Buzan, Barry, Ole Wæver, and Jaap De Wilde. *Security: A New Framework for Analysis*. Boulder: Lynne Rienner Publishers, 1998.

Byrd, William A., and David Mansfield. *Afghanistan's Opium Economy: An Agricultural, Livelihoods and Governance Perspective*. Washington D.C.: World Bank, 2014.

Caiuby Labate, Beatriz, and Pamela Ruiz Flores López. 'Critical Reflections on the National Addiction Surveys (ENAs) in Mexico.' *Drugs: Education, Prevention and Policy* 21, no. 6 (2014): 427–33.

Calderón, Felipe. 'Speech Delivered at the 67th Session of the United Nations General Assembly.' Speech, UN headquarters, New York, September 26, 2012. http://webtv.un.org/meetings-events/general-assembly/general-debate/67th-session/watch/mexico-general-debate-67th-session/1862962046001.

Calderón, Laura, Octavio Rodríguez Ferreira, and David A. Shirk. *Drug Violence in Mexico: Data and Analysis Through 2017*. San Diego: Justice in Mexico, Department of Political Science & International Relations, University of San Diego, 2018.

Campos, Isaac. *Home Grown: Marijuana and the Origins of Mexico's War on Drugs*. Chapel Hill: The University of North Carolina Press, 2012.

Cárcamo, Javiera. *Consumo de Drogas en Detenidos: Estudio I-ADAM 2010*. Santiago de Chile: Fundación Paz Ciudadana, 2011.

Cardona, O. D. 'The Need for Rethinking the Concepts of Vulnerability and Risk from a Holistic Perspective: A Necessary Review and Criticism for Effective Risk Management.' In *Mapping Vulnerability:*

Disasters, Development and People, edited by Greg Bankoff, 37-51. London: Earthscan, 2004.

Carter, Jimmy. '"El Tiempo Disponible para este Trascendental Esfuerzo es Limitado": El Expresidente de EE. UU. y Nobel de Paz Jimmy Carter Escribe Sobre Proceso de Paz en Colombia.' *El Tiempo,* January 13, 2013. https://www.eltiempo.com/archivo/documento/CMS-12512163.

Castillo, Juan Camilo, Pascual Restrepo, and Daniel Mejía. *Scarcity without Leviathan: The Violent Effects of Cocaine Supply Shortages in the Mexican Drug War.* Washington D.C.: Center for Global Development, 2014.

Caulkins, Jonathan P. 'Effects of Prohibition, Enforcement and Interdiction on Drug Use.' In *Ending the Drug Wars: Report of the LSE Expert Group on the Economics of Drug Policy,* edited by John Collins, 16–24. London: LSE, 2014.

Caulkins, Jonathan P., Peter Reuter, Martin Y. Iguchi and James Chiesa. *How Goes the 'War on Drugs?': An Assessment of U. S. Drug Programs and Policy.* Santa Monica, CA: Rand Corporation, 2005.

Center for Legal and Social Studies. *The Impact of Drug Policy on Human Rights: The Experience in the Americas.* Buenos Aires: CELS, 2015.

Chaiken, Jan M., and Maria R. Chaiken. 'Drugs and Predatory Crime.' *Crime and Justice* 13 (1990): 203–39.

Chambers, Robert. 'Vulnerability: How the Poor Cope.' *IDS Bulletin* 20, no. 2 (1989): 1–6.

Chatwin, Caroline. *Towards More Effective Global Drug Policies.* London: Palgrave Macmillan, 2018.

Chawarski, Marek, Richard Schottenfel, and B. Vicknasingam. 'Treatment for Drug Dependence in Asia.' In *Drug Law and Reform in East and Southeast Asia*, edited by Fifa Rahman and Nick Crofts, 271–90. Lanham: Lexington Books, 2013.

Chouvy, Pierre-Arnaud. *An Atlas of Trafficking in Southeast Asia. The Illegal Trade in Arms, Drugs, People, Counterfeit Goods and Natural Resources in Mainland Southeast Asia.* London: I.B. Tauris; Bangkok: IRASEC, 2013.

Chouvy, Pierre-Arnaud. 'The Myth of the Narco-State.' *Space and Polity* 20, no. 1 (2016): 26–38. https://doi.org/10.1080/13562576.2015.1052 348.

Chouvy, Pierre-Arnaud. *Opium: Uncovering the Politics of the Poppy.* Cambridge, MA: Harvard University Press, 2010.

Chouvy, Pierre-Arnaud. 'A Typology of the Unintended Consequences of Drug Crop Reduction.' *Journal of Drug Issues* 43, no. 2 (2013): 216–30.

Collins, John. 'Beyond UNGASS 2016: Drug Control Multilateralism and the End to the "War on Drugs."' In *Militarised Responses to Transnational Organised Crime: The War on Crime,* edited by Tuesday Reitano, Sasha

Jesperson, and Lucia Bird Ruiz-Benitez de Lugo, 1st ed. 2018 edition, 279–97. New York: Palgrave Macmillan, 2017.

Collins, John. 'Development First: Multilateralism in the Post-"War on Drugs" Era.' In *After the Drug Wars: Report of the LSE Expert Group on the Economics of Drug Policy*, edited by John Collins, 9–18. London: LSE, 2016.

Collins, John. 'The Economics of a New Global Strategy.' In *Ending the Drug Wars: Report of the LSE Expert Group on the Economics of Drug Policy*, edited by John Collins, 8–15. London: LSE, 2014. https://www.lse.ac.uk/ideas/Assets/Documents/reports/LSE-IDEAS-Ending-the-Drug-Wars.pdf.

Collins, John. 'The State Department's move to a more flexible diplomatic policy on drugs is a rational approach to a difficult question.' *The LSE US Centre's daily blog on American Politics and Policy*, December 1, 2014. http://bit.ly/1tuVypa.

Comisión Asesora para la Política de Drogas en Colombia. *Lineamientos para un Nuevo Enfoque de la Política de Drogas en Colombia. Informe Final*. Bogotá, May 2015.

Comisión Nacional contra las Adicciones. *Encuesta Nacional de Consumo de Drogas, Alcohol y Tabaco, ENCODAT 2016-2017*. Mexico City: Gobierno de México, 2017.

Commission on Crime Prevention and Criminal Justice. *World Crime Trends and Emerging Issues and Responses in the Field of Crime Prevention and Criminal Justice: Note by the Secretariat*. Vienna: United Nations Economic and Social Council, 2016. https://undocs.org/E/CN.15/2016/10.

Commission on Narcotic Drugs. *Background paper prepared by the United Kingdom of Great Britain and Northern Ireland related to its notification submitted on 23 January to the Secretary-General on the review of the scope of control of mephedrone*. E/CN.7/2014/CRP.11. Vienna: CND, 2014. https://www.unodc.org/documents/commissions/CND/CND_Sessions/CND_57/E-CN7-2014-CRP11_V1401524_E.pdf.

Commission on Narcotic Drugs. *Draft Action Plan on International Cooperation on Eradication of Illicit Drug Crops and Promotion of Alternative Development Programmes and Projects*. E/CN.7/1998/PC/7. Vienna: United Nations Economic and Social Council, 1998.

Commission on Narcotic Drugs. *International Workshop and Conference on Alternative Development in Chiang Rai and Chiang Mai, Thailand, 6–11 November 2011*. E/CN.7/2012/CRP.3. Vienna: CND, 2012. https://www.unodc.org/documents/commissions/CND/CND_Sessions/CND_55/E-CN7-2012-CRP3_V1251320_E.pdf.

Commission on Narcotic Drugs. *Legal Opinion from the Office of Legal Affairs of the Secretariat.* E/CN.7/2015/14. Vienna: CND, 2015.

Commission on Narcotic Drugs. *Making Drug Control 'Fit for Purpose': Building on the UNGASS Decade. Report by the Executive Director of the United Nations Office on Drugs and Crime as a Contribution to the Review of the Twentieth Special Session of the General Assembly.* E/CN.7/2008/CRP.17*. Vienna: CND, 2008. https://www.unodc.org/documents/commissions/CND/CND_Sessions/CND_51/1_CRPs/E-CN7-2008-CRP17_E.

Commission on Narcotic Drugs. *Ministerial Declaration on Strengthening our Actions at the National, Regional and International Levels to Accelerate the Implementation of our Joint Commitments to Address and Counter the World Drug Problem.* Vienna: CND, 2019. https://www.unodc.org/documents/commissions/CND/2019/Ministerial_Declaration.pdf.

Commission on Narcotic Drugs. *Report of the Workshop Portion of the International Workshop and Conference on Alternative Development ICAD, Chiang Rai and Chiang Mai, Thailand, 6-11 November 2011.* Vienna: CND, 2012.

Commission on Narcotic Drugs. *Resolution 57/5. Special Session of the General Assembly on the World Drug Problem to be Held in 2016.* Vienna: CND, 2014. https://www.unodc.org/documents/ungass2016/Background/CND_Res_57_5.pdf.

Commission on Narcotic Drugs. *Updated Information Provided by the International Narcotics Control Board on the Implementation of Commission on Narcotic Drugs resolutions 49/6 'Listing of Ketamine as a Controlled Substance' and 50/3 'Responding to the Threat Posed by the Abuse and Diversion of Ketamine.'* E/CN.7/2014/CRP.2. Vienna: CND, 2014.

Committee on Economic, Social and Cultural Rights. *General Comment No. 14 (2000): The Right to the Highest Attainable Standard of Health (Article 12 of the International Covenant on Economic, Social and Cultural Rights).* E/C.12/2000/4. Geneva: United Nations Economic and Social Council, 2000.

Committee on the Rights of the Child. *General Comment No. 15 (2013) on the Right of the Child to the Enjoyment of the Highest Attainable Standard of Health (art. 24).* CRC/C/GC/15. New York: United Nations Convention on the Rights of the Child, 2013.

Congressional Research Service. *Mexico: Evolution of the Mérida Initiative, 2007–2020.* Washington D.C., updated February 19, 2020.

Congressional Research Service. *U.S. Strategy for Engagement in Central America: Policy issues for Congress.* Washington D.C., updated November 12, 2019.

Cook, Catherine, Jamie Bridge, Susie McLean, Maria Phelan, and Damon Barrett. *The Funding Crisis in Harm Reduction: Donor Retreat, Government*

Neglect and the Way Forward. London: International Harm Reduction Association, 2014.

Cook, Catherine, Maria Phelan, Gen Sander, Katie Stone, and Fionnuala Murphy. *The Case for a Harm Reduction Decade: Progress, Potential and Paradigm Shifts.* London: Harm Reduction International, 2016.

Corda, Raúl Alejandro. 'Imprisonment for Drug Related Offenses in Argentina.' In *Systems Overload: Drug Laws and Prisons in Latin America*, edited by Pien Metaal and Coletta Youngers, 11–20. Amsterdam: Transnational Institute; Washington D.C.: Washington Office on Latin America, 2011.

Corporación Latinobarómetro. *Informe 2018.* Santiago de Chile: Corporación Latinobarómetro, 2018.

Corrales, Javier. 'The Many Lefts of Latin America.' *Foreign Policy*, November–December 2006.

Correa, Catalina Pérez, and Coletta Youngers. *En Busca de los Derechos: Usuarios de Drogas y Las Respuestas Estatales en América Latina.* Mexico City: Colectivo de Estudios de Droga y de Derecho, 2014.

Costa, Antonio Maria. Preface to *A Century of International Drug Control,* by United Nations Office on Drugs and Crime, 3. Vienna: UNODC, 2008.

Count the Costs. *The War on Drugs: Promoting Stigma and Discrimination.* Bristol: Transform Drug Policy Foundation, 2015. http://www.countthecosts.org/sites/default/files/Stigma-briefing.pdf.

Courtwright, David T. *Forces of Habit: Drugs and the Making of the Modern World.* Cambridge, MA; London: Harvard University Press, 2001.

Crespo, Freddy A., and Mireya Bolaños G. 'Delitos Violentos: Entre Los Vapores de la Drogadicción.' *Capítulo Criminológico* 36, no. 3 (2008): 101–41.

Crick, Emily. 'Drugs as an Existential Threat: An Analysis of the International Securitization of Drugs.' *International Journal of Drug Policy* 23, no. 5 (September 2012): 407–14. https://doi.org/10.1016/j.drugpo.2012.03.004.

Crick, Emily, Mark Cooke, and Dave Bewley-Taylor. *Selling cannabis regulation: Learning from Ballot Initiatives in the United States in 2012.* Swansea: Global Drug Policy Observatory, 2014. https://www.tni.org/files/publication-downloads/gdpo6.pdf.

Crick, Emily, Heather J. Haase, and Dave Bewley-Taylor. *Legally Regulated Cannabis Markets in the US: Implications and possibilities.* Swansea: Global Drug Policy Observatory, 2013. https://www.tni.org/files/gdpo1.pdf.

Crofts, Nick, Geoff Monaghan, Steve James, Nicole Turner, and Mohd Zaman Khan. 'Law Enforcement and Drug Policy in Southeast Asia.' In *Drug Law and Reform in East and Southeast Asia*, edited by Fifa Rahman and Nick Crofts, 59–70. Lanham: Lexington Books, 2013.

Cruz, José Miguel. 'The Real Failure in Central America.' *Miami Herald*, July 24, 2014. https://www.miamiherald.com/opinion/op-ed/article1976942.html.

Cruz, José Miguel. 'The Root Causes of the Central American Crisis.' *Current History* 114, no. 769 (2015): 43–48.

Cruz, José Miguel Cruz, María Fernanda Boidi, and Rosario Queirolo. 'The status of support for cannabis regulation in Uruguay 4 years after reform: Evidence from public opinion surveys.' *Drug and Alcohol Review* 37, no. 1 (2018): 429–34.

Cruz, José Miguel, Rosario Queirolo, and María Fernanda Boidi. 'Determinants of Public Support for Marijuana Legalization in Uruguay, the United States, and El Salvador.' *Journal of Drug Issues* 46, no. 4 (2016): 308–25.

Csete, Joanne and Richard Pearshouse. *Detention and Punishment in the Name of Drug Treatment*. New York: Open Society Foundations, 2016.

Dammert, Lucía. 'Drogas e Inseguridad en América Latina: Una Relación Compleja.' *Nueva Sociedad* no. 222 (2009): 112–31.

Daugherty, Arron. 'Ecuador Toughens Drugs Laws, Muddles Policy.' *InSight Crime*, September 10, 2015. http://www.insightcrime.org/news-briefs/ecuador-president-proposes-tougher-punishment-for-microtraffickers.

Dawson, Alexander E. *The Peyote Effect: From the Inquisition to the War on Drugs*. Oakland: University of California Press, 2018.

Degenhardt, Louisa, Bradley M. Mathers, Andrea L. Wirtz, Daniel Wolfe, Adeeba Kamarulzaman, M. Patrizia Carrieri, Steffanie A. Strathdee, Kasia Malinowska-Sempruch, Michel Kazatchkine, and Chris Beyrer. 'What Has Been Achieved in HIV Prevention, Treatment and Care for People who Inject Drugs, 2010-2012? A Review of Highest Burden Countries.' *International Journal of Drug Policy* 25, no. 1 (2014): 53–60.

DeGrandpre, Richard. *The Cult of Pharmacology: How America Became the World's Most Troubled Drug Culture*. Durham: Duke University Press, 2006.

De Boer, John and Louise Bosetti, 'The Crime-Conflict Nexus. Assessing the Threat and Developing Solutions,' Crime-Conflict Nexus Series. United Nations University Centre for Policy Research, May 2017.

De León Beltrán, Isaac, and Juan Carlos Garzón Vergara, *Urban Drug Markets and Zones of Impunity in Colombia*. Amsterdam: Transnational Institute, 2014.

Diaz, Tom. *No Boundaries: Transnational Latino Gangs and American Law Enforcement*. Ann Arbor: The University of Michigan Press, 2009.

Dikotter, Frank, Lars Laaman, and Zhou Xun, *Narcotic Culture: A History of Drugs in China*. Chicago: University of Chicago Press, 2004.

Dolan, Kate, Babak Moazen, Atefeh Noori, Shadi Rahimzadeh, Farshad Farzadfar, and Fabienne Hariga. 'People Who Inject Drugs in Prison: HIV Prevalence, Transmission and Prevention.' *International Journal of Drug Policy* 26, no. 1 (2015): 12–15.

Downing, Thomas E., Aerts, J., Soussan, J., Barthelemy, O., Bharwani, S., Ionescu, C., Hinkel, J., Klein, R.J.T., Mata, L., Martin, N., Moss, S., Purkey, D. and Ziervogel, G. 'Integrating Social Vulnerability into Water Management.' *NeWater Working Paper* No. 5, Stockholm Environment Institute, 2006.

Dube, Oeindrila, and Suresh Naidu. 'Bases, Bullets and Ballots: The Effect of US Military Aid on Political Conflict in Colombia.' Working paper No. w20213, National Bureau of Economic Research, Cambridge, MA, 2014.

Dubove, Adam. 'Argentina's Presidential Hopefuls Aim to Further Militarize Drug War.' *The Pan-American Post*, September 25, 2015. http://panampost.com/adam-dubove/2015/09/25/argentinas-presidential-hopefuls-aim-to-further-militarize-drug-war/.

Dudley, Amy. 'Vice President Biden Travels to Mexico and Honduras.' *The White House President Barak Obama.* March 7, 2012. https://obamawhitehouse.archives.gov/blog/2012/03/07/vice-president-biden-travels-mexico-and-honduras.

Dudley, Stephen S. *Transnational Crime in Mexico and Central America: Its Evolution and Role in International Migration.* Washington D.C.: Migration Policy Institute, 2012.

Durán-Martínez, Angélica. 'Drugs around the Corner: Domestic Drug Markets and Violence in Colombia and Mexico.' *Latin American Politics and Society* 57, no. 3 (2015): 122–46

Durán-Martínez, Angélica. *The Politics of Drug Violence: Criminals, Cops and Politicians in Colombia and Mexico.* New York: Oxford University Press, 2018.

Dutta, Indranil, James Foster, and Ajit Mishra. 'On Measuring Vulnerability to Poverty.' *Social Choice and Welfare* 37, no. 4 (2011): 743–61.

Eakin, Hallie and Amy Lynd Luers. 'Assessing the Vulnerability of Social-Environmental Systems,' *Annual Review of Environment and Resources* 31, no. 1 (2006): 365–94, https://doi.org/10.1146/annurev.energy.30.050504.144352.

Eastwood, Niamh, Michael Shiner, and Daniel Bear. *The Numbers in Black and White: Ethnic Disparities in the Policing and Prosecution of Drug Offences in England and Wales.* London: Release, 2014.

Economic Community of West African States Commission. 'The Thirty-First Session of the Authority of Heads of State and Government: Final Communiqué.' Ouagadougou, Burkina Faso, January 19, 2007.

Economic Community of West African States (ECOWAS). 'ECOWAS Drug Unit Portal.' https://edup.ecowas.int/.

Economic Community of West African States (ECOWAS). 'Forty-First Ordinary Session of the ECOWAS Authority of Heads of State and Government.' Yamoussoukro, Cote d'Ivoire, June 28–9, 2012. https://www.ecowas.int/wp-content/uploads/2015/02/41st-ECOWAS-Summit-Yamoussoukro-28-29-June-20121.pdf.

Economic Community of West African States (ECOWAS). 'Political declaration on the prevention of drug abuse, illicit drug trafficking and organized crimes in West Africa.' Abuja, United Nations Office on Drugs and Crime, December 2008. https://www.unodc.org/westandcentralafrica/en/ecowaspoliticaldeclaration.html.

Economist, The. 'Corruption in Guatemala. Bad apples everywhere.' June 11, 2016. http://www.economist.com/news/americas/21700418-ousted-president-accused-masterminding-kleptocracy-bad-apples-everywhere.

Economist, The. 'The Global Drugs Trade Shifts to West Africa.' November 21, 2019. https://www.economist.com/international/2019/11/21/the-global-drugs-trade-shifts-to-west-africa.

Edith Yunita Sianturi, Rani Andriani (Melisa Aprilia), Myuran Sukumaran, Andrew Chan, Scott Anthony Rush, 2-3/PUU-V/2007 IDCC 16 (October 2007). https://www.hr-dp.org/contents/173.

Edwards, Charlie, and Luke Gribbon. 'Pathways to Violent Extremism in the Digital Era.' *The RUSI Journal* 158, no. 5 (October 2013): 40–7. https://doi.org/10.1080/03071847.2013.847714.

Edwards, Sandra. 'A Short History of Ecuador's Drug Legislation and the Impact on Its Prison Population.' In *Systems Overload: Drug Laws and Prisons in Latin America*, edited by Pien Metaal and Coletta Youngers, 51–60. Amsterdam: Transnational Institute; Washington D.C.: Washington Office on Latin America, 2011. http://www.druglawreform.info/images/stories/documents/Systems_Overload/TNI-Systems_Overload-ecuador-def.pdf.

Ehrenberg, Rachel. 'Engineered yeast paves way for home-brew heroin.' *Nature* 521, no. 7552 (2015): 267–8. http://www.nature.com/news/engineered-yeast-paves-way-for-home-brew-heroin-1.17566.

Eiranova González-Elías, Irina, Ariane Hernández Trujillo, and Ángela Otero Mustelier. 'El ciclo de la violencia en consumidores de sustancias tóxicas.' *MEDISAN* 17, no. 12 (2013): 9081–8.

Eisner, Manuel. 'No Effects in Independent Prevention Trials: Can We Reject the Cynical View?' *Journal of Experimental Criminology* 5, no. 2 (2009): 163–83. doi:10.1007/s11292-009-9071-y.

Eisner, Manuel, and David Humphreys. 'Measuring Conflict of Interest in Prevention and Intervention Research: A Feasibility Study.' In *Antisocial Behavior and Crime Contributions of Developmental and Evaluation Research to Prevention and Intervention*, edited by Thomas Bliesener, Andreas Beelmann, and Mark Stemmler, 165–80. Gottingen: Hogrefe Publishing, 2012.

Elías, José. 'El expresidente de Guatemala, Otto Pérez, ligado a proceso por un nuevo caso de corrupción.' *El País*, July 27, 2016. http://internacional.elpais.com/internacional/2016/07/28/america/1469668078_832754.html.

Ellis, Paul D. *The Essential Guide to Effect Sizes: Statistical Power, Meta-Analysis, and the Interpretation of Research Results*. Cambridge: Cambridge University Press, 2010.

Ellis, Stephen. 'West Africa's International Drug Trade.' *African Affairs* 108, no. 431 (2009): 171–96.

El Tiempo. 'Colombia Pidió Autonomía en Política de Drogas.' *El Tiempo*, May 8, 2015, http://www.eltiempo.com/politica/justicia/colombia-pidio-autonomia-en-politica-de-drogas/15717615.

El Tiempo. '"Perseguimos Cultivadores y Allá El Gringo Metiendo Varillo": Santos.' December 6, 2012. https://www.eltiempo.com/archivo/documento/CMS-12429983.

El Universal. 'Biden Ratifica Postura de EU Contra Legalización de las Drogas.' March 4, 2012. http://archivo.eluniversal.com.mx/notas/834187.html.

El Universal. 'Golpeada por la Droga, Argentina Observa la Experiencia Uruguaya.' May 3, 2014. https://www.eluniversal.com.co/mundo/golpeada-por-la-droga-argentina-observa-la-experiencia-uruguaya-158627-HXEU251017.

Emmers, Ralf. 'Securitization.' In *Contemporary Security Studies*, edited by Allan Collins, 131–43. Oxford: Oxford University Press, 2013.

Enloe, Cynthia. 'Margins, Silences and Bottom Rungs.' In *International Theory: Positivism and Beyond*, edited by Steve Smith, Ken Booth, and Marysia Zalewski, 186–202. Cambridge: Cambridge University Press, 1996.

Erien, Jonathan, and Joseph Spillane. *Federal Drug Control: The Evolution of Policy and Practice*. Philadelphia: Pharmaceutical Products Press, 2004.

Escobar Córdoba, Franklin. *Riesgo Para Cometer Homicidio en Jóvenes Bogotanos. Un Estudio Multimétodo*. PhD diss., Universidad de la Plata, 2006.

Espectador.com. 'Posición del Presidente de JIFE no Representa Opinión de ONU.' December 13, 2013. http://historico.espectador.com/politica/280451/posicion-del-presidente-de-jife-no-representa-opinion-de-onu.

Espinosa, Valeria, and Donald B. Rubin. 'Did the Military Interventions in the Mexican Drug War Increase Violence?' *The American Statistician* 69, no. 1 (2015): 17–27.

European Monitoring Centre for Drugs and Drug Addiction. 'Data and Statistics.' Accessed May 29, 2020. http://www.emcdda.europa.eu/data/stats2015.

European Monitoring Centre for Drugs and Drug Addiction. *European Drug Report 2014: Trends and Developments*. Lisbon: EMCDDA, 2014.

European Monitoring Centre on Drugs and Drug Addiction. *European Drug Report 2019*. Lisbon: EMCDDA, 2019.

European Monitoring Centre for Drugs and Drug Addiction. *France: Country Drug Report 2017*. Luxembourg: European Union, 2017.

Executive Secretariat of the National Public Security System of Mexico. 'Víctimas y Unidades Robadas.' 2020. https://www.gob.mx/sesnsp/acciones-y-programas/victimas-nueva-metodologia?state=published.

Fajardo-Heyward, Paola. 'Understanding the Effect of Security Assistance on Human Rights: The Case of Plan Colombia.' *The Latin Americanist* 59, no. 2 (2015): 3–27.

Falk, Richard. 'Toward a New Geopolitics?' *Foreign Policy Journal*, August 17, 2012, https://www.foreignpolicyjournal.com/2012/08/17/toward-a-new-geopolitics/.

Famuyiwa, Oluwole, Aina F. Olatunji, and Olufunlayo M. Bankole-Oki. 'Epidemiology of Psychoactive Drug Use amongst Adolescents in Metropolitan Lagos, Nigeria.' *European Child & Adolescent Psychiatry* 20, no. 7 (2011): 351–9. https://doi.org/10.1007/s00787-011-0180-6.

Federal Bureau of Prisons. 'Statistics: Offenses.' Data from September 29, 2018. https://www.bop.gov/about/statistics/statistics_inmate_offenses.jsp.

Federal Drug Control Service (FSKN). 'On the narcotics situation in the Russian Federation and the Result of Countering Illicit Circulation of Narcotics (Jan-Mar 2012).' 2012. http://www.fskn.gov.ru/pages/main/prevent/3939/4052/index.shtml.

Federal Law. 'On Narcotic and Psychotropic Substances.' January 8, 1998. In *Russian Law Collection*, 1998. V. 2. Art. 219.

Fedetov, Yuri. 'Yuri Fedotov: "I am surprised that the Global Commission calls for legalization of ecstasy and cannabis",' *Security Index* 17, no. 4 (2011): 25–6, http://www.pircenter.org/media/content/files/0/13406273380.pdf.

Felbab-Brown, Vanda. 'The Coca Connection: Conflict and Drugs in Colombia and Peru.' *Journal of Conflict Studies* 25, no. 2 (2005): 104–28.

BIBLIOGRAPHY

Felbab-Brown, Vanda. *Enabling War and Peace: Drugs, Logs, Gems, and Wildlife in Thailand and Burma.* Washington D.C.: The Brookings Institution, 2015.

Felbab-Brown, Vanda. *Focused Deterrence, Selective Targeting, Drug Trafficking and Organized Crime: Concepts and Practicalities.* Modernizing Drug Law Enforcement Report 2. London: International Drug Policy Consortium, 2013.

Felbab-Brown, Vanda. *No Easy Exit: Drugs and Counternarcotics Policies in Afghanistan.* Washington D.C.: Brookings Institution, 2015.

Felbab-Brown, Vanda. 'The West African Drug Trade in the Context of the Region's Illicit Economies and Poor Governance.' Presentation to Conference on Drug Trafficking in West Africa, in Arlington, Virginia, October 14, 2010.

Felbab-Brown, Vanda. 'What Colombia Can Learn from Thailand on Drug Policy.' *Brookings*, May 4, 2017. https://www.brookings.edu/blog/order-from-chaos/2017/05/04/what-colombia-can-learn-from-thailand-on-drug-policy/.

Felbab-Brown, Vanda, Joel M. Jutkowitz, Sergio Rivas, Ricardo Rocha, James T. Smith, Manuel Supervielle, and Cynthia Watson. *Assessment of The Implementation of The United States Government's Support for Plan Colombia's Illicit Crop Reduction Components.* Washington D.C.: USAID Management Systems International, 2009.

Fielding, Amanda, and Nichola Singleton. *Roadmaps to Regulation: New Psychoactive Substances.* Oxford: Beckley Foundation, 2016. https://beckleyfoundation.org/wp-content/uploads/2016/05/Roadmaps-to-Regulation_NPS_20-06-2016.pdf.

Felbab-Brown, Vanda, and Harold Trinkunas. *UNGASS 2016 in Comparative Perspective: Improving the Prospects for Success.* Washington D.C.: Brookings Institution, 2015.

Financial Action Task Force. *Financial Flows Linked to the Production and Trafficking of Afghan Opiates.* Paris: FATF/OECD, 2014.

Financial Action Task Force. *Second Mutual Evaluation Report of the Russian Federation: Anti-Money Laundering and Combating the Financing of Terrorism.* Paris: FATF/OECD, 2008.

Financial Times. 'Afghan Drugs Crisis.' July 30, 2008.

Flores Pérez, Carlos Antonio. *Historias de Polvo y Sangre: Génesis y Evolución del Tráfico de Drogas en el Estado de Tamaulipas.* Mexico City: Publicaciones de la Casa Chata, 2013.

Fox, Edward. 'US Report on Colombia Cocaine Raises More Questions than Answers.' *InSight Crime*, August 1, 2012, http://www.insightcrime.org/

news-analysis/us-report-on-colombia-cocaine-production-raises-more-questions-than-answers.

Fox, Edward. 'Prison Gang Leaders Order Hit on Police in Venezuela.' *InSight Crime*, November 20, 2012. http://www.insightcrime.org/news-briefs/prison-gang-leaders-order-hit-on-police-in-venezuelan-state.

Franke, Benedikt. 'Africa's evolving security architecture and the concept of multilayered security communities.' *Cooperation and Conflict* 43, no. 3 (2008): 313–40.

Frantz, Douglas. 'The Romeo and Juliet of Economic Transformation.' *OECD Insights Blog*, January 16, 2016. http://oecdinsights.org/2016/01/16/the-romeo-and-juliet-of-economic-transformation/.

French, Howard W. 'Heroin grips poor town in rural China.' *International Herald Tribune*, December 24–26, 2004.

Friedmann, John. *Empowerment: The Politics of Alternative Development*. Oxford: Blackwell, 1992.

Friesendorf, Cornelius. *US Foreign Policy and the War on Drugs: Displacing the Cocaine and Heroin Industry*. New York: Routledge, 2007.

Friman, Richard. *Narco-Diplomacy: Exporting the U.S. War on Drugs*. Ithaca: Cornell University Press, 1996.

Froio, Nicole. 'Brazil's Favelas are in Big Trouble, Despite the World Cup Marketing Push.' *The Guardian*, May 18, 2014. http://www.theguardian.com/commentisfree/2014/may/18/brazil-favelas-big-trouble-world-cup-marketing-police-abuse-killings-security.

Frydl, Kathleen J. *The Drug Wars in America, 1940–1973*. New York: Cambridge University Press, 2013.

Fuller, Thomas. 'Notorious Golden Triangle Loses Sway in the Opium Trade.' *The New York Times*, September 11, 2007. https://www.nytimes.com/2007/09/11/world/asia/11iht-golden.1.7461246.html.

Fundación Ideas para la Paz. *Legalización de la Marihuana Medicinal: ¿Qué Opinan los Colombianos?* Bogotá: Fundación Ideas para la Paz, 2014. http://cdn.ideaspaz.org/media/website/document/5487d40ca0e99.pdf.

Fundación Paz Ciudadana. *Construcción de indicadores de reinserción social de adolescentes infractores de la ley penal*. Santiago de Chile: Fundación Paz Ciudadana, 2010.

Fundación Paz Ciudadana. *Consumo de Alcohol y Delincuencia en Chile*. Santiago de Chile: Fundación Paz Ciudadana, 2003.

Gabrilyants, Mikhail. Adviser to the Head of FSKN. Remarks at the 6th Meeting of the Joint US-Russia Working Group on the Afghan Narcotrafficking, Moscow, October 5, 2015.

Gagne, David. 'Police Violence Continues to Plague Brazil: Report.' *InSight Crime,* November 11, 2014. http://www.insightcrime.org/news-analysis/police-violence-continues-to-plague-brazil-report.

Gallahue, Patrick, and Rick Lines. *The Death Penalty for Drug Offences: Global Overview 2015: The Extreme Fringe of Global Drug Policy.* London: Harm Reduction International, 2015.

Gallahue, Patrick, Fifa Rahman, Ricky Gunawan, Karim El Mufti, Najam U Din, and Rita Felten. *The Death Penalty for Drug Offences: Global Overview 2012: Tipping the Scales for Abolition.* London: Harm Reduction International, 2012.

Garay-Salamanca, Jorge Eduardo, and Eduardo Salcedo-Albarán. *Drug Trafficking, Corruption and States: How Illicit Networks Shaped Institutions in Colombia, Mexico and Guatemala.* Bloomington: iUniverse, 2015.

Garcia-Abreu, Anabela, Isabel Noguer, and Karen Cowgill. *HIV/AIDS in Latin American Countries: The Challenges Ahead.* Washington D.C.: World Bank, 2003.

García Sánchez, Miguel. 'Cultivos Ilícitos y Confianza Institucional en Colombia.' *Política y Gobierno* 21, no. 1 (2014): 95–126.

Garzón Vergara, Juan Carlos. *Consertando Um Sistema Falido: Modernizando a Aplicação Das Leis de Drogas Na América Latina.* Série sobre Reforma Legislativa de Políticas sobre Drogas No. 29. Amsterdam: TNI; London: IDPC, 2014.

Garzón Vergara, Juan Carlos. *Fixing a Broken System: Modernizing Drug Law Enforcement in Latin America.* Amsterdam: Transnational Institute, 2014.

Garzón Vergara, Juan Carlos. *Post-UNGASS 2016: Latin America and Drug Policy Perspectives.* Santiago de Chile: Consejo de Relaciones Internacionales de América Latina y El Caribe, 2017. https://consejorial.org/en/publicaciones/post-ungass-2016-latin-america-and-drug-policy-perspectives-2/.

Garzón Vergara, Juan Carlos. *Tough on the Weak, Weak on the Tough: Drug Laws and Policing.* Washington D.C.: Woodrow Wilson Center, Latin American Program, 2015. https://www.wilsoncenter.org/publication/tough-the-weak.

Garzón Vergara, Juan Carlos. 'Worried about Illegal Drugs? Change the Policy and Think Long-Term.' *Georgetown Journal of International Affairs,* June 26, 2018. https://gjia.georgetown.edu/2018/06/26/illegal-drug-policy/.

Garzón Vergara, Juan Carlos, and John Bailey. 'Displacement Effects of Supply Reduction Policies in Latin America.' In *The Handbook of Drugs and Society*, edited by Henry Brownstein, 482–503. Oxford: John Wiley & Sons, 2016.

Garzón Vergara, Juan Carlos, Marianna Pacheco Olinger, Daniel Rico, and Gema Santamaria. *The Criminal Diaspora: The Spread of Transnational Organized Crime and How to Contain Its Expansion*. Washington D.C.: Woodrow Wilson Center, 2013.

Garzón Vergara, Juan Carlos, and Luciana Pol. 'The Elephant in the Room: Drugs and Human Rights in Latin America.' *SUR International Journal on Human Rights* 12, no. 21 (2015).

Gberie, Lasana. *Crime, violence, and politics: drug trafficking and counternarcotic policies in Mali and Guinea*. Washington D.C.: Brookings Institution, 2015.

Gberie, Lasana, and Camino Kavanagh. *Not Just in Transit: Drugs, the State and Society in West Africa: An Independent Report of the West Africa Commission on Drugs*. Accra: WACD, 2014.

Geneva Declaration Secretariat. *Global Burden of Armed Violence 2015: Every Body Counts*. Cambridge: Cambridge University Press, 2015.

Georgina Wood Committee. *The Georgina Wood Committee Report*. Accra, 2006. http://www.ghananewsagency.org/social/georgina-wood-committee-presents-it-report-to-government-854. Accessed on October 20, 2015. [By September 2020, the reference to the report had been removed from the website.]

Giacomello, Corina. *Women, Drug Offenses and Penitentiary Systems in Latin America*. London: International Drug Policy Consortium, 2013.

Gilligan, James. 'Shame, Guilt, and Violence.' *Social Research: An International Quarterly* 70, no. 4 (2003): 1149–80.

Gilpin, Robert. *The Political Economy of International Relations*. Princeton: Princeton University Press, 1987.

Global Commission on Drug Policy. *Drug Policy and the Sustainable Development Agenda*. Geneva: GCDP, 2018. http://www.globalcommissionondrugs.org/wp-content/uploads/2018/09/ENG-2018_SDGPaper_WEB.pdf.

Global Commission on Drug Policy. *The Negative Impact of the War on Drugs on Public Health: The Hidden Hepatitis C Epidemic*. Geneva: GCDP, 2013.

Global Commission on Drug Policy. *Taking Control: Pathways to Drug Policies that Work*. Geneva: GCDP, 2014. https://www.globalcommissionondrugs.org/reports/taking-control-pathways-to-drug-policies-that-work.

Global Commission on Drug Policy. *War on Drugs: Report of the Global Commission on Drug Policy*. Geneva: GCDP, 2011. http://www.globalcommissionondrugs.org/wp-content/themes/gcdp_v1/pdf/Global_Commission_Report_English.pdf.

Guzzini, Stefano. *The Return of Geopolitics in Europe? Social Mechanisms And Foreign Policy Identity Crises*. Cambridge: Cambridge University Press, 2013.

Godwin, E. 'Drug trafficking menace in Togo.' *Daily Graphic*, March 9, 2009.

Goffman, Erving. *Stigma: Notes on the Management of Spoiled Identity*. Englewood Cliffs: Prentice-Hall, 1963.

Gold, Mark S., Steven T. Gold, and Michael Herkov. 'Drugs and Violence in the USA.' In *Encyclopedia of Violence, Peace, and Conflict*, edited by Lester R. Kurtz, 2nd ed., 590–606. Amsterdam: Academic Press, 2008.

Goldman, Francisco. 'From President to Prison: Otto Pérez Molina and a Day for Hope in Guatemala.' *The New Yorker*, September 4, 2015. https://www.newyorker.com/news/news-desk/from-president-to-prison-otto-perez-molina-and-a-day-for-hope-in-guatemala.

Goldstein, Paul J. 'The Drugs/Violence Nexus: A Tripartite Conceptual Framework.' *Journal of Drug Issues* 39 (1985): 143–74.

Gómez Robledo, Juan Manuel. 'Statement on Behalf of the Government of Mexico by Amb. Juan Manuel Gómez Robledo, Undersecretary of Foreign Affairs for Multilateral Issues and Human Rights: Special Segment on preparations for UNGASS 2016.' Statement delivered at the fifty-eighth session of the CND, Vienna, March 9, 2015. https://www.unodc.org/documents/commissions/CND/CND_Sessions/CND_58/UNGASS_Statements/UNGASS_Statements_9March_PM/16_Mexico_English.pdf.

Goodhand, Jonathan. 'Corrupting or Consolidating the Peace? The Drugs Economy and Post-Conflict Peacebuilding in Afghanistan.' *International Peacekeeping* 15, no. 3 (June 2008): 405–23.

Goodwin, Andrew. *Measuring the Harm from Illegal Drugs: The Drug Harm Index 2005*. Online Report 22/07. London: Home Office, 2007. http://webarchive.nationalarchives.gov.uk/20110220105210/rds.homeoffice.gov.uk/rds/pdfs07/rdsolr2207.pdf.

Gootenberg, Paul. *Andean Cocaine: The Making of a Global Drug*. Chapel Hill: University of North Carolina Press, 2008.

Gootenberg, Paul, ed. *Cocaine: Global Histories*. London: Routledge UK, 1999.

Gootenberg, Paul. 'Cocaine's Long March North, 1900-2010.' *Latin American Politics & Society* 54, vol. 1 (2012): 151–80.

Gootenberg, Paul. 'The "Pre-Colombian" Era of Drug Trafficking in the Americas: Cocaine: 1945–1965.' *The Americas* 64, vol. 2 (2007): 133–76.

Gootenberg, Paul. 'Secret Ingredients: The Politics of Coca in US-Peruvian Relations, 1915–1965.' *Journal of Latin American Studies* 36, vol. 2 (2004): 233–66.

Gootenberg, Paul. 'Talking Like a State: Drugs, Borders, and the Language of Control.' In *Illicit Flows and Criminal Things: States, Borders, and the Other Side of Globalization*, edited by Willem van Schendel and Itty Abraham, 101–27. Bloomington: Indiana University Press, 2005.

Granada, Camilo. 'The OAS and Transnational Organized Crime in the Americas.' In *Transnational Organized Crime and International Security*, edited by Mónica Serrano and Mats Berdal, 95–102. London: Lynne Rienner Publishers, 2002.

Grisaffi, Thomas. *Coca Yes, Cocaine No: How Bolivia's Coca Growers Reshaped Democracy*. Durham, NC: Duke University Press, 2019.

Grupo de Trabajo sobre Mujeres, Políticas de Drogas y Encarcelamiento. *Mujeres, Políticas de Drogas y Encarcelamiento: Una Guía para la Reforma de las Políticas en América Latina y el Caribe*. Washington D.C.: WOLA, 2016. https://www.oas.org/es/cim/docs/WomenDrugsIncarceration-ES.pdf.

Gutierrez, Eric. *Drugs and Illicit Practices: Assessing their Impact on Development and Governance*. London: Christian Aid, 2015.

Haidt, Jonathan. *The Righteous Mind: Why Good People Are Divided by Politics and Religion*. New York: Pantheon Books, 2012.

Hallam, Christopher. *The International Drug Control Regime Hand Access to Controlled Medicines*. Series of Legislative Reform of Drug Policies No. 26. Amsterdam: Transnational Institute; London: International Drug Policy Consortium, 2014.

Hallam, Christopher, and David Bewley-Taylor. 'Mapping the World Drug Problem: Science and Politics in the United Nations Drug Control System.' *International Journal of Drug Policy* 21, no. 1 (2010): 1–3.

Hammersley, Richard. 'Pathways through Drugs and Crime: Desistance, Trauma and Resilience.' *Journal of Criminal Justice* 39, no. 3 (2011): 268–72. https://doi.org/10.1016/j.jcrimjus.2011.02.006.

Hanif, Mohammed. 'Pakistan doesn't owe you a free mansion.' *International New York Times,* May 13, 2016.

Harm Reduction International. *Declaration of Kuala Lumpur: Official Declaration of the 2015 International Harm Reduction conference*. London: HRI, 2015.

Harm Reduction International. *The Global State of Harm Reduction 2014*. Edited by Katie Stone. London: HRI, 2014.

Harm Reduction International. *The Global State of Harm Reduction 2016*. Edited by Katie Stone. London: HRI, 2016.

Harm Reduction International. 'What is Harm Reduction?' HRI, 2010. http://www.ihra.net/what-is-harm-reduction.

Harris, Kamala D. *Gangs Beyond Borders: California and the Fight Against Transnational Organized Crime*. Sacramento: California Attorney General, 2014.

Harrison, Lana. 'The Validity of Self-Reported Drug Use in Survey Research: An Overview and Critique of Research Methods.' *NIDA Research Monograph* 167 (1997): 17–36.

Heath, Edward Allen. 'Mexican Opium Eradication Campaign.' Unpublished master's thesis, California State University, 1981.

Hernández, Ana Paula. 'Drugs Legislation and Prison Situation in Mexico.' In *Systems Overload: Drugs Laws and Prisoners*, edited by Pien Metaal and Coleta Youngers, 60–70. Amsterdam: Transnational Institute; Washington D.C.: Washington Office on Latin America, 2011.

Hernández Tinajero, Jorge, and Carlos Zamudio Angles. *The Law Against Small-Scale Drug Dealing*. Amsterdam: Transnational Institute; Washington D.C.: Washington Office on Latin America, 2009.

Herzog, Marc, and Philip Robins, eds. *The Role, Position and Agency of Cusp States in International Relations*. Abingdon: Routledge, 2014.

Hirschi, Travis, and Michael R. Gottfredson. 'Self-control theory.' In *Explaining Criminals and Crime: Essays in Contemporary Criminological Theory*, edited by Raymond Paternoster and Ronet Bachman, 81–96. Los Angeles: Roxbury, 2001.

Hirschman, Albert. *The Rhetoric of Reaction: Perversity, Futility, Jeopardy*. Cambridge: The Belknap Press, 1999.

Hoaken, Peter. N. S., and Sherry H. Stewart. 'Drugs of Abuse and the Elicitation of Human Aggressive Behavior.' *Addictive Behaviors* 28, no. 9 (2003): 1533–54. https://doi.org/10.1016/j.addbeh.2003.08.033.

Hodes, Cyrus, and Mark Sedra. *The Search for Security in Post-Taliban Afghanistan*. London: Routledge, 2007.

Hope, Alejandro. *Plus Ça Change: Structural Continuities in Mexican Counternarcotics Policy*. Washington D.C.: Brookings Institution, Latin America Initiative, 2015.

Human Rights Council. *Implementation of the Joint Commitment to Effectively Addressing and Countering the World Drug Problem with Regard to Human Rights: Report of the Office of the United Nations High Commissioner for Human Rights*. A/HRC/39/39. New York: United Nations General Assembly, 2018. https://undocs.org/en/A/HRC/39/39.

Human Rights Council. *Report of the Special Rapporteur on Torture and Other Cruel, Inhuman or Degrading Treatment or Punishment, Manfred Nowak: Addendum: Study on the Phenomena of Torture, Cruel, Inhuman or Degrading Treatment or Punishment in the World, Including an Assessment of Conditions of Detention*. A/HRC/13/39/Add.5. New York: United Nations General Assembly, 2010. https://undocs.org/A/HRC/13/39/Add.5.

Human Rights Watch. *Not Enough Graves: The War on Drugs, HIV/AIDS, and Violations of Human Rights*. New York: HRW, 2004.

Human Rights Watch. 'Philippines: Duterte's 'Drug War' Claims 12,000+ Lives.' January 18, 2018.

Human Rights Watch. *'Skin on the cable': The Illegal Arrest, Arbitrary Detention and Torture of People Who Use Drugs in Cambodia.* New York: HRW, 2010.

Human Rights Watch. *Somsanga's Secrets: Arbitrary Detention, Physical Abuse, and Suicide Inside a Lao Drug Detention Center.* New York: HRW, 2011.

Hunt, Paul. *Human Rights, Health and Harm Reduction: States' amnesia and parallel universes.* London: International Harm Reduction Association, 2008. http://www.ihra.net/files/2010/06/16/HumanRightsHealthAndHarmReduction.pdf.

Hurtado, Constanza, and Pilar Larroulet. 'Consumo de Drogas y Validación de Auto Reporte en Cárceles Chilenas.' In *VII Congreso de Investigacion Sobre Violencia y Delincuencia*, 135–47. Santiago de Chile: Fundación Paz Ciudadana, 2012.

Hurtado, Paula. *Consumo de Drogas en Detenidos: Aplicación de la Metodología I-ADAM en Chile.* Santiago de Chile: Fundación Paz Ciudadana, 2005.

Huysmans, Jef. 'Migrants as a Security Problem: Dangers of 'Securitising' Societal Issues.' In *Migration and European Integration: The Dynamics of Inclusion and Exclusion*, edited by Robert Miles and Dietrich Thränhardt, 53–72. London: Pinter Publishers, 1995.

Iberoamérica Central de Noticias. 'Fracasa cumbre centroamericana para despenalizar la droga.' March 26, 2012. http://www.icndiario.com/2012/03/26/fracasa-cumbre-centroamericana-para-despenalizar-la-droga/.

Idler, Annette. 'Narco-Brokers and Financiers: The Key Elements in the Cocaine Business.' *Cocaine Route Programme: Combatting Transnational Organised Crime*, March 2015. http://www.cocaineroute.eu/flows/narco-brokers-financiers-key-elements-cocaine-business/.

Idler, Annette. *Borderland Battles: Violence, Crime, and Governance at the Edges of Colombia's War.* New York: Oxford University Press, 2019.

Idler, Annette. 'Colombia: Organised Crime, Politics, and Convenience,' in *Handbook of Organised Crime and Politics*, edited by Felia Allum and Stan Gilmour. Cheltenham: Edward Elgar Publishing Limited, 2019, 258–74, https://www.elgaronline.com/view/edcoll/9781786434562/9781786434562.00027.xml.

Idler, Annette. 'The Logic of Illicit Flows in Armed Conflict: Explaining Variation in Violent Nonstate Group Interactions in Colombia.' *World Politics* 72, no. 3 (July 2020): 335–76. https://doi.org/10.1017/S0043887120000040.

Idler, Annette. 'Tracing Cocaine Supply Chains from Within: Illicit Flows, Armed Conflict, and the Moral Economy of Andean Borderlands,' in

Cocaine: A Moral Economy, edited by Enrique Desmond Arias and Thomas Grisaffi. Durham, NC: Duke University Press, forthcoming.

Idler, Annette, and James J.F. Forest. 'Behavioral Patterns among (Violent) Non-State Actors: A Study of Complementary Governance.' *Stability: International Journal of Security and Development* 4, no. 1 (2015).

Idler, Annette and Markus Hochmüller, 'Covid-19 in Colombia's Borderlands and the Western Hemisphere: Adding Instability to a Double Crisis,' *Journal of Latin American Geography* 19, no. 3 (2020): 280–88.

Ifediora, Obinna Franklin, and Kwesi Aning. 'West Africa's Ebola Pandemic: Towards Effective Multilateral Responses to Health Crises.' *Global Governance* 23, no. 2 (2017): 225–44.

Igarapé Institute. 'The Homicide Monitor.' Accessed February 2, 2016. https://igarape.org.br/en/homicide-monitor/.

Imbusch, Peter, Michel Misse, and Fernando Carrión, 'Violence Research in Latin America and the Caribbean: A Literature Review,' *International Journal of Conflict and Violence* 5, no. 1 (2011): 88–154.

Ingram, Matthew C., and Karise M. Curtis. 'Violence in Central America: A Spatial View of Homicide in the Region, Northern Triangle, and El Salvador.' In *Crime and Violence in Central America's Northern Triangle: How U.S. Policy Responses Are Helping, Hurting, and Can Be Improved*, edited by Eric E. Olson, 245–84. Washington D.C.: Woodrow Wilson Center, 2015.

Inkster, Nigel. 'Drugs: a war lost in Afghanistan.' *Foreign Policy*, May 29, 2012. https://foreignpolicy.com/2012/05/29/drugs-a-war-lost-in-afghanistan/.

Institute for Criminal Policy Research at Birkbeck University of London. 'World Prison Brief.' https://www.prisonstudies.org/.

Institute for Demography, Migration and Regional Development. *A New Generation of Alternative Development Programs for Elimination of Drug Production in Afghanistan*. Moscow: Institute for Demography, Migration and Regional Development; Belarus: Center for Strategic and Foreign Policy Studies, 2014.

Institute for Health Metrics and Evaluation (IHME). *Findings from the Global Burden of Disease Study 2017*. Seattle, WA: IHME, 2018.

Institute of Law Implementation Problems. 'Justice Atlas.' European University in Saint Petersburg. http://atlasjustice.com/drugmap/region.html.

Instituto de Sociología. *Estudio de prevalencia y factores asociados al consumo de drogas en adolescentes infractores de ley*. Santiago de Chile: Pontifica Universidad Católica de Chile, 2007.

BIBLIOGRAPHY

Instituto Nacional de Estadística y Geografía. *Encuesta Nacional de Victimización y Percepción sobre Inseguridad Pública (ENVIPE) 2018*. Mexico City: INEGI, 2018.

Instituto Universitario en Democracia, Paz y Seguridad. *Observatorio de la Violencia*. Boletín Anual No. 40. Tegucigalpa: Observatorio Nacional de la Violencia, 2016.

Interfax. 'FSKN Has Reported on the Russian Drug Addicts' Preferences.' April 23, 2015.

Interfax. 'FSKN Head Proposed to Allow Courts to Stop Criminal Prosecution of Drug Abusers Who Go Through Treatment.' March 30, 2015.

Interfax. 'FSKN Head Spoke Against Legalization of Soft Drugs.' April 21, 2015.

Interfax. 'FSKN Proposed to Differentiate Punishment for Illicit Drug Storage Depending on the Degree of Public Danger.' March 30, 2015.

Internal Displacement Monitoring Centre. *Global Overview 2015: People Internally Displaced by Conflict and Violence*. Geneva: Internal Displacement Monitoring Centre, 2015.

International Centre on Human Rights and Drug Policy, Joint United Nations Programme on HIV/AIDS, World Health Organization, and United Nations Development Programme. *International Guidelines on Human Rights and Drug Policy*. Essex: International Centre on Human Rights and Drug Policy, 2019. https://www.humanrights-drugpolicy.org/site/assets/files/1/hrdp_guidelines_2019_v19.pdf.

International Conference on Alternative Development 2 (ICAD2). *International Seminar Workshop on the Implementation of the United Nations Guiding Principles on Alternative Development: Chair's Summary*. Bangkok, 2015. https://www.unodc.org/documents/ungass2016/Contributions/IGO/ICAD2/Chairs_Summary.pdf.

International Drug Policy Consortium. *Advocacy Note: On the Road Towards the 2019 Ministerial Segment (Version 2)*. London: International Drug Policy Consortium, 2018.

International Drug Policy Consortium. *IDPC Advocacy Note: Some Initial Priorities for Mr Fedotov, the new Executive Director of the United Nations Office on Drugs and Crime (UNODC)*. London: IDPC, 2010. http://fileserver.idpc.net/library/IDPC%20advocacy%20note%20-%20Appointment%20of%20UNODC%20ED%20FINAL%20VERSION.pdf.

International Drug Policy Consortium. *IDCP Drug Policy Guide: 3rd Edition*. London: IDPC, 2016. https://idpc.net/publications/2016/03/idpc-drug-policy-guide-3rd-edition.

International Drug Policy Consortium. *IDPC Proceedings Document on the 2009 CND and High Level Segment*. London: IDPC, 2009.

International Drug Policy Consortium. *IDPC Response to the UNODC World Drug Report 2012*. London: IDPC, 2012. http://idpc.net/publications/2012/10/idpc-response-to-the-unodc-world-drug-report-2012.

International Drug Policy Consortium. *The International Narcotics Control Board: Current Tension and Options for Reform*. London: IDPC, 2008. http://fileserver.idpc.net/library/IDPC_BP_07_INCB_TensionsAndOptions_EN.pdf.

International Drug Policy Consortium. 'President Sumyai Speaks on Drug Control and Human Rights at the CND.' Last modified November 27, 2018. https://idpc.net/incb-watch/updates/2018/11/president-sumyai-speaks-on-drug-control-and-human-rights-at-the-cnd.

International Drug Policy Consortium. 'Regional Advocacy, East and Southeast Asia.' Accessed November 17, 2015. http://idpc.net/policy-advocacy/regional-work/east-and-south-east-asia.

International Drug Policy Consortium. *Taking Stock: A Decade of Drug Policy: A Civil Society Shadow Report*. London: IDPC, 2018.

International Drug Policy Consortium. *The 2018 Commission on Narcotic Drugs. Report of Proceedings*. London: IDPC, 2018. http://fileserver.idpc.net/library/CND-Proceedings-Report-2018_18.06.pdf.

International Expert Group on Drug Policy Metrics. *Aligning Agendas: Drugs, Sustainable Development, and the Drive for Policy Coherence*. New York: IPI Publications, 2018. https://www.ipinst.org/wp-content/uploads/2018/02/1802_Aligning-Agendas.pdf.

'International Guidelines on Human Rights and Drug Policy.' 2019. www.humanrights-drugpolicy.org

International Narcotics Control Board. 2020. http://www.incb.org/incb/index.html.

International Narcotics Control Board. *Report of the International Narcotics Control Board for 2008*. E/INCB/2008/1. Vienna: United Nations, 2009. https://www.incb.org/incb/en/publications/annual-reports/annual-report-2008.html.

International Narcotics Control Board. *Report of the International Narcotics Control Board for 2011*. E/INCB/2011/1. Vienna: United Nations, 2012.

International Narcotics Control Board. *Report of the International Narcotics Control Board for 2014*. E/INCB/2014/1. Vienna: United Nations, 2015.

International Narcotics Control Board. *Report of the International Narcotics Control Board for 2015*. E/INCB/2015/1. Vienna: United Nations, 2016.

BIBLIOGRAPHY

International Narcotics Control Board. *Report of the International Narcotics Control Board for 2019.* E/INCB/2019/1. Vienna: United Nations, 2020.

International Opium Commission. *Report of the International Opium Commission, Shanghai, China, February 1 to February 26, 1909.* Shanghai: North-China Daily News and Herald, 1909. https://archive.org/details/cu31924032583225.

Irin News. 'Rethinking Thailand's war on methamphetamines.' *The New Humanitarian,* January 13, 2014. http://www.irinnews.org/report/99449/rethinking-thailand-s-war-on-methamphetamines.

Isacson, Adam. 'The US Military in the War on Drugs.' In *Drugs and Democracy in Latin America: The Impact of US Policy*, edited by Coletta Youngers and Eileen Rosin. Boulder: Lynne Rienner Publishers, 2005.

Jelsma, Martin. 'The Development of International Drug Control: Lessons Learned and Strategic Challenges for the Future.' Working paper prepared for the First Meeting of the Global Commission on Drug Policy, Geneva, January 24–25, 2011. http://www.globalcommissionondrugs.org/wpcontent/themes/gcdp_v1/pdf/Global_Com_Martin_Jelsma.pdf.

Jelsma, Martin. 'The INCB vs Uruguay: The Art of Diplomacy.' *Transnational Institute*, December 17, 2013. http://druglawreform.info/en/weblog/item/5214-incb-vs-uruguay-the-art-of-diplomacy#.UrDlNx-34hc.twitter.

Jelsma, Martin. 'TNI Calls for a Wide-Ranging and Open Debate that Considers All Options at UNGASS 2016.' Transnational Institute. Last modified March 11, 2015. https://www.tni.org/en/un-drug-control/cnd/item/6148-tni-calls-for-a-wide-ranging-and-open-debate-that-considers-all-options-at-ungass-2016.

Jelsma, Martin. *UN Common Position on drug policy – Consolidating system-wide coherence.* London: International Drug Policy Consortium, 2019. https://www.tni.org/en/publication/un-common-position-on-drug-policy-consolidating-system-wide-coherence.

Jelsma, Martin. *UNGASS 2016: Prospects for Treaty Reform and UN System-Wide Coherence on Drug Policy.* Washington D.C.: Brookings Institution, 2015. https://www.tni.org/files/download/treaty_reform_drug_policy_ungass2016.pdf.

Jelsma, Martin and Pien Metaal. 'Cracks in the Vienna Consensus: The UN Drug Control Debate.' *Drug War Monitor*. Washington D.C.: Washington Office on Latin America, 2004. http://www.undrugcontrol.info/un-drug-control/cnd/item/2176-cracks-in-the-vienna-consensus.

Jelsma, Martin, Neil Boister, David Bewley-Taylor, Malgosia Fitzmaurice, and John Walsh. *Balancing Treaty Stability and Change: Inter se Modification of the UN Drug Control Conventions to Facilitate Cannabis Regulation.* Washington D.C.: WOLA, 2014.

Jennings, John. *The Opium Empire: Japanese Imperialism and Drug Trafficking in Asia, 1895–1945*. Westport, CT: Praeger 1997.

Jesperson, Sasha. 'Assessing Militarised Responses to Transnational Organised Crime.' In *Militarised Responses to Transnational Organised Crime: The War on Crime*, edited by Tuesday Reitano, Sasha Jesperson, and Lucia Bird Ruiz-Benitez de Lugo, 1st ed. 2018 edition, 1–10. New York: Palgrave Macmillan, 2017.

Johnson, Boris. 'We Are Fighting an Invisible Enemy.' Instagram post, June 3, 2020. https://www.instagram.com/p/CA_CS8GgI38/.

Johnson, Bruce D., Andrew Golub, and Eloise Dunlap. 'The Rise and Decline of Hard Drugs, Drug Markets and Violence in Inner-City New York.' In *The Crime Drop in America*, edited by Alfred Blumstein and Joel Wallman, 164–206. Cambridge: Cambridge University Press, 2000.

Johnston, Lloyd D., Patrick M. O'Malley, Jerald G. Bachman, and John E. Schulenberg. *Monitoring the Future National Survey Results on Drug Use, 1975–2012: Volume I: Secondary School Students*. Ann Arbor: Institute for Social Research, University of Michigan, 2013.

Johnston, Peter, Stephen Schneider, John Neily, Wendy Parkes, and Denis Lachaine. *Developing and Applying an Organized Crime Harm Index: A Scoping and Feasibility Study*. Report No. 011. Ottawa: Public Safety Canada, 2010. http://publications.gc.ca/collections/collection_2012/sp-ps/PS4-99-2010-eng.pdf.

Jones, Branwen Gruffydd. 'Africa and the Poverty of International Relations.' *Third World Quarterly* 26, no. 6 (2005): 987–1003.

Jones, Sam. 'West Africa needs to look at partially decriminalizing drugs, says think tank.' *The Guardian*, June 12, 2014. http://www.theguardian.com/global-development/2014/jun/12/west-africa-decriminalising-drugs-policy-report.

Junger-Tas, Josine, Incke Marshall, and Denis Ribeaud. *Delinquency in International Perspective: The International Self-Reported Delinquency Study (ISRD)*. Amsterdam: Kugler Publications, 2003.

Justice Policy Institute, The. *Substance Abuse Treatment and Public Safety*. Washington D.C.: The Justice Policy Institute, 2008.

Kamarulzaman, Adeeba, and John L. McBrayer. 'Compulsory drug detention centers in East and Southeast Asia.' *International Journal of Drug Policy* 26, no. 1 (2015): S33-S37.

Keefer, Philip, and Norman Loayza, eds. *Innocent Bystanders: Developing Countries and the War on Drugs*. New York: Palgrave Macmillan and The World Bank, 2010.

Keene, Jan. 'A Case-Linkage Study of the Relationship between Drug Misuse, Crime, and Psychosocial Problems in a Total Criminal Justice Population.' *Addiction Research and Theory* 13, no. 5 (2009): 489–502.

Kelman, Jonathan H. C. 'States Can Play, too: Constructing a Typology of State Participation in Illicit Flows.' *Crime, Law and Social Change* 64, no. 1 (August 2015): 37–55. https://doi.org/10.1007/s10611-015-9568-4.

Kenney, Michael. *From Pablo to Osama: Trafficking and Terrorist Networks, Government Bureaucracies, and Competitive Adaptation.* University Park: Penn State Press, 2007.

Kessler, Gabriel. *Sociología del Delito Amateur.* Buenos Aires: Editorial Paidos, 2004.

Khagram, Sanjeev, and Peggy Levitt. *The Transnational Studies Reader: Intersections and Innovations.* New York: Routledge, 2008.

Kilmer, Beau, Jonathan P. Caulkins, Brittany M. Bond, and Peter Reuter. *Reducing Drug Trafficking Revenues and Violence in Mexico: Would Legalizing Marijuana in California Help?* Santa Monica: RAND Corporation, 2010.

Kilmer, Beau, and Gregory Midgette. 'Mixed Messages: Is Cocaine Consumption in the U.S. Going Up or Down?' *The Rand Blog*, April 28, 2017. https://www.rand.org/blog/2017/04/mixed-messages-is-cocaine-consumption-in-the-us-going.html.

Kippenberg, Juliane, and Laura Thomas. *Needless Pain: Government Failure to Provide Palliative Care for Children in Kenya.* New York: Human Rights Watch, 2010.

Kirschbaum, Katrin M., Lisa Grigoleit, Cornelius Hess, Burkhard Madea, and Frank Musshoff. 'Illegal Drugs and Delinquency.' *Forensic Science International* 226, no. 1–3 (2013): 230–4. https://doi.org/10.1016/j.forsciint.2013.01.031.

Kleiman, Mark. 'Surgical strikes in the drug wars: smarter policies for both sides of the border.' *Foreign Affairs* 90, vol. 5 (2011): 89–101.

Klein, Axel, and Blaine Stothard, eds. *Collapse of the Global Order on Drugs: From the UNGASS 2016 to Review 2019.* Bingley: Emerald Publishing, 2018.

Klein, Malcolm W., Cheryl L. Maxson, and Leah. C. Cunningham. 'Crack, Street Gangs, and Violence.' *Criminology* 29, no. 4 (1991): 623–50.

Klevens, Joanne, Ofelia Restrepo, Juanita Roca, and Adriana Martínez. 'Los Escenarios el Delito en Cinco Ciudades.' *Revista de Salud Pública* 1, no. 3 (1999): 245–54.

Knorre, Alexei. *Narcotics Crimes in Russia: Analysis of Court and Criminal Statistics.* Analytical Note. Saint Petersburg: Institute of Law Implementation Problems, European University in Saint Petersburg, 2017. https://

www.openpolice.ru/docs/analiticheskaya-zapiska-narkoprestupleniya-v-rossii-analiz-sudebnoj-i-kriminalnoj-statistiki.

Knorre, Alexei, and Dmitry Skugarevsky. *How MVD and FSKN Fight Drugs: Comparative Analysis of the Two Agencies Effectiveness*. Analytical Notes on Law Implementation. Saint Petersburg: Institute of Law Implementation Problems, European University in Saint Petersburg, 2015.

Kommersant. 'I May Be Saying Scary Things for a Man in Uniform.' September 19, 2018.

Kommersant. 'Medicines Should be Available to Those Suffering from Pain.' April 4, 2016.

Kommersant. '228th in Grams and Terms.' June 18, 2019. https://www.kommersant.ru/doc/3999368?from=doc_vrez.

Kort de, Marcel. 'Doctors, diplomats, and businessmen: Conflicting interests in the Netherlands and the Dutch Indies, 1860-1950.' In *Cocaine: Global Histories*, edited by Paul Gootenberg, 123–45. London: Routledge UK, 1999.

Kozlov, V. 'FSKN is given the capacity to rehabilitate.' *Kommersant*, August 4, 2014.

Kramer, Tom, Martin Jelsma, and Tom Blickman. *Withdrawal Symptoms in the Golden Triangle: A Drugs Market in Disarray*. Amsterdam: Transnational Institute, 2009. https://www.researchgate.net/publication/299978147_Withdrawal_Symptoms_in_the_Golden_Triangle_A_Drugs_Market_in_Disarray.

Krause, Keith, and Michael C. Williams. *Critical Security Studies: Concepts and Cases*. London: UCL Press, 1997.

Kroupnov, Yu., and L. Levinson. 'Is the War on Drugs Lost?' *Security Index* 17, no. 3 (2011): 85–98.

Kuhns, Joseph B., and Tammatha A. Clodfelter. 'Illicit Drug-Related Psychopharmacological Violence: The Current Understanding within a Causal Context.' *Aggression and Violent Behavior* 14, no. 1 (2009): 69–78. https://doi.org/10.1016/j.avb.2008.11.001.

Kushlick, Danny. *International Security and the Global War on Drugs: The Tragic Irony of Drug Securitization*. Bristol: Transform Drug Policy Foundation, 2011.

Lacher, Wolfram. *Organized Crime and Conflict in the Sahel-Sahara Region*. Washington D.C.: Carnegie Endowment for International Peace, 2012.

Lai, Gloria, and Patcharavalan Akbar. 'Thailand amends drug law to reduce penalties and ensure more proportionate sentencing.' IDPC, February 15, 2017. https://idpc.net/blog/2017/02/thailand-amends-drug-law-to-reduce-penalties-and-ensure-more-proportionate-sentencing.

Lampe von, Klaus. 'Withdrawal Symptoms in the Golden Triangle: A Drugs Market in Disarray.' *Trends in Organized Crime* 13, no. 1 (March 2010): 87–108. https://doi.org/10.1007/s12117-009-9084-y.

Lamptey, Afua A. *Tackling the Aftermath of Libya's 'Arab Spring': Addressing the Small Arms Issue.* Accra: Kofi Annan International Peacekeeping Training Centre, 2013. https://media.africaportal.org/documents/Aftermath-of-Libya-1.pdf.

Laohong, King-Oua. 'Drug-Free Communities an Elusive Goal, ONCB Chief Admits.' *Bangkok Post*, November 16, 2015.

Latin American Commission on Drugs and Democracy. *Drugs and Democracy: Toward a Paradigm Shift.* Geneva: Latin American Commission on Drugs and Democracy, 2009.

Le Cour Grandmaison, Romain, Nathaniel Morris, and Benjamin Smith. 'The last harvest? From the US fentanyl boom to the Mexican Opium Crisis.' *Journal of Illicit Economies and Development* 1, no. 3 (2019): 312–29.

Lederach, John Paul. *Building Peace: Sustainable Reconciliation in Divided Societies.* Washington D.C.: United States Institute of Peace Press, 1997.

Lessing, Benjamin. *Making Peace and Drug Wars: Crackdowns and Cartels in Latin America.* New York: Cambridge University Press, 2018.

Lexico Oxford Dictionary. 'Definition of Glocal in English.' 2020. https://www.lexico.com/definition/glocal.

Life Chiang Mai. 'Four Nations Meet in Chiang Mai for Safe Mekong Project.' April 29, 2015.

Lines, Rick. 'A 'Most Serious' Crime? The Death Penalty for Drug Offences in International Human Rights Law.' *Amicus Journal* no. 21 (2010): 21–8.

Lines, Rick, and Damon Barrett. 'Cannabis Reform, "Medical and Scientific Purposes" and the Vienna Convention on the Law of the Treaties.' *International Community Law Review* 20, no. 5 (2018): 436–55. https://doi.org/10.1163/18719732-12341384.

Lines, Rick, Damon Barrett, and Patrick Gallahue. 'The Death Penalty for Drug Offences: "Asian Values" or Drug Treaty Influence?' *Opinio Juris*, May 21, 2015.

Lines, Rick, Damon Barrett, and Patrick Gallahue. 'Guest Post: Has the US Just Called for Unilateral Interpretation of Multilateral Obligations?' *Opinio Juris,* December 18, 2014. http://opiniojuris.org/2014/12/18/guest-post-us-just-called-unilateral-interpretation-multilateral-obligations.

Llorente, María Victoria, and Rodolfo Escobedo. *Lo que Esconden las Cifras: En 2014 Bajaron los Homicidios, Pero Persisten las Dinámicas Criminales.* Bogotá: Fundación Ideas para la Paz, 2015. http://www.ideaspaz.org/publications/posts/1123.

Loader, Ian, and Neil Walker. *Civilizing Security.* Cambridge: Cambridge University Press, 2007.

Lobjakas, Ahto. 'Afghanistan: Multipronged Drug Eradication Effort Set for Helmand.' *RFERL*, January 30, 2007. https://www.rferl.org/a/1074381.html.

Loeber, Rolf, Barbara Menting, Donald R. Lynam, Terri E. Moffitt, Magda Stouthamer-Loeber, Rebecca Stallings, David P. Farrington, and Dustin Pardini. 'Findings from the Pittsburgh Youth Study: Cognitive Impulsivity and Intelligence as Predictors of the Age-Crime Curve.' *Journal of the American Academy of Child and Adolescent Psychiatry* 51, no. 11 (2012): 1136–49. https://doi.org/10.1016/j.jaac.2012.08.019.

López, Denisse. 'El Resultado de la Guerra Contra el Narcotráfico: Más de 61.000 Desaparecidos y Miles de Fosas Clandestinas.' *Infobae*, January 7, 2020. https://www.infobae.com/america/mexico/2020/01/07/el-resultado-de-la-guerra-contra-el-narcotrafico-mas-de-61000-desaparecidos-y-miles-de-fosas-clandestinas/.

López, Germán. 'Mexico Just Took a Big Step toward Marijuana Legalization.' *Vox,* November 1, 2018. https://www.vox.com/world/2018/11/1/18051592/mexico-marijuana-legalization-supreme-court.

López, Julie. 'Guatemala's Crossroads: The Democratization of Violence and Second Chances.' In *Organized Crime in Central America: The Northern Triangle*, edited by Eric E. Olson and Cynthia Arnson, 140–242. Washington D.C.: Woodrow Wilson Center, 2011.

López García, Karla Selene, and Moacyr Lobo da Costa Junior. 'Conduta anti-social e consumo de álcool em adolescentes escolares.' *Revista Latino-Americana de Enfermagem* 16, no. 2 (2008): 299–305.

Lowes, Peter D. *The Genesis of International Narcotics Control.* Geneva: Lib. Droz, 1966.

Lüdke, Fernanda, Silvia M. da Cunha, Lisiane Bizarro, and Débora D. Dell'Aglio. 'Uso de drogas e comportamento antissocial entre adolescentes de escolas públicas no Brasil.' *Trends Psychiatry Psychotherapy* 34, no. 2 (2012): 80–6.

Lund, Christian. 'Twilight Institutions: Public Authority and Local Politics in Africa.' *Development and Change* 37, no. 4 (2006): 685–705.

MacCoun, Robert, Beau Kilmer, and Peter Reuter. 'Research on Drugs-Crime Linkages: The Next Generation.' In *Toward a Drugs and Crime Research Agenda for the 21st Century: Special Report,* 65–96. Washington D.C.: National Institute of Justice, 2003.

MacCoun, Robert, and Peter Reuter. 'Evaluating Alternative Cannabis Regimes.' *British Journal of Psychiatry* 178, no. 2 (2001): 123–28. https://doi.org/10.1192/bjp.178.2.123.

MacCoun, Robert, and Peter Reuter. *Drug War Heresies: Learning from Other Vices, Times, and Places*, RAND Studies in Policy Analysis. Cambridge: Cambridge University Press, 2001.

MacDonald, Ziggy, James Collingwood, and Lorna Gordon. *Measuring the Harm from Illegal Drugs Using the Drug Harm Index: An Update*. London: Home Office, 2006.

MacDonald, Ziggy, Louise Tinsley, James Collingwood, Pip Jamieson, and Stephen Pudney. *Measuring the Harm from Illegal Drugs Using the Drug Harm Index*. Online Report 24/05. London: Home Office, 2005. https://webarchive.nationalarchives.gov.uk/20110218140608/http://rds.homeoffice.gov.uk/rds/pdfs05/rdsolr2405.pdf.

MacGregor, Susan, Nicola Singleton, and Franz Trautmann. 'Towards Good Governance in Drug Policy: Evidence, Stakeholders and Politics.' *International Journal of Drug Policy* 25, no. 5 (2014): 931–4.

Macy, Beth. 'America's Other Epidemic.' *The Atlantic*, May 2020. https://www.theatlantic.com/magazine/archive/2020/05/nikki-king-opioid-treatment-program/609085/.

Madrazo Lajous, Alejandro. 'The Constitutional Costs of the "War on Drugs."' In *Ending the Drug Wars: Report of the LSE Expert Group on the Economics of Drug Policy*, edited by John Collins, 55–60. London: LSE, 2014.

Madsen, Frank G. 'International Narcotics Law Enforcement: A Study in Irrationality.' *Journal of International Affairs* 66, no. 1 (2012): 123–41.

Magura, Stephen, and Sung-Yeon Kang. 'Validity of Self-Reported Drug Use in High Risk Populations: A Meta-Analytical Review.' *Substance Use & Misuse* 31, no. 9 (1996): 1131–53. https://doi.org/10.3109/10826089609063969.

Mahathir, Marina. 'Drug Law Reform in Southeast Asia.' In *Drug law reform in East and Southeast Asia*, edited by Fifa Rahman and Nick Crofts, vii-viii. Lanham: Lexington Books, 2013.

Maizland, Lindsay. 'U.S.-Taliban Peace Deal: What to Know.' Council on Foreign Relations. Updated March 2, 2020. https://www.cfr.org/backgrounder/us-taliban-peace-deal-agreement-afghanistan-war.

Malaysia's Ministry of Home Affairs. *Country Progress Report of Drug Control – Malaysia*. Putraya: Malaysia's Ministry of Home Affairs, 2014. http://www.na.gov.la/files/aifocom11/Doc_for_AIFOCOM/COUNTRY%20REPORT/(11)%20Annex%20M-%20Country%20Report%20of%20Malaysia.pdf.

Mamdani, Mahmood. 'Good Muslim, Bad Muslim: A political perspective on culture and terrorism.' *American Anthropologist* 104 no. 3 (2002): 766–75.

Mangan, Fiona, and Matthias Nowak. *The West Africa–Sahel Connection.* Geneva: Small Arms Survey, 2019.

Manitas, Celina. 'Das Descobertas Privadas Aos Crimes Públicos: Evolução Dos Significados Em Trajectórias de Droga-Crime.' *Revista Toxicodependencias* 63 (2003): 674–706.

Mansfield, David. '"Economical with the truth": The limits of price and profitability in both explaining opium poppy cultivation in Afghanistan and in designing effective responses.' In *Reconstructing Agriculture in Afghanistan*, edited by Adam Pain and Jacky Sutton. Colchester: Practical Action Publishing, draft version, 2007.

Mansfield, David. 'Where have all the flowers gone? The real reasons for the drop in the poppy crop in Afghanistan in 2015.' *Alcis*, October 20, 2015. https://stories.alcis.org/where-have-all-the-flowers-gone-7de7b34e8478#.enfwvwq2ej.

Mansfield, David, and Adam Pain. 'Alternative Livelihoods: Substance or Slogan?' *Issues Papers 14650, Afghanistan Research and Evaluation Unit* (2005). https://doi.org/10.22004/ag.econ.14650.

Mansfield, David, and Adam Pain. 'Evidence from the field: Understanding chaining levels of opium poppy cultivation in Afghanistan.' In *The Politics of Narcotic Drugs: A Survey,* edited by Julia Buxton, 8–30. London: Routledge, 2011.

Manwaring, Max. *Street Gangs: The New Urban Insurgency.* Carlisle: Strategic Studies Institute, 2005.

Marazzi, Alessandro Sassoon. 'Study Calls for Closure of Compulsory Drug Centres.' *The Phnom Penh Post,* January 19, 2017. https://www.phnompenhpost.com/national/study-calls-closure-compulsory-drug-centres.

Marcy, William L. *The Politics of Cocaine.* Chicago: Lawrence Hill Books, 2010.

Marston, Joan. 'Why Should Children Suffer? Children's Palliative Care and Pain Management.' In *Children of the Drug War: Perspectives on the Impact of Drug Policies on Children and Young People*, edited by Damon Barrett, 219–36. New York: IDEBATE Press, 2011.

Martin, Ian, Anita Palepu, Evan Wood, Kathy Li, Julio Montaner, and Thomas Kerr. 'Violence Among Street-Involved Youth: The Role of Methamphetamine.' *European Addiction Research* 15, no. 1 (2009): 32–38. https://doi.org/10.1159/000173007.

Mashal, Mujib. 'Afghanistan's River of Solace.' *International New York Times*, March 10, 2016.

Mashal, Mujib, and Andrew E. Kramer. 'Russia Pulls Back from Cooperating with U.S. on Afghanistan.' *The New York Times,* February 20, 2016. https://www.nytimes.com/2016/02/21/world/asia/russia-pulls-back-from-cooperating-with-us-on-afghanistan.html.

Matthews, Christopher M. 'Justice Department Overruled Recommendation to Pursue Charges Against HSBC, Report Says.' *The Wall Street Journal,* July 11, 2016. http://www.wsj.com/articles/justice-department-overruled-recommendation-to-pursue-charges-against-hsbc-report-says-1468229401.

May, Channing. *Transnational Crime and the Developing World.* Washington D.C.: Global Financial Integrity, 2017. https://www.gfintegrity.org/wp-content/uploads/2017/03/Transnational_Crime-final.pdf.

McAllister, William B. *Drug Diplomacy in the Twentieth Century.* London: Routledge, 2000.

McCoy, Alfred W. 'From Free Trade to Prohibition: A Critical History of the Modern Asian Opium Trade.' *Fordham Urban Law Journal* 28, no. 1 (2000): 304–49.

McCoy, Alfred W. *The Politics of Heroin in Southeast Asia.* New York: Harper & Row, 1972.

McCoy, Alfred W. 'The Stimulus of Prohibition: A Critical History of the Global Narcotics Trade.' In *Dangerous Harvest: Drug Plants and the Transformation of Indigenous Landscapes,* edited by Michael K. Steinberg, Joseph J. Hobbs, and Kent Mathewson, 24–111. New York: Oxford University Press, 2004.

McDermott, Jeremy. 'Militarisation of the Drug War in Latin America: A Policy Cycle Set to Continue?' In *Militarised Responses to Transnational Organised Crime: The War on Crime*, edited by Tuesday Reitano, Sasha Jesperson, and Lucia Bird Ruiz-Benitez de Lugo, 1st ed. 2018 edition, 259–77. New York: Palgrave Macmillan, 2017.

McDonald, Matt. 'Securitization and the Construction of Security.' *European Journal of International Relations* 14, no. 4 (2008): 563–87.

McNeil Jr, Donald G. 'Issue of drug enforcement vs. treatment splits the U.N.' *International New York Times*, October 28, 2015.

McVay, Doug, Vincent Schiraldi, and Jason Ziedenber. *Treatment or Incarceration? National and State Findings of the Efficacy and Cost Savings of Drug Treatment Versus Imprisonment.* Washington D.C.: Justice Policy Institute, 2004. http://www.justicepolicy.org/research/2023.

McWilliams, John C. *The Protectors: Harry J. Anslinger and the Federal Bureau of Narcotics, 1930–1962.* Newark: University of Delaware Press, 1990.

Mead, Walter Russell. 'The Return of Geopolitics.' *Foreign Affairs,* September 15, 2015. https://www.foreignaffairs.com/articles/china/2014-04-17/return-geopolitics.

Medina, Fernando. 'Más Policías para Intentar Frenar el Microtráfico.' *El Comercio*, September 22, 2015. http://www.elcomercio.com/actualidad/policias-microtrafico-droga-ecuador.html.

Mejía, Daniel. *Plan Colombia: An Analysis of Effectiveness and Costs.* Washington D.C.: Brookings Institution, Latin America Initiative, 2014. http://www.brookings.edu/~/media/Research/Files/Papers/2015/04/global-drug-policy/Mejia--Colombia-final-2.pdf?la=en.

Mejía, Daniel, and Pascual Restrepo. *The Economics of the War on Illegal Drug Production and Trafficking.* Documento CEDE no. 54. Bogotá: Universidad de los Andes, 2013.

Mejía, Daniel, and Pascual Restrepo. 'Why Is Strict Prohibition Collapsing? A Perspective from Producer and Transit Countries.' In *Ending the Drug Wars: Report of the LSE Expert Group on the Economics of Drug Policy*, edited by John Collins, 26–32. London: LSE, 2014.

Mejía, Daniel, Pascual Restrepo, and Sandra Rozo. 'On the Effectiveness of Supply Reduction Efforts in Drug Producing Countries: Evidence from Colombia.' Unpublished manuscript, Universidad de los Andes, 2013.

Mena, Fernanda, and Dick Hobbs. 'Narcophobia: Drugs Prohibition and the Generation of Human Rights Abuses.' *Trends in Organized Crime* 13, no. 1 (2010): 60–74.

Mercille, Julien. *Cruel Harvest. US Intervention in the Afghan Drug Trade.* London: Pluto Press, 2013.

Mesoamerican Working Group. *Rethinking the Drug War in Central America and Mexico.* Mexico City: Mesoamerican Working Group, 2013. https://www.ghrc-usa.org/wp-content/uploads/2013/12/Mesoamerica-Working-Group_Rethinking-Drug-War-Web-Version.pdf.

Metaal, Pien, and Coletta Youngers, eds. *Sistemas Sobrecargados: Leyes de Drogas y Cárceles en América Latina.* Translated by Amira Armenta, Beatriz Martínez and Luis Enrique Bossio. Amsterdam: Transnational Institute; Washington D.C.: Washington Office on Latin America, 2010. http://www.dejusticia.org/files/r2_actividades_recursos/fi_name_recurso.192.pdf.

Metaal, Pien, and Coletta Youngers, eds. *Systems Overload: Drug Laws and Prisons in Latin America.* Amsterdam: Transnational Institute; Washington D.C.: Washington Office on Latin America, 2011.

Meyer, Kathyrn, and Terry Parssinen. *Webs of Smoke: Smugglers, Warlords, Spies, and the History of the International Drug Trade*. Latham, MD: Lowman & Littlefield Pubs, 1998.

Meyer, Peter. *U.S. Strategy for Engagement in Central America: Policy Issues for Congress*. Washington D.C.: Congressional Research Service, 2019.

Mikhaylova, Ju.V., A.Yu. Abramov, I.S. Tsybulskaya, I.B. Shikina, N.I. Khaliullin, and E.R. Nizamova. 'Increased drug addiction among children, adolescents and the young in Russia,' *Social Aspects of Public Health*, no. 3 (2014). http://vestnik.mednet.ru/content/view/572/30/lang,ru.

Miller, Fiona, H. Osbahr, E. Boyd, F. Thomalla, S. Bharwani, G. Ziervogel, B. Walker, J. Birkmann, S. Van der Leeuw, J. Rockström, J. Hinkel, T. Downing, C. Folke, and D. Nelson, 'Resilience and vulnerability: complementary or conflicting concepts?' *Ecology and Society* 15(3): 11, 2010; http://www.ecologyandsociety.org/vol15/iss3/art11/.

Miller Llana, Sara. 'Biden in Honduras: US drug policy under scrutiny.' *Christian Science Monitor*, March 6, 2012. http://www.csmonitor.com/World/Americas/2012/0306/Biden-in-Honduras-US-drug-policy-under-scrutiny.

Ministry of Foreign Affairs of the Russian Federation. 'Deputy Foreign Minister Oleg Syromolotov's answer to a journalist's question on drug harm reduction programs, Moscow.' Press release, August 6, 2018. http://www.mid.ru/en/main_en/-/asset_publisher/G51iJnfMMNKX/content/id/3314696.

Ministry of Health of the Russian Federation. 'Position of Ministry of Health of Russia Regarding the Opioid Substitute Therapy.' March 11, 2016. http://www.rosminzdrav.ru/news/2016/03/11/2832-pozitsiya-minzdrava-rossii-v-otnoshenii-zamestitelnoy-opioidnoy-podderzhivayuschiey-terapii.

Ministry of Internal Affairs of the Russian Federation. 'Draft Strategy of State Anti-Narcotics Policy of the Russian Federation through 2030.' January 16, 2020. https://regulation.gov.ru/Files/GetFile?fileid=4b8e646e-9121-4dd0-b0f1-71e5fe668cb8.

Ministry of Internal Affairs of the Russian Federation. 'First Deputy Head of MVD main directorate for drug control Kirill Smurov on the fight against drug-related crimes.' Press release, December 6, 2018. https://xn--b1aew.xn--p1ai/mvd/structure1/glavnie_upravlenija/gunk/novosti/item/15179154/.

Ministry of Internal Affairs of the Russian Federation. 'On the Strategy of State Anti-Narcotics Policy of the Russian Federation through 2030.' January 16, 2020. https://regulation.gov.ru/projects#npa=98716.

Ministry of Justice (of the UK). *Transforming Rehabilitation: A Summary of Evidence on Reducing Reoffending*. London: Ministry of Justice, 2013.

Miron, Jeffrey A. *The Budgetary Implications of Drug Prohibition*. Cambridge, MA: Department of Economics, Harvard University, 2010.

Miron, Jeffrey A., and Katherine Waldock. *The Budgetary Impact of Ending Drug Prohibition*. Washington D.C.: Cato Institute, 2010. http://www.cato.org/pubs/wtpapers/DrugProhibitionWP.pdf.

Mishina, Valeria. 'The War on Drugs is Lost: Global Commission on Drug Policy Invites States to Legally Regulate the Drug Market.' *Kommersant*, September 24, 2018. https://www.kommersant.ru/doc/3750948.

Misse, Michel. 'Illegal Markets, Protection Rackets and Organized Crime in Rio de Janeiro.' *Estudos Avançados* 21, no. 61 (2007): 139–57.

Misse, Michel, and Joana D. Vargas. 'Drug Use and Trafficking in Rio de Janeiro.' *Vibrant-Virtual Brazilian Anthropology* 7, no. 2 (2010): 88–108.

Mithoefer, Michael C., Mark T. Wagner, Ann T. Mithoefer, Lisa Jerome, and Rick Doblin. 'The Safety and Efficacy of ±3,4 Methylenedioxymethamphetamine-Assisted Psychotherapy in Subjects with Chronic, Treatment-Resistant Post-Traumatic Stress Disorder: The First Randomized Controlled Pilot Study.' *Journal of Psychopharmacology* 25, no. 4 (2011): 439–52.

Moffitt, Terry E. 'Adolescence-Limited and Life-Course-Persistent Antisocial Behavior: A Developmental Taxonomy.' *Psychological Review* 100, no. 4 (1993): 674–701. https://doi.org/10.1037/0033-295X.100.4.674.

Morales Rosas, Sabina, and Carlos A. Pérez Ricart. 'Militarización, Obstáculo para la Gobernanza Democrática de la Seguridad en México.' *Revista Colombiana de Sociología* 38, no. 1 (2015): 83–103.

Morris, Kelly. 'Drug Crime and Criminalisation Threaten Progress on MDGs.' *The Lancet* 376, no. 9747 (2010): 1131-23.

Morton, W. Alexander. 'Cocaine and Psychiatric Symptoms.' *Primary Care Companion to the Journal of Clinical Psychiatry* 1, no. 4 (1999): 109–13. doi:10.4088/PCC.v01n0403.

Muggah, Robert, Katherine Aguirre, and Ilona Szabo de Carvalho. *Measurement Matters: Designing New Metrics for a Drug Policy that Works*. Strategic Paper 12. Rio de Janeiro: Igarapé Institute, 2015. http://igarape.org.br/wp-content/uploads/2015/01/AE-12-Measurement-mattes-07h-jan_.pdf.

Muggah, Robert, and John P. Sullivan. 'The Coming Crime Wars.' *Foreign Policy*, September 21, 2018. https://foreignpolicy.com/2018/09/21/the-coming-crime-wars/.

Murillo, Álvaro. 'Miguel Angel Gálvez. Juez a cargo del proceso de Otto Pérez Molina.' *El País*, November 13, 2015. http://internacional.elpais.com/internacional/2015/11/12/actualidad/1447364418_362897.html.

Musto, David F. *The American Disease: Origins of Drug Control.* New Haven: Yale University Press, 1973.

Musto-Dutra, Clara. 'Talking with Elephants. Issue's Framing and Public Opinion Dynamics on the Regulation of Cannabis in Uruguay.' Presentation at the 'Crimes against Reality' event, University of Hamburg, Hamburg, 2015.

Nadelmann, Ethan A. *Cops Across Borders: The Internationalization of U.S. Criminal Law Enforcement.* University Park: Penn State Press, 1993.

Nadelmann, Ethan A. 'Global Prohibition Regimes: The Evolution of Norms in International Society.' *International Organization* 44, no. 4 (1990): 479–526. https://doi.org/10.1017/S0020818300035384.

Nadelmann, Ethan A. 'U.S. Drug Policy: A Bad Export.' *Foreign Policy* 70 (Spring 1988): 83–108.

Naím, Moisés. 'The Drug Trade: The Politicization of Criminals and the Criminalization of Politicians.' Working paper. Prepared for the First Meeting of the Commission Geneva, January 24–25, 2011. GCDPy, 2010.

Nathan, Fabien. 'Natural Disasters, Vulnerability and Human Security.' In *Facing Global Environmental Change: Environmental, Human, Energy, Food, Health and Water Security Concepts*, edited by Hans Günter Brauch, Úrsula Oswald Spring, John Grin, Czeslaw Mesjasz, Patricia Kameri-Mbote, Navnita Chadha Behera, Béchir Chourou, and Heinz Krummenacher, 1121–9. Berlin; Heidelberg: Springer-Verlag Berlin Heidelberg, 2009. https://doi.org/10.1007/978-3-540-68488-6_87.

Nekhezin, V. 'Legalization of Drugs: Russia is Still Against.' *BBC Russian Service*, September 10, 2014.

Newkirk II, Vann R. 'The People Trump's War on Drugs Will Actually Punish.' *The Atlantic*, March 26, 2018. https://www.theatlantic.com/politics/archive/2018/03/killing-drug-dealers-opioid-epidemic/555782/.

Newman, Edward. 'Critical Human Security Studies.' *Review of International Studies* 36, no. 1 (2010): 77–94.

New York Times, The. 'Latin America Rethinks Drug Policies.' May 26, 2015. http://www.nytimes.com/2015/05/26/opinion/latin-america-rethinks-drug-policies.html?_r=1.

Niang, Amy. 'The Imperative of *African* Perspectives on International Relations (IR).' *Politics* 36, no. 4 (2016): 453–66.

Niang, Amy. 'Rehistoricizing the Sovereignty Principle: Stature, Decline, and Anxieties About a Foundational Norm.' In *Recentering Africa in International Relations,* edited by Marta Iñiguez de Heredia and Zubairu Wai, 121–44. London: Palgrave Macmillan, 2018.

Nieto Silva, Carlos José. 'Consumo de Drogas en Tres Etapas de la Vida de Habitantes de Calle de Bogotá: Predictores de Consumo y Comparación con una Muestra de Población Infantil y Adolescente de Brasil.' Master's diss., Universidad Federal de Rio Grande do Sul, 2011.

Nixon, Richard. 'Remarks About an Intensified Program for Drug Abuse Prevention and Control,' Gerhard Peters and John T. Woolley, *The American Presidency Project* (Washington D.C., June 17, 1971), https://www.presidency.ucsb.edu/node/240238.

Nordland, Rod. 'Afghan Graft Hobbles Fight Against Drugs.' *International New York Times*, April 7, 2016.

Norström, Thor, and Ingeborg Rossow. 'Cannabis Use and Violence: Is There a Link?' *Scandinavian Journal of Public Health* 42, no. 4 (2014): 358–63. https://doi.org/10.1177/1403494814525003.

Nossal Institute for Global Health. *Dependent on Development: The Interrelationship between Illicit Drugs and Socioeconomic Development.* Melbourne: Nossal Institute for Global Health, 2010.

Novosti Mail.ru. 'Patrushev: Harm from Narcotics in Russia Equals Health Budget.' February 25, 2013.

Obokata, Tom. 'The Illicit Cycle of Narcotics from a Human Rights Perspective.' *Netherlands Quarterly of Human Rights* 25, no. 2 (2007): 159–87.

Obot, Isidore S. *Prevention and Treatment of Drug Dependence in West Africa.* WACD Background Paper No. 2. Accra: West Africa Commission on Drugs, 2013.

O'Brien, Karen, Linda Sygna, and Jan Erik Haugen. 'Vulnerable or Resilient? A Multi-Scale Assessment of Climate Impacts and Vulnerability in Norway.' *Climatic Change* 64, no. 1 (May 2004): 193–225. https://doi.org/10.1023/B:CLIM.0000024668.70143.80.

Olson, Eric E., ed. *Crime and Violence in Central America's Northern Triangle: How U.S. Policy Responses Are Helping, Hurting, and Can Be Improved.* Washington D.C.: Woodrow Wilson Center, 2015.

Olson, Eric E., and Katheryn Moffat. 'Executive Summary.' In *Crime and Violence in Central America's Northern Triangle: How U.S. Policy Responses Are Helping, Hurting, and Can Be Improved*, edited by Eric E. Olson, 1–17. Washington D.C.: Woodrow Wilson Center, 2015.

O'Mara, Richard, and Sandy Banisky. '80 People Try to Slay a Monster: Drug Conference Draws Participants from 18 Countries.' *The Baltimore Sun*, November 17, 1993. http://articles.baltimoresun.com/1993-11-17/news/1993321086_1_legalization-of-drugs-colombia-national-drug.

Organisation for Economic Co-operation and Development. 'Net ODA.' Data from 2017. https://data.oecd.org/oda/net-oda.htm.

Organization of American States. 'CICAD: Multilateral Evaluation Mechanism (MEM). What is the MEM?' Accessed May 20, 2020. http://www.cicad.oas.org/Main/Template.asp?File=/mem/about/default_eng.asp.

Organization of American States. 'The Economics of Drug Trafficking.' In *The Drug Problem in the Americas*. Washington D.C.: Organization of American States, 2013.

Organization of American States. *The OAS Drug Report: 16 Months of Debates and Consensus*. OEA/Ser.D/XXV.4.1. Washington D.C.: Organization of American States, 2013. https://www.oas.org/docs/publications/LayoutPubgAGDrogas-ENG-29-9.pdf.

Organization of American States – Inter-American Drug Abuse Control Commission. *Hemispheric Report: Evaluation Report on Drug Control: Sixth Evaluation Round*. Washington D.C.: OAS, 2015.

Ortiz, Sara. 'Las Mulas Podrán Ser Consideradas Víctimas.' *El Comercio*, April 24, 2014. http://www.elcomercio.com/actualidad/seguridad/mulas-podran-consideradas-victimas.html.

Osorio, Javier. 'The Contagion of Drug Violence: Spatiotemporal Dynamics of the Mexican War on Drugs.' *Journal of Conflict Resolution* 59, no. 8 (2015): 1403–32.

Oxford Analytica. 'Afghanistan: Narcotics Battle.' October 5, 2010.

Oxford Analytica. 'Pakistan: Intelligence Services.' November 7, 2006.

Paoli, Letizia, Victoria A. Greenfield, and Peter Reuter. 'Change is Possible: The History of the International Drug Control Regime and Implications for Future Policymaking.' *Substance Use and Misuse* 47, no. 8–9 (2012): 923–35.

Paoli, Letizia, Victoria A. Greenfield, and Peter Reuter. *The World Heroin Market: Can Supply Be Cut?* Oxford: Oxford University Press, 2009.

Parameswaran, Prashanth. 'Thailand's Junta to Declare War on Corruption.' *The Diplomat*, May 29, 2015.

Parametría. 'La Legalización de la Mariguana, Apuntes para México (Encuesta Nacional En Vivienda).' February 12, 2014. http://www.parametria.com.mx/estudios/la-legalizacion-de-la-mariguana-apuntes-para-mexico/.

Park, Haeyoun. 'Children at the Border.' *The New York Times*, October 21, 2014. https://www.nytimes.com/interactive/2014/07/15/us/questions-about-the-border-kids.html.

Parra, Jorge. '20 Años de la Despenalización de la Dosis Personal.' *La Silla Vacía*, May 12, 2014. http://lasillavacia.com/node/47362.

Pembleton, Matthew R. *Containing Addiction: The Federal Bureau of Narcotics and the Origins of America's Global Drug War*. Amherst: University of Massachusetts Press, 2017.

Peña Nieto, Enrique. 'Por Un México En Paz Con Justicia, Unidad y Desarrollo.' Palacio Nacional, Ciudad de México, November 27, 2014.

Peoples, Columba, and Nick Vaughan-Williams. *Critical Security Studies: An Introduction*. 2nd ed. London: Routledge, 2015.

Pérez Correa, Catalina, Rodrigo Uprimny, and Sergio Chaparro. 'Regulation of Possession and the Criminalisation of Drug Users in Latin America.' In *After the Drug Wars: Report of the LSE Expert Group on the Economics of Drug Policy*, edited by John Collins, 30–9. London: LSE, 2016.

Pérez Ricart, Carlos A. 'The Role of the DEA in the Emergence of the Field of Anti-narcotics Policing in Latin America.' *Global Governance* 24, no. 2 (2018): 171–93.

Pérez Ricart, Carlos A. 'La Kingpin Strategy: ¿Qué Es y Cómo Llegó a México?,' *Nexos. Prevención y Castigo. Blog Sobre La Política de Seguridad* (blog), October 21, 2019, https://seguridad.nexos.com.mx/?p=1646.

Permanent Mission of the Russian Federation to the International Organizations in Vienna. 'Statement by the Russian President's Special Representative on International Cooperation in the fight Against Terrorism and Transnational Organized Crime, Anatoly Zmeyevsky, at the High-Level Segment of the 57th Session of the UN Commission on Narcotic Drugs, Vienna, March 13, 2014.' Vienna, March 13, 2014.

Pernanen, Kai, Marie-Marthe Cousineau, Serge Brochu, and Fu Sun. *Proportions of Crimes Associated with Alcohol and Other Drugs in Canada*. Ottawa: Canadian Center on Substance Abuse, 2002

Petrosino, Anthony, and Haluk Soydan. 'The Impact of Program Developers as Evaluators on Criminal Recidivism: Results from Meta-Analyses of Experimental and Quasi-Experimental Research.' *Journal of Experimental Criminology* 1, no. 4 (2005): 435–50. https://doi.org/10.1007/s11292-005-3540-8.

Points: The Blog of the Alcohol and Drugs History Society. 'Special Response: Over 100 Researchers and Practitioners Respond to Rod Rosenstein on Safe Injection Sites.' September 20, 2018. https://pointsadhsblog.wordpress.com/2018/09/20/special-response-over-100-researchers-and-practitioners-respond-to-rod-rosenstein-on-safe-injection-sites/.

Pollini, Robin A., Perth C. Rosen, Manuel Gallardo, Brenda Robles, Kimberly C. Brouwer, Grace E. Macalino, and Remedios Lozada. 'Not Sold Here: Limited Access to Legally Available Syringes at Pharmacies in Tijuana, Mexico.' *Harm Reduction Journal* 8, no. 1 (2011): 13.

Posdnyakova, Margarita. 'New Narco-Situation in Russia.' *Review of Russian Foundation for Fundamental Sciences: Humanities and Social Sciences* 2, no. 95 (2019): 77–89. https://doi.org/10.22204/2587-8956-2019-095-02-77-89.

Prados, Luis. 'El presidente de México pide a EE UU mayor control del tráfico de arma.' *El País*, March 5, 2012. http://internacional.elpais.com/internacional/2012/03/06/actualidad/1331000365_099669.html.

Presidencia de la República de Colombia. 'Palabras del presidente de la República de Colombia, Juan Manuel Santos en la XXX Sesión Especial de la Asamblea General de la ONU Sobre el Problema Mundial de las Drogas.' Intervention by President of the Republic of Colombia, Juan Manuel Santos at the Thirtieth Special Session of the UN General Assembly on the World Drug Problem. April 21, 2016. http://es.presidencia.gov.co/discursos/160421-Palabras-del-Presidente-Juan-Manuel-Santos-en-la-XXX-Sesion-Especial-de-la-Asamblea-de-la-Organizacion-de-las-Naciones-Unidas-sobre-el-Problema-Mundial-de-las-Drogas.

Presidencia de la República de México. 'In the World Drug Problem, Let Us Shift from Prohibition Alone to Effective Prevention and Regulation: Enrique Peña Nieto.' Press release, April 19, 2016. https://www.gob.mx/epn/prensa/in-the-world-drug-problem-let-us-shift-from-prohibition-alone-to-effective-prevention-and-regulation-enrique-pena-nieto.

Pudney, Stephen. 'The Road to Ruin? Sequences of Initiation to Drugs and Crime.' *Economic Journal* 113, no. 486 (2003): 182–98.

Qadiry, Tahir. 'Afghanistan, the Drug Addiction Capital.' *BBC Magazine*, April 11, 2013. https://www.bbc.com/news/magazine-22091005.

Quinones, Sam. *Dreamland: The True Tale of America's Opiate Epidemic.* New York: Bloomsbury Books, 2015.

Rahimi-Movaghar, Afari, Masoumeh Amin-Esmaeili, and Behrang Shadloo. *Assessment of Situation and Response of Drug Use and its Harms in the Middle East and North Africa.* Beirut: *MENAHRA*, 2018.

Rahman, Fifa. 'Alternatives to Criminal Justice: Drug Courts, Drug Diversion, and Decriminalization.' In *Drug Law and Reform in East and Southeast Asia*, edited by Fifa Rahman and Nick Crofts, 245–54. Lanham: Lexington Books, 2013.

Rahman, Fifa, and Nick Crofts, eds. *Drug Law and Reform in East and Southeast Asia.* Lanham: Lexington Books, 2013.

Ramírez, María Clemencia. *Between the Guerrillas and the State: The Cocalero Movement, Citizenship, and Identity in the Colombian Amazon.* Durham, NC: Duke University Press, 2011.

Ramsey, Geoffrey. 'The Changing Face of Sao Paulo's "Crackland".' *InSight Crime,* April 29, 2014. http://www.insightcrime.org/news-analysis/the-changing-face-sao-paulos-crackland.

Ramsey, Geoffrey. 'Ecuador Cracks Down on Inhumane Drug Treatment.' *The Pan-American Post,* November 13, 2013. http://www.thepanamericanpost.com/2013/11/ecuador-cracks-down-on-inhumane-drug.html.

Ramsey, Geoffrey. 'Ecuador to Expand Military Role in Fighting Crime.' *InSight Crime,* April 30, 2012. http://www.insightcrime.org/news-analysis/ecuador-to-expand-militarys-role-in-fighting-crime.

Ramsey, Geoffrey. 'Making Rio's Pacification Work: The Limits of UPP Social.' *InSight Crime,* August 22, 2014. http://www.insightcrime.org/news-analysis/rio-pacification-limits-upp-social.

Rashid, Ahmed. *Taliban.* London: Tauris, 2010.

Razavy, Maryam. 'Hawala: An Underground Haven for Terrorists or Social Phenomenon?' *Crime, Law and Social Change* 44, no. 3 (2005): 277–99. https://doi.org/10.1007/s10611-006-9019-3.

Regencia, Ted. 'Senator: Rodrigo Duterte's Drug War has Killed 20,000.' *Al Jazeera,* February 21, 2018.

Reiss, Suzanna. *We Sell Drugs: The Alchemy of U.S. Empire.* Berkeley: University of California Press, 2014.

Reitano, Tuesday and Mark Shaw, 'The Politics of Power, Protection, Identity and Illicit Trade,' Crime-Conflict Nexus Series. United Nations University Centre for Policy Research, May 2017.

República de Guatemala. 'Declaración de Guatemala. CND, 9 de marzo 2014.' Statement of the Guatemalan delegation at the Commission on Narcotic Drugs, March 9, 2014. https://www.unodc.org/documents/commissions/CND/CND_Sessions/CND_58/UNGASS_Statements/UNGASS_Statements_9March_Evening/58_Guatemala.pdf.

Resignato, Andrew J. 'Violent Crime: A Function of Drug Use or Drug Enforcement?' *Applied Economics* 32, no. 6: (2010). https://doi.org/10.1080/000368400322291.

Reuter, Peter, and Alex Stevens. *An Analysis of UK Drug Policy - Executive Summary.* London: UK Drug Policy Commission, 2007.

Reuter, Peter, and Franz Trautmann, eds. *A Report on Global Illicit Drug Market 1998–2007.* Utrecht: European Commission, 2009. https://www.tni.org/files/publication-downloads/global-illicit-markets-short.pdf.

Reyes, Yesid. 'Palabras del Doctor Yesid Reyes, Ministro de Justicia y del Derecho de Colombia, con Ocasión del Segmento Especial del 58 Periodo Ordinario de Sesiones de la Comisión de Estupefacientes.' Speech delivered by Dr Yesid Reyes at the fifty-eighth session of the CND, Vienna, March 2015. https://www.unodc.org/documents/commissions/

CND/CND_Sessions/CND_58/UNGASS_Statements/07_Colombia. pdf.

Rioseco, Pedro, Benjamín Vicente P., Sandra Saldivia B., Félix Cova S., Roberto Melipillán A., and Patricia Rubi G. 'Prevalencia de trastornos psiquiátricos en adolescentes infractores de ley. Estudio caso-control.' *Rev Revista Chilena de Neuro-psiquiatría*. 47, no. 3 (2009): 190–200.

Ritter, Alison. 'Methods for Comparing Drug Policies - The Utility of Composite Drug Harm Indexes.' *International Journal of Drug Policy* 20, no. 6 (2009): 475–9.

Rivera Vélez, Fredy. 'Ecuador: Untangling the Drug War.' In *Drugs and Democracy in Latin America: The Impact of US Policy*, edited by Coletta Youngers and Eileen Rosin, 231–61. Boulder: Lynne Rienner Publishers, 2005.

Robins, Philip. *Middle East Drugs Bazaar: Production, Prevention and Consumption.* New York: Oxford University Press, 2016.

Rodgers, Dennis, Robert Muggah, and Chris Stevenson. *Gangs of Central America: Causes, Costs, and Interventions*. Geneva: Small Arms Survey, 2009.

Rojas-Perez, Isaias. 'Peru: Drug Control Policy, Human Rights and Democracy.' In *Drugs and Democracy in Latin America: The Impact of US Policy*, edited by Coletta Youngers and Eileen Rosin, 185–230. Boulder: Lynne Rienner Publishers, 2005.

Rolles, Steve, George Murkin, Martin Powell, Danny Kushlick, and Jane Slater. *The Alternative World Drug Report*. 2nd ed. Bristol: Transform Drug Policy Foundation, 2016. https://transformdrugs.org/wp-content/uploads/2020/07/AWDR-2nd-edition.pdf.

Rolles, Steve, George Murkin, Martin Powell, Danny Kushlick, and Jane Slater. *The Alternative World Drug Report: Counting the Costs of the War on Drugs*. Bristol: Count the Costs, 2012. http://www.countthecosts.org/sites/default/files/AWDR.pdf.

Rosbusinessconsulting. 'Cabinet of Ministries Has Approved Cultivation of Narcotic Plants for Medicines.' December 26, 2018.

Rosbusinessconsulting. 'A Draft Law to Criminalize Narcotics Propaganda Online Has Been Submitted to State Duma.' July 9, 2020. https://www.rbc.ru/rbcfreenews/5f0707079a79470540e6ef03.

Rosbusinessconsulting. 'Foundation Call for the Ministry of Health to Decriminalize Pain Relieve.' August 24, 2018.

Rosbusinessconsulting. 'FSB Impeded the Work of Two Large Producers of Synthetic Drugs.' July 24, 2018.

Rosbusinessconsulting. 'Russian Court Has Sentenced a Drug Trader for Life for the First Time.' December 21, 2017.

Rotberg, Robert. 'The Little-Understood Connection Between Islamic Terror and Drug Profits.' *The Conversation*, February 16, 2016. http://theconversation.com/the-little-understood-connection-between-islamic-terror-and-drug-profits-53602.

Rudd, Kevin. 'Wresting Order from Chaos.' *The World Today,* June–July 2015.

Ruíz Martínez, Ana Olivia, Marcela Ivonne Hernández Cera, Pedro Joaquín de Jesús Mayrén Arévalo, and Ma. De Lourdes Vargas Santillán. *Family Functioning of Consumers of Addictive Sustances with and without Criminal Behavior.* Mexico City: Universidad Autónoma del Estado de México, Universidad del Valle de México, 2013.

Russell Pasha, Sir Thomas. *Egyptian Service, 1902–1946.* London: John Murray, 1949.

Russia Today. 'Putin: Using Al-Qaeda in Syria like Sending Gitmo Inmates to Fight (EXCLUSIVE).' September 6, 2012. http://rt.com/news/vladimir-putin-exclusive-interview-481.

Russian Government. 'Decree of the President of the Russian Federation no. 507.' July 10, 2014.

Russian Government. 'List of Narcotic and Psychotropic Substances and Precursors, Subject to Control in the Russian Federation.' Enacted by Government decree no. 681 of June 20, 1998. Last updated on March 13, 2020. http://base.garant.ru/12112176/#ixzz6SFc8JlXu.

Russian Government. 'List of Plants, Containing Narcotic or Psychotropic Substances or their Precursors, Subject to Control in the Russian Federation.' Enacted by Government decree no 934 of November 27, 2010. Last updated on August 9, 2019. http://pravo.gov.ru/ipsdata/?docbody=&prevDoc=102135282&backlink=1&&nd=102143353.

Russian Government. 'Statement by Viktor Ivanov, head of State Anti-Narcotics Committee, Director of FSKN.' Statement delivered at the BRICS Ministerial meeting, Moscow, April 22, 2015. http://fskn.gov.ru/includes/periodics/speeches_fskn/2015/0422/094236886/detail.shtml.

Rydell, C. Peter, and Susan S. Everingham. *Controlling Cocaine - Supply Versus Demand Programs.* Santa Monica: RAND Corporation, 1994.

Saens Roja, Mario Alberto, Julio Bejarano, Ronald Alvarado, and Gustavo A. Briceño. 'Privados de Libertad y Drogas: Experiencias en un Régimen de Confianza.' *Medicina Legal* 15, no. 12 (1998).

Sagredo Fernández, Javier. *Nurturing Sustainable Change: The Doi Tung Case 1988–2017.* Bangkok: Mae Fah Luang Foundation, 2017.

Said, Edward W. *Culture and Imperialism.* New York: Random House, 1994.

Said Aly, Abdel Monem. 'The Return of Geopolitics,' *The Cairo Review of Global Affairs*, May 27, 2019. https://www.thecairoreview.com/essays/the-return-of-geopolitics/.

Salazar-Torres, Isabel C., María Teresa Varela-Arévalo, Luisa F. Lema-Soto, Julián A. Tamayo-Cardona, and Carolina Duarte-Alarcón. 'Evaluación de las conductas de salud en jóvenes universitarios.' *Revista de Salud Pública* 12 (2010): 599–611.

Sander, Gen. *The Death Penalty for Drug Offences: Global Overview 2017*. London: Harm Reduction International, 2018.

Santos, Juan Manuel. 'Answers to War.' *New Statesman*, June 13, 2013. https://www.newstatesman.com/politics/politics/2013/06/answers-war.

Schendel, Willem van, and Itty Abraham, eds. *Illicit Flows and Criminal Things: States, Borders, and the Other Side of Globalization*. Bloomington: Indiana University Press, 2005.

Seddon, Toby. 'Explaining the Drug–Crime Link: Theoretical, Policy and Research Issues.' *Journal of Social Policy* 29, no. 1 (2000): 95–107. https://doi.org/10.1017/S0047279400005833.

Sen, Amartya. *Poverty and Famines: An Essay on Entitlement and Deprivation*. Oxford: Clarendon Press, 1981.

Sen, Amartya. *Resources, Values and Development*. Cambridge, MA: Harvard University Press, 1984.

Senate of Canada. 'The Standing Senate Committee on Foreign Affairs and International Trade Evidence.' Declaration by Chrystia Freeland, Canadian Minister of Foreign Affairs, at the Standing Senate Committee on Foreign Affairs and International Trade, Ottawa, May 1, 2018. https://sencanada.ca/en/Content/Sen/Committee/421/AEFA/54008-e.

Serfaty, Edith, E. Casanueva, M. G. Zavala, J. H. Andrade, H. J. Boffi-Boggero, N. Leal Marchena, A. E. Masaútis, and V. L. Foglia. 'Violencia y riesgos asociados en adolescentes.' *Revista Argentina de Clinica Neuropsiquiatrica* 10, no. 3 (2001).

Serrano, Mónica. *El Debate de la Sesión Especial de la Asamblea General de la Organización de las Naciones Unidas sobre el Problema Mundial de las Drogas de 2016*. Mexico City: Instituto Belisario Domínguez - Senado de la República, 2018.

Serrano, Mónica, and Mats Berdal, eds. *Transnational Organized Crime and International Security*. London: Lynne Rienner Publishers, 2002.

Serrano, Mónica, and María Celia Toro. 'From Drug Trafficking to Transnational Organized Crime in Latin America.' In *Transnational Organized Crime and International Security*, edited by Mónica Serrano and Mats Berdal, 155–83. London: Lynne Rienner Publishers, 2002.

Sevastopulo, Demetri, and Katrina Manson. 'Donald Trump Urges Americans to Support "War" on Coronavirus.' *Financial Times*, March 17, 2020. https://www.ft.com/content/f4c7dce8-6883-11ea-800d-da70cff6e4d3.

Seya, Marie-Josephine, Susanne F. A. M. Gelders, Obianuju Uzoma Achara, Barbara Milani, and Willem Karel Scholten. 'A First Comparison Between the Consumption of and the Need for Opioid Analgesics at Country, Regional and Global Level.' *Journal of Pain and Palliative Care Pharmacotherapy* 25, no. 1 (2011): 6–18.

Shadish, William R., Thomas D. Cook, and Donald Thomas Campbell. *Experimental and Quasi-Experimental Designs for Generalized Causal Inference.* Boston: Houghton Mifflin, 2002.

Shanker, Thom and Elisabeth Bumiller. 'U.S. shifts Afghan narcotics strategy.' *The New York Times*, July 23, 2009.

Shaw, Mark. *Illicit financial flows: Illicit narcotics transiting West Africa.* OECD Development Co-operation Working Papers 64. Paris: OECD Publishing, 2019.

Shaw, Mark. 'Soldiers in a Storm: Why and How Do Responses to Illicit Economies Get Militarised.' In *Militarised Responses to Transnational Organised Crime: The War on Crime*, edited by Tuesday Reitano, Sasha Jesperson, and Lucia Bird Ruiz-Benitez de Lugo, 1st ed. 2018 edition, 11–21. New York: Palgrave Macmillan, 2017.

Shaw, Mark. 'West African Criminal Networks in South and Southern Africa.' *African Affairs* 101, no. 404 (2002): 291–316.

Sheehan, Michael J. *International Security: An Analytical Survey.* London: Lynne Rienner Publishers, 2005.

Shirk, David A., and Joel Wallman. 'Understanding Mexico's Drug Violence.' *Journal of Conflict Resolution* 59, no. 8 (2015): 1348–76.

Silva, Jailson de Souza e, and André Urani. *Brazil: Children in Drug Trafficking: A Rapid Assessment.* Investigating the Worst Forms of Child Labour No. 20. Geneva: International Labour Organization, 2002.

Simpson, Mark. 'The Relationship between Drug Use and Crime: A Puzzle inside an Enigma.' *International Journal of Drug Policy* 14, no. 4 (2003): 307–19. https://doi.org/10.1016/S0955-3959(03)00081-1.

Singer, Merrill, and J. Bryan Page. *The Social Value of Drug Addicts: Uses of the Useless.* Walnut Creek, CA: Left Coast Press, 2013. eBook.

Sinha, Jay. *The History and Development of the Leading International Drug Control Conventions: Prepared for the Senate Special Committee on Illegal Drugs.* Ottawa: The Parliament of Canada, Library of Congress, 2001. http://www.parl.gc.ca/content/sen/committee/371/ille/library/history-e.htm.

Smith, Peter H., ed. *Drug Policy in the Americas*. Boulder: Westview Press, 1992.

Spillane, Joseph. *Cocaine: From Medical Marvel to Modern Menace in the United States, 1885–1920*. Baltimore: Johns Hopkins University Press, 1999.

Steinberg, Michael K., Joseph J. Hobbs, and Kent Mathewson, eds. *Dangerous Harvest: Drug Plants and the Transformation of Indigenous Landscapes*. New York: Oxford University Press, 2004.

Stepanova, Ekaterina. *Afghan Narcotrafficking: A Joint Threat Assessment*. Report by Joint U.S.-Russia Working Group on the Afghan Narcotrafficking. New York: EastWest Institute, 2013.

Stepanova, Ekaterina. 'Illicit drugs and insurgency in Afghanistan.' *Perspectives on Terrorism* 6, no. 2 (2012): 4–18.

Stepanova, Ekaterina. *Russia and the Afghan Peace Process*. Program on New Approaches to Research and Security in Eurasia (PONARS Eurasia) Policy Memo no. 618. Washington D.C.: Elliott School of International Affairs, George Washington University, 2019. http://www. ponarseurasia.org/ sites/default/files/policy-memos-pdf/Pepm618_Stepanova_Oct2019. pdf.

Stepanova, Ekaterina. 'Russia and the Search for Negotiated Solution in Afghanistan.' *Europe-Asia Studies*, October 26, 2020, https://www. tandfonline.com/doi/abs/10.1080/09668136.2020.1826908? journalCode=ceas20.

Stevens, Alex. 'Weighing up Crime: The Overestimation of Drug-Related Crime.' *Contemporary Drug Problems* 35, no. 2–3 (2008): 265–90. https:// doi:10.1177/009145090803500205.

Stevens, Alex. 'When Two Dark Figures Collide: Evidence and Discourse on Drug-Related Crime.' *Critical Social Policy* 27, no. 1 (2007): 77–99.

Stevens, Alex, Mike Trace, and David Bewley-Taylor. *Reducing Drug-Related Crime: An Overview of the Global Evidence*. London: Beckley Foundation, 2005.

Stoicescu, Claudia. 'Indonesia Uses Faulty Stats on "Drug Crisis" to Justify Death Penalty.' *The Conversation*, February 5, 2015.

Stoicescu, Claudia, and Gideon Lasco. *10 Years of Drug Policy in Asia: How Far Have We Come?* London: International Drug Policy Consortium, 2019. https://www.aidsdatahub.org/resource/10-years-drug-policy-asia-how-far-have-we-come.

Sustainable Development Goals Fund. 'History.' http://www.sdgfund.org/ history.

Sutin, Angelina R., Michele K. Evans, and Alan B. Zonderman. 'Personality Traits and Illicit Substances: The Moderating Role of Poverty.' *Drug and Alcohol Dependence* 131, no. 3 (2013): 247–51. https://doi. org/10.1016/j.drugalcdep.2012.10.020.

Synnott, Hilary. *Transforming Pakistan: Ways Out of Instability*. London: Routledge and IISS, 2009.

Tate, Winifred. *Drugs, Thugs, and Diplomats: U.S. Policymaking in Colombia. Anthropology of Policy*. Stanford: Stanford University Press, 2015.

Taylor, Arnold H. *American Diplomacy and the Narcotics Traffic, 1900–1939*. Durham: Duke University Press, 1969.

Ten Velde, Liza. *The Northern Triangle's: Drugs-Violence Nexus: The Role of the Drugs Trade in Criminal Violence and Policy Responses in Guatemala, El Salvador and Honduras*. Amsterdam: Transnational Institute, 2012.

Thompson, E. P. 'The Moral Economy of the English Crowd in the Eighteenth Century.' *Past & Present* 50, no. 1 (February 1971): 76–136. https://doi.org/10.1093/past/50.1.76.

Thoumi, Francisco E. 'Competitive Advantages in the Production and Trafficking of Coca-Cocaine and Opium-Heroin in Afghanistan and the Andean Countries.' In *Innocent Bystanders: Developing Countries and the War on Drugs*, edited by Philip Keefer and Norman Loayza, 195–252. New York: Palgrave Macmillan and The World Bank, 2010.

Thoumi, Franciso E. *Debates y Paradigmas de las Políticas de Drogas en el Mundo y los Desafíos para Colombia*. Bogotá: Academia Colombiana de Ciencias Económicas, 2015.

Tibke, Patrick. 'Drug law reform coming to Thailand, but how far will it go?' IDPC, July 16, 2015. http://idpc.net/blog/2015/07/drug-law-reform-coming-to-thailand-but-how-far-will-it-go.

Tilly, Charles. 'War Making and State Making as Organized Crime.' In *Bringing the State Back In*, edited by Peter B. Evans, Dietrich Rueschemeyer and Theda Skocpol. Cambridge: Cambridge University Press, 195, 165–91.

Tinti, Peter. *Illicit Trafficking and Instability in Mali: Past, Present and Future*. Geneva: Global Initiative against Transnational Organized Crime, 2014.

Tokatlian, Juan Gabriel. *Drugs and the Peace Process in Colombia: A Moderate Radical Step*. Oslo: Norwegian Peacebuilding Resource Centre, 2014. https://noref.no/Publications/Regions/Colombia/Drugs-and-the-peace-process-in-Colombia-a-moderate-radical-step.

Tonry, Michael, and Matthew Melewski. 'The Malign Effects of Drug and Crime Control Policies on Black Americans.' *Crime and Justice* 37, no. 1 (2008): 1–44. https://doi.org/10.1086/588492.

Trajtenberg, Nicolas, and Manuel Eisner. *Hacia una Política de Prevención de la Violencia en Uruguay*. Cambridge: University of Cambridge, 2014.

Trajtenberg, Nicolas, and Pablo Menese. 'Self-Control, Differential Association and the Drug–Crime Link in Uruguay in the Context of the Legalization of Marijuana.' *Aggression & Violent Behavior* 46, (2020): 180–9.

Transnational Institute. 'About Drug Law Reform in Ecuador.' *Drugs and Democracy,* June 2016. https://www.tni.org/es/node/22437#:~:text=The%20Law%20on%20Narcotic%20and,the%20process%20of%20being%20replaced.&text=This%20is%20the%20law%20that,of%20narcotic%20and%20psychotropic%20substances%E2%80%9D.

Transnational Institute. 'Infographic: Why is Uruguay Regulating; not Criminalising Cannabis?' Last modified December 10, 2013. http://druglawreform.info/en/publications/item/5183-infographic-uruguays-pioneering-cannabis-regulation.

Transnational Institute. 'International Control of Ketamine: Legal and Procedural Considerations About the Mandate of the Commission on Narcotic Drugs with Regard to Scheduling Decisions Under the 1971 UN Convention on Psychotropic Substances.' Amsterdam: TNI, 2015.

Transparency International. 'Corruption Perceptions Index 2018.' 2019. https://www.transparency.org/cpi201.

Transparency International. 'Corruption Perceptions Index 2019.' 2020. https://www.transparency.org/en/cpi/2019/results.

Turquet, Laura. *Report on the Progress of the World's Women 2011–2012: In Pursuit of Justice.* New York: UN Women, 2011.

Tyazhlov, I. 'Russia is One of the Few Countries where Cases of HIV-Infection and Deaths from HIV-AIDS are on the Rise.' *Kommersant*, May 4, 2015.

Ulyanov, Mikhail. 'Statement of the Permanent Representative of the Russian Federation to the International Organizations in Vienna Mr. Mikhail Ulyanov at the 5th intersessional meeting of the Commission on Narcotic Drugs.' Statement, CND, Vienna, November 7, 2018.

United Nations. *Single Convention on Narcotic Drugs.* New York: United Nations, 1961.

United Nations. *Convention on Psychotropic Substances.* New York: United Nations, 1971.

United Nations. *Single Convention on Narcotic Drugs: As Amended by the 1972 Protocol Amending the Single Convention on Narcotic Drugs, 1961.* New York: United Nations, 1972.

United Nations. *Commentary on the Single Convention on Narcotic Drugs, 1961. Prepared by the Secretary-General in accordance with paragraph 1 of Economic and Social Council Resolution 914D (XXXIV) of 3 Aug 1962.* New York: United Nations, 1973.

United Nations. *Commentary on the Convention on Psychotropic Substances Done at Vienna on 21 February 1971.* E/CN.7/589. Vienna: United Nations, 1976.

United Nations. *Convention Against Illicit Traffic in Narcotic Drugs and Psychotropic Substances.* New York: United Nations, 1988.

BIBLIOGRAPHY

United Nations, and World Bank. *Pathways for Peace: Inclusive Approaches to Preventing Violent Conflict*. Washington D.C.: World Bank, 2018. http://hdl.handle.net/10986/28337.

United Nations Development Programme. *Human Development Report 1990*. New York: Oxford University Press, 1990.

United Nations Development Programme. *El conflicto, callejón con salida: Informe Nacional de Desarrollo Humano para Colombia 2003*. Bogotá: UNDP, 2003.

United Nations Development Programme. *Human Development Report 2013–2014: Citizen Security with a Human Face: Evidence and Proposals for Latin America*. New York: UNDP, 2013. https://www.undp.org/content/undp/en/home/librarypage/hdr/human-development-report-for-latin-america-2013-2014.html.

United Nations Development Programme. *Human Development Report 2014: Sustaining Human Progress: Reducing Vulnerabilities and Building Resilience*. New York: UNDP, 2014. http://hdr.undp.org/en/content/human-development-report-2014.

United Nations Development Programme. *Addressing the Development Dimensions of Drug Policy*. New York: UNDP, 2015.

United Nations Drug Control Programme Legal Affairs Section. *Flexibility of Treaty Provisions As Regards Harm Reduction Approaches*. E/INCB/2002/W.13/SS.5. Vienna: United Nations International Narcotics Control Board, 2002. http://fileserver.idpc.net/library/UN_HarmReduction_EN.pdf.

United Nations Economic and Social Council. *Preparations for the Special Session of the General Assembly on the World Drug Problem: Revised Draft Resolution Submitted by the Chair*. E/CN.7/2016/L.12/Rev.1*. Vienna: United Nations, 2016. https://undocs.org/E/CN.7/2016/L.12/Rev.1.

United Nations General Assembly. *Universal Declaration of Human Rights*. Paris: United Nations, 1948.

United Nations General Assembly. *Resolution S-17/2 on the Political Declaration and Global Programme of Action adopted by the General Assembly at its 17th Special Session, Devoted to the Question of International Co-operation Against Illicit Production, Supply, Demand, Trafficking and Distribution of Narcotic Drugs and Psychotropic Substances*. A/RES/S-17/2. New York, February 23, 1990. https://undocs.org/en/A/RES/S-17/2.

United Nations General Assembly. 'Assembly Special Session on Countering World Drug Problem Together Concludes at Headquarters, 8–10 June.' Press release GA/9423. New York, June 10, 1998. https://www.un.org/press/en/1998/19980610.ga9423.html.

BIBLIOGRAPHY

United Nations General Assembly. *Right of Everyone to the Enjoyment of the Highest Attainable Standard of Physical and Mental Health*. A/65/255. New York, August 6, 2010.

United Nations General Assembly. *Background Note of the Thematic Debate of the 66th Session of the United Nations General Assembly on Drugs and Crime as a Threat to Development*. New York: United Nations, 2012.

United Nations General Assembly. 'General Debate of the 67th Session 25 September 2012 to 1 October 2012.' Last modified October 2012. https://gadebate.un.org/en/sessions-archive/67.

United Nations General Assembly. *Resolution 66/290. Follow-Up to Paragraph 143 on Human Security of the 2005 World Summit Outcome*. A/RES/66/290. New York, October 25, 2012. https://undocs.org/A/RES/66/290.

United Nations General Assembly. *Resolution 68/196. United Nations Guiding Principles on Alternative Development*. A/RES/68/196. New York, February 11, 2014. https://undocs.org/A/RES/68/196.

United Nations General Assembly. *Resolution 68/197. International Cooperation Against the World Drug Problem*. A/RES/68/197. New York, February 18, 2014. https://undocs.org/en/A/RES/68/197.

United Nations General Assembly. *Resolution 69/200. Special session of the General Assembly on the world drug problem to be held in 2016*. A/RES/69/200. New York, January 26, 2015. https://undocs.org/en/A/RES/69/200.

United Nations General Assembly. *Resolution 69/186. Moratorium on the Use of the Death Penalty*. A/RES/69/186. New York, February 4, 2015.

United Nations General Assembly. *Resolution 69/201. International Cooperation Against the World Drug Problem*. A/RES/69/201. New York, February 12, 2015. https://undocs.org/A/RES/69/201.

United Nations General Assembly. *Resolution 70/1. Transforming Our World: The 2030 Agenda for Sustainable Development*. A/RES/70/1. New York, October 21, 2015. https://undocs.org/A/RES/70/1.

United Nations General Assembly. *Thirtieth Special Session: 1st Plenary Meeting*. A/S-30/PV.1. New York, April 19, 2016. https://undocs.org/en/A/S-30/PV.1.

United Nations General Assembly. *Thirtieth Special Session: 2nd Plenary Meeting*. A/S-30/PV.2. New York, April 19, 2016. https://undocs.org/en/A/S-30/PV.2.

United Nations General Assembly. *Thirtieth Special Session: 3rd Plenary Meeting*. A/S-30/PV.3. New York, April 20, 2016. https://undocs.org/en/A/S-30/PV.3.

United Nations General Assembly. *Thirtieth Special Session: 4th Plenary Meeting*. A/S-30/PV.4. New York, April 20, 2016. https://undocs.org/en/A/S-30/PV.4.

BIBLIOGRAPHY

United Nations General Assembly. *Thirtieth Special Session: 5th Plenary Meeting*. A/S-30/PV.5. New York, April 21, 2016. https://undocs.org/en/A/S-30/PV.5.

United Nations General Assembly. *Thirtieth Special Session: 6th Plenary Meeting*. A/S-30/PV.5. New York, April 21, 2016. https://undocs.org/en/A/S-30/PV.6.

United Nations General Assembly. *Resolution S-30/1. Our Joint Commitment to Effectively Addressing and Countering the World Drug Problem*. A/RES/S-30/1. New York, May 4, 2016. https://undocs.org/A/RES/S-30/1.

United Nations Human Rights Office of the High Commissioner. 'Human rights dimension of poverty.' Accessed September 19, 2007. https://www.ohchr.org/EN/Issues/Poverty/DimensionOfPoverty/Pages/Index.aspx.

United Nations Information Service. *Uruguay is Breaking the International Conventions on Drug Control with the Cannabis Legislation Approved by its Congress*. UNIS/NAR/1190. Vienna: UNIS, 2013. https://www.incb.org/documents/Publications/PressRelease/PR2013/press_release_111213.pdf.

United Nations International Drug Control Programme. *World Drug Report*. Oxford: Oxford University Press, 1997.

United Nations Joint Programme on HIV/AIDS, International Labour Organization, Office of the High Commissioner for Human Rights, United Nations Development Programme, United Nations Educational, Scientific and Cultural Organization, United Nations Population Fund, United Nations High Commissioner for Refugees, United Nations Children's Fund, United Nations Office on Drugs and Crime, United Nations Entity for Gender Equality and the Empowerment of Women, World Food Programme, and World Health Organization. *Joint Statement: Compulsory Drug Detention and Rehabilitation Centres*. New York: United Nations, 2012. http://www.unaids.org/en/media/unaids/contentassets/documents/document/2012/JC2310_Joint%20Statement6March12FINAL_en.pdf.

United Nations Joint Programme on HIV/AIDS, International Labour Organization, Office of the High Commissioner for Human Rights, United Nations Development Programme, United Nations Educational, Scientific and Cultural Organization, United Nations Population Fund, United Nations High Commissioner for Refugees, United Nations Children's Fund, United Nations Office on Drugs and Crime, United Nations Entity for Gender Equality and the Empowerment of Women, World Food Programme, and World Health Organization. *Joint Statement: Compulsory Drug Detention and Rehabilitation Centres in the Context of Covid-19*. New York: United Nations, 2020.

BIBLIOGRAPHY

United Nations Office on Drugs and Crime. *Operational priorities: guidelines for the medium term*. Vienna: UNODC, 2003. http://www.unodc.org/pdf/ed_guidelines_mediumterm.pdf.

United Nations Office on Drugs and Crime. *Thematic Evaluation of UNODC Alternative Development Initiatives*. Vienna: UNODC, 2005.

United Nations Office on Drugs and Crime. *Opium Poppy Cultivation in the Golden Triangle. Lao PDR, Myanmar, Thailand*. Bangkok: UNODC, 2006.

United Nations Office on Drugs and Crime. *World Drug Report 2006*. Vienna: United Nations, 2006.

United Nations Office on Drugs and Crime. *World Drug Report 2008*. Vienna: United Nations, 2008.

United Nations Office on Drugs and Crime. *A Century of International Drug Control*. Vienna: UNODC, 2008. https://www.unodc.org/documents/data-and-analysis/Studies/100_Years_of_Drug_Control.pdf.

United Nations Office on Drugs and Crime. 'Political Declaration and Plan of Action on International Cooperation Towards an Integrated and Balanced Strategy to Counter the World Drug Problem.' In *High-Level Segment Commission on Narcotic Drugs*. Vienna: United Nations, 2009. https://www.unodc.org/documents/ungass2016/V0984963-English.pdf.

United Nations Office on Drugs and Crime. *Consumo de Drogas en Población Privada de Libertad y la Relación entre Delito y Droga*. Cuarto Informe Conjunto. New York: UNODC, 2010.

United Nations Office on Drugs and Crime. *La relación delito y droga en adolescentes infractores de la ley*. Quinto Informe Conjunto. New York: UNODC, 2010.

United Nations Office on Drugs and Crime. *The Global Afghan Opiate Trade: A Threat Assessment*. Vienna: UNODC, 2011.

United Nations Office on Drugs and Crime. *World Drug Report 2011*. Vienna: United Nations, 2011.

United Nations Office on Drugs and Crime. *Transnational Organized Crime in Central America and the Caribbean: A Threat Assessment*. Vienna: UNODC, 2012.

United Nations Office on Drugs and Crime. *Transnational Organized Crime in West Africa: A Threat Assessment*. Vienna: UNODC, 2013. https://www.unodc.org/documents/toc/Reports/TOCTAWestAfrica/West_Africa_TOC_COCAINE.pdf.

United Nations Office on Drugs and Crime. *World Drug Report 2013*. Vienna: United Nations, 2013.

United Nations Office on Drugs and Crime. *Global Study on Homicide 2013*. Vienna: UNODC, 2014.

United Nations Office on Drugs and Crime. *Southeast Asia Opium Survey 2014*. Bangkok: UNODC, 2014.

United Nations Office on Drugs and Crime. *World Drug Report 2014*. Vienna: United Nations, 2014.

United Nations Office on Drugs and Crime. *Drug Money: The Illicit Proceeds of Opiates Trafficked on the Balkan Route*. Vienna: UNODC, 2015.

United Nations Office on Drugs and Crime. *Early Warning Advisory on NPS*. Vienna: UNODC, 2015.

United Nations Office on Drugs and Crime. *World Drug Report 2015*. Vienna: United Nations, 2015.

United Nations Office on Drugs and Crime. 'Outcome Document of the 2016 United Nations General Assembly Special Session on the World Drug Problem: Our Joint Commitment to Effectively Addressing and Countering the World Drug Problem.' In *Thirtieth Special Session General Assembly*. New York: United Nations, 2016.

United Nations Office on Drugs and Crime. *Terminology and Information on Drugs*. 3rd ed. New York: United Nations, 2016.

United Nations Office on Drugs and Crime. *World Drug Report 2016*. Vienna: United Nations, 2016.

United Nations Office on Drugs and Crime. *World Drug Report 2017*. Vienna: United Nations, 2017.

United Nations Office on Drugs and Crime. *Afghan Opiate Trafficking Along the Northern Route*. Vienna: UNODC, 2018.

United Nations Office on Drugs and Crime. *World Drug Report 2018*. Vienna: United Nations, 2018.

United Nations Office on Drugs and Crime. *Global Study on Homicide 2019*. Vienna: UNODC, 2019.

United Nations Office on Drugs and Crime. *Transnational Organized Crime in Southeast Asia: Evolution, Growth and Impact*. Bangkok: United Nations, 2019.

United Nations Office on Drugs and Crime. *World Drug Report 2019*. Vienna: United Nations, 2019.

United Nations Office on Drugs and Crime, and Gobierno de Colombia. *Monitoreo de Cultivos de Coca 2014*. Bogotá: UNODC, 2015.

United Nations Office on Drugs and Crime, and Gobierno de Colombia. *Monitoreo de Territorios Afectados por Cultivos Ilícitos 2016*. Bogotá: UNODC, 2017.

United Nations Office on Drugs and Crime, and Islamic Republic of Afghanistan Ministry for Counternarcotics. *Afghanistan Opium Survey 2017: Cultivation and Production*. Kabul: UNODC, 2017.

United Nations Office on Drugs and Crime, and Islamic Republic of Afghanistan Ministry for Counternarcotics. *Afghanistan Opium Survey 2011*. Kabul: UNODC, 2018.

United Nations Office on Drugs and Crime, and Islamic Republic of Afghanistan Ministry for Counternarcotics. *Afghanistan Opium Survey 2018: Cultivation and Production*. Kabul: UNODC, 2018.

United Nations Office on Drugs and Crime Regional Centre for East Asia and the Pacific. *Border Liaison Offices in Southeast Asia 1999–2009*. Bangkok: UNODC, 2010.

United Nations Office on Drugs and Crime Regional Centre for East Asia and the Pacific. *Drug-Free ASEAN 2015: Status and Recommendations*. Bangkok: UNODC, 2008.

United Nations Security Council. *Special Research Report: Emerging Security Threats in West Africa*. New York: United Nations, 2011.

United Nations Security Council. *Statement by the President of the Security Council*. S/PRST/2012/2. New York, February 21, 2012.

United Nations System Chief Executives Board for Coordination. *2nd Regular Session of 2018, New York, 7 and 8 Nov 2018: Summary of Deliberations*. CEB/2018/2. New York, January 2019.

United Republic of Tanzania. *Drugs and Prevention of Illicit Traffic in Drugs Act, Section 16(2)*. Dodoma: United Republic of Tanzania, 1996.

United Nations System Coordination Task Team on the Implementation of the UN System Common Position on drug-related matters. *What we Have Learned over the Last Ten Years: A Summary of Knowledge Acquired and Produced by the UN System on Drug-Related Matters*. New York: United Nations, 2019.

Uprimny, Rodrigo, Sergio Raúl Chaparro, Luis Felipe Cruz, Catalina Pérez Correa, Karen Silva, Gianella Bardazano, and Jorge Paladines. *Curbing Addiction to Punishment: Alternatives to Incarceration for Drug Offenses*. Translated by Hilary Burke. Edited by Coletta Youngers. Mexico City: Colectivo de Estudios Drogas y Derecho, 2015.

Uprimny, Rodrigo, Diana Guzmán, and Jorge Parra. *Addicted to Punishment: The Disproportionality of Drug Laws in Latin America*. Bogotá: Dejusticia, 2012.

US Agency for International Development. *U.S. Overseas Loans and Grants: Obligations and Loan Authorizations: July 1, 1945 – September 30, 2012*. Washington D.C.: USAID, 2012.

US Department of Justice Drug Enforcement Administration. *2014 National Drug Threat Assessment*. Washington D.C.: DOJ, 2014.

US Department of Justice Drug Enforcement Administration. *2015 National Drug Threat Assessment*. Washington D.C.: DOJ, 2015.

US Department of Justice Drug Enforcement Administration. *2018 National Drug Threat Assessment*. Washington D.C.: DOJ, 2018.

US Department of State. 'Foreign Press Centers.' 2020. http://fpc.state.gov/232813.htm.

US Department of State. 'Joint Statement on the Signing of the U.S.–Taliban Agreement.' Media Note, March 6, 2020. https://www.state.gov/joint-statement-on-the-signing-of-the-u-s-taliban-agreement/.

US District Court, Southern District of New York. 'United States v. Oumar Issa, Harouna Touré, and Idriss Abdelrahman.' New York, 2009. http://www.justice.gov/archive/usao/nys/pressreleases/April12/issa/issatoureandabdelrahmanindictment.pdf.

US Government Accountability Office. *Lack of Progress on Achieving National Strategy Goals*. Washington D.C.: GAO, 2015. http://www.gao.gov/assets/680/673929.pdf.

US House of Representatives, Republican Staff of the Committee on Financial Services. *Too Big to Jail: Inside the Obama Justice Department's Decision Not to Hold Wall Street Accountable*. Washington D.C., July 2016. http://financialservices.house.gov/uploadedfiles/07072016_oi_tbtj_sr.pdf.

US Office of National Drug Control Policy. 'Coca in the Andes,' ONDCP, Policy & Research, April 2015.

Valenzuela, Eduardo, and Pilar Larroulet. 'La Relación Droga – Delito: Una Estimación de la Fracción Atribuible.' *Estudios Públicos* 119 (2010): 33–66.

Vertovec, Steven. *Transnationalism. Key Ideas*. London; New York: Routledge, 2009.

Vesti.Medicina. 'Rehabilitation of drug users in Russia will meet new standards.' May 10, 2018. https://med.vesti.ru/novosti/obshhestvo-i-zakonodatelstvo/reabilitatsiya-narkomanov-v-rossii-budet-prohodit-po-novym-standartam.

Vienna Convention on the Law of Treaties, 18232 (1969).

Villarreal-González, María Elena, Juan Carlos Sánchez-Sosa, Gonzalo Musitu, and Rosa Varela. 'El consumo de alcohol en adolescentes escolarizados: Propuesta de un modelo sociocomunitario.' *Psychosocial Intervention* 19, no. 3 (2010): 253–64.

Voice of Russia. 'White Death across Russia.' November 22, 2011.

Wæver. Ole. 'Insecurity, Security and Asecurity in the West European Non-War Community.' In *Security Communities,* edited by Emanuel Adler and Michael Barnett, 69–118. Cambridge: Cambridge University Press, 1998).

Wæver, Ole. 'Securitization and Desecuritization.' In *On Security*, edited by Ronny Lipschutz, 46–86. New York: Columbia University Press, 1995.

Walker III, William O. *Drug Control in the Americas*. Albuquerque: University of New Mexico Press, 1989.

Walker III, William O. *Opium and Foreign Policy: The Anglo-American Search for Order, 1912–1954*. Chapel Hill: University of North Carolina Press, 1991.

Walker III, William O., ed. *Drug Control Policy: Essays in Historical and Comparative Perspective*. University Park: Penn State Press, 1992.

Walmsley, Roy. *World Prison Population List*. 12th ed. London: Institute for Criminal Policy Research and Birkbeck University, 2016.

Walsh, Declan. 'Flower Plower.' *The Guardian*, August 16, 2008.

Walsh, Joahn, Martin Jelsma, Tom Blickman, and Dave Bewley-Taylor. *The WHO's First-Ever Critical Review of Cannabis: A Mixture of Obvious Recommendations Deserving Support and Dubious Methods and Outcomes Requiring Scrutiny*. Washington: Washington Office on Latin America; Amsterdam: Transnational Institute; Swansea: Global Drug Policy Observatory, 2019. https://www.tni.org/en/publication/the-whos-first-ever-critical-review-of-cannabis.

Walt, Stephen. 'The Renaissance of Security Studies.' *International Studies Quarterly* 35, (1991): 211–39.

Ward, Thomas W. *Gangsters without Borders: An Ethnography of a Salvadoran Street Gang*. Oxford: Oxford University Press, 2012.

Washington Office on Latin America. 'UN and US Cocaine Estimates Contradict Each Other.' July 31, 2012. http://www.wola.org/commentary/un.

Washington Times. 'Guinea Narco-State Revealed in TV Confessions.' March 15, 2009. https://www.washingtontimes.com/news/2009/mar/15/guinea-narcostate-revealed-in-tv-confessions/.

Watts, Nick. 'Compulsory Drug Treatment in Southeast Asia – Neither Ethical Nor Effective.' *Global Politics*, May 2, 2015. http://global-politics.co.uk/wp/2015/05/02/compulsory-drug-treatment-in-southeast-asia-neither-ethical-nor-effective/.

Weimer, David. *Seeing Drugs: Modernization, Counterinsurgency, and U.S. Narcotics Control in the Third World, 1969-1976*. Kent, OH: Kent State University Press, 2011.

Werb, Dan, Greg Rowell, Gordon Guyatt, Thomas Kerr, Julio Montaner, and Evan Wood. 'Effect of Drug Law Enforcement on Drug Market Violence: A Systematic Review.' *International Journal of Drug Policy* 22, no. 2 (2011): 87–94. Hhttps://doi.org/10.1016/j.drugpo.2011.02.002.

Western Hemisphere Drug Policy Commission, *Report of the Western Hemisphere Drug Policy Commission*. Washington D.C., December 2020. https://foreignaffairs.house.gov/_cache/files/a/5/a51ee680-e339-4a1b-933f-b15e535fa103/AA2A3440265DDE42367A79D4BCBC9AA1.whdpc-final-report-2020-11.30.pdf.

White House, The. *National Drug Control Budget: FY 2016 Funding Highlights.* Washington D.C.: The White House, 2016.

Williams, Marc Eric. 'The United States and Latin America.' in *Handbook of Latin America in the World*, edited by Ana Covarrubias and Jorge Dominguez, 199–211. New York: Routledge, 2014.

Williams, Michael C. 'Words, Images, Enemies: Securitization and International Politics.' *International Studies Quarterly* 47, no. 4 (2003): 511–31.

Williams, Paul D. *Security Studies: An Introduction*. 2nd ed. London: Routledge, 2012.

Williams, Phil. 'Transnational Organized Crime and the State.' In *The Emergence of Private Authority in Global Governance*, edited by Rodney Bruce Hall and Thomas J. Biersteker, 161–82. West Nyack: Cambridge University Press, 2002.

Williams, Phil, and Roy Godson. 'Anticipating Organized and Transnational Crime.' *Crime, Law and Social Change* 37 (June 2002): 311–55. https://doi.org/10.1023/A:1016095317864.

Windle, James. *Drugs and Drug Policy in Thailand*. Washington D.C.: Brookings Institution, Latin America Initiative, 2015.

Windle, James, and Graham Farrell. 'Popping the Balloon Effect: Assessing Drug Law Enforcement in Terms of Displacement, Diffusion, and the Containment Hypothesis.' *Substance Use and Misuse* 47, no. 8–9 (2012): 868–76.

Working Group on Women, Drug Policies, and Incarceration. *Women, Drug Policies, and Incarceration: A Guide for Policy Reform in Latin America and the Caribbean*. Washington D.C.: WOLA, 2016.

World Bank. *Crime and Violence in Central America: A Development Challenge*. Washington D.C.: World Bank, 2011.

World Health Organization. 'Adolescent Health in the South-East Asia Region.' Adolescent Health. https://www.who.int/southeastasia/health-topics/adolescent-health.

World Health Organization. *Lexicon of Alcohol and Drug Terms*. Geneva: WHO, 1994.

World Health Organization. 'Ketamine: Expert Peer Review on Critical Review Report.' Presented at the 35th Expert Committee on Drug Dependence, Hammamet, Tunisia, June 4–8, 2012.

World Health Organization. 'WHO Expert Committee on Drug Dependence.' Management of substance abuse. 2020. http://www.who.int/substance_abuse/right_committee/en/.

Wright, Richard, Fiona Brookman, and Trevor Bennett. 'The Foreground Dynamics of Street Robbery in Britain.' *British Journal of Criminology* 46, no. 1 (2006): 1–15. https://doi.org/10.1093/bjc/azi055.

Wyn Jones, Richard. *Security, Strategy, and Critical Theory. Critical Security Studies*. Boulder: Lynne Rienner Publishers, 1999.

Wyn Jones, Richard. 'Travel Without Maps: Thinking About Security After the Cold War.' In *Security Issues in the Post-Cold War*, edited by Jane M. Davis, 196–218. Cheltenham: Edward Elgar Publishing, 1996.

Yashar, Deborah J. *Homicidal Ecologies: Illicit Economies and Complicit States in Latin America*. Cambridge: Cambridge University Press, 2018.

Yongming, Zhou. *Anti-Drug Crusades in Twentieth-Century China: Nationalism, History, and State Building*. Lanham: Rowman & Littlefield, 1999.

Youngers, Coletta. 'Behind the Staggering Rise in Women's Imprisonment in Latin America.' *Open Society Foundations Voices*, January 6, 2014. https://www.opensocietyfoundations.org/voices/behind-staggering-rise-womens-imprisonment-latin-america.

Youngers, Coletta. 'Shifts in Cultivation, Usage Put Bolivia's Coca Policy at the Crossroads.' *World Politics Review*, December 5, 2013.

Youngers, Coletta. 'UN Guiding Principles on Alternative Development: Opportunity Lost.' *Open Society Foundations Voices*, November 22, 2013. https://www.opensocietyfoundations.org/voices/un-guiding-principles-alternative-development-opportunity-lost.

Yusuf, Huma. 'The Drugs of War.' *The New York Times*, November 9, 2012. https://latitude.blogs.nytimes.com/2012/11/09/the-war-in-afghanistan-brings-drugs-to-pakistan/.

Zulkifli, Masagos. 'The 36th ASEAN Senior Officials Meeting on Drugs.' Opening speech, Association of the Southeast Asian Nations, Singapore, August 24, 2015.

Zulver, Julia and Annette Idler, 'Gendering the Border Effect: The Double Impact of Colombian Insecurity and the Venezuelan Refugee Crisis,' *Third World Quarterly* 41, no. 7 (2020): 1122–40.

ANNEX
GUIDING QUESTIONS FOR THE CHAPTERS

PART I
1. How did the IDCR come into existence?
2. How can the current drug policy debate be understood from a historical perspective?
3. What has been the historical impact of the IDCR on the drug problem across the globe?
4. How did the US-led War on Drugs interfere with the IDCR?
5. What are the differences in the evolution of the IDCR regarding the various types of drug (especially cocaine and opium)?
6. What are the main reasons explaining why the IDCR has been increasingly called into question?
7. Who have been the main stakeholders in the IDCR? What have been their motivations and incentives?
8. What are the legal parameters that the IDCR imposes on countries? Is there room for flexible interpretation in the treaty framework?
9. How do developments in countries like the United States or Uruguay impact the IDCR?
10. What are the main challenges for drug policy and how can the IDCR face them?
11. What are the possible scenarios for the IDCR and what are the main obstacles and opportunities?

PART II

1. What is the role of the region/country in the illicit drug trade?
2. How has the IDCR impacted drug policy in the region/country?
3. What have been the outcomes of the IDCR in the region/country—main achievements and negative consequences?
4. What is the position of the region/country in the international drug policy debate?
5. How do other countries or international organizations influence drug policy in the region/country?
6. What are the main challenges for drug policy in the region/country and how can the IDCR face them?
7. What are possible scenarios for drug policy in the region/country and what are the main obstacles and opportunities?

PART III

1. How has the IDCR impacted the respective issue area?
2. What are the recent developments and trends in the respective issue area from the drug policy perspective?
3. What are the disagreements and what is the consensus, if any, between and within the countries regarding the respective issue area from the drug policy perspective?
4. From the perspective of this issue area, how is the IDCR related to other international conventions and commitments?
5. What are the mechanisms to coordinate between different agencies, multilateral and regional organizations, and what are the shortcomings thereof, if any?
6. What are the main challenges for drug policy regarding the issue area and how can the IDCR face them?
7. What are possible scenarios for the respective issue area in relation to the IDCR and what are the main obstacles and opportunities?

INDEX